WHERE'S THE 'HUMAN' I
RESOURCE MANAGEI

CW00544666

Managing Work in the 21st Century

Michael Gold and Chris Smith

BRISTOL
UNIVERSITY
PRESS

First published in Great Britain in 2023 by

Bristol University Press
University of Bristol
1-9 Old Park Hill
Bristol
BS2 8BB
UK
t: +44 (0)117 374 6645
e: bup-info@bristol.ac.uk

Details of international sales and distribution partners are available at bristoluniversitypress.co.uk

British Library Cataloguing in Publication Data
A catalogue record for this book is available from the British Library

ISBN 978-1-5292-1379-9 hardcover
ISBN 978-1-5292-1380-5 paperback
ISBN 978-1-5292-1381-2 ePub
ISBN 978-1-5292-1382-9 ePdf

Cover design: Nicky Borowiec
Front cover image: AdobeStock_255745448

Bristol University Press uses environmentally responsible print partners.

Printed in Great Britain by CMP, Poole

Contents

Detailed Contents

List of Boxes, Figures and Tables

Boxes

Figures

Tables

List of Abbreviations and Acronyms

ACAS	Advisory, Conciliation and Arbitration Service
ADCU	App Drivers and Couriers Union
AI	Artificial intelligence
BA	British Airways
BAME	Black, Asian and minority ethnic
BBC	British Broadcasting Corporation
BEIS	(Department for) Business, Energy and Industrial Strategy
BHA	British Hospitality Association
BHS	British Home Stores
BITC	Business in the Community
BMA	British Medical Association
CBI	Confederation of British Industry
Cedefop	European Centre for the Development of Vocational Training
CEE	Central and Eastern European
CEO	Chief executive officer
CGT-FO	*Confédération Générale du Travail – Force Ouvrière* (French General Confederation of Labour – Workers' Force)
CIPD	Chartered Institute of Personnel and Development
CME	Coordinated market economy
CNN	Cable News Network
CSR	Corporate social responsibility
CV	Curriculum vitae
DVLA	Driver and Vehicle Licensing Agency
EFRA	Environment, Food and Rural Affairs (committee)
EHRC	Equality and Human Rights Commission
ELM	External labour market
EM	Electronic monitoring
EQ	Emotional intelligence
ESG	Environmental, social and governance (issues)
ESOP	Employee share ownership plan
ETUI	European Trade Union Institute
EU	European Union
EWC	European Works Council
FCA	Financial Conduct Authority
FRC	Financial Reporting Council
FTSE	Financial Times Stock Exchange (index)
GCSE	General Certificate of Secondary Education
GE	General Electric
GLAA	Gangmasters & Labour Abuse Authority

GM	General Motors
GRI	Global Reporting Initiative
HGV	Heavy goods vehicle
HPWPs	High-performance work practices
HR	Human resources
HRD	Human resource development
HRM	Human resource management
ICT	Information and communications technology
IER	Institute of Employment Rights
IFA	International Framework Agreement
ILM	Institute of Leadership and Management
ILO	International Labour Organization
IPO	Initial public offer
ISO	International Organization for Standardization
IWGB	Independent Workers' Union of Great Britain
JCC	Joint consultative committee
LME	Liberal market economy
MBA	Master of Business Administration
NASUWT	National Association of Schoolmasters Union of Women Teachers
NEET	Not in education, employment or training
NEU	National Education Union
NGO	Non-governmental organisation
NHK	Nippon Hōsō Kyōkai (Japan Broadcasting Corporation)
NHS	National Health Service
NSS	National Student Survey
NUM	National Union of Mineworkers
NYPD	New York Police Department
OECD	Organisation for Economic Co-operation and Development
ONS	Office for National Statistics
PCS	Public and Commercial Services (union)
PGCE	Postgraduate Certificate of Education
PhD	Doctorate of Philosophy
qv	*quod vide* (Latin: 'which see'), in other words, the preceding term is also included in the Glossary so you can look up its meaning
RHA	Road Haulage Association
RHUL	Royal Holloway University of London
RMT	Rail, Maritime and Transport (union)
SACOM	Students and Scholars Against Corporate Misbehavior
SAYE	Save As You Earn (scheme)
SLME	State-led market economy
SMART	Specific, measurable, achievable, relevant, time-bound
T&D	Training and development

TUC	Trades Union Congress
UCEA	Universities and Colleges Employers' Association
UCU	University and College Union
UK	United Kingdom
UN	United Nations
US	United States
VAT	Value-added tax
VET	Vocational education and training
WLB	Work–life balance
ZHC	Zero-hours contract

Notes on the Authors

Michael Gold is Emeritus Professor of Comparative Employment Relations at Royal Holloway University of London (RHUL). He started out as a journalist with Incomes Data Services and Industrial Relations Services but later became a lecturer at the University of Westminster and senior research officer at the National Institute of Economic and Social Research before joining RHUL. Michael's research interests include industrial relations theory, European employment relations, the history of British industrial relations and self-employment. His most recent articles, with Chris Rees, focus on the regulation of employee participation in cross-border takeovers.

Chris Smith is Emeritus Professor of Organization Studies and Comparative Management, Royal Holloway University of London. He has taught at Aston University and held various visiting positions at universities in Australia, Brazil, China and Hong Kong. His research interests include labour process theory, knowledge transfer through transnational firms, comparative analysis of work and professional labour. He has written extensively on work organisation in Japanese overseas companies. He recently published *China at Work* (Palgrave, 2016, with Mingwei Liu), and is currently researching employment relations and the labour process in the UK logistics sector.

Acknowledgements

We both owe an incalculable debt over the years to colleagues and students for stimulating discussions and debates that have informed the arguments and themes reflected in this book. There are too many to name, but we couldn't have written it without you – many thanks! We are particularly grateful to Yu Zheng (Senior Lecturer in Human Resource Management and Asian Business at Royal Holloway University of London) for her contribution to Chapter 19 on human resources (HR) analytics, which lay well outside our competence.

The book itself arose out of our second-year course on HRM in the School of Business and Management at Royal Holloway. It had been running for some years before we took it over, and we gratefully acknowledge the foundations laid by Vidu Badigannavar, Chris Rowley, Axel Haunschild and Neil Conway, and the current work of Chris Rees as well as other lecturers and workshop tutors.

The challenge of presenting our material to critically minded students, few of whom actually aspired to become HR managers, was the inspiration behind our book. Its title, in fact, stemmed from one of our workshops. A student, exasperated by the exploitative labour practices illustrated in one of our case studies, exclaimed: 'So where *is* the "human" in human resource management?' Exactly. The term 'human' in HRM has a rather different meaning from 'human' as in 'humane' or 'empathetic', and we explore this ambiguity throughout the book. We were encouraged in our venture by the heartening comments of three anonymous reviewers who clearly had faith in our approach.

We would like to thank Paul Stevens, Commissioning Editor at Bristol University Press, for his enthusiasm and dedication from the outset, as well as Emma Cook in Editorial and Bahar Muller in Marketing, among other colleagues, for all their help and support. Alison McPherson provided accurate and swift transcription services. We are also grateful to Jan Fraser for carefully checking the manuscript before final submission and to Dawn Rushen for her meticulous copyediting. We take responsibility for any mistakes or errors that remain.

Introduction:
Where's the 'Human' in
Human Resource Management?

The nature of paid work has changed rapidly and dramatically since the beginning of the 21st century, particularly since the global financial crash in 2008–09. The emergence of the gig economy, call centres, agency work, outsourcing, zero-hours contracts, the role of migrant workers in the labour market and 'digital Taylorism' have all been commented on at great length in the media and in popular books. Some commentators have focused on 'bullshit' jobs, that is, jobs allegedly with no intrinsic value (Graeber, 2018), and others on the hi-tech sector (Lyons, 2016). Some examine specific companies, such as Amazon (Geissler, 2018) and Deliveroo (Cant, 2019), others focus more broadly on the gig economy (Kessler, 2018; Prassl, 2018; Woodcock and Graham, 2019), while yet others investigate specifically low-wage sectors (Bloodworth, 2018). A further group analyses how we should respond to the challenges of overwork and automation (Cohen, 2020; Goodhart, 2020; Susskind, 2020), with others exploring the changing political dynamics of work (Dundon et al, 2020; Cruddas, 2021), the potential role for trade unions (Holgate, 2021) and the kind of regulation that's required to improve the employment relationship (Leighton and McKeown, 2020). Some, who are psychologists or therapists, simply focus on advising us on the best ways to survive the messy and sometimes toxic world of office politics (Shragai, 2021; West, 2022).

What all these approaches have in common is a moral charge, expressed in no–holds–barred language that underpins their attempt to expose the factors that lead to worker misery, in particular a combination of falling pay levels, insecurity, persistent organisational change and dehumanisation (Lyons, 2019). Indeed, concerns over the spread of scandalous working conditions in the UK have been reflected in the recent reports of two House of Commons committees, one on British Home Stores (BHS) and the other on Sports Direct. The first, on BHS, 'exposed how capitalism can be worked to the advantage of directors, financiers and advisers at the expense of employees and the wider public interest' (House of Commons, 2016a: 57, para 175), while the second, on Sports Direct, revealed 'some appalling working practices at both the Sports Direct shops and warehouses' (House of Commons, 2016b: 29, para 15). Theresa May MP, then Prime Minister, subsequently commissioned the Taylor Review to make recommendations on the reform of the workplace (Taylor, 2017), which led to the government's *Good Work Plan* the following year (BEIS, 2018). All these investigations centre on the workplace and refer implicitly to the intensifying marketisation of neoliberal economies by way of context, although others explicitly examine the relationship between the degradation of work and the increasingly extractive nature of contemporary – or 'wreckage' – capitalism (Fleming, 2017).

Meanwhile, alongside these broadsides there exists – and has existed for many years – a battery of textbooks on human resource management (HRM) that ostensibly cover the management of employment relations at the workplace. Their focus is rather different from the new-wave exposures, as they examine the issues involved in the management of human resources throughout the traditional hierarchical organisation: recruitment and selection, performance appraisal, reward management, training and development, employee participation and involvement, as well as legal aspects of the employment relationship.

These textbooks share several striking features. Many of them now run to multiple editions, having been originally published in the 1980s or 1990s. For example, Foot et al (2016) is in its seventh edition and dates back to 1996. Bratton and Gold (2017) is in its sixth edition, while Beardwell and Thompson (2017) is in its eighth, both having first been published in 1994. Torrington et al (2014) is in its ninth edition, having first appeared in 1987, while Jackson et al (2017) is in its twelfth, and was first published in 1983. It is unlikely that anyone ever reads them from cover to cover: they are guides to HRM rather than accounts with a coherent explanatory narrative. Their central sections have been largely updated over the years, but within the narrow confines of traditional HRM. Recent developments, such as the emergence of the gig economy, the role of migrant workers in labour markets and the ramifications of the financial crisis, generally appear – if they appear at all – in sections bolted on at the end, apparently as afterthoughts. Furthermore, they are invariably written in line with a management agenda, with some notable exceptions, such as Grugulis (2017) and Wilkinson et al (2021) – although it should be pointed out that more critical analyses generally contain the term 'employee relations' or 'employment relations' in their titles as in, for example, Blyton and Turnbull (2004), Farnham (2015), Bingham (2016) and Dundon et al (2017). This predominant management agenda is not surprising, and nor is noting it a criticism. These textbooks are aimed at students taking courses in HRM at university and/or for professional qualifications, such as those awarded by the Chartered Institute of Personnel and Development (CIPD), with the assumption that they will become human resources (HR) managers.

But how reasonable is this assumption? In our own experience of teaching HRM, there are broadly three types of student who study the subject. Yes, certainly a minority wish to become HR managers. Then there are those who wish to become managers in other areas, such as accounting, marketing or operations, and who need to have an understanding of HRM to be able to function effectively. But a third group of students do not aspire to become managers at all. This group also includes general readers who are interested in finding out more about HRM if only to understand more about the pressures that beset them at work. These people are actually the rest of us who have to earn our own living!

Now, only two types of people don't have to have a paid job with an employer (leaving aside those dependent on welfare benefits or the support of relatives). One type is the self-employed, who traditionally have been freelance and engage with clients on a one-to-one basis, and so are not much concerned with traditional HR issues (although, as we'll see, the notion of self-employment has become increasingly fraught in recent years). The other type has a private income or inherited wealth and so doesn't have to work at all. The rest of us normally have to earn our living as employees on a payroll, and most students will have their own ideas about the kinds of jobs or careers they want. They'll go off and find a job, and at that point HRM will become a really important issue for them because, when we are in an employment relationship, we all find that HR issues crowd in on us – the way we're recruited, how we're promoted, issues of equality and diversity, the way we're paid, how our performance is appraised, how much influence we have over management decisions, and so on. These issues pursue us for the rest of our working lives, which means that HRM is very much a *lived* subject. It's something that we live, whether or not we practise it as managers, and we remain subject to all its constraints and pressures until we retire. Hence it is these people – wage or salary earners, the overwhelming majority of us – who most urgently require analysis to understand what is happening to us at our places of work, as employees now and into the future.

Yet it is exactly at this point that the analysis turns out to be largely missing – analysis that combines the contemporary if partial approach of the popular investigators and journalists with the comprehensive, if dated, approach of the academic textbooks. We need analysis that takes into account the wide range of workplaces opening up in recent years in post-bureaucratic settings, not just those to be found in large-scale hierarchical organisations. And, above all, we need one that examines the HR function not exclusively through the eyes of the managers, who are already professionally well catered for, but also through the eyes of the workers, who – as recent investigators have shown – remain perplexed and powerless, if not increasingly exploited and burnt out. This is not to say, of course, that managers, as wage earners themselves, aren't all those things either (Foster et al, 2019).

The nearest approach to such an analysis currently available is a report published by PricewaterhouseCoopers (PwC) based on a survey of 10,000 people in China, India, Germany, the UK and the US about how they think the workplace will evolve and how this will affect their employment prospects and future working lives (PwC, 2018b). It outlines 'four worlds of work in 2030', which provide an interesting starting point for thinking about work, occupations and HRM in contrasting scenarios that PwC term Blue, Red, Green and Yellow.

The 'Blue World' is essentially the world of large, hierarchical organisations as they are today: 'corporate is king'. Organisations see size and influence as the best way to protect themselves, and some grow more powerful than national economies (as now). Their interests take precedence over corporate social responsibility (CSR). The gap between rich and poor continues to widen, and workers have either a high-paying job or no job (or more likely a precarious one in the gig economy). Workers' performance is continually monitored if they are in the core group of high performers.

In the 'Red World', digital platforms and technology allow those with ideas to flourish: 'innovation rules'. Companies lack any loyalty towards employees: those with skills in demand prosper; those with outdated skills are abandoned. The proportion of full-time workers in companies falls as outsourcing and self-employment grows, favouring the growth of the gig economy.

By contrast, in the 'Green World', CSR has become a business imperative in the context of climate change, waste recycling, diversity management and human rights: 'companies care'. Trust in organisations is central. Workers work for organisations whose values they admire, but their lifestyles are monitored by organisations for sustainability.

Finally, in the 'Yellow World', companies and workers seek greatest relevance and meaning in what they do: 'humans come first'. Workers can work anywhere, thanks to technology (albeit within the limits of their occupation). Collaboration is key, work is fluid, and workers identify with skills/occupations through their professional associations rather than with companies. Work–life balance (WLB) is blurred, but conflicts remain around technology as people won't accept downgrading of their skills.

In each case, the implications for HRM and its future vary. In the Blue World, people remain in demand, but their performance is enhanced through artificial intelligence (AI). Rewards are high, but performance is monitored and WLB remains an issue. In the Green World, HRM comes to focus on wider aspects of 'people and society' and embraces HR, marketing and CSR, among other functions, while in the Yellow World it fosters collaboration and maintaining WLB. However, in the Red World HRM is no longer a separate function, as entrepreneurs rely on outsourced services and automation.

This scenario-based approach to studying HRM has its advantages. It accepts that different forms of organisation and working are likely to coexist for the foreseeable future, and that traditional forms (Blue World) will remain significant, even if they are in longer term decline as outsourcing and digital platforms favour the gig economy (Red World). It indicates, too, that global challenges – most notably climate change – will require organisations to rethink their engagement with environmental issues and sustainability (Green World), while advances in telecommunications that create the ability to work from anywhere allow individuals to collaborate on projects in social-first and community-oriented businesses (Yellow World). The approach also rightly indicates that in each case the role of HRM varies, ranging from its traditional role in the Blue World to, at best, a peripheral role in the Red World. HRM cannot therefore be disembodied from its organisational and technological context, and needs to be embedded in its changing national and global environments.

That said, the PwC approach presents the scenarios in neutral terms. While it does highlight the different conditions that workers are likely to experience in each 'world', it says very little specifically about issues of supervision, monitoring and control, which vary a lot between these 'worlds', especially the *forms* of control (which, of course, have implications for HRM). For example, companies in the Blue and Green Worlds will be monitoring the performance of their workers in direct ways and awarding pay rises in line with performance, but workers in the Red World – who are effectively self-employed gig workers – will have to rely on self-discipline and update their own skills to remain viable in the labour market. Training and development may prove problematic in the Yellow World, too, where responsibility for its provision shifts from the employer to the worker. WLB may prove a challenge, particularly in the Red World, where workers will be more autonomous but dependent on 'selling themselves' to locate clients.

In addition, the scenarios do not consider a range of other developments that influence workers' terms and conditions and their experience of work, such as the continuing role of trade unions, varying management attitudes within each scenario, the part played by social networks in recruitment and discrimination, the nature of emotional labour, and the impact of migration on the demand and supply of workers, among others. Above all, they do not consider the conflictual nature of the interaction between employers and workers that lies at the heart of the employment relationship in capitalist economies, and how it underpins both management action and worker resistance.

This book, then, is designed to fill in these gaps. It is for everyone who is deeply concerned about what is happening to the contemporary working environment, from the meaninglessness of many tasks, to work intensification and bullying. It covers a wide range of work environments, including those outlined by PwC, but also provides a comprehensive overview of the HR function and its impact on workers and managers (as workers themselves). It covers the topics normally included in HR textbooks, but does so from a perspective that gives its central argument a coherence that they generally lack, one that emphasises the 'dynamics of control, consent and resistance at the point of production' (Thompson and Smith, 2010: 11). It explains HRM in terms of its function, which is first to control labour costs, notably pay, fringe benefits and pensions, and second to increase productivity through a range of methods involving supervision and consent, and how they lead to multiple forms of resistance. Our argument places the 'wage–effort bargain' centre-stage in the employment relationship, and examines in depth how the employer seeks to secure a satisfactory standard of work input in exchange for a satisfactory level of remuneration (or not). Its narrative is partisan in that it argues that the issues surrounding HR functions, such as recruitment and selection, appraisal, reward management and employee participation, make sense only when located in the context of the competing interests of employers and workers. Furthermore, much of the misery that apparently characterises many contemporary workplaces – particularly those in post-bureaucratic settings – can be understood more readily once we understand how structural factors, such as the use of digital platforms, free movement of labour and the decline of trade unions, have shifted the balance of power towards employers and undermined collective forms of identity and solidarity among workforces.

Existing HRM theories tend to focus too strongly on the organisation and treat labour as a 'fixed resource' used by the firm for a win–win bargain between employer and employee. We suggest that HRM is facing a different world from the period when the workforce was largely 'fixed' in the large firm through internally secure jobs, established skills, strong unions and tight community bonds between firm and locality. Today there is a greater 'flow' of workers as a result of reduced job tenure, more flexible and insecure forms of working, globalisation of labour markets, higher levels of migration, weaker unions and new ways of employing workers, such as employment agencies and the gig economy. Greater responsibility and risk have been passed down from employer to worker to navigate through the labour market, get training and adapt to trends.

We suggest, therefore, that labour should be seen more accurately as fluid, as a 'flow'. Workers have choices (within significant constraints) over where to work, as well as over their work intensity. Labour is not 'owned' by the firm, and there is always a structural conflict between the two. Under contemporary employment conditions, attachment of workers to the firm has generally weakened. Employers dealing with this 'flow' of labour can pursue different strategies. They can, for example, make work tasks easier to prevent disruption caused by labour turnover, introduce agency workers to match uneven demand or recruit among more diverse groups of workers. Perceiving labour power in this way as a flow 'evokes action and movement' (Smith, 2010: 270). It also draws attention to some key characteristics of labour power (it's human, versatile, dynamic and wilful), which means workers can transform themselves through training and retraining, move or settle with one employer or in one place. They have volition. This is the world we focus on in our book.

Structure of the book

The book is laid out in 19 chapters, divided into three parts. In *Part 1: Where We've Been…* we review the emergence of HRM as a topic and locate it as a particular type of employment relationship, which has a bearing not only on how management views its integration into business strategy, but also on how it engenders specific types of conflict and resistance within organisations. We then take a close look at how national business systems affect the practice of HRM in different countries, and how they are themselves being affected by the emergence of the gig economy. These, in turn, mould trade union activity and management styles.

Our argument is that the operation of the HRM policies generally listed in the standard textbooks is underpinned by management's need to control costs. Throughout the 20th century, the administration of employees evolved through basic forms of record-keeping and advice giving (personnel management), via consultation and negotiations with trade unions (industrial relations), to contemporary means of reward management and performance appraisal based on individualised relationships between managers and employees (strategic HRM). HRM becomes strategic when it is integrated into an organisation's overall business strategy but, as we see, its control mechanisms adapt to a variety of environmental factors, notably the nature of the product or service and its marketing requirements. We analyse why employers have implemented increasingly sophisticated control mechanisms in recent years. Central to our analysis is the employment relationship between employer and worker: the worker is paid a wage or salary, but the amount of effort given in return depends on a wide variety of factors, including skill, training, equipment and motivation. To reduce costs and raise productivity, the employer is continually trying to get the worker to work as hard as possible, while the worker may, in turn, resist the employer's efforts.

In *Part 2: Where We're Heading…* we examine where we seem to be heading, and how HRM is adapting to certain global trends in labour markets, including the rise of 'new' unitarist forms of management in hi-tech companies, the evolving nature of flexible working and the growing significance of service sectors. We also analyse the influence that migrant workers have on the practice of HRM, and company responses to customer campaigns over corporate malpractice and exploitation of workers through the adoption of CSR policies.

Managers adopt varying attitudes towards these trends, but it is clear that old-style supervisory practices, however relevant in hierarchical organisations, have been superseded by the development of the service sector and hi-tech industries, where contracting relations with service providers, integrative cultures and new forms of paternalism have largely taken their place. That said, in lower skilled areas of work – particularly those dominated by the use of digital platforms (the gig economy) – supervision remains close and may involve customer feedback as a supplementary form of control. Migrant workers often play a significant part in these lower skilled areas, and we examine their role, too, in the functioning of HR control mechanisms.

In *Part 3: What All This Means for HRM* we bring these developments together in each of our chapters on particular aspects of HRM practice: recruitment and social networks; discrimination and diversity; pay and rewards; employee participation and involvement; training and development; and work–life balance. We discuss each of these 'standard' HRM topics in the light of our previous analysis of the nature of the employment relationship and the changing dynamics of HRM, including the gig economy, aesthetic and emotional labour, migrant workers and the looming presence of AI.

In our Summary and Conclusions, we provide an overview of the whole book, but we also tuck in a *Part 4*, in which we try to answer our own question in the book title: where's the 'human' in human resource management? We discuss how far innovative HRM is possible within our advanced capitalist societies, focusing on the themes of dignity at work, the role of enlightened employers and owners, the creation of 'new managers', worker ownership and cooperatives, and radical trade unionism. We remain aware that varying national business systems between countries greatly promote or hinder such innovations.

That said, you might notice that we haven't dedicated chapters to certain aspects of HRM as you might have expected. For example, we don't have chapters on the State, international HRM or 'the future of work'. This is because these dimensions are so fundamental to our analysis that they flow through most of the chapters in the whole book, so we've resisted putting them in their own silos. Discussion of the State informs Chapter 5, 'Societal Contexts and Global Trends', where we explore varieties of capitalism and their impact on labour market regulation, as well as Chapters 14, 'Discrimination and Diversity', 15, 'Pay and Rewards' and 16, 'Employee Participation and Involvement', among others. International dimensions of HRM – and its global connections – feature throughout many chapters, notably Chapters 8, 'The "New" Unitarism', 11, 'Migrant Workers', and 12, 'Corporate Social Responsibility'. Our basic point here is that the post-bureaucratic world we describe is about looser forms of economic, social and organisational connections, which involve strong international dimensions that cannot be unravelled from their HR contexts.

The future of work is also present in the very structure of our book, not least in Chapters 6, 'Trade Unions', 18, 'Work–Life Balance' and 19, 'Artificial Intelligence and HR Analytics'. The same message applies: we don't want to isolate 'the future' in one chapter separate from HR processes, but prefer rather to look historically at each HR process, as well as current practice and future trends in, for example, homeworking, especially in the light of the coronavirus pandemic. Institutions are dynamic and systemic shocks can and do occur. That said, in the 'Conclusions', we invite you to speculate for yourself on possible alternative futures. Numerous writers in the past have predicted a range of work futures, and it's instructive to reread them to see what they got right and what they got wrong (see, for instance, Jenkins and Sherman, 1979, 1981; Rifkin, 1995; Leadbeater, 1999). Nevertheless, we feel it's more engaging for you to have a go for yourself in the light of the book as a whole, and to come to your own informed opinions.

★   ★   ★

Having now outlined the key themes in the book, we conclude with a few remaining comments.

There's no one best way to read this book. You may want to read it cover to cover to build up a coherent analysis of HRM as a whole, but you certainly don't have to do so if you don't want to. If you prefer to go straight into some of the standard HRM topics – such as recruitment, diversity, pay, participation, training or flexibility – then you can easily dip into individual chapters without necessarily engaging with the broader context. You'll find that each chapter is stand-alone and accessible and provides a critical overview of the topic under discussion by itself.

In this book we use the term 'worker' to refer to anyone who is dependent on a wage to earn his/her living. This is a broader term than 'employee', that we take to mean someone in regular full-time or part-time employment with one employer or organisation. Our aim throughout has been to use non-sexist language, alternating 's/he' and 'he or she', as well as using 'they' to refer – ungrammatically, but conveniently – to individual non-gender-specific people, such as 'worker' or 'manager'. However, we do make significant use of sources that date back many years when authors (male and female) tended to use only the male pronoun – you need to bear this in mind when reading some of our older quotations. We sometimes use the problematic aggregation 'Black, Asian and minority ethnic' (BAME) as this can be helpful when examining general patterns of discrimination or advantage. However, where data exist and it's important to be specific, we disaggregate into particular minority ethnic or national categories (GOV.UK, 2022).

Our analysis is generally broad-brush as we cover so much ground, but we trust we have given a sufficient number of references for you to chase up any generalisations that particularly interest you. Basically, our hope is that our book will give you a coherent, sound overview of HRM that will encourage you to fill in the details yourself and to refine, criticise or maybe reject our approach – but above all, to reflect on your own experiences of work and HRM.

We also stress throughout the book that the practice of HRM is embedded in national business systems, so it is natural that – as British authors writing for a British publisher – we base much of our material on the UK. Nevertheless, we also use a lot of material from many other countries, not least China and the US, in order to demonstrate the applicability of our analysis of HRM across borders. At the end of the book you'll find a set of 10 case studies that take up many of the themes we cover, as well as a list of films on HRM-related themes that we hope you'll find entertaining but also thought-provoking. HRM is all around us, not least on film! We also include a glossary of key concepts to help you navigate the book more easily.

Finally, we finished writing this book in the middle of the COVID-19 pandemic that swept the world from early 2020. At the time of writing (April 2022), it's impossible to know what lasting effects the pandemic will have on patterns of working, such as homeworking, relative pay levels, sectoral job losses and inequalities in the labour market, among much else. We have not speculated on these possibilities, but we do use boxes inserted into the text to illustrate some of its effects, and three case studies (no 1 on corporate governance, no 4 on homeworking and no 10 on labour shortages) touch on them too. If you'd like to follow up in greater detail, then Eurofound (2021) presents a comprehensive European-wide survey of the impact of the pandemic on employment issues.

PART 1

Where We've Been…

1

What's HRM *Really* About?

So, what is human resource management (HRM) all about? Most textbooks begin by defining HRM as something along the lines of 'the management of people at work', but then soon add that it also has a strategic function – by which they mean that it supports the organisation's business strategy – and that its policies are generally designed to ensure a workforce that is motivated and committed to business objectives. They will then explain something about the ambiguities of the term – and it's true that there is no generally agreed definition – as well as its origins in the US through personnel management and welfare capitalism. For good measure, they will outline some of the more influential models of HRM as well as give an overview of its influence on organisational performance.

This can be confusing. You're confronted with a jumble of definitions, models and theories that can give your brain a battering. So in this chapter we begin from the ground upwards. We examine, first of all, what human resources (HR) managers actually do and the various processes that an organisation requires to deal with its employees, as well as why we need to put the 'human' into HRM. We then move on to examine the principle that underpins the operation of HRM or indeed any system of people management in an organisation, namely, cost control. Cost control is important to any organisation, whether a private company, big or small, a public corporation, or a voluntary body or charity. But in particular, as we'll see, the control of *labour* costs – pay and benefits, pension contributions and so on – is critically important, as labour costs form such a significant proportion of the costs in running an organisation overall. Once we have established cost control as the key principle underpinning people management in general, we'll find that our understanding of what HRM is all about – and particularly its relationship with strategy – will emerge naturally from the discussion.

What do HR managers actually do?

At the most basic level, HR managers are people managers responsible for running a range of processes and activities that organisations need for dealing with their employees. The way to identify these processes is simply to imagine yourself being recruited by a company. You've applied for your first job, or maybe you're moving jobs – what happens to you? Whatever organisation or sector you are interested in, you have to apply and hope you make the shortlist. You'll then go through a recruitment process, which is obviously very much part of the HRM function. You'll fill in an application form, you may be called for an interview and there may be an assessment centre with tests and exercises to evaluate your capacity for

13

the job. Then, if you are appointed, you will have an induction programme and you'll be assessed for any training you may require. HRM will explain your terms and conditions, including your pay, grade, hours of work and promotions process. You'll be told about performance appraisal, how often it takes place and what you have to do to prepare. Your organisation may well also operate various systems for employee participation and involvement, which will give you opportunities to voice your views to management about working conditions and other matters that are important to you. There might be a trade union that negotiates pay and conditions on your behalf, in which case you'll be entitled to join. Handling conflict and resistance is a very important part of HRM as well. Indeed, later on, if you have a grievance at work – or if, unfortunately, your line manager brings a disciplinary case against you – HRM will run the procedures designed to resolve the issue. If you face any particular challenges that may affect your performance – for example, you become a parent or suffer bereavement – again, you'll generally turn to HRM to help you sort things out. Throughout, HRM will be attempting to deal with all these people management issues fairly and in compliance with relevant legislation on, for example, equal opportunities, data protection and health and safety. And at the end of your working life, whether that comes about naturally through retirement or more turbulently through dismissal or redundancy, then again, HRM will be there. At the most basic level, its role is to keep the records, handle the processes and give advice.

The 'human' dimension of HRM

So this is broadly what HR managers do, listed in chronological order as you encounter these processes at work. All these things structure our everyday working environment, and they're all part of what HRM is about. If you are hoping to become an HR manager, you'll study them specifically as management processes (for example, how to conduct a job interview or a performance appraisal, efficient communications or a disciplinary procedure). In the rest of the book we'll be having a closer look at each of these processes, although our objective is to go well beyond management practice in order to understand better how they affect us as individuals and as employees. This is because – as we've stressed – HRM is not just a top-down management process; it's something we experience as human beings and to which we therefore may react favourably or unfavourably. For example, some new system is introduced at work, maybe without consultation, and we resent that change. We feel that it adds unduly to our workload or that it undermines our pay or status, and we may resist it in all kinds of ways. Conflict at the workplace is a serious issue, as it may well impact on our home lives, our sense of identity and security, and our mental health, and in some drastic cases it may even lead to suicide. A central feature of our analysis is therefore to examine why some workplaces seem to be more amenable to managing conflict than others.

Indeed, in the 21st century, the workplace has changed dramatically, and our analysis has to take this into account. The old model of the bureaucratic organisation, embodying long-term employment, a career structure and progress up a pay spine, still exists, of course. Nevertheless, it can no longer serve as *the* business model for HRM as alongside it – in layers, as it were – there now coexist emerging models of people management, involving outsourced workers, zero-hours contracts, the gig economy and extreme levels of employee disposability. There is no longer the 'model' employee working for Ford, or the Civil Service or a hospital. For a start, these organisations have themselves undergone great changes, but where are we to place those working for Uber, Deliveroo or TaskRabbit? Or Amazon? Or Google or Yahoo? Or call centre workers, or domiciliary care providers? Or outsourced service workers, such as accountants or IT technicians? Not to mention workers in the burgeoning service sectors. None of these groups of workers fits the 'standard' model of HRM embodied in HRM textbooks, and so the determination of their pay and working conditions gets overlooked. Our understanding of HRM must find a way to include them too.

In addition, we need to analyse the rotten underbelly of exploitation at work. We use the word 'exploitation' because there are cases of employers who exploit and bully workers and discriminate against them in all kinds of ways, which means that they are extracting work from them under duress in ways that are simply unacceptable. This might involve holding down pay or refusing to respect the law – for example on minimum pay or on hours of work – and taking advantage of their dominant position as an employer to extract more labour from the worker than is actually allowed, or it might involve gangmasters or, at the extreme end, slavery. There are, horrifically, 'modern' forms of slavery currently taking place in the UK as well as in many other countries. Our book will therefore be examining these issues too – this is why it stresses the 'human' in human resource management.

Cost control – and the control of labour costs

How do we make sense of HRM, then, in such a complex and turbulent working environment? Can we identify any principles that underpin people management across all these contexts that might allow us better to understand the dynamics of these complexities and turbulence and where HRM fits in?

We can make a start by considering the organisational context. Any organisation operates in a competitive environment, particularly those in the private sector, but even those in the voluntary or public sectors need to ensure that they are operating efficiently. Milton Friedman, the neoliberal economist, once declared:

> In a free-enterprise, private-property system, a corporate executive is an employee of the owners of the business. He has direct responsibility to his employers. That responsibility is to conduct the business in accordance with their desires, which generally will be to make as much money as possible while conforming to the basic rules of the

society, both those embodied in law and those embodied in ethical custom. (Friedman, 1970)

If we keep, for now, to the private sector, how does a company 'make as much money as possible', or at least maintain itself in the market? The answer to this question involves a discussion of strategy, which we cover next, in Chapter 2, but a successful company needs to position itself distinctively in the market (in terms of factors like price, quality, innovation and service, for example) and embed its strategy into its resources and capabilities. Resources include land, equipment, financial assets and intangibles, such as brand, while 'capabilities essentially lie in the skills and competencies of individuals in the organisation and how those are combined with others' (Hooley et al, 1998: 101). In this way, effective HRM can be viewed as key to the capability of the company.

However, whatever its market strategy, the company must aim to keep its cost structure under strict control, which is where HRM plays a central role from a business angle. Indeed, HRM is arguably the foundation of cost control, because we find that, generally speaking, employment costs for manufacturing companies are somewhere between 20% and 40% of total costs (Adkins, 2019). In the service sector, they are even higher, at 50% to 70%. It is therefore clearly essential to keep labour costs under control and within budget, because if not, the business may find itself undercut by more efficient competitors.

Some costs may be easier to control than others. A company will find it difficult to control the costs of raw materials or supplies, as they may be sourced on world markets and their price is a given. So it may not be able to do much about the price of inputs at all. Technology is likely to be a given, at least in the short or medium term, while repositioning in the market may also prove challenging, again, in the short or medium term. The one factor that the company can aim to control most directly and quickly is the cost of labour – not with total control, but with the greatest control.

This is why HRM becomes such an important feature within business strategy (that word again) because, basically, 'smart' or 'intelligent' HR practices can help to reduce the unit cost of labour. Few organisations actually talk about HRM in terms of costs in this way, but here is a quote from Michael O'Leary, chief executive officer (CEO) of Ryanair, who is known for his colourful language. Asked about his employees, he called them his 'biggest cost', adding: 'We all employ some lazy bastards who needs a kick up the backside, but no-one can bring themselves to admit it' (quoted in Espiner, 2019).

HRM textbooks generally put things rather differently, claiming that 'staff are the company's most important asset', or words to that effect – and there are reasons for this, which we examine later in this chapter. However, what Michael O'Leary is saying here is that staff are also a cost and may be a drain on the organisation if they are not managed properly.

The point he's making, crudely, but succinctly, is the point we are making too: that actually, HRM is about controlling costs. And if you understand that, you begin to understand a little bit more about where HRM is coming from. As we shall see, the ways in which organisations attempt to control labour costs depend very much on a complex variety of factors, such as market position, sector, nature of the technology being used, skill levels of the workers involved, presence of a trade union and much else – and, as noted before, this brings us into a discussion of HR strategy next, in Chapter 2. However, before that, we need to address a concept that is central to our understanding of HR strategy: the concept of unit labour costs.

Unit labour costs

Now, what is a unit labour cost? Imagine for a moment that a firm produces 10,000 units a week of something – it doesn't matter what – and employs 100 workers. These are arbitrary figures – they don't matter, they are just an illustration. This means that the productivity per worker is 100, because you divide 10,000 by 100 and it comes to 100. That's fairly obvious. Then imagine that the firm pays each worker £400 a week with an extra £50 in fringe benefits. Fringe benefits might be, for example, things like a season ticket loan or subsidised food in the cafeteria or parking expenses, but fringe benefits are something else that many companies give their employees. Each worker is therefore being paid the equivalent of £450 a week. This means that the company's total labour cost for 100 workers is going to be £45,000 a week, and that means that the unit labour cost – £45,000 divided by 10,000 – is £4.50. In other words, the cost of producing each unit is £4.50.

This is the first and last time you'll see an equation in this book, and it's not really an equation at all – it's just a kind of way to get your head round the concept:

The unit labour cost will be £45,000/10,000 = £4.50

$$= \frac{E\,(w + f)}{Q}$$

That is, the total number of employees (E) multiplied by their total wage costs (w) plus the total cost of their fringe benefits (f), divided by the total number of units produced each week (Q). This is a fairly elementary example, and we're not claiming that unit labour costs are always easy to calculate – not at all, as we explain further in Chapter 19. Rather, we are making a general point about the way in which labour is factored into producing goods and services (Adkins, 2019).

The question to consider here is: how can HRM serve to reduce unit labour costs? If you think about it, there are only two possible ways you can do it: you can reduce the price of labour (the top line) or you can increase the number of units produced (the bottom line). That's all you can do. In other words, to reduce labour costs, you can either reduce the £450 that you are paying to your workers or you can somehow increase labour productivity. Now, let's have a look at both of those in turn and see how HRM can get involved.

Direct labour costs

What might we do about pay? Imagine we are working for a large company and we're concerned about productivity – our market share is declining and one of the things we're worried about is that we haven't controlled labour costs. Maybe our labour costs in comparison with our competitors are getting out of hand. Maybe they're not competitive any more. What are we going to do about it?

Well, we can't do anything about indirect labour costs, such as employers' pension contributions or National Insurance (social security) contributions, which are legal requirements. That leaves direct costs: wages/salaries and fringe benefits. So we might freeze wages for a while, that is, not increase them. Maybe we can introduce performance-related pay, or a less generous form of it. This goes back to Michael O'Leary's point about the 'lazy bastards'. If some of our staff aren't as productive as we think they should be, maybe one way to get them to produce more is to pay them on a performance-related pay system. We might review fringe benefits and cut them too, for example, by removing subsidised meals from the cafeteria or making employees pay for their parking spaces. This would surely upset the workers concerned, but nevertheless, it's something we might consider. Indeed, Paycor discovered that 65% of companies in the US were looking to re-evaluate benefits in 2021 (Paycor, 2020).

Companies can also change employment contracts. Delivery firms, for example, have moved from a traditional standard employment model to a contractor model. By laying off their drivers and re-engaging them as independent contractors, they have reduced indirect labour costs (such as holiday and sick pay), but at the price of losing workers' trust (Woodcock and Graham, 2019). Contract manipulation of this kind is widespread in the logistics sector, starting in the US with Microsoft, and now spreading across many industries beyond hi-tech companies (van Jaarsveld, 2004).

Another way to control labour costs is to move the work offshore: companies will argue that British workers are too expensive and relocate to Eastern Europe or to Asia in order to save money (see Box 1.1).

BOX 1.1: DYSON MOVES ABROAD

In 2000, Dyson, the manufacturer of domestic appliances, ended production of its bagless vacuum cleaners in Malmesbury, Wiltshire, and moved 800 jobs to Malaysia. James Dyson, the company's founder-owner, at the time blamed soaring manufacturing costs in the UK, specifically the doubling over 10 years of direct labour costs in the Swindon area, where unemployment was zero. The company's performance had also been hindered by a strong pound sterling, and Dyson said that moving abroad would allow him to spend more on research and development (Gow, 2003). In 2019, the company announced that it would relocate its global headquarters from the UK to Singapore.

Moving production from a more expensive to a less expensive country will certainly save money. And then we might also consider whether we should pay more or less than the market rate in the area. This is an important issue because, if you are trying to attract highly skilled workers and you're in a competitive labour market, you may want to pay over the odds to your workers to attract and keep them.

However, the most drastic way to reduce labour costs, especially in the short term, is to declare redundancies, that is, to sack workers or – in management speak – 'let people go' or 'downsize'. In the UK and the US, it is not uncommon to placate shareholders, who may be concerned at falling share values, by cutting the workforce as part of a strategy to restore confidence (see Box 1.2).

BOX 1.2: JOB CUTS AT ROLLS-ROYCE

Warren East became CEO at Rolls-Royce in 2015 at a time of serious crisis for the company. His priority was to convince the City that the company could survive, in which he broadly succeeded, and he then followed up with a plan to cut middle management in an attempt to increase profits.

Rolls-Royce accordingly announced in June 2018 that it would cut 4,600 jobs at a cost of £500 million, including redundancies, which would save £400 million a year by the end of 2020. The plan clearly focused on the interests of shareholders. It illustrates the reaction of a CEO to a corporate financial crisis in the UK by reassuring the City and shareholders that the company had good longer term prospects and then cutting middle management jobs to make it even more profitable. The BBC reported that shares in Rolls-Royce were 'up 4% shortly after midday' on the day of the announcement (BBC News, 2018). In March 2021, it was reported that the company – under further pressure from the COVID-19 pandemic – had cut 7,000 jobs from the total 19,000 in its global civil aerospace division (Jolly, 2021).

A further example is the case of P&O Ferries which in March 2022 sacked 800 workers without consultation to slash labour costs. Peter Hebblethwaite, the company's CEO, stated: 'It was our assessment that the change [in business model] was of such magnitude that no union could accept our proposals' (quoted in Topham, 2022).

Productivity

What might we do about productivity? Productivity is the other dimension – rather than keeping down labour costs, we can try to boost output, but how, exactly? The classic way is to tighten supervision by closely monitoring absence, policing lunch and toilet breaks and clamping down on 'time wasting'. Maybe we need to introduce a new supervisory system to keep workers under tighter control? This might mean introducing electronic devices that monitor work rates of the kind used extensively to monitor workers at Amazon (see Box 1.3). Indeed, electronic monitoring and zero-hours contracts are used by local authorities in the UK to anchor the costs of homecare exclusively in the time that paid carers spend in their clients' homes, thereby squeezing out any time for travel or training and intensifying care labour (Moore and Hayes, 2017).

Or monitoring might mean keeping control of how workers are using their computer systems in the office. Maybe they're booking their holidays or updating their Meta (formerly known as Facebook) pages instead of getting down to writing that report.

BOX 1.3: ELECTRONIC SURVEILLANCE AND PRODUCTIVITY

Two-thirds of employers who responded to a survey conducted by the US Management Association revealed that they monitor their employees' internet connections at work and their online activity even when they are not at work. Forty-five per cent said they tracked content, keyboard strokes and time spent at the keyboard, while 43% reported that they keep and evaluate computer files. Employers conduct electronic surveillance because of worries not only over lawsuits and security breaches but also over productivity. They believe that workers are probably not paying sufficient attention to their paid employment if they spend too much time online (Satariano, 2020).

Online skiving might be an issue, but how do you supervise that without infringing employees' privacy? This is exactly the kind of discussion HRM would have. Furthermore, for each of the HRM processes we noted earlier, we can raise productivity issues:

- Recruitment: Are we recruiting the right people with the right skills mix, or are we wasting time and effort in providing basic training (maybe in computer skills)?
- Talent management: How do we retain people who are talented? Are they moving on too quickly? How do we ensure they have the right level of responsibility?
- Improved job design: Are there ways of reorganising the physical layout of workspace, or of introducing forms of automation, to raise productivity?
- Training: Are employees sufficiently flexible to cover for one another when one is absent or sick? Rather than bringing in an agency worker, maybe it would be more efficient to ensure employees are multiskilled?
- Voice: Maybe improved systems of communication, information and consultation might help to involve employees more satisfactorily at the workplace and make them more proactive to seeking solutions to problems at work themselves?

These are merely some of the measures that the company might want to consider among many others. Not all of them, however, would be considered appropriate in all companies – for example, some hi-tech companies encourage 'churn' among their employees, as they rely on long hours and a burnout culture (points we explore further in Chapter 8). That said, whatever the organisation, it faces the challenge of controlling labour costs in one way or another – keeping down labour costs on the one hand and raising productivity on the other, and thereby, of course, maximising the chances that it survives. Indeed, survival is the bottom line. Whatever an organisation's objectives – profit-maximising, increasing market share or just 'satisficing' (ticking over) – it has to survive, whatever happens (Walker, 2019: 31–5).

BOX 1.4: TESLA AND LABOUR PRODUCTIVITY

In stressing the importance of unit labour costs, we might be accused of ignoring new forms of value, in which firms in hi-tech sectors and the gig economy can see their share price sky-rocket without having made any profits from goods and services, which suggests a disconnection between value creation and production, and therefore the irrelevance of HRM to this process. This so-called 'financialisation' suggests that firms can make money through money markets without actually producing anything. But despite all this hype about crazy share prices, Tesla, one of the craziest with a 'market value of about $632bn, bigger than GM, Ford, Toyota and Volkswagen combined' (*Financial Times*, 2021), nevertheless remains focused on labour costs. Tesla is the only non-unionised US car firm. A campaign for unionisation gained momentum as productivity was ramped up to meet demand (in 2013, the company delivered 22,477 vehicles, rising to just under 510,000 by 2020). Work rates intensified and injuries rose, yet wages remained lower than those in other US car producers:

> In the fall of 2016, José Moran, a Tesla factory employee, reached out to United Auto Workers to ask about starting a union. By early 2017, a group of organisers called it the Fair Future at Tesla campaign. In February 2017, the effort went public when Moran wrote a blog post on Medium entitled, "Time for Tesla to Listen." He said factory workers were constantly getting hurt because the company made them work long hours on machinery that wasn't ergonomically safe. He also said the company had a shortage of workers and kept pushing employees to work faster. He then pointed out that Tesla employees were paid less than other employees in the auto industry and made the case for joining a labor union. "I often feel like I am working for a company of the future under working conditions of the past," Moran wrote in the blog post. (Fernández-Campbell, 2019)

One way or another, this discussion reveals the critical issue that underpins the policy and practice of HRM, namely, the ways in which managers seek to control the workforce to achieve their aims and objectives. This is an issue that goes back to the dawn of industrialisation and the evolution of the modern workplace. One key theorist whose work remains highly relevant today is Frederick W. Taylor (1856–1915). Taylor was an American engineer who originated the principle of 'scientific management', which stipulates that there is one best way to carry out a given task and that it is the manager's role to ensure that the worker concerned carries it out efficiently under close supervision. Taylor devised this principle having observed workers processing pig iron in an iron mill and concluding that productivity could be improved by reorganising work on 'scientific' principles (such as by breaking tasks down into ever smaller units, redesigning work space and streamlining work flows).

These principles became extremely influential in the early 20th century when Henry Ford adopted them in the mass production of motor cars, which successfully reduced production costs and led to dramatic increases in demand. On 'Fordist' assembly lines, supervision is very much top-down. The supervisor monitors the performance of tasks that are delimited and carried out in a certain order and to a certain standard. Even in the 21st century, this model of supervision persists as a kind of archetype: the supervisor as a benign but strict manager who oversees and maybe advises, but who is nevertheless very much in control (Evans and Holmes, 2013).

In reaction, the Hawthorne experiments, conducted by Elton Mayo and his colleagues in the US between 1924 and 1933, revealed that the world of work isn't quite like that, and that workers need to be acknowledged and recognised, as well as controlled (at least, that's the way their work has come to be interpreted, but for a critical review, see Hassard, 2012). They don't want a supervisor to be continually peering over their shoulder and admonishing; rather, they want their tasks and efforts to be appreciated with supervisors taking an interest in what they're doing. This development led to the human relations approach to HRM from the 1930s, reflecting the idea of a worker as a subject who can be manipulated through praise rather than as merely an object to be controlled. This understanding of the role of acknowledgement and recognition underpins the ways in which worker autonomy and trust come to be central concepts in HRM, as well as cruder forms of control. Both scientific management and human relations were anti-union, and assumed good management could substitute for workers having their own voice through independent trade unions, although this assumption was adapted when these ideas travelled out of the US to Europe (Cummings et al, 2017).

We return to these control themes as the book unfolds, and indeed, we find they play a central part in the next chapter, on HR strategy.

Concluding comments

HRM, then, is about two dimensions of control: controlling labour costs and ensuring productivity is rising, or at least not falling. Productivity is a key issue that managers can improve in all kinds of ways, as we've seen. However, the effects of controlling costs and raising productivity may well affect your interests as a worker and the ways in which you engage with your line manager. Changes in work practices may affect your pay, work–life balance and sense of fair treatment, among many other things. Your choices (apart from leaving) are either to suffer in silence or to talk to your manager and do something about them. At that point you're beginning to interact with your company's HR systems. If you see cost control and productivity as the core functions for HRM, then the role of HRM within the company makes much more sense.

Some questions to think about

1. Explain the concept of 'unit labour costs' and why they are so important in HRM.

2. Outline some of the ways in which HR managers might help organisations (a) control labour costs and/or (b) raise productivity.

3. How do you feel about electronic surveillance? Would you be happy if your employer used electronic devices to monitor your work output?

Further reading

Moore, S. and Hayes, L.J.B. (2017) 'Taking worker productivity to a new level? Electronic monitoring in homecare – The (re)production of unpaid labour', *New Technology, Work and Employment*, 32(2): 101–14. [Illustrates the role of electronic monitoring and zero-hours contracts in an attempt to increase the productivity of paid carers.]

Walker, P. (2019) *The Theory of the Firm: An Overview of the Economic Mainstream*, London: Routledge. [Technical introduction to the theoretical understanding of the nature and structure of companies.]

Williams, K., Williams, J. and Haslam, C. (1989) 'Do labour costs really matter?', *Work, Employment & Society*, 3(3): 281–305. [Analysis of the challenges of calculating unit labour costs in British manufacturing – dated, but still relevant.]

2

What's So Special About HR Strategy?

The next step in our quest to discover what human resource management (HRM) is all about is, logically, to ask in greater detail how exactly human resources (HR) managers control labour costs and boost output. Investigating these questions will lead naturally into a discussion about strategy, at which point we'll be much nearer an answer. In this chapter we explore the relationship between personnel management, industrial relations and HRM in order to understand how they feed into the development of strategic HRM. We critically explore the nature of 'strategy', including the ways in which it develops variably as process, practice and culture within institutional frameworks, before examining the 'internal' and 'external' fit of HRM with business strategy and how it leads to forms of 'hard' and 'soft' HRM. These arguably help to explain why some managers view labour as merely a factor of production and others as 'our most valuable asset'. These variations in turn help to explain different approaches to control and productivity.

Personnel management

Personnel management is the earliest form of people management to carry its own name and style. It emerged from the First World War and the development of mass industry in the 1920s, when employers had to coordinate and control large numbers of increasingly skilled workers in immense factories. The basic function of personnel management is operational and process-oriented – to ensure the steady supply of labour at the workplace to guarantee untroubled production of goods and services (this section follows Storey, 1992: 168; and Blyton and Turnbull, 2004: 112). So, when a line manager has a vacancy, personnel are responsible for recruiting the right person quickly. Personnel are also responsible for the payroll and pensions, making sure that workers are paid accurately and on time, and that their social security and pensions contributions are deducted correctly. In addition, they may administer welfare schemes and social clubs, as well as communications systems, such as the organisation's own internal newsletter, as well as employee surveys and other forms of workforce feedback. And, of course, they'll also be responsible for dismissals, redundancies and retirement of employees when they come to the end of their working lives. Throughout, they'll keep staff records of absence, sickness and turnover, among other routine activities. To call them 'routine' is, however, in no way to disparage these activities because, obviously, every organisation needs to carry out these tasks – they're part of the daily life of any organisation and ensure that people are deployed efficiently and that unplanned absences are kept to a minimum.

All these things are critically important, but this kind of personnel function is clearly reactive. It reacts to organisational requirements. For example, in recruitment, personnel are not proactively saying, 'Well, we need a new person of such and such a calibre for this job'. They are waiting for a line manager in another department to come along and ask how to advertise for a new job.

In addition to these reactive functions, personnel managers will also often give advice. For example, it may be that some organisational change is being proposed, such as delayering the organisational hierarchy (taking out layers of management to make it flatter). Such a move may well affect people's career expectations, job grades and pay. So that has to be carefully managed, and personnel are going to be asked about the implications of those changes and maybe how to implement them. Or the introduction of a new technological system within an organisation will undoubtedly affect how people work, the skills required and the kinds of responsibilities involved – personnel may be involved in the consultations. Or there may be a change in labour legislation – for example, the minimum wage goes up or a new law on parental leave comes into effect. How is that going to affect the organisation? Personnel's advice will be sought to ensure the organisation complies. In these senses, personnel are giving advice, but on an ad hoc basis. They are waiting for colleagues in other departments to come and seek advice; they are not giving advice proactively. Personnel in these situations act as a kind of internal consultancy, as a consultant to the organisation, waiting to give advice on whatever questions arise. They remain process–oriented, but with a focus on their organisation's future.

We find that personnel sometimes also have a third role, which is internal regulation. Large, hierarchical organisations in particular have their own internal procedures for employees, often enshrined in staff manuals. Just to give an example, at Royal Holloway University of London (RHUL) (our university), the (electronic) staff manual is 92 pages long. It covers the procedures you have to go through to get things done, such as how to register absence from work; how to apply for promotion or go to a conference; how to purchase things, make travel arrangements or employ casual staff; and all manner of internal regulations. These include grievance procedures (how do you settle a grievance with your line manager?) as well as disciplinary procedures (if our line managers are upset with either of us – for example, if they think we're underperforming – how do they deal with us?).

And, of course, in a unionised setting, there's the issue of the *collective* management of workplace relations. Personnel must inform and consult the recognised trade unions in line with the law and the relevant collective agreements, participate in collective bargaining rounds and ensure the application of the terms and conditions contained in any agreements that are negotiated. Under such unionised conditions, personnel engage in industrial relations, where pay, conditions and internal procedures are the subject of joint regulation. Personnel, then, often have a significant regulatory function within the organisation as well.

Finally, the personnel function might involve change-making. Here we move into a rather different sphere because personnel now become proactive, 'people-oriented' and future-focused. Personnel are no longer simply carrying out everyday functions and waiting to give advice, and nor are they merely responsible for devising and enforcing internal processes and regulations – rather, they are out there, integrated into the organisation's business strategy. At this point, personnel morph into HRM, with HR directors often found on the boards of companies. There was a time when personnel managers were never found at that level. Now, most large organisations will have the HR director on the board which is where strategic or forward-looking decisions are taken (Mayo, 2020). This means that the HR angle is no longer merely reactive but becomes embedded into strategic decisions involving new investment plans, products or marketing schemes, plant closures and redundancies, or indeed the introduction of more proactive HR policies. It is significant, for example, that boards with HR managers are found to have stronger diversity management than firms lacking such board expertise (Mullins, 2018). Consequently, since around the 1980s, we have witnessed the arrival of a whole variety of new HR techniques in companies: assessment centres, performance-related pay, performance appraisal in many guises, various forms of flexible working and employee involvement schemes, many of which are underpinned by attempts to control organisational culture in one way or another.

We return to all these points in later chapters, but for now, we can summarise by stating that personnel management becomes HRM once it's integrated into strategic organisational decision-making systems and its reactive function becomes a proactive, future-oriented function. At least, that's the generally accepted view (Legge, 2005). However, before we examine this claim in greater detail, we can illustrate these findings in Figure 2.1.

HRM and strategy

Figure 2.1 is helpful because it focuses on the distinction between intervention/people orientation and non-intervention/process orientation in personnel matters, and tactical/operational and strategic/future-focused intervention. Obviously, we have to be a bit careful of figures like this, as the world isn't as cut-and-dried and doesn't fall into such neat categories, which actually merge into one another and look much more ambiguous. Nevertheless, Figure 2.1 does help to make everything look more understandable than it otherwise might be, so bear with it for the time being.

The bottom right-hand corner (service providers) indicates old-style personnel management, such as looking after the payroll and making sure the welfare club runs efficiently. It is located on the vertical tactical axis as this function – however valuable – is operationally serving the needs of an organisation and not contributing to its strategy/future. The strategy has already been handed down from above, and personnel is non-interventionist in the sense that it is reacting to events.

Figure 2.1: Four elements of personnel management

Source: Blyton and Turnbull (2004: 112)

The quadrant above that (advisers) is still non-interventionist, but personnel management acquires a strategic/future dimension when it gets involved in giving advice. It is true that when doing so personnel are still not helping to formulate business strategy as such, but nevertheless they are contributing to strategy by responding to a question in an attempt to support it. Advice giving may therefore be seen as form of strategic partnership, although it is non-interventionist.

In the bottom left-hand corner, quadrant 3 (regulator/employee champion) is the function that involves the intervention of personnel in internal regulation. When unions are recognised in the organisation, this quadrant includes industrial relations and the joint regulation of terms and conditions through collective bargaining. Personnel are interventionist, in that they intervene as employee champions in how, for example, disciplinary or grievance procedures are operating, but they are also tactical/operational in that they are not actively contributing to any broader business strategy.

By contrast, only in the top left-hand corner do both strategy and intervention come together (change-maker/change-agent). It is here that HRM makes its entrance. HRM or strategic HRM emerges when the personnel function has developed to such an extent that it is taken seriously by the organisation and the director is generally on the board. The director's views are consulted before business strategies are decided and will feed into the formulation of those strategies. The HR dimensions of new investments, product planning or plant closures will inform decisions from the earliest stages and mould the way in which they are taken, rather than merely being considered during the implementation stages. At this point, personnel management has become genuinely future-focused, and hence turns into HRM.

Figure 2.1 helps us to see our way through the often-confusing terminology that surrounds different forms of people management: personnel management, industrial relations, HRM, strategic HRM. All these different terms slosh around, as it were, and you might be thinking, 'How do they all fit together?' Figure 2.1 should help to explain how all these terms do fit together because it illustrates the different *relationships* that managers foster with employees under different circumstances. In the traditional 'standard' company, personnel management administers the workplace, allowing the routine supervision and monitoring of the workforce. Personnel management acquires an industrial relations function once it deals with a recognised union for the purposes of negotiating pay and other terms and conditions. Strategic HRM begins to develop, generally, but by no means exclusively, in non-unionised workplaces, when employers need to integrate skilled workforces into their business strategies, through individualised techniques (such as performance-related pay and performance appraisal) and culture change designed to enhance employee motivation and commitment. However, we must also note that nowadays terms like 'personnel management' and 'industrial relations' are considered somewhat old-fashioned, so many managers who still perform service-providing and advisory roles are now – in a process of grade inflation – called HR managers, even though they may have few or no strategic responsibilities. Indeed, not every organisation has an HR strategy, and some, particularly smaller, companies merely rely on a general manager for their personnel function.

In the next chapter, we argue that all four quadrants in Figure 2.1 taken together constitute what we refer to as 'employment relations', because, in the end, employment relations are exactly that: the relationship between any employee and their employer or manager at the workplace. And even though the circumstances at the workplace may vary tremendously, this relationship is governed by the employer's requirement to control labour costs, raise productivity and survive. The question, as we'll see, is exactly how they attempt to do so, which will also vary broadly according to which quadrant the organisation fits in.

Anyhow, for now, Figure 2.1 – however oversimplified it may be – does help to highlight key features of the personnel function and in particular to illustrate the way in which the personnel function has developed a strategic dimension morphing as it has done so into HRM. Before we turn to examining the key questions that now arise – notably, how exactly do organisations develop HR strategy and how do HR strategies differ? – we need to make some critical observations about the reality of strategic thinking in the first place.

Strategy: presence, power and types

HR textbooks talk a lot about 'strategy', always assuming that it's a Good Thing – but they don't always analyse what the term really means or implies. Since this book is, above all, about the reality of HRM, we need to look a little more closely at the meaning of strategy.

Presence

The central idea that HRM means the voice of the HR director sitting on the board, which is about the importance of place or *presence* in the hierarchy, is reasonable. But *presence* may simply mean the HR director delivering routine information, ensuring the company complies with new legislation, implementing HR fads and fashions or advising on plans for growth and rationalisation of employment contracts. Insofar as these activities are more future-oriented, for some, they count as *strategic* business (Storey, 1992). These different HR roles can play out in the boardroom, but it's not just the future-oriented stuff that the board looks at. This mythologises what main boards do, suggesting that they sit around thinking up strategy rather than receiving reports and following routines. Smith et al (1990) longitudinally tracked the time devoted to HR issues, especially industrial relations, at Cadbury board meetings, revealing sharp fluctuations in the tabling of HR agenda items depending on the state of relations between management and the unions. In other words, HR roles are set in a dynamic context, not in some elevated heady world of 'strategy'. Schwartz-Ziv and Weisbach (2013: 363), in a survey of board minutes from government-controlled companies in Israel, concluded that: 'boards ... were more likely to receive updates than make decisions, were not presented with alternatives, and almost always voted in line with the CEO'. So we need to be clear that *presence* means being around for all *sorts of activities*. This simply tells us that the peak of an organisation is possibly where 'strategy is done', but the question of how this actually functions is not obvious.

A major problem arises when HR commentators look at the claims HR managers must make in order to justify board presence. This can create an obsession with *strategy* as a golden management activity – and one that eclipses all other activities. This elevation of strategy misunderstands the meaning of the term or reflects simplistic ideas of the military general viewing the battlefield from above the fighting and directing the campaign from on high. If this is case, HR strategy must always be expert, future-focused, long-term and somehow detached from the HRM routine. However, this definition of strategy is outdated. Management academics have theorised and researched strategy for several decades, and the following brief review might help situate the role of HRM when 'being strategic'.

Top-down command

Top-down command models of strategy embrace a classical planning approach that draws on military metaphors where senior management have positional power to look ahead and command (exemplified in Carl von Clausewitz's book *On War*, 1832). This approach looks to Max Weber (1864–1920) and more rationalist understandings of organisations, in which strategies are deliberate, planned and explicit in the sense that they are based on the authority of both expertise and seniority. But Weber's work on leadership also focuses on the authority of 'tradition' (the past) and 'charisma' (the unique leader) (Gerth and Mills, 2014 [1947]). These sources of authority add layers of complexity when analysing the formulation of strategy, as managers who are trying to build coalitions of consensus may also be interacting with the weight of past practice and accommodating the 'vision' of a charismatic leader at the same time. Strategy here is future-oriented, but may be ad hoc and chaotic as the different sources of authority do not always dovetail. In certain cases examined in this book – such as Meta (formerly Facebook) and Sports Direct – powerful owner-leaders embody or personify strategy. They have *power from ownership* rather than narrow expert power, and create what some suggest is a charismatic 'cult of personality' in their corporations that overrides expertise and tradition (Rodriguez, 2019). In the case of Cadbury, the strategic change mapped by Smith et al (1990) was a complex cocktail of direction through ownership authority, a sense of tradition, struggles between different groups of expert managers and the need to adapt to new market trends. All this implies that strategy-making is emergent and messy, not rational.

Types of strategy

Process

An alternative approach to the top-down model is to stress the importance of the 'process' of making strategy, a bottom–up, evolutionary and learning approach (Pettigrew, 1985; Mintzberg, 1987). This questions the assumption that strategies are lying around, fully formed, waiting to be picked up by enlightened leaders. It builds on the idea that strategy-making is a question of politics, of making choices from a range of options. Child (1972, 1997) and Pettigrew (1977) stress that strategy is political, and emerges through a process of argument, power and pressures within the management coalition within large firms. Child's theory of *strategic choice* reacts against the idea that strategies come ready-formed into the organisation from the company's business environment. This theory warns that contingencies, such as sector and technology, should not be seen as determinants of managerial choice. They do not, for example, make company behaviour uniform within its sector (such as car production or supermarkets) or type of technology (such as mass or craft, process or bespoke).

Contingency thinking (to which we return below) can be too deterministic as it tends to remove the will or action choices of managers, assuming that they need only to 'read the environment' to know how to strategise. The situation is actually far more complex. While sector and technology do place structural limits on management, firms within the same sectors often do quite different things, something contingency theory cannot readily explain. For example, firms in the same sector frequently cover several market segments. BMW and Daimler-Benz successfully make cars in all price ranges, yet within an overall quality engineering framework. However, all car companies seem to embrace a universal strategy across all segments of dividing their workforces into a group of 'standard' or regular workers and a group of agency workers with no direct employment (but often lengthy relationships) with the firm, though the proportion of each varies (Jürgens and Krzywdzinski, 2016). In other words, HR strategy does not flow automatically from product markets. It is much more varied and dynamic, but also, for some practices like recruitment in the world's car companies, segmentation may be systemic and universal. Empirical work is always required to examine the relationship between strategy and management practices, such as recruitment, as we really can't read off company practice from sector norms with any confidence.

Practice

Strategy may also be seen as practice, as about 'doing' or agency. In other words, there is no separation between the moment of senior manager strategising on the one hand and then implementation and practicalities on the other. Strategic action is 'something people *do*' (Whittington, 2006: 613). This appears to remove leaders from the picture, as the location of power is no longer related to position or expertise but is, rather, embodied in the daily actions of managers. This stress on activity reminds us of the need to look for strategy within a wider constituency than just senior managers, and to observe how it emerges over time and through managerial interaction. All good points. But the diffuseness of this approach to strategy can be limiting, especially in the sort of owner–manager companies mentioned above, or when strategic change illustrated in the British Airways (BA) example (see Box 2.2) is embodied in the person of a new chief executive officer (CEO). Strategy, in becoming diffuse, becomes less visible and identifiable as it reaches into routines and culture.

Culture

The literature on *strategy as culture* is based on the idea that the identity and values of the firm are a key component of its strategy. That is, strategy is embedded in company values (Pettigrew, 1979) or in a codified ideology that is reproduced and actively managed as company practice (Kunda, 2006 [1992]). Kunda's work on the role of corporate culture within a hi-tech company (NEC) revealed the way in which values were used as part of its strategy to retain expert workers by socialising them into an 'NEC outlook', similar to the way in which Japanese firms propagate a 'Nissan way' or a 'Toyota way' (Elger and Smith, 2005). However, in later research, Barley and Kunda (2006) revealed an alternative to the strategy of building corporate culture to keep these workers, when the tech sector in Silicon Valley began to buy in talent through agencies, the exact opposite to culture as a recruitment strategy, representing a strategic shift from culture to market, and from commitment to flexibility. This sector shift takes us back to looking at strategy as something that arises 'beyond the firm', with companies facing common problems (in this case, labour shortages) but seeking different strategic ways of addressing them. However, when sectors adopt common practices, we are back to looking at *strategy within an environment*.

Institutional context

Institutional approaches to strategy focus on the environmental contexts that determine organisations' choices and the ways in which they act as sifting processes that shape survival pathways. It is the case that organisations in similar areas tend to conform rather than diverge. Why should this be so? In an influential analysis, DiMaggio and Powell (1983) suggest that institutional conformity/ standardisation (or what they call 'isomorphism') arises out of three social pressures: (1) imitation or copying ('mimetic isomorphism'); (2) compulsion or force ('coercive isomorphism'); and (3) adaptation or fitting in with rules/ values ('normative isomorphism'). We can observe these pressures in operation when companies imitate 'good practice' HRM from successful competitors or are required to follow different rules, laws or practices when they move overseas to conform to the host country. This way of thinking suggests that the external environment of the company determines the strategies. For example, a low-cost, mass service or production company will focus on reducing costs, especially labour costs, as its products are price-sensitive. Alternatively, a company targeting the luxury or elite end of the market may be more relaxed about labour costs, as its branded products are not price-sensitive. However, the stock market is never relaxed about labour costs because the structural elements of the employment relationship are more significant for the purposes of maximising shareholder value than strategy as 'market positioning'. We noted this in the case of Dyson (Box 1.1), a high-end producer that nevertheless relocated production to lower cost countries, and in the case of Tesla (Box 1.4), which remains focused on labour costs, despite also being a high-end company. This suggests that strategy may be a *marketing device* that is only superficially related to HRM, so it is too crude to assume a direct correlation between (1) business strategy for marketing positioning and (2) actual HR practices, because Dyson increased its profitability simply by moving production to a lower cost country.

Another institutional approach to analysing the formation of business strategy is to examine the correspondence between national legacies, social frameworks and traditions as a means for shaping HR practice at company level. A simple example, comparing the UK and Japan, helps to make the point (which we return to in Chapter 5, when we examine the role of varieties of capitalism in HRM). Broadly speaking, companies in the UK are comfortable when workers seek promotion and build their careers by moving from one company to another (in technical terms, using external labour markets). By contrast, in large Japanese companies, career building takes place solely within the same company, over a worker's lifetime (in technical terms, using internal labour markets). This contrast is fundamental to how HRM works in Japan, with HR departments not only being much larger than in the UK, but also functioning as central strategic actors in managing company growth (Olcott, 2009). Such historic and fundamental differences feed into strategy formation and practice in UK and Japanese companies respectively.

However, there are problems with this societal approach too, involving levels of analysis and change over time. First, diversity between companies at subnational levels requires us to look at factors such as industry, sector, regional location and the independence of 'strategic choice', that is, leadership within companies that can act *against* national cultural norms (Child, 1972). Second, explaining change within national settings – such as declining union membership across industrialised countries and the emergence of HRM out of personnel management – involves continuities and discontinuities, so it is important to highlight that the nation or country is not a sufficient explanatory framework for understanding the employment relationship. This requires finer levels of analysis.

So how does strategy fit into HRM?

Given these cautionary points, why study HR strategy? What's the point? Historically, it helps us to understand why HRM has evolved as it has and why the contemporary workplace looks the way it does. HRM began to develop in the US and then in the UK in the 1980s and 1990s. As heavy industry declined and was replaced by the service sector, trade unionism and collective employment relationships declined too, and HRM moved in to fill the void (Boxall, 1992). It is therefore not surprising that the literature on HRM began to burgeon around the same time, as observers tried to defend it or explain where it was coming from. Over the same period, much literature began to argue that having an HR strategy was good for business because it helped to control costs, increase productivity and reduce business risks: 'Strategic HR shifted the unit of analysis from individual employees and HR functions to the organisation as a whole and directed research away from employee attitudes and wellbeing to firm performance' (Batt and Banerjee, 2012: 1739). In this way, it links back to our discussion in Chapter 1 about the pressures on organisations to control unit labour costs.

Huselid (1995), for example, considers over a dozen human factors in US companies, such as recruitment, job analysis, performance appraisal, access to grievance procedures, promotion criteria and training, on the one hand, and specific involvement practices, including information-sharing, the use of employee attitude surveys and company incentive schemes, on the other. These practices are often known collectively as high-performance work practices (HPWPs), and form a key element in HR strategy. Huselid concludes that sales levels and shareholder value are much higher when accompanied by HR strategies. Other research has revealed that survival rates of organisations are higher when they have a single HPWP strategy (Welbourne and Andrews, 1996), and that the number of defective products is reduced (Sattler and Sohoni, 1999). Boosting sales volumes and reducing waste clearly raises productivity and helps control costs, so it will help to reduce unit labour costs. Increasing share value helps to ensure the survival of the company by placing it in a better position to resist takeovers, hostile or otherwise.

By contrast, other researchers have found little effect of this type of HR strategy on labour efficiency (Cappelli and Neumark, 2001), and some conclude that moderate improvements in HPWPs may be more effective than higher levels, which are associated with greater stress (Godard, 2001). Yet other researchers criticise HPWPs on the grounds that they may lead to greater work intensification and stress (Ramsay et al, 2000; Kelly, 2004). In addition, some commentators have pointed out the methodological and conceptual dilemmas that these attempts entail (Purcell and Kinnie, 2010). The result is a complex body of knowledge that requires careful interpretation. Cumulatively, the research demonstrates that a positive relationship does exist, although it is not simple (Jiang et al, 2012). A wide range of contextual factors mediates the impact of people on performance: in short, every case is different.

Having introduced these reservations, we need to examine what an HR strategy of this type actually looks like – what does it involve? Broadly, there are three different ways in which this definition of HR strategy is approached in the literature. The first is in terms of 'internal fit' – between different elements of the strategy. The second is 'external fit'– between the ways in which strategies develop within the company and the external product market of that company. And the third focuses on line management integration – the extent to which line managers are allowed responsibility to develop HR policies of their own. But here we concentrate on internal and external fit, starting with internal fit.

Internal fit

We have already established that HRM covers a range of functions, including recruitment and selection, pay systems, training and employee voice. Justifying the idea of *strategic* HRM, certain writers have sought to show that choosing *one set* of HRM policies can have better economic returns than others, and that some cohere better than others in combinations that are not arbitrary – for example, that HR policies in one area, such as recruitment or training, are related to worker consultation. Jeffrey Pfeffer (1998) argues that there are seven practices in HR that are universal:

1. Employment security, making sure that workers feel as if their employment is secure and that they are not going to get the sack next week.
2. Careful hiring, ensuring you get the right person for the job.
3. Decentralising decision–making and integrating self-managed teams into the business.
4. Competitive pay, keeping your pay in line with local markets to avoid people leaving you.
5. Training, ensuring your training is focused and relevant.

6. Reduced status differentials, trying to have a flat organisational hierarchy and ensuring managers are not seen as remote.
7. Information disclosure, keeping employees up to date about the financial wellbeing of the company.

Pfeffer maintains that taken together these policies create what he calls 'internal fit'. The objective of HRM is to ensure that good practices reinforce one another in order to promote the best levels of productivity and competence within the organisation. So, for example, he argues that employment security, high levels of pay and low status differentials reinforce one another as together they all help to motivate people. In other words, if you want to have people who are well motivated in the organisation, you need these three different elements because they fit together. Similarly, he claims that careful hiring, good supportive training and information disclosure are ways to ensure competence at work, adding that decentralised decision-making is a common requirement across all these policies. They are mutually reinforcing in a coherent pattern and not merely isolated elements of personnel, hence the notion of internal fit.

Pfeffer actually goes further than this by claiming that these seven practices are the best policy not only for particular kinds of organisations – such as those in the private sector – but for any organisation, public, private or voluntary. This is therefore often known as a 'universalist' approach. Such an approach to HR strategy claims that there is a universal set of HR policies and practices that should be implemented within an organisation, not just in the UK or the US, but also anywhere in the world. The idea is that these seven HR policies will provide the best fit for an organisation and so provide the best chances for it to prosper.

Now, is this actually the case? Pfeffer is making quite a weighty claim and, in fact, if we look more carefully, we find that things are more complicated. In Box 2.1 we examine the relationship between Pfeffer's practices and Amazon, one of the most commercially successful companies on the planet.

BOX 2.1: AMAZON AND PFEFFER – HOW DO THEY FIT?

Pfeffer advocated a universal 'best way' HRM based on what he saw as seven key HR practices that would work best for all organisations and their workers. The Amazon case is useful for throwing this model under the bus:

1. Employment security: Amazon has high employment insecurity, so the opposite.
2. Careful hiring: Hiring through an employment agency for the majority of workers means Amazon is casual, not careful, so the opposite.
3. Decentralised decision-making: No, Amazon is very top-down and centralised – so the opposite.
4. High compensation: Amazon pays just above the minimum wage, so again, the opposite.

5. Extensive training: There is limited training in specialised jobs at Amazon, but some training for those who accumulate service with the company. So a mixed picture, but more towards limited training.
6. Reduced status differentials: Amazon has strong status distinctions, especially between directly employed and indirect (agency) workers and between workers and supervisors, so again, the opposite.
7. Sharing of financial and performance information: Not at Amazon.

In the Amazon case, then, virtually none of these so-called 'universal' practices is present. Yet Amazon is hugely successful as a business. What this means is that Pfeffer is wrong empirically – there are no universal HR practices, but rather, different ways of doing HRM, and therefore a more contingent approach is empirically stronger. However, Pfeffer might argue that his list is ideal and outlines what would make for better HRM, and so may be defended on those grounds. The Amazon model, from the workers' perspective, is far from ideal. Although efficient by narrow, operational criteria, it remains a stressful place to earn a living (Geissler, 2018). Tight labour markets, increased capital investment and years of union pressure resulted in the first unionisation of an Amazon US distribution centre (Staten Island) in April 2022.

Questioning whether there is one single universal set of HR policies that applies across the board leads us to what is sometimes called the 'contingency approach' to HRM. 'Contingency' means 'dependency'. If something is contingent on something else, it means it's dependent on other things. Accordingly, another body of commentators argues that the idea of a universal set of HRM principles is not really very helpful, and they prefer to look at how organisations adapt HR policies to their own circumstances. In other words, their policies are contingent on something else besides one single prescriptive set of HR policies. We met this approach earlier in this chapter when we looked at institutional approaches to strategy, and the ways in which it is shaped by environmental factors.

External fit

Consideration of this approach brings us to examine the second concept of 'fit' we referred to, external fit, which makes links with the organisation's product markets. This is not really strategy, but rather an investigation of how environments shape or limit what HR managers can do.

Michael Porter (1980, 1985) makes some important points about market strategy, distinguishing between markets that rely on cost leadership, differentiation and specialisation (or niche). For example, Ford, Nissan and Toyota make cheap and reliable cars, so they compete over cost leadership. Mercedes and BMW compete by way of quality in differentiated markets, while Aston Martin, Morgan and TVR produce specialised sports cars and so compete in niche markets. Parallels in UK supermarkets or retail include Asda, Morrison's and Tesco as cheap and cheerful cost leaders, Waitrose in the differentiated market, and Holland & Barrett, which, as a health and wellbeing store, competes very much within its own niche. The same thing applies to airlines: contrast Ryanair and EasyJet, on the one hand, with BA and Cathay Pacific, on the other. Different companies within the same sector – cars, retail or airlines – market their products or services very differently according to their customers and market segments. An interesting idea is that maybe market segment influences the kind of HR strategy – and associated HR policies and practices – that an organisation is most likely to have.

However, as Box 2.2 reveals, this account is too deterministic as it tends to remove the will or action choices of managers, assuming that they need only to 'read the environment' to know how to strategise. In fact, they may seek to move the organisation into another market niche, and in doing so they undermine all the established HR procedures, practices and norms.

BOX 2.2: CONFLICTED STRATEGIES – STRATEGIC CHANGE AT BA

While Ryanair achieves business *focus* as Europe's dominant low-cost mass carrier, meaning its HR strategy is strongly determined by cost reduction, BA has tried to maintain both high-cost and low-cost segments. Some might suggest this confused their business strategy and led to a major dispute with the BA unions, which sought to maintain BA as a 'quality carrier'. Strategic change (here defined as the movement from one market segment to another) was triggered by the appointment in 2005 of a new CEO, Willie Walsh, who had a track record in transforming the Irish airline Aer Lingus and was himself keen on BA 'adopting elements of the LCC [low-cost carrier] model' (Taylor and Moore, 2019: 50). Central to Project Columbus, the management strategy to move BA closer to its LCC rivals (Ryanair and EasyJet), was reduced staffing levels, greater flexibility, inferior terms and conditions and, ultimately, a reduction in labour costs. Casting aside the decades-long tradition of joint regulation at BA, management – personified by Walsh – sought to sideline BASSA (the BA trade union) and implement dramatic changes unilaterally. This inevitably led to major disputes with the unions as 'preventing Walsh from breaking the union was essential for ensuring the maintenance of decent working conditions' (Taylor and Moore, 2019: 71), and what workers saw as defending a quality airline customer experience.

Basically, empirical work is always required to examine the relationship between strategy and management practices, such as recruitment, as we really can't read off company practice from sector norms with any confidence.

'Hard' and 'soft' HRM

This discussion of external fit leads us into making a distinction – a very common distinction in the literature – between 'hard' and 'soft' HRM that will help to bring this chapter to a conclusion. 'Hard' HRM is where you treat workers as just that – hard, a factor of production. Think of the various words in the term 'human resource management'. If you emphasise the *management* of human resources, you think of managers supervising or telling workers what to do. Workers are not treated as individuals but rather as a factor of production within the organisational process, like equipment or machinery: 'From this perspective, the human resource, the object of formal manpower planning, can be just that, largely a factor of production, along with land and capital and an "expense of doing business"' (Legge, 2005: 105). Here you have a model of hard HRM, where you're stressing the management of workers, without much interest in their own thoughts, feelings or aspirations, or the things that make them human. Workers are seen as a cost and as expendable if no longer required, when they can be made redundant.

However, if you think of 'human resource management' with the emphasis on *human*, you get a very different idea, one where you're stressing the human element of the function, and the fact that we all have different thoughts, feelings and aspirations, as well as different aptitudes, skills and requirements at work. This perspective treats employees 'as valued assets, a source of competitive advantage through their commitment, adaptability and high quality (of skills, performance and so on)' (Legge, 2005: 105). This is a model of 'soft' HRM that aims to take into account workers' individuality. It looks at workers as people in a very different way from hard HRM: they are seen as potentially more proactive and motivated.

Here you have two very different ways of looking at workers: the *hard* way, as factors of production and expendable – once you've done your job, then that's it, finish, goodbye; or the *soft* version, which regards workers as adaptable and much more productive, if only you can gain their commitment. There's a polarity there – and we can see it all around us: low-paid and generally low-skilled workers, on the one hand, subject to close supervision and monitoring (often through digital gadgetry); and higher paid and high-skilled workers on the other, who enjoy greater discretion and autonomy at work. Indeed, it is worth pointing out that the basic distinction between hard/soft HRM goes back a long way. In 1974, Alan Fox distinguished between 'low-discretion' roles in industry, involving low-trust relationships, and 'high-discretion' roles, involving high-trust relationships (Fox, 1974). Other writers refer to 'low road' and 'high road' approaches to employment practices as a framework for efforts to improve the quality of work in low-wage employers (Osterman, 2018).

Nevertheless, the broad distinction – that is, between hard/soft HRM, low/high discretion or low/high road – needs to be treated with care. These categories have fluid boundaries and must themselves be refined, as they are largely based on the manufacturing sectors (we'll return to this point in Chapter 10, when we examine HRM in services). The 'hard'/'soft' alternatives are abstractions and not empirically grounded. Still, they are useful for discussing the direction of travel of a sector or company, as in strategic movement at BA (see Box 2.2). In the meantime, we should note that the depiction of HRM as 'hard' or 'soft' is also an oversimplification because these forms may well coexist within the same organisation. It's not that organisations are characterised throughout only by hard or by soft HRM. For example, we tend to think of Amazon as a hard HRM organisation, which depends on low-skilled agency workers who are continually monitored by digital gadgetry (see Box 2.1). However, Amazon also uses elements of soft HRM in its higher levels. The same is true, the other way round, for Google, if we think of it as a soft HRM organisation. Box 2.3 shows that it actually relies on hard elements within its HR strategy when it employs workers on precarious contracts.

BOX 2.3: PROBLEMS COMBINING SECURE WITH PRECARIOUS EMPLOYMENT CONTRACTS

At Google, the company HR model assumes that different groups of workers can be treated differently depending on their skills, scarcity and other supply-side features. Typically, core workers, in research and development, for example, are on stable salaries, while contractors, who are also doing core work but who are brought into the organisation on an ad hoc or casual basis, are on precarious contracts. These contractors, and others on precarious contracts lasting from only two to six months, constitute 54% of Google's global workforce. But this differential structuring of workers' terms and conditions may be challenged by workers and trade unions and become an equity problem. For example, there have been walkouts by Google regular staff over the poor treatment of indirect contract staff, who are not offered benefits like T-shirts and professional development training. Keeping HR strategies separate when workers on different contracts are working together shows the weakness of the contingency approach. Workers may have their own sense of 'universalism' when working alongside each other, and press management to treat everybody in the same way.

Source: Based on Wong (2019)

Furthermore, while low-cost business strategies are generally associated with 'hard' HRM, there is evidence from the airline industry that some pursue 'soft' HR strategies at the same time (Gittell and Bamber, 2010). So we need to be careful in the way we approach notions like hard and soft HRM – they can coexist in layers and they may confound easy associations with types of business strategy. And, of course, we need to be much clearer about which practices count as 'hard' and 'soft' – but that is the task for the rest of this book.

Concluding comments

The key question that we need to finish with is: what forms of HR strategy best suit varying business strategies? The point we are trying to make is that HR strategies are very much part of the business strategy. Their basic aims are to reduce costs, increase productivity and reduce risk as part of that strategy – and hence to achieve the kind of workforce that is required to achieve the business aims of that particular organisation.

Some questions to think about

1. How does *strategic* HRM differ from personnel management and industrial relations? Why might the differences matter in a business context?

2. Evaluate the strengths and weaknesses of approaches to HR strategy, such as the 'universalist' and 'contingency' approaches. How might HR strategy help a firm secure competitive advantage?

3. Would you prefer to work for an employer who used 'hard' HRM or one who used 'soft' HRM? And how would you feel if you were working under a 'soft' HRM system but found yourself alongside others who were working under a 'hard' HRM system?

Further reading

Batt, R. and Banerjee, M. (2012) 'The scope and trajectory of strategic HR research: Evidence from American and British journals', *The International Journal of Human Resource Management*, 23(9): 1739–62. [Its extensive review of literature on HRM confirms its focus on business performance.]

Legge, K. (2005) *Human Resource Management: Rhetoric and Realities*, Basingstoke: Palgrave Macmillan. [A comprehensive and readable analysis of the emergence of HRM.]

Rumelt, R. (2017) *Good Strategy/Bad Strategy: The Difference and Why It Matters*, London: Profile Books. [Case studies of successful and unsuccessful business strategies.]

3

The Employment Relationship

We have been arguing that people management in organisations has evolved from personnel management and industrial relations towards – allegedly – a more strategic role in the workplace through its incarnation as human resource management (HRM). However, the 'fit' between business strategy and actual human resources (HR) policies and practices remains problematic, depending on a wide range of factors including the company's market position, technology and skills requirements. Although HR strategies can be categorised as broadly 'hard' or 'soft' according to the rigour of the supervisory styles that they imply, finding appropriate HR strategies has been likened to the quest for the Holy Grail (Boselie et al, 2005).

So far, so conventional. At this point, however, we need to examine in greater depth a dimension to HRM that is generally glossed over in many standard textbooks. Indeed, we shall argue that the employment relationship itself – that is, the very nature of the relationship between employer and worker in capitalist societies – lies at the heart of all forms of people management, whether personnel management, industrial relations or HRM. It is the way in which this relationship is managed – particularly whether it is managed on a collective or individual basis – that explains the evolution of HRM from the 1980s into the 21st century.

We begin this chapter by exploring the unique nature of labour power and its relationship to the wage–effort bargain – that is, the amount of effort we put into our job to 'justify' the pay we are receiving. As we'll see, determining this bargain with our employer involves a potentially conflictual relationship, which is likely to shift over time (the 'frontier of control'). In law, this relationship is structured through an employment contract (which can take all kinds of different forms), which, in the best circumstances, helps to create trust and discretion between employers and workers. We conclude with a brief overview of the distinction between employment and self-employment, a distinction that has become blurred with the emergence of the gig economy.

We can begin to unravel the complexities of the employment relationship and to understand its significance by thinking of our own experience in paid employment. Think for a moment about the most recent job you've had, whatever that may have been. First, how did you set your terms and conditions – were you merely informed what they were, did you negotiate them, or were they negotiated on your behalf by a union? Second, how did you feel about those conditions – pleased, satisfied or disappointed? Or maybe you took the job because that's all there was? Box 3.1 explores these questions with a really simple, basic example.

BOX 3.1: CLEANING THE CAR

Imagine you are back aged (say) 12 or 13 again and want to earn some pocket money. Your neighbour offers you £10 or £15 to wash her car. You are immediately entering into a very informal employment relationship with your neighbour once you have accepted the money she's offering you. Suppose she offers you £10. You might think, 'Oh, that's good, I'll do that for £10', or you might think to yourself, 'No, that's nothing for washing this SUV, I'm not going to bother' – and so you have the choice of either turning the job down or asking for a higher amount. Are you really going to ask for more, and if so, how much more? But let's assume you accept. The question then is: to what standard are you expected to wash the car? You might hope to do it fairly quickly, but does your neighbour expect you to polish the chrome and vacuum the inside as well? Who says what 'cleaning the car' actually means? And what would you do if she later inspects your work and objects to smears left on the windscreen or car body? Who defines the quality of the work done?

These are the kind of issues that arise – although obviously with far higher stakes – when we begin to unpack the intricacies of the employment relationship.

What is the employment relationship?

The employment relationship is defined here by Lewis et al (2003: 6) as: 'an economic, legal, social, psychological and political relationship in which employees devote their time and expertise to the interests of their employer in return for a range of personal financial and non–financial rewards'.

First of all, then, it is not a simple relationship. It involves economic, legal, social, psychological and political factors:

- Economic, because it's a relationship that requires a wage to be paid.
- Legal, because employment relationships are underpinned by the law of the country through contracts.
- Social, because you may get esteem or rewards over and above the economic rewards of your particular employment.
- Psychological, because there is also a psychological contract, involving trust, or lack of trust, with the employer.
- And political, because it is deeply embedded in the political culture of the country in which it operates. For example, in the case of the UK, Conservative governments have tended to restrict unions' power and influence while Labour governments have tended to increase them; in the US, those roles have been played, respectively, by the Republican and Democrat parties. This is a crude distinction but, broadly speaking, that's how it's worked out.

Labour is not a commodity

The quotation above from Lewis et al (2003) also highlights the two principal agencies involved in the relationship: the employer and the worker. The worker is giving up his or her labour power – physical strength, expertise, skills, knowledge – in exchange for a reward, that is, the pay, fringe benefits, holiday entitlements, pension entitlements and all the terms and conditions you expect from a decent job. So, the relationship involves payment by the employer, on the one hand, and effort from the worker, on the other. Crucially, whatever the particular skills or capabilities the worker possesses, the exchange with the employer can be reduced to a question of *time*: workers sell their labour time, employers hire workers for an agreed time. Workers are 'merchants of time' – that is the universal element all workers sell. But, as we'll show, how this time is utilised involves the frontier of control between sellers and buyers of labour time.

Despite an exchange taking place, labour is not a commodity to be bought and sold in the manner of other factors of production. It is far more complex. We might say more accurately that 'labour is also, but not just, a commodity. It is in this fashion that the maxim ["Labour is not a Commodity"] first appeared and found its way into the 1919 ILO Constitution' (Evju, 2013: 222). This legal ambiguity is more fundamental. For example, a spanner is a tool that is used to tighten components, and it might be used by an electrician, plumber or mechanic, but it's just that, a factor of production. There is demand and supply for spanners, as for any other item of capital equipment. But even though there is clearly demand and supply for labour too, labour is not a commodity like other factors of production, such as capital and land.

What do we mean when we say labour isn't a commodity? First of all, 'labour' isn't a thing or an object: it's all of us, as human beings, with aspirations, hopes and fears, when we are at work. We are not *produced* as wage labourers. We are produced as members of a family. Our parents had children, and we may ourselves choose to have children, and if we do so, it's for the intrinsic reward of having them – it's not, generally, to produce somebody for the labour market! You love your child as an individual, not as a future worker.

Second, when you are at work, you are contributing only quite a small amount of your capacity towards that particular job. For example, if you are working on a computer, you're not using your muscle power. If, on the other hand, you're digging up the road, you're using your muscle power, but probably not a lot of your brain power. However intelligent you are, all you're being paid for is to dig up the road. So all of us, when we're working, are using only a small proportion of our total abilities and capacities, but that small proportion is what our employer is actually paying us for.

Third, labour is variable and adaptable. If you buy any other commodity, such as a packet of crisps or a television set, all you can do normally is to eat them or watch it. But in the case of labour, which is all of us as workers, we have abilities and capacities that can be adapted and enhanced as skills – we can all be trained, retrained and redeployed. In fact, if you work for 30, 40 or 50 years of your life, it's likely that the job you're doing at the end of your career will be very different from the one you were doing at the start. Over your working life you'll probably have done all kinds of things – and every time you change job, your employer will use the different abilities you have to offer, and should train you to do the work efficiently and productively. So we are capable of continually reinventing ourselves, in a way that a spanner or computer or piece of capital equipment isn't. Our ability to adapt ourselves is enormous, and, of course, with technology advancing at the rate it is, so it needs to be.

Finally, we can't send our labour power to work separately from ourselves. If we are carrying out a job or a function, we have to be physically present to do it. Even if you're working in a virtual environment, you're controlling the equipment in order to be there. This means that your personality or your mood can sometimes intrude on the work you're doing. For example, if you're required to help customers who come into a shop to buy various goods, or if you're a flight attendant or a waiter, and you are a sunny, well-disposed kind of person, you'll do quite well. If, on the other hand, you are rather reserved and introspective, you may find the job more challenging. You're perfectly capable of doing it, but your personality may not be as closely engaged with the job as it might be. And, of course, we all have off-days. We all sometimes get out of bed on the wrong side in the morning, yet still have to go to work. We burn the toast at breakfast. We might have discovered that our partner is about to leave us, or that our parents have just gone bankrupt, but none of that is really an issue for our employer. You have to overcome that in order to work. And yet your personal and social life may well seriously affect your ability to carry out the work (points we develop in Chapter 10 on aesthetic and emotional labour). So again, it demonstrates that labour is clearly not like other inert factors of production such as capital and land.

Indeed, effort has a subjective component. When we start a job, we're normally enthusiastic and excited, and keen to learn. Yet as time goes on, maybe we don't find the job exactly as we'd hoped, maybe we have problems with our line manager or colleagues, or we find we are expected to do too much or too little and start feeling resentment, which produces resistance (as we discover in Chapter 4). Our heart isn't in our work any more for one reason or another, and our commitment wavers. This doesn't happen all the time, of course, but we all have peaks and troughs in our social lives, at home, but also at work, and that affects our work. This is something that has to be managed and controlled if you are an HR manager. The ways in which managers try to do so will vary according to the varying circumstances of our work – skilled or unskilled, its location (factories, offices, home, public spaces, virtual environments), number of hours worked, presence of a union, length of service, sector (private, public, voluntary, essential services) and whether we are employed directly or through an agency, among other variables.

Basically, what we're saying here is that, for a whole variety of different reasons, labour is completely different from other factors of production – a key point that will come up over and over again in the course of this book, particularly in the context of the growing predominance of 'emotional labour' at the workplace. As the economy has shifted from manufacturing to service sectors, more and more workers are involved in the customer interface, which means that you have to engage with customers in the way they are expecting. Even though you don't want to smile, you are required to smile as part of the job. All these complex issues about being a human being intrude and affect the level of efficiency that we're able to achieve when at work.

Wage–effort bargain

This idea of extracting labour helps us to understand the notion of a 'wage–effort bargain', which is rather a mouthful, but is a crucial concept in HRM as it links back to our discussion of labour as a commodity or rather, as *not* just a commodity. Imagine you are in an employment relationship with an employer – it might be a bank, a retail outlet, the National Health Service (NHS) or the Civil Service, it might be anything, but you are being employed. Now in that case, you do, of course, have common interests with your employer. There's no question about that. Both your employer and you want your organisation to survive. If it's at all unstable, you might risk losing your job, so you have an economic interest in the success of the organisation you're working for. When redundancies are announced – or even worse, closures – unions (where they exist) will negotiate to prevent them from happening or at least reduce their impact. None of us wants to lose our job or our employer to close down. That, undeniably, is the basic set of interests we have in common with our employer.

Yet at the same time, there are potentially conflictual interests with our employer that we cannot pass over. For example, and this is fairly obvious, a wage or salary is your income and so you want to maximise it to pay your household bills and debts and to do all the things you want to do – going on holiday or whatever. By contrast, to the employer, that same wage or salary is a cost, so employers, naturally, want to reduce costs in the company. That's why, in Chapter 1, we looked at unit labour costs and stressed that companies need to control costs and so reasonably strive to keep down wage and salary costs. There is therefore a tension – an underlying tension – that underpins the employment relationship. Some employers, as we'll see in Chapter 7, deny this. They'll argue that the company is a happy family, a team or a ship, and use the vocabulary of harmony and unison to try and talk up common interests. It's understandable why they do this, but, despite the common interests that do exist within organisations, we can't ignore the underlying conflict and tension.

Effectively, when you enter an employment relationship, you are willingly submitting to the authority of an employer, that is, to the line manager, to tell you what to do in your job: 'the employment relationship is necessarily an *authority relationship* between super- and sub-ordinates, where the employee agrees to accept and follow the "reasonable" instructions of those in positions of authority' (Blyton and Turnbull, 2004: 38; original emphasis).

You broadly know, of course, what your job involves because you applied for it on the basis of an advert or recommendation, and you thought it would suit you, given your abilities, background, interests and qualifications. All the same, when you actually start, you may find that the exact nature of the job will vary, possibly day to day. You'll find new tasks being asked of you, skills to acquire or update, and challenges, such as covering for an absent colleague or having to meet tight deadlines and working long hours to do so. You will find all kinds of things being asked of you, quite legitimately, by the employer, which are too detailed to be covered exhaustively in any contract. The employment contract itself is a limited document. It can't specify absolutely everything that you might be asked to do, and so you have to be prepared, by signing the contract, to carry out the 'reasonable' instructions of your line managers, which very much demonstrates the authority they have over you. The question you may well ask yourself on occasion is where the boundary lies between 'reasonable' and 'unreasonable' instructions. What is reasonable for the manager may not feel reasonable to you.

The wage–effort bargain embedded in the employment relationship, then, involves a power relationship between employer and worker, with the employer attempting to contain the cost and to maximise the productivity of the worker. This relationship also reflects certain further characteristics that need to be highlighted (the following outline follows Blyton and Turnbull, 2004: 36–44).

First of all, the relationship is *ongoing*, whether it lasts many months or years and trust emerges, or whether it lasts just an hour or two (such as when washing the neighbour's car). An agricultural labourer hired by the day to pick fruit has an employment relationship for that particular day, while a civil servant who has worked in a government office for over 40 years has had one over their entire career.

In addition, however, it's an *asymmetrical* relationship. This is a really important point because, in the end, the employer has a higher level of power than the worker, based on control of both economic and legal resources. The employer has greater legal power because, in the end, they are acting on behalf of the shareholder, whose interests in the UK and the US are prioritised under company law. So, for example, if the share price of your company starts to tumble and the board of directors decides it needs to close a plant or declare redundancies, it can legitimately do so in the interests of the shareholders, and you, as an employee, have no say over that, even though you have invested your labour in the company. However much you may protest (and your union, on your behalf), the employer has the ultimate right to sack you, even though that right may be constrained by notification and consultation requirements. In the US, 'employment at will' gives employers absolute or 'divine right' to dismiss workers (Summers, 2000). In other countries, there are notice periods or fixed time for consultation and delays, but ultimately it is accepted that the buyer of labour services has the right to discharge them, as legal power resides with the person doing the hiring (Steinberg, 2003).

The employer similarly has greater economic power than you do as the employee because the employer can rely on a variety of means and processes within the organisation to starve you out, should you decide to go on strike. A dramatic example of this was the miners' strike in the UK in 1984–85 when the National Union of Mineworkers organised a strike against the National Coal Board that lasted a whole year until the miners were, literally, starved back to work because they could no longer exist without an income. If you are dependent on your pay, have no private income and no partner who is working, then in the end, household bills triumph – you have to pay for food, energy, rent, mortgage and living expenses – and you're effectively starved back to work. Now most of the time, of course, the employment relationship does not involve anything like this kind of conflict, but the point we want to establish is that it does *potentially* involve these asymmetries of power. We may go through our entire working life and always have excellent relationships with our line managers and our employers, but that doesn't alter the fact that, underlying it, there is this potential area of tension resulting from the asymmetrical nature of the employment relationship.

That's why we say that the employment relationship is always *potentially a conflictual relationship* – and the key word here is 'potentially'. We do stress this. We are not claiming that it's always going to be conflictual, or that it's necessarily conflictual, only that it is *potentially* so. Paul Edwards calls this relationship 'structured antagonism' (1986, 2018). It involves antagonism because conflict underpins the relationship, and it's structured because the emergence of antagonism reflects a tussle over control. John Eldridge (1998: 140), paraphrasing Baldamus (1961), makes a similar point when he comments: 'by working from the assumption of conflict rather than cooperation, we more readily appreciate the continuing amount of social activity necessary to produce the stability required to make employer–employee relations possible at all'. In other words, if we start from the assumption that the employment relationship is potentially conflictual rather than cooperative, then we understand better the efforts required on all sides to create and sustain harmonious workplaces. It's hard work!

You experience this insight for yourself every time you encounter a point of disagreement with your line manager. As noted, your line manager may well ask you to do things that you don't think are reasonable. The question then is: how are you going to deal with that? Are you going to deal with disagreements by yourself? Are you going to involve your colleagues? Are you going to make a fuss about it? Are you going to bring a grievance? Or are you just going to keep your head down and comply? In the end, are you going to say, well, actually, I need the job, I'm just going to do what my boss tells me to do because I can't afford to lose my job, I need the pay? Those are questions that we all face at some point in our lives, and they may be resolved individually or collectively, or not at all, but they are always there, potentially. We analyse these questions in greater detail in Chapter 4 on conflict and resistance.

BOX 3.2: A SUMMARY OF THE WAGE–EFFORT BARGAIN

The following extract from Hilde Behrend (1957), an analyst of the wage–effort bargain, neatly summarises the particular nature of the employment relationship. When the paper was written, full-time work for regular hours was the norm. Towards the end of the quotation, note her comment concerning 'concealed bargaining about effort intensity' and bear it in mind when reading our next section on the 'frontier of control'.

> Every employment contract (whatever the method of wage payment) consists of two elements: (1) an agreement on the wage rate (either per unit of time or per unit of output), ie, a wage-rate bargain; and (2) an agreement on the work to be done, ie, an effort bargain. The employment contract thus fixes the terms of exchange of work for money. In normal market situations, no difficulty arises in defining the commodity that is being bought, but with labor the difficulty is that the "article" that is being bought is not only difficult to define but impossible to measure. For what is being bought is a supply of effort for performing varying work assignments. Effort, however, is not a substance that can be measured. Only the effect of the application of effort-output can be measured. Effort itself is a subjective experience, like utility. An individual can say whether the effort he expends in performing a particular operation in a fixed time is equal to, greater or smaller than, the effort he expends on another operation in the same amount of time, but he cannot quantitatively define the amount of the difference. In the absence of an agreement on the effort intensity per unit of time that is being purchased, effort intensity can vary between certain limits. Workers will have an upper limit to the amount of exertion they will put out and employers a lower limit to the level of exertion that they will tolerate without firing a worker. There is likely to be *concealed bargaining about effort intensity*, and the entrepreneur is likely to employ various devices of effort control such as supervision and machine pacing. If one postulates that more output means more effort, then it is possible to conclude an effort bargain, and this is essentially what a successful financial incentive scheme does. The worker agrees to raise his output in exchange for the guarantee of higher earnings.
> (Behrend, 1957: 505–6; emphasis added)

In essence, then, our employer buys our labour time, not us as individuals. The employer buys the time we are at work – that is, our 'effort' in the wage–effort bargain – and, over that period, they can require us to comply with 'reasonable' instructions, although the nature of what's reasonable may be open to challenge. And that requirement is based on the power that the employer exerts over us, in both economic and legal terms.

Frontier of control

All this leads us to a further important concept, the 'frontier of control', which dates back to 1919 (Goodrich, 1975 [1920]) and sounds rather dramatic, but basically refers to the boundaries surrounding the space and time within which the wage–effort bargain is contained. In other words, in any employment relationship, there is always a frontier of control between the employer, on the one hand, and the worker, on the other. We can examine this 'frontier' at societal level, when it refers to the regulation of the workplace through market, political and social forces (as we see in Chapter 5 on societal contexts and global trends), but for now, we are restricting ourselves to its narrower meaning, that is, the regulation of the workplace at the workplace by employers and workers (Batstone, 1988).

We argued earlier that the employment relationship is ongoing and asymmetrical. Over the course of the months or years of a specific employment relationship, the frontier of control is likely to shift, depending on the balance of power and influence between the employer and employee (Taylor and Bain, 2001; Hughes and Dobbins, 2020; Upchurch, 2020). As it shifts, conflict may accordingly be provoked or contained, depending on the circumstances. Normally the frontier is unspoken – both sides recognise its boundaries and don't question it. It becomes an issue only when a manager or employee infringes it, when, for example, your manager asks you to do something that you think isn't fair, but then you ask yourself, what am I going to do now? At that point, the frontier of control is broken, and it becomes visible, as illustrated in Box 3.3.

BOX 3.3: THE FRONTIER OF CONTROL AND THE COVID-19 PANDEMIC

The COVID-19 pandemic has highlighted a particularly fraught issue in the frontier of control: when is it reasonable for an employer to demand the return to work of employees, when the health risks of doing so are in dispute?

New figures from the Trades Union Congress (TUC) have revealed that 19% – around one in five – workers is attending their workplace despite being able to do their job from home. The largest driving factor behind this trend, which unnecessarily raises the risk of catching and spreading Coronavirus, was bosses exerting pressure on their staff to physically attend work. Two in five (40%) respondents to a YouGov poll commissioned by the TUC cited this as the main reason they do not work from home. Although the government has repeatedly said that everybody who can work from home ought to be doing so, hundreds of people have complained to their unions that their boss was forcing them to break this rule. But enforcement has been at best inadequate and, too often, non-existent. While headline after headline describes individuals being slapped with hefty fines for breaching lockdown parameters, no employer has been penalised for the same wrongdoing. (IER, 2021)

Box 3.3 illustrates both the power employers have over workers in forcing them where to work as well as their impunity in doing so – the law has not been used against them for breaching lockdown regulations (James, 2021).

Resistance is normal in the employment relationship. While a wage or salary can be agreed in advance of starting to work, the exact amount of effort required to justify that payment, as we have seen, remains hidden. There can be customary norms, a 'going rate' or a 'rule of thumb' for the effort that employers expect, but this shifts over time with the introduction of new competitive pressures and new technology. The pandemic shows that even the location of work (workplace/ home) may prove contentious, so there is an ongoing need to renegotiate or challenge new effort demands as they evolve or are suddenly announced by an employer (Smith, 2006). The fluctuating character of the wage–effort bargain means that both parties will sometimes be in conflict, and resistance to new norms or expectations of effort is the normal outcome of this hidden relationship.

Of course, the frontier of control may also be infringed by an employee. It might be a worker who unreasonably rejects a task, and the manager then has a legitimate grievance against the worker. The real point here is that the frontier of control is continually under negotiation if only implicitly, and an employer might grant concessions in compensation for an extra demand. For example, a client brings forward a deadline for a report, and your line manager requires you to stay late at the office, but maybe allows you to leave early the following day by way of informal compensation. The head of department at your university stems growing resentment at having to attend open days at weekends by formally acknowledging the time commitment by credits on your workload. This is what Behrend means in Box 3.2 by 'concealed bargaining about effort intensity'. Alvin Gouldner (1955, 1965) called this process of give and take an 'indulgency pattern'. What he meant was that some managers don't always strictly enforce rules and don't necessarily ask questions – they act indulgently – provided workers get the work done on time to the required standards. In other words, in a 'good' employment relationship there is this willingness to 'give and take'.

Trust

We can summarise so far by saying that employment relationships can be viewed in both a narrow sense and a broad sense. In a narrow sense, the employment relationship is simply an economic transaction between the worker and the employer, which requires the worker to provide work in exchange for pay, and that's it. The employer and worker barely know one another – there's no genuine relationship at all. However, there is also another notion of the employment relationship that becomes broader as the relationship lengthens, deepens and strengthens. The longer you are employed by an employer, the greater the likelihood that the relationship will become more satisfying to both you and your employer. You will both get to know one another and each other's strange ways, foibles, strengths and weaknesses.

If you have shown the employer that you are trustworthy, that you're somebody who will go that extra mile, that you will do things that are not necessarily required of you by your employment contract, then you will often find that they will repay that by allowing you a degree of indulgence at certain times. If you need to leave early on a particular afternoon because you want to see your child performing in the school play, then a good employer may well agree, and there will be an understanding between you that is not just based on the transaction over wage and effort. These cases show that the wage–effort bargain is always set within a social framework – there's actually a human element to it, which involves customary norms and perhaps trust. 'Trust' really is the useful word here because many employment relationships do not involve trust at all. In the gig economy, there's virtually no trust. Nor is there with zero–hours contracts. But, with more satisfying work, or longer term employment, as you build up deeper relationships, trust becomes much more part and parcel of the employment relationship. So the employment relationship covers a wide variety of different circumstances.

Just as an aside here, we should add that the nature of the employment relationship also varies greatly country by country. We return to this point in Chapter 5, but the contrasts between working in, say, Germany and the UK are marked, because employers, the unions, labour markets and labour law in general operate very differently in each country. The employment relationship is – at the risk of overgeneralisation – more transactional in the UK than in Germany.

Employment contracts

The employment contract – where it exists – is the legal embodiment of the employment relationship, and so has an important role in establishing the contours of the frontier of control and the possibility of trust, if only partially (for an analysis of its evolution in the UK, see Deakin, 2006). The employment contract gives you an overview of the terms and conditions you can expect from your employer. However, the assumption that both employer and employee are free agents in signing the contract may not be the case. It may well be that you, as a worker, are desperate for a job. In that case, you may find yourself agreeing to a lower salary or to worse terms and conditions than you might have wanted. Interns, for example, may be viewed as a form of forced labour (Smith and Chan, 2015). While lawyers and neoliberal economists argue that employers and workers enter an employment contract on a basis of equality, we have seen that in the employment relationship it embodies differences in power too.

The employment contract contains explicit terms and conditions, but also implied terms – for example, the common law responsibility for an employer to provide a safe and healthy working environment. Your employer is required to ensure that unprotected electric wires don't hang off the walls and risk electrocuting you when you enter a room. And then there are also incorporated terms and conditions. For example, labour law and any collective agreement to which the employer is party are also taken as part of the employment contract, and you need to know exactly what they cover. A collective agreement will provide much of the detail of your terms and conditions that are not specified in your contract, while labour law will lay down levels of statutory minimum pay and holiday provisions to which you are entitled (Lewis et al, 2003: Chapter 1). However, it's impossible to tie down everything in the employment contract, which is quite general in scope. You'll find that the nature of your work may change dramatically, and a few years down the line your original contract no longer reflects anything like your current responsibilities. In such circumstances the nature of the wage–effort bargain – and the ways in which you handle the frontier of control – become very significant.

That said, there are many different types of employment contract, and each will greatly influence your terms and conditions. Although we examine them in greater detail in Chapter 9 on flexible working, we highlight their range here in advance as a taster. There are standard or open-ended contracts, which is what we tend to think of the paradigm employment contract. There are also part-time contracts, which may be half time or some other proportion of full time. Fixed-term contracts may be seasonal or casual and last only a few months or longer, and they may or may not be renewable. And then, with a temporary work contract, workers are employed by a temporary work agency and hired out to a client organisation on a service agreement – terms and conditions are determined by the agency, not the client. Some companies, like Amazon, engage a high proportion of their workers through such arrangements as they are easier to adjust numbers of workers up and down, without any requirement to pay statutory redundancy pay as agency workers are *not* employees. And then there are zero-hours contracts, where the employer requires the worker to be on standby whether or not work is available over a particular shift. If you're a courier, for example, you may be on standby over an eight-hour shift and, if there are jobs for you, the employer will text you with the details. The employer is not, however, obliged to give you any work at all, so you may well spend the whole shift not earning a single penny. Now, in Chapter 1, we argued that companies try hard to control unit labour costs. A zero-hours contract is an extreme way of doing so because the employer is saying, if we don't have work for you, we'll not pay you anything even though you are required to be on standby. And link that back to our discussion of the wage–effort bargain, the frontier of control and trust: the employer is paying only for the narrowly defined task, and the balance of power is all with them, with no room for manoeuvre on the part of the worker at all. Such contracts really do favour the organisation's interests in keeping down unit labour costs.

Employment and self-employment

Finally, we need to consider what an 'employee' actually is. Until recently, it was assumed that an employee was somebody employed directly by an organisation or else employed by an agency and then subcontracted to another organisation.

However, the distinction between employment, on the one hand, and self-employment, on the other, has become controversial with the emergence of digital platform companies such as Uber and Deliveroo, among many others, which insist that their workers are self-employed. The crucial point here is that the gig economy has subverted the notion of 'self-employment'. If you're *genuinely* self-employed – for example as a window cleaner or freelance translator or management consultant – you can accept or reject clients, control the fees you charge, and set the hours you work and the time you take off. In other words, you're entirely in control of every aspect of your work. However, the downside of self-employment is you then have to pay your own taxes and your own insurance to cover for sickness or maternity, and you also have to cover yourself for holidays because if you go away, you're not being paid. The upside of self-employment is autonomy; the downside is the pressure of not having a regular pay cheque and having to organise every aspect of your work, such as record-keeping and paying tax. In February 2021 the Supreme Court in the UK ruled that workers for Uber were employed and not self-employed, a significant development to which we return in Chapter 5 on societal contexts and global trends.

As we shall see repeatedly during the course of this book, the concern in contemporary working life is the increasingly unaccountable and often arbitrary command that managers exert over the frontier of control with the consequent risk to trust relationships, with no negotiated or informal comeback for employees. The frontier of control and trust are helpful concepts as they give us a way of analysing what is actually going on at the workplace and the chance to ask ourselves *in whose eyes* something is legitimate or not – that is, whether legitimacy is from the point of view of the employer or the employee.

Concluding comments

The employment relationship is, then, a socioeconomic exchange, but it's not just that, it's not just about wages and effort. It may also evolve into a much more trusting kind of relationship over time. It's codified in the employment contract, which involves explicit and implied terms and conditions. And although in law the employment contract depends on the notion of being a free agent, the employment relationship is based on a balance of power between the employer and employee. Whether that power relationship is collective or individual, a notion of employer authority runs through the employment relationship, and with it the potential for conflict and resistance. Before examining the ways in which the relationship itself is moulded by the institutional and legal frameworks predominant in individual countries, we turn first in Chapter 4 to explore in greater depth its conflictual nature.

Some questions to think about

1. Is labour a commodity? What are the implications of your answer for HR managers?

2. What is your own experience of the 'wage–effort bargain' and how it fits into the employment relationship?

3. What do you understand by the term 'frontier of control' in HRM? Under what circumstances, in your view, might it be reasonable for employers to shift it in their favour, and when might it be unreasonable?

4. How much trust was there between you and your line manager in any job you've had? What types of employment contract are most likely, in your view, to develop trust relationships?

Further reading

Evju, S. (2013) 'Labour is not a commodity: Reappraising the origins of the maxim', *European Labour Law Journal*, 4(3): 222–9. [Analysis of the history of the maxim, 'Labour is not a commodity', that is now enshrined in the Constitution of the International Labour Organization.]

Hughes, E. and Dobbins, T. (2020) 'Frontier of control struggles in British and Irish transport', *European Journal of Industrial Relations*, Available from: https://doi.org/10.1177/0959680120929137 [Illustrates the contemporary relevance of the 'frontier of control' in analysing urban public transport systems in Ireland and the UK.]

Smith, C. (2006) 'The double indeterminacy of labour power: Labour effort and labour mobility', *Work, Employment and Society*, 20(2): 389–402. [Discusses two uncertainties of labour power: *production power*, or wage effort, and *mobility power*, or whether the worker will stay or leave the job.]

4

Conflict and Resistance at Work

In our last chapter, on the employment relationship, we established a significant point: that our employer buys our labour time, not us, as individuals. That is, our employer buys the time when we are at work – our 'effort' in the wage–effort bargain – and, over that period, they can then require us to comply with 'reasonable' instructions, although the nature of what is reasonable may be open to question. We also established that the boundaries around the wage–effort bargain are continually shifting and can be seen as a 'frontier of control'. At its best, however, a long-term employment relationship can lead to high levels of trust on both sides.

In this chapter, we examine more closely the nature of the space and time that we 'sell' as workers to our employer in the form of effort, and how the frontier of control shifts back and forth. Conflict and resistance at work, which are often regarded as abnormal or unnatural by employers, are, in fact, an unavoidable element of the wage–effort bargain, and may fester or erupt when it is contested by either side. Both conflict and resistance may take many different forms, and it is the aim of human resources (HR) managers to try and prevent them from arising in the first place, and to find ways to resolve them once they have. Once we have distinguished between conflict and competition – an important distinction – the rest of the chapter examines common causes of conflict at the workplace and types of resistance, both unorganised and organised, as well as strikes and the implications of conflict for human resource management (HRM).

Conflict and competition

The word 'conflict' tends to imply something bad – we don't like conflict – whereas 'competition' is generally regarded more positively. The difference between the two is important: conflict may arise in a situation where there are incompatible or varying interests between people, particularly at work, which may be difficult to resolve. By contrast, competition generally involves conflict, but within certain boundaries. Competition is controlled because it takes place within certain rules or regulations that everybody accepts. So, a sport or game, such as football, rugby or baseball, is played according to certain rules, and competition takes place within those rules: if you break them, the referee or umpire will discipline you. With conflict, those boundaries are absent, it's something much less structured. The differences between competition and conflict can, of course, sometimes get blurred. Competition may lead to conflict because people – the players – have not accepted the way in which disputes are being resolved, but nevertheless, generally speaking, the distinction is helpful because in a business context competition is generally seen as healthy, while conflict is something to be avoided or dealt with.

Causes of conflict

To stress once again, conflict is not the only dynamic involved in the employment relationship. Employers and managers and workers also have a great deal in common, and it's important to bear this in mind in case conflict seems to be the main driver of organisational activity. We are all interested in the economic viability and survival of our organisation, and there are important win–win areas of HRM that can help both employers and employees, such as well-functioning policies on equal opportunities, health and safety, and training and development. Other areas where cooperation is important include ensuring the efficiency of procedures to handle grievances and disciplinary issues so that disputes at work can be resolved smoothly.

Nevertheless, the general causes of conflict within organisations are varied. Within circles of colleagues, they might include disputes over budgeting, goal differences and role conflict. An academic might, for example, have a teaching role and a research role that occasionally clash: is it more important to give that lecture in person to benefit your students, or to delegate to a colleague so you can attend that seminar to benefit your longer term research projects? There may be a genuine difference in opinion over priorities. Poor communications may cause conflict if your colleagues don't understand your aims and intentions very well, and differentials in power and status may cause jealousies and resentments. Personality clashes – for example between extraverts and introverts – may undermine teamworking and sour working environments. HR managers need to be aware of all these sources of conflict at work and to have strategies to deal with them as best they can.

However, the key source of conflict – the one that underpins the very employment relationship itself – is the one already discussed in Chapter 1: the attempt to control unit labour costs through controlling wages and fringe benefits and raising productivity. This attempt is extremely likely to lead the HR manager into conflict with the workers whose interests are being affected. This arena of conflict, over the wage–effort bargain, is controversial because managers sometimes deny that it exists at all. For this reason, we need to be clear about the specific issues that might create conflict, such as pay, working time and employment security, among others:

- If an organisation is profitable, how are the profits to be distributed? Are they channelled into dividends for shareholders, or pay rises for the workers, or long-term investment in the company? There is a genuine conflict of interest between workers and employers over the way in which profits are allocated.

- Working time is a point of contention. In whose interest is flexible working to be introduced? Employers legitimately require work to be done at a certain time, but workers generally prefer a flexible working environment that allows a decent work–life balance. How do you square that circle?
- Employment security, too, is a serious issue. Organisations may downsize, relocate their operations elsewhere and even close down sections or divisions in order to rationalise production, which will all affect or undermine employment security. How are employers' and workers' interests to be balanced in such situations?

In other words, to use Paul Edwards' term (1986, 2018), there's an inherent 'structured antagonism', or an underlying conflict, between workers and employers that always has the potential to erupt, even though most of the time things run along perfectly well, with workers carrying out their tasks on time as best they can. It's that potential over the failure to give a pay rise, or to allow more flexible work patterns, or to threaten redundancies that may surface and cause tensions (among many other issues too, of course). And where you have conflict at work, you are also likely to get resistance as well. A management policy or practice introduced against the will of a group of workers may well engender resistance. And, of course, the way that managers view that conflict or resistance is going to depend very much on their own perspectives (as we see in Chapter 7 on management styles).

Management-generated conflict

Managers may infringe the 'frontier of control', the accepted norms and values of where roles finish and start at work, inadvertently or deliberately, in all kinds of ways. A poor appraisal that you think is undeserved may leave you feeling upset and demotivated. Being asked to work late at short notice or to come in early without compensation may cause resentment. So may discrimination or unfair treatment, as well as any form of bullying or harassment, or demotion for alleged poor performance. All these different actions, or potential actions, by employers infringe your expectations about what you considered to be acceptable effort for the pay you were receiving.

Employers may also engender conflict in relation to groups of workers, but on a wider scale because it now extends beyond the individual. A new management regime, where supervision becomes more intrusive, is going to cause annoyance. Speeding up tasks – typically on conveyor belts – would cause resentment because it disturbs collectively accepted work patterns. Changing the rate for the job – if management decides that the job is being paid at too high a rate and reduces it – will also be seen as adversarial. The same is true of the withdrawal of overtime: management sometimes relies on overtime to get work done, and workers may rely on working unsociable hours to pay the bills, so if that is withdrawn or reduced, a dispute may arise. It's been known for employers to provoke strikes in order to close a plant, claiming that it is unproductive because it's strike-prone. In a further escalation, employers may lock the gates of a factory in a lock-out and prevent workers from coming into the organisation – the opposite of a strike. And the threat of relocation of a plant elsewhere, and the threat of closures, may have a serious effect on morale, in addition to actual lay-offs and redundancies (Hyman, 1989).

Resistance

There is a wide variety of ways, then, in which employers may inadvertently or deliberately engender conflict, in terms both of individuals and groups and collectivities of workers. In response, the employer risks resistance, which may itself be individual or collective, and organised or unorganised. If asked about the most common form of conflict in organisations, most people in the UK would probably say 'strikes' because a strike is very dramatic. In recent years in the UK, we have witnessed national strikes of junior doctors in the NHS, university lecturers and train drivers. The RMT union on Southern Railway, for example, has been calling strikes since 2016 in protest against changes in duty rosters and the abolition of guards on trains. Strikes are public and so very noticeable, particularly in the service sector, where they have an impact not only on the employer but also on customers and clients – patients in hospitals, passengers on railways and students in universities, for example. Strikes have therefore had a very high profile in the demonology of conflict (Edwards and Scullion, 1982; Hodson, 1995; Thompson and Smith, 2009). However, in 2018 there were only 81 stoppages in the UK, involving 39,000 workers, the second lowest figure since records for workers involved began in 1893 (ONS, 2019a). As this chapter reveals, the forms taken by conflict in organisations are much more diverse than just strikes, and they have become more individualised in recent years. The strike has been replaced by all kinds of individual forms of conflict, which, in many ways, are more expensive and disruptive to employers and – because they are individual – much less noticeable.

This point becomes clearer when we start looking at patterns of conflict/resistance. Figure 4.1 illustrates these patterns, with organised and unorganised forms of conflict/resistance along the vertical axis, and individual and collective forms along the horizontal axis. (We're ignoring here occurrences of interpersonal conflict within organisations, that is, disputes among colleagues or equals, as they don't necessarily affect the power relationships between employers and workers, which is our focus.)

Starting in the top-right hand corner, strikes are organised, generally by trade unions, and they are clearly collective in that they involve groups of workers. Workers may go on strike in favour of a better pay deal or against the introduction of an unwelcome shift system or other threats to established work practices. Strikes are not the only form of organised, collective action. Working-to-rule involves workers doing absolutely everything by the rulebook,

Figure 4.1: Patterns of conflict in organisations – workers

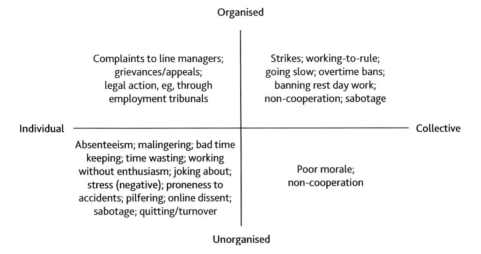

which slows everything down because rules are frequently broken just to keep production moving more smoothly. Going slow involves workers deliberately slowing down the pace of work in order to hinder production. Overtime bans involve just that – refusal to work overtime, which, in some industries, can be extremely significant. Banning rest day working, and not working on Sundays, can also be very disruptive for some industries. Workers may also resolve not to cooperate with management instructions, and even engage in sabotage on an organised basis. 'Sabotage' comes from the French 'sabot', meaning a clog – you took your clog off, shoved it into the machinery and made it grind to a halt. None of us wears clogs anymore, so workers have to be more sophisticated in the way in which they sabotage their work, but with electronic gadgetry and social media everywhere, there are all kinds of ways to do that now. These are all overt forms of resistance, as they are very noticeable (Townsend, 2005; Sewell et al, 2012; Elliott and Long, 2016).

In the top–left hand corner, organised individual forms of conflict include lodging a complaint with your line manager, which is, after all, an expression of resistance to a decision, but just on your own account and through a formal company procedure, which makes it organised. Grievances and appeals may be seen the same way. If, for example, you've been passed over for promotion, you might lodge a grievance because you think you've been discriminated against on the grounds of gender or race. Or you might take legal action through an employment tribunal, as an individual. If you've been unfairly dismissed, maybe you think you've got a case for an employment tribunal. So all these cases are organised, but they are individual, and so contrast with collectively organised cases.

Both forms of organised conflict – that is, collective and individual taken together – may be referred to as disputes, in contrast to the second pair, the unorganised forms, which are more informal and spontaneous.

The bottom left-hand corner, which covers unorganised and individual conflict, includes an amorphous group of forms of resistance, which are particularly interesting because they often go unnoticed, and often deliberately so because workers don't want to bring attention to their misbehaviour or resistance. These forms are often spontaneous, and include the following (listed in no particular order):

- Absenteeism: If you are really fed up at work, you might simply go absent. You might take time off and just not call in to say so. Or you might go absent because of work-related stress.
- Malingering, pretending to be ill when you're not: You are feeling fed up at work, and call in claiming to have a headache or food poisoning and, for the first three or four days, you don't need a medical certificate. After that, you do (in the UK). But for a few days, you might be able to get away with it, particularly if you are not doing so on a regular basis.
- Bad time keeping: You turn up late and leave early, you take a longer lunch break than you should have done, or extend your toilet breaks.
- Time wasting: This can take many different forms, such as booking your holiday or updating your Meta (Facebook) profile on your computer when you should be writing that report or engaged in some genuine professional activity. The more you do it in your employer's time, the less productive you become, which may be difficult for your employer to monitor. Some employers monitor emails and computer usage, but then all kinds of civil liberties issues are involved, which makes disciplinary activity very complex.
- Working without enthusiasm: Working in a half-hearted or unhelpful manner may be particularly disruptive in the services sector where you interact with customers and where your boredom or irritation will undermine service delivery. However, as Box 4.1 demonstrates, workers can find all kinds of ways to express their frustration.

BOX 4.1: PILOTS' FRUSTRATIONS OVER SAFETY CONCERNS FIND UNUSUAL OUTLET

Pilots employed by the New York Police Department (NYPD) had become frustrated at a lack of management response to their concerns about safety. From July 2017, they were required to fly single-engine aircraft in spotting-missions over open water at low altitude and frequently out of radar and radio range, which they considered potentially dangerous. Despite protests, the missions were intensified and, in the end, to express their fury, five pilots flew a spy plane along a flight path ... that was shaped like a gigantic penis. The phallic flight path, which was directed at the head of the NYPD's aviation unit, was revealed by the unit's tracking device. Two of the pilots were later dismissed from the unit and eight more were grounded (Whitehead, 2018).

- Joking about or giving your line manager a nickname: These activities undermine managerial authority and at the same time help a work group to bond and create a sense of shared identity.
- Proneness to accidents: The risks of tripping over things and catching fingers in doors may worsen when workers are dissatisfied at work, which may be a symptom of conflict at work.
- Pilfering: Stealing paper clips and stationery from an organisation may be regarded by workers as low level and justifiable, but it may escalate into serious fraud if it morphs into falsifying expenses.
- Online dissent: Disgruntled workers may vent their workplace grievances through 'gripe sites', work-oriented blogging, online work diaries and Facebook and Twitter, among other means, either as a one-off or as extended campaigns (Richards, 2008b; Thompson et al, 2020).
- Sabotage: A modern form of individualised sabotage is hacking, maybe your boss's computer (not that we know anything about this). Other methods are illustrated in Box 4.2.
- Quitting and turnover: The final way to express your discontent, when all else has failed, is to leave your job: 'Look, I quit, I can't stand this anymore, I'm going somewhere else to find more interesting work and nicer managers.'

BOX 4.2: SABOTAGE AT AMAZON

James Bloodworth, who worked at Amazon for an extended period, notes 'small acts of rebellion' carried out by workers, such as leaving litter or failing to replace mislocated items (Bloodworth, 2018: 49). Heike Geissler, who also worked at Amazon, goes further in listing a variety of ways in which workers could sabotage the company's operations, including hiding products, damaging products badly or subtly, delaying shipments, sprinkling dust inside books or inserting sticky notes with insults directed at the product's buyers. 'And that would be just the beginning', she says (Geissler, 2018: 169).

In the bottom right-hand corner, on a collective or mass basis, if all these things on the left-hand side become endemic, they are going to lead to low morale across the whole workplace or even across the whole company and hence to poor cooperation. So, if allowed to spread, these forms of unorganised, individual conflict can soon become very serious for the organisation and need to be controlled (Richards, 2008a).

Frontier of control

These very disparate forms of resistance share a feature in common: they mostly involve ways in which workers appropriate elements or factors that should belong to the employer (Ackroyd and Thompson, 1999). Analysing them helps us to refine our understanding of the 'frontier of control' that we first met in the last chapter. So, time wasting, absenteeism and turnover are all ways in which you appropriate the *time* of your employer. Or, in other words, the effort that should be for the employer in the wage–effort bargain, the work you should be putting in, you reappropriate for yourself by restricting output, by not giving your best effort or by bargaining over that effort, or maybe even by wrecking it through sabotage.

Or you may appropriate the *product* of your effort, which is actually your employer's. After all, you are engaged to produce that product, but you can appropriate it for yourself in the ways outlined – by pilfering, or by fiddling your expenses, or indeed, by theft. Employers' fear of theft is not so unusual. At Amazon, workers have to pass through airport security systems that detect whether they have stolen anything.

And then the third kind of appropriation, which is more subtle and sophisticated, involves *identity*, which comes back to our earlier discussion (see Chapter 3) on whether labour is just a commodity or not: we argued that no, it isn't, because labour – or labour power – cannot be separated from the person who is actually delivering it. Employers sometimes like to believe that you somehow belong to the company in one way or another during the time you're at work – you're a 'company person' in that you embody the values, roles, norms and standards of the organisation. For them, that is what it is to be an employee. Now, if you resist becoming a 'company person' and instead create your own separate identity as a worker or within a subgroup of workers, then that also is a way of expressing conflict. Take, for example, joking. If you tell jokes about your line manager, you're distancing yourself from them. You're saying, look, my line manager has certain interests, mine are different, and I'm going to tell jokes about them to show that I'm not entering their drama. Class consciousness is perhaps the most historically grounded example – you join a union and identify as working class rather than as a company employee: 'Well, she's the manager, we're the workers.' Such a division creates a sense of identity at work that isn't helpful to the organisation because it draws attention to diverging interests, and the potential for worker mobilisation (Kelly, 1998: Chapter 3). Box 4.3 reveals how even language can be appropriated in this way.

BOX 4.3: APPROPRIATING LANGUAGE AT FOXCONN

When managerial language is highly aggressive and male, and yet a high proportion of the workers are female, adopting the language of the factory (that is, managerial culture) can be both an expression of fitting in *and* resistance, as this insider's account of the management culture in one of Foxconn's Chinese factories reveals:

> In the highly masculinized environment, what happens to the shaping of femininity? ... femininity is ignored and invisible in management practices. Some line supervisors even criticize female characteristics such

as sensitivity and tenderness and thinking these characteristics do not fit masculinized management. Despite management practice, some girls, to protect themselves and fight back, also get rid of some feminine qualities – gentleness, obedience, sensitivity and tenderness – and become more rebellious and bolder. In the workplace, the boundary of conventional gender discourses is constantly challenged by woman workers' "inappropriate" behaviors, such as yelling, cursing, fighting and speaking dirty words. A female worker Lian describes: "I learned nothing in Foxconn except the word 'fuck' [laughs]! In Foxconn, every girl knows how to quarrel, and almost every girl's pet phrase is 'fuck'!" Another female worker Chun said: "Some girls, when they first arrive at Foxconn, didn't know how to fight or curse, but the environment on the shop-floor affects them. Actually, they learn all the dirty words here. No matter what a tender girl you used to be, you will know how to fight and curse people after staying here for two months." (Deng, 2012: 55)

The point here is that you assert yourself through a subculture of language (however distasteful it might appear to some people), and you create a new identity for yourself through an identity of language with your fellow workers. At a very basic level, it's a way of distancing yourself from the factory or managerial discourse.

A further example involves a Japanese company in Telford that tried to introduce a uniform for their British workforce. The workers were not used to wearing a uniform and felt aggrieved that they were being made to identify with the company in a way they didn't like. They were made to wear hats at work, and they subverted the requirement simply by wearing their hat back to front. Now, wearing your hat the wrong way round is trivial, but it clearly annoyed the managers a great deal, as it showed that the workers were not identifying with the employer. It was a way in which the workers kept their identity separate and created a kind of barrier between themselves and their employer (Elger and Smith, 2005).

Yet another example is about music being played on the factory line. A Japanese company, again in Telford, decided that it didn't want music playing on the shop floor. Although there's evidence that playing music while people are working doesn't harm productivity, these particular managers decided unilaterally to turn the music off. The result was that all the workers just walked out (Elger and Smith, 2005). Again, it's a trivial issue. You might think, hats or no hats, music or no music, was it really that important? But the fact is, yes, it was important because it revealed that the managers were crossing a boundary – the frontier of control – which defines, for workers, what is acceptable and what is not acceptable behaviour from a manager. On these occasions, by insisting on the wearing of hats or turning off the music, managers had crossed the frontier and provoked a reaction, a humorous gesture in one case and a walk-out in the other, which would otherwise have looked completely out of proportion to the action. Walking out just because somebody turned the music off seems over the top in relation to the significance of the action, and yet, clearly, it touched a collective nerve, such that all these workers spontaneously just left the factory. In this case the British HR manager was aware of the importance of music on the line, but his Japanese senior manager disagreed, illustrating a clash of shop floor cultural traditions.

Costs of conflict

How much does conflict cost the organisation? After all, the dynamic that underpins HRM, controlling unit labour costs, requires the HR manager to keep down labour costs and raise productivity. What effect do all these different forms of conflict have on labour costs? Well, there are some remarkable figures. The Confederation of British Industry (CBI) has estimated that between 2010 and 2013, strikes cost employers about £400 million a year (Giannangeli and Douglas, 2013). However, stress, which may result from bullying or from other forms of negative behaviour at work, costs around £12 billion a year – again, according to the same source, the CBI (Bullyonline, 2021). You have to read that figure twice – that's billion, not million: £12 billion a year for stress. The cost of strikes simply pales into insignificance alongside that. Figures from the US are no less astronomical. According to the Work Institute (2019: 14), voluntary turnover costs in the US exceeded US$600 billion in 2018, with 77% of resignations preventable by the employer. A further study estimates that something like 70% of business losses in the US are as a result of pilfering (Sauser, 2007). That figure seems astonishing, yet the evidence is there. Although the level may be contested, the research demonstrates that pilfering is a really serious issue for business. In other words, unorganised, individual forms of resistance such as absence from stress, voluntary turnover and pilfering are actually where business has real problems. It's not organised, collective forms like strikes. Indeed, recent figures reveal the lowest levels of strike activity in the UK since records began in the 1890s (we examine the reasons in Chapter 6 on trade unions).

Yet workplace surveys continue to reveal workers' experience of problems. For example, Diamond and Freeman (2001) show that a significant minority of workers endure unfair wages, almost three in ten, and unfair dismissal, bullying and preferential treatment by managers, something like just over 30%. Overall, between 25% and 30% of workers complain about some serious issue at work. These figures are borne out by more recent ones published by the Advisory, Conciliation and Arbitration Service (ACAS). As the name suggests, ACAS runs conciliation services in the UK. So, for example, if you have a problem at work – maybe you're on the minimum wage but aren't being paid properly – what can you do? If your employer fails to help, you can contact ACAS and request initial conciliation – in other words, you ask ACAS to intervene on your behalf. Very often, once ACAS is involved, employers will comply because they know that if you take it any further, it will go to an employment tribunal, and could then become extremely costly for the company, both financially and in terms of public relations. The average compensation award for an unfair dismissal claim in 2017/18 in the UK was £15,007, with the highest compensation award for a discrimination claim standing at £242,130 for disability discrimination (CIPD HR-inform, 2020). Hence there is an incentive for the employer to accept conciliation at an early stage of a dispute.

It is interesting to examine the kinds of complaint that come up involving individual conciliation, that is, conflict expressed by workers as individuals rather than collectively through a union.

Table 4.1: Early conciliation notification forms received (all grounds for complaint)

| | Early conciliation | | | |
| | 2018/19 | | 2017/18 | |
Indicative jurisdictions	Volume	%	Volume	%
Unfair dismissal	34,624	26	29,379	27
Wages Act	33,945	26	28,078	26
Working time (annual leave)	15,340	12	12,895	12
Breach of contract	13,820	10	10,434	10
Disability discrimination	11,674	9	11,186	10
Sex discrimination	8,264	6	6,578	6
Race discrimination	8,256	6	992	1
Public interest disclosure	6,153	5	4,642	4
Redundancy pay	4,278	3	2,889	3
Maternity detriment	4,154	3	3,013	3
Other	18,523		13,410	
Total jurisdictions	**159,031**		**125,081**	
Total notifications	**132,711**		**109,364**	

Source: ACAS (2019: 22)

In 2018/19, just over one-quarter (26%) of cases involved unfair dismissal. Compliance with the Wages Act (minimum pay) involved the same fraction (Box 4.4 highlights the scandal of wage theft). Working time accounts for 12%; breach of contract (failure to carry out one or more terms of an employment contract) 10%; and then disability discrimination, sex and race discrimination came to 21% together; public interest disclosure 5%; and redundancy pay and maternity detriment both on 3%. The total number of jurisdictions is higher than the number of notifications because some conciliations take place under two different headings. For example, if you're not being paid the minimum wage, that's not just a breach of the Wages Act but also a breach of contract, so the conciliation will fall under both headings. The percentages don't add up to 100% either, for the same reason. But the point to underline is that, despite the decline in strikes, significant numbers of problems at work are still coming through to ACAS.

BOX 4.4: WAGE THEFT

The prevalence of wage theft rivals and even surpasses other categories of theft that receive considerably more public attention and law enforcement resources. Employers steal more wages from workers each year than is stolen in "bank robberies, convenience store robberies, street and highway robberies, and gas station robberies combined" (Eisenbrey, 2014). Wage theft is, by many accounts, one of the most common crimes committed in the United States. (Hallett, 2018: 97)

Cases reported to ACAS continue to rise. In the late 1990s and early 2000s, the Labour government, under Prime Minister Tony Blair, introduced new individual rights at work, particularly on protection against discrimination, which meant that the number of cases brought rose because there were more areas of law that the employer could potentially breach. The number of employment tribunal cases peaked in 2006–07 at 132,000 (Dix et al, 2008). This is not early conciliation – you've gone through all that and by now you've actually gone as far as a tribunal, which means that your relationship with your employer has broken down.

By 2013, the Conservative-Liberal Democrat coalition government (2010–15), under Prime Minister David Cameron, felt that the number of these cases was getting out of hand, so it decided to impose a fee to lodge a case. If you'd been unfairly dismissed, weren't being paid the minimum wage or had some other grievance, you had to pay a fee in order to bring your case to the employment tribunal, which was seen by many as grotesquely discriminatory because not only were you suffering a problem at work, a breach of the law, but you were also actually being charged – having to pay upfront – to bring your case to a tribunal. The effect was twofold: first, the number of cases brought to a tribunal fell dramatically because many people simply couldn't afford the fee (the rate stood between £390 and £1,200 depending on the complexity of the case). If your case was that your employer wasn't paying you the minimum wage, or that you'd been unfairly dismissed, these sums were prohibitive. The second effect was a wave of protest from the trade unions that condemned these fees as discriminatory. The issue was referred eventually to the Supreme Court, which, in July 2017, ruled that it was indeed discriminatory to impose fees on people who were bringing a tribunal case, particularly on women, and that the practice was illegal. This was because women faced higher fees: discrimination cases are often complex and cost more than other cases (it is, for example, relatively simple to prove failure to pay the minimum wage since your payslips will show how much you've been paid, but much less simple to prove discrimination). Following the ruling, the government had to repay £32 million to all those who had brought employment tribunal cases since 2013. Since then, ACAS (2019: 12) has once again seen 'a significant increase in the individual dispute resolution caseload'.

Concluding comments

Overall, then, the arena of conflict takes place within the wage–effort bargain, with employers and unions contesting the frontier of control. We must acknowledge that conflicts of interest within the wage–effort bargain are legitimate, and encroachments by managers may lead to resistance on the part of workers, although the forms they take are diverse: they may be organised or unorganised, collective or individual. While defining these forms may sometimes prove difficult and assessing their significance controversial, they should all be considered as 'an intentional, active, upwardly-directed response to managerial controls and appropriation of material and symbolic resources' (Thompson, 2016: 118).

The nature of conflict at work has shifted in balance away from the collective strike, which is in serious decline, and in favour (if that's the word) of individual forms of expression, as borne out in the UK by trends in ACAS conciliation and employment tribunal cases. Indeed, a major survey of disputes and their management in UK workplaces concluded that 'disputes are a ubiquitous feature of organisational life, with the vast majority of firms experiencing some form of conflict in the last 3 years' (Hann and Nash, 2020: Conclusions). That said, the most common disputes involved informal disagreements and traditional disciplinary and grievance cases, with very few involving an employment tribunal, let alone a strike. The key issue is how employers and unions deal overall with conflict, but that requires first a discussion of the institutional, legal and cultural frameworks that mould HR practices in each country (see Chapter 5). We can then analyse the role of employers and unions in context (Chapter 6).

Some questions to think about

1. Give some examples of unorganised individual worker resistance and think about their significance for the workplace. Why should resistance be considered a normal part of the employment relationship?

2. Assess the costs to the employer of not responding to grievances highlighted by workers through different forms of resistance.

3. Wage theft may consist either in employers paying below the statutory minimum wage or in not paying wages at all. Why might this be a growing problem?

4. Have you ever experienced conflict at the workplace? What form did it take? What was the result?

Further reading

Hann, D. and Nash, D. (2020) *Disputes and Their Management in the Workplace: A Survey of British Employers*, ACAS, 30 April, Available from: https://orca.cardiff. ac.uk/132931/1/Published%20Report.pdf [Wide-ranging analysis of recent trends in disputes in the UK.]

Teicher, J. (2020) 'Wage Theft and the Challenges of Regulation', in P. Holland and C. Brewster (eds) *Contemporary Work and the Future of Employment in Developed Countries*, London: Routledge, pp 50–66. [Discussion of increasing numbers of employers not paying workers fully or at all.]

Thompson, P. (2016) 'Dissent at work and the resistance debate: Departures, directions, and dead ends', *Studies in Political Economy*, 97(2): 106–23. [Review of 'the resistance debate', centring contemporary dissenting behaviours in labour process theory.]

Thompson, P., McDonald, P. and O'Connor, P. (2020) 'Employee dissent on social media and organizational discipline', *Human Relations*, 73(5): 631–52. [Examines online dissent and the use of social media to express discontent at work.]

5

Societal Contexts and Global Trends

So far, we've looked at a number of key issues that underpin the conduct of human resource management (HRM) in a fairly abstract way – strategy, the employment relationship and the ways in which conflict finds expression at the workplace through forms of resistance – whereas, of course, in fact they play out in a whole variety of different institutional and cultural settings. Furthermore, there are general trends that emerge in labour markets, such as the growth of more flexible forms of working or the rise of the gig economy, that have universal or systemic reach across many countries. However, there is frequently a tension between such universal trends and local institutional and cultural settings, which we'll examine in this chapter. We'll focus on societal contexts, but also investigate the impact of new international trends, such as the growth of the gig economy.

Given that there are nearly 200 countries in the world, we begin at a more general level, by grouping countries according to common institutional features. These are broadly classified into two different types of political economy: liberal market economies and coordinated market economies. These, in turn, help us to analyse a country's institutions, which can show, for example, the differing roles played by internal and external labour markets in, say, the UK and German systems of HRM. Institutional contrasts also help to explain the strikingly different attitudes towards the regulation of HRM that we find across the industrialised world, although we also look at the ways in which institutions change over time, sometimes rapidly and dramatically. We focus on the emergence of two systemic trends – 'post-bureaucratic' forms of employment and specifically the gig economy – to reveal the likely implications for convergence and continued divergence of HRM in the future.

Institutional structures and cultures

It's obvious that countries vary enormously in their institutional structures and cultures (Kaufman, 2014; Bamber et al, 2017). The most striking differences are things like food, social customs, language and religions, but actually, when we are comparing national business systems, it all goes a lot deeper, particularly when we focus on how employers practise HRM. For example, we might contrast the degree of government intervention in HRM. Some countries go in for much more regulation than others, with the law playing a far greater role in some than in others. France, for example, has a labour code that lays down the whole legal framework for the employment relationship between the covers of just one rather fat book that you can buy from any stationers, while in the UK there is no

71

labour code at all. If you wanted to put one together, you'd have to go through all the different sources of employment rights in Acts of Parliament, statutory instruments and common law going back maybe two hundred years and more.

Countries have very different attitudes towards law and the degree to which law is associated with regulating labour. And, of course, systems of voluntary regulation vary too, that is, the role that trade unions and employers' associations play in setting pay and conditions through collective bargaining, as do the levels at which collective bargaining takes place or, indeed, whether it takes place at all, or whether it has declined in scope so far that pay and conditions are set by individual employers and workers. In Germany and Sweden, for example, employers and unions generally still bargain collectively over pay and conditions at sector level (for example in metalworking, chemicals or banking and finance), while in the UK and US collective bargaining – where it still exists – generally occurs at company level, although most pay and conditions are determined unilaterally by the employer or through forms of performance appraisal of individual workers.

And then there's the question of corporate governance, the degree to which workers are able to influence management decisions at different levels within the company, through forms of representational employee participation, such as works councils or board-level employee representation. Or maybe employers prefer direct employee participation, such as team briefings, staff newsletters and employee surveys. The point is that, if we take any group of countries at all, we can begin to compare them in relation to all kinds of different human resources (HR) practices (Brewster et al, 2019).

When we are examining systems of HRM across countries, we are really comparing and contrasting the nature and the role of three sets of key actors: employers, unions and government. The ways in which they interrelate – and the types and levels of regulation that mould their interrelationships – lead us into a discussion of national business systems, which helps us to understand the principal differences in the operation of HRM between countries. Commentators have focused on a wide variety of these differences, sometimes called 'varieties of capitalism', and we can start by drawing a simple distinction between two types of political economy.

Liberal market economies

First of all, the so-called 'liberal market economies' (LMEs) – the UK and the US, but also Australia, Canada, Ireland and New Zealand – are generally seen as 'shareholder-oriented' economies (Soskice, 1991; Albert, 1993; Hall and Soskice, 2001). This means that their business systems place great importance on the role of the shareholder in determining business strategy and operations. They generally aim to reduce government regulation to give employers as free a hand as possible in running their businesses. These systems tend to have stock markets in which company shares are sold at a high level of volume, and managers tend to be mainly concerned about the level of their share price and its fluctuation, not least because a falling share price is a sign of failure and may open the company to a takeover bid, friendly or hostile. Companies in this situation may resort to redundancies and site closures in order to reduce labour costs and restore the share price. In the case of the UK, the role of the State has been accordingly rolled back since the days of Margaret Thatcher (prime minister, 1979–90) through privatisation, outsourcing and reducing the influence of trade unions. In a variety of different ways, the role of markets has been reasserted since the 1980s after what was seen by the Conservatives as a period of too much State regulation. In the US, Ronald Reagan (president, 1980–88) was associated with similar deregulatory policies.

The employment relationship in LMEs is underpinned by the neoliberal idea that it is independently negotiated between 'free' employers and 'free' workers (Harvey, 2005). It is assumed that there is an equal balance of power between the two and that they are both free to determine, on a free market basis, the wage–effort bargain – that is, the reward that will be paid for the work done. The idea, too, is that new firms are able to enter the market with minimal hindrance, which will help to ensure conditions of perfect competition (Crouch, 2005a). What this tends to mean is that HRM in LMEs relies on external labour markets – basically the idea that labour is freely transferable from one company to another and that many of us, for example, will move (or exit) jobs if we are not happy with them or to gain promotion. This implies that, rather than staying in one company for a long time and getting promotion within that company, we will generally move horizontally between companies, or job-hop. For this reason, too, employers and workers are assumed to have perfect knowledge about pay and conditions, so that you know when you're not being paid at a level commensurate with your merit and you can then leave your job accordingly for another job. The main point here is that LMEs are generally averse to regulation in any form, either through State regulation or through trade unions. Hence LMEs reflect a free market identity that flows through and influences the operation of HRM at all levels.

Coordinated market economies

By contrast, coordinated market economies (CMEs) – notably Austria, Germany, the Netherlands and the Nordic countries – are often called 'stakeholder' economies (Soskice, 1991; Albert, 1993; Hall and Soskice, 2001). This is because their business systems, at least those in the manufacturing sector, acknowledge that a degree of regulation is required to ensure that they operate fairly in the interests not just of shareholders but also a broader range of stakeholders, including workers, banks, customers and other community concerns. The volume of shares is generally traded at a lower level than in LMEs. Large companies such as BMW are often owned by families or by a very small number of owners, which means that they can take a much longer term view of the future. They tend to borrow from banks in order to invest and expand, whereas companies in LMEs tend to issue stocks and shares to raise money and so don't require such a close relationship with them. Bank representatives are often found on the boards of larger German companies, for example, which means that these companies reflect a long-term attitude to capital growth.

CMEs therefore reflect a very different notion of market rationality from LMEs. In Germany, for example, we find that regulation, both by the State but also through trade unions and collective bargaining, is accepted as a means to balance interests between the various stakeholders within the economy (Gold and Artus, 2015). The role of trade unions and works councils is underpinned by legislation that goes all the way back to the 1950s, and considerable emphasis is placed on cooperation between employers and workers, which is sometimes known as 'corporatism'. As noted, German capital has a longer term perspective than that in, say, the UK, not least because the stock market plays a more limited role in the economy, and so capital in Germany has sometimes been described as 'patient' – in other words, it's prepared to wait a long time for returns. It is significant that, between 1985 and 2018, Germany had only 17 hostile mergers and acquisitions while the UK had 385 (Rudden, 2021). The corporate environment in Germany may be seen as less turbulent than that in the UK. For this reason, internal labour markets are more important in German companies than external labour markets. In other words, if you are a worker in a German company, you're more likely to seek promotion by working your way up over many years. This also means that German companies are more likely to look after you during economic downturns. Companies in the UK will, traditionally, make redundancies and close sites to maintain share values. By contrast, German companies will do a great deal to retain workers. Even in a downturn, they seek ways to redeploy or retrain workers, or possibly to introduce short-time working: they'll get their workers to work, say, a four-day week on lower pay rather than sack them. Because German industry has focused on the quality end of the market, German workers are highly trained and productive and so their company doesn't want to lose them. When the upturn in the economy comes, the company doesn't want to have to recruit, train and integrate them again from scratch.

Other varieties of capitalism

As a variant of CMEs, in France and South Korea the State plays a predominantly guiding role in business strategy and – certainly in the case of France – maintains a strong regulatory policy in relation to employment matters. These countries have been termed 'State-led market economies' (SLMEs) (Kang and Moon, 2012). That said, we find that commentators generally focus primarily on LMEs and CMEs, and collapse SLMEs into the latter. However, others distinguish between a broader range of national business systems. For example, Richard Whitley (2000) distinguishes six categories:

- fragmented (such as Hong Kong)
- coordinated industrial district (Italy)
- compartmentalised (UK and US)

- State–organised (South Korea)
- collaborative (Germany)
- highly coordinated (Japan)

Trying to locate China in a 'varieties of capitalism' framework is difficult, as writers place it in different boxes. Lüthje (2015), for example, notes China's correspondence to patterns of corporatism (as in Germany and Japan), while others (Liu et al, 2015) note elements of liberal market capitalism. We can't say that China isn't a society characterised by a 'big State', but it contains both elements, which makes a forced choice between two static models problematic. Zhang and Peck (2016) apply a more nuanced approach to China, which they call 'variegated capitalism', that reflects these multiple facets.

Whichever set of categories we prefer, and we may well have reservations about them, as Box 5.1 suggests, the point is that the employment relationship plays out in a very different context in the UK or the US, on the one hand, from that of, say, China, Germany, France or Japan, on the other, not to mention all the other countries across the world. The basic distinction we have to bear in mind is this question of regulation and the fact that LMEs prioritise shareholder interests and deregulated labour markets, whereas the CMEs – as the name suggests from 'coordination' – favour greater regulation in order to preserve a balance of interests between the various stakeholders involved. So, when we're talking about the employment relationship, we have to look at it in terms of the predominant institutional structures of these different kinds of political economy.

BOX 5.1: HOW CONVINCING DO YOU FIND THE DISTINCTION BETWEEN LMES AND CMES?

In a mixed economy (that is, one characterised by a combination of private and public sectors) there will always be a balance between free market pressures on the one hand, and pressures for government intervention on the other. These pressures coexist, and politicians, economists, employers and trade unions will prioritise the relative merits of the two sides of the balance differently according to their own interests. The free market side prioritises the profit motive, private ownership of business, freedom to set up a business, determination of prices through market forces and general suspicion of regulation. The regulatory or interventionist side prioritises progressive taxation to reduce inequality, government regulation to protect employment standards, taxation to discourage demerit goods (such as pollution) and government provision of public goods (such as education and health).

All mixed economies include a combination of both sides. It's a question of balance and of which side is weightier than the other. Indeed, the balance may change rapidly. In the coronavirus pandemic, for example, even free market-oriented economies allowed far greater government intervention (for example, to support the self-employed and businesses that would otherwise have gone under) in the public interest than they would have normally considered.

That said, LMEs are more free market and CMEs are more regulated, which means that the employment relationship, the notion of the wage–effort bargain, is played out in very different circumstances. That's why, when we're looking at HRM, we have to be very much alive to the institutional pressures on managers and on workers.

How convincing do you find the distinction between LMEs and CMEs overall? One limitation is that it is based on contrasts between manufacturing sectors rather than service sectors, which may operate in a less regulated manner, as we'll see in Chapter 6 when we come to look at union organisation in Germany, for example. In addition, some writers have criticised the distinction as static and Eurocentric, and downplaying forces at the global level by concentrating on dominant players, like the US, Japan and Germany (Hancké et al, 2007). As we have seen, it is difficult to fit China into the typology, so what about other emerging economies, like Brazil, India and Russia? There is a tendency to focus on the *national* economy, thus treating firms as the creatures of the system and giving insufficient attention to the choice they can exercise when developing strategy (Chapter 2). Crouch (2005a) argues that any national system reflects a continuing 'recombination' of elements drawn eclectically from many sources and not necessarily representing any simple model. But even if they don't fit very well, how does an understanding of types and degrees of regulation help to explain the differences between different sorts of countries?

However convincing we find – or don't find – the distinction between LMEs and CMEs, we do tend to discover that managers in different countries will view certain HR practices more or less favourably. For example, a Japanese and a Scandinavian manager will tend to vary in their views on the merits of individual pay systems (Peltokorpi, 2011). As we'll see in Chapter 6 on trade unions, most pay in Scandinavia is determined collectively through sector-level collective agreements in a way that does not apply in Japan, the UK or the US. And that opens up space in the UK and the US for different forms of pay determination, particularly individual performance pay systems. The very reason why individual pay systems have become so prevalent in the UK and the US is exactly because they lack that collective system of pay determination that exists in other European countries.

And it's the same for many other aspects of HRM. For example, workers in the UK – as we have already mentioned – are more likely than workers in Germany or Japan to move from one company to another if they are unhappy at work or if they are seeking promotion. So the way in which we relate to labour markets differs according to the institutional structure of the country we're in. The role of temporary work agencies has increased in the UK more than it has in other European countries because it gives flexibility to employers, allowing them to deregulate the control of the labour supply to a considerable degree. German companies, meanwhile, used to internal labour markets, generally prefer to employ workers directly than at arm's length through agencies (although their use has expanded in recent years). And trade unions and collective bargaining remain controversial in LMEs because employers often view them as an impediment to their ability to pay workers what they want to and hence as a distortion to the free market. By contrast, many employers in Germany and Scandinavia view unions as cooperative partners who actually help to negotiate pay and conditions.

Institutional approaches to HRM

The point we are making here is that HR practices cannot be abstracted from the institutions and cultures in which they take place. When we're looking at HRM, we have to be aware of the national business system in which it's embedded. It's very difficult – even misleading – to examine HRM as if it can be extracted from a particular national business system. An institutional approach, by contrast, leads us into looking behind HR practices, as it were, to discover the key structural elements that determine their outcomes for both workers and managers.

This point becomes clearer if we return to a distinction made earlier in this chapter: the distinction between internal and external labour markets. These terms may sound a little odd when we first see them, but they are very helpful when analysing HRM systems. An *internal* labour market refers to all the workers currently employed in a particular company or organisation. These workers have been successfully recruited, have employment contracts and are on the payroll. Large organisations in particular, which may have hundreds, thousands or even tens of thousands of employees on the payroll, will frequently fill internal vacancies and make promotions through their internal labour markets. They will identify workers who are doing well through performance appraisal systems and then, when a vacancy opens for a promotion, they will appoint them through an internal recruitment system (Doeringer and Piore, 1971; Grimshaw et al, 2001; Camuffo, 2002). The advantage to the worker is that a career structure within the company allows for security of employment and motivation to earn more and gain higher status, while the advantage to the company is that it is familiar with the strengths and weaknesses of the worker involved, so it is promoting a 'known quantity' who already understands the company's objectives, structures and work methods.

You can see here that the role of internal labour markets plays a part in the development of organisational strategy discussed in Chapter 2. If you think of a company that focuses on high-quality goods/services as part of its product strategy, then it clearly requires workers who can deliver that high quality and who are trained to deliver at the high level expected by its customers. And once they are trained to its precise requirements, the company doesn't want to find they are being poached by a rival because they are not being paid or appreciated enough. The point here is that many workers have very company-specific knowledge. A company makes a particular product, or delivers a particular service, and the way in which it does so will be different from even its quality rivals. Therefore, the company-specific skills that are intrinsic to that company – that define its brand – become a resource that you really want to hold on to, because if you lose key workers who have company-specific knowledge, it may take months or years to retrain replacements to the same level.

An institutional perspective on HRM therefore helps us to understand the significance of internal labour markets in developing successful high-end business strategies. In addition, it helps us to explain one of the characteristics of CMEs, notably Germany, where internal labour markets predominate in large organisations because they have specialised in high-quality product market penetration (Windolf, 1986; Bosch et al, 2007). By contrast, the UK, which industrialised very early and had a wide spread of products and services, generally focused on the lower productivity, low-cost end of its markets. And, of course, this thought leads us to consider the role of *external* labour markets in HRM. An external labour market refers to all the workers who might be available in the locality (including virtual localities) for work in the organisation but who are not currently its employees. Before getting their first job, young workers form part of the external labour market, as do registered jobseekers or anyone currently employed in one organisation but who are seeking a job in another. Organisations in LMEs, like the UK and the US, have traditionally relied on external labour markets to fill vacancies at their higher levels than CMEs, like Germany, which generally rely on their own internal labour markets.

Implications for regulation

The varying emphasis on internal and external labour markets has an influence on the ways in which managers view pay determination systems, employee participation and even training and development. After all, the more you value your labour force (internal labour markets), the more likely you are to be concerned about fair pay, voice (that is, your workers' views and opinions) and training. The less you value your labour force (external labour markets, on the grounds that it is relatively easily replaceable), the less likely you are to be concerned about fair pay, voice and training. Of course, both approaches can be combined, and external labour markets can be used to hire in highly qualified workers (Barley and Kunda, 2006).

Let's look at these points in greater detail because they help us tease out certain implications for the conduct of HRM in different countries. For example, in CMEs, where there are strong internal labour markets, we might argue that managers are more likely to regard workers as partners rather than as adversaries, and so might be less hostile to trade unions and collective bargaining because they can see that unions can help to provide a stable industrial relations environment, and hence forward business planning. If you know what your pay levels are going to be for the next three years as a result of a binding collective agreement accepted by your workers as fair and equitable, that helps you plan your labour and business costs. And that, in turn, may make you more likely to accept the role of the State in providing the legal frameworks designed to underpin stable labour markets. Overall, managers in CMEs are more likely to understand the role of regulation in labour markets than those in LMEs, where workers are assumed to be free agents and responsible for their pay by working hard and for their own careers by job-hopping when they choose to (Barley and Kunda, 2006).

Similarly, strong internal labour markets are more likely to encourage more robust employee voice systems (as we'll see in Chapter 16). Those workers who have worked for you for a long time are likely to have developed company-specific knowledge and skills, and you are likely to trust them accordingly. And if you trust them, you're more likely to give them a voice at the workplace. If you look at Germany, the Netherlands and other CMEs, you find a whole range of collective ways in which workers have a voice at the workplace – through information, consultation and negotiation bodies at all levels of the organisation, including board-level employee representation in some countries. If you really regard workers as an asset, if you really feel that they are committed to your company, then you are likely to believe that they also have a voice that should be heard at the workplace. In the UK and other LMEs, we generally find that the collective provision for worker voice is much weaker, with individualised systems of information disclosure (such as team briefings and employee newsletters) more predominant. This is largely because, in HRM systems embedded in external labour markets, managers are more likely to take the view that if you don't like your job, you are free to find another one (Marchington et al, 2005).

Training and development are subject to similar structural pressures (see Chapter 17). If you expect that a worker is going to stay in your company for much of their life, then training makes sense: it enhances skills and productivity. If, on the other hand, you expect the worker to leave after a few years to pursue promotion elsewhere, then you will provide only minimum training, on the grounds that it's wasted – and in the hands of a rival – once they have left. It should come as no surprise, then, to learn that employers spend considerably more on training in Germany than in the UK (Finegold et al, 2000).

So you can see, there are a whole series of implications that arise from adopting institutional approaches towards studying HRM. They lead into various insights about why some countries pursue more individualistic forms of HRM while others pursue more collective forms, which are crucially important to understanding the topic, both domestically and comparatively.

Institutions built on quicksand

Now, having said that, there are, of course, problems with these institutional approaches, some of which we raised earlier in Box 5.1. Although they are actually very fruitful in directing our attention towards certain aspects of HRM that may otherwise get passed over, there are also challenges associated with the institutional approach, not least the fact that institutional structures themselves do not always have the firm foundation they might seem to. Trade unions and collective bargaining, for example, have been around for over 150 years in the UK, but that doesn't mean that they will continue forever. Trade union membership has been in decline across most of the industrialised world since the 1980s, and even in a country like Germany, where sector-level collective bargaining has looked solid for years, it is under threat. One of the problems there, just to give an example, is that new sectors have emerged, like fast food, parcel delivery and information and communications technology (ICT), that aren't actually covered in the traditional identification of sectors. In sectors like supermarket retail, there are now atypical German employers, such as the 'hard discounters' Aldi and Lidl (Wortmann, 2004; Geppert et al, 2015).

Traditional sectors, such as engineering, pharmaceuticals and banking and finance, go back 150 years. By contrast, fast food, parcel delivery and supermarkets are much more recent, so these sectors tend to fall outside institutional structures. New companies, especially US companies, have strongly resisted unionisation and collective bargaining. One issue, then, is the way in which institutions themselves gradually transform over time and, in particular, how competitive pressures can sweep whole industries away altogether (see Box 5.2). Indeed, the State may actively support this process, and a disruptive State may choose to liberalise traditional institutions to reduce regulation. Throughout the 1980s, UK Prime Minister Margaret Thatcher carried out supply-side policies that led to the destruction of traditional industries like coal, iron and steel and shipbuilding; the deregulation of others, such as finance; large-scale denationalisation of the State sector; and a draconian erosion of trade union rights. Their effects have redrawn the context in which HRM is conducted at company and workplace level to this day.

BOX 5.2: LIBERALISATION AND INSTITUTIONAL CHANGE

Nonliberal reforms in a market economy seem to require "political moments" in which strong governments create and enforce rules that individual actors have to follow, even if they on their own prefer not to do so. Liberalisation, by comparison, can often proceed without political mobilisation, simply by encouraging or tolerating self-interested subversion of collective institutions from below, or by unleashing individual interests and the subversive intelligence of self-interested actors bent on maximising their utilities. To this extent, liberalisation within capitalism may face far fewer collective action problems than the organisation of capitalism, and much more than the latter it may be achievable by default: by letting things happen that are happening anyway. (Streeck and Thelen, 2005: 33)

> Streeck and Thelen are arguing here that regulating market economies requires a political opportunity that allows a government to do so. For example, Franklin D. Roosevelt (US president, 1932–44) used the misery of the recession in the 1930s to justify introducing legislation to promote union recognition and a minimum federal wage, while the Labour government in the UK expressed the national mood for social change at the end of the Second World War in 1945 by nationalising major industries, among many other reforms. By contrast, deregulation – or liberalisation – does not require firm collective action but only to allow individuals to pursue their self-interest, 'letting things happen that are happening anyway'.

Following the global financial crisis (2008–09), the president of the European Central Bank stated in 2012 that 'austerity coupled with structural change was the only option for economic renewal in Europe' (Hermann, 2017: 51). Numerous European Union (EU) member states – particularly in Southern and Eastern Europe – accordingly embarked on stringent programmes to cut social expenditure, such as unemployment benefits and pensions, and to introduce labour market reforms that promoted non-standard employment, reduced job security and decentralised collective bargaining. In the context of financial duress, liberalisation or deregulation required very little political mobilisation from governments, just the nerve to face down the protests and opposition that it unleashed.

Brexit – that is, the withdrawal of the UK from the EU – has had a similar disruptive result (although it's true that it involved a referendum). One of the agendas behind Brexit was to remove the EU as a guarantor of employment rights in the UK. Many employment rights in the UK were guaranteed by European legislation, which meant that no UK government could amend, still less repeal, them (Gold, 2009). They were given. Those who adopt a hard-line free market approach to the economy maintain that labour markets operate more smoothly with little or no regulation or at least, without any regulation originating from the EU: they want employers and workers to interact without what they would see as restriction. Outside the EU, and hence outside the authority of the Commission and European Court of Justice to enforce EU legislation, a UK government is now free to amend or repeal employment legislation that had been underpinned by the EU since UK accession in 1973 (legislation that covers areas like working time, temporary work agencies, part-time work and transfer of undertakings, among much else).

Institutions, laws and rights that have been taken for granted for many years may prove to have been built on quicksand, and those who wish to preserve and maintain them need to avoid complacency and remain vigilant.

The emergence of 'post-bureaucratic' employment

Disruption may, however, result not only from employer innovation or broader political intent but also from the development of technologies that create new competitive pressures. The emergence of the gig economy is a prime example of just such a process. Many HRM textbooks are based on institutional approaches to organisations and patterns of work, and tend to assume the enduring nature of bureaucratic forms of employment: workers at the base of an organisational pyramid, with engineers and middle managers occupying the upper levels, and senior management teams at the very top. They therefore tend to miss the significance of the gig economy, which very much falls outside these traditional expectations. Indeed, it disrupts our understanding of a range of features of working that once seemed very familiar, such as self-employment, the worker–customer relationship, commuting and work–life balance, and even the employment contract itself. The point here is not that traditional organisations and work routines aren't still important – yes of course they are, for millions of people. The point is rather that we have to recognise – and integrate into our analysis of what HRM is all about – that certain sectors of employment are in the process of turning more or less swiftly into post-bureaucratic forms of work organisation.

This is not a novel observation. Manuel Castells pointed out in 1996: 'we are witnessing the end of the historical trend toward the salarisation of employment and the socialisation of production that was the dominant feature of the industrial era' (Castells, 1996: 267). What he meant was that, particularly in LMEs, there has been a growth of 'precarious work', and all kinds of casual work that undermines the long-term tendency towards standard employment contracts, regular salaries and work in organisational settings. They have been increasingly replaced by a whole variety of different forms of working, such as fixed-term contracts, temporary work, zero-hours contracts and, more recently, gig work.

These kinds of casualised work patterns generally shift the balance of power towards the employer, who benefits from a more flexible supply of labour. Workers, by contrast, are subject to more contingent forms of working: pay is less regular and more likely to fluctuate, hours of work become less predictable, time spent hanging around may be longer, benefits like holiday pay and sick pay disappear, and it's more difficult to join a trade union. Workers may vary in their response to these conditions. Some might prefer casual work – if you are a student, for example, you might be quite happy with zero-hours contracts because it allows you to study and work at the same time. Indeed, it is likely to suit mainly younger workers or those who are not supporting a family or paying a mortgage or the rent. However, many workers would prefer a regular income, regular hours and other benefits so that they can save and plan their lives in the longer term. Casual work is less likely to allow them to do that as it limits choices. Shorter working hours, after all, mean lower pay. So, there are many disadvantages for some workers, not least because many are forced into casual employment, either because of lack of skills or lack of opportunity, and for them this can be very stressful. In other words, if you have other sources of income and other interests, then a zero-hours contract might be quite helpful to you. If, on the other hand, you're dependent on your income to pay the bills, feed your family and pay the mortgage or rent, then casual work becomes much more difficult because your income is more unstable and it's therefore less easy to plan. It has a lot of downsides (Buchanan, 2004).

What this means is that the traditional features of old-style bureaucratic employment – or hierarchical employment – have tended to erode. Secure, let alone lifetime, employment is scarcer, along with linear careers up an organisational hierarchy. It's more acceptable than ever for people to hop from one job to another. Office locations have become less significant as technology allows more working from home and greater mobility in respect to where work is carried out (a tendency reinforced by the COVID-19 pandemic). Stable workplace communities, with long-term colleagues, are also disappearing, as the workforce becomes more fluid. These trends, it should be noted, all fit into the general employer programme of controlling labour costs as the casualised workforce is actually more controllable because it is more flexible. This is a crucial point because declining loyalty and commitment to organisations actually flows from that, and implicitly creates a new set of assumptions between employer and worker about the nature of the wage–effort bargain. As we saw in Chapter 3, you come to a kind of tacit understanding with your employer about how much effort you put in for your pay, but that may disappear with casualised employment. You're much more likely to cut corners and skive if you're working on a casual basis and don't know your employer, colleagues or performance standards very well. Or, indeed, understandings with your employer over the wage–effort bargain will disappear completely if your performance is monitored by the algorithms set by an online platform (Wood et al, 2019).

Online labour and the gig economy

The development of online labour – and the emergence of the gig economy in its current form sometime around the time of the 2008–09 financial crisis – has added a whole new dimension to the notion of precarious working, which is constantly evolving. Indeed, we refer to the online labour force in a whole variety of different ways: as freelancers or as self-employed (although both terms go back a long way) and, more specifically, as crowd-workers, service providers, agents, sellers or driver-partners (when cab driving) (Kuhn and Maleki, 2017). Whatever the terminology, the conditions under which gig workers function can be devastating, particularly if, for example, they risk their health by continuing to work even when they are ill simply because they lack access to sick pay.

Digital companies themselves, which are central in this emerging post-bureaucratic employment scenario, generally stress the independence of workers. Uber, for example, talks about drivers as entrepreneurs. TaskRabbit suggests you 'become an entrepreneur on our platform'. Handy, an odd-jobs company, denies on its website that it's even an employer, saying it 'simply connects independent service professionals with customers', while its terms of service spell out that the platform is 'solely a venue for communications'.

The question – as we noted in Chapter 3 on the employment relationship – centres on whether gig workers can be seen as genuinely self-employed or not. One helpful way forward is just to ask ourselves, who owns what? The employer, traditionally, owns the factory or the workplace, and will also probably supply any equipment or uniform you need to perform your tasks (Prassl, 2018). The employer also controls the products or services you produce, as well as your pay, hours of work and other conditions (although these may sometimes be negotiated). Workers sell their labour power within the terms of the wage–effort bargain and within the prevailing institutional contexts. So, for example, a teacher operates within the framework of teaching qualifications, educational standards, appropriate lines of authority and so on. In addition, the employer, who pays National Insurance on your behalf, also provides holiday pay, sick pay and a pension. By contrast, if you are genuinely self-employed, then technically you control the clients you accept, the fees you charge and the hours you work. You might decide you're going to work on a Sunday but have Tuesday off if you want to, because no one's breathing down your neck. You can also control (up to a point) where you work. However, you have to provide your own holiday pay, sick pay and pension. Now that is genuine freelance or self-employed status (Buschoff and Schmidt, 2009; Cohen et al, 2019).

However, the status of platform workers is hybrid. Digital workers, despite what Handy, Deliveroo, Uber and all the rest may say, don't have the freedom of the traditional self-employed. You're not able to work where you want – you're told where to work. The platform company will generally decide the area in which you can work and no other. Responsibility for health and safety may become problematic, and the company lays down your rate of pay and won't allow you to turn down clients (Gandini, 2015).

So, for example, we find that the 60,000 or so Uber drivers in the UK are technically self-employed, but actually they have just one customer, namely, Uber, which determines the pace of work, terms and conditions and pay rates. It allows you to turn down one client in a shift, but if you turn down more than one, that's noted and you eventually get struck off the platform. Furthermore, Uber does not provide the cars or pay National Insurance on behalf of its drivers, nor does it award holiday pay, sick pay, pensions or insurance cover. Drivers are required to provide those benefits for themselves. Furthermore, drivers are rated by their customers, and Uber monitors the ratings. So the customer also enters the relationship in a way that can be used by the employer for appraisal purposes. Overall, then, Uber has control over the drivers, which makes it look very much like an employment relationship. Even though Uber claims the drivers are entrepreneurs and self-employed, it is actually controlling their clients, pay, location, working hours, work intensity – the whole thing – so you can't really say that you're an entrepreneur if you're working for Uber (Bloodworth, 2018; Kessler, 2018).

To repeat the point: the status of platform workers is hybrid. It contains elements of both employment and self-employment, which platform companies have –

frankly – used to manipulate the labour process to their own advantage. However, the Supreme Court in the UK ruled in February 2021 that Uber workers have employed status, and so are entitled to holiday pay, a company pension and the national minimum wage (see Box 5.3). Nevertheless, the law in many other countries remains ambiguous about the employment status of gig workers.

> ## BOX 5.3: SUPREME COURT RULES THAT UBER DRIVERS ARE EMPLOYEES
>
> In February 2021, the UK Supreme Court ruled unanimously that Uber drivers are employees under the terms of the Employment Rights Act 1996 and, accordingly, entitled to receive the national minimum wage, annual leave and other basic rights that apply to workers.
>
> Uber had argued that it merely acted as a booking agent for its drivers, who were self-employed 'partners' and therefore not covered by employment rights. The court firmly rejected that claim, ruling rather that Uber has a contract with its passengers and employs drivers to fulfil it.
>
> The ruling supported one made by an employment tribunal in October 2016, brought by two leading organisers of the App Drivers and Couriers' Union (see Box 6.2). Uber may have to pay over £100 million in compensation to around 10,000 drivers affected. No further legal appeals are possible. Frances O'Grady, general secretary of the Trades Union Congress (TUC), stated: 'This ruling is an important win for gig economy workers and for common decency. Sham self-employment exploits people and lets companies dodge paying their fair share of tax.'
>
> Similar cases for employment status are under way at Addison Lee, CitySprint, Deliveroo, Excel Courier and Delivery Company and Hermes, among other platform-based companies.

Concluding comments

The key question we have to ask ourselves when we're looking at the employment relationship is whether we are still in a traditional 'bureaucratic' employment relationship or working on an online platform. What are the implications of one or the other for our ability to control our pay, hours of work, pace and patterns of work, location and clients? And if we are working on a platform, to what extent does it control client interactions and working conditions? The answers in relation to traditional employment relations are those reflected in standard textbooks on HRM, but those in relation to digital platforms are largely open; nevertheless, they need to be integrated into our approach to HRM through our understanding of the wage–effort bargain and the frontier of control. The employment relationship in this new, post-bureaucratic institutional setting remains fluid. That's why, although an institutional approach is central to our understanding of the ways in which the employment relationship plays out in specific countries, we must also remain aware that the institutions themselves are changing and that we don't actually control them, which may have major implications for the power relationship between employers and workers, and indeed, clients.

Institutional frameworks are, then, a key element of HRM, but they are themselves evolving all the time. In the next two chapters we'll examine how trade unions and employers have responded to the challenges presented by the employment relationship in specific settings.

Some questions to think about

1. Has the 'standard employment contract' really reached the end of its life?

2. What is meant by the term 'post-bureaucratic employment'? Give some examples.

3. Have you ever worked in the gig economy? How did you weigh up the advantages and disadvantages by comparison with a 'normal' job?

Further reading

Bloodworth, J. (2018) *Hired: Six Months Undercover in Low-wage Britain*, London: Atlantic Books. [Account of working for Amazon and Uber, as a home care worker and in a call centre.]

Hermann, C. (2017) 'Crisis, structural reform and the dismantling of the European Social Model(s)', *Economic and Industrial Democracy*, 38(1): 51–68. [Analysis of the effects of the financial crisis on labour markets across Europe.]

Streeck, W. and Thelen, K. (2005) 'Introduction: Institutional Change in Advanced Political Economies', in W. Streeck and K. Thelen (eds) *Beyond Continuity: Institutional Change in Advanced Political Economies*, Oxford: Oxford University Press, pp 1–39. [Discussion of types of gradual transformation in advanced economies.]

Whitley, R. (2000) *Divergent Capitalisms: The Social Structuring and Change of Business Systems*, Oxford: Oxford University Press. [Detailed overview and discussion of 'varieties of capitalism'.]

6

Trade Unions

We have established that conflict at the workplace occurs at the frontier of control over the wage–effort bargain, but that the ways in which it plays out depend greatly on the institutional and legal frameworks prevalent in each country. To put it more simply, workers carry out tasks for their employer in exchange for pay, but the nature of the tasks is open to continual reinterpretation by the employer: the amount and quality of the work done, where and when exactly it is done, the equipment and techniques used, the level of training or retraining that's required. Everything goes well while expectations are in harmony between worker and employer, but if they are questioned or undermined, conflict is likely to erupt.

Trade unions have traditionally protected workers in their collective defence of the frontier of control, particularly in the context of the traditional manufacturing company, which, because of the economic significance of manufacturing in 20th-century industrialised economies, tended to dominate industrial relations and human resources (HR) textbooks. In this chapter we discover what a union is, why workers join unions, and the role played by unions in expressing worker voice and determining pay through collective bargaining. We examine unions in their global context, including membership trends and the scope of collective bargaining across different countries, and finish by asking why they continue so often to attract bad publicity in the light of plummeting strike levels. The absence of unions at the workplace has helped create the vacuum into which human resource management (HRM) has moved.

What is a union?

So, what is a union? A classic definition of a union, deriving from Sidney and Beatrice Webb (1920: 1), is: 'a continuous association of wage-earners for the purpose of maintaining or improving the conditions of their working lives'. If we unpack that definition for a moment, 'a continuous association' means that a union is an organisation that persists through time: in other words, it's not a kind of pop-up organisation. Some unions in the UK go all the way back to the 1820s or even earlier, and their origins can be found in the guilds of the Middle Ages (Fox, 1985), so they have a very long history. An 'association of wage-earners' means they are associations of workers, not employers or managers, although managers may themselves join unions as workers. Workers earn their living through selling their labour power, and those who choose to join a union pay their subscriptions on a regular basis to maintain it as a continuous organisation.

Now, that's the other point about a trade union: it's exactly that, it's a trade or a labour union. Workers join 'for the purpose of maintaining or improving the conditions of their working lives': in other words, unions make sure employers don't reduce pay or terms and conditions, but preferably, they also ensure that pay and conditions are improved. Hence unions attempt to negotiate higher pay, longer holidays or improved pensions, or whatever it happens to be, with the employer. Putting this point in the vocabulary of our book, unions attempt to control the frontier of control on behalf of their members by defending or increasing pay levels within the wage–effort bargain, as well by maintaining or reducing the effort required.

Unions, then, unite workers for collective purposes. They're active in the workplace and in the labour market, and they're public in that they may take to the streets to make their case. They are based on associative power, that is, power based on the connectivity of workers working together. That said, there are some myths attached to unions that it's important to debunk. For example, people sometimes think that unions don't allow much individualism, which really isn't true. Individuals within unions have a great deal of say and can make their presence felt in a variety of ways, not least on demonstrations and marches. Another myth is that trade unions involve older, male, unskilled or semi-skilled workers. Again, that's not the case at all, as you can see here from a photo of the junior doctors' dispute in 2016 in the UK.

Figure 6.1 shows that unions are for everybody, for all workers (including junior doctors), for all skill levels, all ages, all ethnic backgrounds – they cover everybody in that sense, not just the stereotypical older male worker.

Figure 6.1: Knowledge workers

Source: iStock.com/janecampbell21

Unions accordingly play various roles. They act as *labour market institutions*, that is, they act within labour markets to try to influence pay, terms and conditions, and the supply and demand for labour.

They also act as *social movements* to improve workers' rights, and we think here of the links between unions and left-wing parties in many countries. In the case of the UK, the unions are major donors and contributors to the Labour Party. Across most of continental Europe, socialist parties have strong links with trade unions, the union forming the industrial wing of the workers' movement, while the socialist party is the political wing in parliament, with the two generally campaigning together (although sometimes amid tensions). Hence unions form part of a more general social movement as well. Unions also act as *interest groups* for workers in particular sectors, such as engineering, construction, banking and finance, local government, health and so on. Unions may often unite to campaign, for example against rising unemployment or the gender pay gap. Unions therefore have multiple roles, all of which are central to the way in which HRM has developed (Gumbrell-McCormick and Hyman, 2013).

Why do workers join trade unions?

Workers join unions for a variety of reasons. IndustriALL Global Union (2019), which represents 50 million workers across 140 countries in manufacturing, mining and energy, lists five key reasons: better wages and benefits; personal protection; equality; health and safety; and solidarity.

In terms of personal protection, a union will represent you as an individual worker. Many people first join a union when they experience a problem at work and want support. For example, suppose you feel you're being bullied or harassed by a line manager – what are you going to do about it? You're hardly going to turn to your line manager to complain, because they are the problem. You'll want somebody independent who will help you to redress what's going on, or to accompany you through a grievance procedure. If you're a member of a union, you'll go to your local representative (sometimes referred to as a shop steward) who will assist you in representing your interests with the employer.

You also, clearly, want to improve your wages and benefits, and – provided it's recognised by your employer – a union will do this on your behalf. It generally negotiates collective agreements with the employer, in a process known as 'collective bargaining', during the course of an annual or a biannual pay round (we come back to this point in the next section). Unions will try to protect existing jobs, and if your company is facing redundancies, closures or restructuring, they will negotiate with the employer to make sure that jobs are preserved within acceptable parameters, or that people are redeployed or retrained or, at the very least, made redundant on acceptable terms. Unions also aim to improve equal opportunities at work, reflecting the diversity of contemporary workforces, and to promote better health and safety. Overall, they seek to influence management's plans. Particularly at an earlier stage of decision-making, if they know that management is proposing a particular area for change, they will try to ensure that the change takes into account their members' interests. For example, imagine your company or organisation is restructuring. Maybe it's decentralising or delayering management hierarchies. That process is certainly going to affect you and your co-workers, whose responsibilities may be altered quite dramatically as a result. Lines of accountability may change, along with grading systems, pay scales and your hopes of promotion. Your union will represent you collectively, so that your group interests in any regrading, redeployment or any knock-on effects during the restructuring are heard and taken into account. So the key point, the reason why workers join unions, is to ensure representation and influence, whether individually or collectively, over issues at work, including, of course, health and safety too. As a result of common activities and campaigns, unions also help to instil a sense of solidarity and identity. For example, the British Medical Association gives junior doctors a sense of professional occupational identity. In the same way, the Royal College of Nursing gives nurses a sense of identity, the Royal College of Midwives does the same for midwives, and so on.

There are, then, a variety of different reasons why workers might want to join a trade union, and if asked, they are likely to give more than one reason. The Trades Union Congress (TUC) has produced its own short video about why workers should join a union, which is well worth watching (see TUC, 2016).

Role of trade unions

Broadly speaking, trade unions play two major roles in people management: a 'voice' role, representing workers at work, and an economic (or 'monopoly') role, helping to determine pay rates.

If we start with voice, as noted, unions represent workers both individually and collectively, and give them a strength that they would otherwise lack (Johnstone and Ackers, 2015). A union rep who accompanies members through a disciplinary procedure, for example, gives them support by helping them to express their views with confidence, and ensuring that processes and rights are properly respected. Union reps who sit on consultative committees and other joint bodies with management can represent the workforce's collective views on matters of concern – from the quality of the food in the cafe to plans on organisational restructuring – that would not otherwise be possible (we pick up these points again later, in Chapter 16, on employee participation). Similarly, union reps can provide a very efficient means of communication for managers. Good managers should be communicating with their employees, both top–down and bottom–up, so that they keep in touch with the workplace. Local union representatives or shop stewards are elected by the workforce with whom they remain very much in touch. These representatives are generally elected or re-elected every year, and will be voted out of office if they fail to represent their members adequately. Hence it's very much in their interests to know what their members are thinking, which means that managers, if they want to know what's going on at the shop floor as well, will try to establish good relations with the union rep who they know will be – or should be – clued up. Box 6.1 illustrates some of the particular ways in which unions have spoken up for their members during the COVID-19 pandemic over the period 2020/21.

BOX 6.1: UNIONS AND THE COVID-19 PANDEMIC

We noted in Box 3.3 that the COVID-19 pandemic had highlighted a serious potential conflict of interests between employers and employees, namely, when it might be reasonable for an employer to demand employees return to work in the context of disputed health risks. Here we see that union membership appears to give employees a degree of protection.

In May 2020, unions representing teachers in the UK urged their members not to engage with plans to reopen schools the following month. The Secretary of State for Education had wanted a phased return to school, but this was opposed by the unions, including those representing support staff, on grounds of risks to health and safety. One union, the National Association of Schoolmasters Union of Women Teachers (NASUWT), cautioned that it would take legal action to defend teachers who felt forced back to work.

Then, in January 2021, following a second lockdown, the same thing happened again. The National Education Union advised its members that it was unsafe to return to school immediately after the Christmas holidays, while the National Association of Headteachers and the Association of School and College Leaders began legal moves against the government to require it to reveal its evidence for its reopening schedule. Schools didn't eventually return until 8 March.

Meanwhile, the Public and Commercial Services union balloted its members for strike action at the UK's Driver and Vehicle Licensing Agency (DVLA) because over 2,000 employees had been required to attend their offices at the DVLA in Swansea (South Wales), with the result that some 560 employees had caught coronavirus over the previous year.

The main function associated with unions is collective bargaining, which has been defined as: 'the process by which trade unions and similar associations, representing groups of employees, negotiate with employers or their representatives, with the object of reaching collective agreements' (Gospel and Palmer, 1993: 15).

'Bargaining' means that you are negotiating on behalf of your members, and 'collective' means you are dealing with all the members of your trade union. So it's the process of establishing an agreement covering pay and conditions for all your members across a particular company or sector. Typically, a union will meet the employer every year to negotiate terms and conditions for all its members covered within the bargaining unit (company or sector). At company level, employers take responsibility for negotiations themselves, but at sector level, employers are presented with an agreement negotiated on their behalf by their employers' association and the union. A sector-level collective agreement is therefore the way in which pay and conditions are harmonised across an entire sector. That's basically what collective bargaining is about: the process by which trade unions and similar associations, representing groups of employees, negotiate with employers, or their representatives, with the object of reaching mutual/ common agreements. It means, obviously, that the unions first have to agree on their demands, for example, a 5% pay rise or a 2% pay rise, or whatever it happens to be. It also means, crucially, that employers have to recognise the unions for the purpose of collective bargaining. This really is the key issue, because if the employer is hostile, the union isn't going to get very far. Employers who dismiss unions as merely an external agency that operates counter to what they might perceive as the harmonious operation of the organisation clearly won't be willing to engage in collective bargaining – indeed, they are unlikely even to recognise a union in the first place. So you may have a union that has members within an organisation (who might be open or secretive about their membership) but it's not recognised by the employer to negotiate on their behalf, a situation that will, of course, create a great deal of tension.

The second principal role played by unions in organisations – the economic (or 'monopoly') role – follows on from this discussion of collective bargaining (Freeman and Medoff, 1984). Through negotiating pay and conditions, unions may have a strong influence over labour costs. We saw in Chapter 1 that wage costs and fringe benefits are a significant element in total organisational costs, so an employer will need good relationships with a union that has influence over the level of such costs. Employers need to keep abreast of thinking within the union, in particular the timing and nature of its pay demands, which may affect the internal economic functioning of the company. A pay agreement that covers pay and benefits, as well as working time, holidays, pensions and much else besides, has major implications for a company's costs and hence continuing viability.

Unions also sometimes have a degree of influence over the supply of labour. The closed shop – where you had to be a union member in order to get a job – is no longer legal in the UK, but it's true that unions may have an effect on labour turnover (the 'exit, voice and loyalty' framework; see Chapter 8). Employers need to recruit workers but also to prevent good ones from leaving. Even though it can no longer affect recruitment, a well-functioning union, with a decent management, may be able to affect turnover by making the company a more attractive place to stay and work. If workers feel that their grievances and problems are acted on through effective consultation procedures, they are more likely to stay than exit, which will reduce turnover (Hirschman, 1970).

For these reasons, then, unions remain significant as representatives of the workforce – giving voice – but also in terms of affecting control over labour costs and the longer term viability of the company. Whether you like unions or not, and whether you approve of them or not (and Chapter 7 reveals a great deal of employer hostility towards them), they have been an essential component in the efficient operation of many organisations and companies in the past, and continue to be so in many today as well.

Unions in a global context

Although this book focuses on HRM in the UK and the US as liberal market economies (LMEs), it's important to consider the global aspect here too, because unions vary considerably in terms of their membership, identities, influence and legal status in different countries across the world. LMEs tend to have more deregulated markets, and so their legal frameworks generally do not support the collective rights of trade unions. By contrast, in many (but not all) coordinated market economies (CMEs), such as Belgium and the Scandinavian countries, unions tend to have higher levels of membership, but even when they don't, they have greater support through the legal and institutional frameworks of their countries. In Germany, for example, the law guarantees the rights of workers to be covered by a collective agreement. By contrast, there's nothing like that at all in the UK. Hence the influence of trade unions in CMEs tends to be more supported by the State than it is in the UK or the US. If we are examining international HRM in particular, we have to be aware of these variations. Regulation varies greatly country by country, and region by region. For example, commentators note the significant contrasts in union organisation in Germany between manufacturing and services. The German 'model' as traditionally outlined – including the central role of the law in underpinning collective bargaining and works councils – is actually largely based on manufacturing, while the service sector is fragmented, with unions more likely to meet employer hostility (especially in US multinationals) and unable to enforce their rights. Hence, contributors to a book on contemporary European trade unionism argue that one of the 'main challenges for German unions today is to build bridges across sectors' (Dribbusch et al, 2017: 216), while their UK counterparts by contrast state that the 'proximate cause of the unions' problems is the UK government' (Coderre-LaPalme and Greer, 2017: 264). Unions in CMEs tend to be more integrated into the national business system than those in LMEs, and that's an important factor from the point of view of HRM in manufacturing (if not in services), because it means that unions have a genuine voice in the company in a way they don't always in, say, the UK or the US.

Union membership

International comparisons are also important when analysing union membership and density of membership (the number of workers who are members of a union expressed as a percentage of the total eligible). Figure 6.2 reveals that in Iceland, nine out of ten workers are members of a union (that is, a 90% density) and in

Figure 6.2: Trade union membership (OECD countries, 2018)

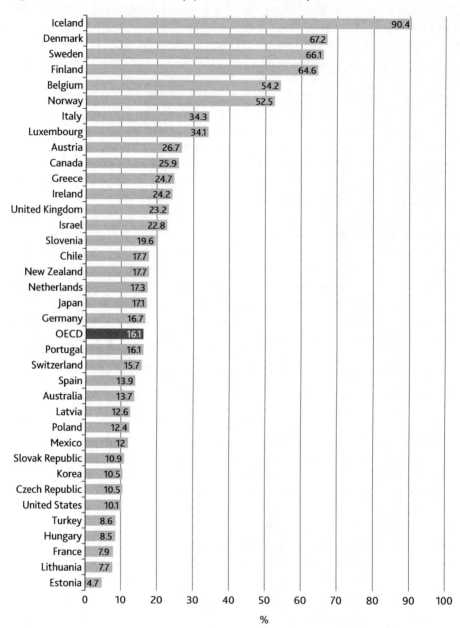

Note: Data refer to 2018 for Australia, Belgium, Mexico and the United States; 2017 for Austria, Estonia, Germany, Ireland, Italy, Japan, Korea, Sweden, Turkey and the United Kingdom; 2016 for Chile, Czech Republic, Denmark, Finland, France, Hungary, Iceland, Lithuania, Netherlands and New Zealand; 2015 for Belgium, Latvia, Norway, Portugal, Slovak Republic, Slovenia, Spain and Switzerland; 2014 for Luxembourg and Poland; 2013 for Greece; 2012 for Israel.

Source: OECD (2019b)

Scandinavia densities generally remain high: in Sweden, 66% of workers who could be a member of a trade union actually are. However, that figure falls quite dramatically in other countries. In Belgium and Norway, densities are over 50%, and in Italy and Luxembourg over 30%. But then densities drop markedly, with the UK on 23%, Germany on almost 17% and the US on 10%. In France, barely 8% are union members. So there's a huge variation in membership densities, which, of course, has a corresponding effect on the role, significance and influence of trade unions in these countries.

A related question centres on the trends in densities over time. Over recent years, there has been a general decline in membership across OECD (Organisation for Economic Co-operation and Development) countries, although it's very variable. In Sweden, density of union membership has fallen, from just under 80% in 1979 to just under 70% now. Denmark and Finland both still have very high numbers of employees in unions, although there has been a small decline. In other countries, however, that decline has been much more marked. For example, in New Zealand, union density has plummeted from around 70% in 1979 to just under 20% in 2018, with a decline in the UK over the same period from just over 50% to 23%, and in the US from around 20% to 10%.

Union membership within countries rises and falls over time. In the UK, for example, it has fluctuated dramatically. Starting in 1892, there was a peak in and after the First World War, but then a decline during the Great Depression, and then, gradually, from about the 1930s all the way up to 1979, a slow but steady increase. After 1979 and the election of Margaret Thatcher as prime minister, there was a steady decline again, although it now appears to have bottomed out. The number of union members rose in 2019 to 6.44 million, the third consecutive year since the low of 6.23 million in 2016 (BEIS, 2020). Indeed, as Box 6.2 illustrates, the conditions for union organisation will remain as long as the conditions for low pay and work intensification remain.

BOX 6.2: LOW-PAID AND GIG WORKERS FORM UNIONS
While union memberships are generally in decline across the industrialised economies, the conditions that underpin their organisation – poor pay, long hours and exploitation – remain as strong as ever, with new ones emerging within the gig economy.

- The Independent Workers' Union of Great Britain (IWGB) was set up in 2012 as a union that grew out of its members' dissatisfactions with Unite and UNISON. Its members are principally low-paid migrant workers who organise in IWGB branches covering, for example, cleaners, couriers, security guards and yoga teachers. It has fought campaigns for the London living wage at the Royal Opera House and retail store John Lewis, among others.
- The App Drivers and Couriers Union (ADCU) was founded in 2020, emerging from a predecessor that had been set up in 2015 to help fight Uber in an

ambitious claim for employment rights (see Box 5.3). It campaigns for better conditions for all couriers and fast-food delivery drivers, including pay rises, employment status and an end to unfair dismissals and deactivations (that is, the deletion of a worker's details from an app for failing to meet targets).

- In 2018, workers in the UK video games industry set up their own union, which is now known as IWGB Game Workers, as a branch of the umbrella IWGB. Their aims include ending the institutionalised practice of excessive/unpaid overtime, improving diversity and inclusion, supporting representation and securing a fair wage for all. Among their reasons for creating the union they state that, while 74% of game workers don't receive overtime, 90% will work extra hours and that 45% of women have experienced some form of bullying or harassment in the industry.
- In May 2020, Uber signed a recognition agreement with GMB (an established union), which is now able to represent up to 70,000 Uber drivers across the UK. The agreement also ensures that Uber drivers will have rights to holiday pay and a pension.

Source: Union websites

A further point about trade unions when examining their influence is the number of unions within a country. In Germany, for example, there are now only eight, while in the UK there are 48 unions affiliated to the TUC, which coordinates them. However, just 12 account for 90% of all members, so union membership is actually more concentrated than it might seem. UNISON, Unite and GMB together have over 3 million members. So, despite the decline in union membership, they remain significant actors in the practice of HRM in the UK, particularly in the public sector.

Confronted by declining membership, unions across all industrialised countries have engaged in campaigns to revitalise their organisation, with distinctions between those advocating partnership arrangements with employers to enhance business performance and those arguing for worker mobilisation and grassroots activity (Ibsen and Tapia, 2017). Some commentators maintain that 'partnership' may function more smoothly in CMEs, like Germany and Sweden, than in LMEs, like the UK and the US (Simms, 2015).

Collective bargaining

As we have seen, collective bargaining takes place at different levels, notably at company level and at sector (or multi-employer) level. The main trend in collective bargaining in the UK (and across the EU, as we see below) has been towards decentralisation. Bargaining at sector level (such as engineering, pharmaceuticals, banking, retail, hotels and catering) has almost vanished in the UK and is now restricted to company level, so individual companies within a sector bargain only for themselves, if they bargain at all (Coderre-LaPalme and Greer, 2017: 248–9). Few sectors – such as engineering construction, local government and universities – are still covered by national agreements. A national agreement means that all workers in that sector are covered by the same pay and conditions across the country. For example, all university lecturers are on the same pay spine. If they move to another university, they know what they are going to get paid because pay and conditions have been negotiated nationally on their behalf by the University and College Union (UCU) and the Universities and Colleges Employers' Association (UCEA).

There are also differences in the *coverage* of collective bargaining in the UK between the public and private sectors (that is, the proportion of workers who fall within the terms of an agreement). The public sector is generally more highly covered by collective bargaining than the private sector. So, if you're working for the Civil Service or local government, it's more likely that your pay is determined by a collective agreement than if you work in the private sector. However, between 2004 and 2011, the coverage of collective bargaining in the UK fell from 17% to 16% in the private sector and from 69% to 44% in the public sector. The decline in collective bargaining in the public sector has therefore been dramatic in recent years, and is almost certainly continuing as privatisation and fragmentation of labour markets proceed. Nevertheless coverage remains significantly above that in the private sector (van Wanrooy et al, 2013: 22).

There are also major variations in coverage between countries, as demonstrated in Figure 6.3. It reveals coverage before the 2008–09 financial crisis (2000/02) and after (2016/18). In Austria and France, the percentage of workers covered by collective agreements remained the same (98% and 94% respectively). This means that if you are a worker in Austria or France, it's almost certain that your pay and conditions will be negotiated on your behalf by a trade union. The same is true for Belgium, Sweden and Finland, where unions remain influential. Even though they have suffered declines in membership and density, they retain the power to negotiate pay and conditions with employers. However, in Ireland and the UK, as well as countries in Central and Eastern Europe, the decline in collective bargaining has been much greater, partly because it doesn't have the legal protection that it does in other countries.

The trends, too, are significant. Decentralisation has taken place across all EU member states (Leonardi and Pedersini, 2018). However, since the financial crisis, there has been a collapse of collective bargaining in countries like Bulgaria (from 56% to 23%), Greece (100% to 26%) and Romania (100% to 23%), with serious declines also in others where the EU imposed swingeing austerity measures, as we noted in Chapter 5 (Hermann, 2017). Generally speaking, Figure 6.3 illustrates an overall decline across Europe, particularly in countries already with a low base, with coverage now ranging from 98% in Austria down to 7% in Lithuania.

Although the situation is complex, the conclusion is that trade unions in LMEs, like the UK and Ireland, as well as those in Central and Eastern Europe, find themselves under increasing pressure. Meanwhile, those in CMEs remain

Figure 6.3: Collective bargaining coverage

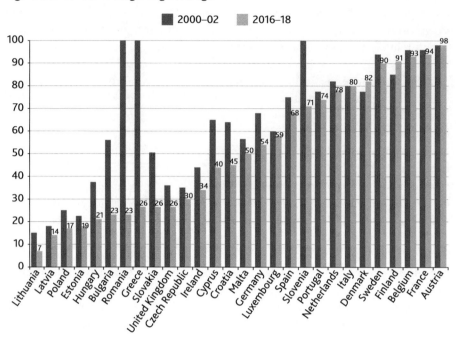

■ 2000–02   ▨ 2016–18

Source: EFJ (2020)

influential because their strength in covering workers through collective bargaining is still largely intact despite the challenges they've faced in recent years in terms of declining membership. Most striking is the case of France, where union membership is 8% (see Figure 6.2) but collective bargaining coverage stands at 94% (see Figure 6.3). And that, of course, is another reason why we study trade unions: when we expand our vision across Europe and the world, we are struck by the great variation in their influence across contrasting institutional and legal contexts.

Why do unions get a bad press?

Before we turn to examine how unions affect management styles, we need to review the main arguments against union activity at the workplace – in short, why unions frequently get such a 'bad press'. Some clues are contained in the analysis above. First of all, neoliberals who believe in the free market view unions as a potential threat as they bargain terms and conditions with the employer, which (in their words) 'distort' wages: wages should be allowed to follow the market, but unions distort the market because they act as an artificial impediment to its free operation. Neoliberals and free market economists accordingly maintain that unions play a negative role in the labour market (see Freeman and Medoff, 1984, for a discussion of this position). This is clearly going to be a matter of opinion. In Chapter 3, we explained why workers could not be seen as factors of production.

We argued that labour isn't a commodity in the way we have markets for other commodities, and therefore to talk about a free market for labour is misleading because the labour market has its own unique properties. The neoliberal view must therefore be disputed.

A related argument is that unions protect 'insiders' (that is, workers with jobs) by safeguarding their terms and conditions and keeping labour costs artificially high, which penalises 'outsiders' (that is, the unemployed). This implies two very different policy options: one is to *reduce the power of insiders*, through anti-union legislation and increased employment insecurity, as practised in the UK; the other is to *increase the power of outsiders* by training, education and promoting greater access to the employment and job securities enjoyed by insiders, as seen in France (Lindbeck and Snower, 2001: 184). In general, employers and governments talk less about levelling up by spreading the benefits of unionisation and rather more about pulling down union benefits in the name of 'market access'.

It has also been argued that, by defending pay within an organisation, unions exclude people who are looking for jobs, because the employer might hire more people at a lower rate of pay than at the higher rate. Some economists therefore contend that unions distort external labour markets as well as internal ones because they prevent the unemployed from finding jobs. However, unions campaign for good wages and training opportunities, such as apprenticeships, for everyone – and never only for the privileged few. For example, the introduction of the national minimum wage in 1999 in the UK didn't lead to unemployment, even though some economists had argued it would price some lower paid workers out of a job. In a review 20 years later, a commentator concluded: 'It was supposed to cost thousands of jobs; instead, it looks like a never-ending good news story' (Howlett, 2019).

A further argument against unions is that they are no longer necessary because employers give such generous pay and conditions. We'll analyse this view in the next chapter on management styles, but, of course, some employers who make an effort to pay above market rates and establish outstanding terms and conditions then claim, 'Look, you don't need a union because we're already giving you the best.' They may have a limited point, but, as we showed in Chapter 3, the employment relationship embodies a wage–effort bargain and an associated frontier of control that contains the potential for conflict, no matter how high pay levels might be.

There is also frequently a political dimension to union unpopularity. Historically they have sometimes been seen as wielding too much political power. There was the so-called 'Winter of Discontent' in the UK in 1978/79, which involved pay demands and a national strike by refuse collectors and local government workers. Rubbish piled up in the streets, and the public suffered major disruption. The causes were complex, but the dispute ended up with the election of Margaret Thatcher in 1979 and anti-union Conservative governments up until 1997. (It must be added that subsequent Labour governments never restored union rights to their pre–1979 levels.) The Conservative ascendancy over this period was at least partly explained by the dislocation caused by the strikes in the late 1970s. In 1979, the public voted for Thatcher who said she'd deal with what the Conservative election manifesto called Labour's "'militants' charter" of trade union legislation' (Conservative Central Office, 1979: 9). However, one commentator, writing for the right-wing think tank the Institute of Economic Affairs, has blogged more recently: 'To my mind the problems in the labour market these days are not caused by trade unionism but by the slow pace of public sector reform, and by excessive and damaging regulation [such as the national living wage and the apprentice levy]' (Shackleton, 2016). In other words, unions' political power – such as it was – is, for him, a thing of the past.

Overall, however, with press ownership concentrated into the hands of a few powerful individuals, many hostile towards trade unions, we should not be surprised that unions receive negative reporting. The media and press focus disproportionally on the 'negative' effects of trade unions (disruption and damage) and rarely on their positive effects (improving wages, conditions and individual life chances). Books on TV coverage of trade unions and disputes (such as Philo, 2014) contrast the language used to describe trade unionists (who are 'demanding', 'confrontational' and 'hostile') with the language used to describe employers (who make 'offers' and are 'compromising'). Bruno (2009: 392) studied press 'bias' through 10 years of reporting on union issues in the *Chicago Tribune*, one of only two daily mass circulation newspapers in the US. The research revealed that reports were 56.7% negative, 36.4% positive and 6.8% neutral. It concluded that the paper 'largely establishes a negative tone in covering the labor movement' (Bruno, 2009: 402). So trade unions literally 'get a bad press' owing to the way newspapers report and distort labour movement issues.

Strikes

That said, we need to examine the issue of strikes more carefully, as many people still associate 'unions' with 'strikes' in the way that they associate 'fish' with 'chips' or 'knives' with 'forks'. Strikes and disruption in production and services may well cause wider hostility towards unions among the general public, although there are, of course, always serious grounds for a dispute – unions don't declare strikes lightly. For example, between 2016 and 2021, strikes in the UK by the Rail, Maritime and Transport (RMT) union (over the abolition of guards) disrupted the rail journeys of passengers, strikes by junior doctors (over shifts) inconvenienced hospital patients, and strikes by university lecturers (over pensions) upset students. In each case, the public – as passengers, patients and students – tend to focus on the disruption caused to their everyday life rather than on the causes of the strike in the first place.

An issue here is the distinction between manufacturing and services. Most of the wealth of the UK used to be produced through manufactured goods – cars, ships, aircraft and a multitude of engineering products. A strike at a car plant, for example, doesn't actually harm the public that greatly, and for a while, the company may well be able to continue supplying its customers from its stockpiles. It's only when you move into a service sector economy – and note that the three examples of strikes given above all affect services – that strikes seriously disrupt clients and customers. A university lecturer who goes on strike is likely to cause anxiety among students who are deprived of lectures and seminars, but students are not the employer; the financial interests of the employer, the university itself, are not immediately affected in the same way that those of a car plant would be.

The challenge for workers in service sectors – such as education, health, hotels and catering, local government and transport, among others – is that the clients (as students, patients, guests, residents and passengers) get inadvertently sucked into the dispute. Rail passengers get sucked into a strike between railway workers and train operating companies, while students get sucked into any dispute between lecturers and universities. That is a particular problem in the service sector, which affects public reaction to strikes and hence, more broadly, towards trade unions. Indeed, as we noted above, the 'Winter of Discontent' in 1978/79 was a dramatic illustration of just this effect, as members of the public had to pick their way through piles of rubbish left mounting up in the streets.

So in terms of public perceptions of unions, we need to analyse the significance of strikes in the UK. In Chapter 4, we saw how prevalent unorganised, individualistic conflicts are in the workplace, with the cost of, say, absence due to stress far outweighing that of strikes. Strikes are still important, however, largely because they remain the most public form of conflict between workers and employers in the economy, and are widely reported when they do occur. But just how serious are strikes in the UK?

The causes of strike activity are extremely complex (Kelly, 1998). They reflect a sense of injustice, require a current of solidarity and leadership, and assume communal attribution of blame for a particular action that's behind the strike – and, of course, they are generally organised by trade unions (although spontaneous walk-outs are not unknown). The definition of a strike is complex, too. The Office for National Statistics (ONS) in the UK defines a strike as a stoppage of work due to an industrial dispute as opposed to a political dispute. The stoppage also has to meet certain thresholds. It must involve at least 10 employees, so if there were only eight or nine involved it wouldn't count. And it must involve a minimum number of hours lost. All this probably underestimates the number of strikes, because a shorter dispute involving fewer workers won't actually get recorded.

Nevertheless, strike data in the UK are astonishing. There has been a phenomenal decrease in the number of strikes since 1975 across all three measures of strike activity: the number of strikes, the number of workers involved and the duration of strikes. In the period 1975–79, there were an average 2,310 strikes a year, involving over 1.6 million workers and leading to the loss of over 11.6 million working days a year. These figures fell steadily to the period of the first Labour government under Tony Blair (1997–2002), when there was an average of 190 strikes a year, involving 278,000 workers and the loss of 518,000 days (Blyton and Turnbull, 2004: 334–5).

Table 6.1, which presents the most recent figures, is even more remarkable. The number of stoppages has remained low and steady since 2010, somewhere between roughly 100 and 150 a year, although it dropped below 100 in 2017 and 2018. The number of days lost reached a peak in 2011 because of a public sector dispute about pensions. Indeed, strike figures are sometimes distorted by a particularly bitter dispute. For example, the increase in working days lost in 2016 compared with 2015 was partly attributable to the junior doctors' dispute in the NHS in England (see Figure 6.1), which accounted for around 40% of the total days lost for 2016. In 2018, the total number lost fell to the sixth-lowest annual total since records began in 1891, with the education sector accounting for 66% of that, mainly because of disputes involving university employees. The number of working days lost in the public sector was the lowest since records for public sector strikes began in 1996. The number of workers involved in disputes in 2018 (39,000) was the second-lowest figure since records for workers involved began in 1893, while the number of stoppages (81) fell to the second-lowest figure since records for stoppages began in 1930. Of course, this situation could change rapidly if economic conditions, such as inflation, worsen dramatically.

Table 6.1: Most recent UK strike data (2010–18)

	Stoppages in progress in year	Workers involved (000s)	Working days lost (000s)
2010	92	133	365
2011	149	1,530	1,390
2012	131	237	249
2013	114	395	444
2014	155	733	788
2015	106	81	170
2016	101	154	322
2017	79	33	276
2018	81	39	273

Source: ONS (2019a)

Concluding comments

Unions have voice and economic implications for the practice of HRM, which is why we study them. Workers join trade unions for a variety of reasons, but the whole discourse around unions tends to become highly polarised, with attitudes on the one side advocating that they need to be resisted at all costs (typically in US companies) and on the other arguing that they can play a constructive and helpful role in the organisation (typically in continental European companies). Overall, ' we are witnessing the lowest levels of strike activity in the UK since records began in the 1890s. However, this is true across all industrialised countries, not just the

UK, and it leads us into our next chapter, which focuses on management styles and how managers deal with trade unions and take advantage of their decline.

Some questions to think about

1. Discuss the case for and against recognising trade unions at the workplace.

2. In the course of an employment crisis, caused, for example, by organisational restructuring or pressures to return to work during a pandemic, would you rather be a member of a union or not? Explain your reasons.

3. What do unions do when they bargain collectively with employers? What are the main trends in collective bargaining across industrialised economies? What explains these trends?

Further reading

Johnstone, S. and Ackers, P. (eds) (2015) *Finding a Voice at Work? New Perspectives on Employment Relations*, Oxford: Oxford University Press. [A wide range of contributions that discuss the challenges facing unions today, mainly in the UK.]

Lehndorff, S., Dribbusch, H. and Schulten, T. (eds) (2017) *Rough Waters: European Trade Unions in a Time of Crises*, Brussels: European Trade Union Institute. [Analysis of the challenges facing trade unions across individual EU member states.]

TUC (Trades Union Congress) (2016) 'What have the trade unions done for us?', February [Video, 4 mins 33 secs], Available from: www.youtube.com/watch?v=lrjySOFLXgg [Not a reading, but a 'watch' – an amusing summary of the reasons to join a trade union, from the TUC's perspective.]

7

Management Styles

In our discussion of the wage–effort bargain in Chapter 3, we pointed out that the concept of the 'frontier of control' – that is, our contested understanding of the amount of effort we have to make to justify the pay we are earning – is helpful because it gives us a way into analysing what is actually legitimate and what is not legitimate behaviour at the workplace, and *in whose eyes*: whether legitimacy is judged from the point of view of the employer or that of the employee.

This observation introduces a degree of ambiguity and uncertainty into the employment relationship; in other words, the employment relationship is no longer something exact, something given. Rather, it shifts and twists according to the balance of power and influence between employer and worker. In Chapter 4 we saw how managers might create conflict at the workplace by attempting to encroach on the frontier of control, and how worker resistance might result in all kinds of forms, organised and unorganised, collective and individual. In Chapter 6, we followed through this discussion of resistance by analysing its expression with specific reference to trade unions: why workers join them and how they organise collective forms of resistance (particularly strikes). All the same, we finished by noting how union membership has declined and how strikes have withered in significance across the industrialised world since the 1970s.

In this chapter we build on this notion of ambiguity in the employment relationship by beginning to analyse management styles and *perceptions* of human resource management (HRM), because we're going to argue that the way in which we *view* HRM is as important as whatever might be construed as its reality. In other words, we have to be aware that a lot of HRM is what goes on in our heads by way of our attitudes, perceptions and value judgements. This requires each of us to become more conscious of the ways in which we perceive HRM and the human resources (HR) function, and especially the role of the employer in managing labour. Where does management's legitimacy in issuing instructions begin and end? This is a prelude to Part 2 of the book, where we begin to examine how HRM has changed as unions have declined, and managers have taken advantage of increasing fragmentation of the employment relationship to drive forward their frontiers of control to produce the characteristics of the contemporary workplace.

In this chapter we tease out some of these points by looking at 'frames of reference': three ways in which employers and employees regard management and labour. You'll find these terms covered quite extensively in the textbooks: unitarism, pluralism and radical perspectives. We'll look at each in turn because each conveys a different perception – a partial view, if you like – of HRM, so to be aware of the totality of the HRM function, we have to get behind each perception. We'll see how they affect our understanding of unions, conflict and the employment relationship itself, as well as the language we use to discuss HRM.

Frames of reference

Let's just start with perspectives, frames of reference, the assumptions we have in our heads at this very minute about certain concepts and terms that we need to disentangle. For example, what is your immediate reaction to the word 'politician'? Do you think of well-meaning, principled people who have the public good at heart and who go into it as a career to help make the world a better place? Or do you, rather, think of a bunch of self-seeking egotists who all have their snouts in the trough and are basically corrupt and in it for themselves? Or points along that spectrum – on the one hand this, on the other hand that?

Or the word 'protestors'? When you see protestors – any protestors – on your smartphone or in the news, what do you think? Do you think they are well-meaning people who are trying to do something for the good of the country, or do you think they're a bunch of agitators who are holding up the traffic? Or maybe you say, well, it all depends on what they are protesting about? Or 'criminals' – are criminals likely to be the product of deprived backgrounds and so deserve rehabilitation? Or are they merely irresponsible individuals who deserve to be locked up as punishment, or something in between?

These questions – and how we answer them – are significant in HRM because human resource management is about people, human beings, all of us, and how we work and are managed – as 'labour' – at work. When we talk about 'labour', we are merely talking about people like ourselves who earn wages or a salary to live, and we all know how difficult we can be at times – argumentative, self-willed and resistant to change. But when we talk about ensuring that 'labour' meets organisational goals, we are thinking in managerial ways. When we look at different ways to achieve those goals, we assume a certain detachment in weighing up the alternatives. In theory and practice, labour is there to be nurtured as an asset or controlled as disobedient and troublesome. However, the human dimension is central to HRM in a way that it's not in, say, accounting or business strategy. It is the core or kernel, if you like, of the subject, so to be alive *to our own perceptions* of each other is critically important. Our perspectives on other people's nature and motivations are the result of immensely complex pressures – our own personalities, family, education, social background, religion or lack of it, friends, peer groups, all these things. Indeed, our perspectives are likely to change as we get older and go to university, and come to experience work and suffer life's various knocks along the way.

Let's take all this further with a specific example from HRM. Here is an image of strikers in Figure 7.1. They happen to be teachers. What do you immediately think when you see them?

Are you interested to know why they're on strike? They must have a reason, mustn't they? Or do you think they ought to be back at work instead of disrupting

Figure 7.1: Teachers' strike (June 2011)

Source: ShutterStock/Matt Gibson

everything? Have you ever been directly affected by a strike, for example on the railways or the buses? How did you deal with that experience? And sometimes employers *lock out* workers as a way to end a strike because temporarily closing the factory prevents workers from coming back, which puts further economic pressure on them to return. What are your views about that?

At the heart of our discussion here about perceptions of strikes there lies (again) the fundamental tension within the employment relationship: failure to secure the active cooperation of the workforce arises from the fundamental tension that exists, and persists, between employer and employee. In Chapter 3 we stressed that the employment relationship is ongoing and unequal, and contains elements of both consent and potential conflict: you, as the worker, are paid a wage, and the wage–effort, the effort part of it, is very much between your employer, supervisor or line manager and you and your motivation in a particular job at a particular moment. There may be rather little agreement about the relationship, with a lot of fluidity in how it's interpreted, and that's really what we're talking about here.

The real question is how we perceive that relationship. This is where we can identify three main perspectives on HRM: unitarist, pluralist and radical. We shall examine each in turn because each in its own way is highly significant when we're analysing the nature of HRM, not least because each reflects a different view of the people to be managed at work and – more broadly – a different view of the contribution that HRM makes to business practice. Bear in mind here that there is no consensus on how many frames of reference there might be, with some writers identifying four (Budd et al, 2021) and others up to nine (Cradden, 2018). Here we stick to the standard three to keep things simple, not least because there is evidence that these go back to the early 19th century in origin (Gold, 2020).

Unitarism

'Unitarism' implies 'one' – it comes from the word 'unit', meaning one thing – so the idea here is of the organisation or the company as a single, unified hierarchy, with senior managers at the top laying down strategy, plans and instructions, and middle and line managers ensuring that they are correctly carried out by workers. That's the basic idea – the idea of a unitary structure. It's based on the manager's right to manage, sometimes termed 'managerial prerogative'. Managerial prerogative in capitalist or neocapitalist societies is based on private property – under company law, private sector companies are owned by shareholders who elect boards of directors to whom they are responsible for carrying out their interests. The principal interest of shareholders is to increase growth in their share capital and to earn dividends from their shares. If the directors achieve these aims, then shareholders are going to be happy. The problem is, if things go wrong and if share prices begin to slide on the stock market, there may be pressure on the company to stabilise, which may well mean that urgent action needs to be taken, such as (as we saw in Chapter 1) cutting labour costs – through redundancies, closing plants, outsourcing work or other means – if not developing new products for the market in the longer term.

Managers with unitarist perspectives believe that a consensus of interests unites workers and managers. Of course, this has some truth. As employees, we don't want our employer to go bust. We're all keen for our company to do well so that our jobs are secure, we receive our pay cheque at the end of the month and we maintain our career progression within the company. However, the unitarist manager goes further in claiming that, because there is this consensus or common interest in wanting the company to succeed, values and objectives are also held in common between managers and workers. The unitarist perspective therefore tends to undermine or deny the *structural* dimension to conflict – such as the tension between wages as a cost and wages as an income – leading the manager confronted by some form of conflict to search for its cause in external agencies or poor communications. So, for example, a unitarist manager confronted by a threat of unionisation or strike action may allege that it has been fomented by outside agitators who do not have the interests of the company at heart. Maybe they're communists or subversives, people who want to bring down the company. Or else they might blame management for failing to communicate adequately with the workers: 'If only they understood what we are trying to do, they would fall into line.' The point here is that when we look at the employment relationship and point out its potential for conflict, the unitarist manager tends to deny any structural element in its cause and focuses only on the areas of consensus or cooperation.

Basically, then, the unitarist manager sees the power relationships within the organisation as unproblematic, and you will often find managers of this persuasion talking about the organisation as a 'ship' or as a 'team' or 'family', which are all designed to highlight the unified nature of the organisation: shipmates work together to ensure the ship reaches its destination safely, teams cooperate to beat the other side, and people like to think that family members all support one another – a powerful fiction that probably runs against much of the evidence!

A key theme that we'll develop throughout this book is that unitarism is, in liberal market economies like the UK and the US, the *default* management perspective. For now, we are going make just one point, which is that unitarism takes various different forms. The most obvious form, *traditional unitarism*, opposes trade unions. Trade unions, after all, represent organised labour and the collective interests of workers, which – as we have seen – often stand in conflict with those of employers. That's what a union does, and so unitarist employers of the old school oppose unionisation. Donald Roy (1980) argues that there are three ways in which traditionalist, unitarist managers can deal with trade unions.

They might use what he calls 'fear stuff'. In this scenario, the employer threatens to dismiss anyone who tries to organise a union at the workplace: 'If you join a union, you're going to lose your job.' Or else the employer ensures that union activists lose favour with their supervisor or don't get promoted. There are all kinds of similar techniques through which an employer can, on an individual basis, deal with union activity. However, they might also make threats on a collective basis to prevent unionisation, for example by relocating a plant, closing it down or outsourcing the work. Other collective threats include laying workers off or refusing pay increases. In yet more extreme cases, employers may attempt to break up unions through violence. Type 'YouTube police attacking strikers US 1930s' into your search engine and you'll find numerous clips of police and hired company thugs breaking up strikes in pre-war US, where there were often running battles between the police and workers who were trying to unionise companies. So, there are a number of different ways in which the employer can instil fear in workers, both on an individual and collective basis, in order to prevent union activity.

Another way unitarist employers traditionally prevent unionisation is through what Roy calls 'evil stuff' – you had 'fear stuff', now you have 'evil stuff'. 'Evil stuff' is where an employer instils hatred of trade unions. Unions are demonised: they have wicked intentions, sinister connections and are mired in corruption. Known union activists may be blacklisted by employers. Construction employers in the UK over many years drew up lists of union activists and circulated them, secretly, to make sure that they would never be employed within the industry (Smith and Chamberlain, 2015). Or the secret services might be used to infiltrate the union movement, which happened in the 1980s when they infiltrated the National Union of Mineworkers during the miners' strike (Beckett and Hencke, 2009: 271).

However, apart from these 'traditional' forms, unitarist employers might use rather more subtle techniques to deter unionisation, known as *sophisticated paternalism* (Sisson and Storey, 2002). The origins of this form of unitarism go back to the paternalist management of certain employers in the 19th century (as we see in Chapter 8). Sophisticated paternalism keeps unions out of the workplace by ensuring that pay and conditions are above sector average and arguing that, as a result, workers gain nothing by joining a union. Having outlined 'fear' and 'evil' stuff, Donald Roy calls this 'sweet stuff'. Examples in the UK include John Lewis and Marks & Spencer, which have successfully excluded trade union recognition by paying above market level wages and conditions within their stores. Similar examples in the US include IBM and Hewlett-Packard (Jacoby, 1997). These employers provide attractive fringe benefits and have improved facilities for staff, such as sports and recreational centres, in the belief that successful businesses require motivated workers. This strategy emphasises the cooperation between worker and employer. Indeed, at John Lewis, the largest cooperatively owned firm in the UK, employees are known as 'partners'.

Finally, more recently, a further form of unitarism – 'new' unitarism – has emerged, which we examine in depth in Chapter 8. This is a unitarist view of the organisation, but it's 'new' in the sense that it manipulates culture within the organisation to secure the compliance and commitment of workers to its objectives. Hi-tech companies, such as Apple, Google and Yahoo!, operate on this basis. As employment became more contingent or precarious from the 1980s, companies, particularly in the hi-tech sector, began to realise that one way to retain highly trained employees was by integrating them into the organisation by making the workplace a fun place to be. Employees are induced to spend long hours at work because work is 'fun'. Many hi-tech companies have developed all kinds of ways to do this – free beer and sweets, games and teambuilding exercises – as part of their HR strategies, to promote the workplace as somewhere that you really want to be because that's where your friends are and where you can enjoy yourself as well as doing your job.

Overall, then, employers can try to keep trade unions out in a variety of ways – ranging from violent strikebreaking to killing with kindness – but they all share the assumption that unions, as external agencies, would damage harmonious relationships within the organisation.

Pluralism

Pluralism, by contrast, presents a rather different view of the organisation. 'Plural' clearly means more than one, which directs our attention to the fact that there's not just one way to look at the organisation: there may be several. So the idea is that managers are there to manage, certainly, but they do so not on the basis of a prerogative that's granted through property rights but rather through persuasion. In other words, if you want workers to carry out instructions and to use their discretion, you have to reason with them. You explain why the instruction has been given, you explain the rationale for the order or the task – you explain why it's part of something that needs to be done for the organisation. Such an approach assumes that potentially differing sets of interests between management and workers need to be mediated by good management. It therefore assumes that the employment relationship may be adversarial or conflictual. This perspective is accordingly in line with the argument we are developing in this book, that the wage–effort bargain involves consensus and cooperation, yes, but conflict too. Pluralists recognise that workers may have values and objectives that differ from those of the organisation, which may potentially cause conflict.

In any organisation there are worker subcultures – workers have their own agendas, gossip, jargon, jokes, stories and nicknames for supervisors, complimentary or otherwise, according to how they get on together. Workers are not the compliant factor of production that unitarists assume. Rather, they interpret situations in their own way, very often on a group basis (a classic illustration can be found in Roy, 1959). Teams will have a view about their work that may not be entirely in line with management objectives. Common values and objectives cannot be taken for granted, which means that conflict is always there, if only in the background, and you need to have procedures to deal with it.

And so, pluralist managers will ensure that there are procedures to channel potential conflict. There are, after all, different ways to handle a worker who has a grievance over, say, hours of work or a sense of discrimination over a failed promotion. A unitarist manager may not take it very seriously, or will tell you to get over it: 'I wouldn't discriminate against you, I'm a decent manager, you know, you should do what you're told.' However, your sense of discrimination may fester because no one is listening to you. In that case, you are going to get more resentful and may eventually leave the organisation. According to a recent survey, 'manager behaviour' was the third most quoted reason for leaving a job, after 'career development' and 'poor work–life balance' (Employee Benefits, 2019). By contrast, a pluralist manager will understand that, in order to deal with grievances, organisations need proper procedures and managers need to listen to employees. This brings potentially damaging conflict caused by resentments out into the open where it can be heard and acted on. And the same goes for disciplinary procedures, after all. Your supervisor may feel that you're not really pulling your weight in your job. A unitarist manager may simply bully you, while a pluralist manager may give you a warning as the first step in a disciplinary procedure against you. The warning will give you the chance to argue your case – maybe you lack the training you need. Your view has to be heard as well as that of your employer.

The pluralist has a broader perspective on the organisation than the unitarist, and will understand that power relations are unequal and may be problematic. Power relations are not as harmonious as the unitarist may think. The period of pluralist dominance in management practice began after the Second World War, not least because the period up to about 1975, globally, was a period of steady growth. Economies were booming, there was full employment, and unions were consequently assertive in demanding pay rises for their members. Employers were relatively weaker and recognised that unions had something to contribute in the workplace. Many managers were inclined to integrate unions into procedures – from collective bargaining and consultation committees to grievance and disciplinary procedures – as a way to help control them, which led to managerial pluralism. This 'classic' pluralism was reflected in the industrial relations theory developed in the US by John Dunlop and Clerk Kerr, and in the UK by Hugh Clegg and Allan Flanders (Heery, 2016), until its eclipse since the 1980s by unitarism (see Box 7.1). As with unitarism, there are different types of pluralism, with more or less awareness of strategic action in relation to union activity (Heery, 2016: 36–69), but for the purposes of our argument here, such differences matter less than the key point that a pluralist framework is one in which workers' interests, organisations and values are legitimate.

BOX 7.1: UNITARIST AND PLURALIST PERSPECTIVES ON THE ORGANISATION

In 2018, Deborah Hann and David Nash carried out a survey of private sector organisations in the UK to investigate employers' perceptions of workplace disputes and how they attempt to resolve them. Their report reveals that 76% of their respondents may be characterised as 'unitarist' and the remaining 24% as 'pluralist' (Hann and Nash, 2020):

> Three-quarters of respondents say that disputes are not inevitable but instead occur as the result of misbehaviour, poor performance or misunderstanding. A further 8% believe that disputes are inevitable, but management strategies and techniques should be derived to try to lessen the impact of such conflict on the organisation and a final 16% embrace disputes as constructive to workplace relations by offering chances to examine, question and adapt routine approaches.

Figure 7.2: Employers' perceptions of workplace disputes

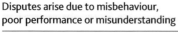

Disputes are an inevitable but unwelcome part of organisational life, which need to be managed — 8%

Disputes are an inevitable and unavoidable part of organisational life and can be constructive to workplace relations — 16%

Disputes arise due to misbehaviour, poor performance or misunderstanding — 76%

Note: *N*=382

Base: All respondents

Source: Hann and Nash (2020: Figure 1)

So, just to recap, the unitarist denies the legitimate origins or the potential for conflict at the workplace, whereas the pluralist is open to the possibility that there are genuine conflicts at work that require expression. In both cases, there are different types of unitarist and pluralist.

Determinants of management styles

A variety of factors might influence management style. However, as other commentators have noted: 'A particular challenge in empirically operationalizing the Frame of Reference model is that its constructs and cause–effect relations are a non-separable mix of objective, subjective, and normative/ideological elements' (Kaufman et al, 2021: 230). Nevertheless, in this section we explore some possibilities.

The study by Hann and Nash (2020) in the UK found that only *sector* had an impact on perspectives, with pluralism rather more predominant in low–paying sectors (see Box 7.2).

BOX 7.2: PLURALISTS MORE LIKELY IN LOW-PAYING SECTORS

In their survey (Hann and Nash, 2020: commentary on Figure 1), Hann and Nash also investigate the determinants of management perspectives (see Box 7.1). They say:

> Organisational perspectives towards disputes are not contingent on organisational demographics or the presence of employment relations stakeholders. The use of an HR function for dealing with HR issues, employee relations specialists and a trade union has no significant impact on the perspective of the employer toward disputes, nor does the size of the organisation or the sector within which it is located. The only variable that had a mildly significant ($p<0.1$) impact on the orientation to disputes was whether the organisation was in a low-paying sector of the economy. A higher proportion of employers in low-paying sectors viewed disputes as inevitable but potentially constructive – the progressive pluralist perspective – than those in higher-paying sectors (21% versus 13%). A possible explanation for this seemingly counterintuitive finding could be that as conflict is more prevalent in the low-pay sectors of the economy ... managers have greater opportunities to see the potential benefits of such disputes.

As they say, this finding does seem 'counterintuitive'. You would have thought that *unitarist* styles of management ('hard' HRM) would be more likely in organisations competing in the low–cost ends of the market, with pluralist styles more likely where you require the commitment of workers in higher paying sectors ('soft'

HRM). However, there are clearly other factors in operation that require further consideration, and research at the level of sector or firm might yield very different outcomes. Indeed, a study of the incidence of these frameworks among employers in four countries (Australia, Canada, the UK and the US) that used survey data from 7,000 workplaces found 'evidence of a large middle range of pluralist type workplaces and smaller groupings of radical- and unitarist-type workplaces toward the bottom and top tails, albeit with somewhat higher concentration in the top unitarist end' (Kaufman et al, 2021: 230).

Besides the role of low-/high-paying sectors and workplace, other factors that influence management styles might include the process of company growth, national context and management education and training. Strong personalities will play a role, too, especially those with a dominant founder. It's doubtful whether Donald Trump's companies or Elon Musk's (see Box 1.4) are known for their pluralism: if you don't agree with them, or if your face doesn't fit, then you're out. Dominant founders or personalities may therefore also have an influence on management styles.

Another possibility is that 'last-resort unitarism' is the core of manager behaviour (Cressey et al, 1985). These commentators argue: 'Companies which are quite different in terms of technologies, products or services, occupational groups and degree of unionisation end up claiming managerial prerogatives – they have to do what they have to do' (Cressey et al, 1985: 132). They add: 'penetrating the flux, contingencies and differing styles of organisational life, the realities of power shape and in a sense identify the limits of pluralism'. This view – that unitarism is a kind of default management setting based on the pragmatic need to 'get the job done' – might help to explain its predominance among British managers revealed by the Advisory, Conciliation and Arbitration Service (ACAS) (see Boxes 7.1 and 7.2). A unitarist approach might simply seem a more efficient style when decisions need to be taken quickly. Consultation brings everybody into the agreement and might improve the quality of decision-making, but, on the other hand, it might seem to take too long. Managers may just prefer to impose business decisions rapidly and top-down when they can.

However, at an international level, it must be stressed that institutional and legal frameworks prove significant too. In coordinated market economies, the law – which generally aims to establish economic consensus among stakeholders – may require employers to negotiate with trade unions or consult workers (as we saw in Chapter 5). Under the system of works councils in Germany, for example, it's not just an option to consult labour, but a legal requirement. The law lays down detailed requirements for employers to inform or consult the workforce and even to codetermine issues with it, with penalties for infringements (see Chapter 16). Such requirements enforce a pluralist perspective, which explains why German employers (for example) are more likely to be pluralist than their UK or US counterparts, although borrowings and hybridity have also been identified (see Pudelko, 2006; Festing, 2012).

In summary, the origins of management styles are complex and depend on a wide variety of factors. Their occurrence is largely an empirical matter, which requires analysis of organisations, sectors and national business systems.

Radical perspectives

We now turn to the third set of perspectives on the organisation: radical perspectives (which are critical, rather than managerial, perspectives). Radical perspectives differ from unitarism and pluralism in that they argue that capitalism is essentially exploitative. Marxists (and others) argue that workers are exploited under a capitalist system of production because they never gain the full product of their labour. Most of that product is creamed off by capitalists in the form of profits that they appropriate, which creates a barrier to workers ever controlling the full fruits of their labour, which means, in turn, that capitalism endemically reflects a conflict of interest between workers and employers. This is known as the 'theory of surplus value'. That view is certainly radical, although taken to its logical end, it is actually revolutionary (see Box 7.3). Basically, it's saying that employers extract profits, seek maximum returns on capital, exploit workers and, accordingly lack loyalty to institutions or countries. They outsource labour to the cheapest areas – wherever they see fit to gain maximum profit for themselves – which means that workers never obtain the full results of their labour. Workers organise in trade unions to defend their living standards and continually fear insecurity and unemployment but, in the end, not even unions are able to protect them from the greater economic and legal power of employers – the capitalist class.

BOX 7.3: A MARXIST VIEW OF THE EMPLOYMENT RELATIONSHIP UNDER CAPITALISM

The following is an extract from a speech given in 1978 by Arthur Scargill, president of the National Union of Mineworkers during the miners' strike (1984–85):

It is a nonsense, it is a fallacy, to believe for one moment that we can live in a capitalist society and attempt to work with it.... I do not believe that the function of our [labour] movement has anything in common with a society which we are committed to end. I therefore assert that the basic contradictions within our society can only be ended if our movement is galvanised in a united fashion against the evils of the society in which we live. The demands enunciated a hundred years ago for the common ownership of the means of production, distribution and exchange are as clear and as true as when they were uttered all those years ago.... There is only one way to advance our movement, there is only one way to advance our class: by taking on the system under which we live. (Scargill, 1978: 4–6)

For a Marxist, then, the employment relationship is *necessarily* unequal as it is controlled by the employer and alienates the workers – separating them from the product of their labour, their tools and the sense of self as social human beings. The wage system disguises the exploitation of the worker; a wage never compensates a worker for the whole product they produce. The full control apparatus within an organisation is exercised by the employer, never the worker. Marxists therefore criticise HRM as a complete waste of time, as a mere sticking-plaster over the gulf that exists between labour on the one hand and employers on the other. What's the point of HRM? Workers and their unions would be better off planning for total social transformation than engaging with their employers, whose interests are necessarily hostile to theirs.

In the UK, Richard Hyman has been central to the application of Marxism to the study of industrial relations (Hyman, 1975; Frege et al, 2011), as has John Kelly, whose work focuses on union renewal and beyond (Kelly, 1998). More broadly, the work of Harry Braverman (1974), which inspired an extended debate on the nature of work and the labour process in capitalist society (Thompson and Smith, 2009; C. Smith, 2015), has made the Marxist approach to the employment relationship much more mainstream. Underlying the approach is the idea that management within capitalist society cannot overcome the contradictions and conflicts that are structural to the system. Hence, management views (pluralism or unitarism, or the various hybrids) are always 'a programmatic choice among alternatives, none of which can prove satisfactory' (Hyman, 1987: 30). This does not mean the end of research on the employment relationship, but rather recognition that capital and labour are in continuous struggle over the production of surplus value, and shifts in the forms of work and employment require constant updating and empirical renewal.

Radical pluralism

Radical perspectives are generally associated with Marxism, but not exclusively by any means. The view of the employment relationship as one based on 'structured antagonism' (Edwards, 1986, 2018) has been called 'radical pluralism' because, while it accepts the potential conflict that underlies the employment relationship, it does not share the (traditional) Marxist belief that revolution is necessarily the outcome of the struggle between employers and workers. Radical pluralists argue that the working class lacks the capacity for whatever reason to overthrow capitalism, and fear that the historical precedents of Communist revolution (as in the Soviet Union) merely lead to alternative forms of bureaucracy and oppression. Alan Fox (1974), the most well-known radical pluralist, advocated the creation of organisational structures that build high-discretion roles rather than low-discretion roles for workers, hence basing employment relationships on trust. Workers can then organise their tasks in more 'self-managed' and 'autonomous' ways (characteristic of many high-discretion professional jobs), hence making them more creative and fulfilling (Gold, 2017).

Perspectives on the employment relationship

In summary, each perspective analysed in this chapter – unitarist, pluralist and radical (Marxist/radical pluralist) – presents a particular view of the employment relationship. Each presents a different view of the nature of conflict in the employment relationship. The unitarist perspective emphasises the cooperative or consensual element in the relationship between employer and worker. The unitarist denies that there is any potential conflict at all. The Marxist perspective does the exact opposite: it stresses only the conflict, arguing that the employment relationship is necessarily conflictual and that there can be no element of consensus between worker and employer at all, which rules out any possibility of cooperation. The pluralist, as the name suggests, takes a rather more nuanced view of the matter and says, well, on the one hand, much of the time there is cooperation, and the fact that industry in Germany, the UK or the US normally operates on a fairly peaceful, stable basis demonstrates that actually workers and employers do have areas of interest – workers do want their employer to succeed. That really is a basic point that needs to be stressed. But at the same time, no one should deny that there is also the potential for conflict. In any organisation, conflict of one form or another is continually rumbling beneath the surface, and it's up to managers, particularly the HR manager, to ensure that it is expressed and channelled in a way that is acceptable, both to the worker and to the employer. If not, resistance emerges in one or more of the numerous forms depicted in Figure 4.1.

While it's possible to see where both the unitarist and Marxist are coming from, HRM – in capitalist economies – is ultimately about the balance of interest between employer and worker, even though the distribution of power very much favours the employer for all the economic and legal reasons analysed in Chapter 3. This is why the radical pluralist will favour attempts to shift the balance towards workers, as far as possible within the system, without endangering the political freedoms that capitalism is assumed to confer. However, this is not to deny the areas of cooperation that may well exist between workers in a well-run organisation and their managers. That's really the point here. But in the end, we all have to work out for ourselves how we view the employment relationship, and whether we adopt a unitarist, pluralist or radical perspective, and which of the various subdivisions within each.

Concluding comments

The most important conclusion from this chapter is that we all need to be aware of our own perspectives. Much of what we discuss in HRM is objective, it's out there in the real world, but much of it is also, frankly, subjective – what's going on in our own heads. It's about how we view and value other people as colleagues and partners or as potential adversaries. This is a significant point because in Part 2 of this book we begin to assess where HRM is going – and one of the issues that emerges is that the unitarist perspective of the organisation is evolving and increasingly dominating the contemporary workplace, with serious consequences.

Some questions to think about

1. Compare and contrast unitarist, pluralist and radical perspectives on HRM. Which do you find most convincing, and why?

2. How will each perspective view a trade union's role in negotiating pay within the organisation?

3. What factors might explain why some managers adopt unitarist perspectives towards their organisation and others adopt pluralist perspectives?

4. What are the limitations of the radical perspectives on the employment relationship (both Marxist and radical pluralist)?

Further reading

Cullinane, N. and Dundon, T. (2014) 'Unitarism and employer resistance to trade unionism', *International Journal of Human Resource Management*, 25(18): 2573–90. [Investigation reveals attachment to a traditional form of unitarism among employers sampled who want to retain absolute control over their company.]

Gold, M. (2017) '"A clear and honest understanding": Alan Fox and the origins and implications of radical pluralism', *Historical Studies in Industrial Relations*, 38: 129–66. [Analysis seeks to restore Alan Fox's 'radical pluralism' as a framework for debates about the need for fairness in the workplace.]

Heery, E. (2016) *Framing Work: Unitary, Pluralist, and Critical Perspectives in the Twenty-first Century*, Oxford: Oxford University Press. [A wide-ranging survey of debates about 'frames of reference' and the employment relationship.]

Roy, D. (1959) '"Banana time": Job satisfaction and informal interaction', *Human Organization*, 18(4): 158–68. [A classic study of subcultures at work.]

PART 2

Where We're Heading...

8

The 'New' Unitarism

In the last chapter, we distinguished between unitarist, pluralist and radical perspectives towards human resource management (HRM). Basically, unitarist managers tend to deny that there is a conflict of interest between employees and employers, while the radical perspective focuses on what it views as the necessarily conflictual relationship between the two. The pluralist, by contrast, argues that the relationship between employees and employers is generally smooth and consensual, but that there is always the potential for conflict just below the surface that can bubble up, given the opportunity.

This chapter focuses on unitarism, specifically, the 'new' unitarism and paternalism, in relation to hi-tech companies in the US, such as Apple, Meta (Facebook), Google and Microsoft, the household names that we all know about (or think we know about) and which many people aspire to work for. It's instructive to have a look at the kind of HRM that they practise, not least because they are at the cutting edge of new trends in HRM.

As noted in Chapter 7, unitarism isn't just one single harmonious set of perspectives. We can distinguish between 'traditional' unitarists, who oppose trade unions and will prevent their organisation by whatever means necessary, sometimes by force, and 'sophisticated' unitarists, including companies like Hewlett-Packard, IBM and Marks & Spencer, that ensure their employees are paid at competitive market rates and enjoy better than average conditions in an attempt to undermine the need for a trade union. In this chapter, we delve deeper into the nature of contemporary forms of unitarism, by examining the meaning and development of paternalism as a management technique, and how it affects workers' 'exit, voice and loyalty' strategies within companies. We then turn to the effects of individualisation at work and the origins of 'new' unitarism in the rapid growth of US hi-tech companies, which embody the further refinement of HRM as a system of control.

Paternalism

To analyse current developments in greater depth, we need first to examine the notion of 'paternalism' and what it means within HRM. The word *pater* is Latin for 'father', so at its most basic it refers to 'the father who knows best', the benign figure who is in control of the family, and who is accordingly obeyed. When applied to HRM, we are referring to the attempt made by employers, going all the way back to the 19th century, to foster a commonality of interests between their workers and themselves by ensuring decent pay, terms and conditions (Ackers,

1998). The aim is to build trust and loyalty with the workforce founded on a two-way effect: the employer, as father-figure, looks out for the best interests of 'his' workers, and the workers, in return, strive to do their best for him. The employer hopes to retain skills that will be required in the longer term, while the workers are guaranteed secure employment. Very often, particularly in the 19th century, labour markets were family-oriented, so father, son and then grandson (and sometimes mother, daughter and granddaughter, until they married) all worked for the same organisation (Smith, 2003). There'd be a family dynasty, not just of the employers, but also of employees, who would be well known by the managers because they had a tradition in the company. Individuals would be recruited not least on account of their family background, and employers then controlled the workplace efficiently, not only through pay, terms and conditions, but also because they knew the workers' strengths and weaknesses, which meant that the company may have acquired a 'family feel' (Smith et al, 1990). This relationship was strengthened, before shares became widely distributed through the stock market, because the owner was frequently also the manager: the two roles, ownership and management, were embodied in the one father-figure.

As a result, workers frequently identified with their company (Drummond, 1995). They would start working for it at an early age and continue until they retired, when the company might award them a gold watch or a clock in commemoration of their long service. Many household-name companies, such as Cadbury, Clarks, Heinz, Rowntree's and Unilever, operated like this, often with religious backgrounds. Cadbury, Clarks and Rowntree's, for example, had Quaker origins (Rowlinson, 1998; Kimberley, 2016). Robert Owen (1771–1858), a textile manufacturer, was a pioneering reformer whose welfare programmes at his New Lanark Mills in Scotland, while acting as a source of inspiration for early socialists, also drew heavily on paternalist ideas (Fox, 1985: 110).

Some of these companies also had strong geographical roots – for example, Cadbury in Bournville (Birmingham), Rowntree's in York and Unilever in Wirral (Merseyside, Lancashire) – where they were embedded in local labour markets, which explains why workers would be recruited from father to son to grandson. This formed the background against which strong relationships between employer and worker could develop in these companies. The worker repays the 'generosity' of the employer through loyalty and hard work: that is the essence of paternalism (Fox, 1985; Morris and Smyth, 1994). But the companies always argued that treating workers well paid off, rejecting the idea that labour was simply a cost to be minimised rather than a resource for long-term investment. Sometimes the employer dominated the local labour market, which shifted paternalism into the more negative realm of a 'company town' with limited employment choices (Varano, 1999; Borges and Torres, 2012). For an oral history of the workers' perspective on paternalism in one community, see Strangleman (2019).

And paternalism often went further than just work. Heinz, the US food manufacturer, had its own baseball team, while Rowntree's organised reading groups for its workers. Paternalist employers took an interest in the physical wellbeing and education of their workers too, as they saw them as people who should improve themselves as well. Some went further still. The Lever Brothers – who founded the company known today as Unilever – established a town, Port Sunlight, in Wirral in 1888, as a model village for their workers. It's still the location of the company's research and development division for health and beauty products. Its houses were desirable places to live – at a time when slum conditions characterised many cities across the UK – because they were well appointed and surrounded by greenery and parks. The Lever Brothers also ensured that the town had its own art gallery, community centre and sports and recreation facilities (all of which exist to this day). This reveals the ways in which they looked after all the interests of their workers, not just their work interests, but also the integrated totality of their potential interests in the arts, leisure and recreation. (If you get the chance, visit the Port Sunlight Museum, as it tells you a lot about 19th-century employment.)

Corporate songbooks are another example of the way in which paternalistic companies attempt to incorporate their workers into the workplace. Some of us might be put off by this prospect of gathering every morning and singing the company song with our colleagues. Nevertheless, these are titles from the IBM songbook (El-Sawad and Korczynski, 2007):

- No 67, 'The IBM Family': 'We are co-workers in IBM – all one big family'.
- No 74, 'IBM, happy men, smiling all the way. Oh, what fun it is to sell our products night and day' (to the tune of 'Jingle Bells').
- No 76, 'The IBM slogan': 'Who are we? Who are we? The International Family. We are T.J. Watson men. We represent the IBM'. (T.J. Watson was the CEO of IBM for a large part of the 20th century, and built the company up into what it is today.)

Notice the repeated use of the word 'family', which is significant, as it underpins the unitarist notion of paternalism and the father as the head of the household, associated with the notion that employers and workers have common aims and interests that override everything else. Some might find this notion cultist and sinister, while others might find it whimsical and benign (see Box 8.1).

BOX 8.1: A VIEW FROM THE TOP

Jason Fried and David Heinemeier Hansson founded a software company, Basecamp, in 2003. They advocate good terms and conditions for their workers – such as single pay grades, three-day weekends in the summer and opportunities for sabbaticals – but they are not fans of paternalism or new unitarism:

> Whenever executives talk about how their company is really like a big ol' family, beware. They're usually not referring to how the company is going

> to protect you no matter what or love you unconditionally. You know, like healthy families would. Their motive is rather more likely to be in a unidirectional form of sacrifice: yours. (Fried and Hansson, 2018: 77)

Exit, voice and loyalty

At this point we need to dig deeper into the issue of worker loyalty and, in particular, to analyse the relationship between exit, voice and loyalty, a combination of terms that help us to understand worker motivation and labour turnover (Hirschman, 1970). The idea here is that if you are a worker and you're dissatisfied with your job, then you can react in one of two different ways. One way is to leave your job – you can *exit*. Exit is a response that leads to high levels of turnover in an organisation. For example, if you don't feel you're being paid enough or getting properly recognised, or if you're not happy with your line manager, colleagues or workload, or indeed anything else, then one alternative is to go, and, of course, many workers do leave their jobs every year, with or without the blessing of their organisation. So, exit is an option if you're dissatisfied.

By contrast, if you have the opportunity – and opportunity is the key issue here – you might choose instead to raise the reasons for your dissatisfaction with your line manager or senior management to try to put things right. As we'll see in Chapter 16 on employee participation and involvement, companies may have a range of mechanisms that allow you to raise your concerns on an individual basis (personal issues), or on a collective basis (broader issues that affect the whole workplace), or both. This chance to express yourself is called *voice*, because the mechanisms allow you to raise your concerns in the expectation that you will be listened to with respect and without fear of recrimination or victimisation. Many companies have grievance procedures to deal with individual issues and some (in the UK) have joint consultative committees to deal with collective issues. In many continental European countries, works councils have a statutory basis, that is, employers are required to set them up under law. The idea is that they help to alert management to problems that are building up so they can be resolved as soon as possible, a valuable way to nip them in the bud. The crucial point, however, is that workers must have the confidence that they're not going to be victimised as a result of raising concerns. If you're functioning in a toxic work environment, you might think, well, if I say something against the employer, maybe I'm going to get bullied or even sacked. Obviously, you need to be certain in your own mind that that won't happen. So, voice mechanisms operate effectively only when there is genuine trust between the employer, on the one hand, and workers, on the other.

And that then leads to the third element under discussion here, which is *loyalty*, and the circumstances under which loyalty may or may not flourish. As we've seen, paternalistic unitarist systems are designed to promote loyalty, which is very much what the employer is after. The idea is that you treat workers well and they repay you with loyalty and stay, which is particularly important if you're keen to retain their skills. The links between voice and loyalty should now be clear: voice is based on trust, which itself engenders loyalty in long-term relationships. Exit, by contrast, is more likely to imply lack of voice and lack of loyalty.

Individualisation

By the later part of the 20th century and into the 21st, many of these voice mechanisms, particularly in liberal market economies, had been undermined by the decline of trade union influence and the introduction of individualised HRM practices, such as individualised pay systems and performance appraisal (Dickson et al, 1988). For example, a performance-based pay system tends to erode some of the bases for loyalty because it risks creating extra grievances at the workplace – you may feel that you're not being paid as well as your colleagues, or that you have been passed over for promotion. Under a paternalist system of HRM, you might have gone to your line manager and talked things over, but with a performance appraisal system, which is based on tick-box tables and indicators, it's more difficult. Individualised HRM introduces more transactional employment relationships than the kind of loyalty-based relationships that characterise paternalistic companies (Tsui and Wu, 2005).

Old-style paternalism as a type of HRM has clearly declined over recent years, not least because of the evolution of professional management. The owner-manager of the 19th century, when ownership and management were embodied in the same person, has largely disappeared and been replaced by the professional manager (Hannah, 2007). As soon as you tease apart the owner (through the shareholder) and the manager (who is employed through the shareholder), then you have the development of a professional management cadre that has no more loyalty to the company than you do, in the sense that the manager is also an employee. Your line manager is not the owner of the company as a paternalistic employer used to be: the manager is, him- or herself, also an employee, and therefore doesn't have that level of loyalty. So that immediately breaks down some of these ties.

In addition, as we've seen, the employment relationship itself is potentially conflictual and may be undermined by any grievance or dispute that erupts and corrodes the trust between the employer and the employee. However strongly rooted paternalism might appear to be, there's always the potential for conflict that might threaten it. And then, of course, workers themselves develop their own subcultures, which are often adversarial and may subvert even paternalistic employment systems.

Old-style unitarism and the 'new' unitarism

There have been major changes within employment structures since the 1970s, which have been well documented. Job security and geographical stability of employment has eroded. The structure of employment has fragmented with the increase in precarious work, part-time work, outsourcing and so on, especially in the UK and the US (Kalleberg, 2011). It's also led to higher levels of job turnover, that is, exit, discussed earlier. If you're not happy with your job, you find another – you go somewhere else (Work Institute, 2019). Now, if levels of turnover start to rise, this is particularly worrying for employers in high-skill sectors. If you want to keep your highly skilled employees, you don't want them leaving for another rival employer, so you have to find ways to keep them. Over recent years, organisational culture has been increasingly developed as a form of control. Many companies, particularly in the hi-tech sector, have tended to do this: 'The cultivation of the corporate workspace as a home-away-from-home, of the hi-tech worker as a playful, emotionally integrated hipster and the corporate team as a cross between a family and a rock band became commonplace' (Turner, 2009: 78).

On the 'dark side', Rodriguez (2019) has said of Facebook (now Meta): 'employees feel pressure to place the company above all else in their lives, fall in line with their manager's orders and force cordiality with their colleagues so they can advance. Several former employees likened the culture to a "cult".' More than a dozen former Facebook employees detailed how the company's leadership and performance review system created a culture where any dissent was discouraged. Employees said that Facebook's ranking performance review system pressurises employees to push out products and features that drive user engagement without fully considering potential long-term negative impacts on user experience or privacy.

Instead of the old-style paternalistic workplace (which is no longer viable), you turn the workplace into a fun place to be, somewhere employees really want to hang out. In the past, paternalism might have taken the form of baseball teams, reading groups or model villages for workers, but that's not quite where it is now. Rather, you create a culture within the organisation that encourages employees to want to be there, where they feel 'cool'.

There have been four developments in the organisation of work that have, arguably, made possible the evolution of this 'new' unitarism and that provide helpful points of contrast with old-style paternalism:

- the nature of labour recruitment and retention
- the differentiation of employment contracts
- the ways in which organisational cultures deal with space and place
- gender and age

Taking *recruitment and retention* first, we noted earlier that old-style paternalism was based largely on successive generations of the family working for the same company. Labour markets were highly localised and drew on immobile workers who lived in set geographical areas, such as Birmingham, Port Sunlight or York. Clearly, that kind of labour force no longer exists. Workers today are extremely mobile and heterogeneous. The idea that we would work for the same company as our parents, let alone our grandparents, would strike most of us as bizarre, if not unthinkable. Hi-tech companies today need to keep highly skilled workers not for their lifetime, as in the 19th and early 20th centuries, but for a short period of time during which they're at their most productive. If you look at the way in which the hi-tech companies operate, you find that people often don't work there for more than two or three years at a time. There's a very high 'churn' of people coming in and out because, as the technology relentlessly advances, you place a premium on recruiting those with the latest skills and most innovative ideas, who displace those who have been around for a while. Hence there is high labour turnover, and the nature of the culture is designed for short-term retention. The culture also favours long hours and extremely intensive working when you're there, which maximises the chances for innovation. The point is that these companies aim for only short-term retention (Lyons, 2016). For example: 'Google is famous for luxe working conditions.... So why does the typical employee only stick around for 1.1 years? Like many tech companies, it's the combination of a hyper-competitive market and the fact that many of the jobs at this company, which has only existed since 1998, are relatively young themselves' (Payscale, 2021).

A further contrast between old-style paternalism and the new unitarism is the role of the *employment contract* itself within the company. As the 19th century advanced, and into the 20th century, workers would have typically had 'standard' full-time employment contracts. This is less often the case now. Core workers with core skills will generally still have such contracts, but much work is now outsourced through supply chains. Hi-tech companies form a hub dependent on a range of satellite companies in which conditions of work and employment are frequently insecure and poorly paid. In a phrase, these outsourced companies involve the 'standardisation of non-standard employment relations' (Cappelli and Keller, 2013: 575). In other words, what used to be seen as non-standard employment, namely, precarious employment, has actually itself become the norm in many outsourced companies. This means that there's a spatial division of labour involved with these companies that didn't exist in the 19th or early 20th centuries, employment contracts having become more fragmented.

Companies in which new unitarism predominates accordingly rely on both internal and external labour markets, with their skilled core workers employed on open-ended standard contracts but many ancillary services provided on a flexible basis by workers in outsourced or external labour markets. This dualistic employment model is embedded deep within the hi-tech sector (Benner, 2002). Google, for example, employs about 121,000 temporary, vendor and contract workers globally (54% of its total workforce) and 102,000 full-time employees, with the two groups treated very differently (see Box 2.3). *The New York Times* (Wakabayashi, 2019) has reported that agency employees are typically paid less and have fewer comprehensive benefits packages than full-time Google staff. These roles span all departments of the company, from chefs to coders. The reality is that the company is merely following the growing trend of tech employers who opt to hire contractors over full-time employees. According to an NPR/Marist poll conducted in 2018, contractors currently make up about 20% of the labour market, with a prediction that they could make up half of the American workforce within a decade (Bergvall-Kåreborn and Howcroft, 2013; Moreno, 2019). Such differential structuring of workers' terms and conditions may be unacceptable to workers and trade unions on grounds of inequality and lead to disputes with management (as we saw in Box 2.3, and examine further below, in the section on 'non-unionism').

Understandings of *space and place* also differ. Under traditional paternalism, employment tended to be locally based, but that is clearly no longer true. Under the conditions of 21st-century technology, with the new unitarism, employees are generally global: there are genuine global labour markets for the kinds of hi-tech skills that we're talking about. Whether you're from Brazil, China, India, Russia or South Africa, provided you have the appropriate skills and attitudes, you may well be sought by one of these companies. This is the very opposite of the local labour markets that were prevalent in previous centuries. And so hi-tech companies employ immigrant workers, who themselves form part of the core labour force because of their high level of skills, even though they lack the same kind of geographical sense of locality that their predecessors would have had in the past. The incidence of immigrant workers, who are mobile, may also encourage higher levels of churn and labour turnover. So that's another contrast, as discussed in Box 8.2.

BOX 8.2: GLOBAL POOL OF LABOUR – YOUNGER AND CHEAPER

Whereas traditional paternalism was a local affair, the labour pool in Silicon Valley is global, drawing workers from across the US and the world. Global labour sourcing is facilitated by the visa system, H-1B, which is designed to fill gaps in the supply of tech workers, but is often used by outsourcing companies to bring in cheaper engineers from India and other countries, allowing outsourced firms to bid for work and undercut existing engineers. As mentioned, there is a dualism within the tech industry, and using foreign engineers is yet another layer of labour to this stratified workforce.

Tech companies depend on the 85,000 foreign workers allowed into the US annually under the H-1B visa programme, a temporary visa intended to bring in foreign professionals with college degrees and specialised skills to fill jobs when qualified Americans cannot be found. A research report by Goldman Sachs estimates that 900,000 to a million H-1B visa holders now reside in the US, and that they account for up to 13% of American technology jobs. American employees face more salary pressure from newcomers who will work for less: 'After 11 years working in the IT department of Northeast Utilities, a

Connecticut-based company now named Eversource Energy, Craig Diangelo was among 220 employees laid off in 2014. Mr Diangelo, was receiving $130,000 a year in salary and bonus, while the Indian H-1B visa-holder who replaced him was on $60,000 a year' (Wakabayashi and Schwartz, 2017).

The final contrast focuses on *gender and age*. In the 19th and well into the 20th century, for many old-style unitarist companies, the opportunity for 'standard' employment was predominantly a male career option as there was often a marriage bar for women who worked (for example, at Cadbury and Unilever). Historically, a woman who worked left her job as soon as she got married on the grounds that she would then be raising a family, and so – because it was assumed her husband, as the breadwinner, would look after her – she would no longer need to work. That condition was made illegal in the UK many years ago, but employment in hi-tech companies remains largely male and young, with allegations of sexism rife (BBC News, 2017; O'Brien and Fiegerman, 2017).

However, the division now centres on age as well as on gender. Workers in hi-tech companies are generally young and will tend to leave early to move on elsewhere: 'Forget about getting booted out when you turn fifty. In Silicon Valley that happens when you turn forty' (Lyons, 2016: 154–5). Older workers are vulnerable to redundancy on the grounds of relative expense or productivity if firms do not want to train them in new technologies. The availability of younger workers, the cost of older workers, the move away from firm-specific or proprietorial technology, the outsourcing of activities and new international recruits hired on H-1B visas all act against firms wanting to invest in training older workers, and in favour of taking younger – more controllable and dependent – workers from universities and the market. In Silicon Valley, 'wages actually start to decline for engineers and managers with more than 24 years' experience' (Benner, 2002: 221). In classical paternalism, length of service is built into the firm. Under new unitarism, youth dominates.

Working in a hi-tech company

Mountain View, Google's headquarters in Silicon Valley, bears a striking similarity to Port Sunlight, Unilever's original headquarters in the Wirral: a river, wide open spaces and work sites that correspond to the main factory at Port Sunlight (Chance, 2017).

However, Figure 8.1 doesn't look like the normal interior of a traditional workplace. If you work for a bank or large multinational, you probably won't see a slide as a substitute for a staircase or escalator. Indeed, other images for Google interiors show fountains and walkways, men pushing a buggy or on bicycles or skateboards or carrying guitars, or with a dog. Google allows pets (and teddy bears). There's a gym, where you are free to exercise when the fancy takes you. And there are art classes – a 21st-century equivalent of the baseball team at Heinz

Figure 8.1: Google as a workplace

Source: ShutterStock/JHVEPhoto

and the reading groups at Rowntree's. There is a vegetable plot at Google, too, in case you want to grow cabbages – what could be more fun than that? Their buses have the company logo to promote group identity as well. Workers are encouraged to air any problems they have and make points at staff meetings to ensure that they feel part of the general organisation.

The overall idea is that you are very much part of a total culture that values your individuality as an employee, one that says, look, do your own thing. If you want to bring in your dog or teddy, then bring them in. If you want to go to the gym, then go to the gym. The working environment is clearly designed to be informal and fun:

> Under the banner "Don't be evil", Brin, Page and Schmidt [the company founders] have encouraged their employees to aim to serve users first and to allow profits to grow from, rather than drive, that process. Some might question the firm's allegiance to that model in the wake of some of its corporate choices, but inside the firm, the argument that Google is changing the world and changing it for the better *encourages employees to align their sense of personal mission with that of the company*. (Turner, 2009: 80; emphasis added)

The point here is that if a company is able to induce its employees to identify with its objectives, values, norms and standards, this helps it to iron out any glitches with them when necessary.

These companies reinforce compliant behaviour with a range of perks or fringe benefits. So, for example, Airbnb give its employees an allowance to stay in any of its properties around the world. Some companies, such as Netflix, LinkedIn and Virgin Management, offer unlimited paid holiday. It sounds like an astonishing benefit to be told by your company, 'Look, you can go on holiday anytime you like and for however long you like.' That sounds like something tremendous that would help to keep you in the company. However, maybe it doesn't quite work out like that. If you look more carefully, for example at Virgin Management, you find that it's actually restricted to just a small number of employees, and very few of them actually take up the benefit. After all, if you really feel part of the company, if you fully identify with its objectives, then why take a holiday? If you're having fun at work, and your friends are your colleagues, the need for a holiday itself gets undermined (Spicer, 2018).

Another fringe benefit at Apple and Facebook is egg freezing. Companies are particularly keen to attract women into the organisation. One issue for women, however, is whether or when to have children. Having children generally involves a career break, and the challenges women face in getting back into their career afterwards may put many put off altogether. So, Apple and Facebook allow women in their employment to freeze their eggs. The Apple statement from 2015 declares: 'We want to empower women at Apple to do their best work of their lives as they care for loved ones and raise their families.' They offer to pay up to £15,000 to store employees' eggs, providing they're covered by an insurance plan. Whether this works or not (and evidence suggests that the success rate for transferring frozen embryos is not very high) is a different matter. The point is that this policy reveals the lengths that companies will go to attract and retain the 'right' staff.

However, there may be disadvantages to all these fringe benefits from the employee's point of view. A BBC report quotes Sandi Mann, a researcher in this area:

> I have spoken to people whose companies provided amazing perks – meals, healthcare, and even alcohol if they had a party at home. The downside is that they feel owned by the company and like they are expected to devote their life to it. They start to have less and less of a life outside, and work can become all-consuming. (Quoted in Lawrie, 2017)

So the downside, from the employee's point of view, is that as you are drawn more and more into this all-encompassing culture, and as you identify more and more with the culture, then your life is inside the organisation, it's not outside anymore, which can come to threaten your general wellbeing. Consulting Glassdoor is very instructive in this respect. Glassdoor is a website that hosts reviews by employees of their company, a bit like TripAdvisor, although for workplaces and not hotels – so if you want to know what it's like to work for a company, consult Glassdoor and you'll get the warts and all. If you look up Google, you find a very mixed bag – what you lose on the swings, you gain on the roundabouts. It's not that Google is a bad employer – far from it. The point is rather that there are disadvantages to all-encompassing employment practices (see Box 8.3).

> ## BOX 8.3: WORKING FOR GOOGLE, ACCORDING TO GLASSDOOR
>
> For example, a current employee, a product manager in London, with five years' service at Google, comments that the pros include 'free food and free gym', but that the cons include 'tough work–life balance and hard work'. A former software engineer, also based in London, lists the pros as 'pay, benefits, work location in Europe, good promotional system and looks good on CV (reason to leave)', but among the cons, 'Horrible management. Bad team spirit. Lack of motivation. Advice to management: address team issues instead of showing pretty graphs and pictures of phones.' A graduate analyst says: 'great people, food and offices, but sucky working hours, no freedom'.
>
> Some of the comments are quite amusing. For example: 'Pros – lots of free muesli. Brunch, working from home, which is handy if you live on Mars.' But then, this respondent's comment is: 'I don't like muesli and the less I see of Mars the better. It's not all that it's cracked up to be – a bit cold and dry and no atmosphere. Advice to management: terraform Mars as quickly as you can to make it liveable.' In other words, make your workplace a genuine liveable place rather than somewhere like Mars.

More systematically, Vourakis (2017) used a dataset with over 67,000 employee comments to review perceptions of working for Google, Amazon, Apple and Microsoft. The aggregated pros included:

- Google: The perks, smart people, free food and good salary.
- Amazon: The ability to learn, their teams, smart people and management.
- Apple: The employee discounts, the products, their teams, the fun environment and the good training.
- Microsoft: Smart people, the products, the salary, the technology and their teams.

The aggregated cons strongly featured poor work–life balance:

- Google: Their teams, the hard work, the projects, office politics and lack of work–life balance.
- Amazon: Lack of work–life balance, the hours and the culture.
- Apple: Lack of work–life balance, the retail store, the customers and the pay.

- Microsoft: Office politics, lack of work–life balance, their team, the hard work and the culture.

These comments reveal that, despite the outstanding benefits, workers resist. As we showed in Chapter 7, we all *interpret* our working environment. The whole point about analysing HRM is that the world of work simply doesn't conform neatly to management's aspirations and expectations. Of course managers have a view, naturally and rightly so, but workers also have their views, they interpret, react and very often resist. These comments reflect a form of resistance even to what might, on the outside, seem like the most wonderful workplace in the world, full of slides and teddy bears, pets and vegetable plots, and all the rest of it. What's not to like? Well, actually, there are clearly things not to like, and in particular, the real question seems to be work–life balance, because hi-tech companies generally expect you to work very long hours, very intensively. People eventually burn out, and that's why you have this churn, this turnover of workers. It's not just because the company needs new blood coming in with new skills at the bottom; it's also because having worked there for two or three years, maybe five at most, you find you have had enough, you just can't cope anymore and need a life outside the company that allows you greater freedom for yourself.

Non-unionism in hi-techs

Historically, very few information and communications technology (ICT) companies accepted trade unions: 'Even in the 1950s and 1960s, when the US labor movement was strong, ICT companies tended to be non-union. Among the leading ICT companies, only NCR, Xerox, and the companies that evolved out of the old Bell System have histories of significant unionization' (Lazonick, 2009: 13). For companies such as IBM, Motorola, DEC and Hewlett-Packard, union exclusion remains an essential part of corporate strategy: 'The development of comprehensive human resource regimes, including company-based mechanisms for employee representation, locked workforces into well-paid, relatively secure employment in factories with comparatively tolerant managerial styles' (Findlay and McKinlay, 2003: 55). Van Jaarsveld (2004: 380) reports:

> some Microsoft high-tech contingent workers formed WashTech [a union] to improve their working conditions and sought support from a traditional labor union through their decision to affiliate with the CWA [Communications Workers of America]. This shows that "new economy" workers still have "old economy" demands for fair wages and benefits and respect in the workplace.

The issues that unions focused on remain relevant today, as Microsoft pioneered agency working to cut labour costs:

> Microsoft offered a benefits package to its full–time employees that far exceeded what agency contractors offered. For example, while full-time employees received performance bonuses and stock options, agency contractors received only overtime pay. Training is vital for high–tech workers to remain competitive [… but while …] Microsoft full-time employees received extensive free training assistance, the agencies provided limited training opportunities. (van Jaarsveld, 2004: 369)

At Microsoft, 'agency contractors also were prohibited from attending morale-building events, shopping in the company store, and using the Microsoft sports fields. These restrictions contributed to the sense of disrespect and alienation many agency contractors experienced in the Microsoft workplace' (van Jaarsveld, 2004: 372).

A union has recently emerged at Google, called the Alphabet Workers Union, after Google's parent company, which now represents more than 600 Google employees and contractors with the support of the Communications Workers of America:

> Unlike traditional unions, this group is a so-called "minority union" and does not have the power to force the company to collectively bargain over pay and benefits. But organizers say that is not the point. This movement, they say, is to examine Google's role in society and help reshape the company's culture. (Allyn, 2021)

Concluding comments

In summary, there are pros and cons with the 'new' unitarism. Even a hi-tech company that has introduced an apparently fun and relaxed working environment can be challenging to work for, particularly in the longer term, and hence find itself subject to criticisms from its employees, who may well resist some of its practices. Work intensity, various forms of inequality and early redundancy, as younger colleagues are recruited with new ideas, may all form issues for dispute. Hi-tech companies make much of their brand image in attracting the right people, but journalistic accounts and the kinds of reports posted on Glassdoor reveal major challenges. Indeed, despite the contrasts between old–style paternalism and the 'new' unitarism drawn in this chapter, the similarities between the two are also quite striking: the principal similarity that unites both forms of unitarism is the assumption that employers and workers share the same aims and objectives at work and perceive the company through the lens of common interests. This assumption is, at best, arguable and, at worst, demonstrably false.

Some questions to think about

1. Discuss the key contrasts between the 'new' and 'old-style' unitarism.

2. Go back to Box 8.1. Do you think Fried and Hansson have a point, or are they being excessively cynical?

3. Would you be tempted to work for a US hi-tech company? What for you, personally, would be the advantages and disadvantages?

4. How useful do you find the comments posted on Glassdoor (see Box 8.3)? Would they help you make up your mind about working for Google, for example, or any other company?

Further reading

Ackers, P. (1998) 'On paternalism: Seven observations on the uses and abuses of the concept in industrial relations, past and present', *Historical Studies in Industrial Relations*, (5): 173–93. [Discussion of the issues surrounding the use of the term 'paternalism'.]

Eggers, D. (2013) *The Circle*, London: Penguin Books. [Unsettling and satirical novel about life within The Circle, a fictional company that runs all your internet activity.]

Farndale, E., Thite, M., Budhwar, P. and Kwon, B. (2020) 'Deglobalization and talent sourcing: Cross-national evidence from high-tech firms', *Human Resource Management*, 60(2): 259–72. [Examination of pressures to localise and globalise the recruitment of science, technology, engineering and mathematics (STEM) candidates into the hi-tech sector.]

Fumagalli, A., Lucarelli, S., Musolino, E. and Rocchi, G. (2018) 'Digital labour in the platform economy: The case of Facebook', *Sustainability*, 10(6): 1–16. [Discussion of 'platform capitalism' and what the authors see as a new technological paradigm based on digital labour.]

Lyons, D. (2016) *Disrupted: Ludicrous Misadventures in the Tech Start-Up Bubble*, London: Atlantic Books. [An insider's account of working for a US hi-tech company.]

9

Flexible Working

Towards the end of the last chapter, we made the point that although hi-tech companies are generally associated with standard employment contracts and secure work ('soft' human resource management, HRM), at the same time they also employ workers on non-standard contracts and rely on companies in their supply chains that use predominantly precarious contracts ('hard' HRM). This is, of course, true in many employment settings. Workers on standard, open-ended contracts work alongside or in a variety of relationships with others whose contracts are more insecure. This observation introduces us to the world of flexible working, a concept that has grown in scope and significance over recent years.

We begin this chapter by examining exactly what is meant by 'flexible working', and how 'standard' employment differs from 'non-standard' employment. This leads on to a discussion of terminology, which can be confusing as different writers use varying terms and concepts to refer to broadly the same things. We then examine types of flexibility (such as numerical, functional and temporal) before assessing their significance within HRM, and asking who actually benefits from flexibility – employers, workers, or both? We present a well-known model of core/peripheral work for critique, and investigate flexible working from the perspective of human capital in order to evaluate its role in human resources (HR) strategy building. We finish by analysing trends in various forms of flexible working – such as part-time, agency work and zero-hours contracts – before concluding the chapter.

'Standard' and 'non-standard' employment

We should start by reminding ourselves what we said about 'post-bureaucratic' employment in Chapter 5. The idea that we all have standard full-time employment and then retire, after many years in the same job, at the age of 65 with a pension – the idea that such a work pattern is typical – has been undermined by changes in economic and social structures and is largely disappearing, certainly among younger workers in the UK and the US. The Organisation for Economic Co-operation and Development (OECD) (2019a: 9) points out that 'non-standard employment is not a marginal phenomenon', with one in seven workers across its member states in self-employment and one in nine on temporary contracts. However, 'standard' employment remains implicit as a benchmark – a kind of 'unmarked' version of what employment is all about – in many traditional accounts of work as well as in many analyses in HR textbooks.

Much has changed in recent years, not least because successive reductions in tariff barriers and quotas under the auspices of the General Agreement on Tariffs and Trade (GATT) and the World Trade Organization (WTO) since 1947 has led to increased economic competition at a global level (Dicken, 2015). This, in turn, has placed mounting pressure on employers in exporting sectors to keep down costs and raise productivity, hence exacerbating the pressures on labour costs outlined in Chapter 1. It's in that general context of change and turbulence that we need to look at this notion of flexibility (Fudge, 2017).

In Figure 9.1, we explain some of what's been happening. The left-hand side illustrates 'traditional' or 'typical' employment, where you find bureaucratic, hierarchical organisations, many of which still exist, of course, in the form of local government, the Civil Service and large multinational companies, where the standard employment relationship still – to some degree – prevails. In these organisations, you will still find full-time, open-ended employment, where you are located in an office and where your employer contributes towards your pension, holiday pay, sick pay or maternity leave. Lifetime employment, then, may still be available if your career manages to avoid the restructuring, outsourcing and redundancies that potentially affect all workplaces. And that observation naturally leads us to examine the right-hand side of Figure 9.1. There you have the changes, the developments in employment relationships that have accelerated over recent years – the emergence of the gig economy, but also pressures towards increasingly precarious employment (Standing, 2011). One of these pressures is the way in which companies have introduced internal markets for their own products and converted divisions into cost centres. The effect on HRM is to make labour costs so much more transparent and apparent. This, in turn, has led to pressures on labour costs within cost centres and has helped drive the

Figure 9.1: 'Standard' and 'non-standard' forms of employment

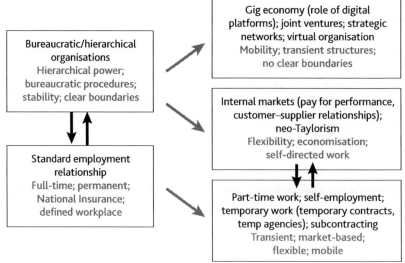

trend towards reliance on all kinds of different flexible employment, including part-time work, use of temporary work agencies, fixed-term contracts, unpaid internships and outsourcing.

Terminology

Before going any further, we need to run through some of the terms used to refer to flexible employment, because terminology varies and may be confusing. 'Standard' work refers to permanent, full-time employment, so 'non-standard' work refers to work that is not permanent or full time. Sometimes the terms 'typical' and 'atypical' (or 'untypical') are used. So, 'non-standard' or 'atypical' work are generic terms that cover all forms of work that's not on a permanent, full-time contract, including part-time work, the use of temporary work agencies, fixed-term contracts, internships, outsourcing and the gig economy, as we'll see shortly.

This point is underlined by further terms that are commonly used to describe atypical and non-standard employment, such as 'casualised', 'contingent', 'irregular' or 'precarious'. These terms draw attention to some notion of uncertainty in the employment relationship. By contrast, terms like 'permanent', 'open-ended', 'regular' and 'full time' exclude uncertainty. 'Permanent' or 'open-ended' means your employment contract is there until you want it to end (unless you are dismissed or made redundant, of course). 'Full time' means just that – you are working a full week or month without any doubt about it. There's something secure, reassuring and certain about these terms. However, as soon as you enter the area of 'casualised', 'contingent', 'irregular' or 'precarious' working, that certainty recedes. The uncertainty may refer to a variety of different aspects of the employment contract: the number of hours worked (part time), the duration of the contract (fixed term), the lack of notice that might be given for its termination (agency work), the uncertainty of payment (zero hours and internships) or the lack of provision for a pension, sick pay or maternity (forms of self-employment used in gig work). Indeed, uncertainty may also involve a combination of these aspects (such as fixed-term part-time work). There may be all kinds of different contingencies that we need to examine. Another related term you'll sometimes see is 'new forms of work'. The idea here is that precarious or contingent working is, in some sense, new. But is that the case? How new is 'new'? We need to question that as well.

Finally, another term that may prove puzzling is 'indirect' employment. 'Direct' employment is when you have a direct employment relationship with your employer. So, for example, you are employed by an organisation, maybe a private company or a public sector organisation or a charity. You have an employment contract with that organisation, you carry out your work tasks and it pays you monthly in return. There's just the two of you – you, as employee, and your employer: that's direct employment, because you are directly employed by your employer. By contrast, 'indirect' employment involves employment through a third party, a temporary employment agency. This 'triangular' employment relationship is illustrated in Figure 9.2. When employers use a temporary agency, they are hiring workers who are employed by that agency, so they have a contractual relationship with the agency to provide the relevant quantity and quality of labour (agency workers may be of all skill levels, including highly skilled, such as nurses and technicians). Hence, if you work as an employee for an agency, you are employed by the agency, not by the company to which the agency has assigned your labour. Your relationship with that company is therefore 'indirect' or 'temporary', because it doesn't actually employ you: you are employed at arm's length through the agency (Forde and Slater, 2005).

Types of flexibility

Figure 9.2: New 'triangular' employment relationship

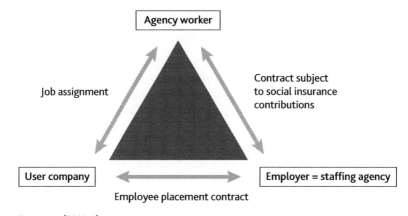

Source: Spermann (2011: 4)

Having sorted out some of the terminology, we now need to examine different varieties of 'flexibility' (Lewis et al, 2003: 50). *Numerical flexibility* is exactly that – flexibility in terms of numbers employed. For example, employment in a particular sector may be seasonal. Agriculture and horticulture employ more workers (such as pickers) at peak harvest time than during the winter, so there is a seasonal dimension to the work. Many builders prefer to work during the summer than during the winter, so even though that doesn't exclude winter work, there may be a greater demand for bricklayers and plasterers during the summer. Or, as Christmas approaches, Santa Claus finds he needs an army of extra helpers in distribution centres and as drivers to assist with Christmas shopping.

Functional flexibility is to do with the nature of the task. In many modern car plants, workers are multiskilled or perform multiple tasks, which is functional flexibility. From the employer's point of view, functional flexibility allows the flexible deployment of workers wherever they are most needed at any particular moment. Rather than having to hire a worker through an agency to cover a temporary vacancy in one area, which is expensive, you can redeploy someone currently surplus elsewhere because you know that they can operate the equipment just as efficiently. So, many employers are keen on functional flexibility while, from an employee's point of view, it means that their employment is more secure because adaptability makes them more valued.

Temporal flexibility covers hours worked. If you're a part-time worker, you are working a fraction of the full-time hours, maybe half time, or whatever it happens to be. Such an arrangement might be important, for example, in a hotel, where cleaning staff are required in the morning to prepare the rooms before guests arrive in the afternoon. A part-time shift that operates in the morning but not in the afternoon would be a good example of such temporal flexibility.

Significance of flexible working

There are a number of positions on flexibility. Some commentators see structural economy-wide shifts away from standard employment, with Castells (1996), for example, arguing that flexibility has become structural, and permanent contracts are over. Others, however, using comparative country data, have shown the persistence of the standard employment contract (Auer and Cazes, 2000). Grimshaw et al (2005) have suggested that the changes to organisational forms and modes of labour deployment (see Figure 9.1) have undermined the open–ended employment contract, and more recent data tend to support the idea of a break or shift away from continuous employment (Kalleberg, 2018). The growth of globalised systems of production, with commodity or value chains, has distributed insecure work internationally and increased the drive to make labour costs more open by rendering contracts within the firm more flexible or by transferring the risk outside the boundaries of the organisation altogether (Fudge, 2017).

Another group of researchers has argued that certain forms of flexible working are linked to the business cycle, so that, for example, workers tend to become self-employed during a boom because work is abundant and they can sell their services more easily if they're self-employed, especially if they have scarce skills in, for example, information and communications technology (ICT) (Barley and Kunda, 2006). However, during a recession, they take cover by going back to work for an employer simply because it's more secure, with a guaranteed pay cheque at the end of each month. When you are self-employed, you can never be quite sure how big that cheque is going to be, which might be acceptable during a boom but not during a recession. Hence trends in self-employment might fluctuate, with the business cycle playing its part (Fevre, 2007; McGovern et al, 2007; Conley, 2008). Others suggest that breaking up traditional forms of employment provokes a reaction from workers and other social actors who seek to return to 'business as usual' and incorporate new forms of flexibility into established institutions (Crompton, 2002).

Another view is that the growth of flexibility has formed part of an ideological project. As neoliberal views about the way in which the economy should be run took hold, particularly under the presidency of Ronald Reagan in the

US (1980–88) and the prime ministership of Margaret Thatcher in the UK (1979–90), it became clear that labour market flexibility isn't only a feature of the labour market, but that it's also an ideology. Supply-side economic policies were introduced over this period in the UK to dismantle alleged rigidities in the operation of the 'free market'. Cutting tax rates, deregulation of financial markets and the injection of competition into the public sector through privatisation, contracting out and the introduction of internal markets comprised part of this neoliberal ideology, while attacking the influence of trade unions and promoting flexible work practices comprised another (Pollert, 1988; Minford, 1991).

There are gender issues here too. Part-time work has traditionally been female work (Pollert, 1988; Crompton, 2002; Bradley, 2016). You can read about female part-time work in the novels of Charles Dickens, George Eliot and Elizabeth Gaskell in the 19th century. The reason is that the traditional woman's role – to stay at home and look after the children – can be combined with part-time occupation as, for example, a seamstress, which can be carried out at home while looking after the family. The traditional family role, with the male breadwinner and the female carer, is one that dovetails neatly with part-time employment patterns. It's why a high proportion of part-time workers, in many 'good' and 'bad' jobs, are women (Warren and Lyonette, 2018).

What becomes clearer, having distinguished between different types of flexibility, is that there are different trends within different types of flexibility, and that its concentration is uneven across sectors and occupations. Indeed, seasonal work goes back to antiquity, while casual work goes back to at least the 19th century (Whiteside, 2019). Other forms, such as functional flexibility and multiskilling, might be more modern, but the reason we examine them is because there is a far higher incidence of flexible working today across industrialised economies than in previous generations, particularly in gig work and growth sectors such as new media, creative and knowledge work (McKinlay and Smith, 2009). Some 85% of workers at Amazon are agency workers, a proportion that clearly suits the company's business model to ensure flexibility of their working arrangements. However, shortages of labour and greater fixed investment have also led Amazon to increase its numbers of directly employed workers, so we need to view flexible working in relationship to ups and downs in the labour market cycle as well.

But the real question here, as always, is that there are two sides to the issue: in HRM, there's the employers' side and there's also the workers' side. The question with flexibility is, who benefits from all this? Is it something that's imposed by management, or is it something that's chosen by workers? Is it something that can benefit workers as well?

Who benefits?

The following quotation makes the critical point that flexible working cuts two ways:

> Casualisation is part of a new regime of the management of labour. It is not one of unlimited choice and flexibility that is mutually advantageous to workers and employers. Rather, it is a regime which fits many workers into the needs of production and service provision by offering only very limited choices to workers. Shorter hours are usually associated with lower pay and lower skilled work. It is primarily undertaken by those with other commitments (eg, carers for children and the elderly and students) or with no other choice (eg, blue-collar workers seeking any kind of alternative to unemployment). (Buchanan, 2004: 20)

Flexible working benefits the employer, most certainly, for the reasons already outlined. However, from the employee's point of view, it can cause uncertainty. Indeed, what's interesting is that – going back to the terminology – employers generally talk about 'flexible working'. Now, 'flexible' is a positive term, isn't it? If things are flexible, then they're adaptable and forgiving, which is good. By contrast, if we talk about 'casual' or 'precarious' work, the term is much more negative. You'll very often find that trade unions and workers talk about 'casualisation', which means the erosion of standard, full-time contracts, while employers will often talk about 'flexible' contracts. Choice of terminology is important because it implies that flexible working is advantageous for employers, but rather less so for employees. So, for example, the quotation above notes that casualised work is 'primarily undertaken by those with other commitments ... or with no other choice'. In other words, people may find themselves forced into precarious work simply because they prefer any work, naturally enough, to unemployment.

A model of core and peripheral workers

At this stage we can draw some of these threads together by presenting a model of these different forms of flexible employment in Figure 9.3. This illustrates the relationship between what its originator, John Atkinson, called 'core' ('standard') and 'peripheral' ('non-standard') work (1984, 1987). It gives us a helpful, coherent overview of how they might all interrelate with one another in an attempt to compare and contrast their various characteristics.

The model goes back to 1984, but it still bears up as a point of departure, even though, as we'll see, there's quite a lot wrong with it. It provides a model of the organisation with, in the middle, this dark grey area of 'core' workers. 'Core' workers are the full-time, permanent employees. They are the people who are traditionally seen as providing the core functions of the organisation.

By contrast, around them, you have a variety of different types of 'peripheral' workers. Peripheral Group I consists of agency workers who are also skilled. In many companies, skilled agency workers work alongside skilled core workers. At Toyota, for example, multiskilled core workers form the foundation of vehicle production at the Derby factory, but about 10% of the total workforce are agency

Figure 9.3: Core and peripheral model

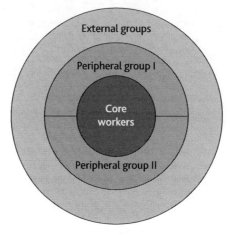

Source: Atkinson (1984, 1987)

workers, who are also highly skilled but who provide a kind of buffer for the core workers. The core workers accept the agency workers because they know that, if there is a fall in demand requiring redundancies, then management will reduce the number of agency workers first, before the core workers (Gold and Rees, 2018). Agency workers, Peripheral Group I, therefore act as a kind of shock absorber for the core workers in many organisations.

Peripheral Group II comprise other types of non-standard workers, so they might be on part-time or fixed-term contracts, but they have a more peripheral relationship with the organisation as they fill less skilled occupations and help provide numerical flexibility. If the company is undergoing a downturn for its product, it can reduce labour costs relatively swiftly by simply failing to renew fixed-term contracts or by reducing the hours of part-time workers, which leaves the core workforce intact.

Finally, round the outside, the External Groups comprise workers who are outsourced. In many organisations, ancillary or support functions, such as catering, cleaning services, grounds maintenance and security, are outsourced to specialist companies that have service contracts with the main company to provide them.

The model presents the notion of a workforce divided between core and peripheral workers, but it also reveals how the periphery is itself fragmented into several different categories of worker. However, it should be noted that the core workers themselves are likely to be functionally flexible. The 3,000 or so core workers at Toyota in the UK are all functionally flexible. When they are recruited, they start work in a particular area, such as assembly, welding or painting, but over time they are trained to acquire all the skills they need to be redeployed across other parts of the factory as and when required, which makes them highly adaptable, efficient and productive.

Human capital

Another way of examining flexible working is to look at the model (see Table 9.1) adapted from Lepak and Snell (1999), which has two dimensions to it: the horizontal focuses on the cost of human capital – how significant is it? In other words, is a certain group of workers highly productive or less productive? The vertical focuses on how distinctive the human capital or skills are that are embodied in this same group of workers – are their skills easily accessible on the labour market, or are they hard to find? If we put those two dimensions together, we find we have a quadrant in which there are four boxes.

Top right, the cost of human labour is significant, that is, workers are multiskilled and central to the company. In other words, they have skills that are not easily available on the labour market. These workers you protect, as they're the ones you really need to maintain your product.

Bottom left are workers with weak skill distinctiveness, that is, workers who are unskilled or semi-skilled. Their skills can be easily found in the labour market and you can replace them, so they are dispensable.

The other two quadrants present hybrid situations. In the top left are skilled positions that may nevertheless have rather low value to the organisation. For example, landscape gardeners are highly skilled – and enhance the quality of the working environment – but they are probably not intrinsically required to create the product. Their services are likely to be contracted out to a specialist.

In the bottom right are positions that can easily be found on the labour market but have high value to an organisation. An example might be cleaning services, which are critical to maintaining health and safety, but may not be particularly highly skilled. These services, too, are likely to be contracted out.

That said, organisations might well pursue different HR policies in relation to these categories of workers. Whether to outsource or not is very much a matter for HR strategy.

Table 9.1: Human capital distinctiveness and cost perspective

	Cost of labour less significant	Cost of labour more significant
Workers with strong skill distinctiveness	Retain within an internal employment relationship as regular employees, or contract with regular contractor	Retain within an internal employment relationship as regular employees
Workers with weak skill distinctiveness	Outsource to general third-party labour market intermediaries, or platform employment	Buy in through specialist labour contractors

Source: Adapted from Lepak and Snell (1999)

Flexible working and HR strategy

The value and uniqueness of human capital – and the role they play in different work settings – is, then, another way to approach the use of flexible working. It also links back to our discussion in Chapter 2 about soft and hard HRM. You'll recall that hard HRM tends to prevail in those companies that focus on low-cost, high-volume production, while soft HRM is associated with more differentiated, high-quality products. Similarly, soft HRM will arguably apply to 'traditional' core workers, because you need to retain them, while hard HR practices will apply more to peripheral workers because they are exactly that, they are peripheral to the main activities and so more dispensable. Soft and hard HR practices may therefore apply to the *kinds* of workers employed in an enterprise. Hence hard and soft HRM are not unique to a particular workplace. They may be found in varying combinations across all organisations in one form or another. It's not that a given organisation is characterised only by hard HRM or only by soft HRM; rather, the combination may depend at least partly on the kinds of skill mixes that are required by the employer.

The Atkinson model of core and peripheral workers has proved immensely influential in providing a terminology to discuss the various kinds of working patterns found in organisations. However, in relation to the 'real world', it can be challenged on several fronts. For example, to repeat an earlier point, core workers in some sectors may themselves be employed on 'peripheral' contracts – or what would be regarded as peripheral in other sectors. So, for example, the predominant form of employment in a hotel may well be part time, with part-time staff acting as 'core workers'. Management will be on standard full-time employment contracts, but they are supervising a core staff who are part time (Nickson, 2013). Furthermore, Geary (1992), in empirical research on US multinational corporations (MNCs) in Ireland, rejects the use of segmentation of workers into different groupings for functional and strategic reasons, as flexible working gave rise to reduced commitment. Elger and Smith (2005) found that Japanese MNCs in the UK initially had all workers on standard employment contracts, but they introduced agency or indirect contracts to manage high labour turnover among non-unionised, low-paid workers and to deal with a fluctuating order book. Google, as we saw in Chapter 8, has seen 'standard' workers walk out over the inequitable treatment of their co-workers on agency and other non-standard employment contracts. Here, the universal solidarity and sense of social justice of these workers challenges the flexible segmentation of the workforce by Google management. What all this means is that flexible working is an interesting idea, but we're still grappling with its realities.

Trends in flexible working

Across the European Union (EU), part-time employment has been quite constant, with 43 million people aged 15 to 64 working part time in 2017. By country, there are higher proportions of workers on part-time contracts in Western Europe than in Eastern Europe (see Figure 9.4). Involuntary part-time work was highest in Greece and other Southern European countries where full-time work was less available. The Netherlands, with half (49.8%) of all employed people aged 15 to 64 working part time in 2017, has consistently been a high user of part-time workers. Economies with about one in four employed part time were Austria (27.9%), Germany (26.9%), Denmark (25.3%), the UK (24.9%), Belgium (24.5%) and Sweden (23.3%).

At the opposite end of the scale, part-time employment accounted for less than 5% of all employment in Bulgaria (2.2%), Hungary (4.3%) and Croatia (4.8%). Low shares were also recorded in Slovakia (5.8%), the Czech Republic (6.2%), Poland (6.6%), Romania (6.8%), Lithuania (7.6%) and Latvia (7.7%)

Figure 9.4: Part-time employment (European Union, 2017)

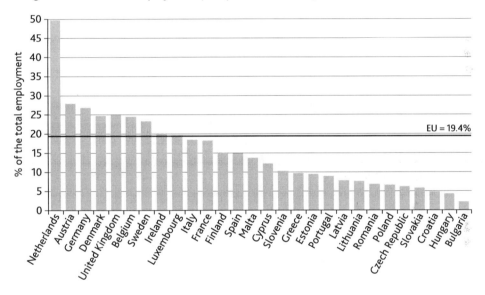

Source: Eurostat (2018a)

Trends in agency working reveal general increases since 1983, with some peaks and troughs. In the case of Spain, for example, there's a spike in the early 2000s and then a drop, but even that remains higher than the figure for the base date. In Denmark, Greece, Japan and Norway the proportion has fallen, and in Belgium, Finland and the UK it has remained fairly static, but elsewhere it has increased substantially. The UK has around 800,000 agency workers (Tomlinson, 2018).

Agency working can bring benefits to everyone concerned, but we need to bear in mind that it is often used to create greater flexibility for the employer without advantages for the worker, as demonstrated in Box 9.1.

BOX 9.1: CAR WORKERS AT THE BMW MINI-PLANT, OXFORD, UK

The BMW plant in Cowley, Oxford, nowadays manufactures BMW Minis (and in the past made Morris Minors). Like Toyota, BMW uses agency workers because they are easily dispensable. In 2009, 850 agency workers were given restricted notice that they were losing their jobs as it was cheaper to reduce agency workers in response to a downturn in demand. 'It's a disgrace. I feel as though I've been used,' said one worker. 'We should have been given one month's notice, not one hour.' The contract staff, who have few employment rights, were brought in to work alongside full-time employees on the production lines. As we have seen, agency workers allow manufacturers to adjust more easily to changes in demand, both up and down.

Tony Woodley, (then) joint leader of the Unite union, said:

> Sacking an entire shift like this, and targeting agency workers who have no rights to redundancy pay, is blatant opportunism on BMW's part and nothing short of scandalous. BMW's parent company couldn't attempt this in Germany because it would be illegal to do so. It is a disgrace, therefore, that workers in this country can be so casually thrown [on] to the dole. (Quoted in Macalister and Pidd, 2009)

The point here is that after two years, a worker on a standard employment contract in the UK is covered by notification and consultation procedures if made redundant, as well as by statutory redundancy pay. However, an agency worker, carrying out exactly the same tasks alongside such a permanent employee, is not. Agency staff have fewer employment rights and allow employers to introduce numerical flexibility according to the demands for their product much more easily than would otherwise be the case. Notice, too, that sacking workers in this way would not have been legal in Germany, which takes us back to the distinctions we were making between liberal and coordinated market economies in Chapter 5.

Zero-hours contracts (ZHCs, or 'no guaranteed hours contracts', the term preferred by the Office for National Statistics [ONS]) are another example of flexible working, and the common element to the terms is the lack of a guaranteed minimum number of hours. From the employers' point of view, zero hours significantly help to control labour costs. If you have workers on call, but don't have any work for them, then you don't pay them. If you're the worker, on the other hand, it can be extremely frustrating to be paid the minimum wage for your hour simply waiting for work that never comes. Riders for Deliveroo and drivers for Uber, among many others who are on call, get paid if the work comes, and don't get paid if it doesn't.

Figure 9.5 shows the incidence of ZHCs in the UK, and its dramatic rate of climb since 2012, with some flattening in recent years. Around 1 million workers are now employed on these contracts, somewhere between 2% and 3% of the total workforce. However, because workers may have more than one job, there are more ZHCs than that. A report by the ONS on ZHCs notes that 'the November 2017 survey of businesses indicated that there were 1.8 million contracts that did not guarantee a minimum number of hours, where work had actually been carried out under those contracts. This represented 6% of all employment contracts' (ONS, 2018a). Koumenta and Williams (2019) show that this contentious form of employment is itself differentiated by the nature of occupational tasks and its overlap with non-standard employment features (such as part time and temporary). They also indicate that ZHCs are highly concentrated in a certain small number of occupations and sectors, with over half of ZHCs found in just ten occupations and over 40% of those working in only two sectors, hospitality and health and social care (Tomlinson, 2018). Figure 9.5 reveals that the rise slowly takes off from around 2009, the time of the financial collapse and recession, when employers were under serious pressure to seek new ways to make workers more flexible (Farina et al, 2020). ZHCs then became much more attractive to employers who might otherwise not have thought about them. However, evidence demonstrates that the general context of employment insecurity concerns workers as much as the actual incidence of ZHCs. Felstead et al (2020: 34) state 'that cutting working hours at short notice is twice as prevalent as zero–hours contracts and triple the number of employees are very anxious about unexpected changes to their hours of work'. In this sense, we always need to look at the context in which new contracts appear.

Figure 9.5: Rise in number of zero-hours contracts in the UK (2000–17)

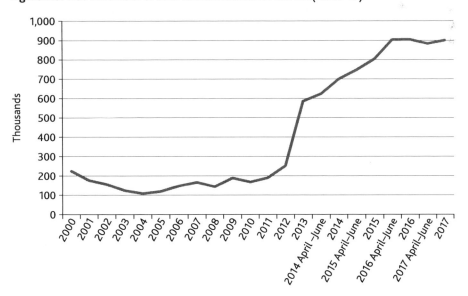

Source: ONS (2018a)

BOX 9.2: NEW ZEALAND BANS ZERO-HOURS CONTRACTS

It has been widely reported that the New Zealand government banned new ZHCs from 1 April 2016, after which date the legislation – the Employment Relations Amendment Act 2016 – requires employers to offer a fixed, weekly minimum number of working hours to their workers, who cannot be penalised for refusing to work longer hours at short notice. It also requires employers to compensate workers if they cancel a shift without reasonable notice.

Restaurant Brands New Zealand Limited, which represents fast-food outlets, subsequently negotiated an agreement with the Unite union to move the sector's 4,000 ZHC workers on to fixed-hours contracts. The Unite union national secretary, Gerard Hehir, declared that the agreement was a win for workers who at last had shifts that were permanently fixed, while Restaurant Brands chief executive, Russel Creedy, said: 'If staff are happy and engaged with the employer, they are less likely to move on' (quoted in Edmunds, 2016). It should be noted that ZHCs haven't actually themselves been banned, 'as it is not necessary to have set hours, however, if you desire set hours per week, they are contractually obligated to give them to you' (Scott and Garland, 2018).

Who is working non-standard employment contracts?

Australian data show that the profile of the non-standard workforce is quite distinctive. Non-standard workers tend to be younger: while younger workers account for less than 15% of the employed, they account for over 40% of non-standard workers. They also tend to be women. Some 60% of part-time workers are women, which may still reflect traditional views about family structure. Hours worked may also tend to be more unpredictable, but then, with certain kinds of non-standard contracts (such as zero hours), that's the whole point (Buchanan, 2004). In the UK, Felstead et al (2020: 41) reported that:

> the experience of insecure working hours and anxiety about unexpected changes to work schedules are also spread more unevenly across social classes, contract types and hours worked. Rarely, for example, do those in the "higher managerial and professional" class report being on a ZHC (0.3 per cent). This compares with one in 20 (5.0 per cent) "routine" workers. The class gradient for other forms of insecurity is not as steep. For example, around one in 12 "higher managers and professionals" (13.8 per cent) report feeling very or fairly anxious about unexpected changes to their work schedule. This compares with 29.8 per cent for "routine" workers.

Workers on non-standard contracts have also tended – with stress on the word 'tended' – to be less skilled. However, this is changing as such contracts are creeping more and more into professional areas as well. A highly skilled occupation such as translation, for example, which used to be carried out within companies in-house by a bank of employed translators, has now almost universally been outsourced to self-employed translators (Fraser and Gold, 2001). Teaching staff in schools are also often employed on fixed-term contracts because of pressure on local government finances (S. Chan, 2013). Yet another area is higher education. Of some 180,000 academics in the UK, one-third (60,000) are on either temporary or fixed-term contracts. Using the terminology outlined in this chapter, there is a core of lecturing staff on standard full-time contracts who work alongside a high percentage of colleagues who are on fixed-term contracts, who provide the numerical flexibility. The same applies to the rise in numbers of adjuncts (temporary lecturers) employed in Australia (Brown et al, 2010) and in the US, where some 73% of all faculty positions are off the tenure track, according to analysis of federal data by the American Association of University Professors: 'for the most part, these are insecure, unsupported positions with little job security and few protections for academic freedom' (Inside Higher Ed, 2018).

Reasons for employers' use of non-standard employment contracts

Employers increasingly rely on non-standard contracts for a variety of reasons. We have already alluded to some of these. One is that a fixed-term contract allows you to buy in specialist skills, but only for a short period of time. Another is that it allows you to respond quickly to fluctuating demand. And it's much easier, quicker and cheaper to dismiss workers contracted to you through employment agencies, which also allows you to screen potential workers who you may wish to recruit. Employers may be able to intensify work, with greater levels of flexibility acting as a threat (Kelliher and Anderson, 2010).

Screening to select the right person for a job – especially a skilled one – can be time-consuming, and making a mistake can prove costly. However, if you employ an agency worker, then the agency has already done the screening for you, and if that worker doesn't fit in for any reason, you inform the agency and they can be removed and easily substituted at no cost to yourself. Hence the expense and risk involved in interviewing and recruitment can be cut by using agency workers.

Employers hiring agency workers can hold out for them the hope that if they perform well and prove themselves, they may then be employed directly on a 'standard' contract. Amazon recruits in this way, with agency workers hired on the basis that their performance may be viewed (although not necessarily) as an extended period of probation. Hence flexible working becomes a management control strategy, with the carrot of standard full-time employment held out to workers on non-standard contracts as an inducement to perform well. Working hard and behaving compliantly may persuade your line manager to convert your precarious contract into a coveted secure contract (Briken and Taylor, 2018).

On the other hand, it may be argued that the downside to non-standard employment contracts is that they can lead to transient work relationships. They might lead to a lack of trust in organisations because a churn of workers coming through agencies means that you're never quite sure who you're working with. The heterogeneity of a workforce – with workers on standard contracts working alongside those on a range of non-standard contracts – may lead to the formation of subgroups and perceptions of unfairness in conditions (recall Box 2.3). This, in turn, may engender a lack of loyalty and commitment, leading to 'exit' as workers with skills in demand move to other companies, and hence to a breakdown of any sense of collective identity. It might also lead to unclear boundaries within organisations – who, for example, is responsible for training? If you're employing an agency worker, training might be seen as the responsibility of the agency or it might be seen as the employer's – or as your own, as the worker (an issue we return to in Chapter 17). There are therefore certain challenges in using flexible work that HR managers need to tackle.

Nevertheless, evidence suggests that many workers on non-standard contracts can be highly committed as well. For example, a case study of casual lecturers in Australia reveals how committed they are to providing optimal teaching for their students, even though their employment conditions may be very trying as some teach at several institutions. One states: 'They're all on different timetables, it's a nightmare – I can't plan, financially speaking. The best I can succinctly say is that it's very harrowing.' But another stresses: 'I'm involved with the students, I really appreciate the students, I love teaching, I love watching their learning process. I get inspired by that. But that's the only thing that keeps me going' (quoted in Brown et al, 2010: 175). For these employees, then, the intrinsic rewards of the job outweigh the challenging working conditions. In other cases, however, there is no guarantee that quality of work might not suffer.

Concluding comments

In conclusion, some will argue that flexible working is here to stay, so we need to ensure that workers on non-standard contracts have income security and 'voice security' too – in other words, that they are involved in procedures that represent workers' interests within the organisation (a topic we return to in Chapter 16). They must also have access to training and retraining and the chance to upgrade their skills as and when required (see Chapter 17). In Europe there have been attempts to provide employers with flexible employment and workers with employment security, best captured in the hybrid word 'flexicurity'. This

> marries two concepts (flexibility and security) that hitherto were seen in opposition. It is indeed hard to believe that these two terms could be subsumed under one roof in a sort of "win–win" game for all when, in reality, the opposing clans (unions and employers) remain armed and suspicious of each other. (Auer, 2010: 372)

By contrast, others will focus on the problems with flexible working, that it leads to a downward spiral of skills within the economy and more transactional employment relationships, where levels of trust and confidence in employees tends to diminish. Indeed, the drive towards non-standard employment is generally stronger where unions are weaker and the State itself is committed to neoliberal policies and values that undermine the protection of these workers.

Flexible employment contracts are certainly entrenched as a feature of labour markets and HR strategies across the industrialised world. Their incidence varies at national and sectoral levels, so always bear in mind that, in HRM, we're always comparing and contrasting sectors, countries and business systems. Some 22 million workers in the UK are still employed on standard full-time contracts, so we can't talk about the end of the bureaucratic organisation by any means. That said, flexible working, in all its manifest forms, has become more significant and dominant, although varying by sector and occupation, which has knock-on effects. The limits to flexible working are the limits to the degree of skills integration within organisations. While organisations are able to integrate those skills, there is a future for non-standard employment through, for example, agency working, but as soon as costs are involved – if agency work comes to be seen as less reliable or efficient than direct employment – employers will react against it.

Basically, flexible working leads to a more dispersed and fragmented workforce, which can lead to tensions in management control systems. The consequences risk including low pay, stress, disengagement from work and higher rates of turnover, as workers on standard and non-standard employment contracts operate alongside one another. The question is whether these risks are significant or not for a given business strategy and its associated HR strategy. The answers are going to be empirical and will depend very much on the particular circumstances of the organisation within its sectoral and national context.

Some questions to think about

1. Define 'functional', 'numerical' and 'temporal' flexibility, and give examples of the ways in which employers use them in the workplace.

2. Have you ever worked on a non-standard employment contract? If so, what type was it? What were its good and bad points?

3. Has the 'standard employment contract' reached the end of its life? Discuss with reference to the growth of flexible working, using examples.

4. Outline the role and consequences for HRM of organisations using employment agencies to adjust swiftly to changes in demand.

Further reading

Forde, C. and G. Slater (2005) 'Agency working in Britain: Character, consequences and regulation', *British Journal of Industrial Relations*, 43(2): 249–71. [Background to the old and new use of agency working and its increasing spread in the UK.]

Fudge, J. (2017) 'The future of the standard employment relationship: Labour law, new institutional economics and old power resource theory', *Journal of Industrial Relations*, 59(3): 374–92. [Global context for the spread of new forms of contracting labour and the state of the standard employment relationship.]

Kalleberg, A.L. (2011) *Good Jobs, Bad Jobs: The Rise of Polarized and Precarious Employment Systems in the United States, 1970s–2000s*, New York: Russell Sage Foundation. [Broad historical review of the rise of more insecure forms of employment in the US.]

Koumenta, M. and Williams, M. (2019) 'An anatomy of zero-hour contracts in the UK', *Industrial Relations Journal*, 50(1): 20–40. [Discussion of flexible forms of employment, focusing on whether they are structural or marginal within societies.]

10

Services and Aesthetic and Emotional Labour

In the last chapter, on flexible working, we noted that the predominant model in human resource management (HRM) remains the 'standard' employment contract based on a form of work traditionally typical of manufacturing. We also noted that the rise of the service sector has tended to favour the increase in non-standard working, so in this chapter we focus on the service sector and how its characteristics affect HRM.

In particular, we build on some of the points made in Chapter 3, about the nature of the employment relationship itself, and the way in which labour is *embodied* – in other words, the fact that we can't separate *ourselves* from our own *labour power*. The labour power that we have is intrinsically part of ourselves; it's part of our bodies. We begin by examining the 'self' and the notion of the self as a social product, where it comes from and what we mean by it, and how it is relevant for HRM in the service sector. We then have another look at the nature of traditional, bureaucratic forms of working, and why they are really not appropriate when discussing the service sector. This leads into examining the various control strategies that management uses in the service sector, which are particularly important when we look at 'emotional' and 'aesthetic' labour. These forms of labour become significant when customers or clients are also involved in the production of a good or a service, meaning that the employment relationship is no longer a matter just for employers and workers (two-party involvement), but for the service user as well (three-party involvement).

We can start by returning to the observation, which we made in Chapter 3, that our labour power is intrinsically part of ourselves.

Figure 10.1 shows some images of bodies. On the left, a muscular arm and a fist clutching a spanner depict a man who is involved in some kind of strenuous manual work. In the middle, the man in a suit staring at a mathematical formula suggests a job that needs brain power – that is, mental abilities of some kind – rather than physical power. And then on the right, you have a young woman who is apparently forcing a smile. That might make us think about cafes or restaurants, where we go as customers to order nice food and drink and want the waiting staff to look happy. So here we have a range of images of labour power, but the key point is that each image represents a *different kind of body* – and that each image conjures up a different kind of notion of the labour power that's required. This chapter examines specifically the question of the physicality of labour and what that might imply for HRM.

Figure 10.1: Body work

Sources: iStock.com/shorrocks, ShutterStock/vectorfusionart, iStock.com/VladimirFLoyd

Construction of the 'self'

We can begin with the 'self'. We talk about the 'self' and constructing the 'self', but what does this mean? Self-awareness arises out of our socialisation, from our childhood, but mainly as we interact with other people. The 'self' isn't something that's objectively given to us. We all have a genetic make-up that we inherit from our parents and grandparents, and we are also socialised in many different ways and accordingly 'become' many different people (Goffman, 1974). We all behave differently in different groups of people – with our parents, friends, colleagues, with our partner – because we experience different expectations from these groups. A teacher who is confident with her pupils in the classroom may find herself much more tentative in a medical consultation with her doctor. Even our language and accent change according to whether we are chatting to friends or in a formal interview. This creation of different 'selves' results from 'reflexivity' – that is, the tendency to reflect on ourselves in a conscious way, which has important implications for HRM. This quotation makes the point rather well:

> The self is a social product, constituted both by spontaneous internal responses and by the processes of self-awareness, self-management and self-display in the context of social interaction. Underlying this definition is a belief in the inherent freedom of individuals to interpret and make meaningful their situation and to create and recreate the sense of self within socially imposed constraints. (Kunda, 2006: 161)

All this has a bearing on our understanding of bureaucratic and post-bureaucratic employment, concepts discussed earlier, in Chapter 5. The standard theory of bureaucracy (associated with the work of Max Weber) states that an efficient organisation is one that delimits tasks within it. It is based on hierarchies, spans of control and clear lines of authority, which ensure that workers understand their place within its overall scheme. And because they know their place, they carry out their allotted tasks that fit in, like the pieces of a giant jigsaw puzzle, with its overall aims and objectives. Weber calls this an 'ideal type' of bureaucracy, and it helps to explain employment structures within the health service, schools and universities and large multinational companies, among many other organisations.

However, later commentators have pointed out that this kind of structure may be very stultifying. Organisational change and improvement require people to be imaginative and creative, so the question centres rather on how imagination and creativity fit into this notion of an ideal type of bureaucracy. This is a good question because they frequently risk getting drummed out of bureaucratic organisations fixated on rule-following and hierarchical control. As long ago as 1940, Robert Merton warned that conformity and following orders made bureaucracies inefficient and unresponsive to change, as the bureaucratic personality lacks the judgement to interpret what may or may not be appropriate action in a dynamic environment (Merton, 1940). William H. Whyte (1956) makes similar criticisms of bureaucratic conformism on the grounds that organisations also require people who can take risks, innovate and deal with uncertainties. Otherwise, they will ossify and fail to progress. And if you want further evidence about the dangers of unthinking obedience and compliance to authority, look up the work of Stanley Milgram on YouTube for the results of some disturbing experiments in the nature of authority.

Balance

Of course, having said all that, organisations do need an element of rule-following, so the real issue is balance. Organisations need workers to understand where they fit in and job descriptions to set boundaries around tasks. At the same time, they need to strike a balance so that there's also enough trust and confidence among their workers to allow for change. Workers have to know they can act as free agents in adapting within certain limits to ensure that the organisation remains innovative and adaptable.

The development of the service sector brings these challenges to a head, as supervision of workers who are dealing directly with customers and clients becomes problematic. Supervisors would find it awkward to monitor shop assistants as they serve customers, or waiting staff as they attend diners in a restaurant, or even lecturers as they teach students, especially if the monitoring might involve correction or even admonishment. Rather, such workers need to be trusted to deliver the required standard of performance without supervision if customers and clients are to remain confident in the level of service provided and to return in the future. Once again, the issue comes down to control mechanisms, but ones that rely on values and self-motivation rather than supervised rule-following.

In Chapter 8 on the 'new' unitarism we examined the ways in which hi-tech companies, such as Apple and Google, among others, try to create strong organisational cultures that promote commitment and motivation by socialising their workers into appropriate value systems. Socialisation becomes the form of control because workers are then self-motivated – they comply, not because the supervisor is breathing down their neck, but because they genuinely want to perform their tasks to the best of their ability as that is the sort of person they have become. Performing well has become part of their identity. The notion of supervision then transforms from the external agency of a supervisor into something that you have within yourself. Supervision is internalised as a set of standards you meet because you believe they reflect the values that give you identity within the organisation.

We can now begin to draw some threads together. In Chapter 3, on the employment relationship, we argued that an employer acquires the capacity of a worker to work, but that the capacity remains open-ended. This is the nature of the wage–effort bargain. You pay somebody a wage, but the amount of effort that they put in for that wage is not given; it can change. The implication of this is that our labour power is necessarily embodied in ourselves. Now, we're all different. We are male or female or maybe transgender, we have different ethnic backgrounds, we are younger or older. Furthermore, some of us are more muscular than others, some of us are better looking (whatever that might mean) – so our labour power comes in a variety of different packages, and those packages are ourselves. They are what make us the people we are, and you can't actually have the labour power without the person. We also discovered in Chapter 1 that HRM is all about controlling unit labour costs, by sourcing labour as cheaply as possible and by finding ways to raise productivity.

It now becomes clear that employers will require certain kinds of control strategies in service work that will be rather different from those appropriate in manufacturing. Andrew Friedman (1977), in a classic formulation, distinguishes between what he calls 'direct control' mechanisms (that is, close monitoring of performance by a supervisor) and 'responsible autonomy' mechanisms (internalising the commitment and motivation of workers). There's a major distinction between the two in that direct control emphasises rule-following and lack of autonomy on the grounds that workers aren't really trusted to carry out their work without supervision, while responsible autonomy emphasises socialisation into organisational standards and values, and the presence of trust.

One of the challenges in discussing HRM – as we've already noted – lies in the different terms that different commentators and writers often use for the same or similar concepts. For example, you might like to consider here the similarities between direct control and 'hard' HRM on the one hand, and responsible autonomy and 'soft' HRM on the other. Yet these different terms are really referring to the same contrast between external and internal control systems: control as an external requirement from a supervisor (hard HRM) and control that is value-centred and internalised by workers (a form of soft HRM). This contrast is critical when we examine HRM in service sectors.

Role of the customer or client

We need to repeat a basic point here. Figure 10.2 shows that the share of employment in the UK between manufacturing (the 'secondary' sector) and

Figure 10.2: UK sectoral shares of employment (1920–2016)

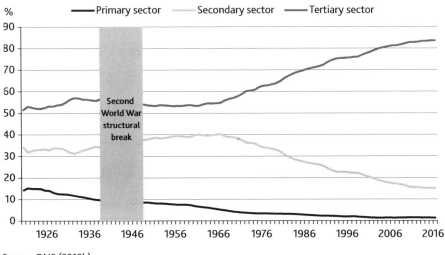

Source: ONS (2019b)

services (the 'tertiary' sector) has been greatly diverging, with agriculture (the 'primary' sector) almost out of sight.

Between 1920 and 2016 employment in agriculture plummeted from 14.3% to 1.3% of total employment; in manufacturing, it fell from 34.2% to 15.1%; but in services it soared from 51.5% to 83.6%. This tendency also reflects trends across other industrialised countries. HRM in manufacturing companies involves just the employer and worker (a dyadic relationship), and generally excludes the customer or client. For example, if you work in a factory canning vegetables, you'll never know the people who've eaten the tin of tomatoes that you've just produced. Once you have finished with the product – anything from a tin of food to a blouse, a car or a laptop – it disappears and you never see it again. Dyadic relationships between employer and worker dominated HRM textbooks for many years, until well after the rise of the service economy.

With service work, however, HRM is characterised by the relationship between not only employer and worker, but also that of customer or client (a three-way, or triadic relationship). In Chapter 9, on flexible working, we came across another triadic relationship when we were looking at agency work: workers are employed by a temporary agency, but then get contracted out to an employer, creating a three-way relationship (see Figure 9.2). With service work, we find a different triadic relationship involving employer, worker and customer or client. The introduction of this third party into the relationship is highly significant, and we must be clear about what this 'third party' exactly refers to. For short hand, we have been referring to 'customers' or 'clients', but our definition is far wider, as we don't just mean somebody who is buying a product. In health services it refers to the patient who is being treated by a doctor or nurse (the worker) within the National Health Service (NHS) (the employer). In transport services it refers to the passenger who is being driven by a bus or train driver (worker) on a bus or rail network (the employer). In universities it refers to the student who is attending a seminar given by a lecturer (worker) in a higher education institution (employer). In all cases, the patient, passenger and student are 'consuming' a 'service' delivered by a worker to a certain standard and at a cost (in the NHS, costs are covered by general taxation and National Insurance, in transport through fares and government subsidies, and in higher education through student fees and, again, government subsidies). Figure 10.2 has demonstrated the importance of employment in the service sectors, and hence the corresponding importance of these triadic relationships in HRM.

Trends towards increasing employment in services consequently underscore employers' increasing need for greater sophistication in employment control mechanisms. A close supervisory system of service workers doesn't make sense. For example, line managers can't stand in the corner of hospital wards to monitor the performance of their nurses. Instead, hospitals expect their staff to reflect the professional standards of the world of healthcare, which means that nurses are 'controlled' through a form of responsible autonomy. The same can be said for shop assistants, train drivers and university lecturers, which is all quite different from the manufacturing sectors.

However, with service work, there are further issues involved. Responsible autonomy in manufacturing (for example in Japanese car plants) differs from that in hospitals, shops, schools, universities and other service workplaces. This is because the third party – the customer, client, patient, passenger, student, or whoever – has also increasingly been brought into the surveillance system. They increasingly form part of the way in which control mechanisms work. For example, in a university, it's no longer just our employer who's hoping that we perform in line with certain standards, but also the students who can assess their lecturers through course feedback forms and the National Student Survey (NSS). Students fill in their responses, which becomes an indicator on the basis of which our performance can be judged. If all our forms say: 'Michael Gold and Chris Smith are a load of rubbish and shouldn't be allowed to teach', then those comments are going to come back to us because our line manager will say: 'Look, you're getting very bad responses from your students – what are you going to do about it? Is it a training matter? Is it a capacity matter? What is actually going on here?' So your opportunity as third-party customer, client, student or whatever to give feedback on the performance of the service provider gives you a lot of say over the employment relationship. Obviously, you are not the employer and yet, as the third party, you have significant influence with the employer. The implications of all this vary according to the nature of the relationship between the third party and service provider. As a passenger, you may not interact with the train driver at all. As a patient in a hospital, your relationship with the nursing staff may last longer, but is still likely to be transitory. As a student, on the other hand, you may have a closer relationship with your lecturers as teachers and advisers.

The role of the third party is also likely to affect recruitment and selection procedures. This is because the criteria may involve not just your skills and abilities, but also how presentable you are in your role. A lecturer may have published cutting-edge research but comes across as incapable of stringing two words together as a teacher. The interview panel may conclude that, however good the candidate's research is, their communication skills are insufficient and so they cannot be appointed. In such a case, subject knowledge alone is not enough – the ability to relate to students (a very different issue from subject knowledge) also enters the field as a criterion for the job.

Aesthetic labour

This observation leads us to consider further, intensely personal criteria that might intrude into service employment, which go well beyond communication skills. We'll examine aesthetic labour first. Imagine you are working in a canning factory or in a car plant. In these kinds of workplaces, you'll have probably been issued a uniform comprising overalls, visor and safety boots. No one is really going to care about your appearance as such, provided you are fit enough to do the job. By contrast, once a third-party relationship is introduced, the appearance of the employee may also then become important. If it does, then we enter the world of aesthetic labour ('aesthetics' refers to the study of beauty or form). Bodily type, gender, emotional control, physical attractiveness and even visible tattoos, among other attributes, start to become important, in a way they don't in a manufacturing job (Timming, 2015). And if you're black, even your hairstyle might be seen as an employment issue (see Box 10.1).

BOX 10.1: CAMPAIGN TO END DISCRIMINATION OVER BLACK HAIRSTYLES

Over one-third of black adults report discrimination at work for wearing their hair naturally, and 25% have been sent home for the same reason. The survey conducted by CROWN UK Fund of 500 black adults and 500 black pre-teens revealed that, overall, 63% had experienced hair discrimination.

In 2020, Unilever, the UK multinational, signed the Halo Code, the UK's first workplace and school code that aims to prevent discrimination against natural afro-textured hair. In addition, Dove, a personal care brand owned by Unilever, launched CROWN UK Fund, an initiative designed to support projects with the same aim, to protect workers and students against forms of hair discrimination (Crowther, 2021).

At this point, management control of service workers can become multidimensional. Service workers can be monitored by supervisors and line managers. They are expected to internalise organisational values and standards through mechanisms that encourage responsible autonomy. And they are subject to feedback on their performance by customers and clients, as this quotation suggests: '"service" shares etymological roots with "servant", "servitude" and "slave" so that it is not surprising that "sales or service workers occupy a social role of implied subordination or even explicit subservience" to customers, who have "the right to define and direct the relationship"' (Korczynski, 2002: 135, quoted in Warhurst and Nickson, 2007b: 786).

In other words, the customer or client becomes a critical part of the employment relationship because, without them, service workers wouldn't have a job at all. It's therefore very much in their interests to ensure that the customer remains satisfied with their performance, which means that the burden of responsibility to turn out in a way that's engaging falls very much on their shoulders. Sometimes employers will make assumptions about what their customers will or will not accept as tolerable appearance (see Box 10.2).

BOX 10.2: BODILY TYPE AND COMPANY IMAGE

'Overweight people are less likely to be hired, have fewer opportunities, are lower paid and often bullied at work', declares Renate van der Zee. 'When Karen gained weight, her boss told her she could no longer work as a receptionist. She was sent to work in the post room instead.... Karen (not her real name ...) worked for a clothing company. She was supposed to wear the company's clothes behind the reception desk. "At one point I reached [UK] size 18, but their clothes only went up to size 14. I asked if I could wear something else – I said I had clothes in the same style. But they made it clear it would be bad for the company's image to have an overweight person in reception."'

Van der Zee points out: 'In the UK, the percentage of obese adults increased from 15% in 1993 to 27% in 2015, by which time 58% of women and 68% of men were designated overweight. All over the world, countless studies reveal that overweight employees face widespread prejudice' (van der Zee, 2017).

Now, clearly, service workers do have agency as well; in other words, they have the ability to choose. Customers, clients, passengers and other third parties don't have a single, uniform effect on service workers, who may resist requirements to modify their appearance or image that they find demeaning. In addition, we have to distinguish between different types of service work – it's not just one homogeneous category. The nature of the customer–client relationship varies greatly according to the kind of service work involved. When we see that term 'service work', we should delve deeper and identify the specific area of service in question.

In all cases we would like to believe that the service worker is happy to be serving the interests of the customer. When we go into a shop, we like to think that the sales assistant is actually pleased to see us and keen to sell us the right product. Of course, for some, even most, of the time, that's true, and workers are positive about serving customers' needs. A McDonald's worker is quoted as saying: 'It's just fun, the people are fun – they make my day, they really do' (quoted in Leidner, 1993: 136). Customer service reps in call centres claim that customer interaction is a source of pleasure: 'When you satisfy a customer you get recognition from a customer'; 'I like talking to people all day'; 'The best part [of the job] is the customer'; 'I like dealing with people, resolving issues, I feel very happy' (quoted in Korczynski, 2001: 93). Housekeeping and room service employees in luxury hotels explain how they are influenced by customer desires, although they have minimal interaction with them (Sherman, 2011). It's difficult to believe that workers feel like this the whole time, but there is evidence that they feel like it at least some of the time. Others, however, looking at working–class men in service work, suggest a conflict between certain masculine values and service (see Box 10.3).

BOX 10.3: CLASS, MASCULINITY AND SERVICE – A CLASH OF VALUES

In research on class and service work, Nixon (2009: 315) found that the older and younger working-class men stressed how hard they found subordination to customer power at the service encounter. The issue of patience, which we can see as a sign of subordination, was central to the men's dislike of interactive service work:

I've got no patience with people basically. I can't put a smiley face on, that's not my sort of thing. (Colin, aged 24, unskilled manual worker)

Bar staff no ... not my cup of tea serving somebody drinks. Don't have the patience for that ... checkout operator, not really good with figures, well, I wouldn't want to do that. Telephone sales, no. Too much talking, I'd lose my patience. (Derek, aged 50, former circuit board assembler)

I was doing retail work, you know, sales assistant, and I just thought I'd change it, go in the warehouse.... The customers treated you like shit and you couldn't say nowt or you'd get sacked ... having to take it all and you just thought, "I ain't taking this". (John, aged 20, warehouse worker)

If someone [a customer] gave me loads of hassle I'd end up lamping them. (Graham, aged 21, unskilled manual worker)

Meanwhile, Figure 10.3 shows workers laughing and joking and playing games with their office chairs. It looks absolutely wonderful, doesn't it? Who wouldn't want to work there?

Figure 10.3: Work is fun – we *have* to have fun

Source: iStock.com/scyther5

Customer control

The 'fun workplace', as we saw in Chapter 8, is often about normative control, the classic unitarist attempt to engage the workforce in management's frame of reference. However, in the service sector there is also customer control, the bringing into employment relations the link to the customer.

This quotation makes the point succinctly: 'Customer control, a continuous yet unobtrusive management form, allows employers access to very direct observations of work performance, while tending to obscure the real locus of power over production. Customer management techniques have helped employers perfect the direction, evaluation and discipline of their subordinates' (Fuller and Smith, 1991: 14). Hence the customer (unwittingly) becomes part of the management system.

This issue has become more acute with the development of automated customer reports. You go to the bank, which is followed up with a text asking: 'How was our service today?' Every online purchase is followed by a text or email requesting you to complete a survey on 'your experience'. Replies are encouraged by the promise of entry into a prize draw. In these ways, employers are continually monitoring the performance of their employees through their customers. The whole point is that feedback then gives the employer indicators on which to appraise the employee's performance and, no doubt, their pay and promotion prospects. This process can, nevertheless, seriously demoralise and demotivate staff. The implication is that customers are always going to submit accurate information back on the service they've had, and this may become problematic. For example, what happens if you have a customer who's racially prejudiced? Or misogynistic? They can start giving very negative feedback on perfectly satisfactory performance simply on the grounds of their prejudice.

In the case of Uber, passengers are asked to assess their drivers on a scale of 1–5. Performance is closely monitored electronically, and Uber will revoke a driver's registration if their score falls below 4.7 (Rosenblat et al, 2016). You therefore see a sign in some Uber cars in the US: 'Free water and gum', which is designed to keep passengers happy. Uber's own website advises drivers to offer water and snacks (Uber, 2022). However, most passengers probably have no idea about the implications of the grading system, so some drivers take the precaution of making sure you know what kind of score to give and what the repercussions would be. The sign might add: 'When drivers fall below a 4.7 score, they lose their ability to drive and provide for their families.' This is because their account is deactivated when ratings fall to 4.6 and below. This illustrates an extreme form of customer control, but digital technology has made it increasingly prevalent:

> Employers, in their search for competitive advantage through consistent service quality, are changing the balance of controls from the direct towards the unobtrusive: seeking to incorporate employees' tacit, inter-personal, affective skills and a degree of self-direction compatible with maintaining overall managerial prerogative. While conceptually the emphasis is on the insertion of customers "as agents in the management circuit" (Fuller and Smith 1991: 11), empirically, the focus is on [rather narrow use of] customer report cards. (Thompson and van den Broek, 2010: 4)

Indeed, there are numerous customer service software packages now that allow employers to track performance ratings of their workers by customers, including Freshdesk, Front, PureCloud, monday.com and Helprace, all of which offer complaint monitoring. In the case of Uber, a simple click of a button by a customer could mean deactivation from the platform for the worker.

However, there are also ways in which platform workers can use customers to evaluate the real demand for work more accurately. Food delivery platforms, for example, want riders on the road, and riders want to ride and not be idle. The food delivery platforms often put out misleading information about the level of demand to get riders out. For the rider, there is no way of knowing if such information is accurate. But Badger (2021), who worked as a rider for his PhD research, quotes another rider, who says:

> I have a baseline restaurant that does food that's rapid to prepare – it's an ice cream parlour – and I know that the estimated delivery time to my house at a really quiet point in the day is 15 minutes. So, if I check back when Mercury [the food delivery platform] tells me it's very high demand and it's still 15 minutes, then I'm fairly confident that they're lying to me. It costs them nothing to get us out on the road and logged in, so they want to make sure they have a surplus of riders all the time. If it says 30–45 minutes to deliver it to my house this means either the ice cream parlour is crazy busy, or, more likely, Mercury is really busy and that extra time represents how long they

think it will take them to free up a rider to be able to take the order. Which for me as a rider, means there's more work than the platform can handle, so there's going to be plenty of work for me if I log in.

By switching roles from worker to customer, the rider can demystify the real demand for work in a setting where information asymmetries between employers and workers are very high.

Differences within service work

We must take care to distinguish between types of service work when tracing the effects of customer control. We can't just talk about 'service work' as such. We can distinguish, for example, between McDonald's workers in a fast-food outlet on the one hand, and, say, insurance workers on the other. While McDonald's workers played a more subordinate role in serving customers, insurance workers 'were told that they controlled their own destinies and were urged to cultivate the qualities of aggressiveness, persistence, and a belief in themselves. While success might require that they take on a deferential manner, it was seen as a matter of skill in manipulating situations, not as servility' (Leidner, 1993: 117).

In other words, insurance workers are led to cultivate aggression in getting customers to buy their products, but not so overtly that the customer perceives their behaviour as such and is put off. That's quite a skill to acquire, and how far it would go in another service sector is a debatable point. Hence the aesthetic labour required from a McDonald's worker is clearly different from the aesthetic labour required from an insurance worker: 'Aesthetic labour is the selling of one's embodied "face", or approved social attributes, to create and preserve a professional and/or corporate image – often described as "looking good and sounding right"' (Sheane, 2012: 145).

How you 'look good and sound right' in one service sector may not be right in another.

Emotional labour

'Looking good and sounding right' leads us, finally, to consider emotional labour, which is related to aesthetic labour, but raises a different set of issues. Aesthetic labour is how you look, how you appear at a particular moment, but emotional labour refers to the way in which you use your emotions to relate to customers and clients. Arlie Hochschild, one of the pioneers in this field, defines emotional labour as 'the management of feeling to create publicly observable facial and bodily display; emotional labour is sold for a wage and therefore has exchange value' (Hochschild, 2012 [1983]: 7). Humans are always emotional, but it becomes 'emotion work' when employers earn money from the emotional labour of workers.

Emotional labour, basically, involves self-discipline and controlling your real feelings at the workplace. The implications of this for the worker depend very much again on the sector. Some examples help to establish this point. A nurse, especially a trainee nurse, might find some sights in hospitals quite repulsive, but can't show the patient that he's repelled by an injury that he's helping to treat in Accident and Emergency. He has to learn to control his reaction of disgust and create a professional persona that is calm and collected in order to instil confidence in the patient. Waiting staff equally have to hide anger and irritation at demanding and thoughtless customers, something that might require real effort in a busy restaurant. A university lecturer has to deliver a class to her students even though her husband might be seeking a divorce or her child is ill in hospital. She dominates her feelings of upset and anxiety because her professional duty is to attend to her students. Shop assistants are meant to be happy and smiley – you'll sometimes see notices saying 'No grouchy staff here!' How serious, though, is the joke? Emotional labour is about control and it's a significant requirement when working in the service sector, with appropriate variations.

Some further examples are compared and contrasted by Hochschild in her book, *The Managed Heart*. She examines the conditions of airline flight attendants and debt collectors. The archetypal image of a flight attendant is of a young, attractive woman who is friendly and closely attentive to the demands of the passengers. Her embodied labour displays beauty, sex and submissiveness. Airlines used to dismiss flight attendants once they reached a certain age on the grounds that they were allegedly 'too old' for the role (a practice now prohibited across the US and the EU). However, a cursory glance at advertisements for airlines or an internet search for 'flight attendants' reveals still today that their stock image remains that of young, smiling women.

By contrast, the role of debt collector embodies an entirely different notion of aesthetic and emotional labour because debt collectors are meant to be the archetypal male – aggressive, brutal, domineering and persistent, someone who is going to terrorise you into paying your debts. The role still involves aesthetic and emotional labour, but is obviously carried out under very different conditions and expectations. Flight attendants and debt collectors are obviously poles apart in their workplace functions; nevertheless, the basic idea in each case is the same, that you have to look a certain way, that you have to 'emote' in a certain way.

Emotional labour exists wherever and whenever management sets standards on what feelings you can and can't display that requires you to conceal or mask how you are really feeling. Management might provide appropriate training to help workers cope with that (Bolton and Boyd, 2003). Company 'smile schools' can be found at one end of the spectrum, although rules of emotional behaviour may prove difficult to teach.

Emotional display is culturally diverse, but pressures of globalisation, international competition and the spread of global US brands, such as Starbucks, KFC and McDonald's, create pressure to express 'standardised' customer care even though cultural norms governing interaction such as eye contact, levels of formality and submissive behaviour vary greatly across the continents. Eye contact, for example, may be seen as friendly in one culture but impolite or forward in another (Tipton, 2008).

At the other end of the spectrum is anger management. For example, if you are working as a tenant liaison officer in a local authority housing department, you may have to deal face to face with people coming to see you about rent arrears. They may frequently be angry and upset because they are in debt and fear eviction. How do you cope with that on a daily basis? Training in anger management might help, because you – as an employee – need to learn techniques to help you handle potentially abusive meetings in order to control your own feelings and ensure you show tenants the respect they deserve. On railway platforms and in shops and elsewhere, you will often see placards that state 'We will not tolerate abuse of our staff', and rightly so, obviously. If you are a customer-facing member of staff, you need to know how to handle potentially abusive situations, although the requirements of your working conditions go well beyond dealing with harassment. They also involve – to a greater or lesser degree – the extent to which you come across as friendly and the extent to which your eye contact and body language are demonstrating interest in the customer: all these things become areas of control. In other words, your ability to empathise and sympathise become marketable features of your labour power. They become part of the way in which you act as an employee, and you may be more or less successful in doing so.

Resistance and unionisation

One difficulty with this discussion of aesthetic and emotional labour is that it tends to underestimate workers' role distance. In Chapter 4, on conflict and resistance at work, we saw that we all tend to resist things that we don't like or don't want to do. Strict requirements for aesthetic and emotional labour may encourage the emergence of subcultures or at least behaviour that is anti-customer or anti-client. A simple example is one of our Chinese students, who worked part time on a beauty counter in a large department store in London and admitted that she would occasionally insult rude customers to her other Chinese colleagues in Mandarin, knowing perfectly well that the customers wouldn't understand. That's a natural way in which employees might show their independence towards unpleasant customers as part of a shared subculture of resistance. We are all capable of finding imaginative ways to demonstrate our resistance to our employers and customers in difficult work situations, although, as we have already pointed out, these situations vary greatly sector by sector, workplace by workplace.

Another difficulty with this discussion is that emotion is transactional. That is, if somebody smiles at us, we tend to smile back. If somebody is aggressive towards us, we tend to be aggressive back. Given that emotional responses are often shared in this way, this becomes an issue for workers. If your customers or clients are polite, then being polite back won't be so hard. The real problem is when they're not polite, and you might find yourself otherwise getting drawn into an argument, which, of course, as the employee, you mustn't. The result for some service workers can be stress and even burnout. Some people may be more able to deal with stressful situations than others, but some kinds of service work can be upsetting (particularly those that focus on the needs of potentially angry or disturbed clients). Many service sector companies support their employees in managing stress, but it remains an issue for many workers (Nixon, 2009).

Finally, we must consider the role of trade unions in service work, and the extent to which service workers are able to organise themselves. Union organisation might be seen as contrary to the kind of persona that service workers are trying to present, who may feel that there are constraints on the kind of collectivism that can be developed when customers and clients are involved in the employment relationship as well. Having said that, many service workers do join unions. Many teachers in the UK belong to the National Education Union, among others, and many lecturers in higher and further education belong to the University and College Union, both of which have been involved in major collective disputes in the recent past. The Royal College of Nursing, which straddles the boundary between union and professional body, and the Union of Shop, Distributive and Allied Workers, have large and active memberships.

Cabin crew at British Airways (BA) are also organised in unions and have been involved in collective disputes following privatisation. Changes in the company, the decline in quality and intensifying pressure at work have distanced cabin crew from their service ethos. One member observes: 'before it used to be your presence, your uniform standard, was very important. That has been taken over by a product ... it's a false performance because you know that you're not going to be able to deliver the standard and quality.... I'll smile at you but I'm just about to hit you with a baseball bat.' Another views customer interaction as part of BA's 'product': 'Hard product is the tangible thing, like seats, trays, cups, the food, in-flight entertainment. Soft is how it's delivered, you, your personality, your interaction.... Yes, I would say we were part of the product. We complement and support the product' (quoted in Taylor and Moore, 2015: 87). Service workers may, then, come to feel as much part of the productive process as any other, at which point their identification with company aims and objectives may come under threat.

Concluding comments

Employment relations in the service sector involve a triadic relationship between worker, employer and customer or client (or whoever the third party happens to be). In many services, the customer has been drafted into control management through various feedback systems, some of them electronic. Service working is everywhere, but the nature of aesthetic and emotional labour remains variable, because it depends on the requirements of individual sectors (from airlines to healthcare, from teaching to debt collection) and on the individual worker's capacity to comply. And the requirements of service work within even one sector – such as catering – will vary globally too, as customer expectations of service in

China or Japan may well vary greatly from those in the US or the UK. Emotional labour cannot be entirely commercialised because we all retain a discretion that allows us to distance ourselves from the kind of work we're doing. However, emotional labour can come under technical control – hence the use of techniques that range from the 'smile machine' to anger management.

The underlying issue here is how service workers manage these roles and their self-image within them. Many of you may find yourselves in these positions, if you haven't already. If you have worked in a bar or restaurant or as a receptionist, for example, you will have your own experience of this kind of employment relationship and the stresses it may create. The way in which we, as individuals, manage that kind of relationship, and our own personal integrity at the same time within the pressures we face as service workers, remains a significant challenge in the workplace.

Some questions to think about

1. Discuss the difference between dyadic and triadic work relations.

2. How might the development of aesthetic and emotional labour in the service sector alter the relationships between employer, worker and customer? Give some examples from your own experience of different service sectors.

3. Think about the ways in which employers attempt to control workers who use aesthetic and emotional labour. Should managers have a say in how employees feel at the workplace?

4. Should there be more transparency and critical evaluation about so-called 'customer control'?

Further reading

Bolton, S.C. and Boyd, C. (2003) 'Trolley dolly or skilled emotion manager? Moving on from Hochschild's Managed Heart', *Work, Employment & Society*, 17(2): 289–308. [Discussion of the different practices of emotional work.]

Nixon, D. (2009) '"I can't put a smiley face on": Working-class masculinity, emotional labour and service work in the New Economy', *Gender, Work and Organization*, 16(3): 300–22. [Review of the gender and class dimensions of practising service work.]

Warhurst, C. and Nickson, D. (2007a) 'Employee experience of aesthetic labour in retail and hospitality', *Work, Employment & Society*, 21(1): 103–20. [A challenge to the idea that service work requires the worker to be subordinate to the customer.]

11

Migrant Workers

In our last two chapters, we analysed flexible working and the significance of service work for human resource management (HRM). In this chapter we turn our attention to the characteristics of many of those who disproportionately work flexible patterns and perform service sector occupations, particularly in lower paid jobs. Migrant labour is an extremely important aspect of HRM, particularly in an age of globalisation, as people increasingly move from one country to another to improve their prospects, send remittances home or seek asylum, among other reasons.

Migration remains a politically controversial issue, but we begin our chapter by establishing that it has always taken place, although increasingly so with the development of global capitalism. We then examine the push/pull reasons for migration as well as the perception of migrant workers as hard working and reliable. We focus on two dimensions of migrant labour that are very important for HRM: (1) the extent to which migrants become integrated into domestic labour markets and workforces; and (2) the reasons why some groups of migrants remain non-integrated and culturally independent. These two categories pose different challenges for HRM, and we explore the issues through case studies of agricultural/horticultural workers, cockle-pickers and workers in fashion retail. We conclude with the observation that we all, as consumers, may unwittingly connive in the exploitation of migrant workers, a point that leads into Chapter 12, on corporate social responsibility.

Patterns of migration

Many of the issues surrounding migration reveal the hidden stories that migrants have to tell about themselves. However, in terms of HRM, we need to focus on the productive capability and the kind of contribution that migrants make to the societies in which they find themselves, and how human resources (HR) managers attempt to manage migrant workers very often alongside domestic workers. The first point to stress is that migration has existed since time immemorial (Harris, 2007), although it has arguably become more pressing as an issue over recent years. In 1970, a time when national economies were more protectionist, there were just under 84.5 million international migrants, then 2.3% of the global population. However, by 2019, following a period of neoliberalism and globalisation, the number had risen to 272 million international migrants, about 3.5% of the global population of 7.7 billion (IOM, 2020). Globally, this is not a major increase in percentages, but there is a concentration of migration into developed economies.

Figure 11.1 summarises the principal migration flows over the 20th century, particularly from emerging countries into industrialised countries. There have been major migrations, particularly to North America, in the earlier part of the 20th century, but also within Europe as a result of two world wars. More recently, there has been migration from the West Indies to the UK, and, as a result of the Vietnam War, emigration from Vietnam. In the 21st century, we continue to witness migration from Africa and the Middle East into Europe, and from Central and South America into North America, largely as a result of conflicts, economic pressures and climate change, among other reasons. Migrants are between one-third and four-fifths of the population in the Gulf States – labour flows following political and economic development (Fargues, 2011). India is the biggest sender of migrants, the US the biggest recipient. What Figure 11.1 demonstrates above all is that migration, however its impacts may be manipulated by unprincipled politicians, is nothing new at all.

Figure 11.1: Major 20th-century migrations

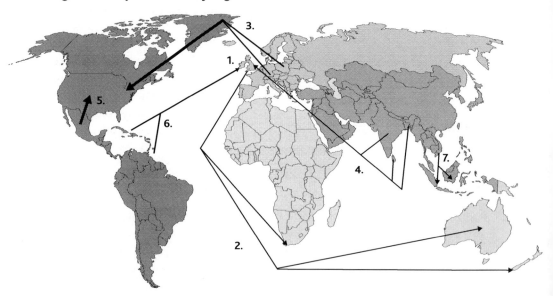

Key:
1. 1918–19: Eastern Europe to USA and Canada
2. 1918: Britain to Australia, South Africa and New Zealand
3. 1940: European Jews to USA
4. 1947: India, Sri Lanka and Pakistan to UK
5. 1950: Mexico to USA
6. 1950–60: West Indies to UK
7. 1975: Vietnam to Malaysia

In 2020, there were 447 million inhabitants living in the European Union (EU) (excluding the UK), of whom 37 million (8.3%) were born outside the EU. This was a lower percentage than most other developed countries (Australia: 30.1%; US: 15.3%; UK: 13.8%) – although if migrants among EU countries were included, the share would rise to 12.2%. In the same year, 8.6 million non-EU citizens were employed in the EU labour market of 189.1 million workers aged from 20 to 64 – 4.6% of the total. The *average employment rate* of the working-age population was lower for non-EU citizens (57.6%) than for EU citizens (73.3%), although many count as 'essential workers' (European Commission, 2021).

In this chapter we focus on migration to and from the UK because this book is being published in the UK, and we have to start somewhere. Figure 11.2 illustrates migration into and out of the UK specifically from other EU member states. It's instructive because migration was one of the main issues in the referendum in June 2016 that led to Brexit (the UK's withdrawal from the EU). We discover, first of all, that there are about 1.2 million UK citizens who live or work in other EU member states, and there are just over 3 million EU citizens who live or work in the UK. So there are major flows of migration in both directions.

Figure 11.2a shows a map of Europe that is distorted according to the number of UK citizens living in those countries. So, for example, we find that Ireland becomes bloated because there are such a large number of UK citizens living there. In the same way, Spain becomes bloated because there are similarly large numbers of UK citizens living in Spain, mainly those who have gone there for retirement. A large number of UK citizens may also be found in Cyprus. On the other hand, in Northern Europe, there are very few – Sweden and the Baltic States have shrunk to almost nothing because they host so few UK migrants. The map therefore illustrates the patterns in which UK migration has taken place.

By contrast, Figure 11.2b shows the number of migrants from other EU countries living in the UK. Poland has swollen because there are comparatively a large number of Poles living in the UK. Spain has also grown, but not nearly as much as Portugal, because there are comparatively more Portuguese in the UK than Spanish. The two-way flow of migration between Ireland and the UK is striking. The Baltic States (Estonia, Lithuania and Latvia) are also very large because of the number of their citizens living in the UK, but Italy is rather small, along with the Nordic countries, because there are rather few. Figure 11.2 therefore draws our attention to the ways in which migratory flows take place. We need to analyse these patterns in order to understand their implications for HRM.

One implication we can note immediately is the effect that Brexit is likely to have on the ability of UK employers to recruit workers from the EU. Some sectors, such as hospitality, will clearly face shortages in labour supply, as Box 11.1 illustrates.

Figure 11.2: EU migration to and from the UK – mapping how UK and (other) EU citizens move between the UK and the rest of the EU

(a) Cartogram showing EU countries resized according to the proportion of UK citizens living there

Brits abroad vs EU migrants
to Britain

High

Low

Number of UK citizens who moved
to an EU country compared to
citizens from that country who
moved to the UK

(b) Cartogram showing EU countries resized according to the proportion of citizens from there living in the UK

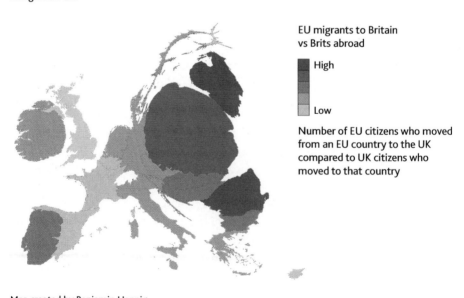

EU migrants to Britain
vs Brits abroad

High

Low

Number of EU citizens who moved
from an EU country to the UK
compared to UK citizens who
moved to that country

Map created by Benjamin Hennig
Source: Views of the World (2017)

BOX 11.1: UK HOSPITALITY SECTOR 'HEAVILY DEPENDENT ON EUROPEAN WORKERS'

The hospitality and leisure industry employs 4.5 million people in the UK over 180,000 businesses. UK Hospitality (the former British Hospitality Association [BHA]) published a press release in 2017 that outlined the challenges it faces over the period until 2029, including a recruitment gap:

> Businesses in the [UK hospitality] sector are anticipating a recruitment gap of over a million jobs by 2029, according to a report by the BHA and KPMG earlier this year, which would mean the industry would need to recruit 60,000 UK workers in addition to sustained recruitment of 200,000 more per annum to meet the demands of growth. Filling these openings would likely be impossible without hiring migrant workers. Firms are heavily reliant on European workers, with half of CEOs reporting their workforce as 25–50% European, with more than a third of those businesses hiring EU citizens to fill 50–75% of their workforce. (UK Hospitality, 2017)

Reasons for migration

Why do people leave their home, family and friends, and their culture and possibly language, to go and live and work abroad in unfamiliar and possibly arduous conditions? There are broadly three sets of individual motivations, or 'pull factors' (Caro et al, 2015). The first set involves 'target earners', people who leave their home country on a temporary basis, probably to earn enough money to send back to their families in the form of remittances. This is a common motivator for some migrants who go to another country – probably one that's more industrialised – for perhaps a year or two, where they hope to earn more than they would have done in their home country.

Second, migrants may be seeking careers with the prospect of longer term or permanent settlement in another country. People, particularly graduates, may wish to pursue an international career when they leave further or higher education and go to work for a multinational company, with the chance for cross-border mobility. Their motivation is rather different from target earners because they are seeking a longer term structural change in the nature of their work through a career abroad.

Finally, there are so-called 'drifters' who, as the term suggests, are those who decide to move from one place to another, earning a living as the fancy takes them. (It should be noted that there are other non-economic reasons for migration, too, such as joining family members, taking educational courses and seeking asylum; see European Commission, 2021.)

Among these motivations, we should also add that some migration is arranged through multinational companies. That is, career-seekers in particular may find themselves engaged on international assignments as expatriates through the company for which they work. It is unlikely that an expatriate is integrated into the local labour market. If you are an expatriate working for a multinational company, you may well find that you live in an expatriate community in another country and that your children (if they travel with you) go to an international school, but then the intention never was that you should integrate into the culture and institutions of your host country (Moore, 2017). On the other hand, other types of migrant may become highly integrated (we return to this question of integration below).

Along with these individual motivations, there are also structural reasons for migration ('push factors'). The world is extremely unequal and characterised by poverty and wars in many regions. We think of conflicts across the Middle East, particularly in Syria, that have created economic, political and social turbulence in those countries and provoked emigration from them. Russia's invasion of Ukraine in February 2022 was predicted to produce between 5–7 million refugees into neighbouring countries (France 24, 2022).

Climate change is undoubtedly motivating emigration from parts of Africa and elsewhere as well. There is also increased demand among employers, particularly in the industrialised countries of Europe and North America, for cheap labour. The two developments coalesce to mean that employers don't have far to look for migrants who will work in certain sectors of the economy, particularly low-paid ones, such as agriculture, care homes, construction, cleaning and hospitality, where there's a continual downwards pressure on pay and conditions to gain cost advantages. And, of course, we connive in this because we, as consumers, buy the goods and services produced by cheap, migrant workers, and so benefit from companies' success in keeping down their wage costs in this way. So the migrant worker, the employer, but also the consumer – that's to say, all of us – form a set of interlocking pressures that result in a system that's generally unequal and hostile to migrant labour.

Perceptions of migrant labour

Figure 11.3 reproduces a chart drawn up by an American steel company, the Central Tube Company, Pittsburgh, in 1925, which lists, down the vertical column, different ethnic and national backgrounds, and along the horizontal row, different occupations that are required in the steel mill. The chart today should come with a health warning, as it is blatantly racist. The colour of the squares depicts the 'racial adaptability to various types of plant work', and are filled in either white (good adaptability), grey (fair) or black (poor).

Across the top row, white Americans rate as 'good' or 'fair' across all jobs and conditions – surprise, surprise – with the clear implication that they can be employed in any job: picking and shovelling, concrete work, hod-carrying, track-repairing, blacksmithing – everything, whether the job involves hot and dry, cold and wet or dusty conditions, among others. The chart ranks 36 nationalities and races in the same way, with widely contrasting results. The Irish and Lithuanians

Figure 11.3: Employment chart of the Central Tube Company, Pittsburgh (1925)

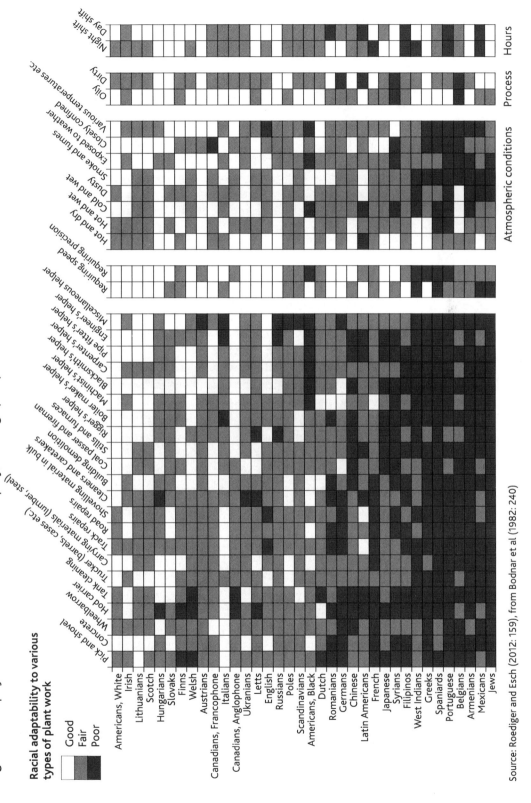

Source: Roediger and Esch (2012: 159), from Bodnar et al (1982: 240)

(in fact, Northern Europeans generally) don't do so badly, but the English feature about halfway down (the Irish, Scots and Welsh fare much better). The English are particularly bad, apparently, at track repairs and shovelling material in bulk. Lower down the chart, there appear workers from Southern Europe and the Middle East, and then West Indians, Greeks, Spaniards, Portuguese and Belgians. Armenians, Mexicans and Jews come out bottom on all these criteria.

Roediger and Esch (2012) document the highly racialised depictions of groups over time, in which emotive claims were made about immigrant and racial groups' cultures, desires, histories, intragroup enmities, physical limitations, work ethics and national characters: 'These claims were articulated by practitioners, such as plantation management experts, "race psychologists", industrial psychologists and engineers. These cheerleaders for racial difference and inferiority can be regarded as the tacticians of modern control systems, categorizing and ranking people, coding spaces and ushering in new supervisory practices' (Smith, 2014: 187). Roediger and Esch (2012) outline many national stereotypes based on crude assumptions: the Germans are seen as 'placid, to love detail, to be effective on precision work'; Italians are considered to be the 'most inefficient of all races' (but later, as the 'most efficient of all races'); the Irish possess a 'cheeriness coupled with occasional terrifying outbursts of authority', making them good foremen; the Greeks and West Indians are believed to be best suited for extremely hot factory jobs because they do well in heat and humidity; and blonds (whites) are well suited to managerial positions because 'their ancestors developed through surviving harsh conditions over centuries'. We could add that, in the construction of the east–west railway in the US, Chinese labourers were intensively employed, as 'their distaste for drunkenness and fighting, as well as their commitment to the work, impressed their employers' (Chiu and Kirk, 2014: 510).

The chart reveals an astonishing way of perceiving immigrant labour, but it dates back only 100 years – and 100 years really isn't that long. While no one would dare produce a chart like this now, the question is how far such attitudes persist, or attitudes like them.

To answer this question, we can examine the way in which temporary employment agencies trade nowadays on alleged national differences when they advertise temporary labour. Interface employment agency, for example, represents women workers from Central and Eastern Europe as: 'intelligent, professionally trained, immaculately groomed, multilingual typists who are qualified in all Microsoft programs … well-mannered, articulate, ideal ephemeral staff, competent in professionally representing the face of your company in any spoken language' (Samaluk, 2014: 170).

Another recruitment agency stresses the likely religion of East European workers: 'Within Eastern Europe, Poles make up 50% of the population eligible to work in the UK – 98% Catholic by faith, strong family values.' The implication is that, as a Catholic, you are likely to have strong family values, and so you are going to be dependable and reliable. You are going to look after your family, and so you will act responsibly and comply with your employer's demands.

That, at least, appears to be the subliminal message (Samaluk, 2014, 2016). The European Recruitment Agency, another contemporary site, says of migrants from Central and Eastern Europe: 'Our skilled workforce are multi-talented, extremely hardworking ... they are ambassadors for their countries.' Here is the idea that an East European is not just a worker, but also a representative of his or her country. The Acorn website boasts 'Polish workers, Polish jobs, Polish full satisfaction guaranteed' and the 'UK's army of Polish workers have the reputation of reliability and fair prices'. Further agencies refer to the 'Polish touch: Polish plumbers, electricians, bricklayers' and so on. 'The reputation of Polish construction workers, nannies and caregivers is so high that other Eastern Europeans sometimes say they're Polish to increase their chances of being hired' (Samaluk, 2014: 171). McGregor (2007), in contrast to this selling of national stereotypes, examines why middle-class Zimbabweans in the UK are working in the social care sector in jobs below their levels of education and training, highlighting gender and racial divisions in labour markets.

All these cases bear witness to ethnic or national stereotyping in one form or another. The whole issue here about the reliability or otherwise of migrant labour isn't just a matter for the Pittsburgh Steel Company in 1925; it's an idea that's still alive and well in contemporary UK. In other words, the perception of migrant labour is complex.

Integration of migrant workers

One reason for this complexity involves the degree to which migrant workers are integrated into the domestic labour market. Employers in the UK and the US often have a preference for migrant workers because they are perceived as being cheaper, more reliable and more hardworking than domestic labour. The reason for this reputation lies with their precarious status in the receiving country. If you're a migrant worker, particularly if you're illegal with no papers, but even if you're legal with everything in order, you may not speak the language very well, or even at all, you may not have much cultural awareness and you may not understand how the various national administrative systems fit together – employment agencies, police, local authorities, taxation and social security, among others – that citizens of the country take for granted. Your unfamiliarity with them places you at a disadvantage on the labour market in relation to domestic workers, and employers can make use of this not just by paying low wages, but also by demanding unsocial hours and imposing poorer conditions (Castles, 2010).

In the early days of a new job, migrant workers, for example working on public transport or in a care home, will be careful to stick to the rules and comply with instructions, because – as migrants – they are likely to feel at a disadvantage in the labour market, particularly if they are in precarious employment and fear dismissal (Baxter-Reid, 2016). However, as they become integrated, they become more like the domestic labour force in adopting the same reference points and behaving in similar ways, not least in speaking up and joining trade unions.

Gradually, the kind of benefit that employers initially hoped for in hiring migrant labour – good behaviour and compliance – dissolves as migrants become absorbed into the predominant norms, standards and values that they find around them in the domestic labour force. This process, which has been called the 'built-in obsolescence of migrants' (MacKenzie and Forde, 2009), is illustrated in Box 11.2.

> **BOX 11.2: MIGRANT WORKERS GRADUALLY FIND THEIR COMFORT ZONE**
>
> Migrant workers don't fully accept the 'good worker' rhetoric for a variety of reasons, including high levels of education, personal aspiration and employers' strategies, such as discrimination. Hazel Baxter-Reid also points out that migrants in time get absorbed into the domestic labour market:
>
> > CEE [Central and Eastern European] workers were clearly the employee of choice [for low-pay employers in the UK] when there were recruitment and retention problems because of their availability and willingness to work. However, the recession resulted in a looser labour market and decreased demand for services. This led employers to expect increased work effort from workers and also reduced the demand for CEE workers. Additionally, all managers noticed a change in work ethic over time: "When they first started coming, I thought they were really keen workers. Superb workers.... But then I found once they get in their comfort zone things change. You find they get into the same league as the rest of them" (Night shift production manager). (Baxter-Reid, 2016: 344)

In other words, migrants aren't essentially more productive or compliant than domestic labour. That advantage, if it is an advantage, begins to disappear over time with their socialisation. Much evidence indicates that migrants (especially second and third generation) integrate into the country and 'normalise' by adopting the attitudes and characteristics of homegrown workers (Piore, 1979; Waldinger and Lichter, 2003; Meardi, 2007; MacKenzie and Forde, 2009; Thompson et al, 2013).

Non-integration of migrant workers

By contrast, there is another category of migrant workers who do not integrate, the so-called 'disembedded' or 'non-integrated' workers, who are particularly at risk of exploitation. This category remains disembedded from the domestic labour force, possibly because of ethnic segregation. Minority ethnic groups often tend to live in the same areas of cities (for example, in the case of London, many Cypriots live in Wood Green, South Koreans in New Malden and Indians in Southall). In these cases, they retain their ethnic identity but are integrated through their employment into the broader London economy. This creates a hybrid situation, where immigrant communities live and work in slightly different circumstances, employed alongside British colleagues during working hours, but going home and socialising with family and friends from the same ethnic background during non-working hours.

However, there are other types of migrant worker who are totally disembedded from wider society. We examine three cases in this chapter: EU migrants in UK agriculture and horticulture; Chinese cockle-pickers in the UK; and Chinese fashion and retail workers in Italy. Each case exposes some of the challenges and risks presented by migrant labour.

EU migrants: agriculture (UK)

Until Brexit on 1 January 2021, migrant workers from the EU had revived significant sectors of the UK economy, not least agriculture and horticulture, which had been largely abandoned by domestic workers. In Lincolnshire, for example, many farms depend on migrant pickers from the EU while in the southwest, flowers are cultivated largely by EU migrants. Domestic UK labour has largely deserted such areas of work because of low pay, lengthy commuting distances and arduous working conditions (Strauss, 2013). This particular type of employment is characterised by spatial segregation – that is, migrants are generally given accommodation on the same farm where they live and work, and so tend to find themselves in geographically isolated rural communities, probably some distance from the nearest town. Hence they form quite homogeneous ethnic and national groupings that are distinctive from the local population and generally made more acute because of language barriers. Many are likely to be 'target earners', or transient workers motivated by the chance to earn more money in a higher wage economy.

Migrant workers in this context use their *mobility power*, if they are able to move, to chase higher wages and better conditions, rather than settling in one location (Smith, 2006; Alberti et al, 2013; Alberti, 2014). Such migrant workers have no real inclination to integrate into the domestic labour market. They have probably been recruited through one of the employment agencies that specialises in Eastern European workers working in agricultural sectors. There will be no opportunity to join a trade union, and rights to employment protection are minimal. There is also the risk that some may be in the UK illegally (especially following Brexit) – and some may even have been trafficked, in which case they have no rights at all unless discovered by the police.

There has been great pressure on supermarkets to reduce costs, which affects terms and conditions in agriculture and horticulture. Price competition among supermarkets on food prices has led to greater intensification of production, particularly in farm work, with long working days, restricted time off and downward pressure on pay (EFRA, 2003). It has also meant employer-dependent accommodation, so workers don't have to commute – they live where they work, which further reduces costs for the employer. Use of temporary agencies also generally squeezes out regular work. As supermarket customers, we all tend to connive in this.

The following comment from a government report, going back to 2003, makes the point that food in supermarkets has to be accurately labelled – for example, with details of additives, preservatives and allergens – as we are rightly concerned about the effects of what we eat and drink on our long-term health.

> Intense price competition and the short time-scales between orders from the supermarkets and deliveries to them put great pressure on suppliers who have little opportunity or incentive to check the legality of the labour which helps them meet these orders. Supermarkets go to great lengths to ensure that the labels on their products are accurate, for example, whether they are organic or contain certain products. We believe they should pay equal attention to the conditions under which their produce is harvested and packed, and label it accordingly. (EFRA, 2003, quoted in Strauss, 2013: 189)

The report specifies that food products should also contain a statement declaring the conditions under which they were produced. It might have to declare, for example, that the workers were paid at the proper rate, that their agreed terms and conditions were observed and that their employer paid the appropriate taxes and insurance contributions. This is an important point because, while we regulate the quality of our food, we don't regulate the quality of the conditions under which workers produce it. And that's because their labour is invisible, we don't see it and we rarely think about the conditions that workers have endured to produce the cheap food and drink that we all like to consume. These are issues we follow up in the next chapter, on corporate social responsibility.

Chinese migrants: cockle-picking (UK)

Deregulation of labour markets in the UK, which accelerated under the Conservative government of Margaret Thatcher in the 1980s, led to the return of gangmasters to UK agriculture following their virtual disappearance by the 1950s. Gangmasters are contractors of labour, mainly in agriculture and horticulture, who recruit mainly migrant workers, and who are often responsible for low or incorrect pay, poor accommodation and the use of undocumented workers, who may or may not be illegal. Debt bondage has become increasingly common in these sectors: workers pay the employer a sum of money, for example, to cover transport costs from their home country to another to work, and then have to pay off their debt through working, which means that until they pay off that debt, they are unable to leave their jobs. The whole point about a 'free market' in labour is that we are all ostensibly able to come and go in our jobs: we can choose which job to accept, whether we want to change employers and to hand in our notice when we wish. However, debt bondage is not free labour, as workers are prevented from leaving and may be subject to threats, harassment and even violence. This conjures up an unpleasant picture (Strauss, 2013).

The second example of non-integrated labour that we examine in this chapter focuses on Chinese cockle-pickers. This is a significant and tragic case, because it involves 23 Chinese cockle-pickers who drowned in 2004 when they were picking cockles from Morecambe Bay (northwest England). It reveals the role of gangmasters in exploiting highly vulnerable groups of workers who had come from an emerging economy, China, to earn money in the UK. In this case, the workers were prepared to take terrible risks that eventually led to their deaths. They were being paid very low wages and were undocumented, conditions that frequently prevail in these transient segments of the labour market.

Cockles are picked by prodding for them with a fork in the sand, and they are then put into a bucket to sell on to the wholesaler. Morecambe Bay is a huge expanse of sand where the tides sweep in extremely rapidly. If you don't understand them correctly, they can catch you miles out on the beach and you're trapped. That's exactly what happened on 5 February 2004, and 23 men and women drowned as a result. The tragedy led to the formation of the Gangmasters' Licensing Authority in 2005, now the Gangmasters & Labour Abuse Authority (GLAA), which requires all gangmasters to be licensed. It became a criminal offence to operate without a licence, and there are penalties imposed if you break the law. The sectors regulated by the GLAA cover agriculture, horticulture, food processing and packaging, and shellfish gathering. Forestry was covered until 2013.

This case demonstrates the role that regulation can play, even in liberal market economies, in improving working conditions. That's what we're really talking about here. Legal gangmasters have to prove to the GLAA that they pay the national minimum wage as well as relevant taxes, National Insurance and value-added tax (VAT) – in other words, that they are integrated into the UK employment and National Insurance systems. They must also show that they don't subject their workers to debt bondage, harsh treatment or intimidation; that they provide suitable accommodation with washing and toilet facilities; that they respect employment rights, including hours of work and time off, as well as health and safety regulations; and also, of course, that they do not employ illegal or undocumented workers. The intention is that, even among disembedded migrant labour, there is a sphere of regulation that's designed to guarantee their pay and conditions.

Evaluation of the effectiveness of the GLAA is rather more difficult. There are around 1,000 licensed gangmasters in the UK. In 2019/20, the GLAA identified 297 potential breaches of its standards, which led to 23 revocations of licence, three with immediate effect (GLAA, 2021: 7). While it removed over 15,000 potential victims from control of their exploiters, only one breach of its standards led to a successful prosecution (GLAA, 2021: 23). Over the period 2008–19, there had been 96 successful prosecutions, with a peak of 26 in 2012, but this rate has since tailed off. The revocation of licences remained fairly stable until 2011, at around 30 a year or more, but has also declined since then. Whether these figures demonstrate effectiveness or not, the formation of the GLAA at the very least means that there is now a mechanism in the UK for investigating gangmasters who are operating without a licence and not guaranteeing the conditions of their workers.

Chinese migrants: fashion and retail (Italy)

The position of non-integrated migrants is also similar in other countries. We now turn to Italy, where we examine the case of Chinese entrepreneurs and workers in Prato in the region of Tuscany. In Prato, there is an industrial district where the Chinese own 50% of all manufacturing businesses, of which 85% is in clothing and fashion (Ceccagno, 2015). This constitutes a high proportion of clothing production in Italy, and has attracted a continuing influx of Chinese workers into the area. Workers sleep on the premises to reduce costs. With no commuting, they can work longer hours because they are on call earlier and can leave later. As a result of this system of low-cost production, it has become difficult for domestic Italian producers to compete as they face higher labour costs and therefore higher production costs.

Above all, this system allows for a kind of 'internal' outsourcing. Outsourcing takes place, typically, when a company manufactures a product in another country to take advantage of lower labour costs. The UK entrepreneur Sir James Dyson provides a well-known example (see Box 1.1). In the case of the Prato industrial district in Italy, there's a kind of internal or local outsourcing that's taking place. Italian retailers contract with Chinese producers within Italy to manufacture garments at a cheaper rate than they would get from domestic Italian producers. So they outsource to non-domestic producers, but within Italy, because this is a self-contained industrial district. In other words, a non-integrated labour force – because the Chinese are disembedded from wider Italian society in a kind of enclave – manufactures garments for the Italian market, and indeed for the international market, at a much lower cost than would be possible elsewhere in Italy. The point is that, again, we generally connive in this because we like to buy cheap clothes. Every time we congratulate ourselves on buying a cheap T-shirt, the reason behind its cheapness is invisible to us – it's been produced by workers who are working long hours on low rates of pay in conditions of inadequate health and safety. Indeed, on 1 December 2013, seven Chinese migrants died in a fire that swept through the building where they worked and lived in the industrial district of Prato, just as 23 cockle-pickers had died in Morecambe Bay (Geddes et al, 2013).

In this particular example of Prato, garment manufacturing has become an area of production that has been *ethnicised*. It's controlled by a particular ethnic group within a dominant culture, with all the consequences that this implies for the disembedding of the workers involved.

Concluding comments

There's nothing strange or unusual about migration. It's always taken place, but it has become politicised for a variety of reasons, largely owing to the rise of populist politics across many countries of the world following the financial crisis of 2008/09. Think of the election of Donald Trump as US president in 2016, for example, or the anti-immigration referendum campaign in the UK that led to Brexit.

Migrant workers very often become integrated into domestic labour markets. After a while, they assimilate dominant norms and values, particularly when they speak the language. For example, a Polish worker employed in Glasgow learns English and is gradually socialised into Scottish work culture, even if they continue to speak Polish at home and prefer Polish food. However, certain groups of workers may remain disembedded and never actually integrate in that way, and they're the ones who are most at risk in HR terms. They form enclaves of what might be termed 'new production systems' in agriculture, horticulture and fashion, among other sectors. These systems are not transient, as they reproduce themselves over time because of the way in which they operate structurally within the economy.

Trade unions have very little influence in such circumstances. Certainly, once immigrants become integrated, then, of course, they may join trade unions along with anyone else. Many Central and Eastern European workers, for example, are members of unions in the UK, but in those areas of employment characterised by non-integrated or disembedded migrants, unions find themselves kept out.

Future trends in migration will depend largely on the immigration policies that national governments pursue. In an age of crisis – such as financial crisis, populist politics, climate change, Brexit and global pandemics – it seems likely that the age of free movement of labour is drawing to an end. The introduction of a points-based immigration system in the UK following Brexit imposes strict limits on immigration into the UK from the EU and the world beyond. Nevertheless, when we examine the conditions of migrants within an HRM or productive context, the question remains how to prevent exploitation. Regulation is one way, with the introduction of the GLAA in the UK as an attempt to come to grips with controlling migrants' conditions.

The role of trade unions and non-governmental organisations is also very important. The next chapter, on corporate social responsibility, examines their role in greater detail, as well as the part that HR managers themselves can play in checking supply chains. When a company locates a new source for its supplies, HRM should be involved in checking their labour conditions, a function of HRM that is currently undervalued and underutilised. Cost and prompt delivery times are not enough – workers' pay rates and terms and conditions must be investigated at the same time. Hence the area of responsibility of the HR manager must extend well beyond the boundaries of their own organisation to cover more broadly the supply chains that feed into its manufacturing or service provision.

Finally, all of us as consumers need to be aware of these areas of potential labour exploitation as well. We connive in exploitation because it's invisible. The labour conditions embodied in the products we enjoy are simply not visible or obvious. Until they are – maybe through a form of labelling, as the UK government report recommended back in 2003 – we need to ask the awkward questions. If we know that workers are paid the going rate and benefit from decent working conditions when we buy that T-shirt or those apples, then that would be a start.

Some questions to think about

1. Why do employers in certain industrial sectors, such as hospitality and distribution, believe that migrant workers have a superior work ethic to locals? Are they right to do so?

2. The sudden decline of European workers in the UK in 2020 (following Brexit and the COVID-19 pandemic) indicates that relying on migration is a risky HR strategy. Do you agree? Why?

3. 'With greater migration in the world economy, we need to get accustomed to a more diverse workforce in all countries.' Consider the HRM implications of this statement.

Further reading

Alberti, G., Holgate, J. and Tapia, M. (2013) 'Organising migrants as workers or as migrant workers? Intersectionality, trade unions and precarious work', *The International Journal of Human Resource Management*, 24(22): 4132–48. [Explores the changing attitudes of trade unions towards migrant workers.]

Anderson, B. and Rogaly, B. (2005) *Forced Labour and Migration to the UK*, London: Trades Union Congress. [Conditions for forced labour are created by employers' demands for ultra-flexible labour, not just cheap labour.]

Meardi, G. (2007) 'The Polish plumber in the West Midlands: Theoretical and empirical issues', *Review of Sociology*, 13(2): 39–56. [Review of the complex motivations for the movement of Polish migrants to one UK city.]

Thompson, P., Newsome, K. and Commander, J. (2013) '"Good when they want to be": Migrant workers in the supermarket supply chain', *Human Resource Management Journal*, 23(2): 129–43. [Use of migrant workers is affected more by requirements of temporal flexibility than any essential features of their labour power.]

12

Corporate Social Responsibility

The last chapter highlighted some of the issues that many migrant workers face when working in the industrialised economies of Europe, North America and elsewhere. This chapter follows on by examining the notion of corporate social responsibility (CSR) and how it fits into human resource management (HRM). It begins by defining CSR and explaining some of its rationales, which might include ethical, moral and legal dimensions, as well as the business case. We then investigate the main instruments for pursuing CSR within organisations: (1) voluntary codes of conduct and (2) compulsory guidelines that may be enforceable, for example, through the International Labour Organization (ILO). We then assess the role of non-governmental organisations (NGOs) and trade unions in promoting CSR, before looking at the ways in which CSR is understood in different kinds of economies. We examine trade union responses to CSR and how they may be involved in monitoring and enforcing CSR policies, before drawing some general conclusions. You may also come across the acronym 'ESG', which stands for 'environmental, social and governance' issues. The main contrast between CSR and ESG is that CSR refers to a business model while ESG refers to the criteria used by customers, clients and investors to evaluate a company's performance.

The European Commission's definition of CSR (2011: 6) draws our attention to one of its principal dimensions: 'the responsibility of enterprises for their impacts on society'. In other words, CSR focuses on ensuring that companies understand that they operate within a general social framework to which they owe certain responsibilities – and that they therefore do not act or carry out their activities purely instrumentally in a kind of bubble of their own creation. In particular, it requires companies to have in place 'a process to integrate social, environmental, ethical, human rights and consumer concerns into their business operations and core strategy, in close collaboration with their stakeholders'. The breadth of these areas of concern is striking. They include, for example, environmental concerns, such as impacts on the natural environment, alongside ethical concerns and human rights, which include prohibitions on using child or slave labour, as well as consumer concerns, that is, responsibilities of care towards those buying products and services. CSR, then, potentially covers a wide variety of different areas and concerns, and needs to be pursued in collaboration with the organisational stakeholders.

Stakeholders are basically anybody with a material interest in the organisation (Freeman, 1984). They include employees and workers because of the wage–effort bargain with their employer – the pay, conditions and security they earn in exchange for the effort they make towards organisational efficiency and productivity. But organisations have many other stakeholders as well, such as the consumers and clients who we met in Chapter 10 when discussing HRM in services. Passengers on the railway, patients in a hospital, householders using gas, electricity or water at home, students at school or in a university – and maybe their parents too – all have a stake in the organisation that is providing the service. As many services have been privatised – such as rail services and the utilities – these stakeholders have been converted into consumers. The same can be said of students in universities: once government grants were abolished in the UK for study in higher education and replaced by tuition fees, the relationship of students to their university became marketised, and their interests shifted from scholarship in itself to value for money and employability.

Subcontractors form another group of stakeholders. Many large organisations contract out ancillary and core services like grounds maintenance, cleaning, security and catering to specialist companies that also then acquire an interest in the viability of their contractor. Suppliers, banks, environmental groups and community associations are also stakeholders. For example, many organisations operate charitable outlets to help improve their local communities, maybe to support young people in need or to care for the elderly.

Finally, in private organisations, there are the shareholders, who are – in liberal market economies (LMEs) (as we saw in Chapter 5) – the key stakeholders. The issue that organisations have to confront is how they create a balance between these stakeholders. In an LME like the UK or the US, which prioritises the interests of shareholders over all other stakeholders, particular measures need to be introduced to protect the interests of other stakeholders. However, in a coordinated market economy (CME), including Germany among other countries in continental Europe, the interests of other stakeholders, particularly employees, are protected structurally through their integration into its legal and social framework. CSR has become particularly visible in LMEs, which are shareholder-oriented, because special mechanisms are required to look after the interests of other stakeholders. CSR has become an attempt by organisations, in particular private companies, to demonstrate that they are paying attention not just to their shareholders, but to other stakeholders as well.

Aspects of CSR

We soon discover, when we explore the nature of CSR in greater depth, that it includes economic, legal, ethical and philanthropic aspects. The economic responsibility of an organisation is to ensure its viability and sustainability over the longer term, or it won't survive. At the same time, it has to ensure that it complies with applicable legislation and regulations in all its locations. It also has to operate in a way that takes into account the ethical standards of the society it's operating in. In 2018, for example, the Nissan board unanimously sacked its chair, Carlos Ghosn, who had been in post for around 20 years and had overseen the company's expansion over that period. He was dismissed for alleged financial irregularities and corruption. The board was very much aware that, if the reputation of its chair were placed in question, he had to go in order to preserve the company's ethical standards (Ghosn later fled to the Lebanon).

A further aspect of CSR is philanthropy, with UK and US companies in particular donating significant sums of money for charitable work. The Bill & Melinda Gates Foundation, for example, which is worth around US$50 billion, is one of the largest charitable enterprises in history, and collaborates with NGOs at a global level with the objective of improving the living conditions of the poor.

These aspects of CSR are sometimes understood as a kind of pyramid, with economic viability at the base, then building upwards with legal compliance, ethical standards and philanthropy at the peak (Carroll, 1991). Alternatively, they are simply regarded as areas or fields of CSR. Business in the Community (BITC) lists them as covering: 'workforce, environment, marketplace, community and human rights' (BITC, 2000).

Rationales for CSR

Organisations introduce CSR policies for a variety of reasons. The first is simply a matter of morality. We noted in Chapter 8, on the 'new' unitarism, that companies like Cadbury, Clarks and Rowntree's were set up in the 19th century by Quaker families not only to manufacture products that people wanted, but also to ensure that their workers were treated well and lived in decent surroundings. The model town of Port Sunlight, today one of Unilever's sites, comprised an entire community around the factory to ensure that workers had comfortable housing and access to the arts, among much else. Although the religious foundations of Quaker companies remain controversial (Rowlinson, 1998; Kimberley, 2016), the moral case for CSR can clearly be made on the religious or humanitarian grounds that one of the roles of a company is to treat workers properly as human beings: CSR is 'the right thing to do'.

Legitimacy is a further rationale. Companies need to show that they are legitimate within the wider society. They are embedded in social values, norms and standards and, as a result, may be seen as more or less legitimate. However, there are boundaries here. For example, Sports Direct is a well-known UK company that fell well short of the standards of treatment of its workers that might have been expected of it, to such an extent that it was investigated by a Parliamentary Inquiry that issued recommendations for ways to reform its corporate governance (House of Commons, 2016b).

And then there is a business case for CSR as well. That is, rather than establishing yourself as a hard-nosed kind of company that doesn't really care about anybody at all, you can make CSR part of your brand if you can demonstrate that your company acts in line with social needs and requirements and looks after its employees. The evidence on whether CSR pays off or not in a business sense is marginally positive (Peloza, 2009), but may risk the suspicion that its adoption merely reflects a cynical ploy designed to improve public relations. Companies not only give to charities, but they might also spend a lot in telling the public about their donations. In Chapter 8, we saw how American hi-tech companies have introduced high standards of conditions for their workforces, which they then portray as part of their corporate image. Consumers may then be attracted to the company and become loyal to its products because they associate with its ethical standards. So that would justify a business case for CSR, as it is something that can be used in publicity as part of the brand. However, we also noted the realities of working in such companies, which can include long hours, stress and burnout.

The websites of many large multinational companies contain statements about CSR, which, you may feel, are designed to impress, to show that they are responsible companies. We examine the realities of CSR next, but in the meantime, we should note that there are clearly a number of rationales for CSR that may well overlap.

Compliance with CSR standards

CSR, then, covers a wide variety of issues such as labour and environmental standards as well as community and human rights. We must now examine issues of compliance and enforcement. CSR may be a matter for a company operating within a purely domestic environment or, in the case of a multinational company, within the global economy. Either way, the whole point about CSR is that it must be enforceable. If it remains merely a statement on a website, it really doesn't mean very much. It might make us all feel nice and warm inside, but if a statement about treating workers in the company and its supply chains properly is just ignored, then it remains nothing more than paying lip-service to a standard. The real issue is enforcement and compliance and ensuring these standards actually make a difference in the workplace and in the environment (Bartley, 2018). The nature of regulation is going to vary, depending on whether it's purely domestic within a country where it's relatively easy to monitor and control legal, ethical and moral standards, or whether it's international, with a multinational company operating across many different borders, when the lines of accountability become that much more difficult to enforce.

Broadly speaking, there are two ways to apply CSR standards: one is through voluntary codes of conduct and the other is through mandatory or compulsory codes.

Voluntary codes

Voluntary codes of conduct comprise company statements, probably posted on their websites, declaring their CSR principles and guaranteeing that they treat their workers correctly, pay the minimum wage and ensure that workers employed in their supply chains are covered by international labour standards. Such voluntary codes of CSR may be promoted by a wide variety of NGOs, as well as by trade unions, which, as we saw in Chapter 6, often play a major role in the internal regulation of companies.

Critically important too is the international dimension of CSR and how it is enforced globally. Numerous international organisations have been involved in drawing up, refining and enforcing CSR guidelines. One of the most well known is the International Organization for Standardization (ISO), based in Geneva, Switzerland, which sponsors ISO 26000, an international CSR framework drawn up in 2010 that outlines 'seven core subjects' that companies need to consider by way of CSR: organisational governance; human rights; labour practices; environment; fair operating practices; consumer issues; and community involvement and development (ISO, 2021). Similarly, the Global Reporting Initiative (GRI), which was founded in the US in 1997, publishes a range of voluntary CSR standards, covering universal, economic, environmental and social (including employment) guidelines (GRI, 2022). Possibly the most well-known set of CSR guidelines is the United Nations (UN) Global Compact, which was launched by the UN in 2000 to offer 'a platform – based on universal principles – to encourage innovative initiatives and partnerships with civil society, Governments and other stakeholders'. The Compact contains 10 such principles based around human rights, labour, environment and anti-corruption. The labour principles are: to guarantee freedom of association and collective bargaining; elimination of forced labour; elimination of child labour; and prevention of discrimination (UN Global Compact, 2021). However, these are all voluntary codes. A company may state in its publicity that it adheres to these codes, but as a consumer or worker, you're never quite sure whether they are really being enforced or not, which is obviously the main point.

One way a company might demonstrate compliance is by producing a video or documentary that demonstrates, through interviews and other evidence, that it really is adhering to the guidelines. For example, Icebreaker, a New Zealand wool company, has produced a series of videos, clearly aware that the garment and fashion industry is known for poor pay and employment conditions. The videos explain how the company monitors the supply chains through which it sources materials and carries out its operations. The first focuses on sourcing fabrics (Icebreaker, 2008a), while the second focuses on sewing (Icebreaker, 2008b). Who actually sewed the clothes you're wearing at the moment? You probably have absolutely no idea. However, this company hopes that – by watching their videos – you will be reassured that the workers who assembled your clothes were not being exploited. Of course, this is not foolproof, not least because conditions can change over time, so we do need to treat company videos with care, and seek further objective evidence to evaluate claims.

NGOs also play a significant role in ensuring company compliance with CSR standards. It is easy to be confused by the sheer number of NGOs that are active in just one area of CSR, such as human rights observance. There are thousands of NGOs across the world that are doing very similar work in highlighting abuses of human rights and labour standards, and trying to improve them, so let's just take one example to start with, Students and Scholars Against Corporate Misbehavior (SACOM). This was an NGO based in Hong Kong (since closed down following the repression of civil society institutions in 2021), which conducted research into multinational companies that operate in China, such as Disney, Foxconn and Walmart, drawing attention to any labour abuses it uncovered. In 2017 it used the launch of a new product by Apple, the iPhone X, to highlight the conditions of the workers who were producing it. We all take advantage of cheap products as consumers, but their cheapness is often at the cost of the pay and conditions of the workers who produce them. SACOM organised an iSlave campaign outside Apple stores, accompanied by this press release:

> iSlave at 10 – 10 years of iSlavery by Apple Global Action demands Apple to stop labour right abuses immediately!
>
> Today (3rd November, 2017) is the releasing date of iPhone X. SACOM, an Hong Kong based NGO, and international activists from Philippines, USA, UK, France, Germany, Austria and other regions have come together and held the iSlave at 10 Global Action Day against Apple's labour abuses during the past 10 years of iPhone production. Activists protested in Apple Shops in their regions and demand Apple to make change immediately. In Hong Kong, SACOM, together with other labour right groups and university students staged a protest at 0830 in Apple Shop, Festival Walk, Kowloon Tong, Hong Kong. (SACOM, 2017)

SACOM's reference to slavery is symbolic: workers making Apple goods are paid, but their wages as a share of profits are very low. However, slavery is increasingly a real and not merely symbolic presence in the world economy. Slavery stands at the furthest extremity of labour exploitation (Kara, 2017), and we tend to think of it as something historical. Yet the UN has set up a website that lists 90 agencies, programmes, NGOs and foundations that are currently working to abolish *contemporary* or *modern* forms of slavery, which is an immensely sobering thought (UN OHCHR, 2021).

According to the International Labour Office (2014: 1): 'Today, about 21 million men, women and children are in forced labour, trafficked, held in debt bondage or work in slave–like conditions.' It estimates that 'the total illegal profits obtained from the use of forced labour worldwide amount to US$150.2 billion per year' (International Labour Office, 2014: 13). Box 12.1 illustrates some of the challenges in eliminating slavery.

BOX 12.1: SLAVERY OR FORCED LABOUR IN SUPPLY CHAINS

Under the Modern Slavery Act 2015, UK companies valued at over £36 million must state on their websites the measures they have taken to eliminate slavery from their supply chains. In the first year of reporting, Marks & Spencer, Sainsbury's and Unilever had taken a lead in compliance with the law, but many other companies were adopting a 'tick-box' response, while 43 were failing in their duties (Cumming, 2017).

And the challenges continue. Cobalt is required to make lightweight rechargeable batteries for electric cars, but 60% of the world's supply is found in the Democratic Republic of Congo, where unregulated mines employ an estimated 40,000 child labourers (Amnesty International, 2016: 28–32). Meanwhile, around 20% of the world's cotton is produced in the region of Xinjiang in China where, according to the Australian Strategic Policy Institute: 'Under conditions that strongly suggest forced labour, Uyghurs [a Muslim minority ethnic group] are working in factories that are in the supply chains of at least 82 well-known global brands in the technology, clothing and automotive sectors' (Xu et al, 2021: 3). Multinational companies may find themselves having to locate alternative supply chains or face an angry public backlash from their consumers if they fail to do so.

Nevertheless, some employers in emerging economies regard bans on child labour as 'part of the wider historic project of Western imperialism in the developing world through which economic resources are extracted from local manufacturers while their perceptions of what constitutes socially responsible behaviour are delegitimized' (Khan and Lund-Thomsen, 2011: 73). This view, that CSR is an indication of enduring post-colonial attitudes, suggests that top-down standards introduced by European and US companies require at the very least close consultation with local representatives before implementation.

Role of trade unions and NGOs

The pressures to enforce these codes often bring trade unions and NGOs together into partnership or relationships that may prove very complex (Gold et al, 2020). NGOs will very often publicise the guidelines or advocate them however they can, but they may rely on trade unions as an enforcement mechanism. This is because unions organise within companies to promote and advance the terms and conditions of their members – clearly, that's the whole purpose of a trade union, as we saw in Chapter 6. Therefore, many NGOs develop quite close, symbiotic relationships with unions in an attempt to evaluate compliance with codes of conduct. NGOs will point out that a particular company has a code of conduct in which it claims that it pays the national minimum wage across its subsidiaries, where applicable, and the union is in a strong position to check whether that's true or not if it organises within the company's subsidiaries across the world.

This is particularly important when it comes to supply chains. It's one thing to be employed directly with a large textiles company, but if the company is reliant on complex supply chains where labour relations themselves are precarious, not to say immoral or sometimes illegal, then it may be difficult for even large companies to monitor them. However, the unions may be in a position to do so. The role of unions in monitoring CSR in supply chains is therefore very important even though, of course, in the end, the NGOs may have a better relationship with consumers (Donaghey et al, 2014). That is, when we, as consumers, are looking at issues relating to CSR, it's probably the NGO's campaign that has caught our attention rather than the union's, because, of course, we're not employees of the company. We have a broader interest, as consumers. The point is that the unions naturally focus on the workers' end of the problem and the NGOs focus on the consumers' end of the problem, and together they can form powerful alliances to shed light on some of the abuses and to campaign to set them right (for examples, see Preuss et al, 2015).

Nevertheless, a point of tension that might exist between unions on the one hand and NGOs on the other is that the unions are generally concerned about the public reputation of the companies in which they organise. One of the interests we have as workers is to ensure the viability of the organisation we work for (as noted in Chapter 3). We obviously don't want it to go bankrupt or cut staff or get a bad reputation because that could jeopardise our jobs. It may prove difficult for a union to publicise unethical activities within an organisation because, in doing so, it might reduce the appeal of the company's product with consumers and damage the longer term prospects of its workers for secure employment. Unions and NGOs accordingly sometimes perform a double act, where the union organises within the company, but it's the NGO that creates the external publicity because the NGO is independent of the company, and its criticisms don't have the same effect on the workers' prospects that those from the union might have had.

Further tensions might also complicate an alliance between a union and an NGO if they have different interests over a particular issue. Take, for example, logging in the Amazon. Many NGOs campaign against uncontrolled logging in the tropical rainforests of Brazil, Indonesia and elsewhere, which, they argue, undermines ecosystems and causes long-term environmental damage. On the other hand, the livelihood of local workers in Brazil may depend on the opportunities to work for a logging company, in which case, the unions come to support logging activities. Hence we have to be aware of the tensions that may exist between NGOs and trade unions in specific circumstances (Rees et al, 2015). Similarly, NGOs advocate the switch away from fossil fuels to clean energy. This will threaten jobs (often well paid) in the carbon-based sectors. Common ground between trade unions and NGOs on this and comparable issues involves planning an economically viable transition of workers from the old to the new economy (Clarke and Lipsig-Mummé, 2020).

In addition, unions are democratic organisations, with officers elected by their members, whereas NGOs are often self-appointed. You may support an NGO and get involved in its campaigns and fundraising activities, but you're not actually a member in the sense of having democratic rights within it. NGOs are largely self-appointed organisations, whereas, as a fee-paying member of a union, you have the right to elect members of its executive and its general secretary. In other words, the internal structure of an NGO is not necessarily democratic, whereas the internal structure of the union is democratic, which may cause tensions over the degrees to which they are accountable, swiftly responsive and regarded as legitimate.

The key issue here is enforcing compliance with voluntary codes of conduct in CSR through the activities of NGOs and trade unions. When they work well together, it's helpful for everybody; however, there are limits to their cooperation as their own legitimate interests and lines of accountability may conflict.

Role of the media

In addition to NGOs and trade unions, the media also provide an important instrument with which to enforce CSR. Contacting the media – such as social media, newspapers, radio or television – can be used to draw attention to all manner of labour abuses, but campaigns today can also create their own websites and post their own YouTube clips, bypassing the mainstream outlets. For example, for a BBC News item on Chinese factory workers working for Apple, see Bilton (2014), and for a six-month *Guardian* multimedia investigation into the way in which some of the world's largest supermarkets used suppliers relying on slave labour in the Thai prawn fishing industry to sell cheap seafood, see Hodal et al. (2014). A Channel 4 report investigated the conditions of Romanian apple pickers in the UK (Kennedy, 2015), while *The New York Times* ran a series on pay and labour conditions in the 2,000 nail bars in the city, raising concerns over 60-hour working weeks, lack of overtime pay, wage theft as the norm, hazardous chemicals at work, failure to pay minimum wages (as little as US$1.50 per hour), and the use of an entirely migrant workforce (Maslin Nir, 2015a, b). In the UK, *The Guardian* (Bland and Makortoff, 2020; Davies and Kelly, 2020) ran a series of articles on illegal sweatshops supplying companies like Boohoo during the pandemic that wiped £1 billion off the share price of the company. Such cases, along with those identified in Box 12.1, demonstrate the ways in which media reports can bring pressure on companies by creating bad publicity and affecting share prices, which they will want to avoid.

Investment and pension funds

We should also note the part played by investment and pension funds in monitoring and publicising CSR-type issues in the UK. Since 2004, self-administered pension funds have been required to have member-nominated trustees on their trustee boards, many of whom are now trade union nominees. Some unions have developed their own guidelines to support their trustees in making ethical decisions about where and how to invest the funds for which they are responsible (Gold, 2008). In addition, investors have, more generally, become concerned at the impact of environmental, social and governance issues on company performance, particularly climate change. Organisations such as Pensions & Investment Research Consultants Ltd are active in providing independent advice to investors with concerns over CSR. Box 12.2 gives an example of how companies operating in the gig economy are likely to come under intensifying scrutiny from investors.

> ## BOX 12.2: INVESTORS CONCERNED AT DELIVEROO'S TREATMENT OF WORKERS
>
> Several large investment funds in the UK announced that they would not participate in the stock market flotation of Deliveroo, the online food delivery company, in April 2021, over concerns at the way in which the company treats its workers. Deliveroo had set out plans for its initial public offer (IPO), the opening sale of its shares to the public, which was projected to raise around £9 billion for the company. However, some of the UK's largest fund managers, including Aberdeen Standard, Aviva Investors, Legal & General and M&G, decided not to invest in the IPO for a number of reasons, including the way in which Deliveroo treats its workers. The head of corporate finance and stewardship at M&G, for example, said that the company's dependence on gig workers made it a risk for investors, adding that the Supreme Court had ruled that employment rights applied to workers at Uber as they were not self-employed contractors (see Box 5.3). He commented: 'Deliveroo's narrow profit margins could be at risk if it is required to change its rider benefits to catch up with peers' (BBC News, 2021b).
>
> The Deliveroo case is merely the latest in a long line of interventions by investment and pension funds in decisions based on CSR-type considerations (Gold, 2008).

Binding instruments

Alongside voluntary codes and instruments we also find binding instruments in CSR, that is, measures that are binding or compulsory. One such instrument is through public procurement. All government, meaning central government and local government (such as the local council where you live) or the European Union (EU), needs to purchase goods and services. Your local council, for example, provides a whole range of services, from schools and care homes, through to libraries, parks, refuse collection, and much else besides. Local councils spend billions of pounds a year on their local infrastructures, financed in the UK largely through Council Tax (a local tax), subsidies from central government and revenues from selling some of their services. Many of these services are provided through competitive tendering – that is, companies will compete for the contract to supply, for example, refuse collection or street cleansing. When a local council circulates such a tender, it can specify that the company that bids must comply with certain labour standards. In other words, local councils can insist that the company that clears the refuse or cleans the streets must guarantee minimum pay, holiday entitlements and so on. The immense purchasing power of government – local, central or European – gives it a great deal of muscle to enforce labour standards, and other standards too. If the council discovers that the company is failing to comply, it has a legal case for prosecuting the company for infringing the terms of the contract. Public procurement, then, is widely used by governments as a means to ensure decent labour standards in a wide variety of different circumstances (McCrudden, 2004).

Otherwise, the International Labour Organization (ILO), established in 1919, is the single most important agency in the field of enforcing international labour standards. The ILO has now ratified 189 Conventions that cover a wide range of global labour standards, with eight fundamental Conventions that focus on the freedom of association and right to organise, collective bargaining, abolition of forced labour and child labour, equal remuneration and discrimination. The ILO has 187 state members and convenes every year to discuss developments and monitor progress. Once a country ratifies a Convention, it becomes binding on that country. If it infringes the terms of a Convention, the ILO can invoke legal processes against it in an attempt to bring it back into line. These processes allow the international community to bring pressure on repressive regimes that are flouting labour standards (ILO, 2021).

At a regional level, the 27 member states of the EU have introduced a common floor of labour rights since its creation in 1957, which is enforced through EU Treaty provisions, some 70 Directives that are binding on all member states and the rulings of the European Court of Justice (Gold, 2009). These basic rights focus on equal opportunities, employment protection, health and safety at work and employee participation, and are designed to guarantee free movement of labour across the member states and to prevent 'social dumping' (the practice whereby companies locate their operations in countries characterised by the poorest labour standards in order to gain a cost advantage). Basic rights have since been supplemented by the development of 'soft law' (such as benchmarking, monitoring and peer review) to promote greater coordination in more 'difficult' areas of employment policy, such as dealing with unemployment, pensions and social inclusion (Gold, 2017). The significance of these policies for CSR is that – within the boundaries of the EU – labour standards can be closely observed and controlled.

Many larger multinational companies have also agreed International Framework Agreements (IFAs) with the trade unions, which are binding across their subsidiaries. There are around 200 or 300 in many household-name companies, which have been listed by the European Commission (2022). These IFAs cover, at global company level, areas like equal opportunities, health and safety and training. IFAs are potentially a powerful framework for CSR as they mean that, within a multinational company, unions can be assured that these minimum standards will be upheld everywhere under their terms. If not, there may be repercussions for the company, not just action from the unions' side, but also a loss of reputation and poor public relations that may damage its interests from the point of view of its marketing. Through IFAs, unions may, at an international level, be able to play an important role in promoting decent labour standards in supply chains (Schömann et al, 2008; European Commission, 2022). At a European level there are a number of European Union Industry Federations, which are affiliated to the European Trade Union Confederation and linked to the Global Union Federations. They monitor companies at EU level and support their member unions, which creates a complex network of agreements and understandings that underpins compliance overall with decent labour standards.

Significance of CSR across countries

The prominence of CSR as a corporate issue varies country by country, according to its national business system. In Chapter 5, we distinguished between liberal market economies (LMEs) and coordinated market economies (CMEs). We pointed out that LMEs (such as the UK and the US) prioritise shareholder interests in decision-making, while CMEs (such as Germany) prioritise broader stakeholder interests, including employees, suppliers and banks. If we accept this distinction as a helpful simplification, we find that the role of CSR in corporate activities varies very much according to the kind of national business system in which it is located.

In LMEs, CSR is often explicit, with company websites and publicity drawing attention to their policies and practices. It has been argued that, in a shareholder-oriented economy, the shareholder is prioritised, so companies have to point out explicitly that they are taking into account the interests of other stakeholders, like employees. In UK or US multinational companies, CSR is often very much part of their self-identity or self-image, with the companies projecting themselves as accountable, responsible and transparent. They have to shout it out, as it were, to emphasise that they are not only taking into account the shareholders in their business strategies (Matten and Moon, 2008; Kang and Moon, 2012).

By contrast, CSR is often implicit in CMEs. In a country like Germany, basic labour standards are already regulated by legislation. Because of the role of trade unions, collective bargaining and works councils, among other aspects of labour-friendly regulation found in CMEs, CSR-type principles (insofar as they cover labour standards) are already embedded implicitly within the fabric of their national business systems and institutional frameworks. This may help to explain why continental companies – Dutch, French, German and Scandinavian – generally don't express the level of interest in CSR that is often found in American and British companies: they would maintain that many of the issues covered by CSR in the UK and the US are already dealt with by the HRM networks that exist in their own systems, not least through collective bargaining and legal regulation (for a discussion of CSR in Germany, see Haunschild and Krause, 2015; for Sweden, see du Rietz, 2015). CSR may therefore be regarded broadly as a phenomenon that arises out of the shareholder-oriented business systems that characterise LMEs.

Trade union attitudes and policies towards CSR

Union interest in CSR similarly depends on the kind of country in which they are organising. It's generally more explicit in the UK and the US than in Germany or the Netherlands. Much also depends on government initiatives on CSR, to which unions may be invited to respond, and on unions' political and religious affiliations. Some unions, such as CGT-FO in France, focus exclusively on their members' interests and view CSR as an unnecessary distraction. The membership profile of a union may affect their attitudes and policies. Some unions that represent members in more technical areas may adopt a broader interest in CSR issues than those that represent mainly unskilled or semi-skilled workers. A 'champion' or official within the union may seek to promote CSR-related issues on the grounds that they are important for its longer term interests and thereby influence its policies.

Unions often express concerns over CSR because it is voluntary and not seen as enforceable. Some maintain that it's fragmented and that its effectiveness depends merely on the company with no standardised framework to guarantee compliance. However, when unions do get involved, particularly through NGOs, their activity generally focuses on verifying the claims of companies. For example, if a company claims to be paying the minimum wage across its subsidiaries and supply chains but then turns out not to be doing so, it then becomes vulnerable to adverse publicity, which is likely to undermine its public relations and customer relations. So unions can use CSR to embarrass companies, sometimes in association with NGOs, if they're not actually complying with their own CSR statements (Preuss et al, 2015).

Concluding comments

In conclusion, companies – especially those based in LMEs – have become increasingly concerned about their CSR presence, maybe for reasons of public relations, as the business case for CSR is not proven. The role of NGOs and unions is extremely important in enforcing CSR practice, although the key question remains the extent to which CSR practice is embedded within companies and their human resources (HR) systems. Monitoring compliance brings together the unions, NGOs and the media, as well as the consumer, meaning all of us. What responsibilities do we all, as consumers, have in enforcing decent labour standards? This question underpins the question we also raised in Chapter 10, on emotional labour. The consumer or customer has also come to play an important role in HRM. We know about the employer, we know about the worker, but what is the role of the consumer within the broader terms of the employment relationship?

This cartoon neatly sums up the issues. It encapsulates much of our thinking in the industrialised economies, like the UK. We do take a lot of these things – growth, wealth, profits – for granted. Yet they're often created for our benefit at the expense of workers who are extremely disadvantaged, particularly in emerging economies. And that's really the issue – although it goes a lot wider than HRM – that we all need to confront.

Figure 12.1: The same boat

Source: Polyp.org.uk

Some questions to think about

1. What is meant by 'corporate social responsibility' (CSR)? Give some examples of CSR in which organisations might get involved.

2. Evaluate the view that strong trade unions are the best way to enforce CSR in the workplace.

3. How far are the conditions under which workers have produced the products we are consuming a matter of *our own* responsibility? How far would you be willing to pay higher prices for products you knew had been sourced ethically?

Further reading

Kara, S. (2017) *Modern Slavery: A Global Perspective*, New York: Columbia University Press. [A first-person investigation into modern slavery across the world.]

Peloza, J. (2009) 'The challenge of measuring financial impacts from investments in corporate social performance', *Journal of Management*, 35(6): 1518–41. [A literature review that uncovers 'a small, but positive, relationship' between CSR and company financial performance.]

Preuss, L., Gold, M. and Rees, C. (eds) (2015) *Corporate Social Responsibility and Trade Unions: Perspectives across Europe*, London: Routledge. [An analysis of the variable meaning of CSR across 11 member states of the EU.]

PART 3

What All This Means for HRM

13

Recruitment and Social Networks

Recruitment is one of the key functions of human resource management (HRM). If you're running any organisation, you need the right workers to start with. Screening and recruiting workers who will be dependable and motivated goes a long way towards making your business or operations a success.

This chapter examines the ways in which organisations recruit as well as the role of social networks in recruitment, which is an area of HRM that is often overlooked or underplayed. We begin by explaining the notion of 'social networks' and by looking at how they are used by jobseekers in particular sectors, such as the creative industries. We then examine the ways in which jobseekers aim to build their reputation in an attempt to improve their employability, particularly by the use of digital media such as LinkedIn. We analyse employers' and employees' rationales for using social networks, before investigating some of the implications of doing so, because there are certain issues involved in how they actually operate in practice.

The opening question is: how do you find a job? Before the internet and digital platforms, you'd read a newspaper known for its job pages and you'd apply for whatever suitable positions you might find advertised in it. Some people, of course, still do. There are also employment agencies you can go to: public ones run by the State, region or local authority; or private recruitment agencies, where you can register your name to be circulated to employers who are seeking candidates in certain areas of expertise. You can sign up to a networking platform. You can also try cold-calling – you can try ringing up organisations out of the blue, and introducing yourself, without any notion of whether or not they have any vacancies. You might strike lucky, but even if you don't, it's a way to get yourself around a bit. But it's not very efficient.

Social networks

Another way to find a job is through your family and friends, and that's really where social networks come in, because one of the most efficient and popular ways to find a job is through people you know, particularly when it comes to your first job (see Box 13.1). This can be particularly challenging because there's a paradox: you need experience to get a job, but then you need a job to get experience – it's a vicious circle, and the issue is how to break out of it. As we'll see, one way is to use family and friends: they know you already and so they will help you find a job.

BOX 13.1: HOW DID YOU FIND YOUR FIRST JOB?

How did you find your first job? Or how do you expect to find one if you don't have a job already? If you're a student, do you have a part-time job? How did you find that? Did you ask family and friends to help you find it? If not, did you reply to an advertisement? If so, where? Or did you find it online?

The basic point here is that your social network is not arbitrary. Your networks are something that have built up throughout the course of your life, through your family, relatives, friends and acquaintances. The social relationships in which we find ourselves are unintentional or unconscious – they are what we find ourselves socialised through and into. However, when we start talking about 'networking', that term is something much more conscious. Social relationships are something we're all born into and we all deal with, but 'networking' is the term given to that process whereby we consciously use our social relationships in order to benefit ourselves in the labour market.

When you start using your social networks to find either your first job or later, promotion within an organisation or career, you're doing so on a coherent and rational basis, and it may help to have the appropriate networking skills. In some areas of employment, particularly project-based work like the creative media and entertainment, the notion of networking is extremely important, not least because there's such a high turnaround of people in this kind of work. Time is very pressurised, and so the way in which workers flow between projects or companies has to be undertaken at great speed and, in order to facilitate that, networking is efficient because you then know exactly the kind of people you're going to approach for a particular job. But, in fact, we find that networks are a very important way in which many people find their work elsewhere too.

We tend to overlook the point that we spend our lives – both social and working – at the centre of our very own complex social networks. When we're looking for a job, we tend to think that we are here, the job is out there, and we may forget or overlook the fact that these networks may intermediate between the two:

> Despite modernization, technology and the dizzying pace of social change, one constant in the world is that where and how we spend our working hours, the largest slice of life for most adults, depends very much on how we are embedded in networks of social contacts – the relatives, friends and acquaintances that are not banished by the never-ending proposals to pair people to jobs by some automatic technical procedures such as national computerized machines. (Granovetter, 1995: 141)

The use of social networks in finding employment is borne out by survey evidence from all kinds of different countries. In a survey of 282 professional, technical and managerial men in Newton, Massachusetts in the US, who found work through social networks, Granovetter (1995) discovered that social contacts, and not information through labour market mechanisms, offered the richest information about jobs. His research built on a long line of anthropological and sociological studies into networks for finding work, especially kinship and family networks, but he applied his analysis to a modern setting comprising professionalised labour, and moved to extend networks away from family structures. Basically, what Granovetter does here is to update preceding work on kinship patterns and social networks in order to show its applicability to modern labour markets.

Evidence from a Panel Study of Income Dynamics in the US (covering 5,000 American families) in 1978 revealed that 43% of black women, 58.5% of black men, 47.1% of white women and 52% of white men had found their current jobs through friends and relatives. A National Longitudinal Survey of Youth (those aged 17–25) in the UK carried out in 1982 showed that 40% had found their current job through contacts. This practice, then, is widespread regardless of gender, ethnic background or age, and nationality. A study in 1985 of 2,003 male workers in the Tokyo metropolitan area found that among those who changed their jobs, 54.6% did so through personal contacts, 31% through formal means and only 8.3% through direct application. Analyses of UK Labour Force Survey data for the period from 2006 to 2009 revealed that social networks were a relatively common method for job search, with one in four people finding work through direct referral from 'hearing from someone who worked there'. This proportion was higher among those with no qualifications, while non–graduates, including jobseekers currently or previously employed in skilled trades, were those most likely to use social networks as a job search method (Green et al, 2011).

While data in Figure 13.1 from the US suggest that the internet is the most popular source for job search (with 34% of the sample using this method), in fact the combined social network data were higher (at 44%). These networks were made up of connections with close friends or family (20%), professional or work connections (17%) and acquaintances (7%). Granovetter (1973, 1983) refers to close friends and family as 'strong ties', and to professional or work connections and acquaintances as 'weak ties'. His influential thesis is that weak ties yield the most useful information to jobseekers because the information and support provided by work colleagues and work acquaintances are more likely to be connected to your occupational preferences.

It's similar in China. The Chinese term *guanxi*, which means 'connection', refers to the way in which you connect with other people to find preferment or a job (Bian, 1994; Huang, 2008). In the case of China, around 80% of jobs for internal migrants are found through family and village networks, a very high proportion (Hare, 1999). This is also true for some research carried out in Chinese towns (Knight et al, 1999). Ko and Liu (2017) demonstrate the exclusive use of social networks for recruiting talent (engineers) in small engineering firms in China.

Figure 13.1: How Americans find work

Roughly one-third of recent job seekers say the internet was the most important resource available to them during their most recent employment search

Among Americans who have looked for a new job in the last two years, the % who ...

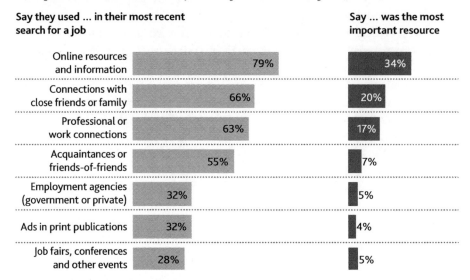

Say they used ... in their most recent search for a job

Say ... was the most important resource

	Used	Most important
Online resources and information	79%	34%
Connections with close friends or family	66%	20%
Professional or work connections	63%	17%
Acquaintances or friends-of-friends	55%	7%
Employment agencies (government or private)	32%	5%
Ads in print publications	32%	4%
Job fairs, conferences and other events	28%	5%

Note: Based on the 34% of Americans who have looked for a new job in the last two years. Survey conducted 10 June–12 July 2015. Sample size = 2,001.

Source: A. Smith (2015)

However, we need to take care over the statistics. Some go back several decades, while, as we saw in Chapter 5, practices may vary considerably by country. For example, country variations in the effectiveness of social capital as a source of recruitment may also reflect the efficiency of other recruitment processes, such as employment agencies that advertise a high proportion of job vacancies (Korpi, 2001). In addition, we need to distinguish between pre-recruitment effects of using social capital, on which we focus in this chapter, and post-recruitment effects, such as whether the use of social networks leads to higher wages and job satisfaction for the worker or decreased labour turnover for the employer. Germany, which is noted for its efficient labour market institutions, reflects a different recruitment setting from, say, the UK or the US. A study of job search in Germany reveals that 'while early research, mainly focussing on the US labour market, found positive correlations between finding a job via social ties and post-hire outcomes ... finding a job via social ties [in Germany] is not related to higher income; yet, weak evidence can be found for higher job satisfaction and a reduction in turnover' (Kossmann, 2016: 1).

We also need to highlight here an issue that we return to later, namely, that there are actually two things going on when we use our social networks to find a job. The first is that, through our network, we are known to our employer; but the second, which is linked to the post-recruitment effects noted, is how competent we are to carry out the job. The problem with social networking arises when people who are not particularly competent get a job simply because of who they know. The old adage 'It's not what you know, it's who you know', may then become a problem for the organisation, which risks getting lumbered with a fool. In addition, if an employer is recruiting for one position, there may be several other employees already in the company who suggest a friend or relative for the job. How does the employer then decide between two or three people proposed out of different social networks? There are issues here, which, as we'll see later on, can present headaches for employers when using networks to fill vacancies.

Social networks are complex because rarely does everyone have equal value or weight – there are always some people who are more valued, trusted or better at finding work. Furthermore, most networks have subgroups containing people with a higher reputation who cut across several such groups (Gandini, 2016). We might say that some people have more 'social capital' than others. Social capital refers to the resources embedded in a person's social relationships (Portes, 1998). These resources can include 'the obligations that people who are connected may feel towards each other, the sense of solidarity they may call upon, the information they are willing to share, and the services they are willing to perform' (Small, 2010: 6). These social resources stem from social connections, and people have to mobilise them – that is, simply having access to good connections does not guarantee their use (Lin, 1999, 2000). 'According to social capital theory, individuals draw upon and utilize these resources to achieve their goals. As a result of the access to and use of these resources, the well-connected benefit compared to those who are not' (Trimble and Kmec, 2011: 166).

Social networks can connect you to work and perform better than responding to adverts. But research suggests that not all social connections have equal value. Those of women and non-white workers do not perform as effectively as going through formal routes. In other words, social networks may be gendered and ethnically based, meaning that women and black workers can be *confined* within social networks of less value for finding work, for breaking into new areas of work or for gaining promotion within occupations (Trimble and Kmec, 2011; Silva, 2018).

Information and influence in social networks

With so many applicants chasing so few jobs, having a bit more information about a particular job can bring you a quantitative advantage. More information might mean more chances of securing a job. Diverse networks provide more leads and more connections. In addition, social networks also provide you with unique information. This is 'insider information' you've gained from informal exchanges, which improves your job search by helping you to complete your application more effectively and by advising you on how to present yourself appropriately to your prospective employer.

And it's not just about gaining informational advantage. Social networks also provide influence. The person providing the information about the job can also be an 'advocate' for the jobseeker. Contacts can exert their workplace influence by 'putting in a good word' for the applicant. In high-status jobs, a high-status sponsor or advocate will add their support or borrowed status to the applicant and boost their chances of securing a job. Without advocating explicitly, high-status contacts can 'signal' to employers that the jobseeker would be a good employee, in part because employers may assume that individuals are connected to others with similar traits.

Reputation

Social networking is particularly important in creative media and entertainment because the rapid turnaround of project work in these sectors means that you come to rely on people you know, people with a good reputation, because you can count on them to do a good job for your next venture (Blair, 2001, 2003).

Networking involves rationalising or systematising your social relationships on a conscious basis to find a job or, in the longer term, to improve your reputation. There's an important distinction between reputation, on the one hand, and trust, on the other, because trust is something that you gain through social relationships: if you trust somebody, it means you know them. For example, if you trust a certain film producer, then it's because you've dealt with them in the past, you've shared a certain history together and you know you can rely on them. If they say they're going to do something, then you know they will do so. That's what trust means – confidence. 'Trust' is therefore a quality specific to relationships we already have. Now, when you are setting out on your first job or career, you are trying to build up networks and relationships in the labour market with people you don't yet know. They don't trust you if only because they don't yet know you, because trust is personal or relational – it is a quality that does (or does not) inhere in a relationship. 'Reputation', by contrast, goes beyond trust because it refers to a transactional relationship rather than to a personal one. Reputation is more arm's length. If you have a reputation, you have a reputation with people who don't necessarily know you. That's the difference from trust. With trust, you know somebody; reputation may precede you. You may have a reputation as somebody who is trustworthy, or untrustworthy, as someone who is a good manager, or 'good with people' or as a good teamworker, or whatever it happens to be. So your reputation spreads more widely than trust. It's a more diffuse set of relationships that you build up, over and above your specific personal trust relationships (Gandini, 2016).

Managing your reputation, therefore, is an important aspect of managing your career, especially if you are self-employed or freelance and depend on contacts for your next project or assignment. This observation leads into a consideration of the role of social media in recruitment and jobseeking strategies.

Social media and recruitment

One of the best-known online networks of professional people is LinkedIn, which, at one level, is a means by which people keep in contact with friends and colleagues across the world. However, it has a much more specialised function, which is directly relevant to recruitment and social networks, as it allows professionals to have a presence in a single digital location where they can post up their educational background, accomplishments and aspirations for the attention of the world at large (LinkedIn, 2014).

This is good news for recruiters. Indeed, the main source of revenue for LinkedIn is recruitment agencies and organisations that are seeking people to fill their vacancies. They pay for a licence to trawl through all the profiles posted up, searching for the kind of candidates they require. They can specify exactly the type of qualifications, experience and skills they are looking for, or any other particular set of criteria they might want to determine, to identify all the possible candidates, who can then be approached.

A distinction can be drawn here between 'passive' and 'active' jobseeking. Active jobseeking is exactly that: you're looking for a job. Maybe you're looking for your first job, or maybe you're a bit frustrated in your current one and fancy a change, so you start actively looking for employment elsewhere. Passive jobseeking occurs when you may be perfectly happy in your job, but a recruitment agency approaches you with invitations to apply for jobs that you hadn't thought about or wouldn't even have considered. For example, a deputy head of a university department may well find herself receiving unsolicited proposals to apply for promotion to head of department elsewhere where there happens to be a vacancy. Or the head of finance in a local authority might be approached to apply for the post of chief executive in another. LinkedIn has, then, both an active and a passive function. It allows you to promote your professional profile – and hence your reputation, which others may endorse – and to create a digital network that goes well beyond the boundaries of your physical network. Such digital platforms therefore build on the notion of social networks by extending them into the virtual world, which enhances your chances of passive jobseeking. By 2020, there were almost 740 million people registered worldwide with LinkedIn, 40% of whom access it on a daily basis.

However, a downside from the employee's perspective is that employers are increasingly screening social media as part of their recruitment process, a practice known as 'cybervetting'. A survey of young people reveals that, on the whole, they are unhappy that their social media profile is being vetted in this way (see Box 13.2).

> ## BOX 13.2: UNHAPPINESS OVER CYBERVETTING
>
> More than half of the employers who use social media screening admit that they have not hired someone because of what they have found online.... Our research evidences that about half of the study participants [undergraduate students] were generally not comfortable with the practice of social media screening.... Overall, the findings speak to the complexity and nuanced nature of individuals' understanding and perception of employers using social media data for job screening. As such, we argue that business ethics in the twenty-first century need to include considerations of job applicants' social media data privacy. (Jacobson and Gruzd, 2020: 185)

Rationales for using social networks

Employers

The advantage of using social networks from the point of view of the employer is, first of all, that it's probably quicker. In the past, as we've noted, a vacancy would have been advertised in a newspaper or trade magazine, and you'd have waited for the applications to arrive by post. You might have waited several weeks for the deadline and then sorted through piles of applications to decide a shortlist, from which you'd have invited the most suitable candidates for interview. Some would drop out, but you'd hold the interviews and offer the job to your first choice, who might then turn it down or hold out for more money, and the whole process would drag on. The use of social networks, where a trusted colleague in your organisation proposes somebody for you, is likely to be a lot quicker and cheaper, and is known as the 'referral method' of recruitment – in other words, an employee refers someone they know to the employer as a candidate for a job (for an example from homecare, see Sticky People, 2017).

Arguably, it's more reliable too – depending, of course, on how the process is handled – because it aims to reduce the risk of failure. Obviously, employers don't want failures, and as an employee, neither, of course, do you – you don't want to end up in a job that you really dislike because you may have felt misled about it. Using social networks might help the employer to reduce the risk of failure by matching skills with the requirements of the vacancy more accurately. This is because networks allow you to filter people more easily – as they are already known to a colleague – and to ensure that they really have the skills and aptitudes needed before they arrive. So, the whole question of training might also be easier for people who have been pre-filtered through some kind of social network, as you already know the areas in which they might require it.

It might be more reliable, too, because, when it comes to making recommendations for employment, your colleagues are also putting their reputations on the line. If they advise you to consider somebody who actually doesn't turn out very well, that may reflect on the quality of their judgement as well, so their concern for their own reputation may also improve the filtering process. None of us wants to propose somebody who is not appropriate for a post. We'll be very careful in making a suggestion to our boss about approaching a certain person because, unless we're fairly sure ourselves, that choice, if it goes wrong, would then rebound on us too.

A strong criticism of recruitment through social networking – to which we return later in this chapter – is that it leads to organisations recruiting in their own image, which can create serious problems. That said, if you work for an organisation that stresses teamworking and you are concerned about getting people who can work well together, then pre-screening through social networks can help you to achieve 'fit' with organisational culture exactly because the candidate has already been vetted by a colleague who knows what's required. After all, with a job advertisement on a website or in a newspaper, there is no screening. A large number of people might apply, who all look very good with the right skills and qualifications but, for all you know, won't fit very well into the organisation for personality or other reasons. The filtering function of social networks can help to reduce the risk of failure and hence the cost of recruitment, a point made by Chinese employers in the following two quotations (Ko and Liu, 2017: 1510):

One senior manager suggested:

> In my experience, the more people … you know, the cheaper and easier it is to find the right people to work for you, because you only need to spend very little or even nothing at all on advertising [job posts].

An entrepreneur made similar remarks:

> I once successfully hired a mould design engineer quickly through a contact [vice president] at xxx [a regional trade association].… It is much cheaper than running a job advertisement for months with no guarantee of finding the right person.

In addition, the use of networks from the employer's perspective can help to build communities at the workplace. Teamworking and company culture (as we saw in Chapter 8) can be important for securing the commitment and motivation of employees in addition to their technical skills and competence. Hence the screening function of networking can help the employer to create communities of workers within the workplace who fit and who are able to work and collaborate together. These particular quotations are from a Chinese engineer, but his nationality isn't really important, as these are views shared by many employers across the world:

> I asked everyone I knew … who had heard about this company, including the person who introduced me to my boss. Apart from the

salary and benefits package, I wanted to know whether the people here [my boss and colleagues] are nice to work with and whether they will take advantage of others or not. Their answers helped me to make the final decision. (Quoted in Ko and Liu, 2017: 1514)

A senior manager added:

I believe we are the best company, with a good reputation for paying engineers a good salary and offering training opportunities. This is simply word-of-mouth, since lots of us who work for this company are from this town…. Therefore, the people here know us [the company] well and also recognize our status in the die-casting industry. (Quoted in Ko and Liu, 2017: 1513)

The employer starts off with candidates from a certain town who turn out successfully, which has steered him in the direction of recruiting from the same location again, because he has come to trust the kind of applicants he has found.

Workers

From the worker's side, there are also advantages to social networking. One, of course, is that it is a helpful way to try and find a job, as we've already seen. It takes its place alongside other techniques, such as replying to advertisements, because your friends and family know you well and may be able to help you find a job.

Social networking may also help to reduce the cost or the problems of a mismatch. One of the worst things about finding a new job is when, after two or three weeks, you know you've made a mistake. You apply for a job that you think is going to be really great, and you arrive and find it's nothing like what you were expecting, maybe because the work is more routine than you'd hoped or because you just don't get on very well with your colleagues for one reason or another. This is really frustrating, because it wastes everybody's time and leads to a great deal of upset, on both your side and on the employer's. Accepting a job through some form of social networking makes it less likely that you will find yourself quitting early because of pre-screening (Callaghan, 1997).

Social networks also allow you to find out more about the job beforehand. In an interview for a job, you'll have the opportunity to ask for more details, such as what it really involves and the pay, terms and conditions, but you don't really know the truth. All organisations (and interview panels) project a certain image of themselves as being a good place to work. You don't discover the realities until your first day. Through your social network, however – that is, through your acquaintances or relatives – you are more likely to find out the real nature of the job in advance, warts and all. An insight into the job from your contact will give you a far more accurate version of the truth about the organisation and working conditions than you would ever get from a job interview. It means that you'll know in advance that you can build on the kinds of skills you've got in an appropriate way.

The use of social networking can also help avoid the demoralisation of getting continually rejected in your job applications. We've all been there. One of the most difficult challenges when submitting your curriculum vitae (CV) for a job is knowing how to make it stand out from the rest. However good you are – however skilled and motivated – the human resources (HR) manager who sifts through all the applications doesn't know you at all. Yours is just one CV among many, you don't know the office politics that might underpin the selection criteria, and if you don't make the shortlist, then you end up rejected. You might ask: what am I doing wrong? Well, maybe you're not doing anything wrong at all. It's just the fact that, for some reason or another, your CV just isn't hitting the mark. This risk is likely to be reduced if you're going for a job where you already know somebody in the company and know the unvarnished truth about the requirements.

Furthermore, as this quotation points out, insider truths might help you as an employee to negotiate your pay and conditions when you start:

> My friend ... told me how much my boss is usually willing to pay for an engineer like me and how much he paid the individual who did the job previously.... I can use this information when discussing my salary with my future boss. (Quoted in Ko and Liu, 2017: 1514)

Knowing the salary of your predecessor will help you greatly if your interviewer asks how much you expect to be paid or, if you are successful, in setting out a realistic amount for negotiation.

Downsides to recruitment through social networking

So far, this chapter has been quite upbeat about the advantages of social networking for both employers and workers. However, we must now examine the downsides as they may have serious implications for employers and workers too.

Cloning within organisations

We can start with the prospect that social networking reinforces cloning within organisations, that is, organisations risk recruiting in their own image. In other words, you have a group of people within the organisation who, rather than looking outside at external sources for appointments, tend to recruit people who look much like themselves. After all, if you are recommended to a company by a colleague or somebody who already works in the company, then that person, by definition, is already an insider, and therefore it's an insider who's recommending somebody to become another insider in a process that snowballs, and so you are likely to be very similar to the person who's recommended you:

your face already fits. We can observe here a self-reinforcing, self-magnifying challenge for organisations, that if they always recruit in the same image, they are likely to reinforce social prejudices and biases within their own structures. A company that is predominantly white and male is likely to recommend to itself and appoint further white, male staff (we noted examples in Chapter 8 on the 'new' unitarism). There may be gender or minority ethnic issues here that are not being confronted.

A good example can be found in football. Some 79% of professional football clubs in England recruit senior administrators through informal mechanisms, including personal recommendation and 'word of mouth' networks (Bradbury, 2011). So, if you are an administrator in football, you have almost a four in five chance of being recruited by somebody who knows you. Only 20% of football managers and administrators are recruited through non-social network means: 'club owners have traditionally exhibited little awareness of the qualifications, experience and competence of minority coaches and tend to recruit coaches from a limited "knowledge bank" of already known applicants from within the dominant (white) social and cultural networks of the football industry' (Bradbury, 2011: 23).

Your opportunities to make a career in football administration are therefore going to be limited if you are not already part of these 'social and cultural networks' – particularly if you are female or from a minority ethnic background. Maybe football is an extreme example, but, actually, such limitations will exist in any organisation that relies on social networks for its recruitment.

The issue revolves around the grounds for recruitment: productivity and effectiveness, or ability to fit in and likeability. The two things aren't the same at all. A candidate could be productive and unlikeable, or unproductive and likeable. In the second case, a candidate could be similar to yourself but lack the cutting-edge of somebody else who might be completely different from you, who you don't know about simply because you're recruiting only through your own limited social networks. This result is known as 'affinity bias' (Shwed and Kalev, 2014). Affinity bias is something that we all suffer from – everybody does. Affinity bias is when we socialise and network with people like ourselves, which means by age, educational background, ethnic background, gender, possibly region and religion, and social class. There are all kinds of these affinity biases that we have to be aware of as HR managers, workers and, indeed, as decent human beings. Network favouritism can reinforce these affinity biases and divert attention from the advantages of recruiting outside our familiar networks.

Pedigree and privilege

A case study of class and the notion of 'pedigree' illustrates many of these issues. Lauren Rivera (2015b) argues that the nature of privilege has changed. In the past, privilege took the form of inheritance, with the owner of a company, for example, handing it on to their sons or daughters, and then grandsons or granddaughters down the line, so companies were retained in the family. Today, however, privilege is transmitted through the educational system. Students in higher education will study for their Bachelor's or Master's degrees, or maybe a Doctorate, but in doing so meet fellow students, some of whom they will continue to know as friends throughout the rest of their lives. Their careers will vary in terms of success. Some may fall by the wayside, but others will become successful in various areas of work, and they may accordingly be able to help them out later on, and vice versa. Attending lectures is therefore only part of what students are doing in going to university, especially at a so-called 'elite' university. However, Rivera (2012: 1016) points out that many working-class students fail to recognise this aspect of their education: 'Working-class students are more likely to enter college with the notion that the purpose of higher education is learning in the classrooms, and invest their time and energy accordingly. But the [fact that] these students focus on academic rather than extra-curriculum pursuits adversely affects their job prospects.'

The advantage of focusing on 'extra-curriculum pursuits' is that socialising with your fellow students may assist you later in your professional life, clearly, but the disadvantage – as we have seen – is that it may also blind you to the benefits of a more diverse workforce. Time and again the people interviewing candidates for jobs in Rivera's study made decisions 'based on subjective issues such as whether a candidate had "polish", "breadth" – and "pedigree"' (Rivera, 2015b: 2). Among 120 employers in elite professional services, Rivera reports that hirers sought candidates who were not only competent but also culturally similar to themselves in terms of leisure pursuits, experiences and self-presentation styles.

'Polish', 'breadth' and 'pedigree' all refer to your social capital. Social capital is an unequally distributed resource – the more elite your contacts, the better. It appears reflected in your implicit skills, such as your worldly knowledge, self-confidence, charm and social ease, all of which are apparently as important in the labour market as your qualifications and technical skills. You may find all this rather depressing, but Rivera's evidence is persuasive. And so, social class – this notion of 'pedigree' is redolent of social class, particularly higher social class – remains a central aspect in recruitment, particularly for elite jobs in accounting, consultancy, the law and finance. The same is true for the UK as well as the US: positions in these professions tend to go to young people who are of a certain class background or from certain universities (Ashley et al, 2015).

Recruitment is, therefore, not just a matter of matching skills to the vacancy. It is partly that, of course, but it's also to do with cultural matching and the affinity bias that underpins much of the process, particularly in the higher level professions. The implication is that qualifications are not the only factors that are important in the job market. Social networks and connections play a major part too.

Personality types and recruitment

Apart from the role of social networks, we can also speculate that having a certain personality type might affect your recruitment chances (see Box 13.3). If you're an extravert, an outgoing sort of person who has little compunction in telling everyone how wonderful you are, then you're in a very different position from somebody who may also be highly skilled and competent, but who is much more of an introvert (Jung, 2016 [1923]). If, for whatever reason, you don't feel comfortable in talking about your achievements and successes and you're reticent about proclaiming your skills, then – in an extravert world – that may prove a difficulty for you.

BOX 13.3: EXTRAVERTS AND INTROVERTS IN JOB INTERVIEWS

Barry Deutsch (2014) argues that: 'Introverts have it really tough in most job interviews. It borders on having the deck stacked against you. It might seem that the hiring manager is playing with a different set of rules in the card game.' Admitting that he is himself an extravert, Deutsch contends that job interviews generally favour extraverts for two basic reasons.

To start with, first impressions generally have an important influence on recruitment panels, which then spend the rest of the interview in validating them. Introverts, by their very nature, may make a poor first impression, coming across as cautious and reticent and not at all as the friendly, outgoing type wanted in a management role. Once introverts get to know you, things can, of course, change – their initial awkwardness disappears and they become as sociable as anyone else. The problem is just that a recruitment panel may assume that their rather uncomfortable first impressions are typical of the introvert's whole personality and behaviour, which would be incorrect but damage their prospects.

Furthermore, questions asked at job interviews require confident, fluent answers. Extraverts are good at self-projection and like to talk and express their views and opinions, while introverts generally prefer to consider the question carefully and think about their answer before replying. Unfortunately, careful consideration may involve a long pause before the answer, which may give the impression of hesitancy and indecision, qualities that will count against the candidate. A recruitment panel is looking for assurance and promptness in responses, which is why introverts may find interviews a challenge.

It's been argued that in the US and other advanced capitalist countries, the extravert personality has now become 'the cultural ideal' (Cain, 2012: 19).

Extravert women and extravert men may both tend to succeed in job applications at the expense of introvert men and introvert women, as Box 13.3 suggests. In a study of graduating college seniors in the US, Caldwell and Burger (1998: 130–1) concluded that: 'the applicant's level of Extraversion was the best single predictor of whether or not the individual received a job offer'.

Concluding comments

We've referred in this chapter to certain advantages of using your social networks to help you find a job, but we must also consider people outside suitable networks or those who find it difficult to make contacts within suitable networks. Indeed, we find that social networks may undermine or hinder equal opportunities policies and our understanding of fairness at work. This is because (as we explore further in our next chapter) the whole point about equal opportunities is that you try to ensure that people, whatever their gender, ethnic background, religion or sexual orientation, among other criteria, are treated exactly the same within the recruitment process. And if they are not, then the process is unfair and may be discriminatory. So discrimination is at least implicit in the way in which social networking operates.

We can highlight here some of the points that we'll develop in our next chapter on diversity. As we'll see, there are various theories to explain discrimination and inequality at the workplace. However, social networking is central to understanding discrimination in the workplace – at least, certain aspects of it – because, once you've got your job, the way in which you then progress through your career has much to do with the connections and linkages that you have forged with others in a position to help or hinder you. Those connections can prove more important, in many circumstances, than your formal qualifications.

The use of these connections helps to explain the 'glass ceiling' – the barrier that many women and minority ethnic groups experience when applying for promotion to the higher levels of the professions (Maume, 1999; Cotter et al, 2001). Women and minority ethnic groups are generally present within the lower ranks of these professions, but occupy very few positions at the highest. For example, there are comparatively few women judges and chief executive officers (CEOs) of large companies. The reason for this discrimination centres surely on the traditional domination of social networks at these levels by older, white men – summarised in that disparaging phrase 'male, pale and stale'. They rise because of their social networks, the ways in which careers are structured (which discourage breaks to raise a family) and affinity bias – the tendency to favour 'people like us'. Affinity bias is key to understanding the origins of discrimination and something we must all be aware of and deal with, not just in recruitment but also across all aspects of HRM. And it clearly helps, too, to be extravert rather than introvert.

Some questions to think about

1. Examine the different ways in which an employer might recruit workers and, in particular, the challenges of using social networks in recruitment. How might an employer ensure that their use of social networks is fair?

2. What are the advantages and disadvantages, from the employee's perspective, of relying on social networks for seeking a job?

3. Have a think about your own social networks. How happy would you be if you had to rely on them to find your first job?

4. What are your views on cybervetting? What steps have you taken (if any) to control your privacy online?

Further reading

Ashley, L., Duberley, J., Sommerlad, H. and Scholarios, D. (2015) *A Qualitative Evaluation of Non-Educational Barriers to the Elite Professions*, London: Social Mobility and Child Poverty Commission. [Report on the role of social class as a ceiling or blockage for accessing elite professions.]

Rivera, L.A. (2012) 'Hiring as cultural matching: The case of elite professional service firms', *American Sociological Review*, 77(6): 999–1022. [Empirical paper on the role of cultural capital or resources for assisting with access to elite jobs.]

Trimble, L.B. and Kmec, J.A. (2011) 'The role of social networks in getting a job', *Sociology Compass*, 5(2): 165–78. [Review of the role of social capital in distributing unequal resources in social networks.]

14

Discrimination and Diversity

In this chapter, we examine discrimination and diversity. We begin by looking at what's meant by discrimination, in particular, the difference between fair and unfair criteria for discrimination. We then turn to the evidence for discrimination on grounds of age, disability, ethnic origin, gender, religion and sexual orientation, among other criteria. Following this, we ask why discrimination actually takes place and investigate some theories to try to explain it. Finally, we look at some of the solutions that human resource management (HRM) puts forward to deal with discrimination at work, and attempt to evaluate their effectiveness.

Fair and unfair criteria for discrimination

The first thing to point out is that we actually discriminate every day, and there's 'good' and 'bad' discrimination. For example, if you are a human resources (HR) manager, you may be faced by 200 applicants for one job vacancy, and you're going to have to sift through them all to make sure you appoint the right person. This is potentially a fraught situation, as we saw in the last chapter on recruitment and selection, as you are having to discriminate between candidates. Nevertheless, it is a form of justified discrimination, because you are legitimately seeking the right candidate for the vacancy. Alternatively, you might be on a promotions committee, with 10 or 20 colleagues in the running for only one possible promotion. How do you cope with that? You need criteria to make the promotion. Or, at the other end of the scale, organisations sometimes 'downscale' or 'downsize', that is, they declare redundancies. How do you select workers for redundancy? In each case, you need appropriate procedures, as these are all everyday issues that HR managers have to contend with: recruitment, promotion and redundancies are part of the job. The question, however, is the criteria. What matters is defining the criteria for discrimination because, basically, there are fair and unfair criteria. For example, if you are appointing or promoting somebody as an accountant, does their skin colour, gender, religion or sexual orientation actually matter? The answer is clearly *no*. You need to appoint 'the best person for the job'. That's what you're trying to do, and the question is, how that objective gets thwarted by other issues that intrude. So the real question, when looking at HR procedures, is: are they fair? And what do we mean by a 'fair' procedure? Because, to emphasise the point, we're discriminating all the time, and the real question is whether we are using fair or unfair criteria.

Unfair criteria for discrimination are generally listed in legislation, and European Union (EU) member states are covered by minimum EU standards (which they may, of course, improve). In the UK, for example, there is the Equality Act 2010, which outlines nine different 'protected characteristics' or criteria on the grounds of which it is unfair to discriminate: age; disability; gender reassignment; marriage and civil partnership (that is, whether the person is married or not married, single or in a partnership); maternity and pregnancy, and whether a woman wishes to start a family; race and racial origin; religion and beliefs, which includes politics; sex; and sexual orientation. If an employer does discriminate on these grounds, then the employee affected will have a basis in law to take the employer to an employment tribunal and, providing the case is proved, claim damages.

Levels of discrimination

When discussing discrimination, we also need to be aware of the levels of discrimination we are referring to, as we often use the word 'discrimination' in quite a loose way. In actual fact, discrimination takes place in a variety of different contexts.

The first context is simply individual. Each of us – and we have to confront this – has our own preferences, stereotypes, ideas about other people, and so on, and we have to be aware of them, a point we stressed in Chapter 7. In other words, there is an individual level of discrimination. For example, a manager might say: 'I don't want to employ an older worker because older workers are less adaptable – they're less able to pick up new skills as easily as younger workers.' That might be his or her own personal view.

One level up from this is what we can call 'organisational' discrimination, which is where the organisation takes a similar view. For example, if you were appointing a bus driver, a manager might claim: 'We can't appoint a woman because women don't have enough stamina to drive buses.' That might again just be the individual manager's view. However, if it is reflected in the organisational recruitment procedures – that is, if the company consistently discriminates against women drivers on the grounds that they lack stamina (or any other grounds) – then this is a form of organisational discrimination. Clearly, individual and organisational forms of discrimination may not match. An individual might have a discriminatory view, but that doesn't mean the view is necessarily reflected by the organisation. The manager who thinks women lack the stamina to be bus drivers may be completely out on a limb in relation to the company, whose policy is indeed to appoint women as bus drivers.

Organisational discrimination may also affect labour markets dominated by company policies that inadvertently discriminate (Pincus, 1996). They may not intend to discriminate, but they do so because of the way in which they've been organised. This may involve forms of indirect discrimination. For example, a shift system that requires workers to be present at 08:00 may indirectly discriminate against women, who still tend to assume most of the caring roles within families. It would place female workers at risk of arriving late at work because other responsibilities in their lives hinder punctuality, while male workers would generally avoid that risk. However, companies can work round this. A survey might reveal that many female workers were taking their children to school at that time, involving a clash of responsibilities. A non-discriminatory response would be to introduce a flexible shift system to allow later arrival and departure times in proportion. That simple example demonstrates how a form of organisational discrimination could be dealt with relatively easily. The allocation of childcare responsibilities between men and women in family units is, of course, another matter, and one we return to in Chapter 18 on work–life balance.

Discrimination may also be institutional. The term 'institutional racism', for example, has been levelled at institutions such as the police force in the UK on the grounds that racism is not just endemic among individual police officers, but is also reflected in the very procedures of the police. This is particularly serious as it's more difficult to confront institutional racism than individual racism (Souhami, 2014). 'Structural' discrimination refers to the discrimination that – for example, in predominantly white societies – non-white citizens face at all levels of social interaction, at school, college, work and in public spaces. This broader scale of discrimination makes it more embedded or structural.

A further form of discrimination, which is in some ways the most insidious, the most difficult to counter, is what's sometimes called 'unconscious bias' (McCormick, 2016). Sometimes we are consciously biased. We may not like people of a certain type, and we have to confront that. But it's even worse when that bias functions at an unconscious level. This appears in the language managers use to evaluate gender. Correll et al (2020: 1022) report that

> men and women are equally likely to be described as having technical ability, while women are viewed as too aggressive and men as too soft. Furthermore, some behaviours, such as "taking charge," are more valued for men than for women: "taking charge" is associated with the highest performance ratings for men but not for women.

Many organisations now, during the recruitment process, won't publish the names of candidates or their age or any personal details when circulating copies of CVs to the interview panel on the grounds they might induce all kinds of stereotypical expectations and hence unconscious bias that we are simply not aware of.

This book has stressed that one of the critical points about HRM is to be self-aware. For example, we need to be aware of our perspectives on the organisation (unitarist, pluralist, radical) and the effects that all kinds of HR procedures – in recruitment and selection, performance appraisal and training and development, among many others – will have on the workers affected, not least their unintended consequences. Being aware of unconscious bias – and confronting it – requires us to be aware of what's going on in our own heads: facing up to our own views, biases, prejudices, predilections and stereotypes. A first step towards dealing with unconscious bias is to be aware of it and to then try to control it when instances arise. But whether unconscious bias training actually reduces bias remains a contentious point (Noon, 2018).

Multiple disadvantage

Discrimination becomes particularly problematic when different forms coincide. The Equality and Human Rights Commission (EHRC) (2010: 26; emphasis added) makes the point rather well:

> The impact of multiple disadvantages in a more competitive labour market, which is less forgiving of low qualifications than a generation ago, cannot be underestimated. Trends are moving in different directions, however: *disabled men are substantially less likely to work than in the past, while the gender gap in employment has almost halved since the mid-1990s, from ten to six percentage points.*

Just focus for a moment on the italicised section of that last sentence. It's saying that discrimination evolves in three ways: some forms may worsen over time, others improve over time, while, of course, others again may remain static. In addition, low skills in the modern economy, where workers have to be ever more adaptable and highly skilled, tend to reinforce certain forms of discrimination, such as gender or ethnic background. However, they are particularly serious when they coincide (see Box 14.1). If you happen to be, for example, a woman with a disability, then disability and gender coincide. If you're a woman with a disability and also from a minority ethnic background, then those factors together coincide to multiply still further the challenges you face in the labour market.

BOX 14.1: PRESSURES ON BAME WOMEN DURING CORONAVIRUS LOCKDOWN

The coronavirus pandemic has highlighted multiple disadvantages as an issue. The pandemic has affected women, minority ethnic groups, people who are low paid and people with disabilities particularly seriously, and even more so people who combine two or more of these disadvantages. Research led by the Fawcett Society (2020) revealed that unequal pressures were experienced at work and at home:

> BAME [black, Asian and minority ethnic] people working from home are more likely to say they are working more than prior to lockdown, with 4 in 10 (41% women and 40% men) agreeing compared with 3 in 10 white people (29% women, 29% men). Nearly half of BAME women (45%) say they are struggling to cope with the demands on their time, compared with 35% of white women and 30% of white men.

Similar findings have been reported in research from numerous other charities and organisations, such as the Institute for Fiscal Studies, the Resolution Foundation and the Runnymede Trust, alongside the Office for National Statistics, the Trades Union Congress and consultancies like McKinsey.

Evidence for discrimination

Patterns of inequality and discrimination in the UK are complex, so the following section (which is based on EHRC, 2019: 34–5, 37–58), merely picks out several areas by way of illustration.

In relation to *gender*, women outperform men in educational attainment at all levels, from GCSEs (the examination taken at the age of 16) all the way up to degree level and PhDs. For example, more women (33.4%) have degree-level qualifications than men (31.7%), and a higher proportion of women (75.1%) achieve a first or upper second than men (70.7%). Even so, the gender pay gap remains a reality. According to the Annual Survey of Hours and Earnings, the median gender pay gap for all employees in Britain in 2017 was 18.8%, down slightly from 19.8% in 2012. So what actually is going on here? It helps to distinguish between horizontal segregation in occupations (when members of one group, such as men, are more likely to be employed in different occupations from women) and vertical segregation (when members of one group, such as men, are frequently employed at a higher level than women in the same occupation or sector).

To take horizontal segregation first, women are underrepresented in apprenticeships in engineering and construction and are more likely to be found in apprenticeships in childcare and hairdressing, which are less well paid. Indeed, women formed the majority of employees in most low-paid sectors, including care work, leisure, sales and customer service, and administrative and secretarial occupations. Furthermore, women occupied 64.6% of jobs in the UK that paid less than the national minimum wage or national living wage (an estimated 1.2% of all jobs). They were also far more likely than men to work part time (42% of women and 13% of men), and more likely to work in insecure employment (9.3% of women and 8.7% of men), which means that they are more likely to be working in temporary work or on zero-hours contracts. Overall, women were less likely than men to work in high-paid occupations (29.4% compared with 32.8%), but they were also far more likely to work in low-paid occupations (36.8% compared with 19.3%). Box 14.2 illustrates that the gender pay gap is reduced if we compare only full-time work, but it still persists.

BOX 14.2: GENDER DIFFERENCES BY OCCUPATION AND SECTOR

Gender pay gaps as they apply to differences in occupation are best identified using comparisons of full-time employees, which controls for the effect of different volumes of part-time employees in an occupation. The gender pay gap for full-time employees in Britain was 9.5% in 2017. The gap was narrower in Wales (6.3%) and Scotland (6.6%) than in England (10.0%). This is likely to reflect that there are more employees in the public sector in Wales, as 32% of employees are employed in the public sector in Wales,

> compared with only 24% in the UK as a whole ... and the public sector has
> a narrower pay gap than the private sector.
>
> In the UK, in all ... major occupational groups, men working full time
> had higher median hourly earnings than women who did so in 2017, but
> the size of the full-time gender pay gap varied considerably. The gap was
> widest for skilled trade occupations (24.8%) and for process, plant and
> machine operatives (20.2%). It was narrowest for sales and customer
> service occupations (3.6%) and administrative and secretarial occupations
> (6.2%). The gap among managers, directors and senior officials and in
> elementary occupations narrowed between 2012 and 2017, whereas the
> gap in professional occupations increased. (EHRC, 2019: 53–4)

Box 14.2 also reveals the significance of sectoral influence on the pay gap. First, women comprise around 65% of the public sector workforce, and even higher proportions in local government and education (TUC, 2012: 3), so the imposition of austerity policies and serious cuts to the public sector since 2010 have had disproportionate effects on women's employment and career prospects. Second, there are major disparities in pay inequality even across the private sector, ranging from high in skilled trades to low in sales and customer services.

If we turn to vertical segregation, women's prospects in high-paid occupations have got better. Although 29.4% of women work in high-paid occupations compared with 32.8% of men, this gap reduced between 2010/11 and 2016/17, from 8.8 to 3.4 percentage points. This improvement is at least partly explained by the appointment of women to the boards of large companies. In 2012, women comprised only 15% of the directors of FTSE 100 companies, but by 2018, this proportion had risen to 29%, while for FTSE 250 companies, the comparable percentages had risen from 9.4% to 23.7%.

Ethnic background raises further issues. In 2016/17, 4.7% of economically active adults in Britain were unemployed, but rates varied considerably by ethnic background, with 13.4% of Bangladeshis and 10.2% of Pakistanis unemployed, but only 4.2% of white British. Between 2010/11 and 2016/17, the percentage of black and white British in insecure employment increased, although Bangladeshis and Pakistanis were twice as likely as white British to find themselves in such employment. Bangladeshis and black British were similarly least likely to be employed in high-paid occupations. On the other hand, black people (38.3%) were more likely to engage in lifelong learning activities than whites (27.5%). Chinese were the greatest achievers, with 42% engaged in lifelong learning and 60.6% with degrees (compared with only 29.7% of whites).

When we examine *religious belief*, we discover that Muslims had the lowest employment rate (50.9% compared with 69.1% for people with no religion), as well as the highest rate of unemployment (11.4% compared with 4.7% overall) and the highest chance of being in insecure employment (18% compared with 9% overall).

And we continue with *disabilities*. As the skill requirements of many jobs have risen over the recent past, disability is likely to affect chances of employment. In 2016/17, 8.1% of young people aged 16–18 were 'not in education, employment or training' (NEETs), but this proportion rose to 16.2% of those with a disability. Indeed, unemployment among disabled people stood at 8.4%, twice the rate of the non–disabled (4.2%). However, employment rates for disabled people vary according to the type of impairment, with less than a quarter of those with learning difficulties, speech impediments or mental health conditions in work.

Finally, Box 14.3 summarises some key points from a report published by the Centre for Ageing Better, which reveals that over a third of people in their 50s and 60s feel at a disadvantage when applying for a job. Note that *age-based discrimination* may compound discrimination against people from minority ethnic backgrounds.

BOX 14.3: OVER A THIRD OF OLDER PEOPLE FEEL AT A DISADVANTAGE WHEN APPLYING FOR A JOB

Researchers found that age-related discrimination may be compounded by other forms of disadvantage. The study showed that people from black and minority ethnic backgrounds were more likely to report recent age-based discrimination than those from white backgrounds (34% versus 18%).

The impact of ageism can be severe. Of those in their 50s and 60s who said they had experienced age discrimination (17%), a third (33%) felt stuck in insecure work, more than two-thirds (68%) said it had affected their confidence, and 43% said it had affected their health and wellbeing. Around three-quarters (76%) were put off applying for jobs, and a third (33%) were put off working altogether or went into early retirement. This is particularly worrying in the current climate, with over-50s being hit hard by job losses during the pandemic, and a second wave of redundancies among this group expected when the furlough scheme ends. Recent figures show that over-50s are twice as likely to fall into long-term unemployment once they lose their jobs compared to younger workers.

Source: Reproduced from an online press release, Centre for Ageing Better (2021)

Theories of discrimination

We now turn to the key question: what actually accounts for discrimination at work? Broadly speaking, we can distinguish four different theories, and we'll go through each one in turn: human capital theory; segmented labour market theory; the 'reserve army of labour' theory; and social network theory. Some prove rather more convincing than others.

Human capital theory

Human capital theory goes back to the 18th-century economist, Adam Smith. It assumes a free market in labour and the lack of any impediments to the way in which employers hire workers, and so argues that any problems in recruitment or skills stem from the employability of the worker. This theory accordingly claims that discrimination occurs because those discriminated against are less productive – in other words, an employer won't employ particular individuals because they are less productive in the labour force, which reflects on them rather than on the employer (Becker, 1993). A focus on human capital assumes that 'all human abilities to be either innate or acquired. Attributes which are valuable and can be augmented by appropriate investment will be human capital' (Schultz, 1981: 21). Such investment can come from the State, companies or individuals. Calculation of the returns on investment in education, on-the-job training, skill-building and healthcare provision give society and the individual both monetary and non-monetary returns on their investments. For example, when the State invests in health and education, it reduces the risks of workers being dependent on State welfare (Blagg and Blom, 2018). At the level of the firm, the HR manager has to decide on training investment – if the training is too broad (such as sponsoring managers to do an MBA), employees may move on after training to cash in on their additional knowledge. Company-specific training may help retain workers, as they can't easily monetise such focused training. In relationship to discrimination, human capital theory has been more micro, stressing the responsibility of individuals to invest in themselves to improve their labour market chances (Bouchard, 1998). The theory would maintain that women are more family-oriented than men, and so do not invest in their education as much as men. Similarly, minority ethnic groups and people with disabilities may have lower levels of education and so face discrimination. That's the basic idea.

When we examine it more closely, however, we discover that this theory is not borne out by the evidence. As noted above, more women (33.4%) have degree-level qualifications than men (31.7%), and a higher proportion of women (75.1%) achieve a first or upper second than men (70.7%). According to the theory, you should not suffer discrimination if you are a woman and have the kinds of skills that employers require, so surely discrimination against women and the gender pay gap should vanish – but they don't.

How convincing is this theory? By placing responsibility for discrimination exclusively on individual employees, it fails to explain why discrimination actually takes place against women. Their qualifications show that they are more highly qualified than men within the UK economy. Closer analysis of this theory, then, shows that it doesn't really stand up.

Segmented labour market theory

We came across segmented labour market theory in Chapter 9 on flexibility, when we examined the contrasts between core and peripheral labour markets. The idea here is quite a simple one, that the economy divides into primary and secondary labour markets. Primary labour markets are those characterised by high-skilled workers. A company requires a number of core employees to manufacture its products or sell its services. In addition, it requires peripheral workers to support the core functions and provide the business with its numerical flexibility and ancillary services, such as catering, cleaning, grounds maintenance and security. The theory assumes that the core, the skilled areas, tend to be populated by more highly skilled workers on permanent employment contracts, while the secondary or peripheral labour markets tend to be populated by women and other disadvantaged segments of the labour market. Segmentation results, according to the theory, because in a downturn, the employer finds it easier and more expedient to dismiss peripheral workers – who may be employed through temporary work agencies or on fixed-term or zero-hours contracts – than core workers. Peripheral workers provide the flexibility in your workforce, because, if you're reducing labour costs, you don't want to make your core workforce redundant, as you depend on them for your central income stream. The idea, then, is that men tend to populate the core, and women and other disadvantaged groups tend to populate the periphery, which is less well paid, less prestigious and less secure – and more expendable.

The question again is whether the theory is borne out by the facts. For a start, do women, for example, or minority ethnic groups, actually choose to work in peripheral areas of employment? Is this a matter of *choice* or *compulsion*? There's no empirical evidence that suggests minority ethnic groups or people with disabilities *choose* to work in a secondary sector. There's little evidence that women generally choose to work in peripheral work either, as most would prefer to work in full-time, permanent employment, although there is evidence that many women, particularly when responsible for raising children, find part-time work often helps them to accommodate a work–life balance in relation to their caring responsibilities. Some writers have suggested that women are more likely to opt for part-time jobs as a choice (see, for example, the 'preference' theory of Hakim, 1995, 2002, and the 'adaptive preference' theory of Leahy and Doughney, 2006). However, other commentators have attacked this view on the grounds that it underplays the importance of forced choice or structural constraints faced by women with children (Ginn et al, 1996). This observation is based on the major assumption that women are the carers and men are the breadwinners, an assumption that can be strongly queried, as we'll see later on in Chapter 18 on work–life balance. Nevertheless, from the point of view of traditional organisational assumptions, this is the kind of scenario that's reflected in segmented labour theory.

The other aspect of this theory to be questioned is whether the core is really so distinct from the periphery (again, see Chapter 9 on flexibility). What is the relationship between core and peripheral workers? Is it really as watertight as implied by the theory? There are some sectors, for example, restaurants, hotels and catering, where the core workers – such as those who service hotel rooms or work in the restaurants – are often seasonal or part-timers. The smaller number of full-time, permanent employees are more likely to be managers (Nickson, 2013). Or the difference between the core and peripheral workers may not be fixed but rather, you move between the groups at different stages of your life. For example, many students take jobs on zero-hours or fixed-term contracts. When not studying, it's convenient for them to earn money by doing all kinds of precarious work. Although they count as peripheral, these jobs meet students' requirements very nicely by allowing them to combine study with work. As soon as they graduate, however, those jobs will no longer appear so attractive, as graduate students are likely to aspire to full-time, permanent posts. At that point, they hope to move from the periphery into a core workforce (Farina et al, 2020).

So, position in either the periphery or core may prove to be fluid. A female worker, who's quite happy to engage in peripheral work when she's younger, may later on become a manager in the core part of the same organisation. Some companies, like Amazon and McDonald's, make a point of recruiting their management teams from peripheral workers who have proved themselves. Over time, shifts like this make the distinction between core and peripheral rather permeable, and so we can't really claim that the two are watertight. Segmented labour market theory contains important insights that are important to pursue, but the relationship between choice and structure, and permanence and change, requires more attention.

'Reserve army of labour'

Another theory, this time with its origins in Marx's work, is that of the 'reserve army of labour'. The theory centres on the idea that in capitalism workers are displaced by mechanisation on a continuous basis, and displaced workers (and those new to the labour force or who struggle to connect to work due to individual attributes or social constraints) can form a reserve of labour that is available to employers to use to dampen wages or break strikes. Labour surpluses, or displaced people from other countries, can also play this role. Whatley (1993: 526), in examining strike-breaking by African-American workers in the US, analyses both the supply side, with employers replacing expensive Europeans with cheaper African-American workers, and the demand side, as class solidarity among white workers excluded black workers who faced racial barriers and made strike-breaking a key entry route into manufacturing work, especially in companies like Ford. 'Many white workers rejected outright the legitimacy of black workers' grievances about racial exclusion from unions and employment'

(Arnesen, 2003: 322), which led to strike-breaking as a legitimate form of action to gain employment.

This theory of discrimination also depends on the nature of the business cycle for some groups, like female workers. It claims that, during the peaks of a business cycle, women will be employed because it's profitable for employers to do so, but that as soon as the business cycle falls into a trough, women are moved out of employment into unemployment, as companies no longer require them. The theory is useful in undermining biological explanations for the exclusion of women, as it stresses employer opportunism and divide-and-rule tactics that govern access to work. But we might ask if there is such fluidity in female employment? Bruegel (1979) suggests that the pattern of women's employment in the UK from the 1970s was more settled and less cyclical, with legislation supporting movement into 'male' domains and dampening the worst effects of wage discrimination seen in early periods. Yet we have seen during the COVID-19 pandemic that married women have borne the brunt of childcare and home education responsibilities and left employment (Alon et al, 2020). The problem with this theory is that there's much more to discrimination than simply the business cycle – the gender pay gap, for example, has persisted over time, even during periods of peak employment. The theory is interesting, but it doesn't really cover the whole story, which brings us on to the last one, which is all to do with social networks.

Social network theory

Social network theory, which we analysed in the last chapter on recruitment and selection, highlights the key point that labour markets are not full of atomised individuals. Labour markets actually reflect tight networks of links and relationships between people. If you're looking for a job, one of your relatives, friends or ex-colleagues may find a vacancy for you. You get appointed because you form part of a social network that acts in your favour because it gets you a job that might have been barred to somebody else from outside your connections. Hence social networks include some people but exclude others, which means it's all to do with who you know and who you don't know. School and university networks also play an important role in this respect. For this reason, organisations that are based on tight social networks tend to be very exclusionist. This is a crucial point, especially in recruitment, promotions and career advancement. For example, almost one in four Pakistani men in the UK drives a taxi for a living. This figure has doubled from one in eight in 1991, and compares to one in a hundred for the whole population (Sarkar, 2019). If you are a young Pakistani man looking for a job, it's very likely that your father, uncle or other relative is already a taxi driver. You become a taxi driver not because you actually aspire to do so, but simply because that's where the vacancies are, they're the contacts who give you the chance to have the job, and you'd rather work as a taxi driver than not at all (horizontal discrimination). This example illustrates the way in which social networks include and exclude, depending on whether you're an in-group or an out-group.

Social network theory therefore provides much insight into the nature of discrimination because in certain key institutions, such as the top FTSE companies, the Civil Service, the judiciary, the police, Parliament and the Army, among others, white male networks have operated – maybe inadvertently through unconscious bias, maybe not – to exclude people who are not white and male. It may be much more difficult, if you're a woman or from a minority ethnic background, to break into the kinds of networks that promote your career within an organisation. So, as you rise up through the organisation, it becomes very clear that, in many cases, the higher you get, the whiter and more male the environment becomes (vertical discrimination). And yet, at lower levels in those same organisations, there may be a great deal of diversity (Clarke and Smith, 2022). Why is it, then, that women and minority ethnic groups aren't rising to the top? Much is to do with social networks and the fact that it's a question of who you know and how you get promoted. Social network researchers argue that, given segregated networks and black and white employees' unequal position in the labour market, employers' reliance on employee referrals reproduces black disadvantage. Analysts of discrimination focus instead on employers' unequal treatment of equally qualified black and white jobseekers – but with the dominance of 'diversity thinking' among HR managers, the persistence of discrimination is often covert, hidden and within informal forms of social networks (Silva, 2018: 741). These sorts of issues are immensely important when we examine the origins and persistence of discrimination.

Policy solutions

What can be done about discrimination? Broadly, there are four sets of solutions. The first one we can discount, as it merely alleges that there isn't really a problem. Frankly, it claims, we don't need to do anything about discrimination because labour markets need to be free, and the ways in which they operate don't require regulation. This is a hands-off, neoliberal, laissez-faire view of the economy that assumes free markets should be left to themselves. That's a possible view and is shared widely by those on the right of the political spectrum (Peck et al, 2010). However, for those who feel that there is a problem – and one that needs to be confronted urgently – other possible solutions do exist. The equal opportunities perspective is designed to ensure that all procedures within an organisation are fair, so that candidates for a position start from the same place and, once inside, are treated equally. The affirmative or positive action perspective advocates equality of outcome rather than equality of opportunity – in other words, it argues that what's important is to ensure that women, minority ethnic groups and other marginalised groups actually achieve the same outcomes as those in the non-discriminated groups. And then, finally, a more recent development is the diversity management perspective, which maintains that we're all different, so we need to manage that diversity in one way or another. We'll examine each perspective more closely in turn.

Equal opportunities

The equal opportunities, or liberal, perspective, which is extremely influential, permeates HRM thinking in the UK and the EU, as well as in many other industrialised countries. The idea is that the law is used to establish equal opportunities policies. So, the law requires employers to pay equal pay for work of equal value and to guarantee equal conditions for categories of worker who are at risk of discrimination. It requires the employer not to discriminate against part-timers, for example, on the grounds that many part-timers are women, and therefore you'd be guilty of indirect discrimination if you did so. It also means that policy-makers will generally seek changes in legislation as a principal means of outlawing forms of discrimination, as Box 14.4 on HRM and the menopause illustrates.

> ## BOX 14.4: HRM AND THE MENOPAUSE
> Many women face lack of understanding and discrimination at work as they experience the menopause. Women report physical discomfort, distraction and anxiety, which may lead to lower levels of concentration, cognitive impairment and mood swings that can, in turn, affect performance at work. In the UK, in July 2021, the House of Commons Women and Equalities Committee launched an inquiry into menopause discrimination. It will examine whether the menopause should become a 'protected characteristic' under the Equality Act 2010 as women are currently tending to bring claims against employers under disability discrimination – and the menopause is not a disability. The chair of the committee, Caroline Nokes MP, has not ruled out changes in the legislation (Topping, 2021).
>
> Meanwhile in June 2021, Girona City Council in Spain became the first to offer eight-hours' menstrual leave a month, provided the time was made up within three months (Kassam, 2021).

HR managers accordingly draw up formal procedures for their organisation, which cover all areas of potential discrimination, such as recruitment processes, job descriptions and evaluation and promotion criteria. If everybody has the same job description when appointed to a particular position, they all benefit from a 'level playing field' for everybody. No matter what your gender, ethnic background or religion may be, you have the same job description. You undergo the same interview process and you are asked the same questions. CVs do not contain names, photos or ages, and interviewers do not ask candidates personal questions, such as their civil status or whether they have children. Those issues are forbidden under equal opportunities procedures, which aim to treat everybody the same. This attempt to create a level playing field means that everybody starts on the same basis, and it forms the basic HR approach to dealing with discrimination (Konrad and Linnehan, 1995).

Affirmative or positive action

A more radical perspective, affirmative or positive action, is based on equal outcomes. It argues that those who are discriminated against in the labour market and workplace require special treatment. Women, minority ethnic groups and people with disabilities all require positive support to bring them up to the same level as those who are not discriminated against. Positive support requires structural interventions, for example, special training or special leadership programmes for women, purely for women, as opposed to both women and men. Affirmative action makes the general assumption that dominant groups – white men, for example – won't give up their positions at higher levels of the organisation without a struggle, so disadvantaged groups need special support. The basic idea is that there are vested interests in organisations that keep organisations the way they are, in favour of non-discriminated groups. An example is the quota legislation adopted by the Norwegian government in 2006 to require 40% female representation on the boards of public and State-owned enterprises by 2008. A number of other European countries have since followed this legal route, although the UK introduced voluntary targets in 2015, currently designed to achieve 33% female representation on FTSE 100 and FTSE 250 companies. Since 2015, all FTSE 100 companies and 96% of FTSE 250 companies have had at least one female director (EHRC, 2019: 56), but this is a weaker performance than countries like France and Italy, which have legally enforceable quotas (ILM, 2021).

Figure 14.1 makes the distinction between equal opportunities and affirmative action rather well. A father (presumably) and his two sons are watching a baseball match over a fence. On the left, they're all standing on the same wooden crate. This is equal opportunities: they're all treated the same. However, you'll notice that the father doesn't actually need the crate and, while the older son certainly does need his, it doesn't actually help the youngest at all. He's standing on the same crate but he's able to watch the match only because there happens to be a crack in the fence – the crate doesn't help him. In fact, equal opportunities, the level playing field, hasn't helped him at all: he's still in a position of disadvantage in relation to the other two. By contrast, the picture on the right depicts affirmative action. You've still got the three crates, but the father doesn't need one, so you leave him out of it – he can still watch over the fence. The older child still requires one crate, but it's the youngest who is the winner here because, with two packing crates, he's now able to watch the match on the same basis as the other two. This signifies equality of outcome. On the left, you have equality of opportunity, while on the right you have equality of outcome: they all end up in the same position.

Figure 14.1: Equal opportunities and affirmative action

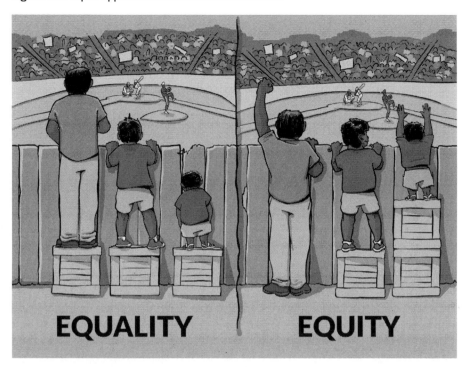

Source: Interaction Institute for Social Change (2016)

Dominant groups may, of course, feel undermined by proposals for affirmative action (Kelly and Dobbin, 1998). In Figure 14.1, no one actually loses out, but some affirmative action policies – such as the introduction of quotas – may leave dominant groups feeling threatened, which presents a challenge to their advocates when trying to have them accepted within organisations (a point we return to below).

Diversity management

Diversity management adopts a further approach towards tackling discrimination. It proposes that, because we are all different, in terms of gender, ethnic origin, educational attainment, and so on, each worker must be treated and valued as an individual. In other words, rather than treating people as stereotypes, you acknowledge their strengths and weaknesses, which you deal with as they come, and you ensure that teams are as diverse as possible, and that training systems are designed to allow people to progress as best they can. The focus is on breaking down stereotypes between people. Diversity management recognises difference and views it as a positive asset, particularly in service-related companies that are outward-facing, where, for example, workers from a particular ethnic background are put in positions where they deal with clients from the same ethnic background.

There is also, then, a business case for diversity (Robinson and Dechant, 1997). The idea here is not just moral but reflects the fact that discrimination restricts the talent pool. This is an important point: if an organisation discriminates against, for example, women, then it is failing to take advantage of their skills, knowledge and understanding (O'Leary and Weathington, 2006).

Assessment

How effective are these policies overall? As always, theory is one thing and practice is something else again. In the UK, almost three-quarters (73%) of organisations have equal opportunities policies of one form or another, but only 20% ever review them (regularity not specified) and only 10% review promotion procedures (Kersley et al, 2006). Things may have changed since 2006, but, generally speaking, it's probably fair to say that organisations, especially larger ones, do have equal opportunities policies because we expect them to do so. The more interesting question is how they are implemented. Are they actually effective?

From a practical point of view, HR managers must ensure that the organisation has embedded fair criteria for making all its HR-related decisions. Fair criteria are transparent, open and debatable and must also avoid indirect discrimination. For example, selecting part-time staff for redundancy may discriminate against women if most part-timers are women. Or a 'last-in, first-out' procedure might discriminate against younger workers if you are declaring redundancies. The workers who joined most recently are likely to be younger than those who have been with a company for longer, so such a procedure might inadvertently discriminate against younger workers. Employees must be informed about equal opportunities and have access to appeals procedures, and the system as a whole must be regularly reviewed to ensure that it is achieving its purposes efficiently and fairly.

The advantages of affirmative action need to be considered carefully, as the policy does guarantee an outcome: improved proportions of categories of worker who otherwise suffer discrimination. However, there are two challenges. First, there is the risk that well-qualified members of the dominant group may get passed over. Take quotas: we noted that in Norway, women must fill 40% of seats on company boards. The arguments for and against this policy must be open and frank. On the one hand, it can be argued that a less well-qualified woman may get appointed over a more well-qualified man purely on grounds of her gender, which could cause resentment. On the other hand, runs the counter-argument, only quotas ensure that women will ever come to fill boardroom positions and allow them to gain the experience necessary to mentor more junior female colleagues and go on to greater responsibility themselves (Bertrand et al, 2014).

The related challenge is that opponents may claim that appointments and promotions are being made solely on the grounds of gender or ethnic background, even though the candidates are not sufficiently qualified. An appointment may be perceived to take place not on grounds of skill or experience, but simply to meet a target. That potential claim is a concern because opponents may allege that such and such a candidate got the job or the promotion merely because 'she was a woman' or reflected 'a certain ethnic background'. Such allegations, if unanswered, may undermine the appointee's authority, and so must be confronted squarely (Furtado et al, 2021).

The Metropolitan Police in London has grappled with these issues, yet, despite all their efforts, only 15% of police officers are from minority ethnic backgrounds, even though 40% of Londoners are from those same backgrounds (Clarke and Smith, 2022). The Metropolitan Police exemplifies some of the challenges that have been met by those organisations that have tried to ensure that their workforces do reflect the population at large, in terms of gender, minority ethnic background and other criteria.

Concluding comments

In summary, we're discriminating all the time. The question is whether it's fair or unfair – and that's the key issue. There are a variety of different theories that explain discrimination, some rather more convincing than others: human capital theory, not very. Social network theory is more plausible, but even then, it can't reflect all the influences and forces that affect working life within organisations. In terms of HRM solutions, equal opportunities policies have proved influential, although we need to query whether equality of opportunity is enough, and whether we shouldn't also be talking about equality of outcome.

Some questions to think about

1. Evaluate the main theories that explain sources of discrimination at the workplace. How convincing do you find them?

2. Some discrimination is a function of the HRM system, such as recruiting through word of mouth or referral. Examine the ways in which an organisation might attempt to reduce or eliminate discrimination.

3. What are your views about affirmative action? How would you assess its advantages and disadvantages? How would you feel if it were applied to you, one way or the other?

Further reading

EHRC (Equality and Human Rights Commission) (2019) *Is Britain Fairer? The State of Equality and Human Rights*, June, London: EHRC, Available at: www.equalityhumanrights.com/sites/default/files/is-britain-fairer-accessible.pdf [Chapter 3, pp 37–58, provides an up-to-date summary of workplace discrimination in the UK.]

Gilbert, J.A., Stead, B.A. and Ivancevich, J.M. (1999) 'Diversity management: A new organizational paradigm', *Journal of Business Ethics*, 21(1): 61–76. [Explores the reasons why diversity replaced equal opportunities as the dominant discourse for discussing inequalities at work.]

Leahy, M. and Doughney, J. (2006) 'Women, work and preference formation: A critique of Catherine Hakim's preference theory', *Journal of Business Systems, Governance and Ethics*, 1(1): 37–48. [Critique of the idea that women with children choose to work part time, rather than make a choice between stark alternatives.]

Noon, M. (2018) 'Pointless diversity training: Unconscious bias, new racism and agency', *Work, Employment & Society*, 32(1): 198–209. [Shines a critical light on the chances for diversity training removing discrimination in the workplace.]

15

Pay and Rewards

Pay and rewards are a central part of an organisation's human resource management (HRM) strategy: getting them right helps to retain and motivate employees, but getting them wrong is likely to lead to undesirable demotivation and labour turnover. In this chapter, we analyse the ways in which managers set objectives for their employees through performance appraisal systems, and assess the advantages and disadvantages of such systems for both employers and employees. We examine reward management itself and how it has evolved, with 'older' systems based on collective bargaining with unions and the 'newer' strategic systems based on individualised methods of performance appraisal. That said, we stress that collective bargaining remains an important aspect of pay determination, particularly in continental European countries, as does the role of government regulation (for example, in the area of statutory minimum pay), which we also investigate, before drawing some conclusions.

This chapter draws together several key themes that have been running throughout the book. In Chapter 1, we pointed out that the control of unit labour costs is one of the principal aims of HRM. Pay and reward systems and performance appraisal are central to the ways in which HRM achieves these aims. In Chapter 2, on strategy, we contrasted varying human resources (HR) strategies, such as 'hard' and 'soft' HRM, in which pay and rewards played a key role. In Chapter 3, which focused on the employment relationship, we introduced the notion of the 'wage–effort' bargain – that is, the bargain that is struck between the worker, who gets paid a wage or salary, and the employer, who expects a certain effort or outcome in exchange. This bargain is often ambiguous because it is very hard to nail down in much detail. However, in terms of the nature of the employment relationship, pay and reward are clearly central. And in Chapter 7, on management styles, we discovered that managers adopting unitarist and pluralist perspectives towards the workplace tended to view pay and reward systems quite differently, with unitarist perspectives favouring individualised systems and pluralist perspectives favouring collective systems.

Broadly speaking, performance management is about controlling worker behaviour through manipulating reward 'resources' (such as pay, employment security, training and promotion). The implementation of reward systems, however, confronts divergent interests and may stir up distrust and conflict. As noted in Chapter 6 on trade unions, pay is a central concern of workplace bargaining and is an arena of major dispute. Overall, then, pay and reward management, and their relationship with performance management, strike at the very heart of the role played by HRM in organisations, whether private or public.

Performance management in unionised settings

Where an organisation recognises a union, pay and conditions will be determined through collective bargaining. The way in which performance management is developed and used within the organisation will itself be a matter for collective agreement, covering matters such as the methods and frequency of performance monitoring. Even where the union may not have much influence over negotiating performance systems, there will, in larger organisations, be grievance procedures through which individual employees can follow through grievances they might have with their employer, and, of course, the other way round – disciplinary procedures, where employers can discipline employees who are not performing as expected. Grievance and disciplinary procedures can themselves be seen as a form of performance management. This is because disciplinary procedures allow managers to intervene to improve what they regard as unsatisfactory performance, even though it's clear by then that their dissatisfaction has reached a late stage. Earlier interventions – such as advice or warnings – have come to nothing, and so they embark on their last resort, a disciplinary, which could end in dismissal.

Performance management in non-unionised settings

By contrast, in non-unionised settings – and, as we've seen, unions in many industrialised countries have been losing membership over recent years – performance will be managed through some form of management by objectives that has been introduced unilaterally by management. As Gilmore and Williams (2013: 225) point out: 'Clear goals will enhance individuals' ability to create precise intention and therefore enable them to define accurately, and act out, the behaviour required to achieve the desired goals.' The basic principle is that your supervisor or line manager ensures that you have clear goals and objectives, so that you know what is expected of you at your place of work. That's really it: a very simple idea that goes back to the work of Peter Drucker (2006 [1954]). However, how that simple idea then gets put into practice is, of course, a different matter.

To function well, management by objectives systems need to answer some basic questions that all workers are going to ask, particularly when starting a new job:

- The first is: 'What am I supposed to be doing?' This is a very good question many of us ask ourselves, even in a job we've been doing for a long time. Job descriptions help, but the requirements of a job alter over time with changing circumstances, and need to be kept under review.
- The second question is: 'How well am I supposed to do the job?' In other words, what are the performance standards I'm required to meet? This question goes back to the wage–effort bargain. Standards may not be clear to you, particularly in a new job. It's not just a matter of carrying out the tasks better or worse, but also of custom and practice and routines ('how we do things here'), that won't be known to you when you start a new job.

- Next is feedback: 'What do you think of my performance?' We all need constructive criticism on how we can do better, so providing feedback in a 'safe', non-judgemental setting is a central aspect of performance management. It requires a trusting relationship between worker and line manager or supervisor.
- Then: 'How will I be rewarded?' This feeds into the whole question of the rewards themselves, and we explore those later in the chapter.
- Finally: 'How can I improve my performance?' As a natural kind of loop, once you've had feedback from your supervisor and you know what the standards are, the next logical question is how you can improve in the future. And, particularly if bonuses are attached to higher levels of performance, you might have a monetary reason for improving, quite apart from the intrinsic psychological ones you might have anyway.

The point about performance management, then, is to answer these very basic questions, and although they are clearly important when you start a new job, they actually remain so throughout your employment, not least as a job evolves around you as conditions at work change (Godard, 2004; Liao et al, 2009; Guest, 2011).

Management by objectives

Supervisors or line managers have to set an individual worker's objectives in line with organisational objectives. So if, for example, the company's objective is to improve its market share by 10% over the next year, each individual in the organisation has to know how they are meant to help achieve that. What does it actually mean for you in the sales or marketing department or wherever you happen to be in the organisation? How do you actually link in with that goal? This is not as simple as it may seem. Liao et al (2009), who examined cases from the service sector, showed that employees at different levels of the organisational hierarchy viewed high-performance work systems very differently. In other words, translating performance into practice is not only a matter of communication but also, more fundamentally, a matter that reflects structural differences of perspective between workers and managers.

So, as an employee, you really do need to participate in the process. There is little point in a manager telling you top-down that you've got to improve your sales by 10% over the next month, without informing you of the basis for that target, where that 10% figure came from. The 10% might be achievable – or it might be absolutely impossible with the resources and staff you have. If so, you need to ensure that the manager understands that, or else there will be repercussions later. Participation, the way in which the manager involves you in setting objectives, is clearly critically important to success.

There also needs to be an ongoing review of progress towards the goal because, a quarter or halfway through the year, it should be clear whether you are on target or not. If you're falling short after specified intervals, you need to make that clear and take remedial action, or you may find, at the end of the year, that you haven't met the goal.

Reviewing progress feeds into the way in which you plan improvements in the future. The Japanese system of *kaizen* (continuous improvement) builds continual, ongoing improvements into the whole production system. Japanese companies integrate continuous improvement into the task cycle, so you are continually suggesting ways to improve it as you go along, on a never-ending basis. Bonuses may be paid according to the value of your improvements, although the precise relationship between improvements and rewards remains uncertain (Elger and Smith, 2005).

From a management point of view, it's important that objectives are clear: theorists have proposed an acronym, SMART, that is meant to help you remember five principles that underpin this clarity (Doran, 1981):

- First of all, they have to be *specific*: You have to state exactly what the goals are. So if you're in the sales department, an instruction to 'increase your sales' would be vague and general, and wouldn't help anybody. The instruction has to be: 'You need to increase your sales by 10%, or by 25%', which is specific and meaningful.
- Objectives should therefore be *measurable*: Even a specific goal is not going to help you if you don't know how to measure it (see Chapter 19 for a discussion of measurability).
- They must also be *achievable*: To be told to double your output over the next year without the resources or means to do so would be demoralising.
- Objectives must also be *relevant* to the organisation: If you want to increase sales in a retail outlet, you need to make sure that the objectives are strictly relevant for that purpose.
- Finally, they have to be *time-bound*, so there has to be a time limit on them: Objectives need to be met within a month, or two months, or a year, or whatever is appropriate. There is little point in declaring, 'We expect this in the future', but not explaining the deadline required.

Here some examples from HRM help to underline the importance of these SMART principles:

- Many organisations run employee satisfaction surveys. If, one year, 85% of your employees say that they are satisfied at work, your HR department might aim to raise that next year to 87%.
- Or you might have problems with labour turnover and decide to ensure it doesn't exceed 3% over the year (excluding retirement).
- Or you might focus specifically on retaining newly recruited staff, as the risk of their resignation is highest after about three months, which imposes a serious cost on the organisation. High levels of wastage might be reflecting on the quality of your recruitment system, which needs improvement.

- Or there may be problems with leadership. The implementation of a new grading or computer system might be posing problems for your project management team. Maybe they require more specialist leadership skills, which would be a task for your training and development department.

If you were an HR manager in an organisation facing these challenges, you could imagine having an appraisal at which you set these kinds of objectives. In each case, you'd need to discuss them in detail with your appraiser and agree specific measures to implement them within a SMART framework. If you can do that, everybody's lives are made easier because shared agreement over objectives avoids any resentment on your part that you're merely being told what to do and obeying orders.

However, there are critics of the use of SMART principles. From an early stage, some were concerned about how they would fit different managerial styles and how they could be set and measured (Jamieson, 1973). Others would argue that, while they might work for short-term objectives, they are less applicable to longer term objectives as they lack flexibility. Indeed, achieving such objectives might be undermined by any number of changing circumstances in the market, social or technological environment. In addition, measuring the achievement of *individual* objectives has become increasingly complex as responsibilities at work grow ever more interdependent and team-oriented in information-driven enterprises (Roth, 2009). And there is also the risk that SMART principles end up becoming little more than an appraiser's tick-box exercise, a kind of mechanical function that deprives projects of any sense of excitement or genuine creativity (Haughey, 2014).

That said, management by objectives has been 'part of corporate dogma for many decades' (Roth, 2009: 36). It's generally accepted in management circles that the communication of objectives is one of its chief benefits. Without an appraisal system, you may work for a large organisation and never really understand where or how you fit in. You just go in at 09:00, you leave at 17:00, you do your work, and you may have lunch with your colleagues, but you don't really know how your input is actually helping the organisation, if at all. Management by objectives at its best helps to clarify your role and to give you some sense of shared purpose. In addition, it should help you continue to improve your performance in relation to those objectives. It may well be that, after a time, you tend to get routinised in a job – you can't see the wood for the trees, and you just do the same thing over and over again. A process of appraisal, provided it is supportive and thoughtful, may well revitalise you in terms of rethinking your input and improving the work process. In such a way it can help to foster systematic improvement across the whole organisation at the same time.

Performance appraisal

And then this takes us to performance appraisal itself. We've agreed the objectives, and after a certain period – three, six, twelve months – we have to meet again to evaluate how things have gone. The search for 'objective appraisals' goes back at least to the 19th century, and probably earlier, and there are various ways to conduct an appraisal (Grint, 1993; Townley, 1993; Cummings et al, 2017).

There is, for example, a rather crude, top-down mechanism, where you meet your appraiser and go through the records to see whether or not you have actually managed to achieve your targets. You may not have much opportunity for explanations, and the appraiser just takes whatever action is required to acknowledge success or sanction failure. This is basically a top-down management communication system. A more satisfactory system is two-way, both top-down and bottom-up. The appraiser evaluates your performance by discussing what's gone well and what hasn't, and also wants your views. All sorts of things might have affected performance that was below par – a period of illness, a bereavement, an unforeseen lack of skills or expertise in a certain area that requires training. Or it might be that you've been lazy and haven't bothered, in which case your appraiser will find out soon enough. Maybe you're demotivated because you feel you've been unfairly passed over for promotion, but if that continues, your line manager might be contemplating a disciplinary procedure against you on grounds of capability. We'll return to this shortly, as the relationship between performance appraisal and discipline, on the one hand, and reward management, on the other, is a controversial one.

Another form of appraisal is called '360 degrees'. Three hundred and sixty degrees is, of course a circle. It means that you get an appraisal not just from your line manager, but also from your colleagues, peers and maybe subordinates, as well as from clients and customers (once again, clients and customers make an appearance in HRM). In other words, a much broader group of stakeholders involved in your job area might be brought into your appraisal process because that is, of course, the idea of 360 degrees, an all-encircling, comprehensive overview of your performance rather than simply your line manager's.

Self-appraisal may also play a role in the process. Your organisation may (actually, should) ask you for your own views about how you've done, and not just expect you to be subjected to the evaluation of your line manager and others. Your own views are important because they require reflection and clearly, any process within an organisation that gets workers to think critically for themselves about what they're doing, as opposed to just doing it automatically, has to be constructive, as it then leads to a greater chance of continuous improvement in the future.

'Performance appraisal', although it's a term we all use, therefore actually covers a variety of different techniques, from the very basic top-down approach right the way through to the sophisticated and time-consuming. Recent UK survey data reveal that the use of performance monitoring for non-managerial staff rose from 43% in 2004 to 70% in 2011 (Findlay and Thompson, 2017).

And since, as we have been arguing throughout this book, perceptions of HR processes are often as important as the processes themselves, it comes as no surprise to discover that perspectives on performance appraisal vary too. A unitarist perspective, reflecting the views of a manager who believes that an organisation is essentially a harmonious entity, is likely to see performance appraisal as generally unproblematic, as merely a process for the line manager to deal with, and hence not such a big thing (Newton and Findlay, 1996). A pluralist perspective might be more complex, because it acknowledges that there are challenges implicit in the processes because workers' interests may differ from those of the line manager, and so require some form of mediation in case of disagreement over performance (Wilson, 2002; Gordon and Stewart, 2009). And then those adopting a radical perspective may reject the principle itself on the grounds that any form of appraisal reflects an essentially exploitative relationship between employer and worker, and so is bound to be unfair to the worker. Appraisal is regarded as merely a form of management control, which explains why its results are so often seen as unsatisfactory (Edwards and Wajcman, 2005).

Some line managers might consider performance appraisal as a waste of time and simply not buy into the whole process. Some might believe that their job is supervision and that appraisal is a waste of their time, in that it prevents them from doing their 'proper' job (whatever that might be). Unless performance appraisal is built into managers' job descriptions and work schedules, and is something that is expected to be part of their job description, you may find that they are quite resentful of carrying out appraisals in the first place. In that case you have a real problem, because if your line manager doesn't even want to be there, then, of course, the quality of their appraisal is going to be pretty poor. Support – meaning training and time allocation – for line managers, as well as making sure that appraisal is part of the job description, is clearly central to making the process a success.

Another problem is that, once appraisal systems are linked to disciplinary or capacity issues, or to pay, they might then clash with certain developmental issues that would better be kept separate. In other words, appraisal, if it's used purely as appraisal, can be a helpful way for line managers to identify weak performance and to discuss with the worker ways to put it right, for example, through training and development. After all, every one of us at some point or another requires skill enhancement or updating to do our jobs better. And the more rapid the pace of change in our sector, the more specialised training and development we need to keep on top of. Appraisal can be really important in identifying these areas, but that role can be undermined if the worker fears that it could endanger a pay rise, or even mean a pay cut, let alone anything else, such as a warning or disciplinary.

However, things are changing, and many large US companies are moving away from formal appraisal systems based on process and ranking towards approaches based on conversation, continuous improvement and coaching. Box 15.1 summarises the position at General Electric (GE), a company once notorious for aggressively ranking its employees.

BOX 15.1: GENERAL ELECTRIC ABOLISHES FORMAL ANNUAL REVIEWS

For decades, General Electric practised (and proselytized) a rigid system, championed by then-CEO Jack Welch, of ranking employees. Formally known as the "vitality curve" but frequently called "rank and yank," the system hinged on the annual performance review, and boiled the employees' performance down to a number on which they were judged and ranked against peers. A bottom percentage (10 percent in GE's case) of underperformers were then fired.

The company got rid of formal, forced ranking around 10 years ago. But now [written in 2015], GE's in the middle of a far bigger shift. It's abandoning formal annual reviews and its legacy performance-management system for its 300,000-strong workforce over the next couple of years, instead opting for a less regimented system of more frequent feedback via an app. For some employees, in smaller experimental groups, there won't be any numerical rankings whatsoever.

With the decision, GE joins other high-profile companies – like Microsoft, Accenture, and Adobe – that have started dumping or have already gotten rid of formal annual reviews.

… Each employee has a series of near-term goals, or "priorities". Managers are expected to have frequent discussions, called "touchpoints", on progress toward those goals and note what was discussed, committed to, and resolved. The app can provide summaries on command, through typed notes, photographs of a notepad, or even voice recordings. The focus isn't on grading how well people are doing, but on constant improvement. (Nisen, 2015)

Whatever the system, we must be certain that our line manager is taking our appraisal seriously, has adequate time and listening skills to pay attention to any issue we might want to raise and, above all, has had sufficient support and training him- or herself. It's not just a matter of putting in a system and expecting line managers to operate it without any further support.

Figure 15.1 illustrates the basic problem. The appraiser is simply covering his own back. He's acknowledging that the employee has done an excellent job, but gives him a 'poor' rating in case he ever needs to sack the unfortunate Asok at some stage in the future. Understanding from Chapter 1 that HRM is all about controlling unit labour costs, it shouldn't surprise us that the line manager may well be required to fire even his best employees at some later date. If you give them poor appraisals, that will be much easier to justify, of course. To add insult to

Figure 15.1: 'Asok, your work has been excellent'

Source: Dilbert, Wednesday 16 April 2003

injury, the appraiser – having read his HRM textbooks – will know that feedback allegedly improves performance, so he assumes that even bad news will improve Asok's motivation. Okay, it's a rather cynical view of appraisal, but nevertheless the cartoon does highlight very succinctly what can go wrong.

Reward management

Reward management may or may not be linked to performance appraisal. Until fairly recently, many managers, technical and supervisory staff were also themselves covered by collective agreements but, as we've seen, coverage of such agreements in many industrialised countries has tended to shrink.

When we talk about rewards, we are talking about extrinsic and intrinsic rewards: extrinsic rewards are pay and conditions, or the material benefits that can be earned in exchange for carrying out the job (the wage–effort); intrinsic rewards, on the other hand, refer to the psychological satisfaction we get from a 'job well done' or a sense of esteem or recognition. Most of us, hopefully, will aspire to both, but they are not at all the same. A highly paid job might be extremely boring and bring little satisfaction. By contrast, a voluntary job might not be paid at all, yet nevertheless provide us with a tremendous sense of being worthwhile. Both qualities are generally combined to a degree: we obviously need to be paid an acceptable rate for the job, but we'll also hope to gain some kind of sense of satisfaction from it too. Most of us would normally avoid a job that is meaningless or lacks any kind of satisfaction (Graeber, 2018).

In this chapter, we are focusing on extrinsic rewards: reward management, in an HRM context, refers principally to extrinsic rewards. We're talking particularly about pay, conditions and fringe benefits, and how the level of reward should be determined: how much do we pay this worker? It's a very basic question. Others follow: what form should payment take? How much should be fixed, and how much should be variable (that is, based on bonuses or commission) or, indeed, should it all be variable? If you're a salesperson, you may earn your money purely through commission, based on the value of the products or services you've sold, in which case your pay is entirely variable and you may have no fixed element at all.

The relevance of our analysis of the wage–effort bargain (in Chapter 3) now becomes apparent. The wage–effort bargain, as we stressed, is ambiguous but based on the authority of the employer. The pay rate is generally predetermined, but only up to a point if it includes a variable element. The effort required in exchange for the pay is certainly ambiguous, as it may vary as working conditions change. Somehow, employers have to set acceptable rates of pay and conditions amid all this ambiguity and variability, and ensure that they maintain motivation at the same time.

A model of reward management must, arguably, cover a number of key elements. Bratton and Gold (2017: 264–70) provide a helpful checklist that can be used to make sure you're not missing anything significant:

- The first point is that the reward system must be linked to the organisation's *strategy* (which we established in Chapter 2). If your company is operating an integrated HR strategy aligned to its business needs, then pay and rewards are a critically important factor. The degree to which reward is tied to performance-related pay or bonus systems, for example, has to be linked to the quantity and quality of high-cost/low-cost output you require from employees in the kind of market that you find yourself.
- Reward *objectives* refer to the employer's concern to recruit workers with the right skills and attitudes, to ensure their commitment to the organisation and to secure their performance, all of which underpin control of unit labour costs. Appropriate extrinsic rewards can promote all three, although employers also need to bear mind the role of intrinsic rewards in this respect.
- The *options* include pay systems that are individual or team-based. Bonuses, for example, may be awarded for individual or team performance. The question is, which is the more appropriate, given organisational strategy and objectives?
- Job evaluation (the process of evaluating jobs in terms of their contribution to organisational objectives) and appraisal systems (some of which we reviewed earlier in the chapter) are two of the *techniques* that HR managers may use to ensure that workers regard the pay system as fair across the whole organisation.
- Finally, *comparability* or *competitiveness* must also be taken into account when drawing up a pay system. Pay is not just a matter internal to the organisation, but it's also one external to it, as employers want to attract and retain workers at the right level without the risk that they may be poached by a rival offering better pay and conditions. Indeed, you might justify paying key members of staff at slightly above the market rate for that very reason.

These are the basic elements that a reward management system must cover. Actual decisions about the detail will vary according to circumstance. It's impossible to make universally applicable proposals. Much will depend on the kind of organisation under discussion, its strategy, market, technological base and local labour market conditions, among other factors.

New or strategic pay paradigm

We have established that the effectiveness of an organisation requires some kind of match between its business strategy and its HR strategy, which, in particular, determines the kind of rewards system it introduces. The 'new' or 'strategic' pay paradigm that has been implicit in much of our earlier discussion has, over recent years, come to focus on the individual and their performance. As trade unions have declined in influence in many (but not all) countries, employers can no longer rely on collective agreements to cover whole sectors of their workforce. As pay has become more individualised, rates have become more fragmented across organisations, although individualisation allows the organisation to become more adaptable and flexible in terms of labour costs, in line with the turbulence in markets. Figures reveal that the proportion of workplaces with merit (or bonus) pay increased slightly overall in the UK, from 40% to 41% from 2004 to 2011, with an increase of 41% to 43% in private workplaces and a steady figure of 17% in the public sector (van Wanrooy et al, 2013: 25). Trends in the public and private sectors are distinct, notably because the public sector remains more highly unionised and resistant to individualised pay systems.

Table 15.1 systematically compares and contrasts the 'old' job-based (or collectively agreed) model of pay determination with the 'new' strategic (or post-bureaucratic) pay model. It displays in tabular form the key differences between the two. The job–based pay model, or the model based on collective agreements, which covers whole sectors of the workforce at the same time, awards a base monthly wage or salary, as well as other conditions, for each job category that's included. For example, anyone can find out the pay and conditions of a lecturer employed in a UK university at a certain point on the pay spine simply by looking them up in the current collective agreement negotiated by the Universities and Colleges Employers' Association (for the employers) and the University and College Union (for the employees). The strategic pay model, by contrast, relies on performance appraisal so that pay is more variable – your pay is adjusted according to whether you meet, or don't meet, your objectives. The more hard-nosed

Table 15.1: 'Old' versus 'strategic' pay models

'Old' job-based pay model	'Strategic' (post-bureaucratic) pay model
Base wage or salary	Variable pay
Based on cost of living and labour market	Based on organisational performance
Evenly distributed between employees	Differentiated
Correlated with length of service	Based on individual performance
Bonuses based on individual performance	Bonuses based on team and organisational performance
Reward flows from behaviour	Reward used as a means of communicating

Source: Adapted from Bratton and Gold (2017: 283)

organisations will reduce pay if you haven't met your objectives, and some may dismiss you altogether if your performance continues to fall below expectations.

Job-based pay models lead to a high level of equality between employees because the collective agreement imposes the same rate for all workers in the particular job category that's covered. The key word here is 'collective'. They're all being paid the same rate because it's assumed that they're all doing the same job and make the same level of effort. However, as soon as you move into an individualised system, any notion of standard pay fragments. Colleagues working side by side generally won't know what the other is being paid, and may well get upset if they find out, particularly if those less well paid are employed through an agency (see Box 2.3).

Bonuses based on individual performance have tended to give way to those based on team performance, while reward based on behaviour – doing the job as best you can – has tended to give way to reward used as a means of communicating. In other words, higher pay is a way in which organisations signal that they regard you as a more highly performing, highly valued colleague than before. So the way in which pay itself is viewed within the organisation may vary according to the predominant pay model.

Possible consequences of strategic pay models for workers

There are, then, distinct contrasts between job-based and strategic pay models. While the strategic pay model appears to allow the organisation greater flexibility in linking pay to individual performance, a number of questions arise from the employee's point of view about its actual operation (Edwards and Wright, 2001).

For example, the new model needs to ensure that team effort is not undermined by individual performance-related pay systems. If the organisation requires teamwork, then the pay model has to reflect team performance, rather than individual performance. And even then, the question arises as to the efficiency of teamwork, given that it can lead to the 'free-rider' problem. The free-rider is the team member who doesn't pull their weight and relies on the others to cover for absence, lack of participation and other forms of poor performance. Teamwork requires careful management to avoid free-riding (Comer, 1995).

Demotivation might also be an unintended consequence of strategic pay models. Commentators note that performance-related pay helps to motivate, but disappointment at missing a pay rise as a result of failure to meet objectives can lead to demotivation and dissatisfaction. The literature focuses on the positive aspects of individualised pay systems, but glosses over their potentially negative aspects, which organisations also need to consider (Tweedie et al, 2019).

It may also be that strategic pay models favour the extravert personality over the introvert (as we saw in Box 13.3). If you are an outgoing, confident sort of person, and you're happy to sell yourself to your line manager and demand a pay rise, your behaviour may well prove successful. By contrast, your unfortunate colleague, who's an introvert and wouldn't say boo to a goose, is far less confident even though equally (or more) competent, and risks getting penalised simply by failure to project him- or herself. A serious implication of this is the effect that confidence and self-projection has on the gender pay gap. Some commentators would argue that individualised pay systems tend to favour confident men as opposed to women, who may lack confidence in promoting themselves (Rubery, 1995; Festing et al, 2015). Whether or not self-confidence is mainly a masculine trait, it is certainly a quality that defines extraverts, so strategic pay models are likely to favour extraverts (male or female) rather than introverts (male or female).

Furthermore, at board level, some would claim that strategic pay models have led to soaring levels of executive pay, and that it's executive power, rather than performance, that explains this growth (Grabke-Rundell and Gomez-Mejia, 2002). This is a complex area, but company remuneration committees have frequently seen fit to pay out enormous bonuses, which bear little or no relationship to performance, and sometimes reflect corporate failure rather than success.

Of course, it must be stressed that the job-based pay model has by no means disappeared. Collective bargaining hasn't vanished in the UK, as we saw in Figure 6.3, let alone in other industrialised countries, such as Austria, Belgium and France, where it remains centrally important for pay determination. Collective systems are still significant and often operate alongside the newer, individualised models.

Low pay, no pay and new insecure models

Even though individualised pay systems are by no means the only game in town, their spread is, however, associated with low pay and insecure payment models. Maury (2020: 810–11) discusses the increase in unremunerated work as payment systems, like zero-hours contracts (ZHCs), increasingly split work into blocks and short shifts spread over the working day interspersed with hours of unpaid waiting, and into piecework paid by the completed task, often demanding additional unpaid labour. In some sectors, such as the creative industries, unpaid work has moved from a feature of early career experience to wider dispersal among those seeking work, especially affecting women (Shade and Jacobson, 2015). But in sectors like care work, ZHCs blur the distinction between paid and unpaid labour, with the introduction of electronic monitoring (EM) obscuring the lines between the two still further:

> In the context of local authority commissioning and constrained budgets, the combination of EM and ZHCs may excise so-called "unproductive" but available labour from homecare. In particular, the minute-by-minute commissioning of care that EM facilitates means the cost of homecare is anchored in the time that workers spend in clients' houses, squeezing out paid travel, time between visits, training and supervision. Paid working time is minimised whilst maximising

the use of unpaid time with resulting intensification of care labour. (Moore and Hayes, 2017: 101)

Work is intensified by stripping out dead time or transferring such time to be borne by the worker. ZHCs tightly match supply and demand, but at the cost of workers suffering uncertainty over pay and wasting time without pay. We saw in Chapter 9 that the 'just-in-time' agency workforce could be employed and stood down at will. Box 15.2 illustrates how this can have an impact on wages.

BOX 15.2: AGENCY STAFF MAY DO THE SAME WORK AS EMPLOYEES, BUT LACK SECURITY AND SUFFER PENALTIES

In a ready-meals factory in the British city of Sheffield, workers stand side by side putting sausages in pots before a depositor adds sauce and a machine adds mashed potato. But there is an invisible divide on this production line: a seam of inequality that runs through the UK and other countries, too.

Some workers are regular employees with 39-hour-a-week contracts, while others are agency staff employed by a third party. If the line shuts halfway through the night, the permanent staff will be redeployed or asked to clean until the end of their shift. The agency staff will be sent home immediately with no more pay but, because the first bus isn't until 5am, most will sit through the rest of the night in the canteen.

When they get home, they will wait for a 10am text message from the agency to confirm the next shift. "It's not fair when they know he's done nights and he's in bed," one regular employee told me of her agency worker colleague on the same production line. "If he doesn't confirm within half an hour, he gets cancelled." (*Financial Times*, 2020a)

Minimum pay legislation

The receding coverage of collective bargaining in many countries has led to downward pressure on pay at the lower ends, which has required governments to intervene to prevent the exploitation of the lowest paid workers. The US introduced a federal minimum wage in 1938, the UK introduced statutory national minimum pay in 1999 and Germany did the same in 2015. While legislation underpins collective determination of pay in many countries, many new sectors – such as fast food, delivery services and the gig economy more generally – now slip through any form of regulation, even in coordinated market economies. This has meant that government regulation of minimum pay has, in recent years, actually become increasingly significant.

Yet the legislation often remains unenforced. Nearly 140 companies investigated by the UK government between 2016 and 2018 had failed to pay £6.7 million to more than 95,000 workers. The companies, which included Tesco, Pizza Hut and Superdrug, responded that the underpayments were historic errors and that employees had been quickly paid back (BBC News, 2020). In addition, some sectors, notably hospitality, rely to a large degree on tipping as a means of employee remuneration, which is also associated with low and insecure pay (Mulinari, 2019).

The COVID-19 pandemic has affected low-paid workers particularly seriously in the UK, because they are most likely to be found in sectors such as hospitality and non-essential retail, where a high proportion of workers are already on the minimum wage. These are the sectors most likely to be shut down in the pandemic, and the workers involved are the least likely to be able to work from home (Powell and Francis-Devine, 2021).

Concluding comments

Overall, individualising the employment relationship has led to the increased use of performance-related HR systems. Performance appraisal can be a helpful means for improving communications between line managers and workers, but only if managers have the requisite training, time and support, and if the appraisal system itself isn't linked to pay determination or to possible disciplinary procedures. If it is, it risks demoralisation on the part of the worker and undermining the whole appraisal system itself. Furthermore, while strategic pay models have become more significant in HR practice, the old job-based model remains important in certain sectors and in certain countries, particularly coordinated market economies. And low pay remains a central issue.

Some questions to think about

1. What are the challenges faced by organisations when they introduce performance appraisal systems? How might managers with pluralist perspectives differ from managers with unitarist perspectives in the kinds of solutions they propose to meet these challenges?

2. How happy would you be to work under a traditional performance appraisal system? In the light of Box 15.1, how do you think they might evolve over the next 10 years or so?

3. What risks do you see (if any) in the replacement of the job-based model of pay determination with newer strategic models?

4. What role should trade unions play in determining pay and conditions? And what role should government play?

Further reading

Guest, D. (2011) 'Human resource management and performance: Still searching for some answers', *Human Resource Management Journal*, 21(1): 3–13. [Overview of the relationship between pay and performance.]

Moore, S. and Hayes, L.J.B. (2017) 'Taking worker productivity to a new level? Electronic monitoring in homecare – The (re)production of unpaid labour', *New Technology, Work and Employment*, 32(2): 101–14. [Empirical investigation into the effects of new technology on monitoring a worker's time in the care sector and the impact on paid and unpaid work.]

Nisen, M. (2015) 'How millennials forced GE to scrap performance reviews', *The Atlantic*, 18 August, Available at: www.theatlantic.com/politics/archive/2015/08/how-millennials-forced-ge-to-scrap-performance-reviews/432585 [Analysis of the pressures traditional appraisal systems are under as generational attitudes change.]

16

Employee Participation and Involvement

In Chapter 15, on pay and rewards, we noted that performance appraisal systems are most likely to succeed when workers are involved in their design, and certainly in their operation. This chapter focuses on employee participation and involvement more generally, and how employers try to involve workers at their place of work in an attempt to make them feel part of the organisation and give them the chance to influence their working conditions and environment. We begin by looking at some theories of employee participation and involvement, as well as the rationales for introducing it. We then turn to types of employee participation, in particular, direct and representational forms. We move on to look at trends in the UK and across Europe to see how far employee participation is a reality, before drawing a few conclusions.

Historically, governments have tended to introduce forms of worker participation as a means of channelling outbreaks of resistance that might otherwise have become more serious (we examined conflict and resistance in Chapter 4). In late 19th-century Germany, for example, legislation to introduce works councils was used to head off the rise of socialism among workers, while in France and Italy, forms of employee representation at the workplace were established immediately after the Second World War as concessions to workers to help undermine the perceived threat of communism. It is striking, too, that interest in employee participation tends to come in cycles, peaking when the economy is strong. When there's full employment, employers are concerned about losing workers, and one way to keep them is to integrate them as far as possible into the company through participation schemes. However, with a downturn and higher levels of unemployment, it would appear employers are rather less interested in forms of participation because they think the labour market will provide enough of a threat to keep workers where they are. Because workers are in a weaker position, it's no longer so important to listen to their views or to consult them (Ramsay, 1977). Maybe this is an oversimplification, but there is some truth in this view. Some forms of participation, such as workers' cooperatives, do periodically emerge at times of economic crisis. In the UK in the 1970s (Gold, 2004) or in the late 1990s and early 2000s in Argentina (Atzeni and Ghigliani, 2007), for example, workers' cooperatives were used in an attempt by workers to save their companies. If a company was being closed down, workers would sometimes take it over to try to save their jobs.

The fundamental issue involved in employee participation is the contrast between exit and voice (a contrast we already met in Chapter 8): the way in which employers attempt to control workers, either by listening and allowing them a degree of influence at the workplace, or else by not really bothering and saying, 'Right, if you're not keen on working here, that's fine – leave.' The options are 'exit', which means turnover, and leaving your job if you're not satisfied, or 'voice', how, if you're dissatisfied, you express your opinions and rectify the problems you've got at work through consultation and negotiation. The basic point here is: to what extent are employers and managers actually going to listen to you and act on your views?

Rationales for employee participation

There are a number of rationales for employee participation. The most fundamental is that, just as those of us who live in democratic societies have political and legal rights as citizens, we should also be able to access rights as employees to protect our interests at work. There appears to be a parallel between our rights as a political citizen and our rights as an employee in relation to our employer. It's a powerful argument: if we have rights as citizens, then we should also have rights as workers. The relationship between political democracy and employee participation is complex and controversial, but it remains central to debates about how to make companies in capitalist societies more accountable to workers and other stakeholders (for a classic analysis, see Pateman, 1975). The growth of migrant workers across the world might, however, dilute this argument slightly, as employers may target migrants for recruitment precisely because they lack democratic or political claims on the workplace.

In addition, there are business rationales for employee participation (Summers and Hyman, 2005: 8–11). All of us would prefer our efforts at work to be recognised, a point demonstrated in the Hawthorne experiments back in the 1920s (see Chapter 1). We are more likely to comply with instructions from a manager who has explained the reasons behind them than with those from a manager who hasn't bothered. Listening to employees' views, and encouraging them to express their ideas, gives them a sense of ownership towards decisions that may affect them and, as a result of that, it may improve their motivation and commitment. The basic psychology of employee participation is really that if we're listened to at work, then we're more likely to be committed and motivated.

A further business rationale for employee participation is behavioural, and goes back to our discussion of conflict and resistance in Chapter 4. Managers recognise that workplaces are often characterised by certain levels of rumbling, unorganised conflict, such as unplanned absences, calling in sick and poor timekeeping. Forms of employee participation may be used to head off resistance by showing that the company genuinely respects and values you as a worker. If you feel respected and valued, then – so runs the argument – you are less likely to go absent. Box 16.1 reveals strikingly high levels of disempowerment among employees in US industry, which convert into low levels of engagement at work.

BOX 16.1: LACK OF ENGAGEMENT IN US INDUSTRY

The economic cost of this disempowerment is enormous. The Gallup organization polls many employees on behalf of their employers, to ask if employees are 'engaged' – as measured by responses to questions about whether at work they feel they have the opportunity to do what they do best, their opinions count, they are committed to quality, and they have opportunities to develop their skills. They have found that the levels of employee engagement in US industry are on average startlingly low: only one-third (33%) of US workers were engaged in 2016. Half of all employees (51%) were 'not engaged' and another 16% were 'actively disengaged'. Other polls show that for fully 55% of private sector workers, their job is 'just what they do for a living', rather than giving them any sense of purpose or identity. Moreover, Gallup has found huge performance differences between those business units in the top quartile of engagement as compared to those in the bottom quartile as concerns safety (70% fewer safety incidents), product quality (40% fewer defects), productivity (17% higher productivity), and even profitability (21% higher) (Adler, 2019: 13).

Evidence certainly suggests that employee participation makes good business sense for employers (Morishima, 1991; Pfeffer and Veiga, 1999; Lawler et al, 2001; Peccei et al, 2005). It shows very firmly that various forms of employee participation can lead to better financial performance, higher levels of discretion at work, greater commitment and motivation, and therefore to improved labour productivity and product quality. Employee participation is also linked to turning out fewer defective products. There is strong overlap here with the evidence we reviewed for the effectiveness of 'high–performance work practices' in Chapter 2 on strategy, as such work practices largely revolve around forms of employee participation.

Dimensions to employee participation

At this stage you might be wondering what employee participation actually looks like. It is helpful to distinguish between a number of different dimensions that it involves. Terms such as 'employee participation', 'employee involvement' and 'industrial democracy' are broad and cover a wide variety of different schemes and techniques. A helpful way to approach the topic is by introducing the 'continuum of participation' (see Box 16.2). Imagine that you are an employee in a company, and your line manager simply gives you instructions, telling you what to do and just expecting you to get on with your job. In a company like that, there's little or no participation at all. Management behaves autocratically, top–down.

BOX 16.2: THE 'CONTINUUM OF PARTICIPATION'

The 'continuum of participation' reflects the degree of worker influence at the workplace or in the company:

- no participation
- disclosure of information
- communication
- consultation
- negotiation
- codetermination
- workers' control (for example, workers' cooperatives)

Source: Adapted from Blyton and Turnbull (2004: 255)

Now imagine that your line manager does give you information about certain aspects of your work. For example, they tell you periodically about the company's financial position, its ideas for new products and upcoming areas of activity that you'll be involved in. They might inform you, for example, about plans for the introduction of a new grading or shift system. Information disclosure is one-way and top–down, but at least you'll feel that you know a little bit about what the company is doing. However, if the system also allows you to ask questions and make your own views known, it becomes two-way, that is, top–down and bottom–up, and can be seen as a form of communication.

Further along the continuum we have consultation, which involves your manager asking explicitly for your views about a workplace issue, generally prior to introducing some form of change. The manager will listen to your views but does not guarantee to take them into account. They might or might not, depending on whether, in their judgement, they support or improve their plans in any way. So, before altering the shift system at work – for example, moving from a two-shift to a three-shift system – your manager might ask for your opinions because, after all, they recognise that you know more than they do about how it actually operates. You'll be able to point out the advantages and disadvantages of the current system and speculate about how the changes might improve or undermine efficiency, how they might affect overtime and their possible knock-on effects on work–life balance, as well as all kinds of things that they might not necessarily have thought about. The manager, however good, doesn't have the same intimate knowledge of the work that you do. Consultation will therefore be really useful in helping them to spot possible glitches in advance and to amend or revise the proposal accordingly. They have to decide: are those good ideas or not? If so, they'll take them into account; if not, they'll ignore them – that's their responsibility (Hall and Purcell, 2012).

The next stage along the continuum is negotiation, which typically involves a trade union and an employer bargaining an outcome that is not known in advance.

However, it might also involve an individual employee negotiating with a manager, for example, over a pay rise. Either way, negotiation contrasts with consultation. With consultation, we know the outcome: management wants to introduce a new HR system of some kind, so the outcome – a new system – is known, and consultation merely involves possible amendments or refinements about how it's done. However, with negotiation, the outcome is not known at all. Collective negotiations with a union are generally known as collective bargaining, which we discussed in Chapter 6 (on trade unions). The union, representing a unionised workforce, meets the management negotiating team for the annual pay round. Maybe it's claiming a 5% increase in pay, to which management responds with a counter-offer of 1%. The union will reject such a low amount because inflation is running at, say, 3%. So what happens then? Nobody can predict the eventual outcome because it's going to depend on the ability of both sides to negotiate with one another for an acceptable outcome on both sides. Management might agree to split the difference and increase its offer to, say, 3%, but on condition that the number of working hours is increased or overtime rates are reduced. The union might agree to limited increases in working hours for certain categories of workers, but on the counter-condition that workplace facilities are enhanced.

Next comes codetermination. Codetermination doesn't exist at all in liberal market economies (LMEs) (such as the US and the UK) but may be found in certain coordinated market economies (CMEs) (such as Germany), where it is exercised through their system of works councils. Codetermination means the right of veto of a works council over certain legally defined areas of managerial policy. Imagine you are working for a company in Germany. Management might announce that it wants to change certain working practices, such as the shift or grading system. Or maybe it wants to introduce a performance-related pay system and so alter the basis on which it pays you. Under German legislation, such a proposal has to be submitted to the works council, which has the right to veto it. That's a collective right laid down in law and cannot be ignored or withdrawn by the employer. Following consideration, the works council may well say no, in which case management must either take back its proposal or amend it for further deliberation by the works council (Gold and Artus, 2015).

Finally, workers' control operates typically through workers' cooperatives, where workers are also the shareholders. In both shareholder and stakeholder models of capitalism, we are familiar with the distinction between management, which represents shareholders, and workers who are employed by the company to supply labour. However, in a workers' cooperative, the workers own the shares themselves. They are both the owners of the organisation, who elect the management board to run it, as well as the workers who work for it – they combine all these roles. The workers are therefore in charge of all strategic decisions, such as investment plans, products and employment, which can sometimes result in some challenging tensions, especially when the cooperative is facing a downturn and needs to take difficult decisions about reducing its own labour costs. Nevertheless, there is much to be said in favour of cooperatives, which form significant sectors of the economy in countries like France and Italy, but much less so in the UK and the US (Michie et al, 2017; Ammirato, 2018).

In summary, then, there are numerous degrees of employee participation, which can be usefully evaluated along this continuum, from very little or no influence at the workplace all the way up to codetermination and workers' control, and everything else in between.

Direct and representative forms of employee participation

It is also important to make a distinction between direct and representative (sometimes called indirect) participation. The rest of this chapter is based on this distinction, which you'll find reflected across the literature on employee participation. The distinction focuses on participation schemes that cover all workers, every one of them in an organisation as individuals (direct), and those that operate through representatives elected through a trade union or staff association (representative).

We'll take direct forms first. Imagine you work for a company where you meet every Monday morning at 09:00 for a team briefing to discuss the coming week's activities. That's a regular slot in your timetable when you and your colleagues go through the work schedules and plans for your department for the week ahead. Or imagine you receive a regular e-newsletter from senior management to keep you abreast of developments at company level, or the company carries out surveys of its staff to gauge the level of their satisfaction at work. Those are forms of direct participation because you are *all* involved in the briefing, or in receiving the e-newsletter, or in replying to the survey.

By contrast, representative forms of participation take place through, as the term implies, representatives of the workers. Again, imagine – and this is a UK example – that you are a member of a trade union (there are around 6 million union members currently in the UK). Your company operates a joint consultative committee (JCC) to help it consult its workforce collectively over issues such as forward planning, financial matters, employment levels, production methods, training, health and safety and welfare, among much else. You have the right to vote for representatives of your union to be on the committee. These representatives will meet management on a regular basis to be consulted over issues of interest to the entire workforce. The difference with direct participation is that those issues will be collective, on which you are likely to have collective interests, such as the ones noted above. The fact is that problems at work very often aren't just individual concerns but collective ones, which entitle you – or should entitle you – to a collective voice. Collective committees of this type are therefore often found in other walks of life too. In universities, for example, student/staff committees bring lecturers and student representatives together to discuss items of joint concern, maybe suggestions for improving courses or to thrash out complaints. A JCC at work and a student/staff committee therefore operate on the same principle: you have an elected representative to take a case forward on your behalf. The basic distinction between direct forms of participation and representative, then, is that one focuses on all workers, as individuals, while the other focuses on representatives to channel collective concerns through committee structures.

Levels of employee participation

So far, we have discussed the continuum of participation and direct and representative forms of participation. A further distinction covers the level at which decisions are taken because traditionally there are a number of levels within an organisation's hierarchy (think back to our discussion of bureaucratic forms of employment in Chapter 5): there's your workplace (maybe an office, or a shop, or location on a factory shop floor); your site (which may consist of multiple workplaces); your division (such as finance, human resource management [HRM], information and communications technology [ICT], marketing or operations management); your company or organisation (which may consist of many sites across your country, or indeed, across the world, if it's a multinational); and your sector (such as banking, engineering, pharmaceuticals or retail). Decisions affecting your working conditions may be taken at any of these various levels. Forms of employee participation therefore need to reflect the levels at which they are taken.

Areas and topics for employee participation

Related to levels of participation are the areas or topics that it covers. There are potentially countless aspects of our working conditions over which we might like to have some influence. At the workplace or site level we find topics like those sometimes disparagingly called 'tea, towels and toilets', in other words, the basic standards of our working environment. These are, of course, very important. If the tea in the canteen is lousy or if the toilets are never clean, that can have a serious effect on morale and needs to be dealt with. On the other hand, they are clearly in a very different category from your pay, or appraisal system, decisions about which will be taken at higher levels, probably the division or company, or indeed, in a different category again from strategic business decisions about investments, product development and restructuring, which will be taken at company board level. So employee participation also involves consideration of the level of the organisation at which it takes place as well as over which topics.

Stage of decision-making

Influence over the stage of the decision is also critical, because we begin with an inkling of an idea about a project, at which stage it is barely formed and still very malleable. Following discussion, the project starts to take a more concrete form. The decision then has to be taken to go ahead with the project or not, and if it does, it has to be implemented and its progress monitored. However, since decisions take place in multiple stages, the question centres on the stage at which workers or their representatives are to be involved – at the very earliest stages of decision-making (at company board level) or only later, at the implementation and monitoring stages (workplace, site or divisional levels)?

Legal basis of employee participation

Finally, employee participation schemes may be based on legal provision, collective agreement or management decision. As we saw in Chapter 5, legal regulation plays a significant role in regulating human resources (HR) practices in CMEs, but only a limited role in LMEs. So we shouldn't be surprised that representative forms of participation are generally required by law across continental Europe but barely at all in the UK and the US, which rely on a 'voluntarist' or lightly regulated approach. (The degree of enforcement is a separate issue, however.) Direct forms of participation, however, are left up to management decision almost everywhere.

You can now see that the term 'employee participation' covers a wide range of different schemes through which employees attempt to exert influence with managers at work: from a team briefing or employee survey all the way up to consultation over the closure of a plant or a new product, or – at board level – an investment strategy designed to take the company into whole new areas or a merger with another company. These are all major issues and might all – depending on the prevailing legislation in the country under review and its levels of unionisation – be subject to some form of employee participation. So, when we see the term 'employee participation', we must immediately try to break it down into its constituent parts. Ask yourself where it lies on the continuum of participation. Does it involve a direct or representative form of employee participation? At what level(s) of the organisation does it operate? Covering which areas or topics? And at which stage of decision-making? All these questions should occur to you to break the notion down into more manageable bite-sized pieces.

The rest of this chapter examines direct and representative forms of participation in greater depth, as this distinction is central in understanding the role each plays in the organisation.

Direct forms of participation

Direct participation is often, but by no means exclusively, associated with unitarist perspectives on the organisation, the idea being that the manager has a certain view of the organisation as a harmonious entity that all the employees share, along with its aims and objectives. Direct forms of participation often therefore reflect unitarist assumptions about the nature of the organisation and the ways in which issues relating to it are phrased. Direct participation is generally initiated by management because it's in management's interests to have a motivated workforce who engage fully (or at least comply) with its interests. Other terms you often see are 'employee engagement' and 'employee involvement', which imply direct forms of participation. These forms of participation focus, to repeat the point, on the individual. Box 16.3 presents a list of possible forms of direct participation, which is not in any particular order or intended to be exhaustive. These forms are often found in combination.

BOX 16.3: FORMS OF DIRECT PARTICIPATION
These forms are often linked to company culture and attitudinal change programmes:

- notice boards
- suggestion schemes
- newsletters/email
- staff surveys
- use of company intranet
- focus groups
- workplace meetings, team briefings
- problem-solving groups, quality circles
- teamwork/task-based involvement
- financial participation.

We have already mentioned team briefings and e–newsletters as a basic way of communicating with employees. Many organisations conduct staff surveys in which they try to find out what their employees really think about working for them, not least because they can then attempt to tackle any gripes or problems that emerge as a way to stem poor morale or labour turnover.

Suggestion schemes give employees the chance to submit their ideas for improving the production process (or anything else). Employees may have all kinds of interesting ideas about how to improve productivity because they know the work, they're doing it; the manager normally isn't so near the point of production, so tapping into employees' ideas is important. In Japanese companies such as Toyota or Nissan, workers are expected to make regular suggestions as part of their policy of continuous improvement (*kaizen*).

Quality circles are also associated with Japanese production methods. Teams of workers don't just manufacture a product; they also take responsibility for its quality at the point of production, and are expected to make ongoing suggestions as to how to enhance it. In other words, quality is guaranteed by the teams of workers themselves, rather than by a separate technical standards supervisor who comes in at the end to detect existing defects.

Teamwork is also a common form of direct participation, but of a rather different kind, because it involves delegating tasks to a team. This allegedly generates synergies and so is more efficient. Teamwork is linked to task–based involvement, where managers give discretion to workers to carry out certain tasks under their own responsibility that, under more traditional work systems, would have required no discretion and close supervision (Carter et al, 2017; Smith and Vidal, 2021). However, teamwork requires expertise and training to operate well. Although widespread, it can lead to stress, which HR managers need to know how to control. Teamwork can be used to pass blame to someone else, and some might claim that it is an effective way to conceal the fact that, individually, we have no idea what we're doing. For some, TEAM stands for 'together everyone annoys me'. Internal team dynamics may prove challenging. It's anecdotally well known that in every group project, one member does most of the work, one has no idea what's going on, the third says they're going to help but never do and the fourth just disappears. This is known as the 'free-rider problem' that has to be managed to prevent demoralisation and disintegration. You can't just introduce teamwork and expect it to run smoothly without supervision (Joyce, 1999).

Financial participation schemes are also covered under direct participation as they give workers – generally, but not exclusively, on an individual basis– a direct, financial interest in their company's success. Employee share ownership plans (ESOPs) create an employee trust that holds and manages individual employee shares in the company. Save as you earn (SAYE) schemes give employees an option to buy company shares at a fixed price after a set period of time. A proportion of their salary is then allocated into the savings fund to pay for these shares. With profit-related pay schemes, a proportion of the worker's pay is linked to the overall profit of the company or business unit. Governments generally give tax incentives for ESOPs and profit-related pay to encourage their spread. Huawei, the Chinese telecommunications multinational, uses financial participation, while Amazon has a financial participation scheme for its permanent workers. John Lewis runs a partnership profit share bonus for all its direct employees (who are known as 'partners'). The underlying assumption here is that workers will be more committed to their company if they have a financial stake in it. This seems to make sense intuitively: if you have a share in your company's profits, then you'll be more committed to improving them as you'll benefit from the proceeds. Or, indeed, if you're awarded shares as a result, you'll be more committed, as you benefit from the dividends and capital growth. However, the impact of ESOPs on employees' actual say in running the companies is minimal (Baddon et al, 1989; Pendleton et al, 1998; Whitfield et al, 2017). A further survey (Diamond and Freeman, 2001) suggests that financial participation is more common among professional and skilled workers than among unskilled workers, and that its effects on motivation and commitment are not that significant. Comparative work by Basterretxea and Storey (2018) revealed positive outcomes for worker ownership, but management attitudes were an important contextual conditioning factor.

It should be noted that direct participation is often associated with programmes to change organisational culture. A company traditionally characterised by high levels of adversarial industrial relations may use forms of direct participation to modify its culture towards a more consensual model, which is more in keeping with higher levels of productivity. Direct participation is generally a characteristic of companies run on 'new' unitarist lines (see Chapter 8).

Indeed, direct participation is often associated with flatter hierarchies and more participative management styles. Semco Partners is often quoted as an example, but this might merely reflect the fact that there are so few instances. Semco is a Brazilian company run by Ricardo Semler, an entrepreneur who decided to introduce very flat hierarchies into the company, where shop floor workers set their own productivity targets and schedules (Semler, 1994, 2001). However, the results have never been verified by social science research, and therefore remain open to question.

Workers' control is, arguably, also a form of direct participation. It's not one that you'll generally find in the textbooks, but if workers run a company in which they own the shares, and can appoint and dismiss the senior management team and take responsibility for all the decisions, from investment and business strategy all the way down to the 'tea, towels and toilets', then that is a workers' cooperative. Ricardo Semler owns Semco, so he remains the director and shoulders final responsibility for everything. In a workers' cooperative, the workers collectively shoulder final responsibility through elected directors. The tension between shareholder and worker interests is resolved through worker ownership. Workers' cooperatives can be seen as an extreme form of direct participation, although rather an unusual one. Nevertheless, they are found across the world and are extremely interesting organisations, not least because they demonstrate an alternative model of how organisations could be run, even in capitalist economies. That said, they are, of course, subject to the same market pressures as any other business, and may go bankrupt and close down if they fail (Taylor, 1994).

Representative forms of employee participation

The other main form of employee participation is representative, which – as we noted earlier – involves workers in electing representatives to represent their views collectively with management, generally on a JCC, works council or some other joint forum. The representatives have a mandate to raise issues and concerns on their constituents' behalf, which allows them protection in law against bullying or victimisation. All industrialised countries give legal protection to union representatives in the course of their duties against dismissal by an employer for representing the collective views, however contentious, of their constituency (that is, those who elected them).

These representative forms of participation generally assume more pluralistic styles of management. Just as direct participation reflects a more unitarist style, so representative forms reflect a more pluralist orientation because they accept that conflict plays a legitimate role within organisations. Worker representatives may be nominated by a union or staff association, but the constituency will be the workforce as defined in the constitution of the forum itself. In most European countries, legislation underpins arrangements for nominations and elections, as well as the powers and remit of the relevant forums, although not in the UK or the US, however, where such arrangements are purely a matter for the employer and the workforce, through its union.

Box 16.4 presents a list of various forms of representative participation, which is not in any particular order or intended as exhaustive. They are often found in combination with forms of direct participation.

BOX 16.4: FORMS OF REPRESENTATIVE PARTICIPATION

Representation may involve trade unions and/or staff associations:

- works councils
- joint consultative committees (JCCs)
- health and safety committees
- board-level employee representation (worker directors)
- (collective bargaining)

We have already discussed works councils in the German context, as bodies that have extensive powers, including codetermination, defined by legislation. JCCs in the UK are bodies that bring management and worker representatives together for the purposes of consultation. Most workplaces in the UK are required by law to set up a health and safety committee to ensure that workplaces are safe (Almond and Esbester, 2018).

Board-level employee representation can be found in 18 of the 27 European Union (EU) member states, notably Germany, France, the Netherlands and the Nordic countries (Gold and Waddington, 2019). These CMEs – or stakeholder model economies – make provision for the election of worker representatives on to the boards of companies (the proportion depends on the country). This means that worker directors are involved at the earliest stages of strategic decision-making by the board, including issues such as investments, new products and restructuring (Gold, 2011). In the UK, the Conservative government invited the Financial Reporting Council (FRC) to revise its Corporate Governance Code to include a new requirement for companies to adopt on a voluntary basis one of three mechanisms for strengthening employee voice: a designated existing non-executive director; a formal employee advisory council; or a director from the workforce. The requirement came into effect in January 2019, but it is weak in comparison with what's in force in other European countries (Rees and Briône, 2021).

We've placed collective bargaining in brackets in Box 16.4 because it is often contrasted with other forms of employee participation. This is because the definition of 'participation' is sometimes limited to information and consultation, although we would argue that collective bargaining is itself a form of participation. Collective bargaining, which covers the negotiation of pay and conditions, may be seen as a technical and discrete area of industrial relations or HRM in its own right. Yet because negotiations can be located on our 'continuum of participation', it seems neater and more logical to include it here. In unionised companies, these forms of participation will involve trade unions, but in non-unionised companies, they may involve staff associations or employee representatives especially elected or appointed for the purpose.

Finally, we should note that the EU has played a significant role in developing representative employee participation across its member states (which, of course, included the UK until Brexit). Three Directives (or binding legal instruments) stand out, covering: European Works Councils (1994), the European Company (2001) and Information and Consultation of Employees (2002), all of which have been integrated into UK legislation (Gold, 2010). The European Works Councils (EWC) Directive requires multinational companies over a certain size to establish an EWC, so that a worker in a multinational operating in the EU has a forum in which to raise specifically EU-level employment issues. By April 2018, there were 1,150 functioning EWCs, covering around 40% of eligible companies. By the same date, there were 534 European companies with operations and employees established under the terms of the European Company Statute and Directive, 74 of which had board-level employee representation (ETUI, 2021). Finally, the Information and Consultation of Employees Directive requires the establishment of domestic works councils in those countries without existing legislation, such as the UK and Ireland. Although it has been enacted in the UK, neither employers nor unions have shown any enthusiasm for implementing its terms (Hall and Purcell, 2012).

Trends in employee participation

Trends in employee participation in the UK are mixed. There has been a decline in joint consultation over recent years in line with the general decline in trade union membership, the coverage of collective bargaining and strike levels. Overall, collective or representative forms of participation have tended to decline, while direct forms of participation have tended to grow in significance.

Table 16.1 depicts the decline in the number of workplaces without JCCs between 2004 and 2011 in private manufacturing, private services and the public sector. It reveals that the number of all workplaces in the UK *without* a JCC rose 12 percentage points from 2004 to 2011: from 64% to 76%. In other words, just under a quarter of workplaces did have a JCC by 2011 and even then, they were concentrated at the higher levels of the public sector. Only 10% of workplaces in private manufacturing had any form of JCC.

By contrast, forms of direct participation have risen quite dramatically. Table 16.2 shows that by 2011, four out of five workplaces had workplace meetings and two-thirds had team briefings. All forms had risen apart from a slight drop in problem-solving groups. There has, overall, been quite a shift towards direct forms of participation, where the manager addresses or communicates with all workers individually rather than through representatives.

Table 16.1: Joint consultative committees (JCCs) in the UK

		No JCC (%)	Workplace JCC (%)	Higher level JCC only (%)
Private manufacturing	2004	87	10	3
	2011	90	6	4
Private services	2004	67	5	28
	2011	80	6	15
Public sector	2004	28	19	53
	2011	37	15	48
All	2004	64	7	28
	2011	76	7	18

Source: van Wanrooy et al (2013: 15)

Table 16.2: Direct participation

Method	2004 (%)	2011 (%)
All-staff workplace meetings	75	80
Team briefings	60	66
Information on workplace finances	55	61
Staff surveys	36	37
Problem-solving groups	17	14

Source: van Wanrooy et al (2013: 18)

The percentages in Table 16.2 show trends but are slightly dated, so Figure 16.1 presents more recent data on direct participation in the UK collected in 2019 (which are not comparable with those in Table 16.2). Surveys of employee satisfaction hold steady at 36%, and solid support remains for other forms of information disclosure and communications.

At this point, you might be wondering about the state of employee participation in CMEs, such as Germany. Surely, with a solid legal framework as a basis, works councils, board-level employee representation and collective bargaining must be in better shape than in an LME like the UK (see Chapter 5)? However, the reality is complex. In 2012, 43% of employees in the West German private sector overall were represented by a works council, with only 36% in the former East Germany, although there were wide variations by sector and company size. Across the whole of Germany, for example, only 6% of workers in small companies (5–50 employees) had a works council compared with 86% in large companies (500 or more employees) (Ellguth and Kohaut, 2013). The coverage of board-level employee representation had also fallen, while collective bargaining coverage had declined in West Germany, from 70% in 1996 to 53% in 2012, and from 56% to 36% over the same period in the former East, although again, with disparities by sector. In Germany, economic pressures from reunification, introduction of

Figure 16.1: Practices that reduce or avoid workplace disputes and promote good relations with employees

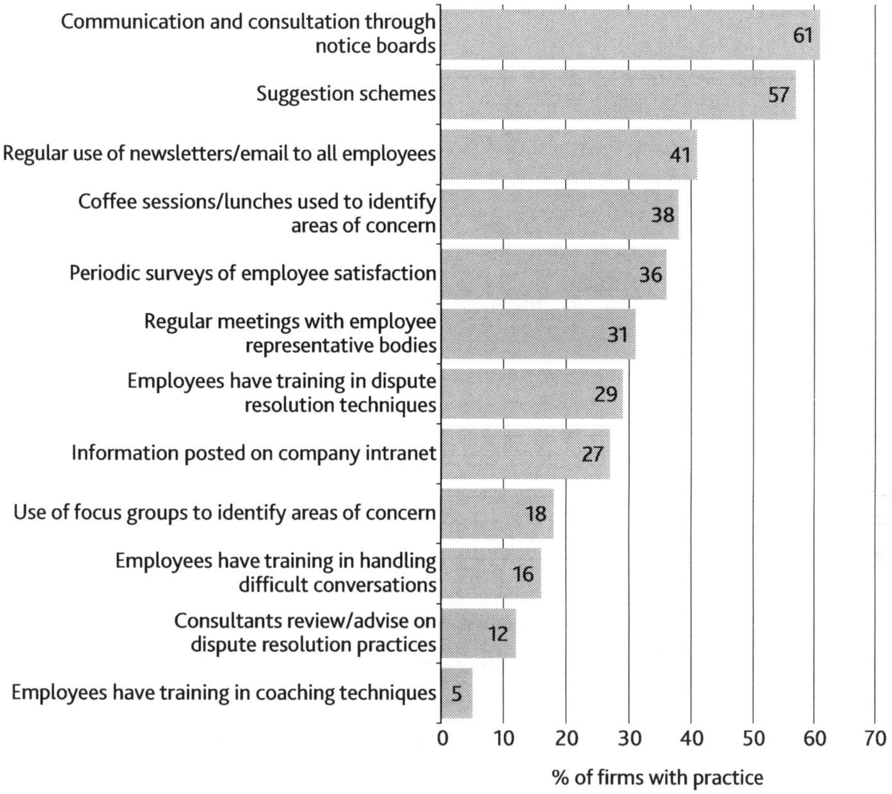

Base: All respondents
Source: Hann and Nash (2020: Figure 13)

greater labour market flexibility and the advent of new sectors (such as ICT, fast food and parcel delivery), often dominated by US multinationals, have also undermined forms of collective worker representation (Gold and Artus, 2015).

Workers' voice in the gig economy

The development of the gig economy raises major challenges for worker participation and involvement, at least in the traditional understanding of these terms. This section, which is based on Heiland (2020), outlines some of them. The central issue is that platforms were initially conceived as markets, with take-it-or-leave-it prices for tasks, and therefore no space for bargaining, employment relations, resistance or collective voice. Heiland (2020: 4) notes that:

> The benefits of this type of working relationship for companies were highlighted by the CEO of CrowdFlower, one of the largest

employment platforms, who said that "before the Internet, it would be really difficult to find someone, sit them down for ten minutes and get them to work for you, and then fire them after those ten minutes; but with technology, you can actually find them, pay them the tiny amount of money, and then get rid of them when you do not need them anymore". (Marvit, 2014)

The employment relationship as understood in the standard employment contract vanishes because platform workers are not only separated from each other in the labour process, but find also that the platforms increasingly set them in direct competition with each other. 'The allocation of orders or working shifts is organised by the platforms by means of internal markets' (Heiland, 2020: 22). Moreover,

> algorithmic management not only undermines the conditions under which workers' voice is created, but also undermines resistance practices and possible representation. Even if forms of workers' voice or active unions exist, they "cannot collectively bargain with an algorithm, they can't appeal to a platform, and they can't negotiate with an equation" (Gearhart, 2017: 13). (Quoted in Heiland, 2020: 24)

But this is only part of the story. In all relations between capital and labour, there is a potential for labour to socialise production through forms of collaboration and coordination. In the gig economy, we can distinguish between riders and drivers (who work on location–dependent labour platforms, or macro platforms, such as Deliveroo and Uber) and freelance platform workers (who work remotely for online sites, or micro platforms, that might be in homes or internet cafes). There are voice opportunities in both formats. With macro platforms, riders can physically meet and virtually cooperate. Micro platform workers, however, are geographically dispersed and can cooperate only online. Yet despite the fragmentation, they are often in quite active contact with each other. Communication via social networks seems to create a degree of social connectedness among the participants. For example, the use of internet forums by micro platform workers is very common: 'According to Yin et al (2016), 90% of workers' communication is organised through such forums. There are numerous websites and threads in which different groups of workers exchange information on different topics' (Heiland, 2020: 28).

As well as discussing work and employment online, workers also change schedules and share work, directly intervening in the labour process: 'In addition to community building and exchange of advice, the forums are used by established workers to re-outsource parts of the jobs assigned to them; subcontracting creates new power structures and dependencies that undermine collective action' (Heiland, 2020: 29).

In addition to communication, there is also self-organisation:

Almost all of the protests and strike action in the different countries were organised by grassroots rider collectives. In many cases, they were supported less by traditional unions and more by rank-and-file unions and networks from the radical left.... With their protests, the riders usually not only focus on one platform, but form solidarity networks with the riders of other platforms and address the working conditions of this kind of platform labour as such – as is also reflected in the names of the various self-organised collectives of the riders. (Heiland, 2020: 33)

Uber provides an example of such self-organisation. We noted in Chapter 10 that Uber can revoke a driver's registration if their score falls below a certain level of passenger satisfaction, which is monitored electronically. In July 2020, the App Drivers and Couriers Union (ADCU; see Box 6.2) launched a legal bid to force the company to disclose the data on which it bases the algorithms that control their employment. ADCU argues that transparency is required to ensure that Uber does not discriminate between drivers (Booth, 2020). In another example, Spanish chambermaids have organised their own union, Sindicato Las Kellys Cataluña, which has set up its own reservations platform to monitor hotels' compliance with the national agreement on pay and conditions. Tourists are able to book a hotel through an app that lists only those guaranteeing decent pay and conditions (Burgen, 2021).

Concluding comments

Given the ambiguity of terms such as employee 'participation', 'involvement' and 'engagement', when required to analyse a specific scheme, it is imperative to break it down into its various dimensions along the lines suggested in this chapter. Who initiated the scheme? Is it an example of direct or representative employee participation? Where is it located on the continuum of participation? At what levels does it function, what topics does it cover and which stages of decision-making does it focus on? Who sets the agenda?

Direct and representative participation are completely different, in terms of their scope, ambitions and functions within an organisation, although they are often found combined. Employee participation involves a continuum of participation that demonstrates the level of influence that workers may or may not have within the scheme. There is evidence that forms of participation do enhance labour productivity in a variety of different ways, but we need to remain critical about this. If we believe that labour isn't a commodity (Chapter 3), then employee participation should, arguably, be an end in itself – a right that all workers should enjoy. Its rationale shouldn't just focus on productivity.

There are costs and risk factors involved in all forms of participation because, while they may help to motivate and create commitment, they also take time and effort to run smoothly and may, of course, result in decisions that don't go your way (mostly if you're a worker). However, employee participation and involvement remain a significant means by which HR managers aspire to control conflict and resistance at the workplace, and by which workers and their representatives aspire to exert influence.

Some questions to think about

1. Would you rather work in a company that operated at least one form of employee participation scheme or in one that didn't? Which form would you feel was most likely to protect your interests at work?

2. Assess the advantages and disadvantages to employers of direct forms of employee participation on the one hand, and representative (or indirect) forms on the other. Give some examples of each form of participation.

3. Why do you think trade unions generally prefer representative forms of employee participation to direct forms?

4. What challenges does the gig economy pose for worker participation and involvement? How might workers overcome them?

Further reading

ETUI (European Trade Union Institute) (2021) *Worker Participation in Europe*, Brussels: ETUI, Available at: www.worker-participation.eu [Well worth browsing, as it's full of information about the state of employee participation across Europe, not just the EU.]

Gold, M. and Waddington, J. (2019) 'Introduction: Board-level employee representation in Europe: State of play', *European Journal of Industrial Relations*, 25(3): 205–18. [Empirical overview of the state of board-level representation across the EU.]

Heiland, H. (2020) *Workers' Voice in Platform Labour: An Overview*, WSI Studies 21, Düsseldorf: The Institute of Economic and Social Research (WSI), Hans Böckler Foundation. [Examination of challenges to voice and opportunities for self-organisation faced by gig workers.]

Whitfield, K., Pendleton, A., Sengupta, S. and Huxley, K. (2017) 'Employee share ownership and organisational performance: A tentative opening of the black box', *Personnel Review*, 46(7): 1280–96. [Analysis of survey data on the decline in the positive links between business outcomes and employee share ownership.]

17

Training and Development

Much of the material we've been discussing so far in this book has been based on the assumption that workers have the appropriate skills to carry out their tasks. So, for example, when contrasting 'core' and 'peripheral' workers in Chapter 9 on flexible working, we made the point that core workers are defined by their key skills, which are seen as central to the activity of the organisation; peripheral workers, whose skills are viewed as more easily replaceable, tend to be employed instead on various forms of 'precarious' contract. There is an assumption here about levels of training, with core workers seen as skilled and adaptable and peripheral workers seen as less skilled and therefore more expendable. As we saw, however, this assumption does not actually hold up because, for example, core workers in catering or hospitality may be relatively unskilled, while agency workers may be highly skilled. Nevertheless, the distinction between skill levels and role in an organisation are significant issues in human resource management (HRM).

In this chapter, we explore the nature of appropriate skills by examining the role of training and development (T&D) in HRM. T&D should be a win–win for both employers and employees: for employers, because the more highly trained your workers are, the more productive they are; and for employees, because the more highly skilled you are, the more likely it is that you can gain promotion in your current job, or if not, seek another job elsewhere, possibly at a higher pay grade. However, it's not quite as simple as that, not least because the source of skills varies from one country to another, and we need to find out who exactly is responsible for providing them. We also need to examine the role of power relationships within organisations that may determine training outcomes, as well as the differences between external and internal labour markets, which we first met in Chapter 5. Internal labour markets generally allow employers to hold on to core workers over a longer period of time, whereas external labour markets generally favour the acquisition of skills outside the organisation and greater flows of workers between companies at different levels. We'll discuss these issues in an international context because different countries present major contrasts in the ways they approach skills attainment and T&D.

Lack of training

We probably think of training as a fairly basic issue in an organisation, but is it really? Think about this comment on the destruction of the Twin Towers in the 9/11 terrorist attack:

> The entire transit system had been privatized, deregulated and downsized, with the vast majority of airport security work performed by underpaid, poorly trained, non-union contractors.... On September 10, as long as flights were cheap and plentiful, none of that seemed to matter. But on September 12, putting $6-an-hour contract workers in charge of airport security seemed reckless. (Klein, 2008: 5)

On 11 September 2001, the World Trade Center in New York was destroyed in a terrorist attack. Two planes were crashed into the Twin Towers, a third into the Pentagon and a fourth intended to destroy another target, possibly the White House. There had been a major breakdown in airport security because the terrorists boarded the planes fully armed and managed to hijack them without, apparently, a great deal of difficulty. Naomi Klein is making the point here that, on 10 September, the day before the murderous assault on the Twin Towers, the notion of airport security didn't seem that important and it was acceptable to pay airport security staff US$6 an hour, a very low rate, in order to carry out airport security duties. However, in the context of the atrocity, on 12 September, the skill of those workers in carrying out their security tasks was cast in a rather different light. Maybe if they had been more highly skilled in forms of vigilance, then some of those hijackers would have been detected and the attacks wouldn't have happened. The notion of training and the level of skills required in a job are very much dependent on the kinds of tasks that workers are required to carry out and the standards expected of them.

Another example is the crash of Air France flight 447 from Rio de Janeiro to Paris in May 2009. An Airbus 330 stalled and killed all 229 people on board. Investigators revealed that the crash had been caused by technical failures and errors made by inadequately trained pilots. They raised the question as to whether pilots are still being adequately trained to fly commercial aircraft by 'stick and rudder', or whether they have become too dependent on computers, a phenomenon known as 'automation addiction'. Following the crash, it was reported that many airlines have begun to retrain their pilots to fly manually (Hosford et al, 2012).

A third example is the Korean ferry disaster in April 2014, in which 304 passengers died. The ferry, MV Sewol, carrying 476 people, capsized. In the inquest, it turned out that the company had spent a derisory US$525 on staff training the year before. The crew on board were mainly temporary agency workers who had never been trained in evacuation procedures in cases of emergency, and were incapable of operating the safety equipment (Kee et al, 2017). So this is another example where lack of training led to a horrific human disaster. Very often, these failures become clear only after some catastrophic incident of this kind.

In the UK, too, scandals have centred on untrained doctors, nurses or teachers. For example, there have been cases where cancer screening has not taken place efficiently in the National Health Service (NHS) because the staff responsible haven't been appropriately qualified, or else untrained staff have been left to insert drips and take blood tests. In schools, untrained or semi-trained classroom assistants have been increasingly taking classes for which they are unqualified (Bach et al, 2006; Houssart, 2013). A lack of training, or undertraining, or inappropriate training are all issues that should bother us because they are found everywhere.

What is training?

What, then, is training? We suggest the following as a fair definition: 'The development of skills, knowledge and attitudes for the future needs of the organisation.' This would seem to be a good place to start, but when we start looking at the definition in more practical terms, it unravels a bit because it uncovers potential conflicts between the interests of the organisation on the one hand, and those of the worker on the other. That's because we all need transferable skills and qualifications. People study for a degree, for example, at least partly because they hope that it will give them the chance to access a better paid job than without a degree. We also appreciate in-house T&D at our place of work. But at the same time, the employer is understandably concerned about costs because, of course, in-house training is a cost, at least in the short term. The employer has to take the employee out of the workplace to complete the training or, for more advanced skills, trainers and specialists may have to be brought in, all of which involves cost.

Although we all need to acquire skills, *cost* is indeed the key point here. For example, from 1998, universities in the UK were obliged to introduce tuition fees for their courses, which currently stand at a maximum £9,250 a year. Students have to take out loans to pay their fees and so go into debt to pay for their degrees. Since the loans have to be repaid, a university degree now represents a significant cost to the student. There is also a level of uncertainty involved because you might wonder: 'What skills should I acquire?' If you're interested in a variety of different subjects, you might look at the job market when you're applying to study for a university degree – or any other qualification – and wonder whether you should specialise in the arts or sciences or social sciences or management, or even HRM. Part of your choice naturally centres on personal interest, what really fires you up, and that's obviously an excellent reason to choose one course rather than another.

But you're probably also thinking about your future job prospects. You're thinking, might I get a better paid job if I do this degree rather than that degree, or if I do an apprenticeship in this or that subject? And you can't really know the answer. You have to decide on the basis of your best analysis of the job market at the moment you're making that decision. Of course, with the job market evolving so rapidly because of the development of all manner of advanced technologies, you simply can't reliably predict what kinds of skills will be most appropriate in even one or two years, let alone in five, ten or twenty. All we *can* say is that we'll need to be adaptable and constantly open to acquiring new skills. So, there is an element of uncertainty in skills acquisition, which is a major issue when we examine T&D. And that's why we may be rather reluctant to bear the cost of our own training – we can never be entirely sure what the return will be.

Skills are, of course, also a collective good. Generally speaking, economists would agree that the more highly skilled a workforce is across a country, the more productive it is, and clearly all countries – both developed and emerging – try to ensure that their workforces are appropriately skilled and adaptable and so fit for purpose for the future demands on the economy. When each of us acquires skills, this activity benefits not only our employer and ourselves as individuals but also, en masse, the whole of society (Crouch, 2005b). The problem is that, in competitive markets, there is an issue about who actually provides the training. Employers will have concerns about costs and may seek to offload them on to government or the employees themselves, not least because, as the rate of technological change accelerates, they may feel that training becomes constant retraining and upskilling.

Types of training

There's an important distinction to be made between qualifications and the skills actually required at work. We can distinguish between Type 1 and Type 2 skills, which helps to make this point (Findlay and Warhurst, 2012). Type 1 skills are those you need to obtain the job in the first place, while Type 2 skills are those you need to do the job once appointed. In other words, there's a distinction between getting your foot in the door through the recruitment process, and then, once you've got the job, your ability to perform it in a competent manner. Type 1 skills reflect the expansion of higher education in the UK over recent years, which has involved a dramatic expansion in the proportion of graduates in annual cohorts of young people. Between 2006 and 2012, the proportion of graduates employed overall in UK labour markets had risen from 30% to 42.3% (Green, 2016: 16). Young people now have much wider access to degree-level courses than in 2000 or 1980, let alone 1960. This means that a degree has increasingly become a prerequisite for getting a job in the first place – in other words, 'employment' has more and more become graduate employment, and more and more jobs require a degree, not least because the cohort is more and more skilled (which itself has consequences).

Type 2 skills are those you require to do the job itself, and graduate trainees soon realise that there are job-specific skills that are too specialised to be taught at university. A university teaches general skills, but the organisation you're working for has very specific requirements – standards, norms, methods – which it has to instil into you during your graduate induction and probation programmes and beyond.

What this means is that employees may end up with a higher level of qualification than they actually need to carry out their particular job, a phenomenon sometimes known as 'credentialism'. In recent years, there has been a wide expansion of graduate employment in the UK – for example, in teaching, certainly, but also in health services. Since 2013, a degree is essential to become a nurse. Similarly, since 2020, all new police officers in England and Wales must be educated to degree level: those intending to join the police must complete either a three-year 'degree apprenticeship', a postgraduate conversion course or a degree. We might dispute whether these inflationary trends are a good thing or not, but that's the way things have gone. Credentialism theory would suggest that 'educational certification is a historical legitimation of advantages that empower degree holders in occupational and organizational recruitment' (Brown, 2001: 20). And in addition to these pressures there's another factor involved here too: requiring degrees for jobs that previously needed none accompanies the decline in internal labour markets and the more secure jobs that allowed reliable assessment of workers within the firm.

There's an issue here, then, about skills that may not necessarily be needed within an organisation but are nevertheless acquired by the workforce. And, of course, by contrast, you do sometimes find that people are performing jobs at a certain level of incompetence. In 2015 '40% of British workers were employed in an occupation for which they did not have the correct qualification' (OECD, 2017: 28): 25% were in occupations that normally require higher qualifications (that is, they were underqualified) and 15% in occupations that normally require lower qualifications (that is, they were overqualified).

These figures reveal an issue here about skills match (or skills mismatch). Training doesn't involve merely ensuring that the organisation employs workers with the skills it requires, but also ensuring that they have exactly the right skills in the right job where they are needed, that is, that their skills and their job match up. The organisation has to skill people up to the level actually required for each task within each job. On the one hand, credentialism is a waste of effort, while on the other, carrying incompetent workers is at best inefficient and at worst dangerous (as the earlier examples of 9/11 and the Korean ferry disaster illustrated). There's a balance, clearly.

Training provision

This leads us on to look at some of the specific problems in training provision. The first one, which we've already mentioned, is: how appropriate, how relevant, is the training to the employer? That's the key issue. If you're the employer and you're paying all this money for training, you have to make sure that it is appropriate for the tasks in hand and to how they are likely to change in the future.

But in addition, as an employer, you want to keep skilled employees. If you've trained them, then you need to make sure you retain them. You don't want to have them poached by your competitor, who does no training but simply pays skilled staff more than you do. All a competitor has to do to attract skilled staff is to pay them a bit more than they earn in the organisation that trained them, which saves all training costs. The issue of poaching, in liberal market economies (LMEs) like the UK or the US, which are characterised by external labour markets, is a concern to employers. Box 17.1 contrasts the position in Germany and the UK.

Because wage rates are generally laid down in Germany by collective agreement, employers are unable to offer higher rates to skilled workers, which undermines their chance to poach. In the UK, where wage rates are fragmented, employers are less likely to train their workers because they risk losing them to a competitor.

BOX 17.1: TRAINING PROVISION IN GERMANY AND THE UK

There is a policy preference in many countries for workplace-based learning. This stems partly from the view that the involvement of the employer, almost by definition, ensures that the training delivered is related to employer demands. It is also more likely to give access to key technologies and work practices in a way that a vocational school might find more difficult. But many countries have struggled to increase participation levels in workplace-based learning in IVET [initial vocational education and training]. This can relate to the structure and regulation of national labour markets. In the German labour market, there is a degree of wage compression resulting from collective bargaining that makes it more worthwhile for the employer to train workers than to leave them unskilled. Because collective bargaining establishes wage rates, it is difficult for employers that do not train to recruit the former apprentices of those companies that do, so there are incentives in place to train people. In contrast, in a relatively unregulated labour market such as that found in UK-England, the amount of risk faced by the employer in training an apprentice is much greater; without the State offsetting that risk through increased funding, employers will tend to invest less in training apprentices. An employer who trains someone, such as an apprentice, is at risk of losing them to another employer (other things being equal) because the non-training employer can pay a higher wage having not borne the training costs. It is certainly the case that increasing participation rates in apprenticeships in UK-England, especially among young people, has been an uphill policy struggle almost from the time modern apprenticeships were first introduced. (Cedefop, 2018: 76)

The real question, then, is how to ensure that the costs of training, as a collective good, are shared among employers in a competitive market. Or, to put it another way, how can that element of competition be overcome in order to ensure that training is provided as a collective good, for the good not just of the individual organisation but, more generally, for society as a whole. This tension between the individual and the collective needs to be resolved.

This, in turn, leads us on to a discussion about who actually provides the training and, broadly speaking, there are a number of different sources (Crouch, 2005b). The first is the *State*. It might seem obvious, at least if you're a rational sort of person, that the State would or should play a major role in providing training, and this does, of course, happen. In Scandinavian countries such as Sweden, for example, the State imposes rules on the levels of training that employers must provide, and ensures that their quality is properly monitored and assessed. Training levies on employers guarantee that everybody is contributing to training funds and stops free-riders from poaching skilled workers from elsewhere. And that is why, in 2017, the UK government introduced an apprenticeship levy on large employers to help meet the costs of training outside the workplace (Cedefop, 2018: 80).

Another source of training provision is through the *professions*. In the UK, for example, to become a doctor, you need a degree in medicine but also membership of the British Medical Association (BMA). Or to become a lawyer, you must have a degree in law but also membership of the Law Society. Increasingly, if you're a translator, you'll have membership of the Chartered Institute of Linguists or the Institute of Translation and Interpreting (which provide continuing professional development), as well as a degree or other professional qualifications in languages. HRM is a good example of professionalisation of this kind because, in the UK, if you want to become a human resources (HR) manager, you increasingly need a professional qualification because most employers, and certainly all large employers, now want you to have a Chartered Institute of Personnel and Development (CIPD) qualification. If you are interested in becoming an HR manager, have a look at what the CIPD does and its qualifications.

Companies do, of course, also provide workplace training themselves, and one way in which they try to avoid poaching by rivals is by giving company-specific training. If your company has developed individualised processes or ways in which it carries out its activities, maybe through particular information and communications technology (ICT) systems that differ from those used by other companies in the same sector, this reduces the risk of poaching because your skills are valuable only within the context of your own company. They're not transferable to a rival who uses very different processes and wouldn't be able to exploit them.

However, such a tactic may prove a risk to the employee. A UK university, for example, recently declared a number of ICT technicians redundant because the systems relating to student records had been changed and their skills, which were very specific to the old system, were no longer required to operate the new one. Redeployment proved unsuccessful, and they were made redundant. Their skills were so specific to the university that, even in the context of higher education ICT, they were unable to find jobs elsewhere. Clearly, workers who have transferable skills that are in demand are in a strong position to request a pay rise, failing which they can carry out a threat to move elsewhere. On the other hand, if the employer has ensured that the processes in which workers are skilled are specific, or maybe unique, to the company, they have nowhere to go. Skill specificity of this type, which allows employers to control key workers, is generally associated with internal labour markets – so it is important to stress that individual companies may try to introduce their own internal labour markets even within national business systems (like the UK's) that generally favour external labour markets.

Along with the State, professions and companies, *employers' associations* may also enforce training standards in particular sectors. In Germany, for example, they lay down and enforce training rules, such as the length of or standards for apprenticeships that are required for young people to become qualified in a particular profession.

Finally, *communities and networks* may participate in training, with Italy being a good example, where small and medium-sized companies collaborate on a voluntary basis to ensure that training is provided on a more collective basis (Crouch et al, 1999).

There are, accordingly, a number of ways in which HR systems can attempt to overcome the tension between the individual and collective provision of training (Tregaskis and Heraty, 2019). Figure 17.1 helps to summarise the discussion. It depicts a cube, a three-dimensional model. First of all, the 'depth' dimension illustrates the practice of learning, which means the way in which skills and training are provided, whether through formal or informal qualifications or through practical experience on the job. This dimension becomes more informal the further towards the rear of the cube it is placed. So, the US (and the UK too, if included) is located in the left-hand corner at the rear, because much training is done on the job, by learning informally from more experienced workers who already do the job (sometimes called 'learning by doing'), rather than through formal training and qualifications.

Then, the vertical axis illustrates standardisation, with low at the bottom and high towards the top, which refers to the extent to which skills are standardised within their provision. The US exemplifies low standardisation, because skills are frequently specific to the company in which they are provided. As noted, the development of company-specific skills is a way in which employers try to retain key workers in countries, such as the UK and the US, that are characterised by external labour markets. Germany and Japan, by contrast, are found at the top because skills are highly standardised within internal labour markets.

The horizontal axis represents stratification, which covers an employee's progress within an organisation and the extent to which they require qualifications to gain promotion. The US again is an example of a training system in which promotions depend on showing flair in the job itself – and making sure that your line manager is aware of your abilities. By contrast, in France – which is diametrically opposed to the US – employers place a high value on formal qualifications. Even if you can do the job, it's very difficult to get a promotion in France if you don't actually have a formal qualification that proves you can do the job (Marsden, 1999). This is a very different way of looking at training. Indeed, it means that in France you also have a high level of standardisation, because qualifications clearly lead to standard levels of skill. After all, university degrees and other qualifications can be compared and ranked, which allows employers to know that they have recruited a certain level of attainment.

Figure 17.1: Different actors in vocational education

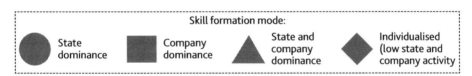

Key: CN: Canada; DE: Germany; FR: France; IN: India; JP: Japan; USA: United States of America
Source: Pilz (2016: 309)

Finally, the shape of each country logo – circle, square, triangle or diamond – reveals the skill formation mode in each country. In France, the State is predominant in the provision of training by ensuring its basic provision through levies. In Japan, the company provides a high level of training through internal labour markets and company-specific skills. In Germany, the State and company dominate, while the US is characterised by voluntary systems, with low intervention through the State or company. Figure 17.1 therefore helps to conceptualise some of the main tensions in the ways in which training is provided.

You can now see that national business systems (outlined in Chapter 5) are key determinants of training systems. Coordinated market economies (CMEs), like Germany and Japan, are characterised by internal labour markets, which have traditionally involved relatively high levels of full-time permanent jobs, length of service and career progression within companies, supported by a long-term commitment to employees and their training and skills. These structures contrast strongly with LMEs, such as the UK and the US, which are characterised by external labour markets and jobs that are less regulated, workers who move more frequently from one company to another, and training provision that is more individualised.

However, it is important to stress that organisations have agency within these business systems, so there is considerable divergence in organisational practice within them. As we noted in the case of the redundant ICT technicians, a university based in the UK may well have a wide choice of skills strategies. A multinational company may have even more choice: operating across a range of different countries, it may also consider a range of options about how to provide training. Indeed, as Box 17.2 shows, migrant workers have been increasingly used in both Germany and the UK to shortcut any training at all.

BOX 17.2: IMMIGRATION AND THE RISKS TO TRAINING

The immigration and integration of refugees in Germany is increasingly viewed as a policy option that might help solve skills shortages, even if this has posed substantial challenge to the authorities in validating the skills of refugees. In the UK, the immigration of young skilled workers has eased many of the skills shortages that would otherwise affect the labour market and VET [vocational education and training] system. However, employers have been accused of not investing in training, because a skilled migrant workforce is easily available to them (the construction and built environment sector is an example). (Cedefop, 2018: 104)

Power relationships

In the case of the UK, as noted in Chapter 6, there has been a decline in trade union membership and influence, which has had an impact on training. In the past, unions negotiated pay and conditions through the process of collective bargaining. These conditions – along with hours of work, holidays, work organisation, and so on – included training, and unions would ensure that it was being provided adequately for its members. So, as trade union membership and influence has generally declined, a bit of a vacuum has arisen over who is responsible for training. In an LME like the UK, allocation of training to workers has been increasingly taken over unilaterally through management (Green et al, 1999; Hoque and Bacon, 2008).

Successive UK governments have recognised this trend, and, realising that there's potentially a significant issue here about lack of skills provision, have tried to revitalise the old apprenticeship schemes. Apprenticeships used to be negotiated between employers and unions in collective agreements, to allow young people to enter employment in a new industry with certain prerequisites regarding the skills they would need to acquire. Figure 17.2 illustrates the number of apprenticeship

Figure 17.2: Apprenticeship starts in Australia, the UK and the US (1998–2017)

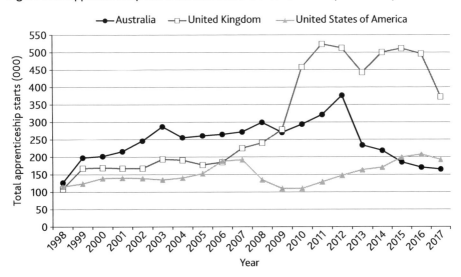

Source: Fortwengel et al (2020)

starts in three LMEs, Australia, the UK and the US, from 1998 to 2017. Research demonstrates that 'successful attempts to renew apprenticeships involved efforts to synchronise government-led and employer-led initiatives, and engaged employer associations, unions and others' (Fortwengel et al, 2020). Merely supplying funding and leaving initiatives up to market forces without concerted coordination was less effective. In Australia and the UK, growth in apprenticeships wavered when their spread into new sectors led to concerns over quality and objectives.

Training and HR strategy

We are now in a position to assess the ways in which skills and training feed into the whole HR strategy of companies, which goes back to Chapter 2. That chapter examined the relationship between HR strategies and company business strategies and how, for example, a low-cost business strategy or a high-end quality business strategy will require different types of human resources. And really, HR strategy, as opposed to HRM as such, is what underpins the achievement of general business strategies. Training becomes critically important in this process because it can give you the competitive advantage that you require. If you start thinking about areas of competitive advantage that companies have (such as customer service, organisational culture or R&D), a number are, in fact, people-related, as know-how and skills mix lead directly to improved productivity. Chapter 10, which covered emotional labour, demonstrated how the service economy places a premium on customer retention, which requires skilled and emotionally sensitive employees to ensure that customers want to come back to the same shop, hotel or restaurant. And that – with all the challenges it poses for the employee concerned – is at least partly a matter of appropriate training. Company culture can also form an area of competitive advantage, which is also HR-related. Hence training becomes a critical element in HR strategy because different business strategies have different implications for training requirements.

'Development' is a further issue. The phrase used in textbooks isn't just 'training' but generally 'development' too and often, specifically, human resource development (HRD). 'Development' often refers – at least in the UK and the US – specifically to management development. That's not so for every country, but basically 'development' refers to the idea that, over time, you need to maintain production levels in line with what's being demanded in a competitive market, and so you need to ensure that you have the specialist skills and processes that allow you to compete with your rivals. It's interesting that the UK, very much a class-based country, distinguishes between 'training' and 'development', with 'development' generally reserved for management tasks. By contrast, in Japan, the difference just doesn't exist. The Japanese don't understand the separate notion of management development, because they see everybody, equally, as requiring both training *and* development (Storey, 1995). Workers in Japanese companies are placed on a single pay spine with a single set of terms and conditions, which also means a single set of training and development provisions. There is no distinction between middle/senior management and 'the workers'. Everybody is treated the same, so the training needs of Japanese companies are much more homogeneous than those of their UK or US counterparts (Dore and Sako, 2002).

Controlling skills

As workers and managers become more skilled, they are able to demand more money, and a threat to leave unless they are paid more becomes potentially serious. Employers deal with this threat in different ways. In Germany and Japan, skills are regarded as a public good and are retained through the operation of internal labour markets (see Chapter 5), and – because they are generally specific to the organisation – they form an integral part of the way in which the organisation sees itself. In the UK and the US, where external labour markets predominate, the cost of higher skills, particularly among management, has been partly dealt with by deskilling. One of the ways to limit the pay claims of higher skilled workers is by gradually deskilling them, by automation or by dividing up their tasks into smaller elements that then become more controllable (Braverman, 1974). Box 17.3 helps to illustrate this point.

BOX 17.3: DESKILLING EVERYDAY JOBS
Think of supermarkets. Cashiers in supermarkets used to ring up purchases manually and calculate change in their heads. Gradually, barcode scanning and electronic tills that calculated change reduced the skills required. And cashless payment has deskilled them further.

> Bank clerks, too, used to deploy a whole range of skills to deal satisfactorily with their customers. However, the arrival of online banking has led to many banks closing their branches as fewer staff are needed.
>
> Black cab drivers in London need to memorise every street in the city before they can qualify to drive a licensed taxi. However, the value of their skills has been undermined by GPS systems that allow rivals like Uber to undercut them.

These simple examples reveal that many tasks within the economy have become deskilled through technology, and what was once a set of skills that allowed you to use your professional discretion and judgement can be divided up very much in the Tayloristic manner (Evans and Holmes, 2013). This process reduces people's skills and allows the employer to pay less.

So far, we've been discussing training very much as if it's a core activity, yet, in Chapter 9 on flexibility, we highlighted the differences between 'core' permanent employment contracts on the one hand, and 'peripheral' contracts on the other. This is a critically important contrast. At the start of this chapter, we saw how, in the Korean ferry disaster, the workers responsible for evacuating the ship in the case of disaster were temporary agency workers who hadn't had the training required to deal with an emergency. With the spread of 'flexible' working, training (or lack of training) has become an increasingly significant issue. There have also been scandals in the UK, for example, in the NHS, which raises similar issues. Hospitals have been affected by MRSA, a bacillus that kills people, as a result of poor levels of hygiene. This is at least partly because outsourced cleaning staff are only responsible at arm's length to the hospital where they're working (Zuberi, 2013). Cleaners were once employed directly by the hospital, which established a clear line of management between the cleaner and supervisor. If the cleaner wasn't cleaning to the required level of hygiene, there would have been warnings and disciplinary action taken, as appropriate. However, outsourced cleaners and those employed on temporary work contracts work at arm's length to the hospital, and so the question arises: who is actually responsible for training – is it the employer, or is it the temporary work agency? These issues become extremely complex.

The question of responsibility becomes particularly important for self-employed workers. One such worker points out the challenges in organising his own training when he's trying to earn a living at the same time:

> One of the biggest things about not working for somebody else is that continued professional development is reliant on you doing it and you organising it. But unfortunately, it takes a back-seat while you are trying to grow business or while you are trying to establish contacts so that, the longer you don't work for someone, the harder it becomes to then go back (John – self-employed). (S. Chan, 2013: 372)

If you're self-employed, then it's not just a question of the cost of training to upgrade your skills but also the *opportunity cost* because, if you take time out to upgrade, you're no longer earning the money that you need to pay the household bills. So at that point, training is not just a professional matter but also an opportunity cost, and the question centres on how you actually pay for it, given that you're simultaneously in full-time self-employment.

Maybe for these reasons there has been a growing tendency in some countries to pass responsibility for training from the collective to the individual, with individuals seen as entirely responsible for their own human capital. Structural changes in labour markets – particularly the rising significance of the gig economy and precarious employment – mean that we simply cannot predict anything five years from now, let alone ten or twenty years ahead. We didn't predict COVID-19, and we cannot imagine the kind of pressures or constraints we'll be working under in the future. Hence individuals, particularly in the UK and the US, are being seen as more and more responsible for their own skills attainment, a trend that's been termed 'ultra-responsible autonomy' through which the worker becomes an 'individual capitalist [and] entirely responsible for his or her economic fate' (Fleming, 2017: 183). The unsettling conclusion is that: 'If you're a loser in the new world of work it must somehow be your fault' (Fleming, 2017: 209).

Concluding comments

By way of conclusion, these following points seem fairly clear. There is a tension between the individual and the collective provision of training, and even when we talk about collective provision, we might be talking about the State, professional associations and/or companies themselves. While training is regarded as a 'win-win', and hence very much part of company strategy, at the same time it is a scarce resource, and the ways in which it's allocated to the right workers at the right time and at the right levels is something that can generate conflict – it's something that needs to be managed with great care. And finally, there are major cross-national differences in all these aspects of training. Within that context, the generic trends that we can observe internationally, with respect to outsourcing, privatisation and the development of all kinds of precarious work, also have major implications for training provision within organisations and its increasing individualisation.

Some questions to think about

1. When employers invest in training a workforce, they can increase the risk that workers move away for higher pay elsewhere. How might HR managers (and policy-makers more generally) seek to restrict this outcome?

2. Examine the main challenges faced by employers in providing training and development for their workers. How might they try to meet these challenges?

3. 'Training should be the responsibility of the employer as they get the benefit of a skilled and trained labour force.' Do you agree? Would you be happy to take responsibility for your own training needs?

Further reading

Bach, S., Kessler, I. and Heron, P. (2006) 'Changing job boundaries and workforce reform: The case of teaching assistants', *Industrial Relations Journal*, 37(1): 2–21. [Examination of the emergence of new occupational categories in education, especially teaching assistants.]

Chan, S. (2013) '"I am king": Financialization and the paradox of precarious work', *The Economic and Labour Relations Review*, 24(3): 362–79. [Analysis of the process of financialisation and how it pushes responsibility for training on to the individual.]

Pilz, M. (2016) 'Typologies in comparative vocational education: Existing models and a new approach', *Vocations and Learning*, 9(3): 295–314. [Review of the comparative national differences in vocational education and training.]

18

Work–Life Balance

The last three chapters have seen you paid, involved and trained, so this one follows up by investigating your work–life balance (WLB), a topic that focuses on how we are meant to balance our working life with our family and domestic responsibilities and leisure time. The pressures have intensified over recent years, not least because of the advent of new technologies. Virtually everyone now has a smartphone, and the way in which employers use smartphones to monitor and to ensure employees' 24/7 availability has become a serious issue.

The chapter opens by looking at the origins of the WLB debate and traditional approaches towards it. We investigate individual employee needs for WLB in terms of social psychology, but also the ways in which different countries embody contrasting approaches towards, for example, the division of labour between men and women. That has an effect on WLB. We'll look at extremes in the workplace, underwork and overwork, and at how companies and legal systems deal with them. We'll also examine the key role of information and communications technologies (ICTs) in evolving discussions about WLB.

Background

The background to WLB debates really revolves around participation rates in the economy and who is working where and for how long. 'Participation rate' is the term used to describe how many people in a particular demographic cohort who are actually working. So if, for example, 70 out of every 100 men aged 15–64 are in paid work, then the participation rate for men is 70%. The other 30 are not at work: they might be unemployed or at home looking after children, or they might have disabilities and can't work – there might be all kinds of reasons why they aren't working. Or they might have their own private income and don't need to work. But participation rates are one way in which we measure the productivity of labour within an economy, and it's generally assumed that the higher the participation rate, the more the economy benefits. However, rates vary greatly from country to country, as Table 18.1 illustrates.

The traditional male breadwinner role – men go out to work while women stay at home and look after the children – has discouraged female employment, but over recent decades industrialised countries have generally tried to increase women's participation rates, which have tended to be lower than men's. Over the period 2010–19, female and combined male/female participation rates had risen in all countries, as had male rates in most countries, apart from Chile, Greece, Mexico, Spain and the US, which registered slight falls. Variation in base rates

Table 18.1: Female, male and all participation rates in selected OECD countries (2010 and 2019), workers aged 15–64

Country	Female participation rates (%)		Male participation rates (%)		All participation rates (%)	
	2010	2019	2010	2019	2010	2019
Australia	70.0	73.9	82.9	83.2	76.4	78.5
Chile	51.8	58.0	77.8	76.8	64.8	67.4
France	65.4	68.2	74.7	75.3	70.0	71.7
Germany	70.8	74.9	82.4	83.5	76.6	79.2
Greece	57.5	60.4	78.3	76.7	67.8	68.4
Iceland	82.7	84.4	88.2	89.4	85.5	87.0
Italy	51.1	56.5	73.1	75.0	62.0	65.7
Japan	63.2	72.6	84.8	86.4	74.0	79.5
Mexico	45.6	48.8	82.4	81.8	63.1	64.6
Poland	58.5	63.4	72.1	77.7	65.3	70.6
Spain	67.1	70.1	81.8	79.9	74.6	75.0
Sweden	76.2	81.1	81.8	84.6	79.0	82.9
Turkey	30.2	38.7	75.4	78.2	52.7	58.5
UK	69.7	74.4	82.4	83.2	76.0	78.8
US	68.4	68.9	79.6	79.5	73.9	74.1

Source: Adapted from OECD (2021: Country tables)

is striking. In 2019, just under six out of ten people aged 15–64 in Turkey were in employment, as against over eight out of ten in Sweden and almost nine out of ten in Iceland. Well under half of women in Mexico and Turkey were in employment, as against over 70% in Australia, Germany, Japan, Spain and the UK, and over 80% in Iceland and Sweden.

However, these increases have been accompanied by falling birth rates in many countries, which has given cause for concern to some governments. In Italy, for example, the birth rate is just about equivalent to the death rate, so there's no growth in population at all. There are fears expressed in some quarters that the more women go out to work, the fewer children they're going to have – and that society suffers as a result (Mills et al, 2008). This is a value judgement that you may or may not agree with, but nevertheless, it's the kind of background against which much discussion about WLB is taking place.

There is also an issue about 'dependency ratios' – the ratios between those at work who are paying taxes and National Insurance and those who are not at work and need to be supported through the country's welfare system. For example, children require education; people who are ill or injured need hospitals; unemployed people need unemployment benefit; and those who are retired receive pensions. Now obviously, children, and those who are sick, unemployed and retired, aren't working, and their income depends on the level of taxation contributed by those at work. If the balance – the dependency ratio – shifts out of equilibrium and there are too many non-workers dependent on too few workers, there are going to be shortfalls in welfare provision that the government will have to address. Governments may, for example, have to raise taxes, increase the State pension age or restrict pension eligibility requirements. Industrialised countries have increasingly had to confront these challenges, especially since the global financial crash in 2008–09 (Vis et al, 2011).

Trends in parenting also affect WLB, much of which is to do with bringing up children and caring responsibilities. Evidence across a range of industrialised countries suggests that mothers are becoming more economically central to family finances, with fathers spending more time raising their children (Sayer and Gornick, 2012; Oláh et al, 2018). Grandparents may get involved, too, if parents have to work long hours (Glaser et al, 2018). One solution for pre-school children is to introduce workplace crèches and to improve childcare facilities, such as nurseries, either privately or through local authorities. However, these solutions are at a cost: non-subsidised private childcare is extremely expensive for parents, while publicly funded nursery schools are, of course, a cost to the community and to the taxpayer. Middle-class families in some societies, such as those on the Pacific Rim, rely on au pairs or live-in maids to look after their children, but it is clearly expensive and cannot easily be replicated in other countries as it may involve issues of immigration and social acceptability. So, these kinds of broad social and public policy issues form the framework within which we have to examine the whole question of WLB within the economy (O'Connell, 2010; Cortes and Pan, 2013).

There are a number of issues here about WLB, how it's organised and paid for, the policy context and what it actually means, which we unpick in the rest of this chapter. Its significance as an issue in HRM is summarised here by John MacInnes, who makes the point that WLB is often regarded as a win–win policy because it is meant to deliver both higher levels of employment (by giving parents greater working-time flexibility) and more time for parenting: 'Work–life balance is regarded as a magic wand simultaneously delivering *both* higher employment *and* more parenting. Hence most governments discuss work–life balance, with "work" meaning formal employment that sustains tax and social security contributions, while "life" means caring and parental responsibilities relevant to labour force reproduction' (MacInnes, 2008: 55; original emphasis).

'Work' as paid employment that delivers revenue to the State is clear enough. However, MacInnes is rather restrictive in the way he refers to 'life', which generally focuses on three non-work factors: self, family and friends. It's assumed that WLB is a particular issue for workers with a partner and maybe children. However, for those without close family, WLB may instead involve friends and a social life. The assumption here is that we all need time to relax and recover, time for ourselves away from a tiring job, sometimes called 'me time'. The nature of the balance will, of course, vary from one individual to another in terms of personal circumstances and interests.

Approaches to WLB

Traditional approaches to WLB involve a number of different elements (Guest, 2002). One is the notion of *segmentation*, the idea that work and life are two separate spheres that don't interact with one another. This reflects the traditional male breadwinner role, where the man goes out to work and provides the income while the woman looks after the family at home but is not in paid employment. This segmentation model is based on agricultural and earlier industrial societies, as illustrated in Box 18.1 by the work of Charles Dickens.

> **BOX 18.1: CHARLES DICKENS AND A SEGMENTED WLB**
>
> Charles Dickens discusses 'work–life balance' in *Great Expectations* (1861) (although the term had not yet been coined). Clerk John Wemmick sees his home as his Castle and states: 'The office is one thing, and private life is another. When I go into the office, I leave the Castle behind me, and when I come into the Castle, I leave the office behind me. If it's not in any way disagreeable to you, you'll oblige me by doing the same. I don't wish it professionally spoken about' (Chapter 25). The issues raised in our chapter here go back, then, to the mid-Victorian period, and no doubt further.

However, there may actually be a *spillover* between 'work' and 'life'. It's often difficult for people to keep their work compartmentalised and not to bring it home, and think and worry about it at home, with implications for their family life. A spillover between the two is not abnormal. The two may also be linked by the notion of *compensation*. For example, you may have a dull, routine job, but compensate by throwing yourself into your social life, or by carrying out voluntary work in your spare time to gain the sense of purpose that you're lacking in your job.

A further relationship is purely *instrumental*. You may work long hours, in a deadbeat, boring job in order to achieve a certain objective – maybe paying off the mortgage, buying a car or saving up for a world cruise. In these cases, you have an instrumental attitude to WLB through which you trade off long hours of tedium in exchange for something else that is important for your family or social life.

However, and this element has increasingly come to frame the discussion around WLB, work and life may actually be in *conflict* with one another, and that's when things become difficult. Maybe you're facing heavy demands in both spheres. You may have a strenuous job that requires long hours at the same time as you are trying to raise a young family who are also time-intensive. Maybe you're a single parent, or your partner is also working. A dual-career relationship places even more pressures on you because you can't count on your partner to be at home when you're at work. And the role of new technology compounds this pressure. Your boss may expect you to be monitoring your smartphone all the time and answering emails, simply to keep up with your job. If you're on holiday or it's the weekend, or if you're out socialising with your friends, this can become an irritating constraint. You're trying to relax with your friends in the pub and you're getting messages asking you to do things well outside 'normal' office hours (van Laethem et al, 2018).

As individuals, we're all different and so are our stress thresholds. Some people can cope better than others. The term 'workaholic' means someone who doesn't mind working all hours or who derives their validation principally from work. There may be certain personality types – achievement-oriented people – who thrive on work, and provided it's genuinely voluntary, the rest of us have to accept that this is the way they are. However, working long hours is often not voluntary. We can use the term 'overworkers' for those who are being overworked, not because they want to be in the office late into the evening, but because they are being required to fulfil some particular project or task. It's the reluctance, or feeling 'I don't want to be here', that causes the conflict in that situation (Guest, 2002; Beckers et al, 2008).

Structural dimensions to WLB

One of the problems with individualistic ways of investigating WLB is that there are limitations in the model. For a start, changes in the nature of the employment structure play a role. Precarious employment – which we examined in Chapter 9 on flexibility – is increasingly significant in the labour market and includes fixed-term contracts, temporary work agencies, zero-hours contracts and the gig economy, among much else. Precarious work deprives workers of their autonomy and leaves little room for WLB. A zero-hours contract, for example, means you are on call to do work that may or may not actually materialise. You're on call, so you're ready for work, but you're not being paid so you can't relax over that period because you're continually thinking: 'Maybe my agency is going to call me with a job' or 'I need to keep checking my app for work'. Hence the fragmentation of contractors and the development of precarious work over recent years has also had an impact on WLB.

Workers in the informal economy are in an even weaker position. There are many workers – some of whom we discussed in Chapter 11 on migration – in all economies, not least industrialised ones, who fall under the official radar because they are not paying tax or National Insurance contributions. According to the International Labour Organization (ILO) (2020: 13): 'Altogether, around 2 billion workers worldwide are informally employed, accounting for 61 per cent of the global workforce.' Workers whose labour is completely unregulated stand no chance of any kind of WLB at all.

In addition, there are gendered divisions of labour. We've already seen this in Chapter 14 on discrimination and diversity when we looked at segmented labour markets, where women tend to be employed in certain types of job rather than men, and vice versa, which produces discriminatory forms of employment. But there is also discrimination between paid and unpaid work. Take housework, for example: shopping, cooking, washing up, hoovering/vacuuming, all those sorts of chores are unpaid housework, but they are nevertheless work – they have to be done, and if they're not, then your house will rapidly look a mess. But that work is not paid (Oakley, 1985 [1974]). By contrast, your paid employment is what pays the bills. Nevertheless, in a household relationship, the woman still tends to take up the unpaid housework and childcare because there is some general expectation that that's what women do – even though they, too, are holding down a paid job. Such a gendered division of housework may well intrude on WLB because, in a heterosexual household, the male partner may be able to come home and relax and watch TV without worrying about all the housework, while the female partner frets until it's all done. The same issue arises with childcare, yet the take-up of shared parental leave, which is meant to improve gender equality in the home and at the workplace, has remained low in the UK (Birkett and Forbes, 2019).

The significance of these issues undoubtedly varies from country to country. As noted in Table 18.1, female participation rates are lower in Southern European countries, such as Greece, Italy and Spain, than they are in Northern European ones, such as Germany, Scandinavia and the UK. This is probably at least partly attributable to the influence of the Orthodox and Catholic churches' traditional views about women's role in society. Family and kinship obligations vary too. Tighter family networks in Southern Europe will also have an effect on patterns of childcare and WLB that is at variance with the looser networks generally found in Northern Europe (Karamessini, 2008).

The international dimension to WLB complicates matters further. If you work for a multinational company, with subsidiaries across the globe, then WLB will be treated in all sorts of different ways according to the business system and culture in which you are functioning. Legal regimes vary, for example, in relation to working hours and, as Figure 18.1 demonstrates, average hours actually worked every year range from 1,356 in Germany up to 2,258 in Mexico (and undoubtedly higher in non-OECD countries).

Even across the European Union (EU) there is considerable fragmentation. The EU Directive on Working Time sets a limit of 48 hours a week, which is quite high and is, in any case, subject to a variety of exemptions in the UK (Benson, 2009: 113–15). In France, there is a 35-hour working week, whereas in other countries it may be 39 hours or higher. Legal constraints on working time will have an effect on the kind of WLB you might expect in a particular country, at least under the law, although cultural aspects, both at national and organisational levels, also shape what is and what is not acceptable practice. Longer working hours are often associated with emerging economies, which may reflect the power and expectations of employers.

Overall, some workplaces might be characterised by rather too little work, and others by too much. Too little work may occur where new technologies allow 'cyberloafing'. Although office output is frequently monitored electronically

Figure 18.1: Average annual hours worked per worker (2017)

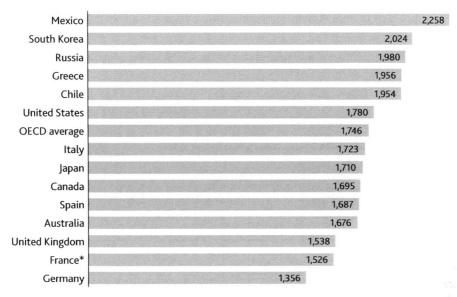

Mexico	2,258
South Korea	2,024
Russia	1,980
Greece	1,956
Chile	1,954
United States	1,780
OECD average	1,746
Italy	1,723
Japan	1,710
Canada	1,695
Spain	1,687
Australia	1,676
United Kingdom	1,538
France*	1,526
Germany	1,356

Note: *Most recent data from 2016.

Source: Feldman (2019)

very tightly, you may nonetheless be able to use your computer to book your holiday or update your Meta (Facebook) page during off-peak moments from processing insurance claims or whatever. Cyberloafing – using the internet to escape work – has grown to such an extent that 'employees generally spend 1.5 to 3 hours of their daily working hours on non–work-related activities' (Paulsen, 2015: 351). By contrast, new technologies in other situations might be used to intensify work (as noted in Box 1.3 and also in Chapter 19). The impact of new technologies can go both ways, but this chapter focuses mainly on overwork and how it might be controlled.

Overwork

Some societies seem to find it difficult to deal with the problem of overwork. In Japan, estimates suggest that around 200 people die a year through overwork, although certain companies have taken steps to prevent it (France 24, 2016). The Japanese word, *karoshi*, means death as a result of overwork and stress. In 2008, relatives of victims organised an exhibition of their suicide notes in Tokyo, which can be viewed in a video clip (NHK World, 2008).

In China, too, overwork is a serious issue. You are not allowed to live and work wherever you want – you can work only where you have a permit to do so (this system is known as *hukou* in Mandarin). It's in the interests of the employer to have a large pool of migrant workers from more rural parts of China who they can bring into the city for productive labour but, if you want to work in a different

Figure 18.2: 'Catbert and mandatory unpaid overtime'

Source: Dilbert, Monday 9 December 1996

place from where you were born, you have to have a permit. As a result, many Chinese companies have industrial dormitories where internal migrant workers come to live and work. It's a total institution, rather like a boarding school or a prison, where you work, socialise, eat and sleep, all in the same place (Goffman, 1973). 'Living at work' in this way can increase working hours as workers live nearby and the working day can be extended to accommodate the demands of orders and managers (see Box 18.2). This 'dormitory labour regime' (Smith, 2003; Ngai and Smith, 2007) is highly productive, but it relies on long hours.

> ## BOX 18.2: LIVE-IN SYSTEMS FORMERLY COMMON IN UK RETAIL
>
> The Chinese are not alone in developing 'living-in' systems. It's not so different from patterns of behaviour that emerged in other countries as they industrialised. Similar factory dormitories were established in the US, and many shopworkers in the UK used to sleep on the premises in the earlier part of the 20th century. Employers paid their workers partly in cash and partly in board and lodging, which gave them a high level of control over their workers' lives. Union campaigns were mounted against the system in the early 20th century, and the living conditions at a drapery emporium became the setting of a play, *Diana of Dobson's*, by Cicely Hamilton, first performed in London in 1908.

The live-in system remains widespread in China. Labour conditions at Foxconn, which manufactures electronic components at factory dormitory complexes across China, are notoriously bad, with a wave of suicides linked to working hours and intensity (J. Chan, 2013; Chan et al, 2020). A Foxconn factory in Zhengzhou, which manufactures half the world's iPhones, employs up to 350,000 workers who live in dorms in a complex known as 'iPhone City' (Jacobs, 2018). An undercover account has revealed details of the surveillance and screening systems that control workers in a Pegatron Apple factory in Shanghai (Tech Insider, 2017).

Once again, we return to the 'invisible face of labour', which we explored in Chapter 11 on migration and Chapter 12 on corporate social responsibility (CSR). Those of us who consume electronic products – virtually all of us nowadays – are generally unaware of the conditions under which these products are manufactured. However, in Chapter 4, we also explored the nature of conflict and resistance at work. Workers will generally try to resist such conditions and, in the case of Foxconn, dormitory consciousness-raising groups and support networks have emerged as ways of dealing with the stress on workers. There is also an emerging independent trade union movement in China, which may, over time, begin to organise workers to negotiate conditions for themselves (Chan and Hui, 2014).

Having said all that, we don't want to claim that everything in Europe is wonderful either. France Télécom has been hit by scandal, with some employees committing suicide because of stress. In 2009, an employee threw herself from her office window having earlier told her father of her fear of changing bosses, the last in a series of changes affecting her working conditions. In 2011, a technician set fire to himself in the company car park having complained to his managers about discontent over his own role at work and what he claimed was management contempt for their staff. These suicides brought the company into the public spotlight over its workplace practices (Waters, 2014).

Regulating working time

Establishing a fair WLB requires, at least partly, regulating and enforcing the length of the working week. Figure 18.3 illustrates the length of the working week, that is, not the statutory working week but the actual hours worked, across member states of the EU.

According to Eurostat, in 2016 full-time employees in the UK worked the longest weekly hours in their main job (42.3 hours), followed by those in Cyprus (41.7), Austria (41.4), Greece (41.2), Poland and Portugal (both 41.1). The shortest working week was in Denmark (37.8 hours), with the next in Italy (38.8), followed by the Netherlands and France (both 39.0), Finland and Ireland (39.1). This is quite a degree of variation, with a full-time worker in the UK working four-and-a-half hours a week more than an average Dane, or around one hour a day more over a five-day working week. Note that Figure 18.1 displays average *annual* hours worked per worker so will take into account, for example, holiday entitlements, while Figure 18.3 shows usual *weekly* hours, so the rank ordering of individual countries may differ.

Taking Europe as an example, we need to examine how different countries attempt to deal with these issues. The law is a good place to start. In 2013, Austria introduced an anti-stress law that requires all employers to have their workplace environment and atmosphere assessed by an occupational psychologist for stress factors, including intrusions into private life, and to enforce stress-reduction measures. The company has to list the stress factors and record the measures it

Figure 18.3: Usual weekly hours in main job for full-time employees in EU (2016)

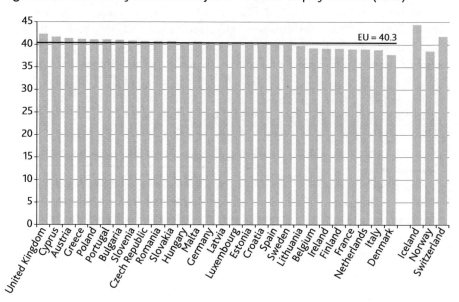

Source: Eurostat (2018b)

intends to take, which are then monitored for evaluation. Germany, following Austria, has also considered an anti-stress law. Fourteen per cent of working days lost in Germany are reportedly due to psychological illnesses such as burnout, a 50% rise in 12 years. Such a heavy increase in the incidence of stress and overwork led the German legislature to ponder a new law to deal with it (Oltermann, 2014). France adopted the El Khomri law (named after Myriam El Khomri, the Minister of Labour), which gave workers the right to disconnect from 1 January 2017. The law requires employers and unions to negotiate the application of this right in companies with at least 50 employees.

Meanwhile, in Belgium and the Netherlands, burnout is a recognised problem at work. Burnout is not just exhaustion, but permanent exhaustion and a sense of hopelessness, a feeling that the situation is never going to end. And this is clearly a serious issue for worker health and safety. Belgian and Dutch legislation requires employers to take action at this point (*The Bulletin*, 2014).

HRM solutions

However, there is much more to working time than legislation, which, after all, has to be enforced. It also requires action from companies themselves and their human resource management (HRM) departments.

At Daimler, you have the right to have all your emails deleted while you're away on holiday so you don't come back to find your inbox crammed with notes, queries and actions you have to take: a two-week holiday means a two-week holiday, without the intrusion of electronic media. Volkswagen has agreed to stop its BlackBerry service from circulating emails outside working hours. If you're working from 09:00 to 17:00, emails won't be sent once you've gone home, so won't clog your inbox overnight. We have all felt dismayed by an email backlog, but these are some simple measures that employers can adopt to deal with it (BBC News, 2012).

Having said that, WLB, particularly in managerial occupations, can prove challenging for companies, not least because it's not always obvious how WLB is going to turn out for individuals (Ford and Collinson, 2011; Murphy and Doherty, 2011). Circumstances vary from one person to another, and stress for one is not necessarily stress for somebody else. Some people might be exhilarated by all this work coming in; others might feel completely overwhelmed by it. Individual differences therefore matter.

WLB is clearly a more urgent issue for employees with caring responsibilities, for example those with children. However, as noted earlier, even if you don't have a family, there is still an issue that needs to be dealt with, namely, 'long-hours cultures' and what's sometimes called 'presenteeism', which may be associated either with being present at work even though you are unproductive, as a kind of status symbol to show how indispensable you are, or with an insistence of coming into work even when you are sick. According to the Chartered Institute of Personnel and Development (CIPD) (2019: 5): 'In a similar pattern to the public sector, four-fifths of private sector organisations have observed "presenteeism" (working when unwell) in their organisation over the last year [2018/19] and a quarter report it has increased during this period.'

If we examine personal circumstances more closely, we soon discover that a number of factors influence our perceptions of WLB. Age is one. Younger workers might be more resilient than older workers, who may tire more easily. Commuting distance might be a factor, too. If you can walk to work because you happen to live round the corner, your position is very different from somebody who has to commute possibly two or three hours each way by train, which can be extremely tiring. Your income bracket and spending commitments are another. Regular spending commitments, such as rent or a mortgage, and/or a family to support, are going to have an impact on the way in which you view your WLB. But your domestic circumstances are critically important, such as whether you have a partner and/or caring responsibilities for children or maybe an elderly or sick relative. There is clearly a wide range of personal circumstances that will affect us in different ways at different times in our lives. For the HRM angle, the issue is how to ensure that policies are flexible enough to take into account the individual circumstances of employees, not just in a global sense.

Actual examples help to make this point. Take Accenture (using evidence from Glassdoor.com, mentioned in Chapter 8 on the 'new' unitarism). At Accenture, people report: 'No work–life balance; working more than ten hours a day; there was a 14th month bonus but that was removed; work–life balance, despite being a tagline of many internal initiatives, is a joke; managers repeatedly ask you to stretch – I told you no work–life balance.' If you are maybe an older worker, with caring responsibilities, you might take these reports into account if you were wondering where to work. If, on the other hand, you were young and didn't have many commitments, then you might not bother so much.

Another example is from Google:

> The downside of Google, that's easy. Everything they do for you is in the interest of keeping you in the office as much as possible. They'll give you breakfast, lunch, dinner (all delicious, no crap). There's gyms, they'll do your laundry, they'll get you a massage, you can play sports, you can bring a pet. So, for some people this is AWESOME. All I see is a bunch of people who are at the office 50–70 hours a week of their own volition, and don't separate their work from their everyday life. (Quoted in Fuchs, 2014: 224)

Maybe working such long hours suits these people, especially if they are young, single and lack commitments. It's probably very exciting and exhilarating. However, if your circumstances change, it may then become a real problem for you, and is no longer very exciting.

Motorola illustrates the ways in which companies can try to manage WLB on an individualised basis. Motorola offers a variety of WLB arrangements, many of which have been long established (McKinlay and Taylor, 2014). The right to work part time on a temporary basis may suit you if you are raising a young family, as you may wish to revert to full-time work as your children grow older. Dependency leave or compassionate leave allows you to look after a relative who's ill or to attend family members' funerals. You may have reservations about private healthcare, but Motorola (and other companies) provide it to allow their employees greater flexibility if they're ill by avoiding NHS waiting lists. Working special, or non-standard, shifts also allows greater flexibility to cover caring responsibilities, such as the daily school run, as you can arrive a little later for work but then leave correspondingly later. Study leave encourages you to update your qualifications. Emergency holiday leave is for the eventuality that annual leave needs to be taken for non-holiday time. And job sharing may help you achieve a better WLB in the longer term. These policies all demonstrate practical measures that HRM can adopt to help improve WLB.

The real question here is – and this reflects the common theme throughout this whole book – what's in it for the employer and what's in it for the employee, and where's the balance? The employer legitimately wants the employee to be working productively, but the employee also wants to make sure that their interests are met satisfactorily, particularly in the context of the COVID-19 pandemic (see Box 18.3).

BOX 18.3: THE COVID-19 PANDEMIC – A SHIFT TO PERPETUAL HOMEWORKING?

Research and advisory company Gartner surveyed 5,000 employees, 550 of whom were customer service professionals, to discover their views about working from home during the pandemic and returning to work afterwards. It commented that, before the COVID-19 pandemic, few organisations offered employees homeworking, which was generally decided on a case-by-case basis for personal reasons. For example, 72% of customer and support services were based almost exclusively at the workplace, with fewer than 10% of employees working from home. However, the pandemic has changed everything. Many service employees have become accustomed to working from home, with about 70% wishing to carry on doing so on regularly. Accordingly, 76% of customer and support services now have between 80% and 100% of their staff working from home. Furthermore, 89% of service leaders predict that somewhere between 20% and 80% of their employees will still be working from home in two years' time. Former biases against working from home organisational models have been undermined because employee performance has remained broadly the same or has even risen in certain cases (Omale, 2021). However, it should be pointed out that the survey focused on technical and professional staff. Key workers, such as those in health and transport services, have very little opportunity to work from home.

Information and communications technology and WLB

The evolution of information and communications technology (ICT) at work over recent years has added a further dimension to discussions around WLB. Managing the role of ICT has become a serious issue in HRM because if, for example, you have a smartphone (or your organisation provides you with one) and you're expected to keep in contact with the office all the time, then this blasts out of the water any distinction between 'work' and 'life' because your work is potentially there at 03:00. The situation is exacerbated if you work for a multinational company across different time zones, and you're expected to respond swiftly to problems that have arisen elsewhere across the globe. 'Work' and 'life' then risk getting inextricably tangled up together.

We have already seen how Daimler and Volkswagen try to deal with these issues, and how French law encourages workers to disconnect. However, even the concept of 'working time' can get blurred. Take commuting and travel time, for example. In the past, commuting time – provided you could get a seat on your train or bus – was time you had to yourself: you could spend the time between leaving home and getting to work reading the newspaper or a book or just staring out of the window. Your employer had very little influence over your travel time. This has now completely changed, and we all now frequently work on the train with our laptops, reading or editing a report, preparing for a meeting, responding to emails – and we're doing all these things for our employer. Research reveals that 'office professionals now work away from their desks 50–90% of their time'. Such 'mobile teleworkers … spend time travelling and/or working at different locations, use ICTs in work [which] involves some level of knowledge intensity and communication with others either internal and/or external to their organisation' (Axtell et al, 2008, quoted in Smith, 2010: 272). Hence, even commuting becomes a time that's controlled by the employer. Felstead (2022) offers a historical and post-pandemic evaluation of remote and hybrid working, and how the dynamics within the employment relationship play out through a more diffuse relationship between working and non-working.

So here's an open question: is there an issue here? And if so, is our smartphone or laptop making our lives easier or more stressful? How does this blurring of 'work' and 'life' affect our wellbeing? These are questions we need to work out for ourselves.

These questions become more urgent if your company gives you a smartphone. The implication is that you are going to be responsive to it, so you need to make the terms under which it's given to you quite explicit and know whether or when you're supposed to reply to messages. Dutch research has concluded that 'intensive smartphone use after work hampers psychological detachment regardless of experienced workplace tele-pressure' (van Laethem et al, 2018: 4), a finding that line managers need to be aware of.

Arnold Bakker, Professor of Work and Organisational Psychology at Erasmus University, Rotterdam, has argued that 'the smartphone had become a Trojan horse through which work infiltrated the home'. He adds: 'It seems difficult, if not impossible, for mobile users to maintain a satisfactory balance between their work and personal life' (quoted in Sample, 2014). In ancient history, the Trojan horse was the device the Greeks used to infiltrate their enemy's city, and the question here – and it's a question, not an answer – is whether the smartphone is a Trojan horse through which WLB is eventually destroyed. The idea is that it infiltrates the home, it's always there, just like the wooden horse that infiltrated Troy. Nevertheless, workers develop strategies – they resist, as we've seen repeatedly throughout this book – to prevent such an infiltration, for example by hiding their smartphone or ignoring calls, but the problem, then, is that, if they're not answering their phone, they may feel guilty about it, and the guilt then itself becomes something that's an issue at work. This is particularly true of self-employed workers (Gold and Mustafa, 2013).

Clarity between line manager and employee is required to ensure that the boundaries between 'work' and 'life' – and particularly those mediated through technology – are well understood and unambiguous, so that both sides know exactly what's expected and what isn't. Lack of clarity, and ambiguity, is what underpins workers' stress and guilt. It's 23:00 but they think, 'Oh, I really should be checking my phone. Maybe my boss has sent me a message – I need to check. If I don't, I'm going get a bollocking in the morning because I haven't answered.' A simple boundary would be to place a limit on the hour after which messages should not be answered, a policy well within the powers of HRM to introduce.

Concluding comments

The background to debates about WLB is a public policy concern over male and female participation rates in the economy. On the one hand, men and women are both increasingly required to work productively within the economy, but on the other, working – or excessive working – crowds out all the other domestic issues in their lives. By 'domestic' we mean not just our family but also our friends, including time for ourselves, time to pursue our own interests and volunteering, and time just to be quiet, to reflect and not to feel continually pressurised by our employer. However, the boundaries around WLB vary dramatically by country and company – with overwork a serious issue in certain places – although some legal systems have responded by attempting to tackle presenteeism and burnout. We saw in Chapter 8 that US hi-tech companies abolish the distinction between work and life – by attempting to integrate life into work, they 'corporatise' life. The US has no legally guaranteed minimum vacation time. Figure 18.1 demonstrated that Americans work longer than Europeans and even longer than the Japanese, who have a long-hours culture. Europe has been at the centre of reducing working hours, increasing female participation in the economy and male participation in the home. It also has employers who aim to regulate the impact of technology, such as smartphones, on private life.

The challenge of WLB is, of course, more acute if you have children, because children are demanding, naturally enough. If you don't have a nanny or an au pair, and if public provision of local nurseries is limited and private childcare is too expensive, then your employer becomes the agency by default through which you have to mediate your WLB. Human resources (HR) policies – and we noted some good examples – must, of course, strike a balance between the employer's and the employee's legitimate interests. The challenges have also been sharpened by trends towards globalisation – with multinational companies operating across multiple time zones – and the rapid emergence of new technologies, which have added a novel and urgent dimension to the whole question of WLB.

Some questions to think about

1. Why is work–life balance an important concept in HRM? How would you assess your own WLB? Outline some of the challenges faced by employers when trying to implement WLB policies.

2. 'Long hours and presenteeism form "part of the job" of many professional and managerial jobs, therefore in choosing these jobs, applicants are directly endorsing work-life imbalance' (Murphy and Doherty, 2011: 252). Evaluate this statement in the light of the WLB literature.

3. 'Information and communications technologies (ICTs) are breaking down the barriers between work and life.' What are the implications of this statement for debates on WLB? Would you feel happy having to reply to your line manager about work matters during evenings, weekends and holidays?

4. How might the aftermath of the COVID-19 pandemic create further inequalities at work by favouring some workers for continued homeworking over others?

Further reading

Guest, D.E. (2002) 'Perspectives on the study of work–life balance', *Social Science Information*, 41(2): 255–79. [Social psychological approach to the different forms of WLB and the increase in conflict models.]

Tech Insider (2017) 'This man worked undercover in a Chinese iPhone factory', Available from: www.YouTube.com/watch?v=5ItLIywwepY [First-hand account of what it's like to work in a huge Chinese factory-dormitory complex.]

Waters, S. (2014) 'A capitalism that kills: Workplace suicides at France Télécom', *French Politics, Culture and Society*, 32(3): 121–41. [Examination of the coercive management workplace regime at France Télécom that led to several workplace suicides.]

19

Artificial Intelligence and HR Analytics

With Yu Zheng

In this chapter, we turn to the significance of automation within labour markets and its increasing penetration of the world of work. We begin by outlining the nature of the three earlier industrial revolutions and their relationship with the fourth, which involves the application of ever more sophisticated levels of artificial intelligence (AI) in the operation of industrial and service sectors. The key questions are how AI will affect the quality of existing jobs, for example through new forms of electronic monitoring and surveillance, and lead to the loss of other jobs, particularly those that are routine. Further questions then arise, relating to which sectors and which groups of workers (age, gender) in which countries are at highest risk. We also need to consider possible constraints on the actual rates of automation as well as differing perspectives on its significance.

Following these broad investigations, the chapter then focuses on a specific application of computer technology to human resource management (HRM) – human resource analytics. This is a branch of HRM that aims to improve the transparency and comparability of human resources (HR) data, to allow for more efficient benchmarking of employee inputs and outcomes, and so enhance productivity. We examine HR analytics as a subject as well as its development and use over recent years. We then look at the problems associated with adopting analytics tools to assess the people side of a business, before considering their advantages and disadvantages. We end by exploring the obstacles to the use of analytic modelling in managing people. Adoption of analytics involves deduction and codification, which may actually turn out to be an opaque way of handling information and making decisions.

The fourth industrial revolution

The economist John Maynard Keynes predicted that by the year 2030 the 'struggle for subsistence' would have been solved and that work would accordingly be shared out as evenly as possible, leading to a 15-hour working week (Keynes, 1931). Writing shortly afterwards, Bertrand Russell speculated on the role of leisure 'in a world where no one is compelled to work for more than four hours a day' (1973 [1935]: 20). Keynes and Russell were both reflecting on the challenges presented by soaring productivity resulting from the first and second industrial revolutions (steam and mass production respectively), challenges that continued with the advent of the third industrial revolution in the 1970s (the advent of the microprocessor). Clive Jenkins and Barrie Sherman, for example, focused on the effects of what they saw as the 'collapse of work' (1979) and the 'leisure shock' (1981), as new technologies were forecast to create rising unemployment across the industrialised world in the 1980s and into the 1990s.

And now we are facing the fourth industrial revolution (Industry 4.0), created by rapid advances in automation and AI, which is provoking similar debates (Ford, 2015; Susskind, 2020). The House of Commons has reflected on both the challenges and opportunities in its analysis of automation and the future of work. On the one hand, it noted that: 'The transition to a more automated workplace and society risks reducing the quality of work, widening existing inequalities and increasing regional disparities' (2019: 53, para 20). On the other hand, echoing the concerns of Keynes and Russell expressed almost 90 years earlier, it suggested that: 'If managed well, the transition to a more automated British workplace should make businesses more productive, improve the supply of high-quality jobs, and support working people to have more leisure time' (2019: 53, para 23).

Automation involves a wide range of technological applications that replace workers with algorithms, computer programs and robots. According to the Office for National Statistics (ONS, 2019c), around 1.5 million jobs in England are at 'high risk' of automation over the coming years, some 7.4% of the jobs of the 20 million people analysed, with 64.9% at 'medium risk'. Concerns of workers, trade unions and policy-makers centre on both the loss of jobs involved and on the quality of the jobs that remain. We've discussed earlier in the book the numerous ways in which employers are using digital platforms to control workers: 'cybervetting' during recruitment, electronic monitoring and surveillance of performance, the use of ambiguous contractual status for gig workers, relying on zero-hours contracts and introducing online tracking devices when transferring work from office to home during the COVID-19 pandemic all stand out as examples. However, as the Taylor Review warned: 'If technology and automation are to enhance human capabilities to maximum effect, they must be created with human factors, tendencies and limitations in mind' (Taylor, 2017: 105).

We have already witnessed the many effects of automation in our daily lives, from ATMs in banks and self-checkouts in shops, online shopping and parcel delivery, ride-hailing apps, to digitalised driving licence and passport applications. Many other effects are more hidden – such as machine translation, keyhole surgery and fraud detection – but they, too, are increasingly shaping our lives. The question that we need to examine is the possible consequences of these developments for HRM: the number and type of jobs that might be affected over the coming years, the sectors and occupations most likely to be involved and the profiles of the workers (age, gender, educational and skills level) most at risk.

The jobs affected

A basic problem lies in predicting just how many jobs might actually be affected. Frey and Osborne (2013: 44) predicted in 2013 that 35% of jobs in the UK could be potentially automated, while in the US 47% were at high risk, 19% at medium risk and 33% at low risk over the 'next decade or two'. Through an analysis of 702 different occupations, they identified three groups of tasks, or 'engineering bottlenecks', that remain difficult for machines to master (2013: 24–8). These include tasks requiring social intelligence (the ability to respond to the emotional cues of others), complex manipulation (the ability to control objects using fine motor skills) and creativity (the ability to conceive novel ideas that push cultural boundaries). On this basis, they categorised occupations on a spectrum from least susceptible to computerisation (such as recreational therapists) to most susceptible (such as telemarketers).

Gardiner and Corlett (2015) agree that 'the "routineness" of jobs is a good explanation for changing employment structures in 16 Western European countries between 1993 and 2010, with the "offshorability" of jobs (how easily they can be moved abroad) also tested but much less important'. They argue that the UK labour market got 'hollowed out' over this period with jobs in the middle ranges – such as secretarial and manufacturing work – most likely to take a hit. By contrast, less routine jobs in customer service roles and social care and healthcare grew in proportion. However, as 'engineering bottlenecks' are overcome, then low-skilled jobs, especially those that require complex manipulation and manual dexterity such as caring, driving and food service in restaurants, come increasingly into the frame for replacement.

Hence there is a general consensus that routine and repetitive tasks are most likely to be automated, meaning that the risks now focus on lower skilled occupations. In England, the ONS (2019c) accordingly identified waiting staff, shelf-fillers and elementary sales occupations at high risk, with medical practitioners, higher education teaching professionals and senior professionals of educational establishments as low risk because they are highly skilled. We noted in Chapter 14 that women tend to be concentrated in lower paid service occupations, so it comes as no surprise that 70.2% of the posts assessed as being at high risk are held by women. The young, too, are seriously affected, with 15.7% of workers aged 20–24 in jobs at high risk, but only 1.3% of those aged 35–39, although the risk then climbs again from the age of 40 (ONS, 2019c).

However, we need to stress that technology does not have an isolated and linear impact, but is rather processed through layers of social structure, with different outcomes. As Martin Krzywdzinski (2021: 502) points out: 'Decisions about the use of technology are made against the backdrop of specific products, production systems, and corporate strategies, but also specific education systems and industrial relations.' His research, which focuses on the automotive industry in three country cases, shows how automation can be reversed and used for different objectives, such as increasing flexibility and reducing labour. It is also critical of the decontextualised nature of technological predictions:

> From a methodological point of view, the analysis shows that deriving automation potentials at the level of individual professions or tasks (eg, Frey and Osborne, 2013) is only of limited use. Rather, the material and technical conditions of automation must be considered at the level of entire manufacturing processes.... Frey and Osborne (2013) expect a 98% probability that assembly workers will be threatened by automation. However, an examination of the assembly processes in the automotive industry shows that the diversity of individual activities ... have so far provided very difficult conditions for assembly automation. (Krzywdzinski, 2021: 527)

This analysis helps to explain why likely impacts vary by country. Economies differ greatly according to the relative weight of their service and industrial sectors. For example, industrial sectors are more susceptible to automation than service sectors but, while France, the Netherlands, the UK and the US have more significant service sectors, they also have a relatively high proportion of jobs within those sectors that could be automated. Research by PricewaterhouseCoopers (PwC) (2018a: 9) reveals that Slovakia (44%) and Slovenia (42%) confront relatively high potential automation rates, while Finland (22%) and South Korea (22%) have lower proportions of jobs that are susceptible to automation. The rate for the UK stands at 32%, for Germany at 37% and for the US at 39%.

Constraints

However, the PwC report (2018a: 36–7) points out that there are a variety of constraints that might affect actual rates of automation. The technology needs to be adapted to real-life business environments, and the business case accepted. In the US 'one additional robot per thousand workers reduces the aggregate employment-to-population ratio by 0.2 percentage points and aggregate wages by 0.42%' (Acemoglu and Restrepo, 2020: concluding remarks). A 0.2 percentage point decline is equivalent to about 400,000 jobs, so much depends on the rate of increase in the number of robots in the US economy. That rate might also be affected by economic constraints: for example, the initial cost of investing in robotisation might make it a high-risk decision. There are numerous legal and regulatory issues that need to be covered, too, for example data protection and, in the case of driverless vehicles, regulations on accident liability. Social acceptance may also prove to be a barrier, with people simply not happy about the use of robots to drive cars or provide healthcare. There may also be concerns about inequalities that emerge, particularly if low-skilled workers do suffer rising levels

Figure 19.1: 'I'm worried about the effects of new technology'

Source: Link and Bunnage (2007)

of unemployment. PwC (2018a: 34–5) also points out, however, that these new technologies may create new jobs, and not just jobs related to themselves but also as a result of the stimulus to productivity, incomes and demand that they lead to. Indeed, it has been argued elsewhere that, although much attention has focused on potential job losses, automation may improve productivity, increase investment in the economy overall and hence boost growth rates (Manyika et al, 2017: Section 3). Of course, whether the boost to creating new jobs will actually outweigh the loss of old ones remains an open question (World Bank, 2019: 18–34).

This book has argued throughout that perceptions of HRM and developments within it are as important as whatever we accept as the 'reality'. Given the sheer unreliability of predictions about the impact of automation on the future number and quality of jobs, it's helpful to summarise here four different approaches to the subject that the Royal Society for the Arts, Manufactures and Commerce (RSA) (Dellot and Wallace-Stephens, 2017: 11–12) has identified. *Alarmists* focus on rising inequality and social tensions as a result of automation. *Dreamers*, by contrast, believe that automation could herald the advent of a new leisure society, in which we are released from the drudgery of work routines. *Incrementalists* argue that automation will lead to the evolution of jobs rather than their elimination, with technology more 'a gradual rising tide rather than a fast-approaching tidal wave'. *Sceptics* claim that only modest innovations remain to be made, as the most significant gains from automation have already occurred.

HR analytics

Having introduced the question of AI in broad terms, we now turn to a specific application to HRM, HR analytics. This is a branch of HRM that aims to improve the transparency and comparability of HR data within an organisation, to allow for more efficient benchmarking of employee inputs and outcomes and so enhance productivity (although, as we'll see, benchmarking by itself is not enough for companies to understand the healthiness of their business). HR analytics can be defined by reference to the following elements:

- Use of statistical techniques to demonstrate the impact of HR activities within the organisation.
- An evidence-based approach to decision-making and the 'people' side of the business.
- Demonstration of the direct links between the importance of people and business outcomes.

The term 'workforce analytics' might therefore be regarded as more accurate, a term that Mark Huselid (2018) has defined as the process involved in understanding, quantifying, managing and improving the role of talent in the execution of strategy and the creation of value. Bear in mind that Huselid is from the US, where 'talent' refers to almost everybody in the organisation. Hence, in effect, he is saying that workforce analytics helps an organisation to ensure that the role of employees is properly integrated into understanding, quantifying and improving the execution of strategy, and that it adds value to a business.

Emotional intelligence

Here's a question to ease us in. Figure 19.2 below depicts an emotion. Do you think the woman looks surprised, shocked, excited or apprehensive?

You might answer 'surprised'. This exercise is an example of a question used for testing emotional intelligence as part of recruitment screening. Companies are

Figure 19.2: Emotional intelligence test

Source: Getty images

increasingly using standard tests to evaluate potential new employees (Deloitte, 2015). Tests are sometimes applied in the very early rounds of recruitment to screen for certain personality traits that the company believes are desirable – one of which, as we saw in Chapter 10, is emotional intelligence. But how do you test someone's emotional intelligence? You can do it face to face, although that could be quite expensive and time-consuming. You can also ask the candidate to interpret another person's expressions or body language, which is the purpose of Figure 19.2 – to show how you relate to the person in the picture. Standard tests can be administered and processed electronically, allowing companies to screen a bigger pool of candidates (Chamorro-Premuzic, 2015).

But is just examining this woman's eyes enough for us to judge her emotion? Actually, rather than 'surprised', some people might say 'excited' or 'apprehensive'. There are various reasons why we might interpret the expression in someone's eyes differently, apart from anything to do with lacking emotional intelligence. If we think about how we relate to another person, we generally try to read their full facial expression as well as their body language. We understand that emotion is often reactive, so it needs to be assessed in context, and a facial expression in one context may not necessarily mean the same thing in another. We also need to be aware that expressions vary between cultures. All these factors contribute to the complexity of the ways in which we, as individuals, read facial expressions. In addition, for the purpose of these tests, companies often use a standard test that has been specially designed and requires an actor to act out specific emotions. And while some actors are extremely good, it may be argued that acting and real emotions are not the same thing. Using standard tests to evaluate individual characteristics or personal traits then creates many potential problems and biases. Indeed, if we are going to use HR analytics to assess individual abilities and performance, we need to know how best to do so in a way that is effective and reduces bias.

Development of HR analytics

There are several terms used for HR analytics, including 'people analytics', 'talent analytics', 'workforce analytics' and 'human capital analytics', all of which are interchangeable. 'Human capital analytics' is probably the earliest term, but 'workforce analytics' is also quite widely used, as noted above. Mark Huselid (2018), one of the key theorists in this field, specialises in high-performance work practices and has developed quantifiable means to assess the effectiveness of HRM systems in improving the productivity and quality of services in a company. His analysis has led him to refer to these analytic tools as 'workforce analytics'. 'People analytics' and 'talent analytics', which are more recent terms, focus more on the people side, but they are still analytics. They attempt to quantify some of the aspects of individual behaviour or the quality of individuals, although it remains arguable as to whether this is achievable or not.

Many companies have also adopted a range of data management and visualisation tools, which are referred to as HR metrics, HR scorecards, HR dashboard or HR information systems. They pull together the human–related data within the company to reveal the healthiness or challenges confronting the HR system in the organisation. This is also referred to as 'digitalisation' of the HR data. Many visualisation tools, such as SQL, Tableau and Python, are widely used to capture and represent trends in HR activities.

Finally, recent development in HR analytics has been driven by big data analysis capacity to provide real-time performance outcomes. For example, Humanyze is one of the big data HR analytics solution providers that relies on tracking online and offline interactions among the workforce to assess organisational efficiency and identify 'blockages' in the workflow. They collect flows of emails, messages and calls among the workforce, and apply algorithms to interpret and map how individuals interact and collaborate with each other. Data collected can also be translated into individual and collective benchmarks of key performance measures. Advances in big data, machine learning and AI have enabled companies to gain new insights into the workforce. HR analytics tools are often involved in using algorithms to track and categorise patterns of human behaviour (Edwards and Edwards, 2019). With assistance of big data and AI, much effort has been made to explore the potential for using these tools to enhance recruitment and selection accuracy, improve workforce diversity and inclusivity, and support employee development and engagement (Eubanks, 2019). Nonetheless, the question of how best to utilise data analytics capacity has fuelled continuous debate between employers and employees across different functions in organisations and across society.

Three dimensions to HR analytics

There are, broadly speaking, three dimensions to HR analytics that companies can develop: diagnostic, predictive and prescriptive (see Box 19.1).

Diagnostic analytics

Diagnostic analytics includes those descriptive indicators that a company can use to assess the robustness of its HRM or the potential problems it has to confront that may be gathered from its HR spreadsheet. This information captures expenditure on human capital, such as salaries, benefits, taxes and National Insurance contributions; on turnaround time of recruitment; and on the effectiveness of management interventions, such as training, among other categories. At the same time, the company will also want to know how well the benefits of this expenditure have been retained within the company, which leads to the second level of indicators, such as the rate of labour turnover. One aspect is voluntary turnover, when individuals choose to leave the company, but it is also important to break turnover down by different types of skill or job because some are easier to replace than others. Such indicators will show how well or badly the company is managing to retain key employees.

Diagnostic analytics also links these indicators together. For example, the quality of leadership within the company refers to its efficiency and responsiveness as well as its ability to replace senior managers internally or externally. These aspects of leadership can be related to levels of employee engagement with the company. So, for example, the percentage of employees responding to staff surveys is linked to issues such as the quality of leadership, with the employee engagement index another key indicator used to measure the robustness of the company's HR system. Diagnostic analytics, then, attempts to identify key indicators to evaluate the system, but also to identify potential causal links between the various indicators.

Predictive analytics

Predictive analytics is a further dimension of HR analytics. In public health, modelling the spread of coronavirus is a good example of predictive analytics, with teams of medical researchers trying to capture future trends in the disease by working out the ways of interpreting patterns of contagion.

In an organisational setting, Oakland Athletics is probably one of the frontrunners in using predictive analytics to measure performance, both of individuals and of teams (Lewis, 2003). It is a relatively small baseball club in the US, with a limited budget, which nevertheless competes in a major league against much wealthier clubs that can identify and buy up first-class players. Although reasonably successful, the club manager's problem was that he was unable to keep his players, as good ones would be scouted away by bigger clubs. He asked an economic modeller to examine the performance of individual players, and then pulled together a group who had potential but who had not yet proved themselves in top-flight baseball. He bought them relatively cheaply and trained them in the team. Although Oakland Athletics did not win the league, it had some successful seasons, which prompted the larger clubs to investigate the ways in which the team had analysed potential, using data to try and predict performance. These methods have since become more prominent in elite sport.

Despite advances in the capacity to process data and generate fine-grained measurement, collective success is seldom a simple aggregation of individual efforts or outputs. In the case of major league baseball teams, further research suggests that league success is a matter of the connections between the players and individual potential (Wang and Cotton, 2018). In other words, the network between the players within the team, and their networks outside the team, may give a stronger indicator of overall team performance. This is due to players' experiences in rival teams leading to a better understanding of competitors' tactics and hence better preparation for the game. Networks, therefore, provide another way of explaining or predicting performance.

Prescriptive analytics

Prescriptive analytics involves the application of mathematical and computational modelling to suggest decision options designed to take advantage of the results of descriptive and predictive analytics. Prescriptive analytics aims to become a more comprehensive approach in data analytics. Prescriptive analytics often specifies both the actions necessary to achieve predicted outcomes and the interrelated effects of each decision – that is, path A leads to one outcome, while path B leads to another. Companies and HR consultancies attempt to predict these outcomes so that management can make informed and evidence-based decisions. In other words, prescriptive analytics offers an estimation of outcomes that differentiates between interventions.

> ## BOX 19.1: DIFFERENCES BETWEEN DIAGNOSTIC, PREDICTIVE AND PRESCRIPTIVE DIAGNOSTICS
>
> To distinguish differences between diagnostic, predictive and prescriptive analytics, let's examine five questions as examples:
>
> 1. What is the absence rate among graduate interns in the department?
> 2. Does outsourcing ICT services save the organisation money?
> 3. Does the in-house training programme reduce employees' intention to leave?
> 4. How satisfied are employees who work in the manufacturing department?
> 5. Which HR scheme has improved employee wellbeing the most?
>
> Questions 1 and 4 can be answered by using descriptive analytics data. Questions 2 and 3 need to be answered by applying predictive analytics techniques. Question 5 requires comparing the impacts of HR interventions, which falls into the territory of prescriptive analytics. Analytics questions should help to build relationships between different aspects of HR, linking the 'people' aspects with the organisation processes, but also linking the 'people' aspects with the execution of corporate strategy and with economic indicators.

The questions we ask often lead to different analytics tools being applied and therefore generating different insights into HR issues as well as recommendations for solutions. This becomes clearer when we think about the example of Oakland Athletics described earlier. If we ask how the quality of the individual players affects the team's performance in league tournaments, the answers will lie in the metrics of individual aptitude, skills and possibly past performance. However, if the question is how the experiences of members of the club playing for rival teams contribute to performance outcomes, as Wang and Cotton (2018) ask in their longitudinal study, the answers will lie in the relational ties among players and supporting staff. The focus of analytics moves to the collective attributes of the clubs. Can you think of other HR analytics questions to probe into what contributes to the league success of a club?

Applying HR analytics

From a practical point of view, using HR analytics to help to resolve a business problem is a complex process, which can be broadly divided into five steps (see Figure 19.3): define the problem or problems (and hence the analytics questions); develop a hypothesis; collect and analyse the data; make recommendations; and implement and evaluate outcomes.

The first step is generally to design the questions for analytics purposes. To define the problem, we must examine the context in which an analytics project is to take place, for example, a firm's comparative advantages, capabilities, strengths and weaknesses, and then identify the gaps in its strategic execution. Both strategic and operational aspects of people management will need to be considered when defining the problem, as well as budget, resources and timeline of implementation. HR analytics is more likely to generate meaningful data and a relationship between different datasets, with specifically defined problem statements.

Once the questions are identified, the second step is to develop some hypotheses, which means establishing the anticipated causal relationships between HR indicators and organisational outcomes. At this stage, we also need to consider using diagnostic analytics to locate the data at different organisational levels that will feed into what is feasible to achieve. Hypotheses direct the data collection and analysis, and also inform the data modelling, which is a process of interpreting, testing and establishing relationships between various indicators.

The third step is to determine the data required for performing analytics. Data need to be sorted, compared and categorised at this stage. A critical reason why HR analytics has not been widely adopted is not lack of data but variance in data quality, which makes it more complicated to draw conclusions based on data collected at different times and from a variety of sources (Minbaeva, 2018). Companies intending to use HR analytics more effectively need to improve data quality, investigate the full range of data sources, and ensure that data are compatible. Attention needs to be paid to both the time when, and the locations where, data have been collected. Longitudinal employee survey data, for instance, are not directly comparable because employees' attitudes towards the same issue can be affected by organisational circumstances and events occurring immediately before the survey.

Figure 19.3: Illustration of the process of applying HR analytics

Source: Y. Zheng

The fourth step is to develop recommendations based on the analysis. It's worth noting here that visualisation of data plays a critical part in building a narrative and gaining support for recommended changes (Diez et al, 2020). Options for recommendations also need to be evaluated in relation to the characteristics of the firm involved, its workforce and its competitive environment. The purpose of HR analytics is not to offer one-size-fits-all solutions, but tailored recommendations, which is where the strength of its evidence-based approach lies. For example, an HR analytics project conducted at an American fast-food chain, Jack in the Box, showed that causes for turnover varied between age groups and types of employment contract, so recommendations for measures to control turnover were adapted accordingly (Schiemann et al, 2018).

Finally, recommendations based on analytics must be implemented and outcomes evaluated. Rather than focusing just on remedial action, evaluation also needs to consider the implications for outcomes and impact. While HR specialists play a central role in making HR analytics an integral management process in organisations, involvement of individuals and departments outside the HR function are critical in implementing the recommended measures and ensuring their effectiveness. HR analytics attempts to probe causal links, predict trends and evaluate which measures have proved effective and which have not, all of which requires input from a range of business functions, such as finance, information and communications technology (ICT), marketing and operations. People from these functions need to be engaged in dialogue and narrative-building, which are powerful tools for implementing the measures recommended, but they also provide the feedback necessary so that modifications can be made.

HR analytics needs to become part of the organisational workflow, in continuously supporting the improvement of data quality and linking its results to existing organisational processes. For example, in an HR analytics project conducted in Maersk Drilling, a multinational offshore drilling operator, researchers found that line managers who were more likely to encourage measures to improve employee engagement were also associated with the improved health and safety of its oil-drilling operations (Minbaeva, 2018). (See also Box 19.2.)

BOX 19.2: NOVO NORDISK – NO ONE-SIZE-FITS-ALL SOLUTIONS

Novo Nordisk is a biomedical manufacturer based in Oslo, Norway. The company has a tradition of encouraging experiment and innovation, taking initiatives and supporting team-based project development. In 2014, Novo Nordisk carried out an HR analytics exercise to measure the performance of its scientists. One surprising finding is that there did not seem to be a causal link between length of service and performance. That was curious because, in the field of research and development, experience is important, and HRM aims to retain a stable workforce. Further analysis of the time spent on different tasks identified many highly experienced and high-performing scientists who were engaged in mentoring and supporting younger colleagues rather than focusing on their own projects. Given that length of service is not a predictor of performance, the company decided not to reshuffle the workplace but rather to introduce a set of digital platforms for sharing knowledge and mentoring, which did, indeed, help to improve performance. The choice made by the company demonstrates how firms contextualise what the data indicate, but also sort out different interpretations of the data, relate the data to the circumstances within the company and encourage experimentation in follow-up actions.

Source: Minbaeva (2018)

Building the HR analytics capability into the organisational structure requires continuous investment in coordination of data collection and organisation, the creation of a culture of inquiry and ensuring a habit of making evidence-based decisions, as well as equipping senior management with tools for action linked to current and future strategic decisions (Levenson, 2018). The case of Vestas, a Danish windmill manufacturing company, makes the point (Minbaeva, 2018). Vestas was trying to understand its workforce diversity (a concept we analysed in Chapter 14). We often say intuitively that a diverse workforce is something positive, but we lack the means to measure the inclusivity of company policies or their impact. Based on analysis of recruiters, the research team at Vestas discovered that female recruiters were more likely than their male counterparts to hire diverse employees. They also found that non-Danish recruiters were more likely to hire employees from diverse backgrounds. Senior management shared this information about good practice and built it into training systems to help raise awareness of unconscious bias and improve the culture of the company. The message here is that the structure of the company needs continuous monitoring and improvement to carry out the advice proposed by HR analytics data.

Summing up so far, application of HR analytics requires firms to consider three elements. The first is data quality, availability and quantity. The second is analytical competence and the skills of both HR specialists and people involved in analytics projects to evaluate statistical visualisation and communications. And the third is the capability to promote actions taken with reference to workforce characteristics, organisational circumstances and the environment to inform organisational-level change.

HR analytics – a fad?

The question arises as to whether HR analytics is just a new fad, a fashion that might just fade away. There is a point here because HR specialists try to demonstrate the value of the work they do and the advice they provide to senior management. Diez et al (2020) liken HR managers to doctors: they are very important, but people go to them only when they have problems. And then HR analytics explains either something that other managers feel they already know or something they do not really want to know in the first place. This is the kind of dilemma that many HR specialists must face up to. So, trying to quantify some of the human aspects of the business – by inserting analytics into the HR arena – seems to form part of their fight-back against marginalisation. That said, HR analytics should at its best allow data to be used more effectively to relate the 'people side' of the business to its 'performance side'.

An example is improving labour productivity. And here we come full circle back to Chapter 1, in which we examined what HRM entails: controlling labour costs, raising productivity and ensuring business survival. A simplified calculation of unit labour costs involves dividing the output by the input. But if you think more carefully, what is output? Is it revenue or sales turnover? Or is it after-tax return? Companies may be using very different data to capture their output. And when you look at input, are you calculating the total number of hours worked, or the size of the workforce, or the investment in HRM? All these are different measures, and they make comparisons more complex. The UK's ONS (2018b) has therefore developed an online tool that allows you to insert relevant data from your business and get a sense of how well your business is doing. Data include elements like sales turnover, various costs and size of workforce. The metrics reveal both a company's productivity and its standing within the given industrial sector in relation to its main competitors. The question remains, however: does such an analytics tool show companies something they do not already know?

Recent developments in HR analytics have built on big data and AI that have promised to uncover insights, although they have also encountered criticisms (Hamilton and Sodeman, 2020). Concerns over the selective bias of the data, the use of predictive algorithms that disproportionately favour (or discriminate against) certain groups of people and the accountability of AI-assisted decisions have led to controversy and public debates. Amazon, for example, invested heavily in developing an algorithm – a set of 'defined steps structured to process instructions/data to produce an output' (Kitchin, 2017: 14) – designed to select software developers, only to find it heavily favoured men over women (Dastin, 2018). This is hardly surprising because the algorithm was merely generalising patterns based on the CVs it was given – and those CVs related to a population of software developers who were predominantly men. After attempts to retrain and correct the algorithm from discriminating against women had failed, Amazon terminated the project. Basically, if you insert sexist, racist or any other kind of prejudice into an algorithm, prejudices simply emerge the other end 'concealed beneath a cloak of objectivity' (Kling, 2020: 183).

During the coronavirus pandemic that began in 2020, many employers have widely adopted homeworking. Some employers introduced an online tracking algorithm to monitor compliance, engagement and productivity of the workers (Harris, 2021). However, while the impact of electronic monitoring on productivity varies, the presence of continuous monitoring can have a negative impact on employee wellbeing (Davidson and Henderson, 2006). Undoubtedly, big data and AI will reshape workplaces. The question of how they can be used to improve the quality of decision-making presents both opportunities and challenges to HR in the foreseeable future.

Concluding comments

When we seek to assess the impact of AI on how we work within companies and organisations, we need to bear in mind that risks vary greatly by sector, groups of worker (skill level, age, gender) and country. We also need to evaluate potential constraints on the actual rates of automation. Our anxieties and hopes about the future depend on our overall perspectives, as so many trends and implications remain a matter of interpretation, not fact.

However, when we focus specifically on HR analytics, we discover that they may help HRM to play a partner role in many business settings, and that they can be used to identify realistic targets, make sense of mega-data and prescribe appropriate management remedies. We need to understand both their potential and limitations, and apply the techniques case by case, aware, too, of the institutional and organisational contexts in which they are being applied.

Some questions to think about

1. Are you an alarmist, a dreamer, an incrementalist or a sceptic with respect to automation and AI? Why?

2. What are the challenges facing HR managers when AI is used in an HR analytics project? How would you advise them to overcome these challenges?

3. How do you think adopting AI in HR analytics will change the debate over whether labour is a cost or an asset in a business?

Further reading

Rasmussen, T. and Ulrich, D. (2015) 'Learning from practice: How HR analytics avoids becoming a fad', *Organizational Dynamics*, 44(3): 236–42. [Practical advice on the application of HR analytics, illustrated in two case studies.]

Tambe, P., Cappelli, P. and Yakubovich, V. (2019) 'Artificial intelligence in human resources management: Challenges and a path forward', *California Management Review*, 61(4): 15–42. [An overview of AI adoption for use in HRM and the challenges it presents.]

Wang, L. and Cotton, L. (2018) 'Beyond Moneyball to social capital inside and out: The value of differentiated workforce experience ties to performance', *Human Resource Management*, 57(3): 761–80. [A reminder that better performance comes from collective efforts and social ties.]

Summary and Conclusions

In this, our concluding chapter, we need to review what we've learned about human resource management (HRM) so far. What really are the key issues that we've come across in all our discussions? And, in particular, how do we answer our own question in the title to this book: where, indeed, is the 'human' in human resource management? First, we summarise the book in broad outline, just to remind ourselves how far we've come. We then change gear, theorising the main issues that have emerged, and in that context, we attempt to examine how HRM might be made more 'human' within capitalist societies.

If you pick up a standard textbook on HRM, you'll find chapters on all its various aspects, but you might be confused by the detail – not being able to see the wood for the trees. The really important thing is to be able to understand the *basic principles* that underpin HRM – *all* HRM – which is where we started. So if you ask us 'What is HRM all about?', we'd say it's about control – management control of employees in so many different ways. You can see it coming through all the different topics we've been discussing in this book – flexibility, reward management, employee participation, discrimination and diversity, and work–life balance. Above all, it keeps coming through in the rapidly changing societal contexts and global trends in HRM, not least in the emergence of the gig economy and the role of digital platforms in managing employment relationships. In all these areas, the central issue remains controlling labour costs, raising productivity and ensuring survival, and how these objectives are followed through at the point of production: in the office, in the factory, in the warehouse, in your gig task, or, if you're a homeworker, at home. If you keep that notion of control in your head as the point of reference, especially if you're finding your way into HRM as a topic, that's as good a place to start as any. And if you don't agree with us, that's fine, but do be clear about your own reasons for disagreeing!

Part 1: Where we've been...

This book has argued that, at its most basic, HRM is about two dimensions of control. One is controlling labour costs, which any organisation has to do. Whether it's in the private or public sector, a charity or a voluntary organisation, labour costs need to be controlled. The other dimension is ensuring that productivity is rising, or at least not falling. Productivity, how you get the best out of labour, is a key issue, and there are many ways you can improve it, as we've seen, for example, by carefully hiring the right people, training them, ensuring diversity, integrating them into management systems through participation schemes, making sure their payment is fair, using performance appraisal systems – all these different human resources (HR) practices boil down to controlling labour costs and raising productivity. Together they ensure that the organisation will survive and continue to provide jobs.

And from your own point of view as a worker, you may find you have issues you want to raise with your employer, so the way in which you engage at work is important. How do you ensure that your pay remains fair? How do you maintain your work–life balance and avoid increasing your stress levels when your employer is arranging next month's duty rosters? How do you avoid discrimination at work? How do you secure a place on that training programme you want to go on? All these issues eventually come back, in one way or another, to controlling costs and raising productivity, and how you manage to fix mutually acceptable outcomes with your line manager. If you see cost control and productivity as the core function for HRM, then much falls into place.

The key question is how HRM fits into overall business strategy and how it helps an organisation maintain competitive advantage over its rivals. The point about controlling costs and raising productivity introduces the notion of unit labour costs. Unit labour costs are basically the total labour cost of producing a good or service, divided by the units produced or delivered. So, if you produce 50 units at a total cost of £50, then one unit costs £1 – and you're trying either to increase the number of units that you're producing or else to reduce their overall cost. Hence the significance of unit labour costs.

This brings us to the heart of the employment relationship and its complexity. For an employer, wages and salaries are a cost, whereas for workers they are income, so there's going to be a certain tension between how each views payment and reward. Basically, all of us as employees would prefer more pay and shorter working hours, while our employers would like the opposite – to pay us less for longer working hours. This structural tension at the heart of the employment relationship is what we call the 'wage–effort' bargain.

The wage–effort bargain is a critically important concept when we analyse the employment relationship and its relationship to HRM. Whatever job we're doing, the employer buys our labour power over a certain period of time and gives us a wage in exchange. The wage or the reward – or the basis on which it is to be paid – is given in your employment contract (at least, by a reputable employer), and remains the same unless you renegotiate it or receive notification that it's to change and you accept the alteration. You're paid a monthly wage or annual salary, and you know what that is. The productivity part of it, on the other hand, is much more fluid – this is the 'effort' part. It is variable because the employer will generally try to gain more 'effort' out of you than you may be prepared for. The idea of employers 'screwing the workers' is a graphic way of making the point, from the workers' point of view, that employers are trying to extract as much from the workers as possible.

The employment relationship in the traditional 'standard' or 'typical' sense of the term (note the inverted commas) is a relationship that is ongoing as it may continue for a considerable period of time. It is also asymmetrical or indeterminate, in that you are being paid a wage in exchange for a degree of effort that can never be precisely or exactly pinned down. Your contract may state that you are required to carry out certain tasks, but in the end, your productivity will vary according to all kinds of other factors (not least the level of trust you share with your line manager). Furthermore, the relationship is, if not overtly conflictual, then at least potentially conflictual. Even the best relationship we have with our line manager may turn a bit sour. If you are given extra work to do at the last minute on a Friday afternoon, you may not be very happy about it. However, if there's already goodwill in that relationship, you may be prepared to go the extra mile. But if you're already feeling fed up or aggrieved, you may turn round to your line manager and refuse and risk the consequences. This idea of potential conflict is therefore always there, at the heart of the relationship. Of course, you might go through your entire working life with great employers and great colleagues, but nevertheless, there is always the risk of conflict because the employer doesn't actually buy *you* – that would be slavery – but rather your time and your effort, and that always creates ambiguity, to say the least.

Which leads us into the notion of strategic HRM and its contrast with personnel management. Personnel management is really the everyday routine work of monitoring labour. It's about keeping records on absenteeism, sickness rates and turnover, and about recruitment and other procedures at a basic, reactive level. By contrast, strategic HRM – however we understand that contentious term 'strategy' – fits proactively into the organisation's overall business context. The 'fit' broadly takes two different forms. One is *internal* fit, where HRM systems are adjusted coherently into a mutually supporting 'whole', since some HR functions fit better together than others. So, for example, a company's need for job security, to retain high-skilled workers, may best be met by well-integrated training and development programmes alongside performance-related pay systems and clearly defined career progression.

The second dimension to 'fit' is *external* fit with business strategy. Any company – it might be an airline, car manufacturer or supermarket – will try to establish itself within a certain niche within its product market. At the high-quality end, it will need workers who can produce a high-quality product or service, while at the low-cost, 'cheap and cheerful' end, it will need less highly skilled workers to produce the product or service. The kind of human resources that are going to be recruited, trained and paid will accordingly vary in line with the business strategy. At the high-quality end, it's claimed, the company will aim to retain a permanent core staff, while at the low-cost end, a company probably won't worry unduly about less competitive pay, labour turnover and maybe some disgruntlement among its workers, as they are relatively easy to replace.

Hence the notion of 'hard' and 'soft' HRM. The clue to the distinction between them lies in how you say the term 'human resource management'. With the stress on 'management' and 'resource', you are referring to hard HRM, which focuses on controlling workers in a strict supervisory system traditionally involving Taylorist-type manufacturing systems, with workers treated as little more than a factor of production alongside land and capital. By contrast, if you say 'human resource management' differently, with the stress on the 'human', then you are referring to soft HRM. Soft HRM focuses on creating trust, commitment and involvement at work, in relationships that produce self-motivation and hence the qualities you require without strict supervision. However, don't get carried away by the distinction. We don't mean to imply that everything is either 'hard' or 'soft'. In the 'real' world, hard and soft HRM often coexist in complex ways within the same organisation.

Nevertheless, it remains an employment relationship: you're still trying to ensure that workers are as productive as possible. It's just that you're doing it in a different way – using different control systems.

Either way, the management of the employment relationship frequently engenders conflict and resistance in one form or another. Conflict, in an HRM setting, has traditionally meant strikes, but there are many other forms of conflict as well, not least unorganised, individual forms, such as absenteeism, calling in sick when you're not sick, or skiving off early. Or you may decide to leave your job as you've tried to change things with your manager and nothing happens. Leaving is, from the employee's point of view, resistance of last resort because, at that point, you just walk out of the door. Stress levels and burnout at work can also reveal conflict at work. And if you look at the figures, you find that days lost through stress cost the country far more than days lost through strikes, yet stress is never seen in quite the dramatic terms that strikes are.

An explanation for this fragmentation and individualisation of conflict and resistance may be found in the changing world of work. In the middle part of the 20th century many workers worked in traditional, 'Fordist' organisations (which, of course, still exist), which were often unionised. However, the increasing significance of post-bureaucratic work organisation in the 21st century has opened opportunities to control the wage–effort bargain that were hitherto unthinkable. The global reduction of trade barriers, market deregulation and the rise of neoliberal ways of thinking among politicians and policy-makers have led to increasing pressures on companies to increase revenues and control labour costs. The emergence of agency working, outsourcing and zero–hours contracts has been underpinned by the use of digital platforms to control workers. The gig economy has led to the (mis)classification of workers as self-employed and to 'digital Taylorism'. Unions find it difficult to organise under such conditions and strike rates have fallen. The specific ways in which worlds of work are regulated depend to a large degree on the national business systems of the countries involved, with institutional and legal frameworks playing a major part in the outcomes. A helpful (if oversimplified) distinction is often made between liberal market economies (LMEs), such as the UK and the US, where governments abstain from intervention in labour markets and unions are weak, and coordinated market economies (CMEs), such as Germany and the Scandinavian countries, where legal frameworks guarantee labour rights at work and the unions are correspondingly more influential.

The role of unions in channelling conflict therefore varies greatly between countries. Coverage of collective bargaining also varies dramatically, as does union involvement in forms of employee participation – but in each case, CMEs generally favour union influence at the workplace while LMEs generally do nothing to assist or protect it. Management attitudes towards trade unions range from hostile to favourable, a point that raises the issue of management styles and perspectives on the employment relationship. Commentators generally distinguish between unitarist, pluralist and radical perspectives. Radical perspectives view the capitalist organisation as necessarily conflictual as it is embedded in unequal class relationships. Pluralist perspectives, on the other hand, see resistance or conflict at the workplace as something to be managed. Pluralist managers are therefore generally more open to trade unions and collective bargaining than unitarists. By contrast, managers with unitarist perspectives see the organisation as a kind of seamless harmony of interests, with conflict the result of agitation or poor communication.

Part 2: Where we're heading…

US hi-tech companies have developed their own forms of 'new' unitarism by combining clan-like cultures to control employees with high levels of turnover and disposability. Trends towards post-bureaucratic work organisation and 'new' unitarism have been underpinned by the increasingly fragmented nature of employment contracts over recent years. The 'standard' employment contract is open-ended, but throughout this book we have observed that many contingent or precarious forms of employment have become more significant, including the use of temporary employment agencies, fixed-term contracts, zero–hours contracts and unpaid internships, among others. They are designed to allow the employer to extract greater flexibility – numerical and functional – out of the workforce. From an employee's point of view, however, handling precarious work can be very stressful, particularly if you have family commitments and need a regular income.

Precarious work has become particularly significant in the service sectors, such as healthcare, hospitality and retail. But these sectors raise further challenges, too, notably aesthetic and emotional labour. Aesthetic labour centres on the appearance of the employee who is dealing with a customer or client, while emotional labour centres on the way in which such employees manage to control their emotions. The point about the service sector is that this third element – the customer or client – enters the employment relationship in a big way. We have defined the employment relationship as the relationship between employer and employee, but in the service sector, the customer or client makes an appearance, centre-stage, too. Many employers use customers as a means to get feedback on their employee's performance, which is then used to monitor the employee – so once again, control becomes an issue.

Migrant workers play a prominent role in the gig economy and in certain service sectors. They can be divided into two different categories that need to be considered separately. The first consists of migrants who become embedded into the domestic workforce and gradually blend in with their domestic colleagues.

The second consists of those migrants who remain disembedded for whatever reason and culturally independent from local labour markets. Each group throws up different HRM challenges. While employers might view the first as a pool of cheap, compliant labour, the second are at greater risk of exploitation as they lack the resources to resist extreme intensification of production. With employer-dependent accommodation too, they may be at risk of modern slavery.

Fears over possible labour exploitation are sometimes reflected in media reports and customer-led campaigns to boycott the products and services involved. The damning publicity may cost sales. Corporate social responsibility (CSR) has become a significant way in which companies, especially multinationals based in LMEs, can be seen to be taking responsibility for their impacts on society. This requires them to integrate consumer, environmental, ethical, human rights and social concerns into their business operations in consultation with their various stakeholders. Although some criticise CSR as mere window-dressing, its rise may be associated with employers' concerns over public perceptions of cost-cutting labour practices and the place of the 'human' in human resource management.

Part 3: What all this means for HRM

HRM, of course, performs certain key functions within the organisation. This part of the book runs through the most important. The first is *recruitment*, which we related to social networks. Ways to find a job include replying to an advertisement or using a job agency, but another is through your own social networks. The downside to this is that it might involve discrimination. Managers are liable to recruit in their own image, a tendency known as 'affinity bias'. Social networks tend to be exclusive and, by being exclusive, they tend, at least implicitly, to be discriminatory, which should give us cause for concern when we think about how they function throughout different areas of HRM.

That concern links into the challenge of *discrimination and diversity*, and how you deal with them at work. A number of theories have attempted to explain discrimination: human capital; segmented labour markets; the 'reserve army of labour'; and social networks. HR solutions include equal opportunities policies, positive action and diversity strategies. These policies are, of course, underpinned by a strong moral dimension, but often reflect a business case for diversity, too, because it ensures that workers are being recruited or promoted on the basis of their abilities and talents alone, and not because they happen to look like you.

Collective bargaining remains central to determining *pay and conditions* in CMEs, but less so in LMEs. In non-unionised workplaces, particularly in LMEs, employers set pay unilaterally or through systems of management by objectives and performance appraisal. There are different forms of performance appraisal, and we commented that one of the challenges is that managers haven't always been trained to apply them properly. Appraisal, then, is not without serious problems but nevertheless, many organisations without unions now use it as a basis for determining pay.

We then examined *employee participation and involvement*, of which there are broadly two different types: one is collective and based on representation through a trade union; and the other is direct, involving the employer communicating individually with the employee, without the intermediary of a trade union or anything else. Each has a rather different function within the organisation – the former is to give the workforce a degree of collective influence over management decisions while the latter is to integrate employees more fully into their organisation.

Training and development are ongoing issues within companies, not least who pays for them and how companies avoid the poaching of their skilled workers. The concern for many companies is that their highly skilled staff, who they have trained, are enticed away by a rival. The role of State funding, the nature of labour markets and companies' own strategies all play a role in its provision, as well as the individual worker, whose own responsibility is increasingly getting stressed.

The issue of *work–life balance* led us full circle back to the question of flexibility, but rather more from the employee's point of view, and how we can avoid, or try to avoid, overwork, stress and burnout, especially in the context of ubiquitous new communications technology. A further theme that pervades this book is the way in which new technologies impinge on the world of work, not least through the gig economy, but also in terms of the way in which we are often wired in to be accessible 24/7 to our employer.

In the last chapter we examined the increasing significance of *artificial intelligence* (AI) on labour markets, and how it might affect both the number of jobs in an economy and also their quality. We also examined the application of *HR analytics* to increasing productivity within companies, as well as various challenges associated with the approach.

We conclude by addressing our own question: where's the 'human' in human resource management? Here we discuss in more theoretical terms the potential future development of HRM in the light of our approach.

Part 4: Innovative HRM within capitalism – what's possible?

We started the book with a discussion about the spread of so-called 'bullshit jobs' since the turn of the 21st century, a pattern seemingly reinforced by the growth of the gig economy and the heavy use of agency and migrant workers. In regard to *trends*, we charted the shift from:

- 'bureaucratic' or standard employment, that is, the national coordination of capitalism, with the workplace as integrated and employment as full time and firm-specific, towards
- 'post-bureaucratic' or non-standard employment, that is, more fragmented, disconnected, market-mediated and flexible forms of coordination, with tiered power relations between employers, workers, clients and customers (Thompson, 2003, 2013).

We also examined the sectoral shift towards service work in many forms (retail, distribution, information and knowledge work). Some service work requires greater capital investment than others, but in general it needs more human beings and has been the space for largely hard HRM (Amazon, Boohoo and Sports Direct, among many others). At the height of trade union membership in the UK in the late 1970s, there were opportunities to increase workers' participation, but moves in this direction were rejected by business in favour of employers and managers 'preserving ultimate managerial prerogative' (Phillips, 2009: 801).

Hard HRM is limiting for the HR manager. The HR profession rests on decades of research into human relations and the advantages of treating workers well. Hard HRM is retrogressive and narrow, with major dysfunctions such as high labour turnover and low commitment. But, it seems, to quote a leading guru of soft HRM, that 'the assholes are winning' (Pfeffer, 2016). With the expansion of service work have come new areas of control for managers – not so much the physical side of work as the aesthetic, emotional and feeling side of the human being, which we looked at in Chapter 10. Or take the unconscious traits and actions of workers secretly tracked by AI, as noted in Chapters 1, 13 and 19. In the US, HR managers have seen their power and scope for action reduced through systematic outsourcing of HR processes to external bodies, the use of the internet for worker–firm interactions and the displacement of risks from the company to individual workers – as in having to buy their own training. In other contexts, HR may still operate as a central management function – in Japan, for example – but this is changing in the light of new competition, such as the gig economy, that HR managers are facing.

With the decline in Fordism, debates have also shifted, from work versus no-work to the type and quality of work available, with a focus on so-called 'good jobs' versus 'bad jobs' (Kalleberg, 2011). However, the good jobs vs bad jobs debate is crushingly limited in ambition. If all good work is secure, unionised and well paid, there is still a lot missing. The advent of the factory and factory work in the 19th and early 20th centuries provoked reformers to imagine new worlds of work – machines doing most of the work and workers putting in only 15 hours of working time per week (Keynes, 1931). But, as we saw in Chapter 18, working hours remain high around the world and work has become both more intensive (producing more per minute) and extensive (with work seeping into home life through new gadgets, increasingly demanding employers and the spread of ever-ready self-employed workers). Karl Marx famously mocked all utopians and those who wanted him to write 'recipes for the cook-shops of the future' instead of engaging in critical empirical analysis of current capitalism (Marx, 1981 [1867]: 99). Nevertheless, there are broad alternative ideals, as in his vision of the end of the specialised division of labour that would enable you – in rural settings anyway – 'to hunt in the morning, fish in the afternoon, rear cattle in the evening, criticise after dinner' (Marx, quoted in McLellan, 1983: 147–8). Today Marx would certainly condemn the brutality of workers having to hold down two or three jobs – something made more pressing with the gig economy – while juggling both work and life and never having the chance to live a working idyll.

Our book builds on the theory of the employment relationship and the nature of the wage–effort bargain, firmly contextualising them within the ways in which the changing structure of capitalism is undermining the traditional labour market institutions that used to regulate capital–labour relations. These new trends reflect the growth of the world's labour pool, the new international division of labour, new technologies (such as apps and platforms) and the growing power of global capital and the relative weakening of the power of labour. These new trends may remove the management function, replacing it instead with labour market intermediaries who contract labour supplies between producers and clients/customers. Market disciplines and different types of labour contracts come to embody the management function without the need for managers. For example, migrant workers may be hired on contracts signed in their home country on terms agreed between international employment agencies and the headquarters of multinational companies, with local HRM in client companies having no role in the contractual process at all, even though they are still responsible for the 'effort bargain'. The separation of wages and labour conditions from the effort bargain alters the employment relationship in fundamental ways. When workers supplied through these agencies have no political stake in the host country, labour institution building grinds to a halt. And when the employer has control not only over labour supply but also over the mobility and movement rights of workers, this alters markedly the terms of the traditional relationship where workers could always once have exited to express grievances (Thompson, 2003; Smith, 2010).

Within a pluralist model, HRM should connect senior management to workers, and be a 'bridgehead' or 'voice of workers' at the senior level – with HR managers contributing an awareness of what workers will and will not accept, what is fair and equitable, what is legal and what can and can't be done in employment relations. HRM can be the champion of 'procedural justice' and fairness. This is the minimum that workers expect the HR manager to do. However, as *organisational* 'experts' the independence of HR managers can always be challenged because, by 'sitting in the middle' between senior management and the workforce, their orientation can have different outcomes. Managers and supervisors, where they provide a technical skill, are selling their labour power through the wage–effort bargain, and are subject to replacement and displacement just like any other group of workers. The collective interests of managers and supervisors can be allied either to senior management or to other workers through 'white-collar' unions or professional societies. But neutrality is difficult to maintain within the firm or organisational arena. For example, HR managers may be duplicitous in conducting workforce surveys, ostensibly to collect workers' views, but in reality providing information to manage discontent better and shore up management authority by ensuring grievances can be contained and displaced.

In addition, outsourcing the HR function turns it from an organisational profession into a fee-based, self-employed 'partner' with senior management.

This seems likely to disconnect HRM further from the workforce and make it more prone to fads and fashions, which can be marketised as products to be sold to companies (see Box C.1).

BOX C.1: THE MARKETISATION OF MINDFULNESS AND MEDITATION

The cultivation of mindfulness, which has been an integral element of Buddhist philosophy for thousands of years, is embedded in a complex set of practices involving ethical behaviour, mental discipline and the development of wisdom. Nevertheless, business consultancies have recently abstracted mindfulness and other practices from their historical and religious roots and sold them back to companies keen to promote employee 'wellbeing' and productivity (Purser, 2019).

Josh Cohen (2020: 176–7) summarises the process as follows:

> Corporate workplaces have become increasingly invested in pressing such fleeting experiences as pure being, including mindfulness meditation and yoga as well as flotation, into their service. If the worker is to be made maximally productive, then the slacker in him must become subservient. The corporate strategy isn't to dismiss the slacker as some loser wandering the streets outside its shiny glass towers but to recognise him as a dimension in all of us. In encouraging the employee to cultivate inner peace, it acknowledges an inertial tendency, an anarchic refusal of the demand to be useful, or, in today's dehumanising parlance, a "net contributor". The clever ruse of sending the employee to a flotation tank during their lunch hour marshals this outlaw region of selfhood for the corporation's own use.

We might want to add that the underlying conditions of workplace stress are not addressed by such practices or classes alone, as 'research by William Fleming of the University of Cambridge on data from 26,471 employees found that various wellbeing and stress management initiatives had "no effect" on mental health' (Howlett, 2021).

Outsourced HRM weakens the 'worker voice' role of HRM, and increases its disconnection as a 'good or honest broker' between senior management and the workforce, as the internal or tacit knowledge of workers' grievances is lost. Outsourced managers can simply no longer get to know the workers. Indeed, outsourcing forms one of the risks that HRM is currently facing as a profession, to which we could add the role of new technologies, like HR analytics, and its future is at stake: 'professions move in many directions rather than the single one implied by the term professionalization' (Abbott, 1991: 355). The future direction of HRM is not entirely clear, not least because the COVID-19 pandemic has opened up new forms of working, notably homeworking, with all the challenges that it represents for both workers and employers (Hodder, 2020; Felstead, 2022).

Meanwhile, the only possible way to enhance the role of workers' voice is to engage it at senior level in making decisions on business. We now look beyond utopianism, into different ways of working and perhaps doing HRM today.

Alternatives and orientation

The changes we are describing can make working and the tasks facing HRM sound hopeless. We have therefore aimed to adopt a critical but positive position throughout. We may be contrasting the old (secure, unionised, widespread coverage of good HRM) with the new (insecure, non-unionised, partial coverage of good work practices), but we don't want to convey the 'good old days' narrative that you might expect from a couple of old white guys. We have been careful to highlight positives and negatives with old and new practices. We outline potential workers' alternatives or solutions that start with the assumption that, given a chance, workers are creative HR 'managers' themselves. This is reflected in the ideas of the Fairwork Foundation, which emphasises good practice principles – sharing, inclusivity, fairness – for online work, and the importance of worker autonomy and control as central to all waged labour (Graham et al, 2020).

We feel that the frequent assumption, that HRM 'looks after the workers', is patronising and misleading. As workers, we can look after each other and organise work in more 'self-managed', 'professional' and autonomous ways, which is characteristic of many professional jobs and proves to be more creative, positive and productive for our wellbeing. 'Self-employment' and freelance working may appear more attractive precisely because they can support more independent and autonomous forms of working, whereas 'being a worker' can be a negative experience, involving being 'managed' or bossed about and treated without respect and dignity.

We want to seek out genuine HR skills and values and remain critical of a 'managers-know-everything' approach, supporting instead autonomy, creativity and self-management for workers. Online information can democratise HR information systems and help support these goals.

Innovative forms of working and handling authority relationships

The book has outlined what it's like to be a worker today. Imagining alternatives to this condition, we sketch out a number of ways in which the humanisation of work has been envisaged. Before doing so, however, we should point out that some reports suggest that younger workers (particularly 'Generation Z') are becoming impatient with the traditional 'world of work' altogether. They are more likely to seek a new job if their employers insist on a return to working full time at the office post-pandemic, a phenomenon that has been dubbed the 'great resignation'. This shift in attitude reflects an 'anti-work' movement that the COVID-19 pandemic has stimulated, with some younger workers turning to online hustles, such as investing in cryptocurrencies or selling online as alternative ways to making a living. The anti-work community on Reddit has risen to over 1 million since it launched in 2013, with half joining since October 2021 (Kaplan and Kiersz, 2021). However, while it's understandable that people want to prioritise their mental health and happiness over getting stuck in toxic corporate cultures and unsatisfying jobs, some might caution against loss of regular income and the risk of embracing another kind of unsustainable lifestyle, one based on 'furiously promoting … e-books, podcasts, vlogs, and online courses' (Bain, 2021; see also Brown, 2022).

Either way, the rest of this chapter focuses on the employer–worker relationship rather than on emerging forms of self-employment, with examples of alternatives drawn from actually existing practices within capitalist societies today (or from the recent past). In that sense they are not utopian dreams. Around each project there is much debate, and space does not permit a full presentation here. But we would encourage readers with an interest in imagining different futures to follow up these projects. They can be divided between those involving a distinct way of organising *ownership relationships* (cooperatives, for example) and those involving different ways of organising the employment relationship, authority and governance within the firm – what we might call *control relationships*. Changing patterns of ownership are perhaps more structural and systemic than changing 'relations' and 'power' between managers and workers, and they do matter (Marsden, 2021). However, within a global economy dominated by capitalist principles, changing either ownership or control relationships is always vulnerable to hostility, incorporation or dilution. Our list below is made with this warning in mind.

Dignity at work

Like the Fairwork Foundation mentioned above, placing a moral value on 'dignity at work' is in the realm of universal recipes for soft HRM, discussed in Chapters 2 and 7. This stream of work focuses on creating the conditions for all workplaces to support dignity in and at work. Bolton (2007) notes the subjective values (autonomy, meaning, self-esteem) and objective elements of *dignity* (access to well-paid work, having a safe and secure working environment free from harassment, and collective and individual voice). Both are well defined and meaningful. Hodson (2001: 5) suggests four challenges to achieving dignity at work, most of which come down to poor management: mismanagement and abuse; overwork; limits on task autonomy; and limits on employee involvement. The COVID-19 pandemic did launch a societal (even global) conversation about 'essential' workers, with public displays of genuine appreciation for them (such as applause, widespread offerings of gifts and expressions of recognition). Such displays are rare in contemporary societies, a reminder that it's those who 'do' and make that are most needed ('essential') in a system that normally celebrates owners, never producers. Research coming out on the COVID-19 experience has, however, also highlighted the abuse of essential workers from frustrated citizens (Hadjisolomou, 2021). But equally, care and wellbeing and solidarity against abuse by workers, managers and customers suggest a new confidence created within the societal designation of workers as 'essential'. Such labelling supports civic power and pride.

This approach can be criticised on the same grounds as the idea of a universal HRM, that the material support for such a prescription is not specified. The project borrows from the idea of a 'moral economy' – it is abstract, normative and prescriptive HRM involving advocacy without defining the agencies or the means that are going to underpin such dignity.

Enlightened employers/owners

The analysis that we have broadly followed in this book, based on the nature of the employment relationship and the wage–effort bargain, suggests that ownership patterns – employers buy labour power, workers sell labour power – are the foundation for the asymmetric relationship and perspectives between employers and workers. This insight allows for not just a single outlook among employers or owners but also diversity and, within that diversity, enables some employers to seek new ways of working. Historically this goes back in the UK to the early factory system, with Robert Owen and the early paternalist employers we looked at in Chapter 8. A rich vein of theorising suggests that 'corporate cultures' can be created to sustain special spaces for democracy, engagement, innovation and making work different from standard capitalist forms of employment.

There is also a structural element to this with self-management and team-based forms of organising celebrated in companies like Zappos, which promotes its company culture that's based primarily on self-governing 'circles', referred to as 'holacracy' (Robertson, 2015; Bernstein et al, 2016). We discussed Semco in Chapter 16, celebrated by its owner for promoting 'workers' control'. The problem here is that owners tend to control the narrative (as at Semco, for example), and since there is little sustained research into innovative corporate cultures, we must be sceptical about such projects. When not centring on employers' narratives, it is the voice of ex-employees that praises (or damns) these corporate cultures, evidence that is open to selection bias. Change can also be a major issue with such 'unique' corporate cultures: what happens when enlightened owners retire, die or sell their company (the sale of Zappos to Amazon for example)? Culture is dynamic, but the dominant narrative gets abstracted from history and change, which risks presenting an inaccurate image of current 'reality'.

At a more everyday level, there are, of course, companies in the UK and the US that recognise the need to embrace the interests of a wider set of stakeholders – employees, communities and broader social concerns – than purely their shareholders. The Purposeful Company, for example, which brings together large companies and accountancy firms, states on its website that: 'Profit is not the purpose of a company, profit is the outcome of identifying and pursuing a purpose that benefits society' (The Purposeful Company, 2022). Since 2015 it has been seeking to support the development of 'purposeful' companies though evidence-based policy proposals on topics such as corporate governance, ownership structures and executive remuneration. The question really centres on how far such honourable intentions can reach within the dominant institutional structures of LMEs like the UK, and we need social science verification of this mission statement.

A more tangible initiative is the living wage campaign, spearheaded in the UK by the Living Wage Foundation, which accredits employers who pay a wage that is based on the cost of living and so meets genuine 'everyday needs – like the weekly shop, or a surprise trip to the dentist' (Living Wage Foundation, 2021). Almost 8,000 UK employers are now accredited, including two-fifths of FTSE companies, with over 250,000 employees having received a pay rise in consequence. As inequalities in incomes and wealth have increased internationally, living wage campaigns have spread across a wide range of sectors and countries (Dobbins and Prowse, 2022).

Another tangible initiative is the campaign to reduce the working week (Coote et al, 2021; Stronge and Lewis, 2021). Reduced working hours without loss of pay would help to address the challenges of work–life balance, give workers greater opportunities to participate at work and, crucially, cut global carbon emissions. Platform London, a UK-based environmental and social justice collective, has calculated that a four-day working week without loss of pay could slash the UK's carbon footprint by 127 million tonnes a year, equivalent to removing 27 million cars from the roads (Platform London, 2021).

Creating 'new managers'

Critical or radical management studies – including training for professional HR management – are based on the assumption that there is a more enlightened mode of organising work, and progressive forms of HRM can emerge from more radical forms of business education. 'New managers' created through this process can do things differently in their workplaces. The problem with this thinking is that students may learn, but not practise what they learn – they learn instrumentally to get a degree, whereas belief in these ideas may be very superficial. But even if 'new managers' are formed in critical management schools of business, they may struggle as early career graduates to influence established organisations that they have to join. The other issue is the security of critical management studies in universities. The University of Leicester, for example, where critical management studies were embedded, has removed all mention of 'critical studies' and promotes only 'conventional management writers and teachers'.

Worker-ownership

Cooperative forms of ownerships are increasing, and high in countries like Spain. In 2022 the UK had 7,237 independent cooperatives employing 250,128 people (Co-operatives UK Ltd, 2022), less than 1% of the working population. We know about some, such as John Lewis in the UK (Cathcart, 2013; Paranque and Willmott, 2014; Storey et al, 2014) and Mondragón in Spain (Johnson and Whyte, 1977; Kasmir, 1996), but how they organise HRM is underresearched. In John Lewis, there is specialisation but also role rotation, sometimes between managers and workers; there are graded salaries, but also shared financial participation. In other cooperatives, for example Suma Cooperative (2021), there is equal pay for all partners, alongside regular job rotation across white-collar and blue-collar roles. There is also evidence that cooperatives could provide fairer working conditions in the gig economy. Food delivery cooperatives Eraman in Spain and Khora in Germany depend on CoopCycle, a bike delivery software cooperative, that has developed a delivery app and support specifically for cooperatives in a move to empower couriers (Atkinson, 2021).

Employees can feel strongly connected and committed to their company through cooperative structures, with resultant benefits particularly in terms of employee engagement, greater levels of employee creativity and ultimately, enhanced productivity gains. While turning workers into 'capitalists' does not, by itself, completely change the 'capital–labour relationship', it does demonstrate a different way of managing authority, power relations and the labour process (Brown et al, 2019). The problem is that cooperatives operate within market economies with the same external constraints as any other business, and therefore have to compete for workers and face rationalising pressures in business downturns. In addition, cooperatives may themselves embrace liberal, socialist and even repressive ideologies, so we always need to look at content and context as well as the organisational form (Iannuzzi and Sacchetto, 2020).

Radical trade unionism

Projects such as Workers' Alternative Plans (Wainwright and Elliott, 1982; Gold, 2004; Gall, 2011) are more explicitly connected with a workers' movement, for example, trade unions, and involve an *extension* of claims on the traditional employment relationship. Workers' Alternative Plans arose out of highly skilled unionised workers demanding control of work in factories where they, and not just management, have technical knowledge. The Lucas Plan, which dates back to 1976, aimed to avoid redundancies by suggesting that workers could produce alternative, non-defence-related products suggested by the workers themselves. The plan was led by UK technical workers, and it remains an inspiration for those looking to extend trade unionism. Management normally has exclusive control over product innovation, but in the Lucas case, shop stewards took centre stage by extending traditional bargaining claims well beyond wages and conditions and challenging managerial prerogatives. The plan gained widespread publicity, but encountered opposition from employers, government and trade unions (McLoughlin, 2017)

More recently, Angry Workers (2020), a political collective, has outlined their experiences in organising workers in factories and warehouses in West London as a call for independent working-class organisation, while Jane Holgate (2021) reminds us that casual work was not abnormal in the UK when workers established the basis of the trade union movement in the 19th century. Her research, which draws on case studies of effective union mobilisation, argues that 'transformational change is not only possible, but within reach'. The challenge facing such campaigns is to move outwards from the locality to implant wider, more generalised and irreversible change.

Country differences

Capitalist social relations are embedded not in abstraction but in countries, whose national institutions exert continuing (path–dependent) influences on work and employment, which means that there are some places that appear to have 'better' jobs and employment conditions than others. It's natural to want to 'learn from' them: to be more like the Germans in training, or more like the Japanese in employment security, or have the French short working week. However, the notion of 'good' jobs and countries is at once too neat and too general. The idea of 'learning between countries' is real, but there is no guarantee that the same practice will look the same in different contexts (Casey and Gold, 2005). That said, different practices highlight diverse but functionally equivalent ways of performing a common action, thus challenging the idea of universal practices and standards that frequently come from dominant countries, like the US. They can also focus attention not only on different 'rules' but also on the benefits of 'good' rules. For example, the attempt in April 2021 to create a self–perpetuating European Super League of elite football clubs from Italy, Spain and the UK highlighted the contrasting structure of German football clubs. Under German Football League rules, German clubs ensure majority control by fans through a rule of 50%+1, which means that they have to demonstrate approval for major decisions by a majority of at least 50%+1 of their registered season ticket holders. German clubs are owned by at least 51% of the fans through democratically controlled supporters' trusts, which have to be given first chance to buy club shares (Bundesliga, 2022).

Final observation

There's one final observation we need to make before we sign off. In this chapter, we've been discussing ways to reform the employment relationship, not to abolish it. You might be wondering whether there are any better, more fundamental ways to overcome the power inequalities inherent in the wage–effort bargain.

Does reform really have to depend on piecemeal changes, such as dignity at work campaigns, enlightened employers and union mobilisation, which will all only ever be partial solutions? The answer takes us – finally – into the dilemma of revolutionary change, which is summarised by Richard Hyman (1975: 203; emphasis in the original): 'Only a total transformation of the whole *structure* of control, at a level which transcends the conventional narrow definitions of industrial relations, can resolve the current contradictions within the organization of work and in social and economic life more generally.'

The dilemma is how to secure that 'total transformation of the whole structure of control'. The revolutions that forged the former Soviet Union or the People's Republic of China in the 20th century failed to abolish the wage–effort bargain, whatever else they achieved. Miklós Haraszti (1977), for example, describes his experiences in the late 1960s and 1970s working on the shop floor of the Red Star Tractor Factory in Hungary, then a member of the Soviet bloc. The conditions – tight supervision, control of piece rates and forms of resistance – reflect Taylorist manufacturing techniques as closely as any that could be found in the UK, the US or any other capitalist country. And our examples of hard HRM in China, which we have used throughout the book (notably in Chapter 18), reveal that the wage–effort bargain is alive and well there too. The dilemmas faced by countries that actually attempt to introduce socialist or communist economies are immensely complex (Kornai, 1992; Nove, 1991).

Many theorists have in any case doubted that revolutionary change necessarily brings improvement or liberation. Hugh Clegg (1960: 29), for example, warned against 'the destruction of democracy, not its improvement', and Alan Fox (1973: 230) – while condemning working conditions under capitalism – believed that 'its master institutions should not be put at serious hazard until there is a high probability of something better replacing them'. Pursuit of this 'something better' remains an ideal of social reform, and falls well beyond the remit of this book. Nevertheless, if you are interested in reform and would like to read some accessible analyses of contemporary capitalism, a necessary precondition for working towards 'something better', you could start with Mazzucato (2019), Dorling (2020) and Carney (2021).

Farewell!

We have been assuming that there are three types of reader of our book (as we pointed out in our Introduction). The first type, probably a minority, want to become HR managers. Generally, if you want to become an HR manager in the UK, you'll need to undertake professional training and gain an appropriate qualification from the Chartered Institute of Personnel Development (CIPD), which will then qualify you. In that case, this book will have given you a different perspective on HRM from the one you'll normally find in the textbooks. Good luck with your career!

The second type of reader consists of those who wish to go into other forms of management, such as accountancy, marketing or operations. Our concluding point to you is that HRM very often gets overlooked by other areas of management, particularly those functioning in LMEs, who discount HRM as they view labour simply as a factor of production. If any of you are going into general management, we hope that some of the points we've been stressing throughout this book – particularly that labour isn't a commodity – have shown you that labour is rather more than that: labour is actually all of us – it's us, people, with aspirations, interests, identities, values and views, who need to be nurtured, protected, cherished and all the rest of it. We're sure that your future experience will confirm to you the importance of understanding and channelling conflict and resistance at work in a constructive way if you are to achieve business success.

The third type of reader is probably the largest group – and it consists of those of you, most of you, who have to work for your living but who don't want to be managers. HRM is unique among management subjects because we all find ourselves – of necessity, unless we're self-employed – in an employment relationship of one kind or another. HRM intrudes into our everyday lives in a way in which accountancy, marketing, operations and other management functions simply don't. So the issues that we've been discussing throughout this book – fair pay, performance appraisal, voice, discrimination and the rest – are ones that you are going to experience throughout the rest of your life while you remain in work. These are not just academic topics – they're lived experiences, ones that all of us have and will experience throughout the course of our working lives. That's really what this book has been all about.

Our final point is this: even if you never work professionally in HRM, we hope that this book has given you some of the ideas, insights and tools to help you understand what's happening to you at your place of work as an employee in the future.

Case Studies

1. POOR CORPORATE GOVERNANCE: THE CASE OF BOOHOO LEICESTER CONTRACTOR FACTORIES

This case illustrates the practice of 'hard' human resource management (HRM) practices and poor corporate social responsibility (CSR) at the supply factories of UK fast fashion brand, Boohoo (Chapters 2 and 12). It examines the weakness of management-controlled corporate governance, and the need to involve other actors (such as non-governmental organisations [NGOs]) in governance practices. It is based on a *Guardian* newspaper investigation (Bland and Makortoff, 2020). The garment industry in Leicester has expanded massively, with home-sourcing trends among online retailers. Accompanying this on-shoring trend have been reports into low wages and poor working conditions in factories, which should also be accessed in relation to this case (Hammer et al, 2015; Hammer and Plugor, 2016). *The Guardian* and *Sunday Times* had found evidence that factories in Leicester were putting workers' health at risk during lockdown (as a result of the coronavirus pandemic), and failing to pay them the minimum wage.

The Guardian article reports the damning review conducted by Alison Levitt QC (2020) on behalf of the fast fashion retailer, who found that allegations of poor working practices in the company's supply chain – initially denied – were 'substantially true'. The 234-page review said that Boohoo's monitoring of the factories was 'inadequate' because of 'weak corporate governance', and called the failure to assess the risk to workers during the coronavirus pandemic 'inexcusable'.

Boohoo accepted the review's recommendations for change in full, and apologised for failing to 'match up to the high expectations we set for ourselves'. Group CEO John Lyttle said the company would be 'a leader for positive change in the city', adding: 'It is clear that we need to go further and faster to improve our governance, oversight and compliance.' Boohoo pledged three reforms:

1. A move to publish a full list of companies in its supply chain.
2. Reducing the number of factories it relies on.
3. Using new ethical suppliers.

Investors reacted positively to Boohoo's promises of reforms, with the company's share price rising 16% following the pledge.

Levitt's review said that the company had failed to provide all the evidence requested. It also found that:

- Founder Mahmud Kamani had told staff in 2018 to 'trade faster, harder and quicker' to push prices in Leicester down, and had for 'too long' been 'allowed to dictate company policy'.
- 93% of suppliers analysed had at least one instance of non-compliance with the company's audits in recent years on issues such as minimum wages and unauthorised subcontracting. Factories were found to have locked fire doors, filthy toilets, buildings in 'deplorable' conditions and 'no wholesome drinking water'.
- Boohoo executives had exhibited an 'occasional lack of frankness', including joint CEO John Lyttle, who failed to mention a trip to 'appalling' factories that he 'could not possibly have forgotten'.
- For long periods Boohoo's on-the-ground audit team for hundreds of suppliers and subcontractors in Leicester consisted of a single person, who told Levitt: 'I admit I'm not a very good admin keeper.... I don't have comprehensive records.'
- Profits were 'prioritised to the extent that the company lost sight of other issues' and 'a series of warning and red flags' were ignored.
- Internal emails warning of social distancing breaches in factories were sent when the pandemic began in March 2020, with one saying: 'This is escalating ... my instinct is this could blow up in our faces.'

The review set out a wide range of findings, concluding that the situation in Leicester had not been allowed to worsen deliberately, but was, instead, the result of 'weak corporate governance'. Concerns over the company's practices dated from well before the pandemic. Levitt said that Boohoo had 'made a significant start on putting things right', and noted that there was no evidence that the company had committed any criminal offences. Levitt was also sharply critical of the authorities in Leicester, and said: 'If the law is not enforced, this sends a clear message that ... the people affected do not matter.'

Leicester Labour MPs Liz Kendall, Jon Ashworth and Claudia Webbe issued a statement describing the findings as 'unacceptable' and accused the government of 'slashing the budgets of the very enforcement bodies that are supposed to keep workers safe'. They called on Lyttle to resign. Andrew Bridgen, Conservative MP for North West Leicestershire who has campaigned on the issue, said he had found Boohoo's previous denials of issues in Leicester 'laughable' and accused the company of 'gaining huge commercial advantage' from turning a blind eye to conditions in the city.

Labour Behind the Label (2020), whose report on Boohoo had first drawn attention to issues in the factories in Leicester during lockdown, said that the company's plans for reform were 'lacking in detail and ambition'.

While Boohoo responded to claims of minimum wage violations in Leicester earlier in 2020 by saying that it was 'shocked and appalled', Levitt concluded that senior directors 'knew for a fact that there were very serious issues' over the treatment of workers there since winter 2019 at the latest. Levitt said that 'somewhat to our surprise' the Boohoo CEO had missed three opportunities to reveal issues arising from a visit to the factories in December 2019, including one that an auditor described as 'the worst that I have seen in the UK', warning that it was 'a major news story waiting to happen'. She said it would be crucial for Boohoo to begin by recognising the humanity of factory workers. Noting that staff she met at Boohoo HQ seemed astonished by the notion that machinists who make the clothes could be invited to the suppliers' 'fabulous parties', she concluded: 'In truth Boohoo has not felt any real sense of responsibility for the factory workers in Leicester and the reason is a very human one: it is because they are largely invisible to them.'

1. The Levitt report says 'Boohoo has not felt any real sense of responsibility for the factory workers in Leicester'. What does this say about the company's HR strategy?

2. Labour Behind the Label, local MPs, national newspapers and local academics had all highlighted the poor working practices in the Boohoo supplier factories before the judge's report, so why hadn't the company acted?

3. What might be the consequences of the three proposed reforms promised by Boohoo?

4. One argument in the CSR literature is that, due to concerns over brand reputation, companies like Boohoo have a vested interest to operate fair supply chains. Do you agree? Why?

Further reading

Hammer, N. and Plugor, R. (2016) 'Near-sourcing UK apparel: Value chain restructuring, productivity and the informal economy', *Industrial Relations Journal*, 47(5-6): 402–16.

2. TRADE UNIONS: COMPANY VERSUS COUNTRY IN THE CASE OF RYANAIR

This case focuses on the role played by varieties of capitalism in human resource management (HRM) (Chapter 5), trade unions (Chapter 6), management styles (Chapter 7) and corporate social responsibility (CSR) (Chapter 12). It focuses on HRM in the low-cost airline carrier, Ryanair, and the very public dispute that took place between its CEO and Danish unions. Ryanair is firmly opposed to trade unions, but Denmark has a high union density. The case examines the ensuing clash.

Ryanair has well over 70 bases across Europe, and as a result, its aircrews are subject to different national conditions and jurisdictions. The company uses 'non-territorial forms of sovereignty ... to redefine employment relations, exert control over labour, and extract surplus value' from its workforce (Harvey and Turnbull, 2015: 308). In other words, it can relocate staff. It also uses bogus self-employed contracts for aircrew to reduce chances for unionisation and to squeeze wages (Harvey et al, 2021). Its low-wage, 'hard' HRM strategy clashes with the high-wage, high-unionisation context of Denmark. In some ways this reflects a clash between liberal and coordinated market economies (Chapter 5).

The case is based on an article in *The Guardian* (Crouch, 2015), 'Ryanair closes Denmark operation to head off union row', and you should also look at Harvey et al (2021) for further discussion of the liberalisation of airlines in Europe and the pressures on wages and de-unionisation. Harvey and Turnbull (2015) suggest that national trade unions are not able to cope with what they call Ryanair's 'sky piracy' and 'trans-nationality', and that what's required is Europe-wide trade unionism to tackle such companies.

The case

Ryanair introduced a service to Copenhagen in 2015. It immediately came under sustained attack from unions and local government for violating workers' rights in the country. There were colourful exchanges in the press and social media involving Ryanair, the unions and even the mayor of Copenhagen. Ryanair organised a press conference in Copenhagen at which some of its pilots praised their working conditions. However, airline unions claimed that these pilots were not on the same contracts as most Ryanair staff, who were paid far worse. Other Ryanair workers went to the media with claims that, in some months, their wages were less than half those paid by local low-cost airlines.

Anders Mark Jensen, vice-president of the Flight Personnel Union that organises pilots and cabin crew in Denmark, said it 'was shocking to the public that this could be happening in our backyard'. Morten Windeløv, who worked for Ryanair from 2007 to 2011, said: 'Ryanair's style is management by fear. There is a widespread disdain for employees; you are not treated with trust or respect as an individual – irrespective of whether you are a pilot or cabin crew. I cannot comprehend that you can be treated like that.'

He went on to say that staff were ordered where to work and when to take holidays, and were under pressure to meet targets to sell merchandise. Pilots compete to save fuel, with their performance disclosed in the crew room for all their colleagues to see. 'Competition at its worst in my opinion,' Windeløv said. Ryanair, which is Europe's largest airline in terms of the number of passengers, said in response to the union's allegations: 'We don't comment on false or second-hand claims made by former pilots. The fact that Ryanair has a waiting list of over 5,000 pilots and cabin crew who wish to join speaks for itself.'

Despite Ryanair's opposition to trade unions, the union won a legal battle in June 2015 when a labour tribunal in Denmark ruled that they could take sympathy industrial action against the airline anywhere in the country, even though the unions had no members among Ryanair staff. In response, in July 2015 Ryanair said it would be withdrawing its bases from the country, thus making any such action illegal. Ryanair would continue to fly in and out of Danish airports, but with planes and staff based in Ireland, Lithuania and the UK. Its Danish staff were relocated. As noted above, Ryanair relocates staff across its European bases to undermine union and legal efforts to support workers in any particular jurisdiction, such as Denmark.

How does Ryanair compare on working conditions and wages?

Danish transport union, 3F, which represents the ground staff, asked an external consultancy to compare working conditions at Ryanair with those of other airlines in Denmark. It concluded that the disposable income of Ryanair employees was DKR 23,000 (about £2,150) lower annually for a cabin attendant (15%). Unions claim the research shows that an extra DKR 37 – about £3.45, roughly half the price of a packet of cigarettes – on each passenger ticket would be enough to pay for decent working conditions and a collective agreement that would uphold custom and practice in relations between unions and businesses in Denmark.

The Irish discount carrier's reputation has gone steeply downhill in Denmark, and the company is solidly in last place in YouGov surveys of corporate reputation. However, in this battle between price and principle, customers are apparently indifferent. A poll reported in a *Guardian* article suggested more Danes would choose Ryanair today than before the dispute with the unions broke out.

Ryanair says it does not negotiate with unions because, for 30 years, its staff have preferred to negotiate directly with the company. The dispute in Denmark demonstrates that 'the Danish model cannot be applied' to the airline industry, it says. This highlights a problem, that multinational companies can circumvent local legislation, which complicates the discussion of national business systems, as discussed in Chapter 5.

Michael O'Leary, boss of Ryanair, told the Danish newspaper *Berlingske* in June 2015: 'If we sign a collective agreement with the Danish unions, we will then be asked to sign 15 French collective agreements, 55 Spanish collective agreements and a lot of Italian collective agreements. We are not going to do that.'

The unions said that if Ryanair carries out its threat to abandon its last base in the country, they will welcome its return to Denmark – but only if the airline agrees to negotiate. 'Our campaign is not to put Ryanair in a bad situation – we are always saying welcome, but please sign a collective agreement with us so we can have fair competition with the other airlines,' Jensen, of the Flight Personnel

Union, said. 'We don't want a Ryanair society in Denmark, we won't let them export it here.'

1. Why doesn't Ryanair wish to negotiate with trade unions?

2. Ryanair is focused on being the top low-cost or budget airline in Europe. This seems to come at the cost of pressing down workers' wages and avoiding trade unions that might improve these wages. Discuss the role of the consumer in this business strategy.

3. Multinational companies can 'shop around' between countries and avoid laws they don't like. What does this pattern of 'regime shopping' mean for a discussion of 'varieties of capitalism'?

4. The notion of CSR assumes that companies are concerned with their reputation, which makes them 'do the right thing'. How does this case fit into this theory of reputation?

Further reading

Harvey, G., Turnbull, P. and Wintersberger, D. (2021) 'Has labour paid for the liberalisation of European civil aviation?', *Journal of Air Transport Management*, 90, Available from: https://doi.org/10.1016/j.jairtraman.2020.101968

3. WORKING IN THE GIG ECONOMY

In Chapter 5, we examined the emergence of the platform or gig economy and its impact on human resource management (HRM). We noted that there were certain objective features of gig work (for example, it is often supplementary work), but that experiences of gig work may vary. The gig economy introduces new contractual relationships, such as zero–hours contracts and employment agencies (Chapter 9) as well as a certain dependence on social networks (Chapter 13). In this case, we examine different types of gig work and how individuals experience these differences. These cases are based on a Chartered Institute of Personnel Development (CIPD) (2017) report on experiences of gig work.

By way of background, there are two types of 'platform' work based on the labour process, which involve:

- location–dependent labour platforms (Type A), such as Deliveroo or Uber (the case of Paul);

- freelance platforms (Type B), such as Upwork or Fiverr (the cases of Mark and Susan).

Type A provides activities that are within a particular area, such as delivering pizza within London, while Type B conforms to labour sourcing with fewer institutional and geographical barriers, and so is less location-specific.

Paul, part-time Deliveroo worker

London-based Paul, age 31, has been balancing his full-time job as a secondary school teacher with working as a Deliveroo delivery rider for the last year to boost his income. Paul has a degree in engineering and worked as an engineer for seven years before deciding he wanted to study for a PGCE in secondary science and become a teacher. He typically works Thursday and Friday evenings and weekends for Deliveroo, averaging about three hours a shift:

> Overall, I would say it has been a positive experience. I started doing it to boost my income and for the exercise. I've found that my salary doesn't go far enough in London and this works really well as an additional supplementary source of income for me. If it was your main source of income, it would not work nearly so well because the work is variable. If I have a slow evening or day at the weekend, it is okay for me, but if you are depending on it then it could be quite stressful.

Paul says he gets paid an average of about £10 an hour, which he thinks is a reasonable rate for the work. However, he is less satisfied with the level of control exercised by Deliveroo:

> You are self-employed but in lots of ways it seems you get treated as an employee. If you turn down two jobs in a row you are automatically logged out of the app. They [the company] also monitor how long you take to do your deliveries and how long you stand about at the restaurants [between accepting jobs].

Mark, freelance working, often through online platforms

Working in the gig economy has been Mark's main source of income for about a year after he left his last permanent job to study for a qualification in languages. Mark now earns about £700 a month from freelance work in the gig economy, mainly through the online platform Fiverr, balancing the work with his studies. He said: 'I could probably earn more if I used other platforms that are out there, but because I'm juggling work with studying, I'm probably doing as much as I can right now.'

Mark offers a range of services through the site, including editing, proofreading, research and report drafting. He likes the Fiverr model, which enables him to bid for jobs he thinks sound interesting and suit his skill-set:

> I bid for work offered on the site. If I'm accepted to do the work, I am emailed an attachment with the requirements. Once I've finished the job, I email it back to the site. There is then a three-day period while the work is reviewed and 14 days before my money clears, which is done through PayPal.

Mark says that the relatively low hourly rate he receives of about £12 an hour from his gigs through Fiverr is partly explained because he is competing with people from all over the world.

'There are people from the USA, China, Switzerland, India, and Indonesia competing for the same work, which is why the hourly rate is so low,' he says. However, he can see a significant upside to the gig economy. 'I would have had very little idea of how to market myself or advertise my services without Fiverr. The gig economy also offers opportunities to people to find part-time work. You can set yourself up without any barriers to entry. The biggest problem for me is the lack of human contact – you are working on your own at your desk at home, which can be a bit isolating.'

Susan, online tutoring

Susan uses a number of online platforms to find work in the evenings as a tutor, which she balances with working part time teaching maths in a secondary school. She started working in the gig economy to provide much-needed supplementary income. She has worked on and off as a tutor since her children were small, and in recent years has used online platforms such as Tutor Hunt and Winchmore Tutors.

Susan works three days a week as a teacher and will combine this with two to three evenings of tutoring work. She charges between £25 and £30 an hour, depending on how far she has to travel, and is able to do a maximum of two tutorials an evening:

> The tutoring is a lot more satisfying than the teaching. I enjoy working with students one to one and feel like I'm making a difference. The teaching [in school] is frustrating and pretty stressful.... Ideally I'd like to stop working but I can't afford to. I've got no work–life balance; I have not got time to exercise and my diet is poor as I haven't got time to plan meals properly. My health is going down the tubes at the moment.

1. Look at the platforms and try to find a profile of the 'typical worker' on the different sites.

2. Full-time or supplementary jobs: does it make a difference if gig work is your main occupation or supplementary to another secure income?

3. 'Working through online platforms means that the worker is exposed in a real sense to a global labour market.' How is that likely to affect your levels of pay and work satisfaction?

4. From the individual case studies, outline the benefits of being an employee, a freelancer or a part-time gig worker?

Further reading

CIPD (Chartered Institute of Personnel and Development) (2017) *To Gig or not to Gig? Stories from the Modern Economy*, Survey report, London: CIPD Publishing, Available from: www.cipd.co.uk/Images/to-gig-or-not-to-gig_2017-stories-from-the-modern-economy_tcm18-18955.pdf

4. HOMEWORKING AND EMPLOYEE SURVEILLANCE

This case, which is based on an article in *Personnel Today* (Fox and Lynch, 2021), examines the remote technological monitoring of workers working from home, a trend that expanded greatly during the COVID-19 pandemic. The case raises issues relating to the frontier of control (Chapter 3); new forms of flexible working (Chapter 9); and the use of artificial intelligence (AI) in employee surveillance (Chapter 19). When introducing or allowing homeworking, employers can: (1) trust workers to continue to work as if they were in the office; (2) use personal control, directly checking workers at home; or (3) use a technical fix to monitor workers remotely. There has been a boom in the use of 'productivity intelligence' software by employers to monitor attendance, effort and hours worked, although evidence suggests it erodes workers' trust.

Employee monitoring

Trade union bodies, such as the UK Trades Union Congress (TUC), opposes such monitoring. Management consultants, such as PricewaterhouseCoopers (PwC), have noted the 'privacy invasion' workers feel from electronic monitoring. The TUC found that 15% of workers had seen an increase in employer monitoring since the start of the pandemic.

Remote employee monitoring software, designed to measure productivity, can track data including the number of mouse clicks, keystrokes, emails, applications used and time spent on particular sites. Commenting on the effects of surveillance on workers, Blumenfeld et al (2020: 47) noted:

> The irony in the expanded use of such tools as a means of enhancing productivity is that, as much research has shown, an organisational culture of mistrust impacts negatively on employee productivity. Hence, surveillance and electronic monitoring of workers and the workplace can undermine the employer's productivity objective in implementing such measures.

Video surveillance and other mediated forms of monitoring and micro management restrict worker autonomy and amplify job strain, and are typically a catalyst to worker resistance, most often expressed through higher absenteeism and turnover. To monitor is to control rather than to trust, and the erosion of trust undermines the consent that the employment relationship rests on.

The California-based company Prodoscore, which monitors emails, work documents and calendar appointments, and even transcribes internet-based phone calls to produce an overall productivity score, was reported by *The Sunday Times* to have seen a six-fold increase in sales since the start of the pandemic. Other providers include Transparent Business, which sends screenshots from employees' computer screens throughout the day to show their boss what they have been doing, and Time Doctor, which uses the camera on work laptops to take photographs of employees roughly every 10 minutes to determine how often they are at their desks. There are now many companies reporting that their employees want to continue to work from home post-lockdown, and many employers – including Dropbox, Twitter and Fujitsu – are actively encouraging them to do so.

What the law says

The UK does not have data protection legislation that specifically addresses the issue of employee surveillance, although there is guidance in, for example, the Employment Practices Code issued by the Information Commissioner's Office.

There are some industries for which employee monitoring is necessary, not just as a tool of management, but in order to achieve legal or regulatory compliance. Firms that are authorised by the Financial Conduct Authority (FCA) must demonstrate that there are processes and safeguards in place to meet regulatory requirements. Regulated firms are required to record telephone and electronic communications of staff engaged in sales and trading.

Monitoring productivity

Employers may want to be more cautious where the justification for increased surveillance relates to productivity or management information rather than regulatory compliance. Article 8 of the European Convention on Human Rights, as incorporated into UK law by the Human Rights Act 1998, provides individuals with the right to respect for private and family life. There hasn't yet been any case law in the European Court of Human Rights on the extent to which monitoring of homeworkers infringes reasonable expectations of privacy. However, given the sharp rise in employees working from home around Europe, it is likely that there will be cases examining this in the future. There must be an appropriate lawful basis for monitoring employees, for example, to increase productivity or to ensure compliance with policies.

The Labour Party has argued that 'people have a right to privacy in their workplace or home – which are increasingly the same' (Fox and Lynch, 2021). There is always a duty of trust and confidence implied in an employee's contract of employment. An employer's monitoring of an employee working from home may constitute a breach of this implied duty, and the employee may be able to bring a claim for constructive dismissal. Employees may also point to the fact that employers have used surveillance data in disciplinary proceedings to support claims to an employment tribunal, for example for unfair dismissal.

Considerations for employers

Organisations, especially those operating internationally across different national legal systems, should consider the following before introducing monitoring software:

- Employers must be transparent and inform employees of their intention to commence employee monitoring, and provide detailed information about the monitoring planned. They should also seek their employees' consent to provide protections.
- There must be an appropriate lawful basis for monitoring employees, for example, increasing productivity or ensuring compliance with policies. The employer's interests must be balanced against the employee's expectations of privacy.
- Employers should act in a justifiable and proportionate manner by ensuring that there is no other suitable option available.
- Safeguards, such as password protection and encryption, should be introduced to prevent abuse. Data must be used only for the purpose for which they were collected.
- Employers must be cautious in limiting monitoring to only certain employees, as this may risk claims of discrimination.

1. What HR strategy are employers using when they employ electronic monitoring?

2. Why does close monitoring cause workers to reduce effort and resist through quitting?

3. Look up some of the companies buying electronic monitoring software (such as Prodoscore, Transparent Business, Time Doctor) and consider if you would want to work for those companies.

4. What does this trend say about the frontier of control and the effort bargain?

Further reading

Blumenfeld, S., Anderson, G. and Hooper, V. (2020) 'Covid-19 and employee surveillance', *New Zealand Journal of Employment Relations*, 45(2): 42–56.

5. MIGRANT WORKERS: REVIEWING THE 'GOOD WORKER' RHETORIC

This case focuses on why employers appear to have preferences for recruiting migrant rather than local workers (Chapter 11). It is based on an article by Hazel Baxter-Reid (2016) who uses three case study organisations, Laundry Co, Hotel Co and Bus Co, which cover the typical sectors in which recent Central and Eastern European (CEE) migrants are employed.

Management expresses a preference for employing CEE nationals and engages with what has been called the 'good worker' rhetoric. This assumes that some workers (in this case, CEE migrants) have an in-built work ethic that is superior to others, typically local or indigenous workers. Baxter-Reid's research, following the work of MacKenzie and Forde (2009), Findlay et al (2013) and Thompson et al (2013), questions the problematic nature of such thinking. The case companies comprise:

- Laundry Co: Part of a large linen hire and laundry company that supplied linen and workwear to clients mainly in the hotel and restaurant sector. The majority of employees performed manual work and were process operators, approximately 80% of whom were new migrant workers.
- Hotel Co: Part of a large hotel and leisure group, with findings reported from the housekeeping and food and beverage departments. Each department had a large proportion of CEE workers, with 90% in housekeeping and 30% in food and beverage.
- Bus Co: Subsidiary of a large bus company and transport group. Only 10% of bus drivers in Bus Co were from CEE countries. Bus Co set up a base in

Warsaw to recruit workers, and could 'order' appropriate numbers of workers at any given time. This is a 'hard' HRM perspective on the recruitment of migrant workers.

Prior to European Union (EU) enlargement in 2004, each case study reported a history of recruitment and retention problems. Managers said that in the past they had relied on: 'young Irish girls, on their summer holidays, looking for a "jolly"' and then 'expensive Spanish agency workers who just wanted to learn English and move on' (executive housekeeping manager, Hotel Co); 'agency workers who were all ex-cons and they were a nightmare' (plant manager, Laundry Co); and 'skilled tradesmen who would float in and out of the bus industry' (training manager, Bus Co). CEE workers were now a fundamental element of each organisation's more targeted recruitment strategy.

Management in Hotel Co and Laundry Co relied on migrant networks to employ existing workers' family and friends, while Hotel Co also advertised job vacancies on a Polish website. Bus Co established a base in Warsaw and advertised throughout Poland for drivers to move to the UK to work.

Managers in all three case studies described employing CEE workers as advantageous. However, when managers were questioned further, there was no real perception of new migrants exerting more effort or of performing the job well. It appears that the main advantage of CEE nationals was related to their availability and willingness to work. Interestingly, migrant workers' perceptions generally corresponded with the managers' definition of a 'good worker'. CEE workers stated that their ability to cope with poor quality jobs distinguished them from domestic workers and contributed to their status as 'good workers': 'I came here because British people didn't want to do that job' (Polish bus driver). Perhaps managers' rhetoric of the 'good worker' shaped CEE workers' work ethic. On the surface it would appear that this was the case, but it's important to question this further by analysing the effort bargain process.

In Laundry Co and the housekeeping department of Hotel Co, migrant workers were subject to strict work-based targets and intensive supervision, which meant they had very little control over the timing and pace of work: 'There are times when management stay behind you and look at what you do. So you feel the pressure.' All CEE workers in Laundry Co and Hotel Co agreed that meeting targets was the most important aspect of their job, yet the work was arduous and it was difficult continually to meet targets. Controlling employee effort in Bus Co was more problematic. Bus routes were chosen by drivers based on their seniority in the depot, which meant that CEE workers were left with the worst routes and most unsociable working hours because they had worked for the company only for a short period of time: 'They don't care about the drivers because they have a lot of drivers, they may fire them and get another one.... I am a nothing' (Polish bus driver).

There was a work–effort conflict in the mind of CEE workers: 'At the beginning I tried to be the best and all that stuff but after three years I realise that the money that they pay us for this job is like a couple of pennies. So I do not owe them anything' (Polish bus driver). In Laundry Co CEE workers felt they were treated differently from domestic workers: 'In my opinion Scottish people are treated better because we [CEE workers] need to meet our targets and some Scottish people don't need to do that. If they [Scottish workers] don't meet targets everything is turned into silence, nobody speaks about it. However, we are threatened with redundancy' (Polish process operator).

Despite this, some new migrants had a good relationship with management and did buy into the rhetoric, which went beyond availability and compliance: 'I am always for the company. When they ask me to work an extra day, I am always here. I never say "no I can't come". I never phone in sick' (Polish housekeeping floor supervisor).

One of the fundamental issues across the case studies, which explained why migrant workers did not buy into the 'good worker' rhetoric, was the lack of recognition for their work and overt discrimination: 'Two controllers are sitting behind the desk and one is telling to another one, whispering "there is no overtime for Polish drivers"' (Polish bus driver). There was a great deal of animosity over CEE workers speaking English: 'I say you are in Scotland, speak Scottish!' (executive housekeeping manager).

1. Summarise the recruitment strategies in the three cases.

2. Was there a clear management rationale for employing migrants in the three cases?

3. Do migrant workers acclimatise to local working practices over time? Why might they do so?

Further reading

Baxter-Reid, H. (2016) 'Buying into the "good worker" rhetoric or being as good as they need to be? The effort bargaining process of new migrant workers', *Human Resource Management Journal*, 26(3): 337–50.

6. CULTURAL MATCHING, RECRUITMENT AND SELECTION: WHAT ARE THE ETHICAL ISSUES?

This case is from an article by Lauren Rivera (2012). It's based on fieldwork in three elite professional organisations: a law firm, an investment bank and a consulting firm. It uses 120 interviews with professionals involved in undergraduate and graduate hiring in these three firms. Salaries at the time were considered top-tier. Typical entry-level salaries for the law firm were US$175,000 to US$330,000; for the investment bank US$70,000 to US$350,000; and for the consulting firm US$70,000 to US$200,000. High salaries and elite status made the firms desirable to entrants. Rivera was interested in exploring the selection criteria used in interviews, especially those considered beyond the formal qualifications and other standard elements required to get to an interview stage for selection. She found that there was a common emphasis on what she calls 'cultural matching' in all three firms (Chapter 13).

'Fitting in' as formal criterion

This notion of cultural matching or 'fit' – defined as perceived similarity to a firm's existing employee base in background, leisure pursuits and self-presentation – was a key driver of evaluation across firms. For example, in the law firm, a partner, Omar (black, male) explained: 'in our new associates, we are first and foremost looking for cultural compatibility. Someone who … will fit in.' Evaluators described 'fit' as being one of the three most important criteria they used to assess candidates in job interviews; the other two were technical and communication skills, and analytical thinking. Over half the interviewees said 'fit' was the most important criterion at the job interview stage. Even evaluators who weren't personally fond of 'fit', such as consultant Priya (Indian, female), frequently reported using it in assessments: 'I don't think [fit] should be [a consideration] at all, it seems to me a very [shakes her head] American thing. But it's what [firms] want, so it's what you do.'

We noted in Chapter 13 the role of social networks in recruitment. However, Rivera's notion of 'fit' was referred to by evaluators as individuals' 'play styles' – how applicants preferred to conduct themselves outside the office – rather than their 'work styles'. In keeping with the discussion of aesthetic labour in Chapter 10, evaluators in these firms focused on notions of 'polish' or 'presence'. Eugene (Asian American, male) fleshed out the distinction between 'fit' and 'client' skills:

> When you are judging someone [to see] if you want to put him in front of a client, the question is to do with how they conduct themselves professionally…. You need someone who speaks in a way that earns your trust, who presents their opinion respectfully but also convincingly…. But in terms of "fit," it's someone that we want on our case team…. You want someone that makes you feel comfortable, that you enjoy hanging out with, can maintain a cool head when times are tough and make tough times kind of fun.

Why did evaluators and firms prioritise cultural fit?

When explaining the importance of fit, evaluators cited the time-intensive nature of their work. With the long hours spent in the office or on the road, they saw having culturally similar colleagues as making rigorous work weeks more enjoyable, although not necessarily more productive or successful. Law firm partner Vivian (white, female) explained: 'When I hire an associate, what I want to know is, is this person someone I could be sitting across the table from at 2am when trying to get a brief done?' Lance (Asian American, male), from the consulting firm, said:

> It seems like we're always at work. We work nights; we work weekends; we are pretty much in the office or travelling. It's way more fun if the people around you are your friends. So, when I'm interviewing, I look for people.... I'd want to get to know and want to spend time with, even outside of work ... people I can be buddies with.

Nicholae (white, male), from the banking firm, explained his justification for emphasising fit:

> A lot of this job is attitude, not aptitude ... fit is really important. You know, you will see more of your co-workers than your wife, your kids, your friends.... So you can be the smartest guy ever, but I don't care. Not only that the person is smart, but that you like him.

Those who were culturally similar were selected to increase their personal enjoyment at work. Fit was also seen to aid retention. Culturally similar candidates were perceived as more likely to enjoy their jobs, be enjoyed by their co-workers, and stay longer.

Banking director Mark (white, male) said: 'We try to hedge our bets. Through the recruiting process, we want to find those people ... who will fit in so that once they get here, they will not leave.' In the face of high turnover, employers also saw creating a tightknit workplace of like-minded people as a selling point to keep attracting new applicants.

How is cultural fit measured in the case studies?

Fit was either the dominant personality of the firm choosing similar workers or the personality of the individual doing the choosing. The divide was somewhat arbitrary:

> A majority of evaluators described firms as having distinct personalities, derived from the typical extracurricular interests and self-presentation styles of their employees. They contrasted "sporty" and "fratty" firms with those that were "egghead" or "intellectual". Some companies

were "white-shoe" or "country club," while others were "gruff" or "scrappy". Evaluators who believed a common personality characterised employees in their firm frequently looked for candidates who fit this image.

A second way evaluators assessed fit was by using the self as a proxy. The logic underlying this method of evaluating fit was that an evaluator represented the firm and its personality. If an applicant had 'fit' with the evaluator, then the applicant would fit with other employees. Carlos (Hispanic, male), from the law firm, explained: 'You ... use yourself to measure [fit] because that's all you have to go on.' Whereas measuring fit by the degree of similarity between candidates' lifestyle markers and firm personality was more common in résumé screens, using the self as proxy was more common in first- and second-round interviews. Evaluators likened ascertaining fit in interviews to selecting romantic partners.

1. Discuss the idea that organisations have a 'personality' and that recruitment is about matching the personality of the individual to the 'personality' of the organisation.

2. 'Fit' here is not simply about how workers are likely to function in the workplace but also socially, after work. How does a long-hours culture and poor work–life balance help overvalue this dimension of fit?

3. What implications for bias and cloning might come through the use of selection on the basis of after-work preferences of individuals?

4. What are the ethical and fairness implications of using cultural fit for selection?

Further reading

Rivera, L.A. (2012) 'Hiring as cultural matching: The case of elite professional service firms', *American Sociological Review*, 77(6): 999–1022.

7. ARTIFICIAL INTELLIGENCE: THE END OF BIAS, OR JUST THE START OF A NEW SET OF BIASES?

This case is taken from a *New York Times* (Cain Miller, 2015) article, 'Robo recruiting'. We noted in Chapter 19 that artificial intelligence (AI) has been used in areas like screening for recruitment – automating the process of sifting the many applications that popular companies receive. Hiring is critical to firms, and selection would seem to require human attention and judgement, making it a less obvious target for automation. On the other hand, all selection procedures are subject to biases, whether conscious (selecting only from certain schools or universities) or unconscious (favouring male over female applicants, for example). AI might therefore offer the chance to make this process more 'objective' by removing human fallibility and so make it a useful additional tool for human resource management (HRM) (the 'fairness' principle). On the other hand, it might introduce yet another type of selection bias.

There are numerous start-ups that use AI tools for 'blind hiring' on grounds of its fairness principle, including Entelo, Textio, Doxa, GapJumpers, Xor.ai and Avature among many more that are trying to tap into the lucrative hiring market. Have a look at these when addressing the questions at the end of this case. Some of these companies target candidates to aid their sifting and selection of firms, aggregating data from company evaluation sites, like Glassdoor, which specialises in gathering profiles of companies for those seeking career moves.

'Every company vets its own way, by schools or companies or résumés,' said Sheeroy Desai, co-founder and chief executive of Gild, which makes software for the entire hiring process. 'It can be predictive, but the problem is it is biased. They're dismissing tons and tons of qualified people.'

Some people doubt that an algorithm can do a better job than a human at understanding people. 'I look for passion and hustle, and there's no data algorithm that could ever get to the bottom of that,' said Amish Shah, founder and chief executive of Millennium Search, an executive search firm for the tech industry. 'It's an intuition, gut feel, chemistry.' He compared it to meeting his wife for the first time.

Yet some researchers say notions about chemistry and culture fit have led companies astray. This is because many interviewers take them to mean hiring people they'd like to hang out with (Rivera, 2015a).

Using applicants' data from social media platforms

As we saw in Chapter 13, social networks – 'who we know' – heavily inform recruitment. Does the use of automated processes overcome this bias? Recruitment companies recommend that human resources (HR) managers use structured interviews in which they ask the same questions of every candidate and assign tasks that simulate on-the-job work – and rely on data.

Gild, for instance, uses an employer's own data and publicly available data from sources such as LinkedIn or GitHub to find people whose skills match those that the company is looking for. It tries to calculate the likelihood that people would be interested in a job and suggests the right time to contact them, based on the trajectory of their company and career.

Mr Desai said that Gild finds more diverse candidates than employers typically do. In tech, it finds more engineers who are women and older and who come from a wider variety of colleges and socioeconomic backgrounds. 'If you have white, young male engineers, who are they going to know?' Mr Desai said. 'White, young male engineers.' More than 80% of the technical employees at most tech companies are men, and less than 5% are black or Latino (Molla and Lightner, 2016).

One engineer had applied twice to Rackspace, a cloud computing company, unsuccessfully. As an army veteran who worked in public radio with no high school degree or professional programming experience, he did not fit the pattern that Rackspace was looking for. But Gild suggested him based on the software he had been writing on his own, and he was hired.

Tech companies and gender representation

Women engineers are underrepresented in hi-tech (Chapter 8). 'At Twitter, for instance, just 10% of technical employees are women, and at Facebook and Yahoo, it's around 15%' (Molla and Lightner, 2016). Some women and minorities in tech describe an unwelcoming culture (Miller, 2014), and in response to the criticism, tech companies have begun publishing their diversity data and pledging to make changes.

So far, Doxa has uncovered aspects of working at companies that are rarely made public to jobseekers (Doxa, 2022). The data, from anonymous employee surveys, include what time employees arrive and leave, how many hours a week they spend in meetings, what percentage they work nights and weekends, and which departments have the biggest and smallest gender pay gaps.

Another service, Textio, uses machine learning and language analysis to analyse job postings for companies like Starbucks and Barclays. Textio uncovered more than 25,000 phrases that indicate gender bias, said Kieran Snyder, its co-founder and chief executive. Language such as 'top-tier' and 'aggressive' and sports or military analogies such as 'mission-critical' decrease the proportion of women who apply for a job. Language like 'partnerships' and 'passion for learning' attract more women.

So where do humans fit if recruiting and hiring become automated? Data are just one tool for recruiters to use, people who study hiring say. Human expertise is still necessary. And data are creating a need for new roles, like diversity consultants who analyse where the data show a company is lacking and figure out how to fix it.

Moreover, HR managers need to be aware that algorithms can have bias built in – past practice, facial and voice recognition – using the past as a predictor of good future outcomes are all subject to reproducing 'business as usual': 'People will also need to make sure the algorithms aren't just codifying deep-seated biases or, by applicants who have certain attributes, making workplaces just as homogeneous as they were before' (Miller, 2015).

1. The premise of the new start-ups is that they can automate hiring, and 'software can do the job of hiring staff more effectively and efficiently than people can'. Comment on the underlying idea in this statement that machines *replace*, rather than *complement*, people.

2. The assumption behind a lot of AI and automation debates is that somehow technology is 'neutral' and 'unbiased'. What are the problems with this proposition?

3. Using the case of female presence in the technology sector, discuss in what ways using AI software may and may not overcome such underrepresentation.

4. Discuss how language used in companies can impact recruitment.

Further reading

Rao, R. and Hill, B. (2019) 'How is the role of AI in talent acquisition evolving?', Cornell University, ILR School site, Available from: https://digitalcommons.ilr.cornell.edu/student/231

8. RECRUITMENT, PROMOTION AND RACIAL DISCRIMINATION IN THE METROPOLITAN POLICE SERVICE

This case looks at racial discrimination. We noted in Chapter 14 that there are different forms of discrimination and that we have witnessed in recent years a general decline in explicit, direct, conscious discrimination/bias, but a rise in indirect, hidden, unconscious discrimination/bias as the law and social norms have changed. This case focuses on racial discrimination in the London Metropolitan Police Service (the Met), and draws from various sources but particularly the work of André Clarke (2018) and Clarke and Smith (2022). This work looks at the conscious efforts of the Met to increase diversity of recruitment against the background of underlying and persistent unconscious discrimination in promotion chances. Both the level of discrimination, organisational and institutional, and the hidden mechanisms that foster discrimination, namely, social networks among the white incumbents of senior positions, are highlighted.

The first black police officer in the Met, Norwell Roberts, was recruited in 1967. Here he explains what happened the first day he arrived at his first posting at a police station in East London, and his subsequent experiences:

My reporting sergeant said to me: "look you N*****, I'll see to it you never pass probation" and I didn't think anything at all. This is just the way it was then, you know. I had buttons ripped off my uniform, my pocket books were torn up, my car tyres were slashed, my car was towed away several times. (Quoted in Clarke, 2018: 123)

From these bleak origins, tackling explicit racial discrimination inside the Met has been a slow process. After a series of damning reports, the Macpherson Inquiry into the murder of Stephen Lawrence, a black teenager killed in 1993 by a racist white gang, labelled the Met 'institutionally racist' (Macpherson, 1999: para. 46.27). Thereafter there was an effort to increase the recruitment of black, Asian and minority ethnic (BAME) officers. Clarke and Smith (2022) note:

> Strategies to widen recruitment of BAME police officers have increased numbers (3,029 BAME constables in 2018, out of a total Met force of 34,073 [12.5%]). However, these figures remain unbalanced in comparison to the population they serve, which continues to increase in terms of ethnic and national diversity (40.2% BAME in London in 2018). In addition to the slowness of attracting BAME into the service, turnover rates have been reported to be higher amongst BAME officers, this exacerbating a persistent problem of under-representation.

A 2020 BBC File on 4 report (BBC, 2020) into racism in the police found police forces in England and Wales were in the middle of an unprecedented recruitment drive to add 20,000 new officers by March 2023, providing an opportunity to improve diversity. But the assumption that, by adding numbers at junior ranks, the Met and other police forces will become more diverse as these officers progress up the ranks of the organisation has not proved accurate. Clarke and Smith (2022) have shown that the upper echelons of the Met lack racial diversity, with only one non-white chief officer out of 29 in 2018. As well as blocked career progression, the File on 4 report quoted Home Office figures for 2019 indicating that many specialist positions continue to be dominated by white officers. There were only two minority ethnic officers among 184 in the mounted police; 15 out of 734 dog handlers; and 11 among 426 detectives in special investigations teams. It seems entry is only the first step. While there are many avenues into lucrative and senior ranks within the Met, social networks are used to ensure that they remain 'white' places. Clarke and Smith (2022) emphasise that social networks, along with implicit and institutional racism, combine to 'reproduce white' in the Met.

The File on 4 report asks whether the way black and Asian officers are currently treated is likely to prove a barrier to attracting suitable candidates, and whether merely increasing their numbers in lower ranks will improve their representation in senior ranks. The programme revealed data, collected by the National Black Police Association, that minority ethnic officers represented 14% of all officers under misconduct investigation and over 20% of inquiries that had progressed to a misconduct or gross misconduct hearing, despite representing less than 7% of all officers.

Underrepresentation at this senior level might reflect the lack of mentors and other BAME officers in senior positions, which means they 'are disadvantaged in their efforts to achieve leadership positions, because there are fewer ethnically similar individuals in powerful positions with whom they can form homophilous ties' (Wyatt and Silvester, 2015: 1245). Alongside the importance of social bonds and networks for progression, there remains the issue of institutional racism, that is, the conscious or unconscious racial biases in recruitment and promotion mechanisms within the organisation that reproduce existing white dominance (Souhami, 2014).

This case throws up several issues, such as the persistence of impersonal, institutional discrimination; the importance, but limitations, of challenging racism by increasing diversity through widening recruitment; the role of misconduct cases as way of blocking career progression; the higher labour turnover of BAME officers, who are more likely to experience career frustration and therefore quit; and the powerful role of social networks, examined in Chapter 13, in reproducing white domination of senior and high-status positions within the Met.

1. Why does increasing diversity of recruitment at the junior officer level not diversify the Met at higher levels?

2. Examine the role of social networks within the Met as an explanation for continued racial discrimination with respect to career progression and movement to high-status jobs for non-white officers.

3. In the context of an organisation described as 'institutionally racist', why do you think black and minority ethnic officers have higher levels of misconduct investigations?

4. How might the Met change its internal policies to make the organisation genuinely diverse and fair to all officers?

Further reading

Clarke, A. and Smith, C. (forthcoming) 'Reproducing white: The Chief Officers' Club in the Metropolitan Police Service', *Work, Employment & Society* [in submission].

9. UNILEVER AND A REDUCTION IN THE WORKING WEEK

This case examines a trend to reduce long-hours working by cutting the working week. Several examples are discussed, in particular Unilever, based on a *Financial Times* article (2020b). Flexible working (Chapter 9) and work–life balance (Chapter 18) are central to the discussion.

The case

Unilever will give the push for a four-day working week one of its biggest boosts yet when the consumer goods group launches a year-long trial of the practice in New Zealand. The company behind Lipton tea and Dove soap announced in November 2020 that it would start paying its 81 staff in New Zealand for five days while letting them work four. After 12 months, Unilever says it will look at the lessons the experiment offers for how the rest of its 155,000 employees work. 'I've got colleagues all over the world who are saying "Please don't stuff this thing up because we want to have a go at it sometime in the future"', said Nick Bangs, Unilever's New Zealand managing director.

Mr Bangs told the *Financial Times* that most of his staff sold or distributed Unilever goods, and he was 'very conscious' that more thought would be needed to introduce a four-day working week at manufacturing sites. The company does not carry out manufacturing in New Zealand. His colleagues would still have to produce the same output, he added, but if they ended up working four very long days 'then we've completely missed the point'. 'This is about changing the way we work,' he said. The group's move is among the most ambitious efforts so far to test a practice that advocates say makes workers happier, healthier and more productive.

Other cases

A number of large companies have begun trials in the past two years, even though critics argue that the practice would send many businesses into a loss. Microsoft said employee productivity rose when it offered a four-day week in August 2019 to its staff in Japan, home to some of the world's longest working hours (Kleinman, 2019). US burger chain Shake Shack also started trialling the measure in 2019 to see if it could help to recruit and retain staff (Eadicicco, 2019). Mr Bangs of Unilever said he had been inspired by Andrew Barnes, founder of Perpetual Guardian, a New Zealand estate planning company. It drew global headlines in 2018 when it said that giving its 240 staff a day off at full pay for eight weeks had led to such big productivity gains it was making the change permanent.

Supporters of a four-day working week point to research suggesting that the financial benefits of more productive and healthier staff are significant. The system's ability to cut sickness levels and recruitment costs while boosting staff retention and efficiency could help save UK businesses £104 billion a year, a report from Henley Business School (2019) has argued.

However, some suggest the scheme is hard to implement. In London, the Wellcome Trust biomedical research foundation concluded in 2019 that it could not even conduct a trial of the four-day week without 'an unacceptable disruption' to its business. Mr Bangs said the COVID-19 pandemic had shaken traditional thinking about working practices, but it had not been the main driver of a trial for which Alan Jope, Unilever's chief executive, had offered 'overwhelming support'. Mr Jope said in January 2021 that he did not think Unilever would ever go back to a time when 100% of office workers' time was spent in the office. 'We see a hybrid future of work, where people might spend a couple of days in the office and two or three days at home or working remotely,' he said. 'This has unlocked tremendous productivity and flexibility in the Unilever team.'

In the US, 15% of the 60,000 US companies that participated in the Society for Human Resource Management's survey conducted in April 2019 said they offer a four-day working week of 32 hours or fewer, which is up from 13% in 2017 and 12% in 2018 (Society for Human Resource Management, 2019). Furthermore, the organisations that have implemented this shorter working week didn't report a decrease in productivity or revenue, the study says. What is not clear is whether wage costs are cut when working time is cut. The importance of the Unilever experiment is that hours are cut but not salaries and benefits. It is easy to cut both, but the point is to work smarter, not more cheaply.

Unilever's trial ran from December 2020 to December 2021. The firm is working with Sydney's University of Technology (UTS) Business School researchers to measure how performance fares.

Unilever, which employs around 155,000 people globally, has been active in New Zealand for more than 100 years. Its operations are focused on import and distribution. All 81 employees there are eligible to participate.

Uniqlo's parent company, Fast Retailing, was reported in June 2015 to be introducing a policy to allow some of its employees to work four-day weeks. About 10,000 of Uniqlo's full-time employees in Japan were allowed to take schedules with three-day weekends and longer workdays. The rationale for shortening the working week was a familiar one, aimed at improving full-time employee retention, since employees who want more personal time often choose to become part time. The shortened schedules were available to in-store employees and, if the test run went well, might be rolled out to headquarters and other stores. Employees who took advantage of the schedule would work four 10-hour days that included the weekend, then enjoy three days off. However, there have been no reports of the follow-up study – a problem with many such cases, an announcement to the press, but no follow-ups.

In 2018 the Japanese Labour Ministry survey found that 6.9% of privately owned companies with 30 or more full-time employees had introduced some kind of shorter working week, such as four-day working. A decade earlier, the figure was 3.1%.

1. Working smarter can often translate as working harder or more intensely. The Unilever manager said that if workers ended up working four very long days, 'then we've completely missed the point'. How might HR managers try to avoid this problem?

2. What are the benefits to the company and the worker of cutting the working week?

3. In Chapter 18 we noted that working hours varied across the world, but that trends were towards longer working hours. Why aren't more companies adopting the Unilever approach?

4. Unilever are taking an 'evidence-based' approach to the working week. What are the advantages of this approach?

Further reading

Delaney, H. and Casey, C. (2021) 'The promise of a four-day week? A critical appraisal of a management-led initiative', *Employee Relations: The International Journal*. Available from: https://doi.org/10.1108/ER-02-2021-0056

10. LORRY DRIVER SHORTAGES

This case looks at labour supply in UK road haulage or trucking, specifically with respect to heavy goods vehicles (HGVs), as industry bodies suggest there was a shortage of 100,000 drivers in 2021. This affected the supply chain to supermarkets and many other sectors, and pressure was increasing on the Conservative government to act. The case covers several themes such as reward management (Chapter 15); migration (Chapter 11); and the fall out for labour supply following Brexit, the UK's exit from the European Union (EU), which created new barriers for EU workers entering the UK labour market (Chapter 11). Additionally, the COVID-19 pandemic massively restricted the free movement of people across Europe while also increasing the demand for the transport of goods as consumers moved online at an unprecedented rate. It also concerns trade unions (Chapter 6) and training (Chapter 17).

Responses to market pressures from employers, unions and, above all, the UK government pulled in different directions. Government pushed for increased wages, whereas employers wanted permission for migrants to come to the UK on temporary visas to address the labour shortage. Some HGV companies use third-party drivers to improve profit margins. Outsourcing to continental drivers was common prior to Brexit. Unionisation has been in decline for many years, with deregulation and growth in self-employment eating away at union membership

(Smith, 2001; Viscelli, 2016). However, many big employers, such as UK supermarkets, contract to companies with unionised workers. Historically, in the US and the UK, wages in road haulage had been some of the highest for manual workers, but the move to self-employment intensified competition and depressed wages, increased labour turnover or churn, and reduced the attractiveness of the job to potential recruits. These are problems that underpin the current issues of labour shortage discussed in the case.

Background and issues

Labour shortages in road haulage are a long-standing problem. A range of factors are at play, including an ageing workforce (the average age of HGV drivers is now 53), the price of obtaining the mandatory driver Certificate of Professional Competence (around £3,000) and the wages and conditions of work. The recruitment crisis was highlighted in a 2016 report from the government's Transport Select Committee, which attributed the driver shortage to:

> many years of under-investment in recruiting and training to replace existing drivers as they retire; a relative reduction in availability of suitably qualified drivers from elsewhere in the EU; and drivers who moved to other sectors not returning to the industry as demand picks up. An estimated 35,000 drivers retire each year, with only 17,000 thought to start out in the industry annually. (UK Parliament, 2016)

The reasons for the shortage of drivers in 2021

The body representing the industry, the Road Haulage Association, surveyed hauliers and gave the following reasons for the problem: drivers retiring; Brexit; tax changes; workers moving to other jobs (turnover); poor pay; and COVID-19. Brexit and workers leaving the industry (retirement and labour turnover) were the top reasons (BBC News, 2021a). The issue of high levels of labour churn is common in the sector (Smith, 2001; UK Parliament, 2016). The tax changes referred to make it more expensive for drivers from elsewhere in Europe to work or be employed in the UK. And the reform of the IR35 rules – or how people working off the payroll pay tax – is designed to prevent workers setting up limited companies and paying less tax and National Insurance while working, in effect, as an employee.

Different perspectives on the shortage of drivers

A number of policy proposals have been made to help resolve the problem:

1. Train more British drivers: The shortages will push up wages and force changes in the working conditions and therefore the labour market will 'sort out' shortages. The question is, will this address the immediate problems?

2. Invite foreign drivers to return to the UK by changing visa rules: This goes against the idea of Brexit and the government's aim to increase well-paid jobs and labour productivity, and returns to what is perceived to be a 'broken model' of low-paid migrants running sectors of the economy. The government agreed to 5,000 temporary visas for continental drivers, but they had a limited take-up. EU drivers do not seem to be attracted to work in the UK on these temporary visas. Sarah O'Connor (2021) quoted one such driver: 'Why would you want to go to Britain, jump all these hoops, face all this hostile environment, if you could go to Ireland or Holland and earn more, be respected, drive on nicer motorways with nice truck stops, and be a free European citizen, not a second-class citizen?'

3. Change the working conditions to lengthen the working day to allow drivers to do more hours and therefore get more work out of the existing workforce: The UK government extended drivers' working day by one hour above the current legal limit in response to the current problems, but does this help in the longer term? What are the health and safety implications of adding an extra hour to the lorry driver's working day? How attractive will it be to potential young drivers to enter an industry where long working hours just got longer?

4. Change the loads (cabotage rules) (GOV.UK, 2021) that foreign drivers are allowed to carry so they can make more trips in the UK: Under Brexit-agreed rules, EU drivers can make only two pick-ups or drop-offs each week. In October 2021 the government proposed new plans, which would allow drivers to make unlimited deliveries or collections within a 14-day period. What impact would this have on UK haulage companies and independent drivers? Rod McKenzie, from the Road Haulage Association, said: 'The government has been talking about a high-wage, high-skill economy, and not pulling the lever marked "uncontrolled immigration", and to them this is exactly what it looks like' (BBC News, 2021a).

5. Invest in technology to have automatic or driverless vehicles and therefore cut the need for drivers altogether: This might be only a very long-term solution to the shortage of drivers.

6. Bigger road haulage companies and supermarkets, such as Tesco and Sainsbury's, have unionised drivers (Unite represents around 50,000 drivers in these sectors) and were offering new entrants higher starting salaries to attract new workers into the industry in the light of shortages: This could create two-tier wages for workers. The main union for lorry drivers, Unite, threatened strike action to challenge this two-tier model and demanded better pay and working conditions for *all* drivers. 'The treatment of drivers across the board has been nothing short of a disgrace,' said Unite general secretary Sharon Graham: 'Now is the time for action not words. It's time for employers to pay workers a proper rate

for the job' (Gillett, 2021). Unions have more bargaining power in times of labour shortages, and wages generally rise under such conditions.

7. Fast-track training to increase the speed at which British-based workers can become HGV drivers and contact with retired drivers: A BBC report stated:

> Ministry of Defence examiners will be brought in to increase the number of HGV driving tests. There will be free intensive "boot camps" to train 5,000 people to become HGV drivers, with another 1,000 to be trained through courses funded by the adult education budget. The government is also writing to nearly one million drivers who hold an HGV licence to encourage them to return to the industry. (Gillett, 2021)

The Road Haulage Association, however, argues that basic training does not produce experienced workers, which takes time and can't be rushed.

Critically discuss each of these proposals as ways to deal with the issue of labour shortages:

1. Existing companies should train more British drivers – the shortages will push up wages and force improvements in working conditions, which will attract drivers.

2. By increasing the number of visas to allow more foreign workers to access the UK, the pool of available drivers will rise to meet the increased demand.

3. Trade unions need to put pressure on employers (through strike action) to use the current shortage of drivers to increase pay, as higher wages will ultimately attract more workers into the sector and resolve shortage issues.

4. Change the rules around hours of work, to increase the time current drivers are allowed to work, and solve the shortage problem by lengthening the working day of current drivers.

Further reading

Belzer, M.H. and Sedo, S.A. (2018) 'Why do long distance truck drivers work extremely long hours?', *The Economic and Labour Relations Review*, 29(1): 59–79.

List of Films About Human Resource Management

The following films, listed in date order, cover one or more of the following broad themes:

- discrimination and diversity
- migration and integration
- resistance/reaction to unemployment:
  - formation of cooperatives
  - finding alternative employment
  - individual endeavour
  - individual decline
- role of consultants
- strikes
- technological change
- trade union corruption
- trade union organisation
- whistleblowing
- working conditions.

The list is by no means meant to be exhaustive – let us know if you'd like to propose any additions!

Strike (*Stachka*) (directed by Sergei Eisenstein, 1925) with Grigoriy Aleksandrov and Ivan Klyukvin: Oppressed factory workers take strike action in pre-revolutionary Russia. (1h 35m)

Metropolis (directed by Fritz Lang, 1927) with Brigitte Helm: A vision of the city and working conditions in the year 2000 from the perspective of the 1920s. (2h 33m)

Black Fury (directed by Michael Curtiz, 1935) with Paul Muni (originally banned in several US states): Looks at US labour relations as a Pennsylvanian coal miner forms a breakaway union and takes on corrupt owners and strike-breakers. (1h 34m)

Modern Times (directed by Charlie Chaplin, 1936) with Charlie Chaplin and Paulette Goddard: A light-hearted view of Taylorism in what looks like a Ford factory. (1h 27m)

Chance of a Lifetime (directed by Bernard Miles, 1950) with Kenneth More and Basil Radford: Dissatisfied workers in a small factory set up a cooperative, but a currency crisis destroys their credit and threatens bankruptcy. (1h 29m)

The Man in the White Suit (directed by Alexander Mackendrick, 1951) with Alec Guinness and Joan Greenwood: Connivance of management and unions to perpetuate inefficiencies and halt technology. (1h 25m)

On the Waterfront (directed by Elia Kazan, 1954) with Marlon Brando: Union corruption in New York's docklands. (1h 48m)

I'm All Right, Jack (directed by John Boulting, 1959) with Peter Sellers: Satire on trade unions and corrupt management practices in postwar British industrial relations. (1h 45m)

The Angry Silence (directed by Guy Green, 1960) with Richard Attenborough: A worker defies an unofficial strike call, becomes a strike breaker and is given the silent treatment by workmates. (1h 35m)

The Big Flame (directed by Ken Loach 1969) with Norman Rossington and Godfrey Quigley: BBC drama focusing on the decision by striking workers in the Liverpool Docks to occupy their workplace and run the operation themselves. (1h 25m)

Leeds United! (directed by Roy Battersby, 1974) with Lynne Perrie: BBC drama about the struggle of female textile workers in Leeds for equal pay. (1h 54m)

The Price of Coal: Meet the People (directed by Ken Loach, 1977) with Kath and Tony Storey: BBC drama about preparations for a royal visit to the fictional Milton colliery. (1h 15m)

Blue Collar (directed by Paul Schrader, 1978) with Harvey Keitel and Richard Pryor: Oppressive weight of factory life and car workers exploited by their own union. (1h 54m)

Norma Rae (directed by Martin Ritt, 1979) with Sally Field and Beau Bridges: US textile worker turns union activist. (1h 54m)

9 to 5 (directed by Colin Higgins, 1980) with Jane Fonda, Dolly Parton and Lily Tomlin: Three female employees live out their fantasies of having revenge on their autocratic boss. (1h 49m)

The Life and Times of Rosie the Riveter (directed by Connie Field, 1980) with Lola Weixel and Margaret Wright: Documentary about the lives of women who worked in American industry during the Second World War. (1h 5m)

United Kingdom (directed by Roland Joffé, 1981) with Ricky Tomlinson and Colin Welland: BBC TV Play for Today examines left-wing politics on a northern council, set against industrial decline and unemployment. (2h 25m)

Brazil (directed by Terry Gilliam, 1985) with Jonathan Pryce and Robert De Niro: A look at bureaucracy laced with cruelty, fantasy and satire. (2h 12m)

Gung Ho (directed by Ron Howard, 1986) with Michael Keaton: A clash of values and culture when a Japanese auto firm buys a closed car factory in an American town with high unemployment. (1h 52m)

Matewan (directed by John Sayles, 1987) with Chris Cooper: Labour troubles and violent clashes between police and striking miners in Virginia in the US. (2h 15m)

Friends & Enemies (directed by Tom Zubrycki, 1987) with Vince Lester: A documentary about the strike by a thousand power workers against the South East Queensland Electrical Board in 1985 in protest against the introduction of contract worker hire. (1h 28m)

Prejudice (directed by Ian Munro, 1988) with Grace Parr and Patsy Stephen: Impact of legislation on discrimination in Australia, gender in newspapers and ethnicity in healthcare. (1h 36m)

Riff-Raff (directed by Ken Loach, 1991) with Robert Carlyle and Emer McCourt: The story of Stevie, a construction worker, and his girlfriend, an unemployed pop singer, serves to show the living conditions of the British working class. (1h 35m)

Spotswood (directed by Mark Joffe, 1991) with Anthony Hopkins: An efficiency expert examines work practices in a Melbourne shoe factory that tries to introduce drastic changes. (1h 35m)

Hoffa (directed by Danny DeVito, 1992) with Jack Nicholson, Danny DeVito and Armand Assante: Story of Jimmy Hoffa, the infamous leader of the US Teamsters Union. (2h 20m)

Brassed Off (directed by Mark Herman, 1996) with Tara Fitzgerald, Ewan McGregor and Pete Postlethwaite: A local community is pitched against the backdrop of the UK miners' strike and pit closures in 1984–85. (1h 48m)

The Full Monty (directed by Peter Cattaneo, 1997) with Robert Carlyle and Tom Wilkinson: Six unemployed steel workers form a male striptease act. (1h 31m)

Human Resources (*Ressources humaines*) (directed by Laurent Cantet, 1999) with Jalil Lespert and Jean–Claude Vallod: Against the backdrop of the 35-hour working week, a business school graduate becomes involved in economic and familial politics. (1h 40m)

Billy Elliot (directed by Stephen Daldry, 2000) with Jamie Bell and Julie Walters: Set against the 1984–85 miners' strike, a young boy is torn between his unexpected love of dance and the disintegration of his family. (1h 50m)

The Navigators (directed by Ken Loach, 2001) with Dean Andrews and Thomas Craig: Five Sheffield rail workers react to the privatisation of the railway maintenance organisation for which they all work. (1h 36m)

Mondays in the Sun (*Los Lunes al Sol*) (directed by Fernando León de Aranoa, 2002) with Javier Bardem and Luis Tosar: A group of middle-aged shipyard workers in Northern Spain try to come to terms with redundancy. (1h 53m)

Burnt Out (*Sauf le respect que je vous dois*) (directed by Fabienne Godet, 2005) with Olivier Gourmet and Dominique Blanc: The stresses of corporate culture set in the context of a thriller. (1h 30m)

Faith (directed by David Thacker, 2005) with Christine Tremarco and Jamie Draven: Drama of family conflict set against the background of the miners' strike, 1984–85. (1h 42m)

Kinky Boots (directed by Julian Jarrold, 2005) with Chiwetel Ejiofor and Joel Edgerton: A drag queen comes to the rescue of a man who, after inheriting his father's shoe factory, needs to diversify his product to survive. (1h 47m)

On a Clear Day (directed by Gaby Dellal, 2005) with Brenda Blethyn and Peter Mullan: An unemployed Glaswegian shipbuilder determines to salvage his self-esteem by swimming the English Channel. (1h 35m)

Last Train Home (directed by Lixin Fan, 2009) with a cast of migrant families: Workers return home from an industrial Chinese city to their homes in rural villages for the New Year. (1h 25m)

She, a Chinese (directed by Xiaolu Guo, 2009) with Lu Huang and Geoffrey Hutchings: A young woman on a trip from East to West escapes from her provincial Chinese village. (1h 43m)

Up in the Air (directed by Jason Reitman, 2009) with George Clooney and Vera Farmiga: A 'careers transition consultant' travels around the country firing people, until his company grounds him. (1h 49m)

Made in Dagenham (directed by Nigel Cole, 2010) with Sally Hawkins, Bob Hoskins and John Sessions: Dramatisation of the 1968 Ford sewing machinists' strike at the Ford Dagenham assembly plant. (1h 53m)

The Internship (directed by Shawn Levy, 2013) with Vince Vaughn and Owen Wilson: Having been recently made redundant, two older salesmen find themselves internships at Google, but then have to compete with much younger and savvier applicants for full-time posts. (1h 59m)

Two Days, One Night (*Deux jours, une nuit*) (directed by Jean-Pierre Dardenne and Luc Dardenne, 2014) with Marion Cotillard and Fabrizio Rongione: Sandra returns to work following a bout of depression to discover her colleagues have voted to take a bonus at the expense of her job. She has just one weekend to change their minds. (1h 35m)

Pride (directed by Matthew Warchus, 2014) with Bill Nighy, Imelda Staunton and Dominic West: A London-based group of gay and lesbian activists raise money to support the families of striking miners during the miners' strike of 1984–85. Based on a true story. (1h 59m)

The Nothing Factory (*A Fábrica de Nada*) (directed by Pedro Pinho, 2017) with José Smith Vargas and Carla Garvão: Workers occupy a Lisbon lift factory, which the owners intend to close, leaving the workers redundant. Based on a true story. (2h 57m)

Corporate (directed by Nicolas Silhol, 2017) with Céline Sallette and Lambert Wilson: An investigation is launched after an employee of an industrial food company commits suicide at work following what turns out to be deliberate corporate strategy to remove uncooperative/underperforming workers. (1hr 35m)

In the Aisles (*In den Gängen*) (directed by Thomas Stuber, 2018) with Franz Rogowski and Sandra Hüller: A loner with a criminal past takes a job as a fork-lift truck driver in a large supermarket in the former East Germany. (2h 5m)

Men on the Dragon (directed by Sunny Chan, 2018) with Francis Ng, Chan-Leung Poon and Tony Tsz-Tung Wu: A group of workers in a tech company in Hong Kong join their company's dragon boat team hoping that it will help them survive a round of lay-offs, but, in fact, their male bonding underpins their subsequent decision to go on strike. (1h 32m)

Sorry to Bother You (directed by Boots Riley, 2018) with LaKeith Stanfield and Tessa Thompson: A black call centre worker, who works in telemarketing, has to choose between his own individual success within the organisation and solidarity with his colleagues when they go on strike. (1h 52m)

The Plan that Came from the Bottom up (directed by Steve Sprung, 2018): A documentary about workers at Lucas Aerospace who, in 1976, proposed a strategy to shift their company's production from armaments to socially useful products. (3h 32m)

American Factory (directed by Julia Reichert and Steven Bognar, 2019) with Jumming 'Jimmy' Wang, Robert Allen and Sherrod Brown: A documentary about a Chinese billionaire who reopens a General Motors factory in Ohio that closed in 2008, and the clash of cultures as the plant gradually re-establishes itself. (1h 50m)

Sorry We Missed You (directed by Ken Loach, 2019) with Kris Hitchen, Debbie Honeywood and Ross Brewster: An unskilled worker, in debt, takes the chance to become a self-employed delivery driver, but the stress brings the family to breaking point. (1h 41m)

The Assistant (directed by Kitty Green, 2019) with Julia Garner and Matthew Macfadyen: A day in the life of a young female assistant as she endures the pressures of a sexually abusive boss and toxic office culture. (1h 27m)

I Never Cry (Jak najdalej stad) (directed by Piotr Domalewski, 2020) with Zofia Stafiej: The challenging life of a Polish migrant worker is explored through multiple perspectives, especially his daughter and left-behind family, and his employer, workmates and overseas partner. (1h 38m)

Minari (directed by Lee Isaac Chung, 2020) with Steven Yeun and Yuh-Jung Youn: A Korean-American family moves from California to Arkansas to live the American dream, and learns how to integrate into a remote rural setting. (1h 55m)

Nomadland (directed by Chloé Zhao, 2020) with Frances McDormand and David Strathairn: A widow, who loses her job in Nevada, buys a recreational vehicle (RV) and travels the country searching for seasonal work, which includes a job at Amazon. (1h 47m)

Between Two Worlds (Ouistreham) (directed by Emmanuel Carrère, 2021) with Juliette Binoche, Hélène Lambert and Léa Carne: Based on French journalist Florence Aubenas' undercover investigation, *Le Quai de Ouistreham*, the film exposes conditions among cleaning workers. (1h 46m)

Boiling Point (directed by Philip Barantini, 2021) with Stephen Graham and Vinette Robinson: Shot in one take, the film tracks how the staff of a top London restaurant deal with multiple crises in the course of a single evening. (1h 32m)

Glossary of Key Concepts

We use the abbreviation (qv) to refer to a term that is defined elsewhere in the Glossary; *quod vide* (Latin: 'which see').

Aesthetic labour   Refers to the 'look' a worker presents or embodies as a person, and the linking of that look with the 'brand' or market positioning a service company is trying to project, for example a luxury hotel or restaurant. By hiring a certain type of aesthetic labour, a company can project a certain brand image (such as, for example, dynamic, smart, young).

Agency work   Employment agencies are businesses that mediate between employing firms (clients) and workers, and they make money by finding workers for clients. They are labour market intermediaries. Agency work is a form of indirect working because in contrast to having an employment contract (qv) directly with an employer, the worker finds work circuitously through an employment agency.

Atypical/typical employment   See **Standard/non-standard employment**.

Binding/non-binding instruments   In corporate social responsibility (CSR) (qv), binding instruments are measures that compulsorily require companies to act in line with certain norms and standards, often as part of State or public procurement policies, before being allowed to compete for government contracts. A non-binding instrument is a measure that is adopted voluntarily that has no mandatory effects on the company.

Capitalism   Describes a political economy in which ownership of property is held in private hands, not by the State or other collectives (although nationalisation is compatible with capitalist mixed economies). Owners of capital (shareholders) increase their wealth (accumulate more capital) through employing the means of production (machinery and labour), which is put to work for the purpose of generating profit. Free waged labour requires capital (and a labour process [qv]) to earn a wage. Waged labour is human and it cannot be stored or converted into productive labour except through a labour process. Capital is more liquid and can be converted into the form of money, machinery and commodities. But to expand or accumulate, capital also requires waged labour. In this sense, labour and capital are bound together in capitalism.

Career   The concept of continuous employment (qv) in one bounded occupation or profession that gives continuity and meaning to a person's working life and in which they acquire additional skills as the occupation evolves.

Codetermination   May be found in certain coordinated market economies (CMEs) (qv), such as Germany, where it is exercised through works councils. It involves their right to veto certain statutorily defined areas of managerial policy, such as methods of remuneration, organisation of working time and the use of equipment to monitor employees.

Collective bargaining   The process by which trade unions (qv) and similar associations negotiate with employers in order to reach a collective agreement, that is, an agreement on pay and working conditions that applies to the group (collectivity) of workers represented by the trade union.

Commodity status of labour   Whereas commodities may be either raw materials (such as coal or iron ore) or manufactured products (such as cars or mobile phones), workers are neither a raw material nor a manufactured good. Workers are instead 'produced' through families who do not, however, have children 'for the market'. Workers sell labour services or labour power, which is variable and adaptable as workers can be retrained. Labour power is an embodied (qv) commodity because, as individuals, we have to present ourselves at work, even though what we are selling may represent only a fraction of our potential as human beings, such as our muscles/physical skills, mental abilities or appearance and emotions.

Conflict   Employers and workers have to cooperate because production and providing services cannot occur without employers first hiring workers, and workers cannot survive economically without being employed. Maintaining production and services may then unite employers and workers because the continued survival of the business depends on continued cooperation. However, although workers typically know in advance of an employment relationship (qv) the wages or salary they will be earning, they do not know precisely the effort required to earn them. This structural uncertainty forms the basis of conflict at work.

Consultation   Involves management in requesting workers' views about a workplace issue prior to taking a final decision about it. Management will listen to their views, but does not guarantee to take them into account. Consultation is more active and two-way than disclosure of information (qv), but a weaker method of involvement than negotiation (qv).

Contingency theory   Suggests that organisational structures and practices (including HR practices) will vary according to the product market or technological context in which a firm operates. For example, those in mass production markets are likely to have vertical, command structures, while those in custom or niche product markets would require flatter, more dynamic organisational structures. From this arises the idea of strategic fit (qv), that organisations need to match their internal structures with the external business environment. Contingency theory is generally contrasted with universalism (qv).

Contingent/flexible/peripheral/precarious work   All mean broadly the same thing, but the terms have different connotations. 'Contingent' is neutral as a description, while 'flexible' is more positive (from an employer's perspective) and 'peripheral'/'precarious' are more negative (from a worker's perspective). 'Peripheral' work is the term generally associated with the 'flexible' firm (qv). The use of these terms is another reminder that our understanding of HRM is underpinned by our frames of reference (qv). Broadly, they are all forms of atypical (qv) or non-standard employment (qv), which involve work that is irregular by time, employer and location. *Casual work* is infrequent or seasonal work that does not last for a working year. *Indirect employment* involves a worker contracting with an employment agency (qv) that then indirectly finds them work with the client firm, a situation that contrasts with contracting directly with the employer. *Informal work* involves cash-in-hand or day labouring work that has high temporal insecurity. *Zero-hours contracts* are employment contracts (qv) where hours fluctuate from week to week, thereby creating intense instability of working hours and therefore wages. They are used widely in the UK but are illegal in many countries (such as Switzerland) and limited in others (such as New Zealand).

Continuum of participation   Reflects the degree of worker influence at the workplace or in the company and, in ascending order of influence, comprises: management prerogative (no participation) (qv); disclosure of information (qv); consultation (qv); negotiation (qv); codetermination (qv); and workers' control (qv).

Control   See **Management control**.

Cooperation   See **Conflict**.

Coordinated market economies (CMEs)   See **Varieties of capitalism**.

Deskilling   Tasks or jobs can be often be broken down into smaller and smaller parts, and automation/mechanisation can replace human labour. Deskilling was advocated by F.W. Taylor as a form of management control (qv). Deskilling can also mean the substitution of less skilled workers for higher skilled workers in order to 'deskill' a job.

Development   A form of training (qv) that goes beyond the job in itself, and often applies – at least in the UK and the US – specifically to management development, in a process designed to create 'change-makers' adept in promoting strategic organisational change.

Direct employee participation   Refers to the methods management uses to engage workers individually in their workplace or organisation. Direct participation is also sometimes known as 'engagement' or 'involvement'. With these methods, management communicates directly with each worker, sometimes top-down (for example through newsletters) and sometimes two-way, which allows or encourages a response (for example through employee surveys or question-and-answer sessions at team briefings).

Direct labour costs   In welfare economies, labour costs are both direct (the wages the employer pays the worker) and indirect (such as National Insurance and pension costs), which the worker receives as benefits when ill, on maternity leave or unemployed (insurance), or as delayed wages once retired (pension). Indirect costs can be high, but by using agency workers, a proportion can be passed on to the employment agency or worker.

Disclosure of information (communications)   Managers disclose information when they inform workers about their intentions, but do not invite or expect workers to contribute to their decisions. In the UK, there are legal obligations on managers to disclose certain categories of information, such as notice periods when making workers redundant, but these are limited. By contrast, in Germany, works councils have statutory rights to much broader categories of information, such as the company's financial situation, investment programmes, regradings and dismissals.

Discrimination   Occurs when a group of people is treated differently, and usually in an unequal and unfair way, relative to others. In the UK, the law specifies protected characteristics (qv) that defend the individual concerned from negative or unfair treatment, whether direct (open) or indirect (hidden). See also **Policy interventions to counter discrimination**.

Diversity   A looser term than discrimination (qv), suggesting that 'differences' beyond protected characteristics (qv) should be encouraged to make the workforce as inclusive as possible to reach a wider market for the organisation's services or products. Diversity policies may risk undermining the weight of structural and institutional discrimination by playing down the differences between categories of discrimination through encouraging a sense of equivalent weighting between all types of difference.

Embodied labour (body work)   The growth of service employment and the commercialisation of personal services (such as body piercing and tattoo parlours) has induced researchers in HRM to move away from exploring skills related to cognitive or manual dexterity and to refocus on so-called 'soft skills' (such as appearance, attitudes, emotions, feelings, looks and self-presentation). This refocusing has led to the study of aesthetic labour (qv) and emotional labour (qv).

Emotional labour   A concept developed by Arlie Hochschild (1973), this is a type of 'work' that is generally not paid, as it is assumed to be embodied in particular physical body types, typically female for caring work (such as flight attendants) or male for work involving threats of violence (such as debt collectors). Training involves 'feeling rules' that specify how workers should interact with customers, such as reassuring or smiling.

Employment   Employment status gives authority to the employer and their agents, such as line managers and supervisors, over the employee to determine pay and conditions, and any other accompanying legal or trade union negotiated entitlements, such as time off for training, holidays, pensions, sickness and other benefits. The legal side of being an employee has been highlighted because self-employment (qv) as a non-employee (such as an independent contractor or freelancer) has expanded with the growth of the gig economy (qv), and employers seek to reduce unit labour costs (qv) by converting their workforce into non-employee status.

Employment agency   See **Agency work**.

Employment contract   The employment contract, where it exists, is the legal document that embodies the employment relationship (qv), and so has an important role in establishing the contours of the wage–effort bargain (qv) and the frontier of control (qv), but only partially. It merely gives workers an overview of the pay, terms and conditions that they will expect from their employer.

Employment relationship   This is more open-ended than a sales or market relationship because a buyer of labour services (employer) and a seller of labour services (worker) 'meet' not in a marketplace but in a workplace, where the sale of the worker's labour services or labour power, which can be extremely variable, is exchanged for a definite income or wage. The employment relationship is: *ongoing* (while pay may be agreed in advance, effort is not laid down precisely and shifts); *asymmetrical* (the employer has greater legal and economic power than the worker); and *potentially conflictual* (both in terms of individual and collective grievances). It is therefore fundamentally about control.

Exit, voice and loyalty framework   This framework is used to lay out the choices workers have in the employment relationship (qv) where, if dissatisfied with an employer, the worker can quit or leave one employer (*exit*) to seek to gain a better contract with another. Trade unions (qv) seek to give workers influence (*voice*) in the management of the employment relationship, to ensure workers' interests are expressed collectively. Employers may also try to convince workers that they share the same interests to create a sense of *loyalty*.

External fit   See **Strategic fit**.

External labour market   The use of an external labour market refers to the practice of recruiting people who are not currently employed in the firm or organisation, who work for other firms or who are entering the labour market for the first time, such as school leavers or university graduates. Relying on recruitment through an external labour market implies that employers prefer to 'buy' workers at the required level of skill, rather than train them themselves.

Flexibility   There are various forms of flexible working that an organisation may introduce. *Numerical flexibility* refers to hours of work, such as working part time or job sharing. *Functional flexibility* involves multiskilling, to ensure that workers are able to carry out more than one task/job/role/occupation at their workplace so that they can be redeployed easily in case of need (such as holiday absence of a fellow worker). It contrasts with the deskilling (qv) advocated by F.W. Taylor in his 'scientific management'. *Temporal flexibility* focuses on the management of time and the matching of workers (supply) with the precise need (demand) for work, as in flexible rostering in supermarkets or the use of temporary work agencies. And *spatial/geographical flexibility* involves workers moving across borders or regions to carry out jobs, such as Eastern European migrant workers doing service or agricultural jobs in the UK.

Flexible firm   It has sometimes been assumed that the ideal type employment pattern is a mix of permanent (core) and temporary/insecure (peripheral [qv]) contracts that form the 'flexible firm'. Various forms of employment flexibility (qv) may be found in the so-called 'flexible firm'. However, the term 'flexible firm' has been criticised for its pejorative language, as 'peripheral' implies something unimportant and marginal, and for its imprecision.

Flexicurity   A hybrid term combining both 'flexibility' (qv) and 'security' (qv), which is the European attempt to seek a win–win for workers and employers embracing flexible forms of employment and better protection for workers on new, and potentially insecure, contracts. It has been embraced by the European Union (EU) (and HRM writers in the UK and the US) and adopted in many European countries, but many critics suggest it is a flawed and fundamentally contradictory concept seeking to reconcile that which cannot be reconciled.

Frames of reference   A way of 'seeing the world'; in the case of HRM, a way of seeing the roles that managers and workers should play in the world of employment relationships (qv). The same event can be interpreted or understood in very different ways depending on our frame of reference and how we filter the facts about it. We can broadly reduce these alternatives to three frames of reference for understanding the employment relationship: unitarism (qv), pluralism (qv) and radicalism (qv).

Frontier of control   Reflects the ever-shifting balance of power between employers and workers over the wage–effort bargain (qv). Employers develop strategies to increase workers' effort, while workers develop strategies for resistance (qv). The frontier of control involves an ongoing struggle, as the competitive nature of capitalist economies means that new competitors, technologies and ways of managing are always evolving to challenge the status quo.

Gig economy/online labour/platform economy   The gig economy essentially reduces the employment relationship (qv) to a transactional buyer–seller relationship, with apps as the technological fix that broker exchanges between the two parties. New companies built on apps, such as Uber (ride-hailing) and Deliveroo (food delivery), have virtually no directly employed workers but command high share values. Some companies call the workers using their app 'independent contractors'. However, the casualised work patterns in the transactional gig economy generally shift the balance of power towards the 'employer' or app owner, who benefits from a more flexible supply of labour. Workers, by contrast, are subject to more precarious (qv) forms of working: pay is less regular, hours of work become less predictable, benefits such as holiday and sick pay disappear, and it's more difficult to join a trade union, although new forms of resistance (qv) are emerging. The status of platform workers may be seen as 'hybrid', as neither employment (qv) nor self-employment (qv), but containing elements of both, which platform companies have manipulated to their own advantage. The legal status of gig workers is still unclear in the UK – and in many other countries too.

'Good worker' rhetoric (migrant workers)   An assumption is sometimes made that migrants are 'good workers', that is, that they have a stronger work ethic than local workers and that they are more willing to work hard and put up with tough conditions, poorer pay and longer working hours. This is a constructed category, which often reflects stereotypes of particular nations, such as 'the Chinese are hard-working' or 'Polish people are friendly'.

'Hard'/'soft' HRM   Alternative ways of treating the worker – as an object or instrument to be used (hard HRM) or as a human being to be developed (soft HRM). Hard versions lead to less 'people-friendly' policies including tighter control and supervisory systems. Soft versions, by contrast, regard workers as individuals, adaptable and much more productive, if only you can gain their commitment.

High-performance work practices (HPWPs)   Originate from so-called 'lean production', the application of Japanese production techniques, notably teamworking, continuous improvement and task delegation to workers. They are sometime referred to as 'high-investment' and 'high-commitment' practices. They assume, following a long history of 'best practice' thinking, that there is an ideal set of work practices that produce optimal performance in terms of output and, more dubiously, high levels of worker commitment.

Homeworking   The COVID-19 pandemic has reset the rules around the practice of homeworking, and the phrase 'working from home' has raised issues around controlling homeworkers, their productivity and how feasible homeworking is for different occupations.

Human capital   The education, training and work experiences that a person (or population) undergoes can be described as 'human capital', which correlates with salary: the higher our human capital, the more highly qualified and skilled we are, and so the more likely we are to have a higher salary.

Human resource management (HRM)   Began to replace personnel management (qv) as a term in the UK in the 1980s. In addition to the traditional functions of personnel management, it is generally accepted today that HRM focuses in particular on strategy (qv) and that HR directors form part of the senior management team with responsibility for current and future outcomes for the company.

Hybrid working   A term that emerged from the COVID-19 pandemic, this is a type of flexible working (qv) where employees split their time between the employer's workplace and working remotely, whether at home or somewhere else with internet access that is not their place of work. The hybrid part relates to the geographical split or divide. Some countries are enacting laws to give employees the right to hybrid working. Employers and employees have both positive and negative attitudes towards hybrid work.

Indirect labour costs   See **Direct labour costs**.

Individualisation   There is a generic trend in the industrialised world away from collective bargaining (qv) towards individual pay and rewards, especially in the private sector. Individualisation is gradually replacing collective approaches to HRM, including the increasing use of direct (qv) forms of employee involvement and the role of employment tribunals in channelling individual grievances, the number of cases having soared in the UK in recent years as strike levels have plummeted.

Industrial relations   The branch of employment relations (qv) that analyses the collective activity of employees and employers, especially through the role of trade unions (qv), collective bargaining (qv) and industrial disputes, such as strikes (qv). Industrial relations managers specialise in liaising with the unions recognised within the company. They are now generally known as HR managers as the role of unions has declined and the HRM agenda has expanded.

Institutional approaches to human resource management (HRM)   Suggest that HR practices cannot be abstracted from the institutions and cultures in which they develop and take place. When we're examining HR practices, we have to be aware of the *national* business system (qv) in which it's embedded. It's very difficult – even misleading – to examine HRM as if it can be extracted from a particular national business system. If we do so, we risk reflecting the dominant US-centric model of HRM and assuming that *this is the world*.

Integration/non-integration of migrant workers   Many migrants become citizens in the country they move to, and within one or two generations integrate into their new society, following the so-called 'melting pot' idea that whatever the diversity of origins, a standard citizen can be moulded through migration. However, in many societies, regardless of citizenship, discrimination (qv) can remain, especially towards black and minority ethnic groups in predominantly white societies. Non-integration is the result.

Internal fit   See **Strategic fit**.

Internal labour market   The use of an internal labour market refers to the practice of recruiting people from within the firm or organisation rather than seeking to source from the external labour market (qv). In organisations or countries characterised by the use of internal labour markets, we witness 'cohort recruitment', with entry into the organisation occurring at fixed times, when entry-level positions are open for school leavers and new graduates. Countries like Japan favour internal labour markets, and mid-career job moves are traditionally considered a sign of disloyalty and discouraged.

Labour process   Refers to activity that transforms a natural object or raw material into a useful product that satisfies a human need. What Karl Marx (1981 [1867]: 284) called the 'simple elements of the labour process' consist of human labour, the object on which work is performed, the instruments or tools used to perform that work and a purpose or goal. Capitalist societies are basically organised to satisfy the owners of the instruments of production, raw materials and finished products, which typically means making profit or financial gains through the labour process.

Liberal market economies (LMEs)   See **Varieties of capitalism**.

Management by objectives   Links the performance of managers and employees to achieving targets, which might include financial indicators, such as share value or output at organisational level, or more specific indicators at workplace level, such as reducing rates of absenteeism or turnover in an HR department. Individual workers' objectives will be closely linked to organisational objectives and regularly monitored through performance appraisal (qv).

Management control   Because employers and workers are unable to agree about the nature of the wage–effort bargain (qv) and the frontier of control (qv), management develops numerous forms of control to convert hired labour time into productive time. They include *personal control*, where the line manager directly exercises face-to-face supervision, and *deskilling* (qv). *Administrative or bureaucratic* control involves the use of regulations to direct tasks and practices, where rule-following has become an abstraction of personal supervisory control. *Technical control* occurs where technology determines the direction and pace of production. *Cultural, normative and value-based forms of control* suggest that employers may use labour power more productively by engaging with it rather than by directing it. Management may also use *surveillance* techniques, such as monitoring devices, to control workers, although in the UK, the law requires employers to inform staff that they are in use.

Management prerogative (no participation)   Refers to the manager's right to manage, which, in capitalist societies, is based on private property. Under company law, private sector companies are owned by shareholders who elect boards of directors to whom they are responsible for carrying out their interests. In liberal market economies (LMEs) (qv), shareholder interests are paramount, so unitarist (qv) perspectives – which prioritise management prerogative – are generally more commonly found among managers there than in coordinated market economies (CMEs) (qv), which take account of a wider range of stakeholders, not least workers. Accordingly, companies in LMEs are more likely to be located towards the 'no participation' end of the continuum of participation (qv) than those in CMEs.

Multiple disadvantage   Occurs when an individual has a combination of protected characteristics (qv), such as a black woman with disabilities, who is covered by three of them, and therefore faces the likelihood of combined or multiple discrimination (qv) in the labour market and at the workplace.

National business systems   See **Varieties of capitalism**.

Negotiation   When it involves representational (or indirect) employee participation (qv) it is closely associated with pluralist frames of reference (qv), in that it is based on the legitimate right of workers and their trade unions (qv) to pursue their own interests construed differently from those of management. Unions engage in collective bargaining (qv) over pay and conditions, which is a form of negotiation, although negotiation may also take place between individual workers and managers in the context of management by objectives (qv) and setting performance targets. Individualised negotiations of this sort are extremely limited in scope in comparison with collective bargaining.

'New' unitarism (neo-paternalism or new paternalism)   New unitarist approaches to HRM have been adopted by modern US hi-tech companies, such as Apple, Meta (Facebook), Google, Microsoft and Yahoo!, that seek to build trust (qv) with their employees by paying high wages, developing corporate cultures and offering benefits beyond a simple economic transactional model. However, unlike traditional paternalism (qv), new unitarism seeks to use workers' time intensively in the short term.

Overwork   Involves working excessive hours, which is common in many companies or societies with normalised 'long-hours cultures'. Long working hours can result in 'burnout' – the physical and mental exhaustion of the employee. The Japanese word *karoshi* means death as a result of overwork.

Paternalism   Traditional paternalism is a form of unitarism (qv) that rests on the idea of the employer as a 'father-figure' who 'looks after' his workers, often for a whole working lifetime. The word *pater* is Latin for father, so, at its most basic, it refers to the father who knows best, the benign figure who controls the family and is accordingly obeyed. In the 19th century, paternalism was relatively common, as non-wage benefits (such as training, sickness and holiday benefits) were at the discretion of the employer and not legal entitlements. With the rise of the welfare state, expansion of universal education and the growth of trade unions (qv), it became increasingly seen as old-fashioned to seek 'entitlements' from employers as a 'gift' and not as a right. It survives in the form of 'new' unitarism (qv).

Performance appraisal   The process of assessing an individual's performance against goals or objectives set in meetings between the employee and line manager/supervisor. Assessment involves the line manager in evaluating performance indicators gathered from management sources as well as, possibly, colleagues, customers and suppliers in so-called '360 degree' appraisals, which cover 'all-round' assessment.

Performance management   That branch of HRM that links individual rewards with organisational performance. It involves coordinating individual skills with organisational goals through management by objectives (qv) and performance appraisal (qv).

Personnel management   There is no real difference between personnel management and HRM in some countries. However, in the UK, personnel managers focused principally on organisational record-keeping, provision of advice and conducting industrial relations (qv) – in those companies where trade unions (qv) were recognised – until the 1980s, when the term was gradually replaced by the US designation, 'human resources manager'. Today 'human resources' (HR) is in common usage.

Pluralism   A frame of reference (qv) that – derived from the word 'plural', or more than one – suggests there may be several different ways of looking at the organisation. Pluralists argue that managers are there to manage, certainly, but they're there to do so on the basis of persuasion rather than management prerogative (qv) that's granted through property rights, as in the case of unitarism (qv). Pluralism therefore assumes that potentially differing sets of interests implicit in the wage–effort bargain (qv) need to be mediated by good management because the employment relationship (qv) may be adversarial or conflictual. Workers need to express their grievances collectively, for example through a trade union (qv), which the pluralist recognises as legitimate both in the workplace and in wider society.

Policy interventions to counter discrimination There are a variety of ways in which governments and employers have attempted to tackle discrimination (qv) at the workplace and in labour markets. *Equal opportunities legislation* makes it illegal to discriminate against individuals with protected characteristics (qv), although its implementation has been criticised along with its failure to come to grips with the hidden nature of discrimination. *Affirmative or positive action* is a more radical approach that may set quotas for discriminated groups to overcome institutional or societal barriers, although it risks alienating dominant groups by so doing. *Diversity management* (qv) focuses on improving opportunities for all individuals, not just minority groups, by recognising difference as a positive asset and promoting the business case for diversity, not just the moral case, namely, that discrimination reduces the potential talent pool.

'Post-bureaucratic' employment 'Employment' (qv) in the latter part of the 20th century traditionally meant by default typical or standard employment (qv), namely, possession of an open-ended, full-time employment contract (qv). This model of employment was also sometimes called 'bureaucratic' or 'secure', because it involved a long-term career (qv) and promotion from within, based on internal labour markets (qv). By the start of the 21st century, this model had fragmented, particularly in liberal market economies (LMEs) (qv), in favour of what is sometimes termed 'post-bureaucratic' employment (qv) involving rising levels of contingent work (qv). Organisations have become increasingly involved in managing a bundle of different employment contracts, many of which are contingent. Post-bureaucratic employment also covers the emergence of more recent working arrangements, such as zero–hours contracts and the gig economy (qv).

Presenteeism A form of management control (qv) based on having to *display* loyalty to your line manager or company through being present at work, especially after the 'typical' working day (09:00 to 17:00) is finished. It is not necessarily linked to greater employee productivity.

Protected characteristics Protected characteristics of workers in UK legislation (Equality Act 2010) cover: age; disabilities; gender reassignment; marriage and civil partnership (that is, whether the person is married or not married, single or in a partnership); maternity and pregnancy, and whether a woman wishes to start a family; race and racial origin; religion and beliefs, which includes politics; sex; and sexual orientation. It is unlawful for an employer to practice discrimination (qv) against a worker in any of these nine categories.

Radicalism The 'radical' perspective is a frame of reference (qv) that differs from unitarism (qv) and pluralism (qv) in that it views the employment relationship (qv) from a wider political economy perspective, arguing that capitalism (qv) is itself essentially exploitative. Marxists (and others) argue that workers are exploited under capitalist systems of production because they never gain the full product of the wage–effort bargain (qv). Radical pluralism (qv) has been developed by a group of analysts who, while accepting the potential conflict (qv) that underpins the employment relationship, do not share the (traditional)

Marxist belief that revolution is necessarily the outcome of the struggle between employers and workers.

Radical pluralism   A frame of reference (qv) that – like radicalism (qv) – accepts that conflict (qv) underpins the employment relationship (qv) in capitalist societies. Radical pluralists share their analysis of capitalism (qv) as exploitative with Marxists, but reject the (traditional) Marxist view that class struggle will necessarily lead to its overthrow through working–class revolution. Alan Fox (1974), the most well-known radical pluralist, advocated the creation of organisational structures that build high–discretion roles rather than low-discretion roles for workers, hence employment relationships based on trust (qv). Workers can then organise their tasks in more 'autonomous' and 'self-managed' ways (characteristic of many high–discretion professional jobs), hence making them more creative and fulfilling.

Recruitment and selection   Recruitment covers methods to attract the most suitable workers into the organisation, such as advertising in newspapers or online, or the use of social networks (qv). Selection is the subsequent process of choosing the best candidate to fill the post from among those who have been recruited.

Representational (or indirect) employee participation   Representational forms of participation are methods that involve workers in electing representatives to represent their views collectively with management, generally through a trade union (qv). They are also sometimes known as 'indirect' participation because the union mediates between the individual worker and management. Representatives meet management regularly on joint bodies such as joint consultative committees, works councils, health and safety committees or, in some countries, the company's supervisory board. In liberal market economies (LMEs) (qv), the decline of union membership has led to a similar decline in the role of representational forms of employee participation where it generally lacks statutory backing, but in coordinated market economies (CMEs) (qv) it remains stronger on account of its legal foundations. In unitary frameworks (qv), managers are hostile to representational participation, but in pluralist frameworks (qv) it plays a crucial role in the organisation's HRM.

Reputation   The status or position within a social network that extends beyond the people we know directly. In construction, creative industries and the gig economy (all project-based work, where jobs are short term and people need to compete for new work regularly), among others, maintaining reputation means maintaining opportunities to be offered work.

'Reserve army of labour'   Capitalist societies do not achieve full employment, as there are always reserves of the underemployed or unemployed who are made redundant through technological displacement or societal discrimination. Karl Marx argued that this 'reserve army of labour' functioned to hold wages down, break industrial disputes and weaken worker solidarity. The reserve army includes those with protected characteristics (qv), such as women and minority ethnic workers. Critics of this view argue that capitalist economies have achieved full employment at least over certain periods; policy interventions to counter discrimination (qv) can bring workers with protected characteristics into regular employment; and labour markets are able to absorb technologically displaced workers.

Resistance   Conflict between employers and workers is normal in capitalist economies and may provoke different forms of resistance among workers. Resistance may be organised, for example, when a strike or working to rule is coordinated or led by a trade union, or unorganised when workers just walk out of the job as a result of an act of perceived injustice or breach of the frontier of control (qv). Resistance may also be either collective, when it involves a group of workers who share the same sense of injustice or grievance, or individual, when it involves the grievance of a single or isolated worker.

Reward management   May be linked to performance appraisal (qv). Rewards themselves may be extrinsic or intrinsic. *Extrinsic rewards* are our pay and conditions, or material benefits that we earn in exchange for carrying out our job (the wage–effort bargain [qv]). *Intrinsic rewards* refer to the psychological or subjective satisfactions we get from our job, such as a sense of a 'job well done', or esteem or recognition. These are personal rewards and cannot be easily quantified.

Segmented labour market theory   Divides labour markets into various parts or segments, principally primary and secondary labour markets (see also flexible firm [qv]). Primary (or core) labour markets offer well-paid, secure employment, which is generally unionised and traditionally occupied by skilled, qualified and often white male workers. Secondary labour markets, by contrast, offer jobs that are insecure and poorly paid and are often occupied by workers with lower levels of education and skills, who have protected characteristics (qv). The approach does not focus on the individual's assets, capabilities and motivations (as does human capital (qv) theory), but rather, on the way in which social groups are treated in society. A criticism of the approach is that it does not explain much, although it does offer a more refined description of the character of the labour market.

Self-employment   The fastest growing category of employment in the UK (and many other countries). Following the financial crisis in 2008–09, many employers began to transfer existing employees to self-employment status to reduce labour costs, especially indirect labour costs (qv). The growth of the gig economy (qv) has further expanded this process, generating so-called 'independent contractors', who are often referred to as 'disguised' or 'false' self-employed, as many aspects of their working life remain controlled by a dominant authority, as in standard employment status.

Social capital   The stock or value of all a person's connections. High social capital means that people have a 'bank of connections' that helps them find work at the level they want. Attending a public school or elite university helps to increase the value of social capital, but social networks (qv) among peer groups may do so too.

Social exclusion   A common problem with connection-based recruitment that relies on social networks (qv) is that it is exclusive: people with links to those inside an organisation get information about work and employment chances, while those without such links cannot. Such a situation is unfair to those wishing to work in those organisations and sectors but who lack the 'right connections' and information.

Social media   Used for finding work online or through platforms such as LinkedIn, but they should not be confused with social networks (qv). Social networks are exclusive, while social media are more inclusive. Recruiters and head-hunters use social media to make money from recruitment.

Social networks   The exclusive connections we accumulate through family, friends, colleagues and acquaintances. Each individual has unique social networks. Connections can help with activities such as recruitment and selection (qv). However, social networks may reinforce discrimination (qv), by including and excluding. Social networks help explain the hidden or taken-for-granted norms that indirectly and unconsciously perpetuate discrimination.

'Soft' HRM   See **'Hard'/'soft' HRM**.

Standard/non–standard employment   Standard or typical employment refers to the traditional understanding of employment in the latter part of the 20th century that generally involved an open-ended, full-time employment contract signed by the employer and the generally male worker that often expired only on his retirement. It may also be called regular or secure employment. Such an arrangement was the default understanding of the employment contract (qv), hence it was known as standard or typical. However, the development of 'post-bureaucratic' (qv) employment (qv) and the gig economy (qv) has dramatically fragmented the structure of labour markets in the 21st century, particularly in liberal market economies (LMEs) (qv), but elsewhere too. This has led to the growth of forms of employment that appear to be non–standard or atypical (interchangeable terms that express the contrast with work that is more or less regular and secure).

Strategic fit   A concept associated with contingency theory (qv), that an organisation needs to match its internal structures with the external environment. *Internal fit* involves ensuring that all HR policies are joined up so, for example, recruitment, rewards, training and participation systems are mutually reinforcing (that is, have internal fit). *External fit* involves ensuring that a company's internal set of HR practices matches the requirements of its market and business environment. To achieve this, the company has to identify its market strategy: (broadly) cost leadership, differentiation or specialisation.

Strategy (HRM)   Involves the direction of the organisation, and managing and shaping the future, which is, of course, unknown. By being strategic, management make assumptions about the future, which adds to the mythic power of being a manager or leader – they somehow know the future, like a priest or fortune teller (Cleverley, 1973). Typically, such visions of the future involve 'following a trend', such as advocating outsourcing business functions and making jobs more contingent (qv), which has been common in recent neoliberal times. (See also **contingency theory** and **universalism**.)

Strikes/industrial disputes   A strike is a collective withdrawal of labour by workers, who may stop working normally to put pressure on an employer if the process of collective bargaining (qv) fails to result in an agreement. Strikes are usually organised by a trade union (qv), but they may be spontaneous, unofficial and/or illegal. They may be small scale and local to the particular workplace, widespread across a whole industry or even 'general' across an entire country. A victory can increase workers' confidence and help them to push back against management more generally, but when workers are defeated, employers may take the chance to reorganise employment to take advantage of their demoralisation. Strikes can be measured by comparing the *number* that take place across a country or sector, the incidence of *working days lost* as a result and the *total number of workers* involved. It is important to be clear, however, that strikes are only one form of resistance (qv) at the workplace, and nowadays a minor one at that.

Third-party employment relationships   See **Triadic employment relationships**.

Trade unions   The classic definition of a trade union, deriving from Sidney and Beatrice Webb (1920: 1), is: 'a continuous association of wage-earners for the purpose of maintaining or improving the conditions of their working lives'. 'Wage-earners' (workers) form their own continuous associations (unions) in order, collectively, to bargain for improved pay and conditions. Trade unions also represent workers who have individual grievances, but their core activity is collective bargaining (qv) and expressing collective views and opinions.

Training   Most jobs require time to acquire the skills or dexterity to perform at the level or speed required in the labour process (qv). Training is the development of attitudes, knowledge and skills for the current and future needs of the organisation. Training has an applied element: general education may be part of it, but training is more applied and specific as it is linked to an occupation, or keeping up with changes taking place within an occupation. Training is a private good, in that it benefits the individual, but also a public good, as it also benefits wider society. Societies with high levels of trained workers are more productive than those without.

Triadic employment relationships   The triangular (or triadic) employment relationship adds the 'customer' or 'client' to the normal dyadic employment relationship (qv) between employers and workers. This addition is sometimes framed in terms of 'customer control', and the role played by customers in contributing information to management control (qv) over workers through rating sites or apps (internal and external platforms that quantify the 'customer experience' and put customers in a potential power position over employees, contractors and managers). This relationship is especially strong in the service sector, but many areas of employment include customer reviews as a way of monitoring employee (and management) performance. Another type of triadic relationship is referred to when employers recruit labour indirectly using employment agencies (qv). In this meaning, the three elements of the employment relationship are workers, employment agencies and the client companies that recruit workers from the agencies.

Trust The status that you have within your social networks (qv), that is, within the circle of people or connections you know personally or directly. Being trusted means your circle can provide access to resources like jobs. In an employment relationship (qv), trust requires a significant length of service or repeat transactions to develop. In transactional work situations, such as those involving contingent work (qv), length of service is not normally accumulated with one employer/client, so there is little basis on which a trusting relationship can evolve. An employer's trust in an employee reduces the cost of monitoring and increases the chances of greater productivity and efficiency. An employee's trust in an employer reduces the cost of job search and may help to promote the meaningfulness of work. However, owing to the inherent instability of the wage–effort bargain (qv), maintaining trust may prove challenging. For this reason, trust is often contrasted with exit, voice and loyalty (qv).

Typical/atypical employment See **Standard/non–standard employment**.

Unit labour costs Defined as the average cost of labour per unit of output produced. They are calculated by multiplying the total number of employees (E) by their total cost of their wages (w) and fringe benefits (f), and dividing the result by the total number of units produced each week (Q). So, if you spend £10,000 a week on labour costs and produce 1,000 units, you are spending £10 on labour for each unit. Your unit labour costs are therefore £10 (although in practice the calculations may be much more complex). Controlling unit labour costs is central to HRM.

Unitarism A frame of reference (qv) that – derived from the word 'unit', or 'one' – views the organisation as a single, unified hierarchy, with senior managers at the top deciding on strategy, and middle and line managers ensuring that workers correctly carry out their instructions. Unitarism is based on the concept of management prerogative (qv), or the manager's right to manage, which, in capitalist societies, is based on private property: under company law, private sector companies are owned by shareholders who elect boards of directors to whom they are responsible for carrying out their interests. Managers with unitarist perspectives believe that a consensus of interests unites workers and managers, which, of course, is true to some extent: as employees, we're all keen for our company to do well so that our jobs are secure. However, the unitarist manager goes further in claiming that, because of this common interest, values and objectives are also held in common between managers and workers. Unitarism therefore tends to deny the structural dimension to conflict (qv) that results from the wage–effort bargain (qv), and so leads the manager to seek its causes in union agitation or poor communications.

Universalism Proposes that there is only one, the right or best, set of HR practices, which, accordingly, ought to be applied to all organisations in all market and technological circumstances. It reflects the resource-based theory of the firm, which suggests people are the key competitive resources, and so ensuring 'good' HR practices to retain employees is critical for the success of the firm. Jeffrey Pfeffer is a management writer who proposes a list of key HR practices as a universal recipe for successful management, based largely on Japanese experience. Universalism is generally contrasted with contingency theory (qv).

'Varieties of capitalism' 'Varieties of capitalism' theory (sometimes known as 'national business systems' theory) is a well-known institutional approach to HRM (qv). Although complex in its detail, it boils down to making a distinction between two dominant types of capitalism: liberal market economies (LMEs) (qv), such as the UK and the US; and coordinated market economies (CMEs) (qv), such as Germany and Japan, although there are also profound differences between these two. Theorists associated with 'varieties of capitalism' include Michel Albert, David Soskice, Peter Hall and Richard Whitley.

Wage–effort bargain Refers to the level or quality of effort a worker puts into a job in exchange for the wages or salary they receive. This sounds straightforward, but it isn't. Effort depends on the individual, and although the work requirements to do a job may specify the output expected, such as the number of items produced per hour, the effort made by one worker to complete a job cycle may vary greatly from the effort made by another (depending, for example, on application, aptitude, experience and training). Effort may be measured fairly easily for some jobs in agriculture or manufacturing, where output can be rewarded with simple piece rates. However, for most service sector jobs and more complex occupations, output cannot be easily measured and measuring wage–effort becomes fraught and ambiguous. In these cases, the employer is likely to want to create trust (qv) at the workplace in order to create a committed and loyal workforce.

Workers' control A form of ownership (such as workers' cooperatives) that dissolves the formal separation of the employer from the worker by converting everyone working in the enterprise or cooperative into co-owners. There are significant cooperative sectors in countries like France and Italy, but this form of ownership also sometimes emerges when firms fail, and owners abandon production facilities or fixed capital. In such circumstances, workers may occupy their workplace and attempt to restart the business. Workers' control is therefore located at the end of the continuum of participation (qv) with greatest worker influence over the business.

Work–life balance The relationship between paid work and private life, and the suggestion that the individual (or society) can somehow achieve a perfect trade-off between the two spheres, underpins the idea of work–life balance. Many workers gain intrinsic satisfaction from their occupation, which they don't view as alienating or oppressive. For others, however, work is merely a 'means to an end', an instrumental way of earning wages for the purposes of paying the bills and surviving, which creates the divide between working and not-working.

References

Abbott, A. (1991) 'The order of professionalization: An empirical analysis', *Work and Occupations*, 18(4): 355–84.

ACAS (Advisory, Conciliation and Arbitration Service) (2019) *ACAS Working for Everyone, Advisory, Conciliation and Arbitration Service, Annual report and accounts 2018–19*, 18 July, HC 2197, Available from: https://assets.publishing.service.gov.uk/government/uploads/system/uploads/attachment_data/file/821879/acas-annual-report-web-2018-2019.pdf

Acemoglu, D. and Restrepo, P. (2020) 'Robots and jobs: Evidence from US labor markets', *Journal of Political Economy*, 128(6): 2188–244.

Ackers, P. (1998) 'On paternalism: Seven observations on the uses and abuses of the concept in industrial relations, past and present', *Historical Studies in Industrial Relations*, 5: 173–93.

Ackroyd, S. and Thompson, P. (1999) *Organizational Misbehaviour*, London: Sage Publications.

Adkins, W. (2019) 'How to calculate the employee labor percentage', Small Business, 31 January, Available from: https://smallbusiness.chron.com/calculate-employee-labor-percentage-15980.html

Adler, P.S. (2019) *The 99 Percent Economy: How Democratic Socialism Can Overcome the Crises of Capitalism*, Oxford: Oxford University Press.

Albert, M. (1993) *Capitalism Against Capitalism*, London: Whurr.

Alberti, G. (2014) 'Mobility strategies, "mobility differentials" and "transnational exit": The experiences of precarious migrants in London's hospitality jobs', *Work, Employment & Society*, 28(6): 865–81.

Alberti, G., Holgate, J. and Tapia, M. (2013) 'Organising migrants as workers or as migrant workers? Intersectionality, trade unions and precarious work', *The International Journal of Human Resource Management*, 24(22): 4132–48.

Allyn, B. (2021) 'Google workers speak out about why they formed a union: "To protect ourselves"', NPR, 8 January, Available from: www.npr.org/2021/01/08/954710407/at-google-hundreds-of-workers-formed-a-labor-union-why-to-protect-ourselves?t=1612201555376

Almond, P. and Esbester, M. (2018) *Health and Safety in Contemporary Britain: Society, Legitimacy, and Change since 1960*, London: Palgrave.

Alon, T.M., Doepke, M., Olmstead-Rumsey, J. and Tertilt, M. (2020) *The Impact of COVID-19 on Gender Equality*, Working Paper 26947, April, Cambridge, MA: National Bureau of Economic Research.

Ammirato, P. (2018) *The Growth of Italian Cooperatives: Innovation, Resilience and Social Responsibility*, London: Routledge.

Amnesty International (2016) *'This Is What We Die For': Human Rights Abuses in the Democratic Republic of Congo Power the Global Trade in Cobalt*, London: Amnesty International.

Angry Workers (2020) *Class Power on Zero-Hours*, Hendon: PM Press UK, Synopsis available from: www.angryworkers.org/2020/03/17/introduction-class-power-on-zero-hours

Arnesen, E. (2003) 'Specter of the black strikebreaker: Race, employment, and labor activism in the industrial era', *Labor History*, 44(3): 319–35.

Ashley, L., Duberley, J., Sommerlad, H. and Scholarios, D. (2015) *A Qualitative Evaluation of Non-Educational Barriers to the Elite Professions*, London: Social Mobility and Child Poverty Commission.

Atkinson, J. (1984) 'Manpower strategies for flexible organisations', *Personnel Management*, 16: 28–31.

Atkinson, J. (1987) 'Flexibility or fragmentation? The United Kingdom labour market in the eighties', *Labour and Society*, 12: 87–105.

Atkinson, S. (2021) '"More than a job": The food delivery co-ops putting fairness into the gig economy', *The Guardian*, 11 May, Available from: www.theguardian.com/world/2021/may/11/more-than-a-job-the-meal-delivery-co-ops-making-the-gig-economy-fairer

Atzeni, M. and Ghigliani, P. (2007) 'Labour process and decision-making in factories under workers' self-management: Empirical evidence from Argentina', *Work, Employment & Society*, 21(4): 653–71.

Auer, P. (2010) 'What's in a name? The rise (and fall?) of flexicurity', *Journal of Industrial Relations*, 52(3): 371–86.

Auer, P. and Cazes, S. (2000) 'The resilience of the long-term employment relationship: Evidence from the industrialized countries', *International Labour Review*, 139(4): 379–408.

Axtell, C., Hislop, D. and Whittaker, S. (2008) 'Mobile technologies in mobile spaces: Findings from the context of train travel', *International Journal of Human-Computer Studies*, 66(12): 902–15.

Bach, S., Kessler, I. and Heron, P. (2006) 'Changing job boundaries and workforce reform: The case of teaching assistants', *Industrial Relations Journal*, 37(1): 2–21.

Baddon, L., Hunter, L., Hyman, J., Leopold, J. and Ramsay, H. (1989) *People's Capitalism? A Critical Analysis of Profit-Sharing and Employee Share Ownership*, London: Routledge.

Badger, A. (2021) 'Labouring at the interface: Exploring the rhythms and resistances of working in London's food delivery gig economy', PhD thesis, Royal Holloway University of London.

Bain, I. (2021) 'Can a work-free life really work? Why Gen Z's new trick of "idling" fails to convince i's millennial', *i-news*, 24 November, Available from: https://inews.co.uk/inews-lifestyle/work-free-life-can-work-gen-z-idling-fails-convince-millennial-1314987

Baldamus, W. (1961) *Efficiency and Effort: An Analysis of Industrial Administration*, London: Tavistock Press.

Bamber, G.J., Lansbury, R.D., Wailes, N. and Wright, C.F. (eds) (2017) *International and Comparative Employment Relations: National Regulation, Global Changes*, London: Sage Publications.

Barley, S.R. and Kunda, G. (2006) *Gurus, Hired Guns, and Warm Bodies: Itinerant Experts in a Knowledge Economy*, Princeton, NJ: Princeton University Press.

Bartley, T. (2018) *Rules without Rights: Land, Labor, and Private Authority in the Global Economy*, Oxford: Oxford University Press.

Basterretxea, I. and Storey, J. (2018) 'Do employee-owned firms produce more positive employee behavioural outcomes? If not why not? A British–Spanish comparative analysis', *British Journal of Industrial Relations*, 56(2): 292–319.

Batstone, E. (1988) 'The Frontier of Control', in D. Gallie (ed) *Employment in Britain*, Oxford: Blackwell, pp 218–47.

Batt, R. and Banerjee, M. (2012) 'The scope and trajectory of strategic HR research: Evidence from American and British journals', *The International Journal of Human Resource Management*, 23(9): 1739–62.

Baxter-Reid, H. (2016) 'Buying into the "good worker" rhetoric or being as good as they need to be? The effort bargaining process of new migrant workers', *Human Resource Management Journal*, 26(3): 337–50.

BBC (2020) File on 4: *Racism in the Police*, 28 June, Available from: www.bbc.co.uk/programmes/m000kgtl

BBC News (2012) 'Volkswagen turns off Blackberry email after work hours', 8 March, Available from: www.bbc.co.uk/news/technology-16314901

BBC News (2017) '100 Women: Sexism in tech is like "a thousand little cuts"', 2 October, Available from: www.bbc.co.uk/news/av/world-41444679/100-women-sexism-in-tech-is-like-a-thousand-little-cuts

BBC News (2018) 'Rolls-Royce announces 4,600 job cuts', 14 June, Available from: www.bbc.co.uk/news/business-44479410

BBC News (2020) 'Tesco, Pizza Hut and Superdrug in minimum wage fail', 31 December, Available from: www.bbc.co.uk/news/business-55491925

BBC News (2021a) 'How serious is the shortage of lorry drivers?', 15 October, Available from: www.bbc.co.uk/news/57810729

BBC News (2021b) 'More big investors shun Deliveroo over workers' rights', 26 March, Available from: www.bbc.co.uk/news/business-56515498

Beardwell, J. and Thompson, A. (2017) *Human Resource Management: A Contemporary Approach* (8th edn), Harlow: Pearson Education Ltd.

Becker, G.S. (1993) *Human Capital: A Theoretical and Empirical Analysis, with Special Reference to Education*, Chicago, IL: University of Chicago Press.

Beckers, D.G., van der Linden, D., Smulders, P.G., Kompier, M.A., Taris, T.W. and Geurts, S.A. (2008) 'Voluntary or involuntary? Control over overtime and rewards for overtime in relation to fatigue and work satisfaction', *Work & Stress*, 22(1): 33–50.

Beckett, F. and Hencke, D. (2009) *Marching to the Fault Line: The Miners' Strike and the Battle for Industrial Britain*, London: Constable.

Behrend, H. (1957) 'The effort bargain', *ILR Review*, 10(4): 503–15.

BEIS (Department for Business, Energy & Industrial Strategy) (2018) *Good Work Plan, December 2018*, Cm 9755, Presented to Parliament by the Secretary of State for Business, Energy and Industrial Strategy, London: HM Government, Available from: https://assets.publishing.service.gov.uk/government/uploads/system/uploads/attachment_data/file/766167/good-work-plan-command-paper.pdf

BEIS (2020) 'Trade Union membership, UK 1995–2019: Statistical Bulletin', 27 May, Available from: https://assets.publishing.service.gov.uk/government/uploads/system/uploads/attachment_data/file/887740/Trade-union-membership-2019-statistical-bulletin.pdf

Belzer, M.H. and Sedo, S.A. (2018) 'Why do long distance truck drivers work extremely long hours?', *The Economic and Labour Relations Review*, 29(1): 59–79.

Benner, C. (2002) *Work in the New Economy: Flexible Labor Markets in Silicon Valley*, London: John Wiley & Sons.

Benson, E. (2009) 'Employment Protection', in M. Gold (ed) *Employment Policy in the European Union*, Basingstoke: Palgrave Macmillan, pp 93–118.

Bergvall-Kåreborn, B. and Howcroft, D. (2013) '"The future's bright, the future's mobile": A study of Apple and Google mobile application developers', *Work, Employment & Society*, 27(6): 964–81.

Bernstein, E., Bunch, J., Canner, N. and Lee, M. (2016) 'Beyond the holacracy hype', *Harvard Business Review*, 94(7): 1–26.

Bertrand, M., Black, S.E., Jensen, S. and Lleras-Muney, A. (2014) *Breaking the Glass Ceiling? The Effect of Board Quotas on Female Labor Market Outcomes in Norway*, NBER Working Paper 20256, Cambridge, MA and Örebro: National Bureau of Economic Research, Örebro University School of Business.

Bian, Y. (1994) 'Guanxi and the allocation of urban jobs in China', *The China Quarterly*, 140: 971–99.

Bilton, R. (2014) 'Apple "failing to protect Chinese factory workers"', BBC News, 18 December, Available from: www.bbc.co.uk/news/business-30532463

Bingham, C. (2016) *Employment Relations: Fairness and Trust in the Workplace*, London: Sage Publications.

Birkett, H. and Forbes, S. (2019) 'Where's dad? Exploring the low take-up of inclusive parenting policies in the UK', *Policy Studies*, 40(2): 205–24.

BITC (Business in the Community) (2000) *Winning with Integrity: A Guide to Social Responsibility*, London: BITC.

Blagg, K. and Blom, E. (2018) *Evaluating the Return on Investment in Higher Education: An Assessment of Individual- and State-level Returns*, September, Washington, DC: Urban Institute.

Blair, H. (2001) '"You're only as good as your last job": The labour process and labour market in the British film industry', *Work, Employment & Society*, 15(1): 149–69.

Blair, H. (2003) 'Winning and losing in flexible labour markets: The formation and operation of networks of interdependence in the UK film industry', *Sociology*, 37(4): 677–94.

Bland, A. and Makortoff, K. (2020) 'Boohoo knew of Leicester factory failings, says report', *The Guardian*, 25 September, Available from: www.theguardian.com/business/2020/sep/25/boohoo-report-reveals-factory-fire-risk-among-supply-chain-failings?CMP=Share_iOSApp_Other

Bloodworth, J. (2018) *Hired: Six Months Undercover in Low-Wage Britain*, London: Atlantic Books.

Blumenfeld, S., Anderson, G. and Hooper, V. (2020) 'Covid-19 and employee surveillance', *New Zealand Journal of Employment Relations*, 45(2): 42–56.

Blyton, P. and Turnbull, P. (2004) *The Dynamics of Employee Relations* (3rd edn), Basingstoke: Macmillan.

Bodnar, J., Simon, R. and Weber, M.P. (1982) *Lives of Their Own: Blacks, Italians, and Poles in Pittsburgh, 1900–1960*, Campaign, IL: University of Illinois Press.

Bolton, S.C. (2007) 'Dignity *in* and *at* Work: Why It Matters', in S.C. Bolton (ed) *Dimensions of Dignity at Work*, London: Routledge, pp 3–16.

Bolton, S.C. and Boyd, C. (2003) 'Trolley dolly or skilled emotion manager? Moving on from Hochschild's Managed Heart', *Work, Employment & Society*, 17(2): 289–308.

Booth, R. (2020) 'Uber drivers in legal bid to uncover app's algorithms', *The Guardian*, 20 July, p 15, Available from: www.theguardian.com/technology/2020/jul/20/uber-drivers-to-launch-legal-bid-to-uncover-apps-algorithm

Borges, M.J. and Torres, S.B. (2012) 'Company Towns: Concepts, Historiography, and Approaches', in M.J. Borges and S.B. Torres (eds) *Company Towns: Labor, Space, and Power Relations across Time and Continents*, New York: Palgrave Macmillan, pp 1–40.

Bosch, G., Rubery, J. and Lehndorff, S. (2007) 'European employment models under pressure to change', *International Labour Review*, 146(3–4): 253–77.

Boselie, P., Dietz, G. and Boon, C. (2005) 'Commonalities and contradictions in HRM and performance research', *Human Resource Management Journal*, 15(3): 67–94.

Bouchard, P. (1998) 'Training and Work: Some Myths about Human Capital', in S.M. Scott, B. Spencer and A.M. Thomas (eds) *Learning for Life: Canadian Readings in Adult Education*, Toronto, ON: Thompson Educational Publishers, pp 128–39.

Boxall, P.F. (1992) 'Strategic human resource management: Beginnings of a new theoretical sophistication?', *Human Resource Management Journal*, 2(3): 60–79.

Bradbury, S. (2011) 'From racial exclusions to new inclusions: Black and minority ethnic participation in football clubs in the East Midlands of England', *International Review for the Sociology of Sport*, 46(1): 23–44.

Bradley, H. (2016) 'Gender and Work', in S. Edgell, H. Gottfried and E. Granter (eds) *The Sage Handbook of the Sociology of Work and Employment*, London: Sage Publications, pp 73–92.

Bratton, J. and Gold, J. (2017) *Human Resource Management: Theory and Practice* (6th edn), Basingstoke: Palgrave Macmillan.

Braverman, H. (1974) *Labor and Monopoly Capital: The Degradation of Work in the Twentieth Century*, New York: Monthly Review Press.

Brewster, C., Mayrhofer, W. and Farndale, E. (eds) (2019) *Handbook of Research on Comparative Human Resource Management*, Cheltenham: Edward Elgar.

Briken, K. and P. Taylor (2018) 'Fulfilling the "British way": Beyond constrained choice – Amazon workers' lived experiences of workfare', *Industrial Relations Journal*, 49(5–6): 438–58.

Brown, D.K. (2001) 'The social sources of educational credentialism: Status cultures, labor markets, and organizations', *Sociology of Education*, Extra Issue, pp 19–34.

Brown, R.K., McQuaid, R., Raeside, R., Dutton, M., Egdell, V. and Canduela, J. (2019) 'Buying into capitalism? Employee ownership in a disconnected era', *British Journal of Industrial Relations*, 57(1): 62–85.

Brown, S. (2022) *Get Rich or Lie Trying: Ambition and Deceit in the New Influencer Economy*, London: Atlantic Books.

Brown, T., Goodman, J. and Yasukawa, K. (2010) 'Academic casualization in Australia: Class divisions in the university', *Journal of Industrial Relations*, 52(2): 169–82.

Bruegel, I. (1979) 'Women as a reserve army of labour: A note on recent British experience', *Feminist Review*, 3(1): 12–23.

Bruno, R. (2009) 'Evidence of bias in the Chicago Tribune coverage of organized labor: A quantitative study from 1991 to 2001', *Labor Studies Journal*, 34(3): 385–407.

Buchanan, J. (2004) 'Paradoxes of significance: Australian casualisation and labour productivity', Paper prepared for ACTU, RMIT and *The Age* Conference 'Work Interrupted: Casual and Insecure Employment in Australia', Melbourne, 2 August.

Budd, J.W., Pohler, D. and Huang, W. (2021) 'Making sense of (mis)matched frames of reference: A dynamic cognitive theory of (in)stability in HR practices', *Industrial Relations*, Available from: https://doi.org/10.1111/irel

Bulletin, The (2014) 'Burnout legally recognised in Belgium', 2 September, Available from: www.thebulletin.be/burnout-legally-recognised-belgium

Bullyonline (2021) 'Stress and health', Available from: www.timfieldfoundation.org.uk/index.php/health/6-stress-and-health

Bundesliga (2022) 'German soccer rules: 50+1 explained', Available from: www.bundesliga.com/en/news/Bundesliga/german-soccer-rules-50-1-fifty-plus-one-explained-466583.jsp

Burgen, S. (2021) 'Spanish hotel booking app to show working conditions of staff', *The Guardian*, 1 September, p 26, Available from: www.theguardian.com/world/2021/sep/01/five-stars-for-staff-working-conditions-on-new-hotel-booking-app

Buschoff, K.S. and Schmidt, C. (2009) 'Adapting labour law and social security to the needs of the new self-employed: Comparing the UK, Germany and the Netherlands', *Journal of European Social Policy*, 19(2): 147–59.

Cain, S. (2012) *Quiet: The Power of Introverts in a World that Can't Stop Talking*, London: Viking.

Caldwell, D.F. and Burger, J.M. (1998) 'Personality characteristics of job applicants and success in screening interviews', *Personnel Psychology*, 51: 119–36.

Callaghan, G. (1997) *Flexibility, Mobility and the Labour Market*, Aldershot: Ashgate.

Camuffo, A. (2002) 'The changing nature of internal labor markets', *Journal of Management and Governance*, 6(4): 281–94.

Cant, C. (2019) *Riding for Deliveroo: Resistance in the New Economy*, Cambridge: Polity.

Cappelli, P. and Keller, J.R. (2013) 'Classifying work in the new economy', *Academy of Management Review*, 38(4): 575–96.

Cappelli, P. and Neumark, D. (2001) 'Do "high performance" work practices improve establishment-level outcomes?', *Industrial and Labor Relations Review*, 54(4): 737–75.

Carney, M. (2021) *Value(s): Building a Better World for All*, Glasgow: William Collins.

Caro, E., Berntsen, L., Lillie, N. and Wagner, I. (2015) 'Posted migration and segregation in the European construction sector', *Journal of Ethnic and Migration Studies*, 41(10): 1600–20.

Carroll, A.B. (1991) 'The pyramid of corporate social responsibility: Toward the moral management of organizational stakeholders', *Business Horizons*, 34(4): 39–48.

Carter, B., Danford, A., Howcroft, D., Richardson, H., Smith, A. and Taylor, P. (2017) 'Uncomfortable truths – Teamworking under Lean in the UK', *The International Journal of Human Resource Management*, 28(3): 449–67.

Casey, B. and Gold, M. (2005) 'Peer review of labour market programmes in the European Union: What can countries really learn from one another?', *Journal of European Public Policy*, 12(1): 23–43.

Castells, M. (1996) *The Rise of the Network Society*, Oxford: Blackwell.

Castles, S. (2010) 'Understanding global migration: A social transformation perspective', *Journal of Ethnic and Migration Studies*, 36(10): 1565–86.

Cathcart, A. (2013) 'Directing democracy: Competing interests and contested terrain in the John Lewis Partnership', *Journal of Industrial Relations*, 55(4): 601–20.

Ceccagno, A. (2015) 'The mobile emplacement: Chinese migrants in Italian industrial districts', *Journal of Ethnic and Migration Studies*, 41(7): 1111–30.

Cedefop (European Centre for the Development of Vocational Training) (2018) *The Changing Nature and Role of Vocational Education and Training in Europe, Volume 3: The Responsiveness of European VET Systems to External Change (1995–2015)*, Cedefop Research Paper no 67, Luxembourg: Publications Office, Available from: http://data.europa.eu/doi/10.2801/621137

Centre for Ageing Better (2021) *Too Much Experience: Older Workers' Perceptions of Ageism in the Recruitment Process*, 23 February, Available from: www.ageing-better.org.uk/sites/default/files/2021-02/too-much-experience.pdf

Chamorro-Premuzic, T. (2015) 'Ace the assessment', *Harvard Business Review*, 93(7/8): 118–21.

Chan, C.K.C. and Hui, E.S.I. (2014) 'The development of collective bargaining in China: From collective bargaining by riot to party state-led wage bargaining', *China Quarterly*, 217: 221–42.

Chan, J. (2013) 'A suicide survivor: The life of a Chinese worker', *New Technology, Work and Employment*, 28(2): 84–99.

Chan, J., Seldon, M. and Ngai, P. (2020) *Dying for an iPhone: Apple, Foxconn and the Lives of China's Workers*, London: Pluto Press.

Chan, S. (2013) '"I am King": Financialisation and the paradox of precarious work', *Economic and Labour Relations Review*, 24(3): 362–79.

Chance, H. (2017) *The Factory in a Garden: A History of Corporate Landscapes, from the Industrial to the Digital Age*, Manchester: Manchester University Press.

Child, J. (1972) 'Organizational structure, environment and performance: The role of strategic choice', *Sociology*, 6(1): 1–22.

Child, J. (1997) 'Strategic choice in the analysis of action, structure, organizations and environment: Retrospect and prospect', *Organization Studies*, 18(1): 43–76.

Chiu, H.B. and Kirk, A.T. (2014) '"Unlimited American power": How four California newspapers covered Chinese labor and the building of the Transcontinental Railroad, 1865–1869', *American Journalism*, 31(4): 507–24.

CIPD (Chartered Institute of Personnel and Development) (2017) *To Gig or not to Gig? Stories from the Modern Economy*, Survey report, London: CIPD Publishing, Available from: www.cipd.co.uk/Images/to-gig-or-not-to-gig_2017-stories-from-the-modern-economy_tcm18-18955.pdf

CIPD (2019) *Health and Well-Being at Work*, Private sector, April, London: CIPD, Available from: www.cipd.co.uk/Images/health-and-well-being-2019-private-sector-summary_tcm18-55947.pdf

CIPD HR-inform (2020) 'The latest tribunal statistics for April to June 2018', Available from: www.hr-inform.co.uk/news-article/employment-tribunal-claims-continue-increasing-quarterly-statistics-reveal

Clarke, A.T. (2018) 'British Bobby Physiognomies: A Qualitative Approach to Comprehending the Reasons for Such Poor Representation of BMEs within the NPCC Ranks of the London Metropolitan Police Service', Doctoral thesis, Royal Holloway University of London.

Clarke, A.T. and Smith, C. (forthcoming) 'Reproducing white: The Chief Officers' Club in the Metropolitan Police Service', *Work, Employment & Society* [in submission].

Clarke, L. and Lipsig-Mummé, C. (2020) 'Future conditional: From just transition to radical transformation?', *European Industrial Relations Journal*, 26(4): 351–66.

Clegg, H. (1960) *A New Approach to Industrial Democracy*, Oxford: Basil Blackwell.

Cleverley, G. (1973) *Managers and Magic*, Harmondsworth: Penguin.

Coderre-LaPalme, G. and Greer, I. (2017) 'Dependence on a Hostile State: UK Trade Unions Before and After Brexit', in S. Lehndorff, H. Dribbusch and T. Schulten (eds) *Rough Waters: European Trade Unions in a Time of Crises*, Brussels: European Trade Union Initiative (ETUI), pp 245–70.

Cohen, J. (2020) *Not Working: Why We Have to Stop*, London: Granta.

Cohen, R.L., Hardy, K. and Valdez, Z. (2019) 'Introduction to the Special Issue: Everyday self-employment', *American Behavioral Scientist*, 63(2): 119–28.

Comer, D.R. (1995) 'A model of social loafing in real work groups', *Human Relations*, 48(6): 647–67.

Conley, H. (2008) 'The nightmare of temporary work: A comment on Fevre', *Work, Employment & Society*, 22(4): 731–6.

Conservative Central Office (1979) *The Conservative Manifesto 1979*, April, London.

Co-operatives UK Ltd (2022) 'Homepage', Available from: www.uk.coop

Coote, A., Harper, A. and Stirling, A. (2021) *The Case for a Four-Day Week*, Cambridge: Polity.

Correll, S.J., Weisshaar, K.R., Wynn, A.T. and Wehner, J.D. (2020) 'Inside the black box of organizational life: The gendered language of performance assessment', *American Sociological Review*, 85(6): 1022–50.

Cortes, P. and Pan, J. (2013) 'Outsourcing household production: Foreign domestic workers and native labor supply in Hong Kong', *Journal of Labor Economics*, 31(2): 327–71.

Cotter, D.A., Hermsen, J.M., Ovadia, S. and Vanneman, R. (2001) 'The glass ceiling effect', *Social Forces*, 80(2): 655–81.

Cradden, C. (2018) *A New Theory of Industrial Relations: People, Markets and Organizations after Neoliberalism*, New York: Routledge.

Cressey, P., Eldridge, J. and MacInnes, J. (1985) *'Just Managing': Authority and Democracy in Industry*, Milton Keynes: Open University Press.

Crompton, R. (2002) 'Employment, flexible working and the family', *British Journal of Sociology*, 53(4): 537–58.

Crouch, C. (2005a) *Capitalist Diversity and Change*, Oxford: Oxford University Press.

Crouch, C. (2005b) 'Skill Formation Systems', in S. Ackroyd, R. Batt, P. Thompson and P. Tolbert (eds) *The Oxford Handbook of Work and Organisation*, Oxford: Oxford University Press, pp 95–114.

Crouch, C., Finegold, D. and Sako, M. (1999) *Do Skills Matter? A Political Economy of Skill Formation in Advanced Societies*, Oxford: Oxford University Press.

Crouch, D. (2015) 'Ryanair closes Denmark operation to head off union row', *The Guardian*, 17 July, Available from: www.theguardian.com/business/2015/jul/17/ryanair-closes-denmark-operation-temporarily-to-sidestep-union-dispute

Crowther, T. (2021) 'Dove Launches the CROWN UK Fund to help end hair discrimination', PopSugar, 5 January, Available from: https://uk.finance.yahoo.com/news/dove-launches-crown-uk-fund-135850176.html

Cruddas, J. (2021) *The Dignity of Labour*, Cambridge: Polity.

Cumming, E. (2017) 'Shoppers must ask why goods are cheap ... they're probably made by slaves', *Evening Standard*, 20 October, pp 12–13.

Cummings, S., Bridgman, T., Hassard, J. and Rowlinson, M. (2017) *A New History of Management*, Cambridge: Cambridge University Press.

Dastin, J. (2018) 'Amazon ditched AI recruiting tool that favored men for technical jobs', Reuters, 11 October, Available from: www.reuters.com/article/us-amazon-com-jobs-automation-insight-idUSKCN1MK08G

Davidson, R. and Henderson, R. (2006) 'Electronic performance monitoring: A laboratory investigation of the influence of monitoring and difficulty on task performance, mood state, and self-reported stress levels', *Journal of Applied Social Psychology*, 30(5): 906–20.

Davies, R. and Kelly, A. (2020) 'More than £1bn wiped off Boohoo value as it investigates Leicester factory', *The Guardian*, 6 July, Available from: www.theguardian.com/business/2020/jul/06/boohoo-leicester-factory-conditions-covid-19

Deakin, S. (2006) 'The Comparative Evolution of the Employment Relationship', in G. Davidov and B. Langille (eds) *Boundaries and Frontiers of Labour Law*, Oxford: Hart, pp 89–108 [Also published as CBR Working Paper No 317, Available from: www.cbr.cam.ac.uk/wp-content/uploads/2020/08/wp317.pdf]

Delaney, H. and Casey, C. (2021) 'The promise of a four-day week? A critical appraisal of a management-led initiative', *Employee Relations: The International Journal*, 44(1): 176–90, Available from: https://doi.org/10.1108/ER-02-2021-0056

Dellot, B. and Wallace-Stephens, F. (2017) *The Age of Automation: Artificial Intelligence, Robotics and the Future of Low-Skilled Work*, September, London: Future Work Centre, Royal Society for the encouragement of Arts, Manufactures and Commerce, Available from: www.thersa.org/globalassets/pdfs/reports/rsa_the-age-of-automation-report.pdf

Deloitte (2015) *Global Human Capital Trends*, Westlake, TX: Deloitte University Press.

Deng, Y. (2012) 'Gender in factory life: An ethnographic study of migrant workers in Shenzhen Foxconn', PhD, Hong Kong Polytechnic University, Available from: https://theses.lib.polyu.edu.hk/handle/200/6959

Deutsch, B. (2014) 'Introverts are set-up for failure in job interviews', LinkedIn, 2 July, Available from: www.linkedin.com/pulse/20140701230002-7589947-introverts-are-set-up-for-failure-in-job-interviews

Diamond, W. and Freeman, R. (2001) *What Workers Want from Workplace Organisation*, London: Trades Union Congress.

Dicken, P. (2015) *Global Shift: Mapping the Changing Contours of the World Economy*, London: Sage Publications.

Dickson, T., McLachlan, H.V., Prior, P. and Swales, K. (1988) 'Big blue and the unions: IBM, individualism and trade union strategy', *Work, Employment & Society*, 2(4): 506–20.

Diez, F., Bussin, M. and Lee, V. (2020) *Fundamentals of HR Analytics: A Manual on Becoming HR Analytical*, Bingley: Emerald.

DiMaggio, P.J. and Powell, W.W. (1983) 'The iron cage revisited: Institutional isomorphism and collective rationality in organizational fields', *American Sociological Review*, 48(2): 147–60.

Dix, G., Forth, J. and Sisson, K. (2008) *Conflict at Work: The Pattern of Disputes in Britain since 1980*, ACAS Research Paper Ref 03/08, London: Advisory, Conciliation and Arbitration Service.

Dobbins, T. and Prowse, P. (eds) (2022) *The Living Wage: Advancing a Global Movement*, London: Routledge.

Doeringer, P. and Piore, M.J. (1971) *Internal Labor Markets and Manpower Analysis*, Lexington, MA: Heath.

Donaghey, J., Reinecke, J., Niforou, C. and Lawson, B. (2014) 'From employment relations to consumption relations: Balancing labor governance in global supply chains', *Human Resource Management*, 53(2): 229–52.

Doran, G.T. (1981) 'There's a SMART way to write management's goals and objectives', *Management Review*, 70(11): 35–6.

Dore, R.P. and Sako, M. (2002) *How the Japanese Learn to Work*, London: Routledge.

Dorling, D. (2020) *Slowdown: The End of the Great Acceleration – And Why It's Good for the Planet, the Economy, and Our Lives*, New Haven, CT: Yale University Press.

Doxa (2022) 'Find tech companies where female employees thrive', Available from: www.doxascore.com

Dribbusch, H., Lehndorff, S. and Schulten, T. (2017) 'Two Worlds of Unionism? German Manufacturing and Service Unions since the Great Recession', in S. Lehndorff, H. Dribbusch and T. Schulten (eds) *Rough Waters: European Trade Unions in a Time of Crisis*, Brussels: European Trade Union Institute, pp 197–220.

Drucker, P. (2006 [1954]) *The Practice of Management*, New York: Harper Business.

Drummond, D.K. (1995) *Crewe: Railway Town, Company and People, 1840–1914*, Aldershot: Scholar Press.

Dundon, T., Cullinane, N. and Wilkinson, A. (2017) *A Very Short, Fairly Interesting and Reasonably Cheap Book About Employment Relations*, London: Sage Publications.

Dundon, T., Martínez Lucio, M., Hughes, E., Howcroft, D., Keizer, A. and Walden, R. (2020) *Power, Politics and Influence at Work*, Manchester: Manchester University Press.

Du Rietz, S. (2015) 'Sweden', in L. Preuss, M. Gold and C. Rees (eds) *Corporate Social Responsibility and Trade Unions: Perspectives across Europe*, London: Routledge, pp 169–84.

Eadicicco, L. (2019) 'Companies from Microsoft to Shake Shack have experimented with a shorter, 4-day workweek – and most of the time, it's had incredible results', *Business Insider*, 10 November, Available from: www.businessinsider.com/microsoft-shake-shack-4-day-work-week-productivity-life-balance-2019-11?r=US&IR=T

Edmunds, S. (2016) 'No more "zero hours" deals for Restaurant Brands staff', Stuff.co.nz, 11 October, Available from: www.stuff.co.nz/business/industries/85183967/no-more-zero-hours-deals-for-restaurant-brands-staff

Edwards, M. and Edwards, K. (2019) *Predictive HR Analytics: Mastering the HR Metric* (2nd edn), London: Kogan Page.

Edwards, P.K. (1986) *Conflict at Work: A Materialist Analysis of Workplace Relations*, Oxford: Blackwell.

Edwards, P.K. (2018) *Conflict in the Workplace: The Concept of Structured Antagonism Reconsidered*, Warwick Papers in Industrial Relations, No 110, Coventry: Industrial Relations Research Unit, University of Warwick, Available from: http://hdl.handle.net/10419/197743

Edwards, P.K. and Scullion, H. (1982) *The Social Organization of Industrial Conflict*, Oxford: Blackwell.

Edwards, P.K. and Wajcman, J. (2005) *The Politics of Working Life*, Oxford: Oxford University Press.

Edwards, P.K. and Wright, M. (2001) 'High-involvement work systems and performance outcomes: The strength of variable, contingent and context-bound relationships', *International Journal of Human Resource Management*, 12(4): 568–85.

Edwards, R.C. (1979) *Contested Terrain: The Transformation of the Workplace in the Twentieth Century*, New York: Basic Books

EFJ (European Federation of Journalists) (2020) 'The great decline of collective bargaining in the EU in the last 20 years', 21 February, Available from: https://europeanjournalists.org/blog/2020/02/21/the-great-decline-of-collective-bargaining-in-the-eu-in-the-last-20-years

EFRA (Environment, Food and Rural Affairs Committee) (2003) *Fourteenth Report*, London: House of Commons.

Eggers, D. (2013) *The Circle*, London: Penguin Books.

EHRC (Equality and Human Rights Commission) (2010) *How Fair is Britain? First Triennial Review: Executive Summary*, London: EHRC, Available from: www.equalityhumanrights.com/sites/default/files/how-fair-is-britain-executive-summary.pdf

EHRC (2019) *Is Britain Fairer? The State of Equality and Human Rights*, June, London: EHRC, Available from: www.equalityhumanrights.com/sites/default/files/is-britain-fairer-accessible.pdf

Eisenbrey, R. (2014) 'Wage theft is a bigger problem than other theft – But not enough is done to protect workers', Economic Policy Institute, 2 April, Available from: www.epi.org/publication/wage-theft-bigger-problem-theft-protect

Eldridge, J. (1998) 'A benchmark in industrial sociology: W.G. Baldamus on *Efficiency and Effort* (1961)', *Historical Studies in Industrial Relations*, 6: 133–61.

Elger, T. and Smith, C. (2005) *Assembling Work: Remaking Factory Regimes in Japanese Multinationals in Britain*, Oxford: Oxford University Press.

Ellguth, P. and Kohaut, S. (2013) 'Tarifbindung und betriebliche Interessenvertretung: Ergebnisse aus dem IAB-Betriebspanel 2012', *WSI Mitteilungen*, 4: 281–8.

Elliott, C.S. and Long, G. (2016) 'Manufacturing rate busters: Computer control and social relations in the labour process', *Work, Employment & Society*, 30(1): 135–51.

El-Sawad, A. and Korczynski, M. (2007) 'Management and music: The exceptional case of the IBM songbook', *Group & Organization Management*, 32(1): 79–108.

Employee Benefits (2019) 'Employee retention: Top 5 reasons employees leave their jobs', 8 November, Available from: https://employeebenefits.co.uk/employee-retention-top-5-reasons-employees-leave-their-jobs

Espiner, T. (2019) 'Michael O'Leary: Ryanair's outspoken boss', BBC News, 4 February, Available from: www.bbc.co.uk/news/business-46364169

ETUI (European Union Trade Institute) (2021) *Worker Participation in Europe: The Gateway to Participation Issues in Europe*, Brussels: ETUI, Available from: www.worker-participation.eu

Eubanks, B. (2019) *Artificial Intelligence for HR: Use AI to Support and Develop a Successful Workforce*, London: Kogan Page.

Eurofound (2021) *Living and Working in Europe 2020*, Luxembourg: Publications Office of the European Union, Available from: https://skills4industry.eu/sites/default/files/2021-05/Eurofound_2021_Living%20and%20Working%20in%20Europe%202020.pdf

European Commission (2011) *A Renewed EU Strategy 2011–14 for Corporate Social Responsibility*, COM(2011) 681 Final, Brussels: European Commission.

European Commission (2021) *Statistics on Migration to Europe*, 10 December, Available from: https://ec.europa.eu/info/strategy/priorities-2019-2024/promoting-our-european-way-life/statistics-migration-europe_en

European Commission (2022) 'Database on transnational company agreements', Available from: http://ec.europa.eu/social/main.jsp?catId=978&langId=en

Eurostat (2018a) 'How common – and how voluntary – is part-time employment?', Eurostat News, 8 June, Available from: https://ec.europa.eu/eurostat/web/products-eurostat-news/-/DDN-20180608-1?inheritRedirect=true&redirect=%2Feurostat%2F

Eurostat (2018b) 'How many hours do Europeans work per week?', Eurostat News, 25 January, Available from: https://ec.europa.eu/eurostat/web/products-eurostat-news/-/DDN-20180125-1

Evans, C. and Holmes, L. (eds) (2013) *Re-Tayloring Management: Scientific Management a Century On*, Farnham: Gower.

Evju, S. (2013) 'Labour is not a commodity: Reappraising the origins of the maxim', *European Labour Law Journal*, 4(3): 222–9.

Fargues, P. (2011) 'Immigration without inclusion: Non-nationals in nation-building in the Gulf states', *Asian and Pacific Migration Journal*, 20(3–4): 273–92.

Farina, E., Green, C. and McVicar, D. (2020) 'Zero hours contracts and their growth', *British Journal of Industrial Relations*, 58(3): 507–31.

Farnham, D. (2015) *The Changing Faces of Employment Relations: Global, Comparative and Theoretical Perspectives*, London: Palgrave.

Fawcett Society (2020) 'Impact on BAME women: Pressures at work and home', News and press releases, 8 June, Available from: www.fawcettsociety.org.uk/news/impact-on-bame-women-unequal-pressures-at-work-and-home

Feldman, S. (2019) 'Who works the most hours every year?', Statista, 30 April, Available from: www.statista.com/chart/12449/who-works-the-most-hours-every-year

Felstead, A. (2022) *Remote Working: A Research Overview*, London: Routledge.

Felstead, A., Gallie, D., Green, F. and Henseke, G. (2020) 'Unpredictable times: The extent, characteristics and correlates of insecure hours of work in Britain', *Industrial Relations Journal*, 51(1–2): 34–57.

Fernández-Campbell, A. (2019) 'Elon Musk broke US labor laws on Twitter', *Vox*, 30 September, Available from: www.vox.com/identities/2019/9/30/20891314/elon-musk-tesla-labor-violation-nlrb

Festing, M. (2012) 'Strategic human resource management in Germany: Evidence of convergence to the US model, the European model, or a distinctive national model?', *Academy of Management Perspectives*, 26(2): 37–54.

Festing, M., Kornau, A. and Schäfer, L. (2015) 'Think talent – think male? A comparative case study analysis of gender inclusion in talent management practices in the German media industry', *The International Journal of Human Resource Management*, 26(6): 707–32.

Fevre, R. (2007) 'Employment insecurity and social theory: The power of nightmares', *Work, Employment & Society*, 21(3): 517–35.

Financial Times (2020a) 'What a ready-meals factory tells us about hidden inequality', 20 October, Available from: www.ft.com/content/674054ea-d8d4-40bc-95a2-bce902636654

Financial Times (2020b) 'Unilever to test 4-day working week in New Zealand', Available from: www.ft.com/content/fc3e1d5a-5abc-4de4-a1b5-b40c5c09620d

Financial Times (2021) 'Sociology not technology will decide the electric car race', Available from: www.ft.com/content/fa585fe6-3c69-4e12-b3bb-d48560fbdbb2?shareType=nongift

Findlay, A., McCollum, D., Shubin, S., Apsite, E. and Krisjane, Z. (2013) 'The role of recruitment agencies in imagining and producing the "good" migrant', *Social & Cultural Geography*, 14(2): 145–67.

Findlay, P. and McKinlay, A. (2003) 'Union organising in "Big Blue's backyard"', *Industrial Relations*, 34(1): 52–66.

Findlay, P. and Thompson, P. (2017) 'Contemporary work: Its meanings and demands', *Journal of Industrial Relations*, 59(2): 122–38.

Findlay, P. and Warhurst, C. (2012) *More Effective Skills Utilisation: Shifting the Terrain of Skills Policy in Scotland*, SKOPE Research Paper No 107, Cardiff: SKOPE, Cardiff University.

Finegold, D., Wagner, K. and Mason, G. (2000) 'National skill-creation systems and career paths for service workers: Hotels in the United States, Germany and the United Kingdom', *International Journal of Human Resource Management*, 11(3): 497–516.

Fleming, P. (2017) *The Death of Homo Economicus: Work, Debt and the Myth of Endless Accumulation*, London: Pluto Press.

Foot, M., Hook, C. and Jenkins, A. (2016) *Introducing Human Resource Management* (7th edn), Harlow: Pearson Education Ltd.

Ford, J. and Collinson, D. (2011) 'In search of the perfect manager? Work–life balance and managerial work', *Work, Employment & Society*, 25(2): 257 73.

Ford, M. (2015) *The Rise of the Robots: Technology and the Threat of a Jobless Future*, New York: Basic Books.

Forde, C. and Slater, G. (2005) 'Agency working in Britain: Character, consequences and regulation', *British Journal of Industrial Relations*, 43(2): 249–71.

Fortwengel, J., Gospel, H. and Toner, P. (2020) 'Apprenticeship schemes in new sectors especially fraught and may put apprenticeship "brand" at risk', King's College News Centre, 27 January, Available from: www.kcl.ac.uk/news/apprenticeship-schemes-new-sectors-fraught-brand-risk

Foster, W.M., Hassard, J.S., Morris, J. and Wolfram Cox, J. (2019) 'The changing nature of managerial work: The effects of corporate restructuring on management jobs and careers', *Human Relations*, 72(3): 473–504.

Fox, A. (1973) 'Industrial Relations: A Social Critique of Pluralist Ideology', in J. Child (ed) *Man and Organization: The Search for Explanation and Social Relevance*, London: George Allen & Unwin, pp 185–231.

Fox, A. (1974) *Beyond Contract: Work, Power and Trust Relations*, London: Faber and Faber.

Fox, A. (1985) *History and Heritage: The Social Origins of the British Industrial Relations System*, London: Allen & Unwin.

Fox, R. and Lynch, E. (2021) 'Employee surveillance: Getting the balance right', *Personnel Today*, 22 January, Available from: www.personneltoday.com/hr/employee-surveillance-getting-the-balance-right

France 24 (2016) 'Worked to death: Japan questions high-pressure corporate culture', 15 December, Available from: www.youtube.com/watch?v=Y0-jpm5l_dY

France 24 (2022) 'Russian invasion risks displacing more than 7 million Ukrainians, says EU crisis commissioner', 27 February, Available from: www.france24.com/en/europe/20220227-europe-must-prepare-for-millions-of-ukrainian-refugees-eu-commissioner-says

Fraser, J. and Gold, M. (2001) 'Portfolio workers: Autonomy and control amongst freelance translators', *Work, Employment & Society*, 15(4): 679–97.

Freeman, R.B. and Medoff, J.L. (1984) *What Do Unions Do?*, New York: Basic Books.

Freeman, R.E. (1984) *Strategic Management: A Stakeholder Approach*, Boston, MA: Pitman.

Frege, C., Kelly, J. and McGovern, P. (2011) 'Richard Hyman: Marxism, trade unionism and comparative employment relations', *British Journal of Industrial Relations*, 49(2): 209–30.

Frey, C.B. and Osborne, M.A. (2013) 'The future of employment: How susceptible are jobs to computerisation?', Oxford Martin Programme on Technology and Employment, 17 September, Available from: www.oxfordmartin.ox.ac.uk/downloads/academic/The_Future_of_Employment.pdf

Fried, J. and Hansson, D.H. (2018) *It Doesn't Have to Be Crazy at Work*, London: HarperCollins.

Friedman, A.L. (1977) *Industry and Labour: Class Struggle at Work and Monopoly Capitalism*, London: Macmillan.

Friedman, M. (1970) 'A Friedman doctrine – "The social responsibility of business is to increase its profits"', *The New York Times*, 13 September, Available from: www.nytimes.com/1970/09/13/archives/a-friedman-doctrine-the-social-responsibility-of-business-is-to.html

Fuchs, C. (2014) *Digital Labour and Karl Marx*, London: Routledge.

Fudge, J. (2017) 'The future of the standard employment relationship: Labour law, new institutional economics and old power resource theory', *Journal of Industrial Relations*, 59(3): 374–92.

Fuller, L. and Smith, V. (1991) 'Consumers' reports: Management by customers in a changing economy', *Work, Employment & Society*, 5(1): 1–16.

Furtado, J.V., Moreira, A.C. and Mota, J. (2021) 'Gender affirmative action and management: A systematic literature review on how diversity and inclusion management affect gender equity in organizations', *Behavioral Sciences*, 11(2), Available from: https://doi.org/10.3390/bs11020021

Gall, G. (2011) 'Contemporary workplace occupations in Britain: Motivations, stimuli, dynamics and outcomes', *Employee Relations*, 33(6): 607–23.

Gandini, A. (2015) 'The rise of co-working spaces: A literature review', *Ephemera. Theory and Politics in Organization*, 15(1): 193–205.

Gandini, A. (2016) *The Reputation Economy: Understanding Knowledge Work in Digital Society*, London: Springer.

Gardiner, L. and Corlett, A. (2015) 'Looking through the hourglass: Hollowing out of the UK jobs market pre- and post-crisis', PowerPoint presentation, March, London: Resolution Foundation, Available from: www.resolutionfoundation.org

Gearhart, D. (2017) 'Giving Uber Drivers a Voice in the Gig Economy', in M. Graham and J. Shaw (eds) *Towards a Fairer Gig Economy*, London: Meatspace Press, pp 13–15.

Geary, J.F. (1992) 'Employment flexibility and human resource management: The case of three American electronics plants', *Work, Employment & Society*, 6(2): 251–70.

Geddes, A., Craig, G., Scott, S., Ackers, L., Robinson, O. and Scullion, D. (2013) *Forced Labour in the UK*, York: Joseph Rowntree Foundation.

Geissler, H. (2018) *Seasonal Associate*, South Pasadena, CA: Semiotext(e).

Geppert, M., Williams, K. and Wortmann, M. (2015) 'Micro-political game playing in Lidl: A comparison of store-level employment relations', *European Journal of Industrial Relations*, 21(3): 241–57.

Gerth, H.H. and Mills, C.W. (eds) (2014 [1947]) *From Max Weber: Essays in Sociology*, London: Routledge.

Giannangeli, M. and Douglas, H. (2013) 'Strikes during coalition government's reign have cost British economy £400m', *Daily Express*, 20 October.

Gilbert, J.A., Stead, B.A. and Ivancevich, J.M. (1999) 'Diversity management: A new organizational paradigm', *Journal of Business Ethics*, 21(1): 61–76.

Gillett, F. (2021) 'Lorry driver shortage: Government to lift rules on foreign haulier deliveries', BBC News, 15 October, Available from: www.bbc.co.uk/news/uk-58921498

Gilmore, S. and Williams, S. (2013) *Human Resource Management*, Oxford: Oxford University Press

Ginn, J., Arber, S., Brannen, J., Dale, A., Dex, S., Elias, P., et al (1996) 'Feminist fallacies: A reply to Hakim on women's employment', *The British Journal of Sociology*, 47(1): 167–74.

Gittell, J.H. and Bamber, G.J. (2010) 'High- and low-road strategies for competing on costs and their implications for employment relations: International studies in the airline industry', *International Journal of Human Resource Management*, 21(2): 165–79.

GLAA (Gangmasters and Labour Abuse Authority) (2021) *Annual Report and Accounts, 1 April 2019 to 31 March 2020*, HC 1099, 10 February, Nottingham: GLAA, Available from: www.gla.gov.uk/media/6843/glaa-annual-report-and-accounts-2019-20-web-accessible-version-100221-dated-7-january.pdf

Glaser, K., Stuchbury, R., Price, D., Di Gessa, G., Ribe, E. and Tinker, A. (2018) 'Trends in the prevalence of grandparents living with grandchild(ren) in selected European countries and the United States', *European Journal of Ageing*, 15(3): 237–50.

Glassdoor (2021) 'Companies and reviews', Available from: www.glassdoor.com/Reviews/company-reviews.htm

Godard, J. (2001) 'High performance and the transformation of work? The implications of alternative work practices for the experience and outcomes of work', *Industrial and Labor Relations Review*, 54(4): 776–805.

Godard, J. (2004) 'A critical assessment of the high-performance paradigm', *British Journal of Industrial Relations*, 42(2): 349–78.

Goffman, E. (1973) *Asylums: Essays on the Social Situation of Mental Patients and Other Inmates*, Harmondsworth: Pelican.

Goffman, E. (1974) *The Presentation of Self in Everyday Life*, Harmondsworth: Pelican.

Gold, M. (2004) 'Worker mobilization in the 1970s: Revisiting work-ins, co-operatives and alternative corporate plans', *Historical Studies in Industrial Relations*, 18(1): 65–106.

Gold, M. (2008) 'A silent revolution? The role of trade union trustees in occupational pension funds in the UK: Lessons from the 1970s and 1980s', *Historical Studies in Industrial Relations*, 25/26(1): 141–76.

Gold, M. (2009) 'Overview of EU Employment Policy', in M. Gold (ed) *Employment Policy in the European Union: Origins, Themes and Prospects*, Basingstoke: Palgrave Macmillan, pp 1–26.

Gold, M. (2010) 'Employee participation in the EU: The long and winding road to legislation', *Economic and Industrial Democracy*, 31(4s): 9–23.

Gold, M. (2011) '"Taken on board": An evaluation of the influence of employee board-level representatives on company decision-making across Europe', *European Journal of Industrial Relations*, 17(1): 41–56.

Gold, M. (2017) 'The European Union: A Case of Advanced Regional Integration', in T. Edwards and C. Rees (eds) *International Human Resource Management*, London: Prentice Hall, pp 46–68.

Gold, M. (2020) '"Frames of reference" in Victorian England: What Elizabeth Gaskell's *North and South* reveals about perceptions of the employment relationship', *Journal of Industrial Relations*, 63(2): 126–48.

Gold, M. and Artus, I. (2015) 'Employee Participation in Germany: Tensions and Challenges', in S. Johnstone and P. Ackers (eds) *Finding a Voice? New Perspectives on Employment Relations*, Oxford: Oxford University Press, pp 193–217.

Gold, M. and Mustafa, M. (2013) '"Work always wins": Client colonisation, the erosion of work–life boundaries and the anxieties of self-employed teleworkers', *New Technology, Work and Employment*, 28(3): 197–211

Gold, M. and Rees, C. (2018) *Direct Participation in the UK: Country Report*, Direct Project VS/2016/0305, Brussels: European Commission – DG Employment, Social Affairs and Inclusion.

Gold, M. and Waddington, J. (2019) 'Introduction: Board-level employee representation in Europe: State of play', *European Journal of Industrial Relations*, 25(3): 205–18.

Gold, M., Preuss, L. and Rees, C. (2020) 'Moving out of the comfort zone? Trade union revitalization and corporate social responsibility', *Journal of Industrial Relations*, 62(1): 132–55.

Goodhart, D. (2020) *Head, Hand, Heart: The Struggle for Dignity and Status in the 21st Century*, London: Allen Lane.

Goodrich, C.L. (1975 [1920]) *The Frontier of Control: A Study in British Workshop Politics*, London: Pluto Press.

Gordon, M.E. and Stewart, L.P. (2009) 'Conversing about performance: Discursive resources for the appraisal interview', *Management Communication Quarterly*, 22(3): 473–501.

Gospel, H. and Palmer, G. (1993) *British Industrial Relations*, London: Routledge.

Gouldner, A.W. (1955) *Patterns of Industrial Bureaucracy*, London: Routledge & Kegan Paul.

Gouldner, A.W. (1965) *Wildcat Strike*, New York: Harper & Row.

GOV.UK (2021) 'Government set to bolster supply chains by extending cabotage rights', Available from: www.gov.uk/government/news/government-set-to-bolster-supply-chains-by-extending-cabotage-rights

GOV.UK (2022) 'Writing about ethnicity', Available from: www.ethnicity-facts-figures.service.gov.uk/style-guide/writing-about-ethnicity

Gow, D. (2003) 'Dyson profits from Malaysian move', *The Guardian*, 8 November, Available from: www.theguardian.com/business/2003/nov/08/4

Grabke-Rundell, A. and Gomez-Mejia, L.R. (2002) 'Power as a determinant of executive compensation', *Human Resource Management Review*, 12(1): 3–23.

Graeber, D. (2018) *Bullshit Jobs: A Theory*, London: Allen Lane.

Graham, M., Woodcock, J., Heeks, R., Mungai, P., van Belle, J.P., du Toit, D., et al (2020) 'The Fairwork Foundation: Strategies for improving platform work in a global context', *Geoforum*, 112: 100–3.

Granovetter, M. (1973) 'The strength of weak ties', *American Journal of Sociology*, 78(6): 1360–80.

Granovetter, M. (1983) 'The strength of weak ties: A network theory revisited', *Sociological Theory*, 1(1): 201–33.

Granovetter, M. (1995 [1974]) *Getting a Job: A Study of Contacts and Careers*, Chicago, IL: University of Chicago Press.

Green, A.E., De Hoyos, M., Li, Y. and Owen, D. (2011) *Job Search Study: Literature Review and Analysis of the Labour Force Survey*, Department for Work and Pensions Research Report, 726, London: Department for Work and Pensions.

Green, F. (2016) *Skills Demand, Training and Skills Mismatch: A Review of Key Concepts, Theory and Evidence*, August, London: Foresight, Government Office for Science, Available from: https://assets.publishing.service.gov.uk/government/uploads/system/uploads/attachment_data/file/571667/ER4_Skills_Demand__Training_and_Skills_Mismatch_A_Review_of_Key_Concepts__Theory_and_Evidence.pdf

Green, F., Machin, S. and Wilkinson, D. (1999) 'Trade unions and training practices in British workplaces', *ILR Review*, 52(2): 179–95.

GRI (Global Reporting Initiative) (2022) *A Short Introduction to the GRI Standards*, Amsterdam: GRI, Available from: www.globalreporting.org/media/wtaf14tw/a-short-introduction-to-the-gri-standards.pdf

Grimshaw, D., Marchington, M., Rubery, J. and Willmott, H. (2005) 'Introduction: Fragmenting Work across Organizational Boundaries', in D. Grimshaw, M. Marchington, J. Rubery and H. Willmott (eds) *Fragmenting Work: Blurring Organizational Boundaries and Disordering Hierarchies*, Oxford: Oxford University Press, pp 1–38.

Grimshaw, D., Ward, K.G., Rubery, J. and Beynon, H. (2001) 'Organisations and the transformation of the internal labour market', *Work, Employment & Society*, 15(1): 25–54.

Grint, K. (1993) 'What's wrong with performance appraisals? A critique and a suggestion', *Human Resource Management Journal*, 3(3): 61–77.

Grugulis, I. (2017) *A Very Short, Fairly Interesting and Reasonably Cheap Book About Human Resource Management*, London: Sage Publications.

Guest, D.E. (2002) 'Perspectives on the study of work–life balance', *Social Science Information*, 41(2): 255–79.

Guest, D.E. (2011) 'Human resource management and performance: Still searching for some answers', *Human Resource Management Journal*, 21(1): 3–13.

Gumbrell-McCormick, R. and Hyman, R. (2013) *Trade Unions in Western Europe: Hard Times, Hard Choices*, Oxford: Oxford University Press.

Hadjisolomou, A. (2021) 'Customer abuse in the era of COVID-19: A comparative analysis between the UK and Cyprus food retail sector', Paper to the 2021 ILPC Conference, Available from: www.ilpc.org.uk

Hakim, C. (1995) 'Five feminist myths about women's employment', *British Journal of Sociology*, 46(3): 429–55.

Hakim, C. (2002) 'Lifestyle preferences as determinants of women's differentiated labor market careers', *Work and Occupations*, 29(4): 428–59.

Hall, M. and Purcell, J. (2012) *Consultation at Work: Regulation and Practice*, Oxford: Oxford University Press.

Hall, P.A. and Soskice, D. (2001) 'An Introduction to Varieties of Capitalism', in P.A. Hall and D. Soskice (eds) *Varieties of Capitalism: The Institutional Foundations of Comparative Advantage*, Oxford: Oxford University Press, pp 1–68.

Hallett, N. (2018) 'The problem of wage theft', *Yale Law & Policy Review*, 37(1): 93–152.

Hamilton, R.H. and Sodeman, W.A. (2020) 'The questions we ask: Opportunities and challenges for using big data analytics to strategically manage human capital resources', *Business Horizons*, 63: 85–95.

Hammer, N. and Plugor, R. (2016) 'Near-sourcing UK apparel: Value chain restructuring, productivity and the informal economy', *Industrial Relations Journal*, 47(5–6): 402–16.

Hammer, N., Plugor, R., Nolan, P. and Clark, I. (2015) *A New Industry on a Skewed Playing Field: Supply Chain Relations and Working Conditions in UK Garment Manufacturing*, Leicester: Centre for Sustainable Work and Employment Futures, University of Leicester.

Hancké, B., Rhodes, M. and Thatcher, M. (2007) *Beyond Varieties of Capitalism: Conflict, Contradictions, and Complementarities in the European Economy*, Oxford: Oxford University Press.

Hann, D. and Nash, D. (2020) *Disputes and Their Management in the Workplace: A Survey of British Employers*, ACAS, 30 April, Available from: https://orca.cardiff.ac.uk/132931/1/Published%20Report.pdf

Hannah, L. (2007) 'The "divorce" of ownership from control from 1900 onwards: Re-calibrating imagined global trends', *Business History*, 49: 404–38.

Haraszti, M. (1977) *A Worker in a Worker's State*, Harmondsworth: Pelican Books.

Hare, D. (1999) '"Push" versus "Pull" Factors in Migration Outflows and Returns: Determinants of Migration Status and Spell Duration Among China's Rural Population', in S. Cook and M. Maurer-Fazio (eds) *The Workers' State Meets the Market: Labour in China's Transition*, London: Frank Cass, pp 45–72.

Harris, J. (2021) 'Homeworking sounds good – Until your job takes over your life', *The Guardian*, 7 March, Available from: www.theguardian.com/commentisfree/2021/mar/07/homeworking-job-takes-over-life-office-grind-remote-working

Harris, N. (2007) 'The Economics and Politics of the Free Movement of People', in A. Pécoud and P. de Guchteneire (eds) *Migration without Borders: Essays on the Free Movement of People*, Paris and New York/Oxford: UNESCO Publishing and Berghahn Books, pp 33–50, Available from: www.auca.kg/uploads/Migration_Database/Publications/MWB_PDF-libre.pdf_eng.pdf

Harvey, D. (2005) *Neoliberalism: A Brief History*, Oxford: Oxford University Press.

Harvey, G. and Turnbull, P. (2015) 'Can labor arrest the "sky pirates"? Transnational trade unionism in the European civil aviation industry', *Labor History*, 56(3): 308–26.

Harvey, G., Turnbull, P. and Wintersberger, D. (2021) 'Has labour paid for the liberalisation of European civil aviation?', *Journal of Air Transport Management*, 90, Available from: https://doi.org/10.1016/j.jairtraman.2020.101968

Hassard, J.S. (2012) 'Rethinking the Hawthorne Studies: The Western Electric research in its social, political and historical context', *Human Relations*, 65(11): 1431–61.

Haughey, D. (2014) 'A brief history of SMART goals', ProjectSmart, 13 December, Available from: www.projectsmart.co.uk/brief-history-of-smart-goals.php

Haunschild, A. and Krause, F. (2015) 'Germany', in L. Preuss, M. Gold and C. Rees (eds) *Corporate Social Responsibility and Trade Unions: Perspectives across Europe*, London: Routledge, pp 66–82.

Heiland, H. (2020) *Workers' Voice in Platform Labour: An Overview*, WSI Studies 21, Düsseldorf: The Institute of Economic and Social Research (WSI), Hans Böckler Foundation.

Heery, E. (2016) *Framing Work: Unitary, Pluralist, and Critical Perspectives in the Twenty-first Century*, Oxford: Oxford University Press.

Henley Business School (2019) 'Four better or four worse?', Available from: https://assets.henley.ac.uk/defaultUploads/Four-Better-Four-Worse-Henley-Business-School.pdf?mtime=20190701093655

Hermann, C. (2017) 'Crisis, structural reform and the dismantling of the European Social Model(s)', *Economic and Industrial Democracy*, 38(1): 51–68.

Hirschman, A.O. (1970) *Exit, Voice, and Loyalty: Responses to Decline in Firms, Organizations and States*, Cambridge, MA: Harvard University Press.

Hochschild, A.R. (2012 [1983]) *The Managed Heart: Commercialization of Human Feeling*, Los Angeles, CA: University of California Press.

Hodal, K., Kelly, C., Lawrence, F., Stuart, C., Remy, T., Baqué, I., Carson, M. and O'Kane, M. (2014) 'Slave labour in Thai prawn fishing industry', *The Guardian*, 10 June, Available from: www.theguardian.com/global-development/video/2014/jun/10/slavery-supermarket-supply-trail-prawns-video

Hodder, A. (2020) 'New technology, work and employment in the era of COVID-19: Reflecting on legacies of research', *New Technology, Work and Employment*, 35(3): 262–75.

Hodson, R. (1995) 'Worker resistance: An underdeveloped concept in the sociology of work', *Economic and Industrial Democracy*, 16(1): 79–110.

Hodson, R. (2001) *Dignity at Work*, Cambridge: Cambridge University Press.

Holgate, J. (2021) *Arise: Power, Strategy and Union Resurgence*, London: Pluto Press.

Hooley, G., Broderick, A. and Moller, K. (1998) 'Competitive positioning and the resource-based view of the firm', *Journal of Strategic Marketing*, 6(2): 97–115.

Hoque, K. and Bacon, N. (2008) 'Trade unions, union learning representatives and employer-provided training in Britain', *British Journal of Industrial Relations*, 46(4): 702–31.

Hosford, M., Effron, L. and Battiste, N. (2012) 'Air France Flight 447 crash "didn't have to happen", expert says, ABC News, 5 July, Available from: https://abcnews.go.com/Blotter/air-france-flight-447-crash-didnt-happen-expert/story?id=16717404

House of Commons (2016a) *BHS. First Report of the Work and Pensions Committee and Fourth Report of the Business, Innovation and Skills Committee of Session 2016–17*, HC54, 25 July, Available from: www.publications.parliament.uk/pa/cm201617/cmselect/cmworpen/54/54.pdf?utm_source=54&utm_medium=module&utm_campaign=modulereports

House of Commons (2016b) *Employment Practices at Sports Direct, Third Report of Session 2016–17 of the Business, Innovation and Skills Committee*, HC219, 22 July, Available from: www.publications.parliament.uk/pa/cm201617/cmselect/cmbis/219/219.pdf?utm_source=219&utm_medium=module&utm_campaign=modulereports

House of Commons (2019) *Automation and the Future of Work, Twenty-third Report of Session 2017–19*, Business, Energy and Industrial Strategy Committee, HC 1093, 18 September, Available from: https://publications.parliament.uk/pa/cm201719/cmselect/cmbeis/1093/1093.pdf

Houssart, J. (2013) '"Give me a lesson and I'll deliver it": Teaching assistants' experiences of leading primary mathematics lessons in England', *Cambridge Journal of Education*, 43(1): 1–16.

Howlett, E. (2019) 'Two decades on, has the minimum wage worked?', *People Management*, 28 September, Available from: www.peoplemanagement.co.uk/long-reads/articles/two-decades-minimum-wage-worked#gref

Howlett, E. (2021) 'Wellbeing classes do not improve workers' mental health, research suggests', *People Management*, 26 August, Available from: www.peoplemanagement.co.uk/news/articles/wellbeing-classes-do-not-improve-workers-mental-health-research-suggests

Huang, X. (2008) 'Guanxi networks and job searches in China's emerging labour market: A qualitative investigation', *Work, Employment & Society*, 22(3): 467–84.

Hughes, E. and Dobbins, T. (2020) 'Frontier of control struggles in British and Irish transport', *European Journal of Industrial Relations*, Available from: https://doi.org/10.1177/0959680120929137

Huselid, M.A. (1995) 'The impact of human resource management practices on turnover, productivity, and corporate financial performance', *Academy of Management Journal*, 38(3): 635–72.

Huselid, M.A. (2018) 'The science and practice of workforce analytics: Introduction to the HRM Special Issue', *Human Resource Management*, 57(3): 679–84.

Hyman, R. (1975) *Industrial Relations: A Marxist Introduction*, London: Macmillan.

Hyman, R. (1987) 'Strategy or structure? Capital, labour and control', *Work, Employment & Society*, 1(1): 25–55.

Hyman, R. (1989) *Strikes*, Basingstoke: Palgrave Macmillan.

Iannuzzi, F.E. and Sacchetto, D. (2020) 'Outsourcing and workers' resistance practices in Venice's hotel industry: The role of migrants employed by cooperatives', *Economic and Industrial Democracy*, Available from: https://doi.org/10.1177/0143831X20960227

Ibsen, C.L. and Tapia, M. (2017) 'Trade union revitalisation: Where are we now? Where to next?', *Journal of Industrial Relations*, 59(2): 170–91.

Icebreaker (2008a) 'Transparent Supply Chain – Chapter 4: Fabric', Available from: www.youtube.com/watch?v=w31knfaMzkE

Icebreaker (2008b) 'Transparent Supply Chain – Chapter 5: Sewing', Available from: www.youtube.com/watch?v=lUstiZBvs5w

IER (Institute of Employment Rights) (2021) 'One in five going into workplace unnecessarily, as bosses pile on pressure', 12 February, Available from: www.ier.org.uk/news/one-in-five-going-into-workplace-unnecessarily-as-bosses-pile-on-pressure

ILM (Institute of Leadership and Management) (2021) 'Should UK boardrooms have tougher gender quotas?', March, Available from: www.institutelm.com/resourceLibrary/should-uk-boardrooms-have-tougher-gender-quotas.html

ILO (International Labour Organization) (2020) *World Employment and Social Outlook: Trends 2020*, Geneva: ILO, Available from: www.ilo.org/wcmsp5/groups/public/---dgreports/---dcomm/---publ/documents/publication/wcms_734455.pdf

ILO (2021) 'Home page', Available from: www.ilo.org/global/lang--en/index.htm

IndustriALL Global Union (2019) 'Five reasons to join a union', 1 February, Available from: www.industriall-union.org/5-reasons-to-join-a-union

Inside Higher Ed (2018) 'A non-tenure-track profession?, Available from: www.insidehighered.com/news/2018/10/12/about-three-quarters-all-faculty-positions-are-tenure-track-according-new-aaup

Interaction Institute for Social Change (2016) 'Illustrating equality vs equity', 13 January, Available from: https://interactioninstitute.org/illustrating-equality-vs-equity

International Labour Office (2014) *Profits and Poverty: The Economics of Forced Labour*, Geneva: International Labour Office, Available from: www.ilo.org/wcmsp5/groups/public/---ed_norm/---declaration/documents/publication/wcms_243391.pdf

IOM (International Organization for Migration) (2020) *World Migration Report 2020*, Available from: www.un.org/sites/un2.un.org/files/wmr_2020.pdf

ISO (International Organization for Standardization) (2021) *Discovering ISO 26000*, Available from: www.iso.org/files/live/sites/isoorg/files/store/en/PUB100258.pdf

Jackson, S., Schuler, R. and Werner, S. (2017) *Managing Human Resources* (12th edn), Oxford: Oxford University Press.

Jacobs, H. (2018) 'Inside "iPhone City", the massive Chinese factory town where half the world's iPhones are produced', *Business Insider*, 7 May, Available from: www.businessinsider.com/apple-iphone-factory-foxconn-china-photos-tour-2018-5?r=US&IR=T

Jacobson, J. and Gruzd, A. (2020) 'Cybervetting job applicants on social media: The new normal?', *Ethics and Information Technology*, 22: 175–95.

Jacoby, S.M. (1997) *Modern Manors: Welfare Capitalism since the New Deal*, Princeton, NJ: Princeton University Press.

James, P. (ed) (2021) *HSE and Covid at Work: A Case of Regulatory Failure*, London: Institute of Employment Rights.

Jamieson, B.D. (1973) 'Behavioral problems with management by objectives', *Academy of Management Journal*, 16(3): 496–505.

Jenkins, C. and Sherman, B. (1979) *The Collapse of Work*, London: Eyre Methuen.

Jenkins, C. and Sherman, B. (1981) *The Leisure Shock*, London: Eyre Methuen.

Jiang, K., Lepak, D.P., Hu, J. and Baer, J.C. (2012) 'How does human resource management influence organizational outcomes? A meta-analytical investigation of mediating mechanisms', *Academy of Management Journal*, 55(6): 1264–94.

Johnson, A.G. and Whyte, W.F. (1977) 'The Mondragón system of worker production cooperatives', *Industrial and Labor Relations Review*, 31(1): 18–30.

Johnstone, S. and Ackers, P. (eds) (2015) *Finding a Voice at Work? New Perspectives on Employment Relations*, Oxford: Oxford University Press.

Jolly, J. (2021) 'Rolls Royce reports £4bn loss as Covid crisis shakes jet-engine maker', *The Guardian*, 11 March. Available from: www.theguardian.com/business/2021/mar/11/rolls-royce-reports-4bn-loss-as-covid-crisis-shakes-jet-engine-maker

Joyce, W.B. (1999) 'On the free-rider problem in cooperative learning', *Journal of Education for Business*, 74(5): 271–4.

Jung, C.G. (2016 [1923]) *Psychological Types; or the Psychology of Individuation*, London: Routledge Classics.

Jürgens, U. and Krzywdzinski, M. (2016) *New Worlds of Work: Varieties of Work in Car Factories in the BRIC Countries*, Oxford: Oxford University Press.

Kalleberg, A.L. (2011) *Good Jobs, Bad Jobs: The Rise of Polarized and Precarious Employment Systems in the United States, 1970s–2000s*, New York: Russell Sage Foundation.

Kalleberg, A.L. (2018) *Precarious Lives: Job Insecurity and Well-Being in Rich Democracies*, London: John Wiley & Sons.

Kang, N. and Moon, J. (2012) 'Institutional complementarity between corporate governance and corporate social responsibility: A comparative institutional analysis of three capitalisms', *Socio-Economic Review*, 10(1): 85–108.

Kaplan, J. and Kiersz, A. (2021) 'Inside the rise of "antiwork," a workers' strike that wants to turn the labor shortage into the new American Dream', *Business Insider*, 25 November, Available from: www.businessinsider.com/what-is-antiwork-workers-quit-dont-work-strike-better-conditions-2021-11?r=US&IR=T

Kara, S. (2017) *Modern Slavery: A Global Perspective*, New York: Columbia University Press.

Karamessini, M. (2008) 'Continuity and change in the southern European social model', *International Labour Review*, 147(1): 43–70.

Kasmir, S. (1996) *The Myth of Mondragón: Cooperatives, Politics, and Working Class Life in a Basque Town*, New York: State University of New York Press.

Kassam, A. (2021) 'Spain's public sector trailblazers seek to lead way on menstrual leave', *The Guardian*, 30 December, Available from: www.theguardian.com/world/2021/dec/30/spain-public-sector-trailblazers-seek-lead-way-menstrual-leave

Kaufman, B.E. (2014) *The Development of Human Resource Management across Nations*, Cheltenham: Edward Elgar.

Kaufman, B.E., Barry, M., Wilkinson, A., Lomas, G. and Gomez, R. (2021) 'Using unitarist, pluralist, and radical frames to map the cross-section distribution of employment relations across workplaces: A four-country empirical investigation of patterns and determinants', *Journal of Industrial Relations*, 63(2): 204–34.

Kee, D., Jun, G.T., Waterson, P. and Haslam, R. (2017) 'A systemic analysis of South Korea Sewol ferry accident – Striking a balance between learning and accountability', *Applied Ergonomics*, 59: 504–16.

Kelliher, C. and Anderson, D. (2010) 'Doing more with less? Flexible working practices and the intensification of work', *Human Relations*, 63(1): 83–106.

Kelly, E. and Dobbin, F. (1998) 'How affirmative action became diversity management: Employer response to antidiscrimination law, 1961 to 1996', *American Behavioral Scientist*, 41(7): 960–84.

Kelly, J. (1998) *Rethinking Industrial Relations: Mobilization, Collectivism and Long Waves*, London: Routledge.

Kelly, J. (2004) 'Social partnership agreements in Britain: Labor cooperation and compliance', *Industrial Relations*, 43(1): 267–92.

Kennedy, S. (2015) 'Supermarkets launch investigations over migrant exploitation', Channel 4 News, 19 October, Available from: www.channel4.com/news/supermarkets-exploitation-investigation-launched

Kersley, B., Oxenbridge, S., Dix, G., Bewley, H., Bryson, A., Forth, J. and Alpin, C. (2006) *Inside the Workplace: Findings from the 2004 Workplace Employment Relations Survey*, London: Department of Trade and Industry.

Kessler, S. (2018) *Gigged: The End of the Job and the Future of Work*, New York: St Martin's Press.

Keynes, J.M. (1931) 'Economic Possibilities for Our Grandchildren', in J.M. Keynes (ed) *Essays in Persuasion*, London: Macmillan, pp 358–74.

Khan, F.R. and Lund-Thomsen, P. (2011) 'CSR as imperialism: Towards a phenomenological approach to CSR in the developing world', *Journal of Change Management*, 11(1): 73–90.

Kimberley, J. (2016) 'Edward Cadbury: An Egalitarian Employer and Supporter of Working Women's Campaigns', in P. Ackers and A.J. Reid (eds) *Alternatives to State Socialism in Britain: Other Worlds of Labour in the Twentieth Century*, London: Palgrave Macmillan, pp 153–77.

Kitchin, R. (2017) 'Thinking critically about and researching algorithms', *Information, Communication & Society*, 20(1): 14–29.

Klein, N. (2008) *The Shock Doctrine: The Rise of Disaster Capitalism*, New York: Random House.

Kleinman, Z. (2019) 'Microsoft four-day work week "boosts productivity"', BBC News, 4 November, Available from: www.bbc.co.uk/news/technology-50287391

Kling, M.-U. (2020) *QualityLand*, London: Orion Fiction.

Knight, J., Song, L. and Huaibib, J. (1999) 'Chinese Rural Migrants in Urban Enterprises: Three Perspectives', in S. Cook and M. Maurer-Fazio (eds) *The Workers' State Meets the Market: Labour in China's Transition*, London: Frank Cass, pp 73–104.

Ko, W.W. and Liu, G. (2017) 'Overcoming the liability of smallness by recruiting through networks in China: A Guanxi-based social capital perspective', *International Journal of Human Resource Management*, 28(11): 1499–526.

Konrad, A.M. and Linnehan, F. (1995) 'Formalized HRM structures: Coordinating equal employment opportunity or concealing organizational practices?', *Academy of Management Journal*, 38(3): 787–820.

Korczynski, M. (2001) 'The Contradictions of Service Work: Call Centre as Customer-Oriented Bureaucracy', in A. Sturdy, I. Grugulis and H. Willmott (eds) *Customer Service: Empowerment and Entrapment*, London: Macmillan, pp 79–101.

Korczynski, M. (2002) *Human Resource Management in the Service Sector*, Basingstoke: Macmillan.

Kornai, J. (1992) *The Socialist System: The Political Economy of Communism*, Princeton, NJ: Princeton University Press.

Korpi, T. (2001) 'Good friends in bad times? Social networks and job search among the unemployed in Sweden', *Acta Sociologica*, 44(2): 157–70.

Kossmann, R.W. (2016) *Effectiveness of Social Capital in the Job Search Process*, SOEP Papers on Multidisciplinary Panel Data Research, No 823, Berlin: Deutsches Institut für Wirtschaftsforschung, Available from: http://hdl.handle.net/10419/130577

Koumenta, M. and Williams, M. (2019) 'An anatomy of zero-hour contracts in the UK', *Industrial Relations Journal*, 50(1): 20–40.

Krzywdzinski, M. (2021) 'Automation, digitalization, and changes in occupational structures in the automobile industry in Germany, Japan, and the United States: A brief history from the early 1990s until 2018', *Industrial and Corporate Change*, 30(3): 499–535, Available from: https://doi.org/10.1093/icc/dtab019

Kuhn, K.M. and Maleki, A. (2017) 'Micro-entrepreneurs, dependent contractors, and instaserfs: Understanding online labor platform workforces', *Academy of Management Perspectives*, 31(3): 183–200.

Kunda, G. (2006 [1992]) *Engineering Culture: Control and Commitment in a High-Tech Corporation*, Philadelphia, PA: Temple University Press.

Labour Behind the Label (2020) *Boohoo and Covid-19: The People Behind the Profits*, Available from: https://labourbehindthelabel.org/report-boohoo-covid-19-the-people-behind-the-profit

Lawler, E.E., Mohrman, S.A. and Benson, G.S. (2001) *Organizing for High Performance: The CEO Report on Employee Involvement, TQM, and Re-Engineering, and Knowledge Management in Fortune 1000 Corporations*, San Francisco, CA: Jossey-Bass.

Lawrie, E. (2017) 'Job perks: Are these the best freebies in the world?', BBC News, 27 September, Available from: www.bbc.co.uk/news/business-40976787

Lazonick, W. (2009) 'The new economy business model and the crisis of US capitalism', *Capitalism and Society*, 4(2): 1–70.

Leadbeater, C. (1999) *Living on Thin Air: The New Economy*, London: Viking/Penguin.

Leahy, M. and Doughney, J. (2006) 'Women, work and preference formation: A critique of Catherine Hakim's preference theory', *Journal of Business Systems, Governance and Ethics*, 1(1): 37–48.

Legge, K. (2005) *Human Resource Management: Rhetoric and Realities*, Basingstoke: Palgrave Macmillan.

Lehndorff, S., Dribbusch, H. and Schulten, T. (eds) (2017) *Rough Waters. European Trade Unions in a Time of Crises*, Brussels: ETUI.

Leidner, R. (1993) *Fast Food, Fast Talk: Service Work and the Routinization of Everyday Life*, Berkeley, CA: University of California Press.

Leighton, P. and McKeown, T. (2020) *Work in Challenging and Uncertain Times: The Changing Employment Relationship*, London: Routledge.

Leonardi, S. and Pedersini, R. (eds) (2018) *Multi-Employer Bargaining under Pressure: Decentralisation Trends in Five European Countries*, Brussels: ETUI.

Lepak, D.P. and Snell, S.A. (1999) 'The human resource architecture: Towards a theory of human capital allocation and development', *Academy of Management Review*, 24(1): 31–48.

Levenson, A. (2018) 'Using workforce analytics to improve strategy execution', *Human Resource Management*, 57(3): 685–700.

Levitt, A. (2020) *Independent Review into the Boohoo Group PLC's Leicester Supply Chain*, 24 September, Available from: www.boohooplc.com/sites/boohoo-corp/files/final-report-open-version-24.9.2020.pdf

Lewis, M. (2003) *Moneyball: The Art of Winning an Unfair Game*, New York: Norton & Co.

Lewis, P., Thornhill, A. and Saunders, M. (2003) *Employee Relations: Understanding the Employment Relationship*, London: FT/Prentice Hall.

Liao, H., Toya, K., Lepak, D. and Hong, Y. (2009) 'Do they see eye to eye? Management and employee perspectives of high-performance work systems and influence processes on service quality', *Journal of Applied Psychology*, 94(2): 371–91.

Lin, N. (1999) 'Social networks and status attainment', *Annual Review of Sociology*, 25: 467–87.

Lin, N. (2000) 'Inequality in social capital', *Contemporary Sociology*, 29: 785–95.

Lindbeck, A. and Snower, D.J. (2001) 'Insiders versus outsiders', *Journal of Economic Perspectives*, 15(1): 165–88.

Link, J. and Bunnage, M. (2007) *The Modern Toss Guide to Work*, Basingstoke: Boxtree.

LinkedIn (2014) 'Workers of the world, log in', *The Economist*, 16 August, Available from: www.economist.com/business/2014/08/18/workers-of-the-world-log-in

Liu, M., Bentley, F.S., Evans, M.H.T. and Schurman, S.J. (2015) 'Globalization and Labor in China and the United States: Convergence and Divergence', in A. Chan (ed) *Chinese Workers in Comparative Perspective*, Ithaca, NY: Cornell University Press, pp 44–68.

Living Wage Foundation (2021) 'For the real cost of living', Available from: www.livingwage.org.uk

Lüthje, B. (2015) 'Exporting Corporatism? German and Japanese Transnationals' Regimes of Production in China', in A. Chan (ed) *Chinese Workers in Comparative Perspective*, Ithaca, NY: Cornell University Press, pp 21–43.

Lyons, D. (2016) *Disrupted: Ludicrous Misadventures in the Tech Start-Up Bubble*, London: Atlantic Books.

Lyons, D. (2019) *Lab Rats: Why Modern Work Makes People Miserable*, London: Atlantic Books.

Macalister, T. and Pidd, H. (2009) 'Uproar in Cowley as BMW confirms 850 job cuts at Mini factory', *The Guardian*, 16 February, Available from: www.theguardian.com/business/2009/feb/16/bmw-mini-job-cuts

MacInnes, J. (2008) 'Work–Life Balance: Three Terms in Search of a Definition', in C. Warhurst, D.R. Eikhof and A. Haunschild (eds) (2008) *Work Less, Live More? Critical Analyses of the Work–Life Boundary*, Basingstoke: Palgrave Macmillan, pp 44–61.

MacKenzie, R. and Forde, C. (2009) 'The rhetoric of good workers versus the realities of employers' use and the experiences of migrant workers', *Work, Employment & Society*, 23(1): 142–59.

Macpherson, Sir William (1999) *The Stephen Lawrence Inquiry Report*, February, Cm 4262-I, London: HMSO. Available from: https://assets.publishing. service.gov.uk/government/uploads/system/uploads/attachment_data/ file/277111/4262.pdf

Manyika, J., Lund, S., Chui, M., Bughin, J., Woetzel, J., Batra, P., et al (2017) *Jobs Lost, Jobs Gained: What the Future of Work Will Mean for Jobs, Skills and Wages*, 28 November, McKinsey & Company, Available from: www.mckinsey.com/ featured-insights/future-of-work/jobs-lost-jobs-gained-what-the-future-of- work-will-mean-for-jobs-skills-and-wages

Marchington, M., Grimshaw, D., Rubery, J. and Willmott, H. (2005) *Fragmenting Work: Blurring Organizational Boundaries and Disordering Hierarchies*, Oxford: Oxford University Press.

Marsden, D. (1999) *A Theory of Employment Systems: Micro-Foundations of Societal Diversity*, Oxford: Oxford University Press.

Marsden, D. (2021) 'Patterns of organizational ownership and employee well- being in Britain', *British Journal of Industrial Relations*, 59(4): 988–1019.

Marvit, M.Z. (2014) 'How crowdworkers became the ghosts in the digital machine', *The Nation*, 5 February, Available from: www.thenation.com/article/ archive/how-crowdworkers-became-ghosts-digital-machine

Marx, K. (1981 [1867]) *Capital, Volume 1, 2nd Preface to Capital*, Harmondsworth: Penguin.

Maslin Nir, S. (2015a) 'The price of nails', *The New York Times*, 7 May. Available from: www.nytimes.com/2015/05/10/nyregion/at-nail-salons-in-nyc- manicurists-are-underpaid-and-unprotected.html

Maslin Nir, S. (2015b) 'Perfect nails, poisoned workers', *The New York Times*, 8 May, Available from: www.nytimes.com/2015/05/11/nyregion/nail-salon- workers-in-nyc-face-hazardous-chemicals.html

Matten, D. and Moon, J. (2008) '"Implicit" and "explicit" CSR: A conceptual framework for a comparative understanding of corporate social responsibility', *Academy of Management Review*, 33(2): 404–24.

Maume, D.J. Jr (1999) 'Glass ceilings and glass escalators: Occupational segregation and race and sex differences in managerial promotions', *Work and Occupations*, 26(4): 483–509.

Maury, O. (2020) 'Between a promise and a salary: Student–migrant-workers' experiences of precarious labour markets', *Work, Employment & Society*, 34(5): 809–25.

Mayo, S. (2020) 'HR at the top table', *Strategic HR Review*, 19(6): 259–65.

Mazzucato, M. (2019) *The Value of Everything: Making and Taking in the Global Economy*, London: Penguin Books.

McCormick, H. (2016) *The Real Effects of Unconscious Bias in the Workplace*, Chapel Hill, NC: UNC Kenan-Flagler Business School, Available from: https://teammates.atriumhealth.org/-/media/human-resources/documents/ new-teammates/unc-white-paper-the-real-effects-of-unconscious-bias-in-the- workplace-final.pdf

McCrudden, C. (2004) 'Using public procurement to achieve social outcomes', *National Resources Forum*, 28(4): 257–67.

McGovern, P., Hill, S., Mills, C. and White, M. (2007) *Market, Class, and Employment*, Oxford: Oxford University Press.

McGregor, J. (2007) '"Joining the BBC (British Bottom Cleaners)": Zimbabwean migrants and the UK care industry', *Journal of Ethnic and Migration Studies*, 33(5): 801–24.

McKinlay, A. and Smith, C. (2009) *Creative Labour: Working in the Creative Industries*, London: Palgrave.

McKinlay, A. and Taylor, P. (2014) *Foucault, Governmentality, and Organization: Inside the Factory of the Future*, London: Routledge.

McLellan, D. (1983) *Karl Marx: His Life and Thought*, London: Granada.

McLoughlin, K. (2017) 'Socially useful production in the defence industry: The Lucas Aerospace combine committee and the Labour government, 1974–1979', *Contemporary British History*, 31(4): 524-45.

Meardi, G. (2007) 'The Polish plumber in the West Midlands: Theoretical and empirical issues', *Review of Sociology*, 13(2): 39–56.

Merton, R.K. (1940) 'Bureaucratic structure and personality', *Social Forces*, 18(4): 560–8.

Michie, J., Blasi, J.R. and Borzaga, C. (eds) (2017) *The Oxford Handbook of Mutual, Co-operative, and Co-owned Business*, Oxford: Oxford University Press.

Miller, C.C. (2014) 'Technology's man problem', *The New York Times*, 5 April, p 1, Available from: www.nytimes.com/2014/04/06/technology/technologys-man-problem.html?module=inline

Miller, C.C. (2015) 'Robo recruiting: Can an algorithm hire better than a human?', *The New York Times*, 25 June. Available from: www.nytimes.com/2015/06/26/upshot/can-an-algorithm-hire-better-than-a-human.html

Mills, M., Mencarini, L., Tanturri, M.L. and Begall, K. (2008) 'Gender equity and fertility intentions in Italy and the Netherlands', *Demographic Research*, 18(1): 1–26.

Minbaeva, D.B. (2018) 'Building credible human capital analytics for organizational competitive advantage', *Human Resource Management*, 57(3): 701–13.

Minford, P. (1991) *The Supply Side Revolution in Britain*, Aldershot: Elgar/Institute of Economic Affairs.

Mintzberg, H. (1987) 'The strategy concept I: Five Ps for strategy', *California Management Review*, 30(1): 11–24.

Molla, R. and Lightner, R. (2016) 'Diversity in tech', *Wall Street Journal*, 10 April, Available from: http://graphics.wsj.com/diversity-in-tech-companies

Moore, F. (2017) 'Recruitment and Selection of International Managers', in T. Edwards and C. Rees (eds) *International Human Resource Management*, London: Pearson, pp 208–29.

Moore, S. and Hayes, L.J.B. (2017) 'Taking worker productivity to a new level? Electronic monitoring in homecare – The (re)production of unpaid labour', *New Technology, Work and Employment*, 32(2): 101–14.

Moreno, J. (2019) 'Google follows a growing workplace trend: Hiring more contractors than employees', *Forbes Magazine*, 31 May.

Morishima, M. (1991) 'Information sharing and collective bargaining in Japan: Effects on wage negotiations', *Industrial and Labor Relations Review*, 44: 469–85.

Morris, B. and Smyth, J. (1994) 'Paternalism as an Employer Strategy, 1800–1960', in J. Rubery and F. Wilkinson (eds) *Employer Strategy and the Labour Market*, Oxford: Oxford University Press, pp 195–225.

Mulinari, P. (2019) 'Weapons of the poor: Tipping and resistance in precarious times', *Economic and Industrial Democracy*, 40(2): 434–51.

Mullins, F. (2018) 'HR on board! The implications of human resource expertise on boards of directors for diversity management', *Human Resource Management*, 57(5): 1127–43.

Murphy, F. and Doherty, L. (2011) 'The experience of work–life balance for Irish senior managers', *Equality, Diversity and Inclusion: An International Journal*, 30(4): 252–77.

Newton, T. and Findlay, P. (1996) 'Playing God? The performance of appraisal', *Human Resource Management Journal*, 6(3): 42–58.

Ngai, P. and Smith, C. (2007) 'Putting transnational labour process in its place: The dormitory labour regime in post-socialist China', *Work, Employment & Society*, 21(1): 27–45.

NHK World (2008) 'Death from overwork in Japan', 16 September, Available from: www.youtube.com/watch?v=fj9N52lRTAQ

Nickson, D. (2013) *Human Resource Management for Hospitality, Tourism and Events*, London: Routledge.

Nisen, M. (2015) 'How millennials forced GE to scrap performance reviews', *The Atlantic*, 18 August, Available from: www.theatlantic.com/politics/archive/2015/08/how-millennials-forced-ge-to-scrap-performance-reviews/432585

Nixon, D. (2009) '"I can't put a smiley face on": Working-class masculinity, emotional labour and service work in the New Economy', *Gender, Work and Organization*, 16(3): 300–22.

Noon, M. (2018) 'Pointless diversity training: Unconscious bias, new racism and agency', *Work, Employment & Society*, 32(1): 198–209.

Nove, A. (1991) *The Economics of Feasible Socialism Revisited*, London: HarperCollins Academic.

Oakley, A. (1985 [1974]) *The Sociology of Housework*, Oxford: Basil Blackwell.

O'Brien, S.A. and Fiegerman, S. (2017) 'Silicon Valley finally faces a reckoning with sexism', CNN Business, 9 August. Available from: http://money.cnn.com/2017/08/09/technology/culture/silicon-valley-sexism/index.html

O'Connell, R. (2010) '(How) is childminding family like? Family day care, food and the reproduction of identity at the public/private interface', *The Sociological Review*, 58(4): 563–86.

O'Connor, S. (2021) 'Temporary lorry driver visas are a symptom of government failure', *Financial Times*, Available from: www.ft.com/content/73fb9887-055f-4a5b-89b1-5df0c37ecc2b

OECD (Organisation for Economic Co-operation and Development) (2017) *Getting Skills Right: United Kingdom*, 20 November, Paris: OECD, Available from: https://read.oecd-ilibrary.org/employment/getting-skills-right-united-kingdom_9789264280489-en#page1

OECD (2019a) *The Future of Work, OECD Employment Outlook 2019, Highlights*, Paris: OECD, Available from: www.oecd.org/employment/Employment-Outlook-2019-Highlight-EN.pdf

OECD (2019b) 'Trade union density' (Data by theme/Labour/Trade unions and collective bargaining/Trade union density), Available from: https://stats.oecd.org

OECD (2021) *OECD Labour Force Statistics 2011–2020*, Paris: OECD, Available from: https://read.oecd-ilibrary.org/employment/oecd-labour-force-statistics-2021_177e93b9-en#page59 (NB Statistics for 2010 no longer available as range has been updated).

Oláh, L.S., Kotowska, I.E. and Richter, R. (2018) 'The New Roles of Men and Women and Implications for Families and Societies', in G. Doblhammer and J. Gumà (eds) *A Demographic Perspective on Gender, Family and Health in Europe*, Cham: Springer, pp 41–64.

Olcott, G. (2009) *Conflict and Change: Foreign Ownership and the Japanese Firm*, Cambridge: Cambridge University Press.

O'Leary, B.J. and Weathington, B.L. (2006) 'Beyond the business case for diversity in organizations', *Employee Responsibilities and Rights Journal*, 18(4): 283–92.

Oltermann, P. (2014) 'Germany ponders ground-breaking law to combat work-related stress', *The Guardian*, 18 September, Available from: www.theguardian.com/world/2014/sep/18/germany-law-work-related-stress

Omale, G. (2021) 'Customer service and support leaders must understand employee desires on key aspects of work from home to help shape strategy moving forward', Gartner, 18 February, Available from: www.gartner.com/smarterwithgartner/future-of-work-from-home-for-service-and-support-employees

ONS (Office for National Statistics) (2018a) 'Contracts that do not guarantee a minimum number of hours', 23 April, Available from: www.ons.gov.uk/employmentandlabourmarket/peopleinwork/earningsandworkinghours/articles/contractsthatdonotguaranteeaminimumnumberofhours/april2018

ONS (2018b) 'How productive is your business?', 6 July, Available from: www.ons.gov.uk/employmentandlabourmarket/peopleinwork/labourproductivity/articles/howproductiveisyourbusiness/2018-07-06

ONS (2019a) 'Labour disputes in the UK: 2018', 17 May, Available from: www.ons.gov.uk/employmentandlabourmarket/peopleinwork/workplacedisputesandworkingconditions/articles/labourdisputes/2018

ONS (2019b) 'Long-term trends in UK employment: 1861 to 2018', 29 April, Available from: www.ons.gov.uk/economy/nationalaccounts/uksectoraccounts/compendium/economicreview/april2019/longtermtrends inukemployment1861to2018

ONS (2019c) 'Which occupations are at highest risk of being automated?', 25 March, Available from: www.ons.gov.uk/employmentandlabourmarket/peopleinwork/employmentandemployeetypes/articles/whichoccupationsareat highestriskofbeingautomated/2019-03-25#:~:text=When%20considering%20 the%20overall%20risk,are%20low%20skilled%20or%20routine

Osterman, P. (2018) 'In search of the high road: Meaning and evidence', *ILR Review*, 71(1): 3–34.

Paranque, B. and Willmott, H. (2014) 'Cooperatives – Saviours or gravediggers of capitalism? Critical performativity and the John Lewis Partnership', *Organization*, 21(5): 604–25.

Pateman, C. (1975) *Participation and Democratic Theory*, Cambridge: Cambridge University Press.

Paulsen, R. (2015) 'Non-work at work: Resistance or what?', *Organization*, 22(3): 351–67.

Paycor (2020) 'The biggest cost of doing business: A closer look at labor costs', 24 December, Available from: www.paycor.com/resource-center/a-closer-look-at-labor-costs

Payscale (2021) 'The least loyal employees', Available from: www.payscale.com/data-packages/employee-loyalty/least-loyal-employees

Peccei, R., Bewley, H., Gospel, H. and Willman, P. (2005) 'Is it good to talk? Information disclosure and organisational performance in the UK', *British Journal of Industrial Relations*, 43(1): 11–39.

Peck, J., Theodore, N. and Brenner, N. (2010) 'Postneoliberalism and its malcontents', *Antipode*, 41: 94–116.

Peloza, J. (2009) 'The challenge of measuring financial impacts from investments in corporate social performance', *Journal of Management*, 35(6): 1518–41.

Peltokorpi, V. (2011) 'Performance-related reward systems (PRRS) in Japan: Practices and preferences in Nordic subsidiaries', *International Journal of Human Resource Management*, 22(12): 2507–21.

Pendleton, A., Wilson, N. and Wright, M. (1998) 'The perception and effects of share ownership: Empirical evidence from employee buy-outs', *British Journal of Industrial Relations*, 36(1): 99–123.

Pettigrew, A.M. (1977) 'Strategy formulation as a political process', *International Studies of Management & Organization*, 7(2): 78–87.

Pettigrew, A.M. (1979) 'On studying organizational cultures', *Administrative Science Quarterly*, 24(4): 570–81.

Pettigrew, A.M. (1985) *The Awakening Giant: Continuity and Change in Imperial Chemical Industries*, Oxford: Blackwell.

Pfeffer, J. (1998) *The Human Equation: Building Profits by Putting People First*, Boston, MA: Harvard Business School Press.

Pfeffer, J. (2016) 'Why the assholes are winning: Money trumps all', *Journal of Management Studies*, 53(4): 663–9.

Pfeffer, J. and Veiga, J.F. (1999) 'Putting people first for organisational success', *Academy of Management Executive*, 13: 37–48.

Phillips, J. (2009) 'Business and the limited reconstruction of industrial relations in the UK in the 1970s', *Business History*, 51(6): 801–16.

Philo, G. (2014) *The Glasgow Media Group Reader, Vol II: Industry, Economy, War and Politics*, London: Routledge.

Pilz, M. (2016) 'Typologies in comparative vocational education: Existing models and a new approach', *Vocations and Learning*, 9(3): 295–314.

Pincus, F.L. (1996) 'Discrimination comes in many forms: Individual, institutional, and structural', *American Behavioral Scientist*, 40(2): 186–94.

Piore, M.J. (1979) *Birds of Passage: Migrant Labor and Industrial Societies*, New York: Cambridge University Press.

Platform London (2021) *Stop the Clock: The Environmental Benefits of a Shorter Working Week*, May, Available from: www.youtube.com/watch?v=281hhBbI0e0

Pollert, A. (1988) 'Dismantling flexibility', *Capital & Class*, 12(1): 42–75.

Porter, M.E. (1980) *Competitive Strategy: Techniques for Analysing Industries and Competitors*, New York: The Free Press.

Porter, M.E. (1985) *Competitive Advantage: Creating and Sustaining Superior Performance*, New York: The Free Press.

Portes, A. (1998) 'Social capital: Its origins and applications in modern sociology', *Annual Review of Sociology*, 24(1): 1–24.

Powell, A. and Francis-Devine, B. (2021) *Coronavirus: Impact on the Labour Market*, Briefing Paper 8898, 25 March, House of Commons, Available from: https://commonslibrary.parliament.uk/research-briefings/cbp-8898

Prassl, J. (2018) *Humans as a Service: The Promise and Perils of Work in the Gig Economy*, Oxford: Oxford University Press.

Preuss, L., Gold, M. and Rees, C. (eds) (2015) *Corporate Social Responsibility and Trade Unions: Perspectives across Europe*, London: Routledge.

Pudelko, M. (2006) 'A comparison of HRM systems in the USA, Japan and Germany in their socio-economic context', *Human Resource Management Journal*, 16(2): 123–53.

Purcell, J. and Kinnie, N. (2010) 'HRM and Business Performance', in P. Boxall, J. Purcell and P. Wright (eds) *The Oxford Handbook of Human Resource Management*, Oxford University Press, pp 533–51.

Purposeful Company, The (2022) 'A company's *reason for being*', Available from: https://thepurposefulcompany.org

Purser, R.E. (2019) *McMindfulness: How Mindfulness became the New Capitalist Spirituality*, London: Repeater Books.

PwC (PricewaterhouseCoopers) (2018a) *Will Robots Really Steal Our Jobs? An International Analysis of the Potential Long-Term Impact of Automation*, London: PwC, Available from: www.pwc.com/hu/hu/kiadvanyok/assets/pdf/impact_of_automation_on_jobs.pdf

PwC (2018b) *Workforce of the Future: The Competing Forces Shaping 2030*, PwC Global, Insights and Case Studies, Available from: www.pwc.com/gx/en/services/people-organisation/publications/workforce-of-the-future.html

Ramsay, H. (1977) 'Cycles of control: Worker participation in sociological and historical perspective', *Sociology*, 11(3): 481–506.

Ramsay, H., Scholarios, D. and Harley, B. (2000) 'Employees and high-performance work systems: Testing inside the black box', *British Journal of Industrial Relations*, 38(4): 501–31.

Rao, R. and Hill, B. (2019) 'How is the role of AI in talent acquisition evolving?', Cornell University, ILR School site, Available from: https://digitalcommons.ilr.cornell.edu/student/231

Rees, C. and Briône, P. (2021) *Workforce Engagement and the UK Corporate Governance Code: A Review of Company Reporting and Practice*, London: Financial Reporting Council, Available from: www.frc.org.uk/getattachment/56bdd5ed-3b2d-4a6f-a62b-979910a90a10/FRC-Workforce-Engagement-Report_May-2021.pdf

Rees, C., Preuss, L. and Gold, M. (2015) 'European Trade Unions and CSR: Common Dilemmas, Different Responses', in L. Preuss, M. Gold and C. Rees (eds) *Corporate Social Responsibility and Trade Unions: Perspectives across Europe*, London: Routledge, pp 202–22.

Richards, J. (2008a) 'The many approaches to organisational misbehaviour: A review, map and research agenda', *Employee Relations*, 30(6): 653–78.

Richards, J. (2008b) '"Because I need somewhere to vent": The expression of conflict through work blogs', *New Technology, Work and Employment*, 23(1–2): 95–110.

Rifkin, J. (1995) *The End of Work: The Decline of the Global Labor Force and the Dawn of the Post-Market Era*, New York: Putnam Publishing Group.

Rivera, L.A. (2012) 'Hiring as cultural matching: The case of elite professional service firms', *American Sociological Review*, 77(6): 999–1022.

Rivera, L.A. (2015a) 'Guess who doesn't fit in at work', *The New York Times*, 30 May, p 5, Available from: www.nytimes.com/2015/05/31/opinion/sunday/guess-who-doesnt-fit-in-at-work.html?module=inline

Rivera, L.A. (2015b) *Pedigree: How Elite Students Get Elite Jobs*, Princeton, NJ: Princeton University Press.

Robertson, B.J. (2015) *Holacracy: The New Management System for a Rapidly Changing World*, New York: Henry Holt & Company.

Robinson, G. and Dechant, K. (1997) 'Building a business case for diversity', *Academy of Management Perspectives*, 11(3): 21–31.

Rodriguez, S. (2019) 'Inside Facebook's "cult-like" workplace, where dissent is discouraged and employees pretend to be happy all the time', CNBC, 8 January, Available from: www.cnbc.com/2019/01/08/cnbcs-salvador-rodriguez-inside-facebooks-cult-like-workplace-where-dissent-is-discouraged-and-employees-pretend-to-be-happy-all-the-time.html

Roediger, D. and Esch, E. (2012) *The Production of Difference: Race and the Management of Labor in US History*, Oxford: Oxford University Press.

Rosenblat, A., Levy, K.E., Barocas, S. and Hwang, T. (2016) 'Discriminating tastes: Uber's customer ratings as vehicles for workplace discrimination', *Policy & Internet*, Available from: https://papers.ssrn.com/sol3/papers.cfm?abstract_id=2858946

Roth, W.F. (2009) 'Is management by objectives obsolete?', *Global Business and Organizational Excellence*, 28(4): 36–43.

Rowlinson, M. (1998) 'Quaker employers', *Historical Studies in Industrial Relations*, 6: 163–98.

Roy, D.F. (1959) '"Banana time": Job satisfaction and informal interaction', *Human Organization*, 18(4): 158–68.

Roy, D.F. (1980) 'Fear Stuff, Sweet Stuff and Evil Stuff: Management Defences against Unionization in the South', in T. Nichols (ed) *Capital and Labour*, Fontana, pp 395–415.

Rubery, J. (1995) 'Performance-related pay and the prospects for gender pay equity', *Journal of Management Studies*, 32(5): 637–54.

Rudden, J. (2021) 'Volume of hostile merger and acquisition (M&A) take-overs in Europe between 1985 and 2018, by country', Statista, Available from: www.statista.com/statistics/1043178/number-of-hostile-takeovers-in-europe-by-country

Rumelt, R. (2017) *Good Strategy/Bad Strategy: The Difference and Why It Matters*, London: Profile Books.

Russell, B. (1973 [1935]) *In Praise of Idleness*, London: Unwin Books.

SACOM (Students and Scholars Against Corporate Misbehavior) (2017) 'iSlave at 10 – 10 years of iSlavery by Apple, Global Action demands Apple to stop labour rights abuses immediately!', Press release, 3 November, Available from: http://sacom.hk/2017/11/03/press-release-islave-at-10-10-years-of-islavary-by-apple-global-action-demands-apple-to-stop-labour-right-abuses-immediately

Samaluk, B. (2014) 'Racialised "Price Tag": Commodification of Migrant Workers on Transnational Employment Agencies' Websites', in M. Pajnik and A. Floya (eds) *Work and the Challenges of Belonging: Migrants in Globalizing Economies*, Cambridge: Cambridge Scholars Publishing, pp 154–77.

Samaluk, B. (2016) 'Migrant workers' engagement with labour market intermediaries in Europe: Symbolic power guiding transnational exchange', *Work, Employment & Society*, 30(3): 455–71.

Sample, I. (2014) 'Are smartphones making our lives more stressful?', *The Guardian*, 18 September, Available from: www.theguardian.com/technology/2014/sep/18/smartphones-making-working-lives-more-stressful

Sarkar, M. (2019) 'In a taxi, stuck or going places? A Bourdieusian intersectional analysis of the employment habitus of Pakistani taxi drivers in the UK', Doctoral dissertation, University of Leeds.

Satariano, A. (2020) 'How my boss monitors me while I work from home', *New York Times*, 7 May, Available from: www.nytimes.com/2020/05/06/technology/employee-monitoring-work-from-home-virus.html

Sattler, L. and Sohoni, V. (1999) 'Participative management: An empirical study of the semiconductor manufacturing industry', *IEEE Transactions in Engineering Management*, 46(4): 387–98.

Sauser, W.I. (2007) 'Employee theft: Who, how, why and what can be done?', *SAM Advanced Management Journal*, 72(3): 13–25.

Sayer, L.C. and Gornick, J.C. (2012) 'Cross-national variation in the influence of employment hours on child care time', *European Sociological Review*, 28(4): 421–42.

Scargill, A. (1978) *A Debate on Workers' Control*, IWC Pamphlet no 64, Nottingham: Institute for Workers' Control.

Schiemann, W.A., Seibert, J.H. and Blankenship, M.H. (2018) 'Putting human capital analytics to work: Predicting and driving business success', *Human Resource Management*, 57(3): 795–807.

Schömann, I., Sobczak, A., Voss, E. and Wilke, P. (2008) 'International framework agreements: New paths to workers' participation in multinationals' governance?', *Transfer: European Review of Labour and Research*, 14(1): 111–26.

Schultz, T.W. (1981) *Investing in People: The Economics of Population Quality*, Los Angeles, CA: University of California Press.

Schwartz-Ziv, M. and Weisbach, M.S. (2013) 'What do boards really do? Evidence from minutes of board meetings', *Journal of Financial Economics*, 108: 349–66.

Scott, S. and Garland, I. (2018) 'An exploration of zero hour contracts in modern day Britain', The Aberdeen Law Project, 31 January, Available from: https://abdnlawproject.com/blog/2018/1/30/zero-hour-contracts-hero-hour-contracts

Semler, R. (1994) 'Why my former employees still work for me', *Harvard Business Review*, 72(1): 64–71.

Semler, R. (2001) *Maverick! The Success Story behind the World's Most Unusual Workplace*, London: Random House.

Sewell, G., Barker, J.R. and Nyberg, D. (2012) 'Working under intensive surveillance: When does "measuring everything that moves" become intolerable?', *Human Relations*, 65(2): 189–215.

Shackleton, L. (2016) 'We need a new kind of trade unionism', Institute of Economic Affairs, 29 April, Available from: https://iea.org.uk/blog/we-need-a-new-kind-of-trade-unionism

Shade, L.R. and Jacobson, J. (2015) 'Hungry for the job: Gender, unpaid internships, and the creative industries', *The Sociological Review*, 63: 188–205.

Sheane, S.D. (2012) 'Putting on a good face: An examination of the emotional and aesthetic roots of presentational labour', *Economic and Industrial Democracy*, 33(1): 145–58.

Sherman, R. (2011) 'Beyond interaction: Customer influence on housekeeping and room service work in hotels', *Work, Employment & Society*, 25(1): 19–33.

Shragai, N. (2021) *The Man Who Mistook His Job for His Life: How to Thrive at Work by Leaving Your Emotional Baggage Behind*, London: W.H. Allen.

Shwed, U. and Kalev, A. (2014) 'Are referrals more productive or more likeable? Social networks and the evaluation of merit', *American Behavioral Scientist*, 58(2): 288–308.

Silva, F. (2018) 'The strength of whites' ties: How employers reward the referrals of black and white jobseekers', *Social Forces*, 97(2): 741–68.

Simms, M. (2015) 'Union Organizing as an Alternative to Partnership: Or What to Do When Employers Can't Keep Their Side of the Bargain', in S. Johnstone and P. Ackers (eds) *Finding a Voice at Work: New Perspectives on Employment Relations*, Oxford: Oxford University Press, pp 127–52.

Sisson, K. and Storey, J. (2002) *The Realities of Human Resource Management: Managing the Employment Relationship*, Buckingham: Open University Press.

Small, M.L. (2010) *Unanticipated Gains: Origins of Network Inequality in Everyday Life*, New York: Oxford University Press.

Smith, A. (2015) 'Searching for work in the digital era', Pew Research Center, 19 November, Available from: www.pewresearch.org/internet/2015/11/19/searching-for-work-in-the-digital-era

Smith, C. (2003) 'Living at work: Management control and the dormitory labour system in China', *Asia Pacific Journal of Management*, 20(3): 333–58.

Smith, C. (2006) 'The double indeterminacy of labour power: Labour effort and labour mobility', *Work, Employment & Society*, 20(2): 389–402.

Smith, C. (2010) 'Go with the Flow: Labour Power Mobility and Labour Process Theory', in P. Thompson and C. Smith (eds) *Working Life: Renewing Labour Process Analysis*, London: Palgrave, pp 269–96.

Smith, C. (2015) 'Continuity and change in labor process analysis forty years after labor and monopoly capital', *Labor Studies Journal*, 40(3): 222–42.

Smith, C. and Chan, J. (2015) 'Working for two bosses: Student interns as constrained labour in China', *Human Relations*, 68(2): 305–26.

Smith, C. and Vidal, M. (2021) 'The Lean Labor Process: Global Diffusion, Societal Effects, Contradictory Implementation', in T. Janoski and D. Lepadatu (eds) *The Cambridge International Handbook of Lean Production: Diverging Theories and New Industries around the World*, Cambridge: Cambridge University Press, pp 150–76.

Smith, C., Child, J. and Rowlinson, M. (1990) *Reshaping Work: The Cadbury Experience*, Cambridge: Cambridge University Press.

Smith, P. (2001) *Unionization and Union leadership: The Road Haulage Industry*, London: Routledge.

Smith, P. and Chamberlain, D. (2015) *Blacklisted: The Secret War between Big Business and Union Activists*, Oxford: New Internationalist Publications.

Smith, V. (2014) 'Review of David R. Roediger and Elizabeth D. Esch: The production of difference: Race and the management of labor in US history', *Administrative Science Quarterly*, 59(1): 187–9.

Society for Human Resource Management, The (2019) *Leave and Flexible Working*, Available from: www.shrm.org/hr-today/trends-and-forecasting/research-and-surveys/Documents/SHRM%20Employee%20Benefits%202019%20Leave%20and%20Flexible%20Working.pdf

Soskice, D. (1991) 'The Institutional Infrastructure for International Competitiveness: A Comparative Analysis of the UK and Germany', in A.B. Atkinson and R. Bruneta (eds) *The New Europe*, London: Macmillan, pp 45–66.

Souhami, A. (2014) 'Institutional racism and police reform: An empirical critique', *Policing and Society*, 24(1): 1–21.

Spermann, A. (2011) *The New Role of Temporary Agency Work in Germany*, IZA DP No 6180, November, Bonn: Forschungsinstitut zur Zukunft der Arbeit/ Institute for the Study of Labor.

Spicer, A. (2018) 'The ugly truth about unlimited holidays', *The Guardian*, 5 June, Available from: www.theguardian.com/money/shortcuts/2018/jun/05/the-ugly-truth-about-unlimited-holidays

Standing, G. (2011) *The Precariat: The New Dangerous Class*, London: Bloomsbury Academic.

Steinberg, M.W. (2003) 'Capitalist development, the labor process, and the law', *American Journal of Sociology*, 109(2): 445–95.

Sticky People (2017) 'Employee referral schemes in homecare: Improving recruitment in social care', 20 January, Available from: www.youtube.com/watch?v=yCmgqbESG1s

Storey, J. (1992) *Developments in the Management of Human Resources*, Oxford: Blackwell.

Storey, J. (ed) (1995) *HRM: A Critical Text*, London: Routledge.

Storey, J., Basterretxea, I. and Salaman, G. (2014) 'Managing and resisting "degeneration" in employee-owned businesses: A comparative study of two large retailers in Spain and the United Kingdom', *Organization*, 21(5): 626–44.

Strauss, K. (2013) 'Unfree again: Social reproduction, flexible labour markets and the resurgence of gang labour in the UK', *Antipode*, 45(1): 180–97.

Stronge, W. and Lewis, K. (2021) *Overtime: Why We Need a Shorter Working Week*, London: Verso.

Strangleman, T. (2019) *Voices of Guinness: An Oral History of the Park Royal Brewery*, Oxford: Oxford University Press.

Streeck, W. and Thelen, K. (2005) 'Introduction: Institutional Change in Advanced Political Economies', in W. Streeck and K. Thelen (eds) *Beyond Continuity: Institutional Change in Advanced Political Economies*, Oxford: Oxford University Press, pp 1–39.

Suma Cooperative (2021) 'Homepage', Available from: www.suma.coop

Summers, C.W. (2000) 'Employment at will in the United States: The divine right of employers', *University of Pennsylvania Journal of Business Law*, 3(1): 65–86.

Summers, J. and Hyman, J. (2005) *Employee Participation and Company Performance: A Review of the Literature*, Work and Opportunity Series No 33, York: Joseph Rowntree Foundation.

Susskind, D. (2020) *A World Without Work: Technology, Automation and How We Should Respond*, London: Allen Lane.

Taylor, M. (2017) *Good Work: The Taylor Review of Modern Working Practices*, July, London: Royal Society for the Encouragement of Arts, Manufactures and Commerce. Available from: https://assets.publishing.service.gov.uk/government/uploads/system/uploads/attachment_data/file/627671/good-work-taylor-review-modern-working-practices-rg.pdf

Taylor, P. and Bain, P. (2001) 'Trade unions, workers' rights and the frontier of control in UK call centres', *Economic and Industrial Democracy*, 22(1): 39–66.

Taylor, P. and Moore, S. (2015) 'Cabin crew collectivism: Labour process and the roots of mobilization', *Work, Employment & Society*, 29(1): 79–98.

Taylor, P. and Moore, S. (2019) *Cabin Crew Conflict: The British Airways Dispute 2009–11*, London: Pluto Press.

Taylor, P.L. (1994) 'The rhetorical construction of efficiency: Restructuring and industrial democracy in Mondragon, Spain', *Sociological Forum*, 9(3): 459–89.

Tech Insider (2017) 'This man worked undercover in a Chinese iPhone factory', Available from: www.youtube.com/watch?v=5ItLIywwepY

Teicher, J. (2020) 'Wage Theft and the Challenges of Regulation', in P. Holland and C. Brewster (eds) *Contemporary Work and the Future of Employment in Developed Countries*, London: Routledge, pp 50–66.

Thompson, P. (2003) 'Disconnected capitalism: Or why employers can't keep their side of the bargain', *Work, Employment & Society*, 17(2): 359–78.

Thompson, P. (2013) 'Financialization and the workplace: Extending and applying the disconnected capitalism thesis', *Work, Employment & Society*, 27(3): 472–88.

Thompson, P. (2016) 'Dissent at work and the resistance debate: Departures, directions, and dead ends', *Studies in Political Economy*, 97(2): 106–23.

Thompson, P. and Smith, C. (2009) 'Labour power and labour process: Contesting the marginality of the sociology of work', *Sociology*, 43(5): 913–30.

Thompson, P. and Smith, C. (2010) 'Debating Labour Process Theory and the Sociology of Work', in P. Thompson and C. Smith (eds) *Working Life: Renewing Labour Process Analysis*, Basingstoke: Palgrave Macmillan, pp 11–28.

Thompson, P. and van den Broek, D. (2010) 'Managerial control and workplace regimes: An introduction', *Work, Employment & Society*, 24(3): 1–12.

Thompson, P., McDonald, P. and O'Connor, P. (2020) 'Employee dissent on social media and organizational discipline', *Human Relations*, 73(5): 631–52.

Thompson, P., Newsome, K. and Commander, J. (2013) '"Good when they want to be": Migrant workers in the supermarket supply chain', *Human Resource Management Journal*, 23(2): 129–43.

Timming, A.R. (2015) 'Visible tattoos in the service sector: A new challenge to recruitment and selection', *Work, Employment & Society*, 29(1): 60–78.

Tipton, F.B. (2008) '"Thumbs-up is a rude gesture in Australia": The presentation of culture in international business textbooks', *Critical Perspectives on International Business*, 4(1): 7–24.

Tomlinson, D. (2018) 'The UK's tight labour market and zero hours contracts', Resolution Foundation, 21 February, Available from: www.resolutionfoundation. org/comment/the-uks-tight-labour-market-and-zero-hours-contracts

Topham, G. (2022) 'P&O Ferries boss admits firm broke law by sacking staff without consultation', *The Guardian*, 24 March, Available from: www. theguardian.com/business/2022/mar/24/po-ferries-boss-says-800-staff-were-sacked-because-no-union-would-accepts-its-plans

Topping, A. (2021) 'Equality laws could be changed to protect women in menopause, says MP', *The Guardian*, 18 August, Available from: www. theguardian.com/society/2021/aug/18/equality-laws-could-be-changed-to-protect-women-in-menopause-says-mp

Torrington, D., Hall, L., Taylor, S. and Atkinson, C. (2014) *Human Resource Management* (9th edn), Harlow: Pearson Education.

Townley, B. (1993) 'Performance appraisal and the emergence of management', *Journal of Management Studies*, 30(2): 221–38.

Townsend, K. (2005) 'Electronic surveillance and cohesive teams: Room for resistance in an Australian call centre?', *New Technology, Work and Employment*, 20(1): 47–59.

Tregaskis, O. and Heraty, N. (2019) 'Human Resource Development: National Embeddedness', in C. Brewster, W. Mayrhofer and E. Farndale (eds) *Handbook of Research on Comparative Human Resource Management*, Cheltenham: Edward Elgar, pp 184–99.

Trimble, L.B. and Kmec, J.A. (2011) 'The role of social networks in getting a job', *Sociology Compass*, 5(2): 165–78.

Tsui, A.S. and Wu, J.B. (2005) 'The new employment relationship versus the mutual investment approach: Implications for human resource management', *Human Resource Management*, 44(2), 115–21.

TUC (Trades Union Congress) (2012) *Women's Pay and Employment Update: A Public/Private Sector Comparison, Report for Women's Conference 2012*, London: TUC, Available from: www.tuc.org.uk/sites/default/files/tucfiles/womenspay. pdf

TUC (2016) 'What have the trade unions done for us?', February, Available from: www.youtube.com/watch?v=lrjySOFLXgg

Turner, F. (2009) 'Burning man at Google: A cultural infrastructure for new media production', *New Media & Society*, 11(1–2): 73–94.

Tweedie, D., Wild, D., Rhodes, C. and Martinov-Bennie, N. (2019) 'How does performance management affect workers? Beyond human resource management and its critique', *International Journal of Management Reviews*, 21(1): 76–96.

Uber (2022) 'How to improve ratings', Available from: https://help.uber.com/driving-and-delivering/article/how-to-improve-ratings?nodeId=b7625579-3e02-42ae-b7ad-8795f0b36bd4

UK Hospitality (2017) 'Perfect storm on the way for UK hospitality industry: Consumers to face increasing prices', Press release, 5 June, Available from: www. hospitalitynet.org/news/4083064.html

UK Parliament (2016) 'A driver shortage?', Available from: https://publications. parliament.uk/pa/cm201617/cmselect/cmtrans/68/6805.htm

UN Global Compact (2021) *The World's Largest Corporate Sustainability Initiative*, Available from: www.unglobalcompact.org/what-is-gc

UN OHCHR (Office of the High Commissioner for Human Rights) (2021) 'List of agencies, programmes, NGOs and foundations working on contemporary forms of slavery', Available from: www.ohchr.org/EN/Issues/Slavery/ UNVTFCFS/Pages/SlaveryList.aspx

Upchurch, M. (2020) 'Time, tea breaks, and the frontier of control in UK workplaces', *Historical Studies in Industrial Relations*, 41: 37–64.

van der Zee, R. (2017) 'Demoted or dismissed because of your weight? The reality of the size ceiling', *The Guardian*, 30 August, Available from: www. theguardian.com/inequality/2017/aug/30/demoted–dismissed–weight–size– ceiling–work–discrimination

van Jaarsveld, D.D. (2004) 'Collective representation among high-tech workers at Microsoft and beyond: Lessons from WashTech/CWA', *Industrial Relations: A Journal of Economy and Society*, 43(2): 364–85.

van Laethem, M., van Vianen, A.E.M. and Derks, D. (2018) 'Daily fluctuations in smartphone use, psychological detachment, and work engagement: The role of workplace telepressure', *Frontiers in Psychology*, 9(1808): 1–12. Available from: https://doi.org/10.3389/fpsyg.2018.01808

van Wanrooy, B., Bewley, H., Bryson, A., Forth, J., Freeth, S., Stokes, L. and Wood, S. (2013) *The 2011 Workplace Employment Relations Study*, London: Department for Business, Innovation and Skills, Available from: www.gov.uk/ government/uploads/system/uploads/attachment_data/file/336651/bis–14– 1008–WERS–first–findings–report–fourth–edition–july–2014.pdf

Varano, C.S. (1999) *Forced Choices: Class Community and Worker Ownership*, Albany, NY: State University of New York Press.

Views of the World (2017) *EU migration to and from the UK*, 3 March, Available from: www.viewsoftheworld.net/?p=5360

Vis, B., van Kersbergen, K. and Hylands, T. (2011) 'To what extent did the financial crisis intensify the pressure to reform the welfare state?', *Social Policy & Administration*, 45(4): 338–53.

Viscelli, S. (2016) *The Big Rig*, Los Angeles, CA: University of California Press.

Vourakis, A. (2017) 'Analyzing employee reviews: Google vs Amazon vs Apple vs Microsoft', Towards data science, 27 April, Available from: https:// towardsdatascience.com/analyzing-employee-reviews-google-vs-amazon-vs- apple-vs-microsoft-4dc3c036666b

Wainwright, H. and Elliott, D. (1982) *Lucas Plan: A New Trade Unionism in the Making*, London: Pluto Press.

Wakabayashi, D. (2019) 'Google's shadow work force: Temps who outnumber full-time employees, *The New York Times*, 28 May, Available from: www.nytimes. com/2019/05/28/technology/google-temp-workers.html

Wakabayashi, D. and Schwartz, N.D. (2017) 'Not everyone in tech cheers visa program for foreign workers', *The New York Times*, 5 February, Available from: www.nytimes.com/2017/02/05/business/h-1b-visa-tech-cheers-for-foreign-workers.html

Waldinger, R. and Lichter, M.I. (2003) *How the Other Half Works: Immigration and the Social Organization of Labor*, Los Angeles, CA: University of California Press.

Walker, P. (2019) *The Theory of the Firm: An Overview of the Economic Mainstream*, London: Routledge.

Wang, L. and Cotton, L. (2018) 'Beyond Moneyball to social capital inside and out: The value of differentiated workforce experience ties to performance', *Human Resource Management*, 57(3): 761–80.

Warhurst, C. and Nickson, D. (2007a) 'Employee experience of aesthetic labour in retail and hospitality', *Work, Employment & Society*, 21(1): 103–20.

Warhurst, C. and Nickson, D.P. (2007b) 'A new labour aristocracy? Aesthetic labour and routine interactive service', *Work, Employment & Society*, 21(4): 785–98.

Warren, T. and Lyonette, C. (2018) 'Good, bad and very bad part-time jobs for women? Re-examining the importance of occupational class for job quality since the "great recession" in Britain', *Work, Employment & Society*, 32(4): 747–67.

Waters, S. (2014) 'A capitalism that kills: Workplace suicides at France Télécom', *French Politics, Culture and Society*, 32(3): 121–41.

Webb, S. and Webb, B. (1920) *The History of Trade Unionism*, London: Longmans, Green & Co.

Welbourne, T. and Andrews, A. (1996) 'Predicting the performance of initial public offerings: Should human resource management be in the equation?', *Academy of Management Journal*, 39(4): 891–919.

West, T. (2022) *Jerks at Work: Toxic Coworkers and What to do About Them*, London: Ebury Edge.

Whatley, W.C. (1993) 'African–American strikebreaking from the Civil War to the New Deal', *Social Science History*, 17(4): 525–58.

Whitehead, J. (2018) 'NYPD pilots fly penis-shaped route in $4M plane to annoy boss', *Independent*, 2 August, Available from: www.independent.co.uk/travel/news-and-advice/nypd-pilots-penis-flight-path-spy-plane-route-james-coan-safety-a8474106.html

Whiteside, N. (2019) 'Casual employment and its consequences: An historical appraisal of recent labour market trends', *Historical Studies in Industrial Relations*, 40: 1–26.

Whitfield, K., Pendleton, A., Sengupta, S. and Huxley, K. (2017) 'Employee share ownership and organisational performance: A tentative opening of the black box', *Personnel Review*, 46(7): 1280–96.

Whitley, R. (2000) *Divergent Capitalisms: The Social Structuring and Change of Business Systems*, Oxford: Oxford University Press.

Whittington, R. (2006) 'Completing the practice turn in strategy research', *Organization Studies*, 27(5): 613–34.

Whyte, W.H. (1956) *The Organization Man*, New York: Simon & Schuster.

Wilkinson, A., Dundon, T. and Redman, T. (2021) *Contemporary Human Resource Management: Text and Cases* (6th edn), London: Pearson.

Wilson, F. (2002) 'Dilemmas of appraisal', *European Management Journal*, 20(6): 620–9.

Windolf, P. (1986) 'Recruitment, selection, and internal labour markets in Britain and Germany', *Organisation Studies*, 7(3): 235–54.

Wong, J.C. (2019) 'Google staff condemn treatment of temp workers in "historic" show of solidarity', *The Guardian*, 2 April, Available from: www.theguardian.com/technology/2019/apr/02/google-workers-sign-letter-temp-contractors-protest

Wood, A.J., Graham, M., Lehdonvirta, V. and Hjorth, I. (2019) 'Good gig, bad gig: Autonomy and algorithmic control in the global gig economy', *Work, Employment & Society*, 33(1): 56–75.

Woodcock, J. and Graham, M. (2019) *The Gig Economy: A Critical Introduction*, Cambridge: Polity.

Work Institute (2019) *2019 Retention Report: Trends, Reasons and a Call to Action*, Franklin, TN, Available from: https://info.workinstitute.com/hubfs/2019%20Retention%20Report/Work%20Institute%202019%20Retention%20Report%20final-1.pdf

World Bank (2019) *World Development Report 2019: The Changing Nature of Work*, Washington, DC: World Bank, doi:10.1596/978-1-4648-1328-3.

Wortmann, M. (2004) 'Aldi and the German model: Structural change in German grocery retailing and the success of grocery discounters', *Competition & Change*, 8(4): 425–41.

Wyatt, M. and Silvester, J. (2015) 'Reflections on the labyrinth: Investigating black and minority ethnic leaders' career experiences', *Human Relations*, 68(8): 1243–69.

Xu, V.X., Cave, D., Leibold, J., Munro, K. and Ruser, N. (2021) *Uyghurs for Sale: 'Re-Education', Forced Labour and Surveillance beyond Xinjiang*, Policy Brief Report No 26/2020, Canberra: Australian Strategic Policy Institute, Available from: www.aspi.org.au/report/uyghurs-sale

Yin, M., Gray, M., Suri, S. and Vaughan, J.W. (2016) 'The Communication Network within the Crowd', in J. Bourdeau (ed) *Proceedings of the 25th International Conference on World Wide Web*, Montreal, Canada, 11–15 May, Geneva: International World Wide Web Conferences Steering Committee, pp 1293–303.

Zhang, J. and Peck, J. (2016) 'Variegated capitalism, Chinese style: Regional models, multi-scalar constructions', *Regional Studies*, 50(1): 52–78.

Zuberi, D. (2013) *Cleaning Up: How Hospital Outsourcing Is Hurting Workers and Endangering Patients*, Ithaca, NY: ILR Press.

Names Index

References to tables, figures and boxes are in *italics*.
Names of organisations are in the subject index.

Subject Index

References to tables, figures and boxes are in *italics*.
There is a separate names index.